Abraham Eraly, who was born in Kera
in Madras and the United States. He
Throne (originally published by Penguin India as *Emperors of the Peacock Throne*), which is also available in Phoenix paperback. He lives near Madras.

By Abraham Eraly

Gem in the Lotus
The Mughal Throne

GEM IN THE LOTUS

The Seeding of Indian Civilisation

ABRAHAM ERALY

PHOENIX

A PHOENIX PAPERBACK

First published in Great Britain in 2004
by Weidenfeld & Nicolson
This paperback edition published in 2005
by Phoenix,
an imprint of Orion Books Ltd,
Orion House, 5 Upper St Martin's Lane,
London WC2H 9EA

Originally published by Penguin Books India in 2000

1 3 5 7 9 10 8 6 4 2

Copyright © 2000 Abraham Eraly

The right of Abraham Eraly to be identified as the
author of this work has been asserted by him in accordance
with the Copyright, Designs and Patents Act 1988.

All rights reserved. No part of this publication may be
reproduced, stored in a retrieval system, or transmitted,
in any form or by any means, electronic, mechanical,
photocopying, recording or otherwise, without the prior
permission of the copyright owner.

A CIP catalogue record for this book
is available from the British Library.

ISBN 0 75381 854 X

Printed and bound in Great Britain by
Clays Ltd, St Ives plc

www.orionbooks.co.uk

Why does the wind not cease?
Why does the mind not rest?
Why do the waters, seeking truth,
Never ever cease?

— ATHARVA-VEDA

Take up thy bow, the Upanishad, a mighty weapon,
Fit in thine arrow sharpened by devotion,
stretch it on thought allied with resoluteness –
this is the target, friend,
the Imperishable. Pierce it!

— MUNDAKA UPANISHAD

CONTENTS

ACKNOWLEDGEMENTS

This book was written when I was living alone and in near total isolation in an outback suburb of Chennai – in a village really, where there were, it seemed to me, as many buffaloes as men – with virtually no social or familial contacts. It was a forced *tapas* for this reluctant and unlikely but mulish hermit.

However, I have to gratefully acknowledge the help of Nancy Gandhi, who, as she did with my last book, went through my manuscript with a fine-toothed comb, correcting inconsistencies and errors in grammar and spelling, thus saving me endless hours of toil.

I am equally beholden to Ravi Singh and Anjana Ramakrishnan, my editors at Penguin, for their encouragement and editorial support. To David Davidar, the CEO of Penguin Books India, I owe a particular debt of gratitude, for sanctioning a generous advance on this book even before a word of it was written, which enabled me to concentrate on my work without worrying too much about where to find money for my daily gruel.

This book bears no dedication, but if I were to dedicate it to anyone, it would be to the memory of the great Indologists of the last three centuries, from William Jones in the eighteenth century to D.D. Kosambi in our own times. To encounter their devotion to scholarship, incisive intelligence, unfailing fairness, and the sheer monumentality of their achievement has been a humbling experience to this reteller of history. But for their pioneering work in translating and analysing ancient Indian texts, I could not possibly have written this book, even if I had laboured on it for a whole lifetime.

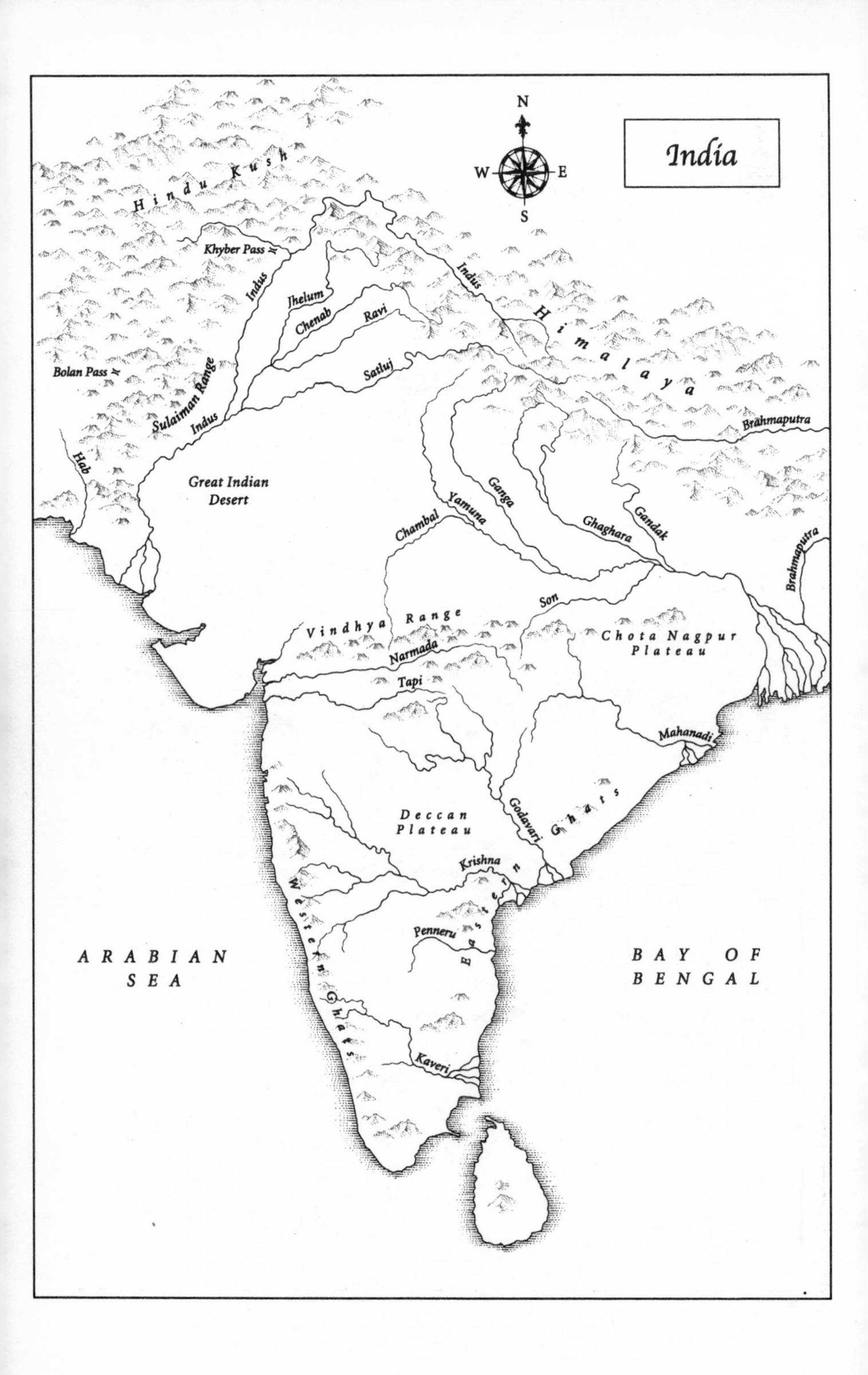
India
N
W
E
S
Hindu Kush
Khyber Pass
Indus
Jhelum
Chenab
Ravi
Satluj
Bolan Pass
Sulaiman Range
Indus
Hab
Great Indian Desert
Indus
Himalaya
Brahmaputra
Ganga
Yamuna
Chambal
Ghaghara
Gandak
Brahmaputra
Son
Vindhya Range
Chota Nagpur Plateau
Narmada
Tapi
Mahanadi
Deccan Plateau
Godavari
Eastern Ghats
Krishna
Western Ghats
Penneru
Kaveri
ARABIAN SEA
BAY OF BENGAL

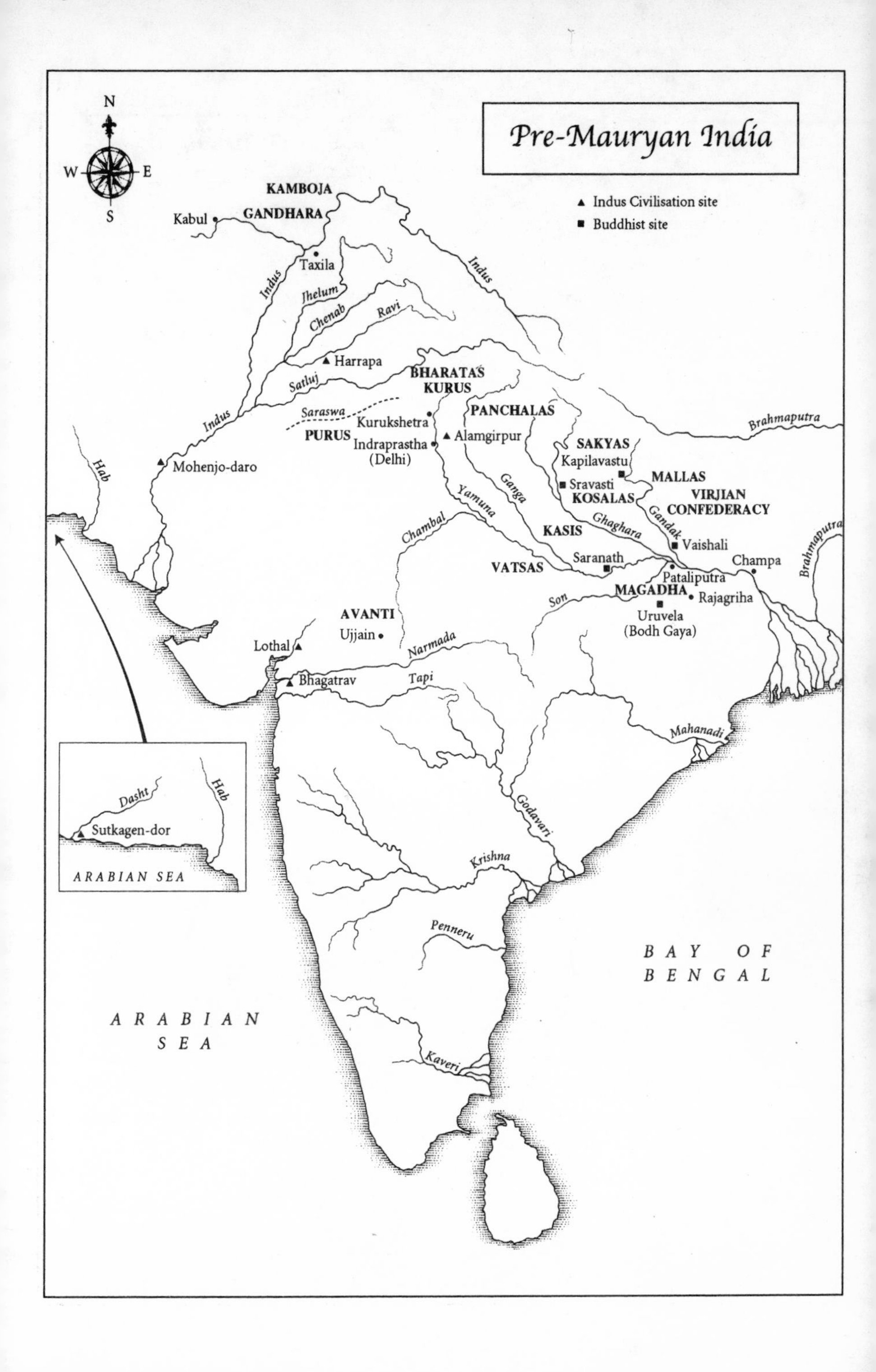

Pre-Mauryan India
N
W
E
S
Indus Civilisation site
Buddhist site
KAMBOJA
GANDHARA
Kabul
Taxila
Indus
Jhelum
Chenab
Ravi
Harrapa
Satluj
BHARATAS
KURUS
PANCHALAS
Saraswa
Kurukshetra
PURUS
Indraprastha
(Delhi)
Alamgirpur
Brahmaputra
Hab
Mohenjo-daro
SAKYAS
Kapilavastu
MALLAS
Sravasti
KOSALAS
VIRJIAN
CONFEDERACY
Ganga
Yamuna
Gandak
Ghaghara
Chambal
KASIS
Vaishali
Saranath
Champa
VATSAS
Pataliputra
MAGADHA
Rajagriha
Son
Uruvela
(Bodh Gaya)
AVANTI
Ujjain
Lothal
Narmada
Bhagatrav
Tapi
Mahanadi
Dasht
Sutkagen-dor
ARABIAN SEA
Godavari
Krishna
Penneru
BAY OF
BENGAL
ARABIAN
SEA
Kaveri

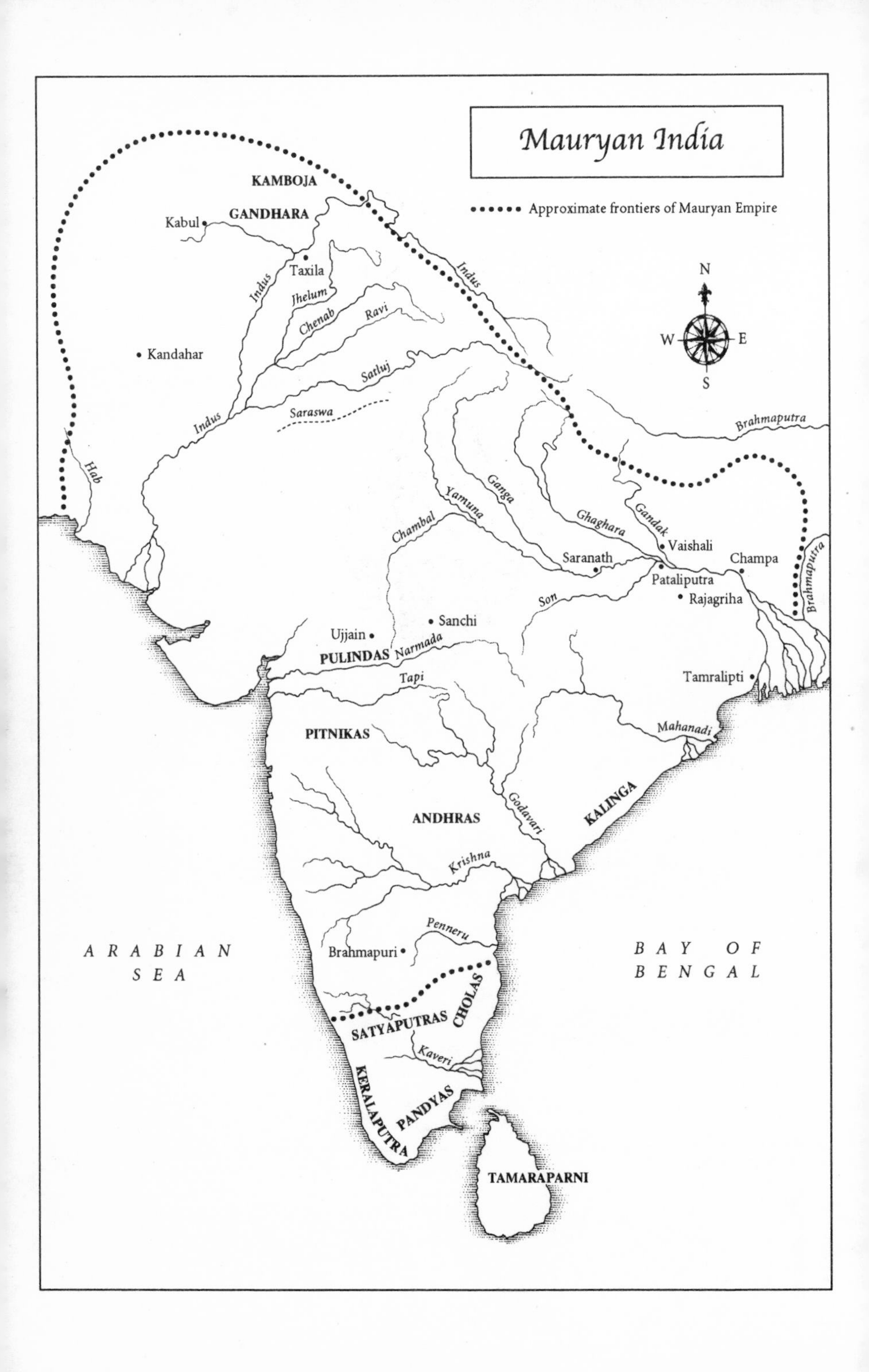

Mauryan India
Approximate frontiers of Mauryan Empire
N
S
E
W
KAMBOJA
GANDHARA
Kabul
Taxila
Indus
Jhelum
Chenab
Ravi
Kandahar
Satluj
Saraswa
Indus
Hab
Indus
Brahmaputra
Ganga
Yamuna
Ghaghara
Gandak
Vaishali
Chambal
Saranath
Champa
Pataliputra
Rajagriha
Brahmaputra
Son
Sanchi
Ujjain
PULINDAS
Narmada
Tapi
Tamralipti
Mahanadi
PITNIKAS
ANDHRAS
Godavari
KALINGA
Krishna
Penneru
Brahmapuri
ARABIAN SEA
BAY OF BENGAL
CHOLAS
SATYAPUTRAS
Kaveri
KERALAPUTRA
PANDYAS
TAMARAPARNI

Chapter One

THE GENESIS

THE ROSE-APPLE LAND

In the beginning there was no India. All the landmass of the earth then lay huddled together in protocontinents in the lap of the idling primeval sea. Around 170 million years ago this cluster of continents began to break up and drift apart, because of the movements of the crustal plates jacketing the semi-molten interior of the earth, a geological process called plate tectonics. In the process, some 100 million years ago, a huge and roughly triangular chunk of land broke off from the eastern flank of Africa above Madagascar, and, pivoting slightly anticlockwise, began a millennially slow, 4000-odd-kilometre-long slide north-north-eastward across the ancient Tethys Sea, bearing a stark, crystalline massif like a granite sail. Eventually, after about a forty-million-year-long ocean journey, it docked into the soft underbelly of the sprawling Asian landmass, to become the land that would be known many aeons later as India.

The underthrust of that impact, sluggish but relentless, penetrating through the sedimentary flesh of the Asian belly, upheaved, in the course of several million years, rocks from the depths of the sea and the land, and reared the Himalayas, the youngest, largest and highest mountain range on earth. At the same time, as the land heaved and rose in a sort of earth wave, it left, along the entire length of the mountains, an immense marshy trough, which slowly sank under the sea. Then, as the snows and glaciers that covered the Himalayas melted, great rivers with hundreds of tributaries, bringing millions of tons of silt daily, descended from the mountains into the lagoon, gradually, over millions of years, filling it with detritus and alluvium, and building up, layer by layer, the Indo-Gangetic Plain, a gift of the Himalayas.

All this happened in very recent geological times, long, long after the formation of the earth some 4.6 billion years ago, and it all happened in a wink of cosmic time, though over many millions of earth years. It was only during the Pleistocene Epoch, between a million and ten thousand years ago, that the present broad physical features of India became finally established. Even then the geodynamic forces involved were not entirely exhausted. Kashmir, once a vast lake, has since turned into a garden valley.

Many centuries later, the forestland off Bombay subsided into the sea, and as recently as 1819, an extensive tract of land in Gujarat, including the fort of Sindree, slid under the sea in an earthquake. It was presumably in some such cataclysm that the ancient and renowned port city of Poompuhar on the Coromandel Coast slumped into the sea, probably around the sixth century AD. Calamitous earthquakes still occasionally convulse northern India, as the Indian plate continues to push and grate against Asia. The Himalayas are still rising.

The Himalayas are estimated to be currently growing at the rate of about six millimetres a year – rising seven millimetres and eroding one millimetre – and are believed to have risen about 1.4 kilometres in the last 1.5 million years. The mountains stretch 2,400 kilometres east-west like a massive, jagged rampart along the northern rim of the subcontinent, their north-south width varying from about 200 to about 400 kilometres, and covering a total area of nearly 600,000 square kilometres. As many as thirty of its peaks rise to well over 7,600 metres, with Mount Everest, the highest peak in the world, measuring 8,848 metres. The Himalayas are the abode of snow, as their name indicates, and have the most extensive snowfields and glaciers outside the polar region, of over 45,000 square kilometres.

The bulk of the Himalayas however lies below the snow line, in three distinct earth-swells, each uplifted in widely different periods. The first to form, around sixty million years ago, was the snow-topped Great Himalayas (average elevation: 6,000 metres), then the Lesser Himalayas (maximum height: 4,600 metres), and finally, about seven million years ago, the Outer Himalayas (maximum height: 1,500 metres). At their far ends, the mountains abruptly fold southward and stretch towards the sea, thus sealing off India effectively from the rest of Asia. Mountains also run along the entire coastline of India, and this gives the subcontinent a sequestered appearance, which is reinforced by the wide seas bordering peninsular India. Only in the north-west do the mountains dip in a few places to yield land passages into India – the Khyber Pass near Peshawar, a thirty-two-kilometre-long serpentine defile, and far to the south of it, near Quetta, the Bolan Pass, and still further south, the Gomal Pass. There is also a corridor into India from Iran along the Makran coast, but this route, through countless treacherous sand-hills and mangrove swamps flanked by bald, gaunt mountains, is so forbidding that it is almost impassable, though it was used by Alexander the Great on his retreat from India in 325 BC, and was frequented by hardy Arab traders in the Middle Ages.

The land thus enclosed by the mountains and the seas is so vast and of such great geo-biological diversity that it is usually described as a subcontinent. From Kashmir in the far north to Kanyakumari (Cape Comorin) at the southern tip, India stretches some 3,200 kilometres, and it has a width of about 2,900 kilometres from the Hindu Kush in the north-west to the Assam mountains in the north-east, a total area of about 4.2 million square kilometres in the five nations – Pakistan, India, Nepal, Bhutan and Bangladesh – into which the subcontinent is now divided.

These political divisions are however mere accidents of history, and have no physical basis whatsoever. Geographically, India falls into three broad regions – the mountains of the north, the peninsular plateau in the south, and the Indo-Gangetic Plain in between. Of these, the northern mountain range was the crucial determinant in moulding life in India, defining and guarding its frontiers, regulating its climate and thus texturing the disposition of its people – as Curtius Rufus, a Roman chronicler of the first century AD, wisely comments, 'The character of the people is here [in India], as elsewhere, formed by the position of their country and its climate.' The Himalayas also provided a spectacular celestial playground for the multitudinous gods and goddesses of India, an ideal setting for its luxuriant mythical lore.

At the foot of the great mountains lies the Indo-Gangetic Plain. This tract has been the main theatre of historical action in India, even though it makes up only a small part (about 18 per cent) of the land area of the subcontinent. A narrow ribbon of land, the maximum width of the Indo-Gangetic Plain is only about 320 kilometres, but it is 2,400 kilometres long, and has an area of nearly 800,000 square kilometres. It is one of the largest, deepest, and most fertile stretches of alluvium in the world, its depth varying from about 1,300 metres to over 1,800 metres. It took millions of years for the plain to fill up and dry out, and it was only around six thousand years ago that the area finally became suitable for human habitation. But its soil, rich with the wash of the mountains, is splendidly congenial for agriculture, and it was here that the great civilisations, religions and empires of India flourished.

The whole of this plain was once lush with vegetation, but in early historical times the scene changed somewhat, when its south-western region gradually turned into a desert (the Great Indian Desert) and acquired a distinctive life-cycle of its own. The monsoon that annually rejuvenates much of India generally passes over the desert merely raking the dunes and spreading the sand, without precipitating much rain. The rivers that once watered the region, including the great river Saraswati, which the Vedic poets exultingly called the mother of rivers, and on the banks of which the Rig-veda was composed, are today lost in the sands of Rajasthan. The Luni, rising from the Ana Sagar Lake near Ajmer and flowing into the Rann of Kuchch, is today the only living river of Rajasthan, but its water is salty over much of its course, and the river itself turns into a trickle in rain-deficient years.

To the south of the Indo-Gangetic Plain, the Vindhya Range marks off peninsular India, which constitutes the bulk of the Indian landmass. This is the chunk of land that broke off from Africa, and it has the same rock stratification and fossil remains of flora and fauna as those of Africa, Australia, South America and Antarctica, all of which were once parts of a supercontinent called Gondwana.

Peninsular India, one of the most ancient crust-blocks of the earth, has a geological history quite different from that of the still-evolving northern India. While the northern plains and mountains have all been beneath the sea during most of their geological history, the peninsula has been land for over 500 million years, since the Cambrian Period. The region is geologically quite stable, though not entirely free of earthquakes, and its physical features have remained largely unchanged through all the convulsions of the earth over millions of years. Its hills and mountains were not upheaved like the Himalayas, but are relict mountains, adamantine portions of the plateau that have withstood the weathering of ages and erosion by wind and water. The soil of peninsular India, unlike the rich alluvium of the northern plains, is laterite (the hard clay formed by the granulation of rocks) and has little fertility. Groundwater resources are also negligible in the peninsula, and on the whole the region does not favour agriculture, though parts of the coastal land, as well as the alluvial plains along the river valleys, give good yield, and the black soil of the northern Deccan is ideal for cotton cultivation.

The Vindhya Range lies transverse at the head of the peninsula, pressing against the Indo-Gangetic Plain. One of its outliers, the Rajmahal Hills, advances close to the Ganga at Teliyagarhi, near the point where the river turns south at the border of Bengal; far to the west, another outlier, the Aravali Range, strikes north-eastward from Gujarat, an ancient, stubby, callused finger of the peninsula jabbing at Delhi through the yielding soil of the Indo-Gangetic Plain. Nestling close to the Vindhyas on the south is the Satpura Range, and in between them flows the Narmada river, the conventional dividing line between northern and southern India. At the western end of the Satpura, at a right angle to it, lies another great mountain range, the Western Ghats, which runs down the coastline all the way to the narrow southern tip of India, where it is joined by the Eastern Ghats, a relatively low and discontinuous range that lies along the eastern coast of the peninsula.

The elevation of peninsular India has a slight eastward tilt, so its great rivers – Godavari, Krishna and Kaveri – though originating in the Western Ghats, close to the Arabian Sea, flow a great distance east across the width of the plateau to drain into the Bay of Bengal. The only major west-flowing river in the region is the Narmada. These peninsular rivers are of great antiquity, and have kept their placid courses over millions of years.

In contrast, the Himalayan rivers have often dramatically changed their beds. The Indus and the Ganga, it is believed, were in the beginning a single river, which arched along the foot of the northern mountains from sea to sea, draining into the Arabian sea in the west as well as into the Bay of Bengal in the east. It was then as much a lagoon as a river, into which innumerable Himalayan feeder streams emptied. This gargantuan river was cleaved by post-Himalayan earth movements into two separate, diverging river systems, the Indus and the Ganga. Later there were other disjunctions and conjunctions – the Saraswati, geologists conjecture, was abducted by the Yamuna in early historical times, and the Yamuna itself, once part of the Indus system, was later constrained to change its southward course and flow east towards the Bay of Bengal.

The Yamuna and the Ganga rise close to each other from Himalayan glaciers, the Yamuna from the Yamunotri Glacier west of Bander-punch, the Monkey-tail Mountain, and the Ganga a mere twenty-five kilometres to the east of it, from an ice-cave called Gaumukh, Cow's Mouth, at the snout of a glacier. The two great rivers – 2,510 (Ganga) and 1,370 (Yamuna) kilometres long – run companionably close together for several hundred kilometres in a south-easterly direction before joining at Allahabad to become one river named Ganga. Further down, in Bengal, the Ganga branches into many rivers to flow into the sea, and in the process gets entwined with the Brahmaputra, another great Himalayan river.

The Brahmaputra, 2,900 kilometres long, rises in the Plateau of Tibet near Mount Kailas, the abode of Hindu gods, and runs a great distance east along the northern flank of the Himalayas in Tibet, before turning sharply south into Arunachal Pradesh in India; it then snakes west into Assam, and finally south into Bangladesh, there to join the Padma, a distributary of the Ganga for the short run to the Bay of Bengal. The Ganga-Yamuna-Brahmaputra river systems hang from the neck of the Himalayas like the strands of an askew necklace, their broad estuary a braided pendant.

The Indus, the river that gave India its name, is 3,060 kilometres long, and is the largest river of the subcontinent. Though originating close to the Brahmaputra in Tibet, it takes the opposite course, and runs north-west for about 800 kilometres through Tibet and Kashmir, before taking a sharp turn south by cutting through a precipitous, 5,200-metre-deep gorge. It then swerves west again for a short distance, and finally turns south, to leave the mountains and enter the Punjab plains, from there to flow cool and blue through the scorching desert sands of Sind into the Arabian Sea.

*

Early Aryans in India were quite conscious of the geographic distinctiveness of their new homeland, and described it as *Himachala Setu paryantam*, the land stretching from the Himalayas to the southern seas, and in their proprietary pride they named the land Bharat, after their legendary royal hero. 'The land that lies north of the ocean, and south of the snowy mountains is Bharat, for there dwell the descendants of Bharata,' states the *Vishnu Purana.* But Indians had never, till modern times, called their land India, or called themselves Indians. The name India is derived from the Sanskrit term *sindhu,* meaning 'river', specifically the Indus. Ancient Persians mispronounced *sindhu* as Hindu, and used it to refer to the Indus as well as to the Indus Valley, and later to the whole subcontinent. The Greeks turned the Persian word Hindu into Indus, and from that Europeans in late medieval times derived the name India.

Ancient Sanskrit writers usually spoke of India metaphorically as a lotus flower, but they had no interest in factual geographical knowledge. Unlike the Chinese, who were expert geographers, and whose topographic maps date back to the second century BC, Indians were on the whole inclined to dream up cosmographies, rather than to draw realistic maps. They maintained that the earth was a flat disk with a golden mountain, Mount Meru, at its centre and four continents around it in the four directions. Of these, the southern continent was called Jambudvipa, land of the rose-apple tree, of which India, set off by the Himalayas, was held to be the southern part, though India itself was often called Jambudvipa.

There are several variations of this notion, one of which describes the continents (seven of them) as lying in concentric circles around Mount Meru, each girded by a distinct ocean, one of salt (around Jambudvipa), another of treacle, others of wine, ghee, milk, curds and fresh water. These and other such whimsical ideas persisted even after it became known to Indian astronomers, early in the Christian era, that the earth was spherical. The astronomers, instead of repudiating the myths, sought to integrate them with scientific facts by treating Mount Meru as the earth's axis. Gradually, however, as pilgrims, travellers, traders and conquering armies traversed the land, a more realistic picture of India emerged. Kalidasa, the great Sanskrit poet of the early fifth century AD, for instance, shows in his works considerable knowledge of the geography of India, and gives precise and detailed descriptions of its features, probably having travelled extensively in the country.

The other great civilisations of the ancient world – the Chinese in the east, the Persians, Greeks and Romans in the west – had some knowledge of India's topography, though their depictions were often grossly distorted. Typically, Ptolemy's map showed India squashed and horizontally distended, stretching east from the mouth of the Indus. However, Megasthenes, a Greek official in India in the fourth century BC, described the country fairly accurately as a rhomboid. India was known to the Chinese of the second century BC as Yin-tu (Hindu) and later as Thian-tu; sometimes they simply called it Magadha, and at other times described it as the kingdom of Brahmins. 'This country in shape is narrow towards the south and broad towards the north,' stated an ancient Chinese writer; 'and the people's faces are of the same shape as the country.'

Climatic conditions in India have great diversity, as is to be expected in a land of subcontinental size and stretching over twenty-nine parallels of latitude. In broad terms, the Indo-Gangetic Plain has a continental climate of extremely hot summers and severe winters, while the eastern and western coasts are tropical, and the peninsular plateau subtropical; the Greater Himalayas are arctic, but western Rajasthan is a searing desert, where temperatures rise as high as 54 degrees centigrade in summer. Similar extremes also mark rainfall – on an average, the desert receives less than 13 centimetres of rain a year, but Cherrapunji in north-eastern India gets an overbountiful 1,109 centimetres of rain, and is the second wettest place on earth, after Mount Waileale in Hawaii.

In all this, the Himalayas play a decisive role, climatically insulating India from the Asian mainland by barring the entry of the arctic winds of Central Asia and the Tibetan Plateau, and preventing the exit of the moisture-laden monsoon winds blowing in from the seas. The monsoons, the south-west monsoon in summer and the north-east monsoon in winter, so totally dominated life in India until modern times that the passage of time itself was reckoned in terms of the monsoon – *varsha*, rain, also means year in Sanskrit.

The monsoons are essentially the seasonal elaborations of the daily alternation between land and sea breezes along the coast due to the unequal warming of the land and the sea. During the summer months of March, April and May, when the northern hemisphere tilts toward the sun due to the shift of the earth's axis, northern India and Central Asia receive more of the sun's heat than the equatorial Indian Ocean, and this causes temperatures to rise over the land and drop over the sea. The land in heat then lures and draws over itself the heavy, moisture-laden monsoon winds from the sea. Then, as the lowering clouds roll over the warm land, convection currents lift them to the cooler upper atmosphere, where they condense and pour their bounty over the thirsting land – a simple yet awesome annual rejuvenative rite, of which the Rig-vedic poet sang:

Like a cow the lightning lows and follows,
mother-like, her youngling,
When the rain-flood hath been loosened.

This, the first rainy season of the year, is called the south-west monsoon, and lasts about four months, from June to September. It enters India in two branches, one from the Arabian Sea and the other from the Bay of Bengal. The Arabian Sea branch reaches the southern tip of Kerala in the first week of June, then advances along the Western Ghats and splits into two unequal streams. The smaller of these streams vaults over the Ghats (after pouring rain copiously along the mountain slopes and over the coastal plain) and blows across the peninsula (yielding only meagre rain there) to pass over to the Bay of Bengal. Meanwhile the main Arabian Sea stream, blowing north along the Ghats, splits again, sends one branch funnelling into central India through the Narmada valley, while the other branch crosses the Gujarat coast, yields some rain there, then whips through the desert of Rajasthan with a dry, mocking howl, and heads for Punjab.

In the meantime, the Bay of Bengal branch of the monsoon also splits into two. One stream advances into Myanmar, while the other crosses the Bengal coast and drenches the Assam mountains with the heaviest rainfall in India. Then, unable to cross the high mountains, it wheels westward and sweeps towards Punjab, showering rain along the Himalayan slopes. On reaching Punjab, it combines with the Arabian Sea stream that has streaked over Gujarat and Rajasthan, and together they precipitate heavy rain over the entire north-western India. All this activity mostly leaves out the Gangetic Plain, which then forms a low-pressure trough, drawing monsoon rains into itself as well as over Orissa and Madhya Pradesh. By the end of June, the monsoon is active over virtually the entire subcontinent.

By mid-September, the land/sea temperature equation begins to reverse, as rain cools the land, and the earth gradually shifts its axis again to tilt the southern hemisphere to the sun. The monsoon then slowly retreats, introducing dry wintry weather over much of India by mid-October. In the process, the dominant low pressure system over India shifts to the Bay of Bengal, and that drives the retreating monsoon towards the south-eastern region of the peninsula, which has been so far largely bypassed by the rains. In October and November the retreating monsoon (called the north-east monsoon in its new avatar) yields the heaviest showers of the year over much of Karnataka, Tamil Nadu and Andhra Pradesh, often bringing cyclonic storms in its wake.

Ancient Greek travellers believed that it was the bountiful rain and the humid, torrid climate of India that enabled so many life forms to proliferate and thrive luxuriantly in India, as nowhere else in the world. But the beginning of life in India is much older than the monsoons, older than India itself, and is part of the story of the evolution of life on earth. When the supercontinent Gondwana broke up, the drifting Indian plate carried a substantial complement of the plants and animals of the mother continent, and these life forms continued to evolve in the floating landmass, adapting themselves to the new environment into which they were being carried. This was the age of dinosaurs and mammoths, of giant flying birds and dragonflies. But as yet there were no human beings.

Nor did man evolve in India. It was in Africa that the critical evolutionary divergence that separated man from apes took place, some five to seven million years ago. This process led, a few million years later, to the emergence of a genus called *Homo*, which had an erect posture, and had probably learned to use fire, and to make crude stone tools. These clever animals proliferated and spread from Africa into Europe and Asia, including India, and from them evolved, some 300,000 years ago, the first true human types, whom we in self-adulation call the *Homo sapiens*, meaning, literally, wise man. And finally, some 40,000 years ago, emerged man himself, physically identical to modern man in every respect.

Much of this evolution took place outside India. But creatures of the *Homo* genus seem to have entered the Indian subcontinent soon after they evolved – stone artefacts that are over two million years old have been excavated in the north-western Himalayan foothills, the oldest find of its kind in Asia. During the Glacial Periods, when the oceans froze and much of Europe and Asia was covered with ice, India would have been a fairly agreeable habitat for primitive man, as the Himalayas protected the land from the severity of the cold. Later, during the Old Stone Age, man apparently spread into peninsular India, for artefacts of this age have been found in several places there, but none at all in the Indo-Gangetic Plain, which was an uninhabitable marsh at this time.

Despite all these finds, the story of early man in India remains obscure, as archaeologists arrange and rearrange shards of evidence, often sharply disagreeing with each other about what happened where and when. No skeletal or fossil remains of Old Stone Age men have been found in India, and there is hardly any cultural information about them. We do not know who these people were, or whether they were the same people who lived in different parts of India and at different times. Some primitive drawings and paintings have been found in rock shelters in southern India and Baluchistan, but they are of uncertain age.

The only certain relics of Old Stone Age men in India are their stone tools, the hand-axe and the cleaver, made of quartzite pebbles. This technology, because of its rudimentary nature, was the same among primitive peoples everywhere in the world, and remained virtually unchanged for scores of centuries. Human progress was so slow at this stage that it was almost non-existent – it took man over 20,000 years to advance from the Old Stone Age to the Middle Stone Age, and about 3,000 years to advance from that stage to the New Stone Age. Yet, over these great lengths of time, the distinctions between one age and the next are defined only in terms of minor refinements in making stone tools! Today these gains seem pathetically slow and utterly insignificant, but it was these very minute, tremulous advances that culminated in leading man, slowly and falteringly, to civilisation.

The life of man in the Old Stone Age, in India as elsewhere, was barely distinguishable from that of animals – though more cunning than other animals, and capable of responding creatively to challenges, man still lived like an animal among other animals, hunting in packs and gathering food. Then, sometime between the ninth and seventh millenniums BC, along the fertile crescent arching from Egypt to the Persian Gulf, he began to take charge of his environment – take charge, in fact, of his own destiny. Instead of depending on the chancy yield of hunting and gathering, he now began to domesticate plants and animals, thus assuring and controlling his food supply. The adoption of agriculture required man to be rooted to land, so he gave up nomadic life and settled in village communities. Security of food and security of life led to the rapid expansion of human population, and this enabled man to spread out across far horizons, tighten his dominance over other animals, and in time turn the earth into his personal fief.

Villages and townships now began to appear. The wheel was invented, and carts made. So also boats. Man now produced pottery, wove garments, made tools and weapons of metal, and built houses and shrines. And, being at last free from total preoccupation with physical survival, and having the leisure and the inclination to turn to non-material concerns, he now began to dream up poetry, religion, perhaps even rudimentary philosophy. From casual doodles, he developed art. And he invented writing, the visible language, so he could accumulate knowledge over generations. He also set up political institutions and laid down civic laws. And, most important of all, human behaviour, instead of being governed by instinct, now came to be gradually regulated by formal social conventions. Man thus ceased to be just another animal on earth. Man became human.

And so began the civilisation of man. Once the process began, progress was rapid, compared to the slow, imperceptible cultural evolution over the previous several millenniums. In time the settlements of farmers and pastoralists spread from the Middle East to the Iranian Plateau and Central Asia, and from there, around the sixth millennium BC, into the Indian subcontinent, first into the upland valleys on the Sind-Baluchistan border, and then, a couple of thousand years later, into the Indus Valley.

The racial make-up of early Indians is uncertain. The earliest inhabitants of India were, it is presumed, Negritos, who were fairly common in India until early medieval times – they are frequently represented in Gupta sculptures and Ajanta frescoes – but have since become almost extinct. They are today found only in the Andaman Islands in small numbers. Proto-Australoids probably followed Negritos into India, and this racial type is still found among the aboriginals of India, though often admixed with other races.

It is generally believed (though this is by no means certain) that the people who first brought farming to India and developed an urban civilisation were a Caucasoid sub-race called the Mediterraneans, who spoke a proto-Dravidian language, the precursor of Tamil and other modern south Indian languages. Dravidians – or, more accurately, Dravidian language speakers – in ancient times lived in large numbers all over India, but were gradually crowded out into southern India by Indo-Aryans, another Caucasoid sub-race, who entered India in the second millennium BC. Still later, in historical times, came several other races, turning India into one of the greatest ethnographical museums of the world. All these races blended together so thoroughly over the centuries that today it is virtually impossible to find any pure racial types in India, except perhaps among some aboriginal tribes in the deep jungles. But broadly speaking, Aryo-Dravidians are today prominent in UP, Bihar and Rajasthan; Caucasians in Punjab and Kashmir; Turko-Iranians in the north-west; Mongoloids along the Himalayan fringe, in Bengal and parts of Orissa; and Dravidians in southern India.

All these distinctions based on language and race are in the final analysis superficial – scientists, on the basis of DNA tests, have concluded that all the people of the world are the descendants of a single woman who lived in East Africa perhaps about 150,000 years ago, and are all brothers and sisters to each other. Similarly, modern linguists trace all the 4,000 or so languages in the world today to a single parent language, which originated in some unknown remote past and was last spoken some 12,000 or 15,000 years ago. Early man had no language anywhere in the world, only rude, monosyllabic animal grunts, and it was from this that the parent human language evolved. And from this parent language branched several ancient protolanguages.

These early languages had virtually no grammatical structure, but were merely sets of words or compound sounds, which in time developed into syntactic languages. Each race, living in relative isolation in different regions of the earth, then developed its own distinctive language, so that genetic clustering of early prehistoric populations closely matched language clustering. Later, these racial mother tongues themselves branched into new languages – as clans within the race spread out into new areas, lost contact with each other and intermingled with other people, their speech over a period of time mutated into distinct dialects, and eventually developed into mutually unintelligible languages.

That was how India, subjected as it was to successive waves of migrations and invasions, came to be the teeming linguistic jungle that it is today, having, according to a linguistic survey conducted in the early twentieth century, as many as '225 distinct languages in addition to dialects.' Indians even in prehistoric times were a polyglot people, as indicated by skeletal remains of different racial types found in Harappa and Mohenjo-daro, the earliest cities of India.

ENIGMA OF THE INDUS VALLEY

Nothing in the long recorded history of India gives even a faint hint of it having had a beginning like the Indus Civilisation. When Harappa and Mohenjo-daro, the celebrated metropolises of the civilisation, were first excavated in the 1920s, the mystery was even greater, for the civilisation had then seemed to hang suspended wondrously full-blown in time and space, without any links whatsoever, neither precedence nor sequence. Subsequent archaeological discoveries have established the existence of numerous spatial and temporal connections of the civilisation. Still, much of its mystery remains.

Aristobulus, a Macedonian general in Alexander's army that invaded India in the fourth century BC, seems to have been the first person ever to record seeing the Indus ruins. Unfortunately, his chronicle of Alexander's campaigns has been lost, but Strabo, a first century BC–AD Greek historian, quotes him as stating that, during Alexander's harried retreat down the Indus, 'when he was sent upon a certain mission, he saw a country of more than a thousand cities, together with villages, that had been deserted.' These could only have been the abandoned Indus settlements, for post-Indus urbanisation was not yet old enough or extensive enough (certainly not in Sind) to leave so many ancient ruins, even if we discount Aristobulus's fabulous figure by 99 per cent to a realistic ten or less.

But we cannot be certain of what exactly Aristobulus saw. Well over 2,000 years would pass before we would get the first authentic report on the Indus ruins. This was in the travelogue of Charles Masson, an Englishman, who in 1826 noted that he saw in Harappa 'a ruinous brick castle having remarkable high walls and towers.' But there was no follow-up on that discovery. Thirty years later, another Englishman, William Brunton, an engineer, also came across the ruins of Harappa. The British, who had annexed Punjab a few years earlier and were at this time engaged in laying a railway line from Karachi to Lahore, had great difficulty in procuring, in that stoneless country, the ballast they needed for the track. Then someone told Brunton (who was in charge of building the northern section of the track) about Harappa, and he, in shocking contrast to the patient and dedicated work of many of his compatriots to conserve India's heritage, seized on the ancient city as a brick quarry. The ruins were well over 3,000 years old, but this was not known then. Harappa was for Brunton just another pile of ruins, in a country littered with ancient ruins. Besides, Indians themselves had shown scant regard for their heritage – local peasants had been plundering bricks from Harappa for centuries to build their humble homes, and in Mohenjo-daro Buddhists had long ago built a stupa with the bricks quarried from the ancient city.

Fortunately, not all was lost. Enough of the cities would remain to engage the curiosity of archaeologists for very many decades, and for them to wrangle endlessly over the interpretation of their finds. And, in a way, Brunton's vandalism was what eventually led to the discovery of the Indus Civilisation. By a happy chance, Alexander Cunningham, an officer of the Royal Engineers, who would be later known as the father of Indian archaeology, was at this time stationed in Karachi, and he, on learning about Harappa from Brunton, visited the site and collected several artefacts. But even he did not realise the true value of the discovery, and there was no further exploration of the Indus Valley for the next sixty-odd years. It was only in 1920, during the tenure of Sir John Marshall as the Director-General of Archaeological Survey of India, that excavation at Harappa began in earnest. Two years later, R.D. Banerji of the Archaeological Survey of India discovered Mohenjo-daro. Subsequently several new sites, settlements of varying sizes, were identified and excavated, establishing the pattern of evolution of the Indus Civilisation. 'India,' declared Marshall, 'must henceforth be recognised ... as one of the most important areas where civilising processes were initiated and developed.'

The initial civilising impulse came to India from the Middle East through Iran, Afghanistan and Baluchistan, leading to the establishment of agrarian settlements along the piedmont region on the western border of the Indus Valley around 7000–6000 BC. Mehrgarh on the Bolan River south of Quetta in Baluchistan was one such settlement, which presents us with 'the earliest ... evidence to date of an early agricultural settlement on the edge of the Indus plains,' states Allchin. Baluchistan in prehistoric times was not the desolate and forbidding country that it is today, but a verdant, river-laced land of agricultural bounty. It was a pleasant home for settlers, and they lived there in small farming communities for a couple of thousand years. Then, around the middle of the fourth millennium BC, because of environmental changes or the pressure of growing population, these communities began to spread out to the Indus Valley, advancing in slow stages and founding settlements along the way.

The establishment of farming settlements in the Indus Valley was the decisive turning point in the history of civilisation in India, for it was the tension between challenge and opportunity in the new environment that released human creativity and set man on the path of rapid material and cultural progress. In the mountain valleys of Baluchistan and Afghanistan human settlements were tiny and secluded, seldom more than a couple of acres in extent, with limited economic and political potential. But now, in the vast, open expanse of the Indus Valley, settlements could spread out and become integrated with each other to establish cultural homogeneity and political cohesiveness over a wide area. Further, the rich alluvium of the Indus Valley, renewed annually by river floods, was ideal for agriculture, and produced plenty of food surplus, and this in turn enabled a good number of people to withdraw from direct food production, move on to live in cities, and occupy themselves with crafts and trade, religion and politics.

These were major advantages. Without agricultural abundance, cities could not have come into existence, indeed civilisation itself would not have been possible. But the Indus Valley also confronted man with a major problem. The river floods that nourished the land also at times destroyed crops and settlements. Means therefore had to be devised to harness the river and protect the settlements. This required not only technological innovation but also the organisation of society and government in new ways to promote and enforce civic cooperation and discipline. New value systems and work ethic, also new religious institutions, had to be developed to integrate the new society.

The Indus Civilisation rose out of man's response to these exigencies. In this process, it is probable that the Indus people did receive some cultural and technological stimulus from the older cities of Mesopotamia, with which they were in contact, but the civilisation they created was essentially an indigenous response to an indigenous situation. It was very much a product of the native soil, and the stages of its evolution over a period of several centuries can be traced at many far-flung settlements in the Indus Valley, in Sind as well as Punjab.

At its height, the geographical reach of the Indus Civilisation covered about 1.3 million square kilometres, an area far more extensive than that of the modern state of Pakistan. Its domain stretched south from the Himalayan foothills of Punjab down to the mouth of the Indus, and from there eastward and westward along the sea coast – eastward into Gujarat up to Bhagatrav at the mouth of the Narmada, and westward along the Makran Coast up to Sutkagen-dor on the Dasht river. Apart from Harappa and Mohenjo-daro, numerous other sites of the civilisation have been identified along the Indus and its tributaries and the now dry Saraswati, mostly tiny hamlets measuring no more than 90 metres by 60 metres, but also a few urban centres. The easternmost site excavated is at Alamgirpur, across the Yamuna north-east of Delhi, probably a very late settlement.

There is some uncertainty about the dates of the Indus Civilisation.

Archaeologists had initially assigned to it a broad 1,000-year lifespan, from 2500 to 1500 BC, by coordinating its dates with the known chronology of the Mesopotamian Civilisation. These dates have been subsequently modified on the basis of radiocarbon dating to assign the mature phase of the civilisation a lifespan of about 800 years, roughly from 2500 to 1700 BC, preceded by several centuries of slow evolution and followed by a couple of centuries of rapid decline.

The Indus Civilisation reached its peak around the middle of the third millennium BC, and was then stabilised and homogenised at that level, by enforcing standardisation in culture over its entire vast area. Progress beyond that stage was apparently viewed as inconceivable or unnecessary, and any deviation from the established norms as pernicious. Mohenjo-daro, notes Stuart Piggott, passed through 'nine phases of rebuilding ... often interrupted by disastrous river floods, but from the top to the bottom of the accumulated layers of debris no change can be detected in the content of the material culture, and it is reasonable to suppose that the less tangible elements of the people's lives were similarly unmodified.'

The level of conformity required was, for that ancient age singularly rigid and comprehensive. From pottery vessels to stamp-seals and script, from the dimensions of bricks and the system of weights and measures to urban planning, near-absolute uniformity was maintained throughout the Indus region for many centuries. It is not known who set these standards or how they were enforced, but the establishment of the totalitarian order was, according to Allchin's assessment, the culmination of a 100-year period of 'paroxysmal change' around 2500 BC. The imposition of the new order seems to have initially involved the use of force, at least in some places – at two centres, Amri and Kot Diji, early settlements were burned down to rebuild them according to the new urban norms. But once set, standards were internalised by society as immutable conventions or religious prescripts, so that no further coercion was required to enforce conformity. Indus society was peaceful and orderly. Quiescent, in fact.

Who created this unique civilisation? We are not certain. Not many human remains have been found at the Indus cities, but they obviously had mixed populations, as revealed by skeletal evidence as well as stone and metal sculptures. The social structure of the Indus Valley, Piggott conjectures, was made up of a Proto-Australoid and Negrito underclass, a dominant class of Mediterraneans (commonly associated with the earliest agricultural settlements in West Asia and Egypt) with an admixture of Alpines, and occasional foreigners like Mongols. The Proto-Australoids and Negritos, who had preceded the Mediterraneans into India, probably lived according to their own tribal ways in the countryside or along the periphery of the Indus settlements, rarely in the settlements themselves, just as primitive tribes and untouchables would live at the outskirts of villages and towns in India in later times.

There is strong circumstantial evidence to indicate that the Mediterraneans of the Indus Valley spoke a Dravidian language. The oldest form of the term Dravida is said to be Dramila or Dramiza, and it is possible that the pre-Hellenic people of the eastern Mediterranean region, known to Herodotus as Termilai, were Dravidians, and that they brought civilisation to India. The pastoral Brahui tribe of Baluchistan, who speak a proto-Dravidian dialect, is believed to be a vestige of the ancient Dravidian migration into India from West Asia. Significantly, southern Baluchistan was known in classical times as Gedrosia, 'the country of the dark folk'. Further, as S.K. Chatterji argues, the 'survival of Dravidian vocables in the place-names of Northern India ... [and] the presence of a strong Dravidian element in the Aryan language' from Vedic times on, as well as the references to non-Aryan tribes in Vedic literature, all point strongly to the probability that Dravidian people were predominant in Punjab and the upper Gangetic Valley in prehistoric times, and that they were the people whom Aryans displaced. It is also quite likely that the Dravidian elements found in the early Brahminical religion were derived from the Indus people.

The trans-Indian connection of the Dravidian language is a matter of speculation – some linguists believe that it is related to the Finno-Ugrian family of languages of Eastern Europe, while others maintain, perhaps with greater justification, that it is truly cognate to the Elamite language spoken in southern Iraq and Iran. There are also some who claim that the Indus language was proto-Sanskrit, but this surmise has more to do with sentiment than with facts or reason. The Rig-vedic culture, as Romila Thapar points out, did not extend to Sind, which was the main centre of the Indus Civilisation. 'Both early Indo-European and Indo-Aryan speakers are almost wherever they are identified, associated with horses and related cultural traits, such as horse furniture, horse-drawn chariots and horse burials,' observes Allchin. 'The virtual absence of any evidence of these things in the Indus Civilisation makes it most unlikely that the language of Harappan inscriptions can have been a form of Proto-Indo-Aryan.' The balance of probability therefore is that the Indus people were Dravidians.

But there is no certainty about this. The clue to the puzzle about the true identity of the authors of the civilisation lies hidden in the Indus script, which has not been convincingly deciphered so far. There are no bilingual or long inscriptions to facilitate the reading of the script – the average number of signs to a text in the script is only five, and no inscription has more than twenty or so symbols. Because of the fragmentary nature of the Indus writing and other related difficulties, unless there is some major new discovery, the Indus script seems likely to remain undeciphered, leaving much of the mystery about the civilisation unresolved.

Writing is said to have been first developed in Sumeria around 6000 BC, but we do not know when it was adopted in the Indus Valley. The earliest date assigned to an Indus inscription is 2600 BC, but the script had apparently been in use long before this time, as indicated by its advanced features, such as a relatively small number of symbols, a total of only about 400 signs (consisting of about 250 symbols and their variants) compared to the 900 characters of the Early Dynastic Sumerian script. In its final form, the Indus script was evidently a wholly local creation, for it has no discernible resemblance to any other known script. Scholars are generally agreed that it was a logo-syllabic script – a mixture of word and phonetic signs – and that it was written in the boustrophedon method, in which the first line runs from right to left, and the subsequent lines alternately from left to right and right to left. Once codified, the script remained unchanged for several centuries, like much else in the Indus Civilisation. In all, well over 3,000 Indus inscriptions have been discovered, about 90 per cent of which are from Harappa and Mohenjo-daro, most of them incised on seals, but quite a few on seal impressions as well. Inscriptions have been found also on metal, bone and ivory artefacts, as well as on pottery and stoneware.

Mohenjo-daro and Harappa, the 'twin capitals' of the Indus state, were some 600 kilometres apart, but were connected by the Indus river system. Harappa, on the east bank of the Ravi about 160 kilometres down the river from Lahore, is today about 10 kilometres from the river, but in prehistoric times it was on the riverbank. The city, scholars speculate, could be the Hariyupiya mentioned in the Rig-veda, where the god Indra won a decisive battle for Aryans – 'At Hariyupiya he smote the vanguard of the Vrcivants, and the rearfield fled frightened,' gloats the Vedic poet. Another tradition, recorded by Cunningham, has it that Harappa was founded by Raja Harappa, 'who claimed the husband's privilege on every marriage,' and was consequently destroyed by divine wrath.

No such spicy legend envelopes Mohenjo-daro, though Kosambi believes this could be the city of Narmini mentioned in the Rig-veda as having been burned down by god Agni. The name Mohenjo-daro is of uncertain origin but is thought to mean the Mound of the Dead. The city, about 320 kilometres north of Karachi, today lies nearly 5 kilometres from the Indus on its western bank, but was once probably on the eastern bank, or, as Piggott suggests, on a tongue of land between two branches of the river, the tract being known locally as 'the island'. The two metropolises were, by prehistoric standards, immense in size and population, each having a circuit of over 4 kilometres, with Mohenjo-daro probably having a population of over 35,000, and Harappa somewhat less. The exact limits of the Indus cities are not identifiable, because of the erosion of the ruins over the centuries.

Harappa and Mohenjo-daro were probably very early settlements, and the remnants of their evolutionary stages might be lying beneath their excavated levels. Archaeologists have not been able to reach their lowest strata, as they are well below the present water table, river silt having raised the Indus plain by about 9 metres over the centuries. If indeed such early settlements existed, it is quite possible that they were demolished and rebuilt during the mature phase of the Indus Civilisation, as evidence elsewhere suggests. The cities as we see them today are not rustic settlements that grew haphazardly into metropolises, but laid out according to well-established precepts of town planning.

Both the cities were built to virtually identical plans, on roughly 1.6-square-kilometre-areas along riverbanks, and each had, on its original riverside, a towering and heavily fortified citadel built on an immense artificial terrace. The citadel, a looming, awe-inspiring structure visible from miles around in that open landscape, was the seat of the lords of the land. To the east of the citadel, and set slightly apart from it, was laid out the lower city. Remnants of what appears to be city walls have been found at Mohenjo-daro and a couple of other sites, but these were probably meant primarily for flood protection, being too low for defence.

A major concern of the Indus Valley town planners was to protect the cities, especially their citadels, from floods, for the Indus is devastating in spate during the monsoon, when it often carries nearly a million tons of silt a day. As the awestruck Rig-vedic poet would observe,

> *When the streams of rain pour thund'ring from cloud,*
> *the Sindhu onward rushes like a bellowing bull.*

Alexander's army in the fourth century BC was also witness to the havoc caused by river floods, during which, reports Strabo, 'cities situated on the top of mounds became islands.' Harappa being on an Indus tributary, the embankments built there against inundation seem to have been adequate, for there is no sign of any serious flood damage there, but Mohenjo-daro on the main river is layered at intervals with deep sections of alluvium, indicating that the city was ravaged by floods several times.

But the river silt that covered Mohenjo-daro also preserved its architectural history, so the city has yielded maximum information about the Indus Civilisation. Here the lower city was laid out in neat blocks, with its two main streets running north-south, bisected at right angles by two somewhat narrower east-west streets. Other streets further divided the city into a gridiron of blocks. Several of these blocks have been excavated, and it is believed that there were in all 'twelve major building blocks in three rows of four, east to west ... Within the main blocks was an irregular network of small roads, lanes, and alleys roughly following the general lines and dividing the blocks into individual houses,' notes Piggott. The main streets of Mohenjo-daro were grand avenues, about 9 metres wide, but the secondary streets were rather narrow, and some of the lanes were just 1 metre broad. The streets were not paved. Nor were they, not even the main avenues, tree-lined – there was something about the dry, baked-brick stolidity of the city that precluded the gaiety of avenue trees.

Mohenjo-daro had impeccable sanitation arrangements, and was probably the cleanest city in the prehistoric world, cleaner than even most modern Indian cities. Its streets were flanked by covered brick sewage channels, which were provided at intervals with manhole covers for clearing them. Sewage from houses emptied into street drains through earthenware pipes or through chutes, and the system was so intelligently conceived that rain water and sewage from houses were 'not permitted to flow into the street drains direct, but had first to enter a sump or cess-pit in which was deposited the solid matter,' notes Earnest Mackay, an archaeologist who excavated Mohenjo-daro under Marshall. 'When the sump was three-fourths full, the water flowed into the main drains, and by this method the street drains were prevented from overflowing.' The drains however were not carried outside the city, but emptied into soak pits, which were cleared periodically.

Equal care was taken for the disposal of household garbage, which was conveyed through chutes built into the walls of houses into brick bins outside, from where it was presumably cleared by municipal sanitation workers. There were public dustbins on side streets. 'The whole conception shows a remarkable concern for sanitation and health without parallel ... in the prehistoric past,' comments Piggott. To enforce civic regulations and to prevent crime, there were police check-posts along the main streets, 'small single rooms, placed mostly on corner sites with their doors in important thoroughfares,' as Wheeler describes them. Big Brother was everywhere. There was, as Piggott comments, 'a terrible efficiency' about the Indus Civilisation.

The Indus cities were divided into three distinct zones. Politico-religious institutions were concentrated in the citadel, while the lower city was a mixed zone of residences and commercial establishments. Polluting industries like the kilns of brick-makers and potters were located outside the city, as were cemeteries.

The citadel, built along the western edge of the city and oriented on a north-south axis, dominated the Indus cities, rising (in Harappa) to over

14 metres above the surrounding plain, nearly as tall as a five-storeyed building. A rough parallelogram structure, 421 by 197 metres, its length twice that of its width, the citadel was built on an approximately 7-metre-high rectangular platform of mud-brick and clay. The platform was protected against floods by a massive mud and mud-brick embankment, nearly 14 metres wide at the base and sloping upwards, which in turn was secured by a battered baked-brick revetment.

Over the embankment, and integral to it, were built the ramparts of the citadel, with bastions, salient towers and lofty gateways. It is not clear what these defences were for. There is no evidence of any dominant military establishment in the Indus cities, or any indication of serious assaults on them, except at the very end of their history. Could it be then that the lofty platform of the citadel and its elaborate ramparts were more for the display of the pomp and majesty of the rulers and their gods, than for defence? Perhaps the fortifications originally served a primarily military purpose, but later, during the secure, mature phase of the civilisation, ceremonial and ritual functions became more important.

There is in Harappa, according to Piggott, evidence of 'ceremonial terraces and a processional way leading up from a ramp or flight of steps to the actual gateways [of the citadel], the terraces being provided with guard-rooms at the outer angles.' Similarly, in Mohenjo-daro there is a 6.7-metre-wide grand flight of stairs that rises from the plain to the citadel, with a well at its foot and a small bathroom at its top, 'as though suggesting the need for lustration before entering the precinct of the citadel,' notes Mortimer Wheeler, who worked on the Indus sites in the mid-1940s. The buildings in the citadel have a distinctly religious or ceremonial character. This is evident in Mohenjo-daro, where a number of citadel structures have been excavated, but the citadel in Harappa, vandalised by brick-robbers, is so ruined that it is impossible to ascertain the plan of the buildings there.

A curious structure of obviously religious nature in the Mohenjo-daro citadel is the Great Bath, a pool in a cloistered courtyard, somewhat like the Hindu temple tanks of later times. Measuring about 12 metres by 7 metres, and about 2.5 metres deep, the Great Bath is quite a prehistoric engineering marvel. It was kept watertight by lining its floor and sides with two layers of close-fitting, carefully trimmed baked bricks set on edge in gypsum mortar, with a 2.5-centimetre-thick skin of bitumen sealer between the two layers. A high, corbelled conduit was provided at its north-west corner to drain the tank. At the northern and southern ends of the tank, there are flights of steps, originally with timbered treads set in bitumen, leading down to the floor of the tank, and there is a low platform at the base of the steps in the north, meant for some ritual purpose. The courtyard around the tank is neatly paved with bricks, and on its three sides are a set of small rooms, in one of which is a large well which supplied water to the tank.

Directly across a lane from the Great Bath on the north is another curious structure, a block of eight small bathrooms with a brick staircase in each room, which was in some way connected with the rituals in the bath complex. To the east of the Great Bath is a long, monastery-like building, with a cloistered court and a suite of rooms, often described as The College, which Mackay, who excavated it, thought was 'the residence of a very high official, possibly the high priest himself, or perhaps a college of priests.' A short distance to the south of these structures is another large, twenty-pillared building, a durbar hall or *mandapam* of sorts.

Among the prominent structures in the Indus cities are the state granaries. These are massive structures, designed with skill and care, for they were the state treasuries of the age, in which taxes and tributes in grain were stored. The granary in Mohenjo-daro, a huge timber edifice covering an area of over 1,000 square metres, was built, as befitting its importance, within the citadel complex itself, and was among the earliest structures built there. In Harappa, the granary was built outside the citadel, but close to it on the north. It was also close to the riverbed, with access from the riverside, indicating that grain was possibly transported to it in boats.

Adjacent to the granary in Harappa is a work area for husking grain, five neat rows of circular platforms built around massive, sunken wooden mortars, in which grain was pounded with long wooden pestles. Eighteen such platforms, concentric rings of baked bricks laid on edge, each about 3 metres in diameter, have been excavated so far, with remains of wheat, barley and husk still sticking in their hollows, and their bricks worn smooth by the bare feet of the workmen who laboured there some four thousand years ago. To the south of this work area, right next to the citadel wall, are two parallel rows of detached, two-roomed workers' barracks, enclosed within a common compound wall. In Mohenjo-daro also there are similar coolie-lines, in the north-west corner of the lower city, close to the citadel.

The grey, joyless regimentation and bleak functionality that mark the coolie-lines also characterise the town planning and domestic architecture of the Indus cities. 'The wide expanse of bare brick structures, devoid of any semblance of ornament ... [bears] in every feature the mark of stark utilitarianism,' comments Marshall. Everything was efficient and well-ordered in the Indus cities, most remarkably so, but there was little scope for artistic flourishes or individual creativity in this bloodless, precision-engineered society. All houses, though they varied greatly in size, were of similar design. 'One house is so like the other,' comments Mackay.

The poor in the Indus cities had to make do with tiny, one or two-roomed tenements, and the very poor, Mackay conjectures, 'did not live in the city at all, but lived outside in daub-and-wattle huts of which no trace remains.' But the merchant princes of the cities lived in palatial mansions of over 300 square metres, with dozens of rooms and several courtyards and entrances. Some of the larger houses were probably occupied by joint families, or were residential-cum-commercial establishments, with business or manufacturing units along the street, and residential quarters at the back, around a courtyard, or on the upper floor, an arrangement clearly identifiable in one of the excavated buildings in Mohenjo-daro. The city probably also had lodges or caravanserais for itinerant merchants, such as the large building that Mackay described as 'some kind of hostel for pilgrims or travellers.'

The Indus houses were designed for clean, comfortable living, but not for luxury or aesthetic indulgence. Even in the residences of the affluent, the house fronts were bare and featureless, with the street doors tucked furtively into side alleys and guarded by watchmen in cubicles at entrances. The blank severity of the facades of houses was not relieved even by windows – though there were windows in the interior walls of houses, there is little evidence of them in the exterior walls; if they were there at all, they were mere slits and were placed high. Walls were covered with mud plaster internally, but seldom externally. Mackay fancies that there could have been carved wood verandas and screens, or ornamental brickwork, on the upper floors of buildings, but such decorative displays seem unlikely and out of character in the Indus cities. Mohenjo-daro and Harappa were essentially burgher cities, and reflect the drabness and parsimony of the middle-class, their homes unpretentious though comfortable.

As in Sumer, houses in the Indus cities were built around courtyards, on two or three sides of which were rooms of varying sizes, including bathrooms, with street doors opening into the courtyard. Animals might also have been kept in the courtyards, for feeding bins have been found there. Baked bricks were generally used for construction, though sun-dried bricks were at times used for internal walls or for raising floor levels. The outer walls of large houses were often about 1.5 metres thick, and were battered, presumably to bear the weight of upper floors. Beam-holes indicating upper storeys have been noted in some buildings, and stairways – usually steep and narrow, with steps as high as 38 centimetres but only about 13 centimetres wide – leading to upper storeys or flat roofs were common. Timber was presumably used extensively in the construction of upper floors, for a considerable amount of charcoal has been found in the debris of the fire-destroyed Mohenjo-daro. Piggott, following Mackay, speculates that 'the flat roofs of houses were covered with bamboo and rush matting coated with mud and earth to form a solid waterproof layer.'

The ceilings of the Indus houses were low, only about 1.8 metres high, as the evidence of beam-holes indicates. But that was enough. The Indus people were not tall – the height of the Mediterranean male was only about 1.6 metres and of the Proto-Australoid about 1.5 metres. Doorways were nearly of the same size as in later Indian homes, about 1 metre wide, though a few were as broad as 2.4 metres, probably because these houses doubled as commercial establishments. Flat timber lintels normally capped doorways, though some were corbelled. Floors were of beaten earth or bricks. Most houses had party walls, but some were separated by a foot of space, which was bricked up at either end for security.

The concern for civic and personal hygiene was a major characteristic of the Indus Civilisation. Nearly all the houses, even two-roomed tenements, had their own bathrooms or bath areas, their floors paved with bricks laid four or five courses thick, using sawed bricks (instead of bricks straight from the mould) so they could be laid close, to keep the floors watertight. For corners, 'L'-shaped bricks were used for a perfect fit. Bathrooms were usually built on the street-sides of houses, with their floors sloping to one side, so water could drain into the public sewerage system or into private soak-pits. The polish of bare feet on bathroom floors gives us a rare and momentary peep into the private moments of Indus citizens.

There is no agreement among scholars about the lavatory system in Indus homes. According to Piggott, privies were 'practically unknown' in Indus cities. Marshall on the other hand thought that there could have been latrines, or at least urinals, on the first floor, from which fluid waste was carried by terracotta pipes in brick casing, a view with which Mackay concurred, adding that the tiny doorless chambers on the ground floor probably served as cesspits for privies. Daya Ram Sahni, one of the contributors to Marshall's report on Mohenjo-daro, claims that in one house he found 'two well-built privies ... the small square platform in front of which was used for ablutions.' And Wheeler reports that 'in some houses a built seat-latrine of Western type is included on the ground or first floor, with a sloping and sometimes stepped channel through the wall to a pottery-receptacle or brick drain in the street outside.'

Water supply to the cities was from wells, which were constructed with the customary thoroughness of the Indus Civilisation, and were lined with wedge-shaped bricks, on which can be seen the grooves cut by the friction of the ropes by which water was drawn. And on the paved floor around the wells are slight, smooth depressions left by water pots. The wells had no parapet around them for safety, but only a coping of a few inches, probably because most wells were quite small, mere pits in fact, some only about 60 centimetres across, so there was little danger of anyone falling into them. Even the larger wells, with diameters of over 2 metres, were probably not hazardous, as they were quite shallow, the water table being high.

The rich had private wells in their houses, but most people used public wells, which were numerous and often placed in blind alleys between two houses. Little clay cups have been found strewn near some of these public wells, which, according to Piggott, indicates the prevalence of the traditional Hindu taboo on drinking twice from the same cup. Little would change in India over the millenniums.

PRIEST-KINGS AND MERCHANT PRINCES

In Mohenjo-daro, at a depth of about 1.5 metres under rubble and alluvium, was found a small but important stone bust of a bearded man, commonly described as the priest-king. He has an air of sullen authority about him, and is dressed in a trefoil-patterned mantle, presumably the regal vestment. This is the only material evidence we have that is directly associated with the Indus rulers, and even here the identification is entirely hypothetical.

The Indus rulers have left their mark on every facet of life in the valley, but have themselves remained anonymous. We are not even certain of their form of government. Hereditary monarchy, however, can be ruled out. Kings are by nature self-exalting, and express themselves in building grand palaces, mausoleums and other monumental structures, of which there is no evidence in the Indus cities. The persistence of uniform citadel architecture in widely separated cities over many centuries also excludes the possibility of royal authority, which is susceptible to individual whims. Moreover, there is no indication of a dominant military presence in the Indus Valley, such as we would expect in a monarchy, the king being primarily a warlord.

There was in fact a surprising absence of emphasis on warfare in the Indus Civilisation, and its military technology was inferior to that of other contemporary civilisations. Though weapons such as axes, spears, arrow-heads and daggers of copper and bronze, stone maces, and baked clay pellets for slings have been found in the Indus Valley, most of them were not made well enough to be effective as instruments of war, and were probably used only for ceremonial purposes or for hunting. Spearheads, for instance, were 'unaccountably primitive in form, thin and broad in the blade without any strengthening midrib, and with a tang instead of a socket,' notes Marshall. There were no swords. Arrows were rare, and there is no trace of any defensive armaments like shield, body armour and helmets. Obviously, military concerns had low priority in Indus society. Kings could not have thrived in such an environment.

With monarchy excluded, the most credible hypothesis about the Indus government is that it was a theocracy, rule by a small endogamous, socially exclusive, priestly class or caste, headed by a priest-king or a council of high priests. The example of Mesopotamia, where priest-kings ruled, also favours this conclusion. It is unlikely that the Indus Civilisation would have had a political system radically different from that of the civilisations in its neighbourhood. 'The lords of Harappa administered their city in a fashion not remote from that of the priest-king or governor of Sumer and Akkad,' comments Wheeler. 'In Sumer, the wealth and discipline of the city-state were vested in the chief deity, i.e. in the priesthood or a priest-king. The civic focus was the exalted temple, centre of an elaborate and carefully ordered secular administration under divine sanction.'

'The texture of the Harappa civilisation has a strongly theocratic tinge,' observes Piggott. The uniformity that Indus society and polity maintained over the centuries, and the relatively effortless and non-coercive enforcement of civic regulations in Indus cities, imply the internalisation of customs, practices and regulations by the people through long habituation, such as usually found in theocracies, in which temporal institutions assume the nature of an immutable cosmic order. This accounts for the passivity and conservatism of Indus society.

Even more puzzling than the nature of the Indus government is the nature of the Indus state. 'The Indus Civilisation,' Wheeler confidently asserts, 'exemplifies the vastest political experiment before the advent of the Roman Empire.' This hypothesis, it is argued, best explains the uniformity of material culture and civic regulations throughout the geographical area of the civilisation, and the near total identity in the layout and architecture of Harappa and Mohenjo-daro, the presumed twin capitals of the empire. But there are equally persuasive arguments against the imperial hypothesis – the Indus domain was too extensive to be ruled effectively by a centralised authority in prehistoric times, given the vast distances involved and the slowness of primitive transportation. It would, for instance, have taken a messenger well over a month to travel from Harappa to Mohenjo-daro. Some scholars have therefore postulated that the region was divided into two (or more) independent city-states, as in Mesopotamia.

There are however difficulties with this concept too. If the Indus Valley was divided into independent city-states, why is there no evidence of conflict between them, as in Mesopotamia, though aggrandisement is a universal characteristic of political authority? Furthermore, how could total uniformity of culture and civic regulations, such as in the Indus Valley, have prevailed in a competitive political environment, that too over several centuries? There was evidently some sort of unified socio-political authority over the entire area of the Indus Civilisation. It therefore seems highly probable that the region was divided into autonomous (but not independent) city-states under the suzerain authority of a priestly caste, which enforced socio-political order and cultural uniformity.

*

The Indus government, whatever its actual nature, was appropriate to the prevailing environment, and its legitimacy was validated by the security and prosperity enjoyed by the people. This prosperity comes as a surprise to the modern visitor in the region, for a good part of the Indus Valley, especially the area around Mohenjo-daro, is today dismally arid, laboriously reclaimed for cultivation through modern irrigation systems. As Piggott graphically describes the scene, immediately to the north of Mohenjo-daro, 'in the dreary country around Larkana, the soil is so impregnated with salt that, drying in the summer heat that rises to 120° [fahrenheit] in the shade, it has a brittle shining crust that crushes beneath the step like a satanic mockery of snow. The whole landscape is whitened, and forms a dead background to the ugly stunted trees and grey-green bushes that stud the plain.'

The scene in prehistoric times was however quite different. Sind was then within the range of the south-west monsoon, and was lush with vegetation, yielding ample surplus agricultural produce to feed the huge populations of its cities. The abundance of water in the region is indicated by the numerous wells in Mohenjo-daro. And it was the prevalence of heavy rains that necessitated the construction of an elaborate drainage system in the city, and required houses to be built of baked bricks, instead of sun-dried bricks vulnerable to water erosion. Indeed, the very fact that baked bricks could be made in vast quantities in the Indus Valley proves that wood for kilns was plentiful in the neighbourhood. Evidently, there were dense jungles around the periphery of the cities at this time, and this is corroborated by the depiction of wild animals like tigers, elephants and rhinoceroses on Indus seals. 'The river Hydrotes (Ravi), the banks of which are covered with dense forest, abound with trees not elsewhere seen, and are filled with peacocks,' notes ancient Greek historian Curtius in his account of Alexander's invasion of India.

The challenge that the Indus people faced was of taming the rivers, not of water scarcity. To deal with this problem, they, we should assume, would have set up, with their usual efficiency and skill, a system of dikes and canals. We have, however, no actual evidence of any irrigation works. Nor do we have much knowledge of the farming methods of the Indus people, for hardly any of their agricultural implements – which were no doubt made of wood, adequate to till the alluvial soil – have survived. But there is evidence that they used the plough, for a ploughed field was discovered by archaeologists under building debris at Kalibangan, and terracotta models of ploughs have been found at some Indus sites. The harrow, however, was probably more commonly used than the plough in the Indus Valley, as noted by Alexander's men in the region in the fourth century BC. 'The land,' reports Strabo, 'while still but half dried, is sown, and though only scratched into furrows by any sort of digging instrument, it nevertheless brings what is planted to perfection and yields excellent fruit.'

The Indus people cultivated a variety of crops – wheat and barley principally, but also pulses, sesame, linseed, and several fruits, as well as cotton. Rice does not seem to have been grown. They also harvested the river, probably the sea too, for fish – a potsherd from Harappa shows a man walking on a riverbank, carrying fishing nets on a pole held across his shoulder. Several animals were domesticated and bred by the Indus people: humped and humpless cattle, buffaloes, goats, sheep, domestic fowl, also perhaps pigs, asses, possibly even elephants. Cats and dogs were kept as pets – millenniums fall away and a diverting domestic incident in prehistoric Sind merges into our own childhood memories when we read that at Chanhu-daro a brick was found 'over which, when soft and unbaked, a dog had chased a cat, both leaving their characteristic foot-prints.'

Farming in the Indus Valley was probably regulated by a centralised authority. Trade and industry certainly were, by standardising weights and measures and systematising production techniques, either by official diktat or by rigid craft and trade conventions. Bricks, for instance, were everywhere made to one ratio – width twice that of height, and length twice that of width – and in three roughly standard sizes, the most common dimensions being about 30 by 15 by 7.5 centimetres.

This standardisation, though it facilitated production and trade, was not entirely a good thing, for it stifled innovation and progress by turning production methods into sacrosanct routines. Not surprisingly, craft technology in the Indus Civilisation, in contrast to its organisational sophistication, was rather backward. Tools like chisels, knives and razors were without the strengthening midrib, and axes were of the simple, flat type, without shaft-holes, despite the proficiency of the Indus people in the techniques of casting and forging. This low level of technology is all the more surprising because the Indus people had access to knowledge of better production methods and designs, such as in Sumer. They chose to ignore these advanced techniques, presumably because they held their own methods as inviolable.

A fair amount of the production in the Indus Valley, in agriculture as well as industry, but especially in industry, was for trade, not for domestic consumption, though the Indus households no doubt produced, as in all pre-modern societies, some goods (cloth for instance) for their own consumption. Even in small Indus settlements there were large crafts industries, whose output exceeded local needs and was meant at least partly for export. Commercial production was well-organised in Indus cities, by concentrating different trades and manufacturing activities in different city zones, and encouraging craft specialisation. A bead factory, where all activities related to bead making were concentrated, has been excavated at Lothal, an Indus trading station in Gujarat. But no major workshops have been found so far in Mohenjo-daro or Harappa, though in Harappa an industrial area for copper working has been found north of the citadel. Craftsmen's residences usually doubled as their workshops, and their families, along with apprentices, constituted the work force, as everywhere in the ancient and medieval world. Probably there was also some slave or bonded labour, at least in public service.

Cotton cloth was clearly a major item of manufacture and trade in the Indus Valley – numerous spindle-whorls have been found in Indus houses, and in Mohenjo-daro archaeologists came across a silver vase with bits of red-dyed cotton cloth sticking to its side. Ivory working also seems to have been an established Indus craft – a couple of elephant tusks have been found among the skeletons of a group of people, ivory workers presumably, overtaken and slaughtered by invaders in Mohenjo-daro. Other common Indus craft products were metal wares in copper, bronze, lead, gold, electrum, and silver; querns, bowls and blades in stone; beads of semi-precious stones, metals, shell, paste and ivory; stone sculptures; pottery; faience products like beads, inlays and seals; stoneware ornaments; terra-cotta figurines, and so on.

Curiously, despite the high demand for baked bricks, no brick kilns have been discovered within the Indus cities; these, as well as pottery-kilns, were probably located outside the cities, to avoid air pollution. Pots, occasionally hand-made but generally wheel-turned, were well made, though lacking in variety and artistry. The Indus people did not use iron – like their contemporaries in the Middle East, they belonged to the Bronze Age, when copper and bronze were the only metals used for making tools and weapons. Household utensils were mostly of earthenware, rarely of copper and bronze, but cutlery was generally of metal, though there were some pieces of stone as well, such as the flake knife of chert. Also in common use were stone dishes, bowls, vases, toilet-boxes and burnishers. Silver and gold were used for ornaments.

Some of these Indus craft products were traded in the Middle East, especially in Sumeria. We do not know when the trade contact between the Indus and Sumerian civilisations began, but by the Akkadian period in Sumer (2370–2100 BC) this trade was well established, and it continued to be active until about the second quarter of the second millennium BC. Several Sumerian inscriptions refer to a city named Meluhha, a port generally believed to be at the mouth of the Indus, but which could very well be Mohenjo-daro itself, which was well placed to command both land

and sea trade. It is significant that most of the Indus seals (used to identify traders and their goods) were found in Mohenjo-daro, as much as 68 per cent, compared to the mere 19 per cent from Harappa, and 13 per cent from all the other sites together.

Trade in the Indus Valley seems to have been dominated by a class or caste of professional merchants, probably the Panis mentioned in the Rig-veda as the 'greedy and selfish' adversaries of Aryans – according to Kosambi, the Indian terms *vanik* (trader), Baniya (trading caste), *pana* (coin) and *panaya* (trade goods and commodities) are derived from their name. It is quite likely that a group of these traders had settled in Sumer, for Indus-style engraved seals and other artefacts have been found there. One sealing even has the imprint of coarse cloth on its back, so cotton was probably a major item of export from India, as in later times – cotton in early historic times was known as *sindhu* (the old name for the Indus) in Mesopotamia. It is not clear what else the Indus people exported to Sumeria – quite possibly wood, ivory, inlay and beads – and it is even less clear what they imported from there, for there is little evidence of Sumerian goods in the Indus Valley. Nor do we know much about the nature of the Indus trade with other regions, though it is likely that, in addition to trade with Sumeria, Indus people traded with other centres of civilisation in the Middle East and Central Asia, as well as with other regions of India.

The Indus people used both land and the sea routes for their long-distance trade. Overland, they carried on extensive trade through Baluchistan, travelling in caravans of pack oxen or donkeys. Ox-carts (clay models of which are common finds at Indus sites) were also extensively used for transport, but mostly on the plains. The prehistoric Indus carts were heavy, lumbering contraptions, with near-solid wheels and a wheelbase of about a metre, and were of the same type as those found in the region in modern times. For personal travel the affluent in the Indus cities seem to have used an *ekka*-type covered trap, drawn by a pair of oxen. It is unlikely that the Indus people had horse-drawn carriages; though bones of horses have been found at a couple of Indus sites, the animal does not seem to have been in common use, and is not represented in any drawing or engraving, except in one doubtful terracotta representation found at a high level in Mohenjo-daro.

For river and sea transport, Indus traders used sailing ships, as Babylonian evidence indicates. But representations of ships are extremely rare in Indus artefacts. There are, however, two engravings – a terracotta amulet and a stone seal – which clearly show ships, with high prow and stern and a cabin in the middle, probably made of bamboo or some such reed. The Indus was a treacherous river to sail on, because of its shifting sand-banks, but there would nevertheless have been considerable river transport at this time between riverine settlements, as well as coastal shipping southward to

Gujarat and westward to Mesopotamia. Harbour facilities were particularly conspicuous in Lothal, where a dockyard and a wharf have been excavated. The dockyard, ingeniously designed with a spillway and a locking device, had artificial channels connecting it to the Bhogava, a tributary of the Sabarmati. Several stone anchors have been found in the dock basin. The wharf, constructed of brick, stretched over the entire eastern side of the town, and had alongside it a high platform on which were warehouses or granaries.

Long-distance trade brought the Indus people into contact with diverse civilisations, but they seem to have maintained these as only business relationships, with no cultural overtones, their ingrained conservatism insulating them against what they probably considered as cultural contamination. This frigidity of the Indus Civilisation has led some scholars to regard it as a fossilised civilisation, and to trace to it, as Piggott has done, the 'innate conservatism of thought that is repeated through the centuries' of Indian history. Piggott overstates the case. 'There is,' observes Wheeler, 'no doubt that the so-called uniformity of the Harappan culture in depth has been exaggerated, and is due as much to archaic methods of research as to any inherent conservatism in the ancient craftsmen.' This comment places the conservatism of the Indus Civilisation in proper perspective, but does not deny it. Progress in prehistoric societies was everywhere imperceptibly slow, but even in such an environment, the conservatism of the Indus cities seems particularly rigid and sterile.

The Indus people evidently had no urge to go adventuring beyond their familiar horizon, and would not even adopt the superior technologies they came across – their own system worked entirely to their satisfaction, so there was no need to trouble themselves with innovations. Being sheltered by the great mountains from much of the racial and political convulsions of Central Asia and the Middle East, they had enjoyed a secure and comfortable life for many centuries, and this induced inertia in them, which in turn led to the calcification of the civilisation. There was no challenge to force change.

The Indus Civilisation remained stagnant during its entire mature phase. There was no significant cultural or material progress during those long centuries, and the only change we notice is decay towards the end. But even in its decay, the basic character of the civilisation does not seem to have changed. Its decay was without decadence. The civilisation just broke down, like old machinery.

GODS OF THE VALLEY

The Indus civilisation carried with it to its grave the key to many of its mysteries. There is no clear evidence even on the Indus religion, even though religion apparently played a crucial role in Indus society. No temple has been excavated at any Indus site. A couple of structures in Mohenjo-daro are thought possibly to be temples, but the identification is highly doubtful. It is also considered possible that the Buddhist stupa of historic times built at the highest (and presumably the most sacred) spot of the Mohenjo-daro citadel mound might be overlying some prehistoric temple, but the possibility is remote. Temples apart, not even any clearly identifiable major religious object has been found anywhere in the Indus region. All this is surprising, considering the (presumed) theocratic nature of the Indus polity, and the prominence of temples in the related Sumerian Civilisation.

Several reasons have been advanced to explain this anomaly: that the temples were built of wood and have perished; that the Indus religion, like the Vedic religion, was based on magical rites and sacrifices, not on the worship of high gods in congregational temples, and so on. None of these explanations are quite convincing. It has also been suggested that the Indus religion was unstructured and was centred on household shrines, but this seems most unlikely in view of the highly regulated and homogenised nature of everything else in Indus society.

The only plausible explanation for the absence of any distinct temple structure in the Indus cities is that the citadel itself was a temple complex, from which the priest-king or a conclave of priests ruled the state. Public rites and religious processions of high ceremony, such as are usually associated with priestly rule, were evidently important in Indus society, and were conducted in the citadel. Processional ways and ceremonial terraces have been identified at the Harappa, Mohenjo-daro and Kalibangan citadels. One Indus seal has been found to depict what seems to be a religious pageant, a file of four persons carrying tall staffs bearing, in succession, a brazier, a unicorn, a banner and an unidentifiable (damaged) fourth emblem. The citadel, writes Wheeler, 'presents an aspect of combined or undiscriminated religious and secular administration.'

The Great Bath in the Mohenjo-daro citadel, it is generally agreed, had some ritual purpose, sacred ablutions perhaps. It could not have been merely for bathing, for most houses in the city had their own bathrooms, and the river was close by as well. Noting this, Kosambi speculates that 'it was part of the ritual for men [in the Indus cities] not only to bathe in the sacred water but also to cohabit with the female attendant representatives of the mother goddess to whom the citadel complex belonged. This is not far-fetched. The temples of Ishtar in Sumer and Babylon had similar practices ...' Perhaps. On the other hand, it could also be that the Great Bath was meant only for ritual purification, and that it signifies that the Indus religion, like later Hinduism, was taboo ridden.

The most tantalising of all the sources of information on the Indus religion are the seals, but these are subject to varying interpretations, as their script remains unread. The one certainty about the seals is that, whatever their function, and whatever the meaning of their inscriptions, the figurative engravings on them are of religious significance. Sculptures and figurines also provide us with further clues about the Indus religion.

Archaeologists have presumed to see some later Hindu deities and practices in the artefacts of the Indus Civilisation. Marshall, for instance, maintains that the three-faced, ithyphallic figure depicted in some Mohenjo-daro seals is 'recognisable at once as the prototype of historic Shiva.' The figure, wearing an elaborate horned head-dress, many strands of necklaces and a girdle, but otherwise naked, sits on a low bench in a typically pyramidal yogic posture, legs doubled up laterally to rest flat on the bench, sole against sole, and arms (laden with bangles up to shoulders) stretched out to rest on knees, fingers drooping. The image, surrounded by many animals and itself of a ferocious visage, could indeed be a depiction of Shiva as Pasupathi, the Lord of Beasts, who is sometimes portrayed with three faces. But such Shiva seals have not been found in Harappa, except for a crude sealing with a central squatting figure, which is considered to be a Shiva representation.

Shiva images are also not found in terracotta figurines, which are predominantly of the type that Marshall identified as the mother goddess. Such goddesses are commonly associated with fertility cults and were widely worshipped in ancient societies. But unlike the big-breasted, broad-hipped Venus figures found all over Europe, the pinched Indus figurines are hardly the fecund maternal type, and are unlikely to have been representations of the mother goddess. These coarsely-made figures, nude except for a girdle around the waist, most of them wearing a 'peculiar fan-shaped head-dress with pannier-shaped appendages,' have been found in large numbers in Harappa and Mohenjo-daro, in nearly every house in fact. They were probably votive figures, or charms to ward off evil, which would account for their crude appearance. Significantly, male terracotta figurines are rare, while, on the other hand, the so-called mother goddess is not represented at all in seals or stone sculptures.

There is good reason to believe that the Indus people were phallus worshippers. The Rig-veda refers to Indra as overrunning a rich 'city with a hundred gates' belonging to the worshippers of the phallus, *sisna-deva*, and this supports the surmise that Shiva (worshipped in Hinduism in the form of the phallus) was a chief deity of the Indus people. The prevalence of fertility cult in the Indus Civilisation is thought to be further indicated by the stylised representations of the *linga* (phallus) and *yoni* (vulva) found at Indus sites. Most of the presumed *lingas* are small, some as small as 2.5 centimetres made of shell or faience, but some are as large as 60 centimetres and made of stone or alabaster. A few are explicitly phallic, but not all the polished cylindrical stones could have been *lingas*, or all the ring-shaped stones *yonis*. Oddly, *linga* and *yoni* were never found together at any Indus site.

The most unusual fertility-cult-related Indus artefact is an oblong sealing found in Harappa, which depicts a nude woman lying on her back, with her legs spread out and bent, and from whose vulva a plant (or 'a scorpion or even a crocodile,' some scholars fancy) issues. Another seal, found at Chanhu-daro, shows, as Allchin describes it, 'a recumbent figure with female genitalia exposed and a sprout emerging from the head; over this prone figure stands a rearing gaur. The beast is shown (uniquely among Harappan seals) as ithyphallic and is evidently about to copulate with the recumbent female.'

Human sacrifice was often associated with fertility cults in the prehistoric world, and this seems to have been prevalent in Indus society as well. A Harappan sealing shows what appears to be a scene of human sacrifice – a man with a peculiarly shaped short sword, somewhat like the one carried by south Indian temple oracles, stands menacingly over a seated woman, who seems to be possessed or in a trance, her hair dishevelled and her arms raised in supplication.

Animals as totems, or as objects of veneration, were important components of the Indus religion. Figurines of animals were probably carried in processions, for some of them were found to have a hole at the base, to attach them to nails or poles. About three-quarters of the Indus terracotta figurines represent animals, mostly the humped bull, but also the buffalo, rhinoceros, monkey, elephant, and so on, and occasionally birds, but never the cow. Many of the animals depicted in the Indus seals and terracottas are mythical or composite creatures; there are also several man-headed animals, bearded and horned. In most primitive cultures, horns were a symbol of divinity, 'a badge ... of superhuman powers,' as Marshall puts it.

Animal form gave man the persona of the animal, and that was considered desirable, for animals were generally more powerful and more beautiful than men.

The most remarkable animal seen in Indus artefacts is the unicorn, found in many of the seals and sealings of Mohenjo-daro. The unicorn – and sometimes the bull and the one-horned rhinoceros – is generally shown with a 'sacred brazier' next to it, signifying its hallowed nature; some seals even show thin lines rising from the brazier, evidently to indicate smoke. The snake was also probably an Indus cult object; it is often represented in pottery paintings, and a carved figure of a snake has been found in Harappa.

Trees or tree spirits were also venerated, and tree motifs are common in Indus seals, especially the pipal, the fig tree commonly held sacred in India. One seal depicts a nude deity, horned and with thick, long plaits of hair, standing between the branches of a pipal tree, being worshipped by a similarly adorned devotee kneeling before it. The ceremony is watched by a man-headed goat, and is attended by a row of seven pigtailed women wearing elaborate headdresses, and, according to Wheeler, 'perhaps engaged in a ritual dance.' The worshipper and the attending women wear sprigs on their heads, marking it as a celebration of vegetal fertility and regeneration.

The vegetable world ever renews itself, and this was a matter of envy and wonder for primitive man. Unable to reconcile himself to his mortality, man therefore invented a life after death for himself. This he did quite early in his history, as evidenced by the high prominence given to burial rituals in most prehistoric cultures. In contrast, the attitude of the Indus people (as in later India too) towards death seems to have been rather casual. Not much is known about their burial customs, and what little is known is quite ordinary and colourless. There was no Pharaonic grandness about the Indus Civilisation, and it built no great mausoleums. Not even any graves with rich burial goods have been found in the Indus Valley. In fact, the Indus graves all seem to have been of the common people. We do not know where the ruling class and the merchant princes were buried. Perhaps they were cremated.

Burial of the whole body was the normal Indus practice, but partial burials of skeletons removed from elsewhere were also known. The only Indus cemetery found is at Harappa, just outside the city limits. Here the bodies, sometimes wearing their ornaments, were buried fully extended, with the head usually to the north, along with a number of pottery vessels, usually about fifteen to twenty but sometimes as many as forty, presumably containing provisions to sustain the deceased in the afterlife. Small, pointed goblets were found in several graves, and in one grave, at the feet of the body, a small pottery lamp and the bones of a fowl. Occasionally, make-up articles like copper mirrors and small rods for applying antimony to eyes were considerately placed in the graves. Just ordinary requirements of ordinary people. There was nothing extravagant about the Indus people, either in life or in death.

The vagueness of evidence about the Indus religion has led to a lot of airy speculation about its influence on later Indian beliefs and practices, and there has been a general tendency to credit to the Indus people all those elements of Hinduism that cannot be directly attributed to Aryans. 'All the material of a religious nature recovered at Mohenjo-daro and Harappa appears to be characteristically Indian ... Iconic and aniconic cults existed side by side, and were just as compatible five thousand years ago as they are in the Hindustan of today,' states Marshall. 'This religion of the Indus people was the lineal progenitor of Hinduism.' And Kosambi asserts that 'there is every reason to believe that a good deal of the Indus art and hieroglyphics are intimately connected with Tantric motifs of Hinduism which first began to be openly recorded about the sixth century AD, having been profoundly secret mysteries till that time.' Some scholars even ascribe to the Indus people the yoga system and the Sankhya philosophy underpinning it, seeing these complex concepts in the tenuous evidence of a few small seals with their undeciphered script and mysterious engravings!

None of these claims can be substantiated. But it seems fair to assume that the Indus religion, like much else in that civilisation, was fairly sophisticated, and functioned at different levels to serve different classes of people according to their cultural needs and mental capacity, as most advanced religions do. And it is quite probable that the Indus civilisation greatly influenced the evolution of religion in India, though what precisely that influence was cannot be proved.

RIGOR MORTIS

It was on the whole a good life in the Indus cities. The people there probably lived a more orderly, more secure, perhaps even less exploited life than in any other prehistoric civilisation. 'Except for occasional floods, there must have been little to upset the humdrum routine of these busy communities of traders,' comments Mackay. Theirs was a life of smug and placid contentment. But archaeologists often also speak of the drab utilitarianism of the Indus Civilisation, its 'competent dullness' which Piggott found 'repellent'. The Indus Valley was a land of plenty, but its culture was barren.

So goes the common view. And this view might be substantially true. But the drabness of the Indus Civilisation can be, and often has been, exaggerated. How can we judge a culture solely by its bare, time-eroded material remains? We know nothing certain about the intangibles of the life of these people, nothing about their dreams and fears, the songs they sang, the stories they told, the lore of their gods and heroes. The literature of the people, which would have recorded such matters, has not survived. We do not even know whether they had any literature.

The Indus people were certainly not joyless automatons. Even the scanty evidence we have indicates that there was music and dance, wine and revelry in the cities. Festive scenes are found depicted in their engravings and figurines. One seal shows a man beating a drum and people dancing, and a male terracotta figurine has something like a tambourine hanging from its neck. There were probably restaurants or taverns in the Indus cities. Some of the large rooms found in prominent locations in Mohenjo-daro, one with a flight of steps to the street and another with a kitchen adjoining it, were thought to be restaurants by Mackay; they had shallow, conical depressions on the floor to hold pots – of liquor?

The Indus people amused themselves with games like dice and marbles. Perhaps they gambled. Stone marbles, several dice and a brick on which rectangles had been incised to mark out a game – with the home square marked with crossed lines – have been found in the Indus Valley. Their dice, made of pottery, were cubical, not oblong as in later India, and the numbers on them were marked differently: one was marked opposite two, three opposite four, and five opposite six, instead of the opposite sides adding up to seven as in modern dice. They also used casting bones, either for play or for divination; these were as common as dice, and were sometimes found in groups of three. Hunting was also a common sport among them, for engravings show men shooting antelopes and goats with bows and arrows. For women, fetching water from the public well was as much a pastime as a chore – at some of the wells, brick platforms were thoughtfully provided for women to sit and chat.

Indus children had numerous toys, mostly made of baked clay – toy men and women; cattle and birds mounted on wheels, some with waggling heads; sliding monkeys with the braking device of a bent perforation to stop it at will by tightening the rope on which it slid; rattles; whistles shaped like birds; models of household articles, of oxen yoked to carts, and so on. A tiny, *ekka*-like cart made of copper, just 5 centimetres high, was discovered in Harappa. Perhaps Indus children also kept pets, for small terracotta cages have been found at some sites.

There was probably not much furniture in the Indus homes, but two models of chairs have been identified among the toys found in Mohenjo-daro, and it is likely that chests of wood, possibly also beds and stools, were common, according to Mackay. But not a single article of their furniture has survived.

Mackay believes that most of the cooking in Indus homes was done in courtyards, though houses also had small kitchens. Cooking was usually done on a raised platform of brick, but large houses had, as in India even in later times, brick channels on the floor to burn firewood under cooking vessels. Saddle-querns and curry-stones to grind grain and herbs, and rolling-pins of pottery and stone, were common kitchen equipment. The staple food of the people consisted of cereals like wheat and barley (but not rice), which was eaten with meat and fish, and was supplemented with fruits, milk and dairy preparations. *Silajit*, a substance commonly used in Indian medicine, was, according to Mackay, identified in Mohenjo-daro.

Little is known about the clothes of the Indus people, but they seem to have dressed differently according to their social status. Most people went virtually naked. Terracotta figurines show women naked except for a short loincloth, men without even that. But the elite, if we are to go by sculptural evidence, wore embroidered robes, which were tucked under the right arm and thrown over the left shoulder. No footwear is shown in figurines or seals, and none has been found by excavators.

Men as well as women wore their hair long. Women usually wore it plaited and tied at the end with a bow, but sometimes they let it cascade loose at the back, or coiled it into elaborate coiffures. Often they wore high headdresses that rose 'fan-like from the back of the head,' as Mackay describes it. Ornamental pins, bodkins and combs of bone and ivory were used to dress the hair, and numerous such pieces have been found in Mohenjo-daro. Men normally wore their hair combed back from the forehead, using a fillet to bind it; at the nape, the hair was either cut short or coiled into a chignon or allowed to fall loose. Occasionally they wore caps. The high fashion among men was to shave the upper lip while keeping a short, clipped beard, as in prehistoric Sumer. A large number of razors of different shapes, some quite small, have been found in the Indus Valley, and they were probably used by men as well as women.

For the Indus people, dressing up meant adorning the body with ornaments, not wearing elaborate clothes. They wore hardly any clothes, but were loaded with ornaments – both men and women wore necklaces, fillets, armlets and finger-rings; in addition, women wore girdles, earrings and anklets, probably also nose-studs. The rich had ornaments of gold, silver, ivory, faience and semi-precious stones, but the poor had to make do with copper, shell, bone and terracotta. Women covered their entire left arm with bangles, usually made of shell, but wore only a couple of bangles on the right (working) arm. Nothing much is known about the make-up they used, but evidently they applied kohl to their eyes, and used mirrors of burnished copper.

In Harappa, a vast jewellery hoard of gold and semi-precious stones, nearly 500 pieces, was found hidden in a hole dug beneath a coolie-line tenement, probably the stash of a master thief. The necklaces and girdles were made of several strings of beads, their rows kept parallel with spacers of bronze and copper. Marshall writes of 'a singularly beautiful necklace ... made of soft green jadeite beads with disks of gold in between, producing the effect of a bead-and-reel moulding, with pendant drops in front of agate-jasper.' A favourite ornament of women in Mohenjo-daro was the necklace made of long tubular beads of cornelian.

Personal hygiene was a fetish with the Indus people. Numerous cakes of baked clay, 4 to 10 centimetres across, were found in Mohenjo-daro, many of them in drains. Some of these probably served the same purpose as toilet paper, for cleaning up after defecation, but others, with a smooth, rounded back, and the front flattened and made rasp-like by pricking it, were clearly flesh-rubbers.

The Indus cities were like highly organised beehives – everything there was spick-and-span and hygienic, all the systems worked with smooth efficiency, and there was a high degree of civic discipline. Too much discipline, in fact. There were no frills, no extravagances. Inevitably, no artistic effervescence either. There was, writes Piggott, 'a dead level of bourgeois mediocrity in almost every branch of the [Indus] visual arts and crafts,' for the artist there had to work within the 'narrow limits of traditional forms, fossilised over the centuries into a rigid, inescapable mental prison.'

There are only a handful of art objects of the Indus Civilisation that are noteworthy – the engravings on some of the seals are brilliant, and a couple of statuettes and a few figurines are of some merit, but that is about all. And these pale into insignificance when compared to the grand accomplishments of ancient Mesopotamia and Egypt. 'Of ornament for ornament's sake there is next to none, and what trifle there is, is not of a high order,' notes Marshall.

The one art form in which the Indus people excelled was in engraving seals. Some of the 'seals', as Marshall thought, were probably used as amulets, but most of them were undoubtedly stamp seals of commercial purpose, which were, notes Piggott, 'pressed directly on to the soft material used for sealing, in the normal manner of a modern seal or signet-ring.' The seals are mostly tiny, ranging from about 1.5 to about 6 centimetres square, and many of them are almost replicas. Apart from brief inscriptions, the seals also bear engravings of men, animals and plants, and these are of considerable interest for what they incidentally reveal about life in the Indus Valley. A few of the seals have complex designs, depicting mysterious rituals or myths. Some engravings, such as of a man grappling with a tiger, attempt to tell stories.

Usually small and square, occasionally oblong or round, but rarely cylindrical, the seals were made usually of steatite, often with a 'perforated boss at the back for handling and suspension.' Their motifs are conventional, and their quality varies, but the best of them, as Wheeler notes, are 'little masterpieces of controlled realism.' Especially impressive are the engravings of the humped and dewlapped bull, which are executed with such verve that, as Piggott puts it, they seem 'monumental for all their miniature size.' In contrast, human figures are depicted in a casual, summary manner.

The skill and finesse evident in the Indus seals are rarely seen in stone sculptures. But these sculptures were undoubtedly of considerable civic importance, as evident from the fact that a large proportion of them in Mohenjo-daro was found in the citadel. Stone for carving was rare in the Indus Valley and had to be brought from great distances, and therefore would have been used solely for special purposes. Very few stone sculptures have been found in the Indus Valley, just thirteen, and most of them are badly damaged or weathered. Two are of uncertain origin. All are small in size. The best known of them is the 18-centimetre-high steatite bust of a stout, heavy-jowled, middle-aged man – often described as the priest-king – wearing an embroidered robe of trefoil design and a smug, faintly disdainful expression. His eyes, long and heavy-lidded, are half closed; his nose is high bridged and prominent, his forehead narrow and receding, his lips fleshy. He wears a spruce, well-groomed beard, with a shaven upper lip, and his hair, parted in the middle and combed back neatly, is held in place by a diadem worn high on his forehead, with a round jewel (now missing) on it directly above the nose. There is a similar jewel on the armlet he wears on his upper right arm. Two holes have been drilled on either side of his neck, probably to hold a metal necklace.

The statue, though found close to the surface in Mohenjo-daro, at a depth of only about 1.4 metres, belongs unmistakably to the Indus Civilisation. But there is some uncertainty about the age of another fine statue, the red sandstone torso of a voluptuously plump young man found in Harappa. It is a tiny piece, only about 10 centimetres high, and a mere fragment, without head or legs or arms, but the subtle and sure realism of its modelling, the tactile delicacy of its contours – the soft swell of its abdomen, the dimpled sensuality of its buttocks – are quite alien to the hieratic formalism of Indus art. Stylistically it looks rather like a Kushana sculpture of the early Christian era, but its sculptural technique – of fitting arms and head separately with metal pegs, and the use of inlay for nipples – as well as the stone used, are unlike that of any Kushana work.

From Mohenjo-daro comes the bronze statue of a nude, Proto-Australoid nymphet, with budding, tumescent breasts and a slender body, possibly a dancer. Her left leg is slightly raised, perhaps, as Marshall thought, to beat time to music, as she strikes a saucy, sullen pose, right arm impudently on the hip, left arm on the flexed left knee, head thrown back. Her hair is dressed carefully, but she is totally naked, except for a short chain with heavy pendants around the neck, a large number of bangles on the left arm and a couple of them at the wrist and elbow of the right arm. The statue, without feet and ankles, and just 11.5 centimetres high, is not beautiful in the conventional sense, but has a strangely sensuous charm.

Apart from stone sculptures, the Indus people made models of animals in faience, tiny figurines of sheep, monkeys and squirrels, 'which at their best and within obvious limitations are little masterpieces of craftsmanship,' observes Wheeler. They are carefully executed, the medium itself compelling care. It is possible that Indus craftsmen were expert wood carvers as well, but none of that work, if there was any, has survived.

Far more common than stone and faience statuettes, in fact ubiquitous at Indus sites, are terracotta human and animal figurines. But all these are crudely made, perhaps reflecting the culture of the common people, and are interesting only for what they tell of the life of the people, not for their artistic merit. About 75 per cent of the terracottas represent cattle, generally humped bulls; most of the rest are of women, but there are also a few masks (probably used as charms to avert evil), several clay models of carts, and suchlike. There are very few male figures in clay. 'The features and general modelling [of human figures] are the crudest; the eyes and breasts are circular pellets, the nose beak-like, and the mouth an applied strip of clay with a horizontal gash,' notes Wheeler. Some of the figurines, especially of the standing women, seem to have been used for burning oil wicks or incense pellets in the pannier-like cups of their headdresses, for they have smoke stains in them.

The Indus pottery too has little artistic merit, and is mostly plain and severely utilitarian. Only a few are decorated, that too in an unrefined, exuberant style, probably the work of untrained commoners. 'They are usually painted in a sprawling, slapdash technique which covers all the available area of the vessel in an irregular mass of foliage and tendrils, among which birds (sometimes peacocks) and less frequently animals take their place,' comments Piggott. 'It is an untidy, luxuriant style, and has nothing of the formalism and sense of precise patterning found in so much of the Baluchistan pottery.'

The lack of creative elan in arts and crafts in the Indus Civilisation was a symptom of its greater malaise of the desiccation of spirit. Indus society was an over-organised society, in which the maintenance of the system had become an end in itself, and the purpose of setting up the system had receded into the background or had been forgotten altogether. Consequently, the system had become sterile, incapable of responding to new challenges, and ultimately ineffectual in serving its basic purpose of sustaining society. The Indus Civilisation was thus reduced to a state of rigor mortis, long before it actually perished in violence at the hand of invaders. The final act was only a *coup de grâce.*

The signs of urban decay were all too evident in the final phase of Indus history. Authority, which had so effortlessly asserted itself for many centuries, became effete, and citizens brazenly flouted civic regulations once held inviolable. Building standards fell, and some of the buildings now encroached into streets. Lanes become choked, zonal regulations were disregarded, and pottery kilns, once kept out of the city, moved in. One kiln was even built right in the middle of a street. The sewerage system collapsed. There was at this time considerable turbulence in the countryside, and people swarmed into the cities, seeking security or livelihood. In this unsettled environment, trade atrophied and agriculture declined, and cities became impoverished and hopelessly overcrowded. Affluent neighbourhoods turned into tenements, as great mansions were partitioned into many small rooms to house the migrants. Law and order broke down, so some streets had to be blocked with thin walls, for security. People began to bury their valuables.

Coinciding with these adversities, but probably long preceding them, occurred certain environmental changes that would slowly turn the fertile lower Indus plain into a wasteland, and destroy the agricultural base of the Indus Civilisation. Strabo quotes Macedonian general Aristobulus as stating that during Alexander's ten-month-long voyage down the Indus in the fourth century BC, 'they saw rains nowhere, not even when the Etesian (monsoon) winds were at their height.' The analysis of pollen deposited in the bed of the now dry Laukaransar Lake by Gurdip Singh has shown that the Indus region went through a major drought around 1700 BC, probably caused by a shift of the monsoon away from the region. Some scholars consider that the deforestation caused by the extensive cutting down of trees to fire the bricks needed for the periodical reconstruction of flood damaged cities like Mohenjo-daro was a major factor in bringing about climatic changes, but this seems to be an exaggeration. There certainly would have been some environmental degradation because of brick-making, but its effect could have been only marginal, for the Indus people often used old bricks for new buildings, and in any case the population of the Indus cities was not large enough to do any great damage to the woodland beyond their immediate periphery.

A far greater cause for environmental changes was the tectonic disturbances that took place around this time. The Indus region, states Strabo on the authority of Alexander's generals, was 'quite subject to earthquakes.' These upheavals seem to have caused major floods in the Indus Valley, for thick layers of silt were found deposited in the upper strata of Mohenjo-daro. The ever shifting course of the Indus would have been another major threat to riverine settlements – the capriciousness of the Indus was noted by Alexander's men a millennium later, and would remain a problem even in late medieval times, as Mughal chronicles show. The long-term effects of the geological changes were even more serious, resulting in the eastward diversion of some of the rivers that flowed through Punjab, Rajasthan and Sind, and the eventual drying up of the Saraswati, leading to the gradual salination of the soil in Sind.

All this happened at a time when the old West Asian civilisations were breaking up, because of the great people movements in the region, which would eventually engulf the Indus Valley as well. The destruction of the ancient cities of the Middle East led to the collapse of the flourishing Indus trade with the region; trade with Sumer, for instance, ceased early in the second millennium BC. In the end it was just one crisis after another for the Indus people. It sapped their energy, snapped their will. So when the decaying cities came under the attack of a youthful new people from across the mountains, most probably Aryans, in the middle of the second millennium BC, they did not have the vitality, nor perhaps the military skill, to defend themselves.

The Indus people were well aware of the imminent menace, for migrant tribal hordes had already swept into Baluchistan long before they debouched into the plains, and refugees from the uplands had been flooding into the Indus Valley for many decades. Rana Ghundai in the Zhob Valley near Quetta was burned down and occupied by invading tribes. In the Indus Valley itself, some of the outlying settlements were abandoned in panic, as people taken by surprise fled for their lives, with women leaving their cooking vessels scattered at fireplaces, for prying archaeologists to mull over a few thousand years later. The fleeing people set up temporary homesteads elsewhere, but these too were abandoned in a short while, as the foe advanced. There was at this time a dramatic shift of Indus population from Sind and western Punjab towards eastern Punjab and Haryana, because of the turbulence in the west and the growing aridity of the lower Indus region. At several places, a new type of pottery, apparently that of the victors, appears over the ashes of the torched Indus settlements. Terracotta models of horses and camels now make their appearance for the first time.

The migrants did not overwhelm the Indus Valley in one fell swoop. It was a slow inundation. The early migrants probably did not even directly attack the urban centres, but occupied the countryside. This was enough to strangulate the Indus cities, as the loss of control of the food-providing countryside made them unsustainable, precisely at a time when people were crowding into them and they needed increased supplies of food.

Presently, it was the turn of the cities. Their threat came from the west. In defence, the fortifications in the north-western corner of the citadel in Harappa were 'reinforced by an additional salient, and the two entrances of the western gate system were wholly or partially blocked,' notes Piggott. But there was really nothing much that the Indus people could do to prevent being overrun. They had no great military tradition and do not seem to have maintained a strong army. All they could do was run for their lives. 'They,' says the Rig-vedic poet with spitting contempt, 'like emasculates with men contending, fled.'

The final onslaught was sudden, at least in Mohenjo-daro, and caught the people unawares as they went about their daily chores. As raiders stormed into the city, the people fled in terror, but many were cut down in the streets. Some were butchered as they huddled in their homes. A lone man was done to death in a lane. A group of nine, five of them children – probably a family of ivory workers, for they had with them two elephant tusks – hid in a shallow pit, but were slaughtered. At a public well, four persons, probably women, were drawing water, when they heard the commotion outside and rushed out, but were butchered, two of them on the steps leading to the street, the other two just outside. Harappa seems to have been spared such a gory end, probably because the people there had fled before the attackers arrived, for the only sign of violence there is a mass of human skulls and other bones of some twenty people found at the outskirts of the city.

As Harappa and Mohenjo-daro, the taproots of the Indus Civilisation, perished, the outlying settlements they nourished also withered, and the unified Indus Civilisation collapsed into fragmented cultures. In some places, pre-urban local cultures replaced the Indus culture. Even Lothal in Gujarat, though far from the path of the ravagers, gradually went into decline, though here there was, as Allchin notes, 'a more substantial continuity of population and culture as a whole.' It was a sad end for a peaceable people, who did not keep their spirit up.

Who were the migrant tribes? Evidence points to Aryans, though they probably drove other people before them into the Indus Valley. Circumstantial, literary and linguistic evidence indicates that Aryans, passing through West Asia, arrived in India, overpowered the Indus people, and took their lands. But there is little material evidence to back up this inference, except perhaps Wheeler's identification of Aryan artefacts in Harappa.

Archaeological evidence on what happened to the routed Indus people is scanty, but Vedic literature, as well as subsequent socio-cultural developments, indicate that in Punjab many of them continued to live subordinate to Aryans, though quite a few of them no doubt fled eastward across the Satluj into the Gangetic Valley. From Sind the people probably fled southward into Gujarat, and from there into the Deccan and southern India. Some of the Indus people seem to have fled even to the west in their blind scramble for safety, probably to take refuge with the Dravidian-speaking people of Baluchistan. As a Rig-vedic hymn has it:

The foolish, faithless, rudely-speaking niggards,
without belief or sacrifice or worship,
Far away hath Agni chased those Dasyus,
and, in the east, hath turned
the godless westward.

Southern India would eventually be the new domain of the Indus people, but for many centuries they would remain prominent in northern India too, where there were substantial Dravidian communities as late as Mughal times, especially in Bihar and Madhya Pradesh, where even today there are Dravidian speaking pockets. But the Indus people generally suffered economic and cultural regression after the collapse of their civilisation, being driven into jungles and kept ever on the move by the advancing waves of Aryans, while Aryans, settling in the fertile northern plains, advanced in civilisation.

There was no cultural affinity at all between Aryans and the Indus people – the very things that distinguished the Indus people were what Aryans found contemptible. Despising the urban lifestyle, Aryans did not even care to occupy the cities they overran. Often they simply set fire to Indus settlements – the Rig-veda repeatedly glorifies Agni for burning down the settlements of the dark-hued people. The Indus cities thus became ghost cities, and in time acquired their present names signifying their blighted fate: Mohenjo-daro in Sindhi and Lothal in Gujarati are said to mean 'the place of the dead'. Slowly the earth moved in to bury the cities and rear giant funeral mounds over them. A photograph of Mohenjo-daro before its excavation shows it as an ugly, leprously eroded, rubble-strewn sandy hillock on a barren, sun-baked plain, with a few spiky scrub-plants huddling in one corner of the mound's lower slope. It is a scene of utter desolation, with absolutely no sign of life anywhere.

Soon there would not be even any memory of the Indus Civilisation. Urban culture would have to be reinvented in India several centuries later. The great achievements of the Indus people in town planning were lost forever, and India would not again achieve that level of excellence until modern times. But while the material gains of the old culture were lost, its intangible residues still pervaded the land, and would in time percolate into Aryan society, despite all the victor's scorn for the ways of the vanquished. And out of that process would emerge the hybrid, polymorphic culture and religion of India, with its complex social structure and myriad gods and beliefs.

Chapter Two

VEDIC INDIA

INDRA'S LEGIONS

The scene now shifts briefly to Central Asia. Down the ages this region has been the epicentre of the human cataclysms that time and again altered the course of history and transformed civilisations the world over. The first of these great eruptions took place around the middle of the fourth millennium BC, when some unknown disturbance – environmental changes perhaps, or just the growing pressure of men and cattle on land – loosened the cluster of Indo-European tribes from their habitat, like an avalanche loosening snow and ice on the mountain slope, and sent them rolling across the Eurasian continent. A virile, dynamic, warlike people, they proliferated and spread rapidly, and within a couple of millenniums dominated most of the land stretching all the way from India in the east to the British Isles in the west.

The location of the original home of Indo-Europeans is a subject of lively and occasionally fanciful debate – it has been claimed, for instance, that they came from the North Pole around 6000 BC, or even that India itself was their home – but the consensus among scholars is that they came from Central Asia, probably from the steppes north of the Caspian Sea at the divide of Europe and Asia.

From Central Asia, some of the marauding Indo-European tribes swarmed westward into Europe and were lost for several centuries in that land without history, but other bands of the race swept south-west and south-east, into Anatolia and Iran, and from there, over several centuries, advanced into the Middle East and India, and overwhelmed the ancient and decaying civilisations there. Of these diverse tribes, one group, those who settled in the Iranian plateau, called themselves Aryans – the only branch of Indo-Europeans known to take that name – and christened their land Ariana, the home of Aryans, later to be known as Iran.

The term Aryan was probably a tribal name initially, but in time it came to mean 'nobleman' or 'master', in contradistinction to the indigenous people whom Aryans subjugated. In the mid-nineteenth century AD the name came to be applied commonly to all Indo-European people, and it then took on a distinctly racist overtone. Since then scholars have been generally reluctant – especially after the Second World War, as a reaction to Nazi ethnocentrism – to ascribe any racial significance to the term. What gives the Aryan people a collective identity, it is argued, is their common language, not their racial make-up.

But this is true only of the modern world. The situation was quite different in early prehistoric times, when people of the same race generally lived together in the same region, spoke the same language and shared the same culture. We should therefore assume that ancient Aryans, apart from having a common language – the proto-tongue that was the mother of Sanskrit, Persian, Greek, Latin, Celtic, Teutonic and Slavic – also belonged to a common racial stock. There was definitely an Aryan race once, a people who were conscious of being ethnically and culturally distinct. But as the race split and the tribes scattered, they, by intermixing with diverse local people, and through the slow process of physical adaptation to new environments, began to diverge genetically and culturally.

In Iran, Aryans split again in the closing centuries of the third millennium BC, and one branch moved eastward into Afghanistan and Baluchistan, and, still pressing on, squeezed through the narrow passes of the Hindu Kush and the Sulaiman Range, and entered the Indus Valley around 1500 BC. India was not, however, a conscious destination for them – they could not have had any clear prior knowledge of the land they were moving into, and were not in any case an organised political power deliberately seeking conquest. Rather, they were a nomadic people wandering into whichever land that sun and water and grass, opportunity and impulse – their own and that of their cattle – took them, without any serious premeditation. There was no planned Aryan invasion of India, only a haphazard migration spread over several centuries. They came in waves that were part of a tidal movement, but each group moved of its own volition. Probably later, as Aryan clans and tribes banded together to occupy particular regions, the migration became more deliberate, though not yet organised enough to be termed an invasion.

The Iranian and Indian Aryans were kinsfolk; they shared a common culture, spoke dialects of the same language, and worshipped common gods like Indra, Varuna, Mitra, Savitr, Soma and Agni. It is however probable that there were already some cultural differences between the two groups when they lived as neighbours in northern Iran, and that was the reason why they parted company and went their separate ways. Once they split, the great mountains kept them segregated, and their divergence widened, as there were major differences in the physical and cultural environment of India and Iran. In time the gods of one group became the devils of the other: the Indian term *deva* for god came to mean demon in Iran, and the Iranian term *ahura* (*asura*) for god came to mean devil in India. This cultural alienation further deepened in the sixth century BC, when Zarathustra swept away the old gods in Iran. Thereafter Agni (Fire) was the only common deity worshipped by the two nations.

In India, Aryans lost all memory of their ancient wanderings through Central Asia, Iran and Afghanistan. There are no references to these adventures even in their earliest literature, the Rig-veda, except a few faint echoes here and there, as in summoning 'Agni from afar,' or in speaking of Indra as 'the hero of our ancient home.' One hymn recalls that 'Indra ... our youthful friend ... led Turvasa, Yadu from afar.' That is about all.

The Rig-veda however reverberates with the sound and fury of the Aryan occupation of the Indus Valley, a savage tale of slaughter and destruction. The chief Aryan victims in India were a people they called Dasas or Dasyus (whose name later came to mean helot, just as Slav came to mean slave in German) and Panis (who were, according to the Rig-veda, rich, deceitful and covetous – probably the dominant trading community in the Indus cities). The natives, says the Rig-veda, possessed great wealth, were 'adorned with arrays of gold and jewels,' and lived in fortified strongholds. Aryans viewed their forts with disdain as *krishna-garbha*, sanctum of the black people, and described the people themselves as dark-complexioned, flat-nosed and 'bull-lipped,' having a strange speech, worshipping strange gods, and performing strange rites.

The differences in physical appearance were an easy means for Aryans to distinguish themselves, but they were also separated by fundamental cultural differences. The term *anasa* (noseless) used to describe Dasas occurs only in one passage in the Rig-veda, and even there it could be, as Sayana interprets the term, a reference to their unintelligible speech rather than to the shape of their nose. In two other passages Dasas are described as *mridhravacha* (of alien speech), a term used for Panis as well. The Rig-veda speaks of Dasas also as *avrata* (without rites), *anyavrata* (of strange rites), *ayajya* (non-sacrificers), *abrahma* (without prayers), *anindra* (without Indra), and so on. They were phallus worshippers, and practised sorcery, a 'godless art' of 'wiles and magic' involving the use of 'magical devices,' and it is against them that the Rig-vedic hymnist invoked the wrath of Agni:

Destroy with your heat the workers of magic;
destroy with your power the evil spirits;
destroy with your flames the idolaters;
burn to nothingness the murderous scoundrels!

We know the story of the Aryan occupation of Punjab only from the point of view of the victor, but on the whole it seems to have been an easy passage for them. On the approach of Aryans, the natives, says the

Rig-vedic poet, 'fled like kine unherded from the pasture, each clinging to a friend as chance directed.' The sedentary and peaceable mercantile people of the Indus cities had no means to withstand the raw ferocity of the predators careering down the mountains. Besides, Aryans had superior military technology. Their warriors stormed into battle in horse-drawn combat chariots – a mode of warfare unknown to the Indus people – and their footmen wielded lethal socketed axes as well as ribbed daggers and swords of bronze, perhaps even of iron, while the Indus people fought on foot using flimsy copper or bronze weapons. The charge of the chariot horse, says the Rig-veda, was irresistible as it swooped down 'as a hungry falcon ... and at his deep neigh, like the thunder of heaven, the foemen trembled in fear.'

The only advantage that the Indus people had over Aryans was that they lived in fortified cities. But the Aryan occupation of the surrounding agricultural lands would have made the cities indefensible, by depriving them of essential provisions. Aryans probably had also acquired some expertise in capturing forts by the time they arrived in India, for the Rig-veda speaks of battering down fortifications 'with deadly weapons.' Indra, the chief Aryan god, aptly bears the proud appellation Purandara, Destroyer of Forts – he 'rends forts as age consumes a garment,' gloats a Rig-vedic poet in an evocative but mismatched metaphor, while another hails him for having 'overthrown the twice ten kings of men, with sixty thousand nine and ninety followers ... Thou goest from fight to fight intrepidly, destroying castle after castle here with strength.'

In this exploit, Indra was aided by Agni, the fire god. 'For fear of thee fled the dark-hued races, scattered abroad, deserting their possessions, when, glowing ... thou Agni didst light up and rend their castles,' extols the Rig-veda. Aryans also demolished dams (or embankments) of rivers to flood fields and cities – Indra, states the Rig-veda, smashed the demon Vritra who 'lay like a great snake across the hill-slope,' so 'the stones rolled away like wagon wheels' and the waters 'flowed over the demon's inert body.'

In the Rig-vedic times the Aryan homeland was Punjab, the tract stretching westward from the Saraswati to the Kabul river. They knew the Himalayas, but not the Vindhyas. Punjab was at this time called Sapta Sindhu, the land of seven rivers. Two of these seven rivers, Drisadwati and Saraswati, later dried up, leaving only five rivers, so the region later came to be known as Punjab, the land of five rivers. The Rig-veda mentions in all twenty-five rivers – Yamuna is mentioned in three passages, but Ganga only once, in a late hymn – but the most sacred river of the early Aryans was Saraswati, which they revered as *sindhu-mata*, the mother river. Sang the hymnist:

Marked out by majesty among the mighty ones ...
guide us, Saraswati, to glorious treasure:
refuse us not thy milk,
nor spurn us from thee.

Vedic Aryans were a rustic people. They had no urban culture, and disdained to occupy the cities they overran. Instead, they settled in scattered villages in Punjab, living in humble cottages of wood and reed. There was little in common between their way of life and that of the Indus people. However, the antipathy and conflict between the two races seem to have been short-lived, as the natives docilely yielded – as Indians invariably would throughout history – lordship to the invader. There is no mention in the later Vedic literature of Aryan battles against Dasas and Panis, but only of the clashes between the various Aryan tribes themselves.

The Indus people lost power and wealth to Aryans, but in some respects they prevailed over their conquerors. Though Vedic literature continued to speak with contempt about the natives and their ways, behind that facade the two races quietly intermingled, each influencing the other, with the Indus people exerting on Aryans the same kind of civilising sway that the Aegeans had on the Hellenic Greeks. This resulted in the modification of every facet of Aryan life, even of their language. Aryan religion especially was transformed in the process. There was also a fair amount of racial interbreeding.

But more than all these, what fundamentally changed the Aryan civilisation in India was the gradual transformation of the economic base of Aryan society, from a primarily pastoral to a primarily agrarian economy. People now abandoned their nomadic ways for a settled life. And in this new environment of relative security of life and abundance of food supply, the Aryan population grew exponentially, and they began to spread out further and further into the subcontinent.

By the end of the second millennium BC, Aryans in India were on the move again. From their settlements in Punjab they advanced east through the sub-Himalayan valleys, initially to settle in the cool highlands north of the Ganga, and then to spread gradually southward to cover virtually the entire Indo-Gangetic Plain. The Ganga now replaced the Saraswati as the sacred river of Aryans – even in the Yajur-veda there is no mention of the Indus and its tributaries.

The Aryan colonisation of the Gangetic Valley was a slow and arduous process, because of the impenetrable virgin forests covering the entire region. The valley was virtually uninhabited at this time, as the pre-Aryan people of India did not have the implements to clear the forest, and even Aryans, despite their superior iron equipment – iron came into common use around this time – could do so only with difficulty. Burning down the forest was easier than cutting it down, and this was favoured by Aryans. 'Agni thence went burning along the earth to the east, and priest Gotama Rahugana and king Madhava Videgha followed after him, as he was burning along,' states the *Satapatha Brahmana*, telling the story of the Aryan occupation of the Gangetic Valley. Fire was the divine collaborator of Aryans, and the Rig-vedic poet sings praises of him as a great martial hero:

Urged by the wind he spreads through dry wood
as he lists, armed with his tongues
for sickles, with a mighty roar.
Black is thy path, Agni, changeless, with
glittering waves, when like a bull thou
rushest eager to the trees.

With teeth of flame, wind-driven, through the
wood he speeds, triumphant like a bull
among the herd of cows,
With bright strength roaming to the everlasting
air: things fixed, things moving
quake before him as he flies.

For a while the eastward advance of Aryans was halted by a river they called Sadanira, the ever-flowing river, probably the Gandak, a northern tributary that joins the Ganga near Patna. This river was hard to cross, and the land beyond it was marshy. 'Even in late summer this river ... rages along; so cold is it, not having been burnt over by Agni,' says the *Satapatha Brahmana*. 'At that time [the land to the east of this river] was hardly cultivated, being marshy, as it had not been burned down by Agni ... Nowadays, however, it is well cultivated, for Brahmins have caused (Agni) to taste it through sacrifices.'

There were no substantial Aryan settlements beyond the Indo-Gangetic plain, though they would later filter into southern India in thin strands through the forbidding Vindhyas. The vast plains of northern India, once a salty lagoon but now a lush and marvellously fertile alluvial basin, was land enough for them. They settled there in prosperous agrarian communities, naming the tracts they occupied after their own tribes: Kuru, Panchala, Kosala, Malla, Chedi and so on. The middle-northern India, the stretch of land from Kurukshetra to Prayag (Allahabad), now became Aryavarta, the abode of Aryans, in the place of Punjab, their Rig-vedic homeland, which they now scorned as *mleccha-desa*, alien country. And in this new home, in the early centuries of the first millennium BC, Aryan culture, synthesising with the Indus culture, mutated and begot Indian civilisation.

THE VEDIC CORPUS

For a long span of well over a thousand years, from the collapse of the Indus Civilisation to the establishment of the Magadhan Empire, we have no material relics for the study of Indian history. There are no ruins of cities, no monuments or inscriptions. The only archaeological evidences for this vast stretch of time are a few tools and potsherds. But this dearth of material evidence is more than compensated for by the vast and marvellously rich body of Vedic literature, a literary legacy unparalleled in any other ancient civilisation. The Vedas, though scriptural works, are a cornucopia of data on life in ancient India.

There are however no dateable events in Vedic literature, and the dates of the texts themselves are uncertain. A major problem in dating Vedic literature is that, for all its immense volume, it was entirely composed and transmitted orally, and was not written down for very many centuries. Aryans had no script when they arrived in India – there is no mention of writing in the Vedas, Brahmanas or Upanishads – and it is not known when they actually took to writing. It is likely, according to Keith, that they acquired this art sometime soon after 800 BC, but Buhler thinks that they did so only as late as 500 BC. What is certain is that they had developed a sophisticated script of their own – the Brahmi, from which all Indian scripts are derived – long before the Mauryan times, for Asokan inscriptions of the third century BC show long familiarity with writing. The original source of the Brahmi is unknown. Possibly, as some hopefully maintain, it was derived from the Indus script, or, more probably, it was based on an early north Semitic (Phoenician) script. We cannot be certain.

If the script was indeed derived from the Semites, Indians transformed it completely, elaborating the twenty-two borrowed Phoenician symbols into the forty-six letters of the Brahmi script, and arranging them, as Macdonnell observes, 'in a thoroughly scientific method, the simple vowels (short and long) coming first, then the diphthongs, and lastly the consonants in uniform groups according to the organs of speech with which they are pronounced. Thus the dental consonants appear together as *t, th, d, dh, n,* and the labials as *p, ph, b, bh, m* ...' It is, Basham states, 'the most scientific script in the world.'

The Aryan writing materials were birch bark, leaves of the birch tree, and palm leaves. As these were perishable, Indian manuscripts older than the fourteenth century AD are extremely rare. The oldest surviving manuscript, a fragmentary Pali text on birch bark found in a monastery in Taxila, is not much older than the fifth century AD, which is also the approximate date of the oldest extant Sanskrit manuscript on birch bark. The earliest known palm-leaf Sanskrit manuscript belongs to the sixth century AD. Hsuan Tsang, the Chinese Buddhist pilgrim who was in India in the seventh century AD, saw palm leaves being commonly used for writing everywhere in India, but their use had obviously begun many centuries earlier, as evidenced by a copper-plate inscription of the first century AD shaped like a palm leaf. Occasionally, cotton or silk, or thin strips of wood or bamboo were used for writing, while important documents were inscribed on copper plates. Parchment was never used for writing in India. Paper came into use only in the thirteenth century.

To prepare for writing, the palm leaf – usually the leaf of the talipot palm – was dried, cut into even strips, rubbed smooth and given a coat of size. The inner bark of the birch tree was also similarly prepared. A neat round hole was made at the centre of the leaves – for large books, two holes at either end – to tie the leaves together. The book was bound by placing the manuscript pile between two thin strips of wood (sometimes lacquered and painted) with holes matching those of the leaves, and tying them together with a thread drawn through the holes. The book was usually kept wrapped in a coloured or embroidered cloth. Ink (*masi,* made from lampblack or charcoal) and reed pen (*kalama*) were used for writing in northern India, but in the south a fine point stylus was used to scratch letters, which were then rubbed over with powdered lampblack or charcoal. The earliest specific mention of the use of ink in India is in a second century BC inscription at a Buddhist relic mound, but probably it was used as early as the fourth century BC, as ancient Greek sources indicate.

Even after Indians acquired the art of writing, the Vedas were not written down for many centuries. The priestly class stoutly opposed the transcription of the Vedas, in order to protect their monopoly of sacred knowledge and to prevent the texts from falling into the hands of the lower castes. It is not known when these works were first reduced to writing, but some texts at least were available as manuscripts in medieval times and were studied by Muslim scholars; some were even translated into Persian, as Mughal prince Dara did with the Upanishads. Presumably, in ancient India too there were violations, or attempted violations, of the injunctions against writing down the sacred texts, for the *Mahabharata* warns that those who commit the Vedas to writing would be condemned to hell, a threat that would not have been necessary if there was no danger of the rule being breached.

But such transgressions, if any, were effectively suppressed. For well over two thousand years, the voluminous Vedic literature was transmitted entirely by word of mouth. Yet it was, in an astounding feat of mnemonic ingenuity and discipline, preserved in its original form by generations of Brahmin scholars. Unlike the legends and tales of the Puranas and Epics, which were much altered and added to in the course of time, no liberties were taken in transmitting the Vedas, as the scriptural nature of their contents – hymns, prayers and ritual prescriptions – ensured their inviolability.

Extraordinary precautions, involving complex and laborious learning processes, were taken to safeguard the purity and correctness of the Vedas. The texts were often memorised in five different ways – first, in their given form, as sequential words making verses or sentences; then each word separately in its independent form, by a routine called *pada-patha*; thirdly, as overlapping pairs of words (*karma-patha*: ab, bc, cd ...); fourthly, in a braided form (*jata-patha*: ab, ba, ab ...); and, finally, in a complex braided form (*ghana-patha*: ab, ba, abc, cba, abc ...). In addition to all this, cross-reference manuals were provided to check the correctness of what had been learned – *Pratisakhya Sutras* that showed 'exactly all the changes necessary for turning the Pada into the Samhita text,' and *Anukramanis* (indices) that listed the contents of the Rig-veda under various headings, and furnished 'calculations of the number of hymns, verses, words and even syllables' in the book.

These elaborate and diligent methods assured that the Vedas were, through endless repetition, etched in the memory of the learner as indelibly as words engraved on stone by the endless tapping of the chisel. Not only was it essential to remember the text correctly, but it was also of cardinal importance to pronounce the words precisely, for their very sounds were believed to have 'magical significance that could be varied only at the peril of the individual reciter.' States the *Mahavagga*, an ancient Buddhist text: 'The Brahmins of today chant over again and repeat, intoning or reciting exactly as had been intoned or recited.' Speech, *vac*, according to the *Taittiriya Brahmana*, was a sacred faculty, which had to be revered as 'the firstborn of truth, the mother of Veda.' Says the Rig-veda: 'When ... men first sent forth the earliest utterance of speech, giving names to things, then was disclosed a jewel treasured within them, most excellent and pure.'

To forget what was learnt was considered by ancient Indians a sin as grave as the murder of a friend or a Brahmin. The very first hymn of the Atharva-veda is for the retention of sacred learning:

Come again, lord of speech,
together with divine mind;
lord of good, make it stay
in me, in myself be what is heard.

Yet, despite all the reverential care taken to prevent errors in transmitting the Vedas, we cannot assume that no one ever made a mistake in learning them. It was inevitable that the intrusions of temper, mood or illness, of the teacher or the learner, would occasionally vitiate Vedic teaching and learning, and that fallible human memory would in some cases scramble the stored data. The puzzling obscurity of many Vedic passages, even in the midst of simple hymns, cannot all be due to the peculiarities of the original composition, but must be at least in part due to faulty learning and reproduction. But apparently these corruptions were confined to the early evolutionary stages of the Vedas. Once they settled into their sacrosanct scriptural forms, there were no further changes over the centuries. In the case of the Rig-veda, for instance, when it was finally written down, 'the readings of the different manuscripts were found to have been preserved perfectly, syllable for syllable the same,' notes O'Flaherty.

The corpus of Vedic literature consists primarily of the four Vedas (the Rig, Sama, Yajur and Atharva Vedas) and the Brahmanas (expository ritual texts attached to each of the Vedas, 'dealing with the minutiae of sacrifice'). These are called *sruti* (heard: revealed) texts, and to these are commonly added the Aranyakas and Upanishads, metaphysical treatises. Supplementary to these are the *smriti* (remembered: traditional) texts comprising the Sutras and Sastras, which explain the scriptures and prescribe social norms and family rituals. And finally, there are the Vedangas (Limbs of the Vedas), the background studies required for the proper understanding and practice of Vedic religion – phonetics, metrics, etymology, grammar, astronomy and instructions about the correct performance of sacrifices. To this body of sacred literature it is convenient to add the Epics (*Ramayana* and *Mahabharata*) and the Puranas (Olden Tales), even though they have numerous later interpolations and are of varying sacredness.

None of these works can be precisely dated. There are no real synchronisms in the Rig-veda by which the date of its composition can be determined, so Max Müller used a 'sort of philological dead-reckoning' to assign the text to 1200–1000 BC. Others assign a broad 500 years for its composition, the period between the arrival of Aryans in Punjab around 1500 BC and their advance into the Gangetic Plain around 1000 BC. In all likelihood, the text was given its final form towards the end of this period, when Aryans were living along the upper course of the Saraswati south of Ambala.

The Yajur and Sama Vedas were compiled in the succeeding couple of centuries, and after that the Atharva-veda. The Brahmanas are thought to have been composed between 800 and 600 BC, and the earliest Upanishads towards the end of this period. The *Mahabharata* got its final form only around the fourth century AD, though it contains a good amount of material that is many centuries older. The oldest portions of the *Ramayana* were probably composed in the sixth century BC, but much matter was added to it later. The Puranas, like the Epics, had long gestations, beginning in the pre-Christian era and going on until about the fifth century AD. The Sutras were probably composed between the sixth and second centuries BC, but they also contain later interpolations; the Sastras belong to the early centuries of the Christian Era.

The term *veda* means knowledge – the Vedas are books of knowledge, not knowledge in the common sense of the term, but sacred knowledge, such as of hymns, chants, rituals and magical formulas. They are liturgical works meant for the use of priests, not for general edification. Of the four Vedas, the oldest and the most sacred is the Rig-veda, a book of hymns to be recited at rituals. The Yajur-veda deals with sacrificial formulas; the Sama-veda is a book of liturgical chanting, while the Atharva-veda is a book of charms, prayers and spells. The first three Vedas deal with high rituals, and are, as Bloomfield observes, the three parts of a trio 'whose melody is carried by each in turn.' The Atharva-veda is altogether different in content and purpose – it is not a book for high priests, but for shamans dealing with the everyday problems of man.

The Rig-veda is a compendium of 1,017 primary and 11 supplementary hymns, making a total of 1,028 hymns. The number of stanzas in the hymns varies from three to forty-eight, and there are in all nearly 154,000 words in the Rig-veda. The hymns are in fifteen different metres, seven of which are frequent, with three of the metres accounting for about four-fifths of all stanzas. A favourite metre of the Rig-vedic poet was Gayatri, consisting of three lines of eight syllables each, in which was composed the hymn that bears the name of its metre:

Tat Savitr vareniam
bhargo devasya dhimahi
dhiyo yo nah pracodayat –

Let's reflect on the divine
splendour of Lord Savitr,
so he may quicken our minds.

The hymns of the Rig-veda are arranged in ten books (*mandalas*), but only the ninth book has a unity of subject, the Soma sacrifice. The Soma hymns were, it would seem, originally scattered in the preceding books, but when the Rig-veda was finally collated, these hymns were taken out of them to make a separate, exclusive Soma book. The closing book, the tenth, was evidently composed last, for it shows familiarity with the other books and is linguistically somewhat different; it also marks a slight shift in Aryan religious concerns by entering into cosmogonic and philosophical speculations. There are some repetitions in the Rig-veda – stanzas eight to eleven of the second hymn of the seventh book, for instance, are identical with stanzas eight to eleven of the fourth hymn of the third book. Nearly half the Rig-vedic hymns are addressed to just three deities, Indra, Agni and Soma, so there is a good amount of duplication of images and ideas in them.

The Rig-veda is held to be a revealed text, and hence immutable, but nowhere does it speak of itself in those terms. In fact, the Rig-vedic poet calls himself a *karu*, meaning labourer or artisan, and speaks of his work as *taksh*, meaning 'to hew'. The text certainly was not originally considered unalterable, and many alterations, additions and deletions of hymns were made in it before it took its final hallowed form. The evidence of this is in the Rig-veda itself, which speaks of ancient hymns and later additions:

With sacrifice and wish have I brought Indra ...
Him magnified by ancient songs and praises,
by lauds of later time and days yet recent.

Tradition attributes the compilation of the Vedas to Veda-vyasa, but this appellation is more a descriptive title (vyasa means compiler) than a real name. Veda-vyasa is certainly a mythical figure, but some sage, or, more probably, a group of sages did indeed perform the task attributed to him, and they no doubt exercised their editorial discretion in selecting the hymns. The Sakala text they produced came to be accepted as definitive, and it is the only full text of the Rig-veda that exists today. But even after the text was finalised, there were evidently attempts to rework the hymns, for the *Satapatha Brahmana* specifically warns that the bid by some to alter the text was unacceptable. At one time there were probably several versions of the Rig-veda, as indicated by the existence of two fragmentary texts, the Valakhilya (eleven hymns, which are inserted in the eighth book of the Rig-veda as supplementary hymns) and Bashkala (thirty-six hymns, most of which are, says Ghosh, 'spurious fabrications, inserted in various places in the Sakala text'). In the sixteenth century AD one Raghunandana is said to have forged a passage into the Rig-veda to justify sati.

Who were the Vedic poets? Four of the ten books of the Rig-veda – the first, eighth, ninth and tenth – are compilations of hymns by diverse sages. The other six books are each attributed to a different sage, like Vasistha, Visvamitra and so on, and were presumably composed by them and their descendants over several generations. They are clan books. Not all these sages were Brahmins – the entire third book of the Rig-veda, for instance, was composed by the family of Visvamitra, a Kshatriya. The information about the sages and their patrons is found in the Rig-veda itself, in the *dana-stutis*, hymns in praise of the munificence of patrons. Of the mode of composition of the hymns, the Rig-veda says:

> *The sages fashioned the word in their mind,*
> *sifting it as with sieves the corn is sifted ...*

The Rig-vedic hymns 'are not simple ballads of primitive pastoral tribes,' comments Iyengar, but complicated and designedly literary compositions of the sacerdotal class, based on well-defined metrical schemes of an elaborate and fully developed system of poetics. They use an 'artificially archaic' language, which Macdonnell describes as 'the scholastic dialect' of the priestly class. It was not the tongue of the common people. What this language was called in Vedic times is not known, but after it was stereotyped in the fourth century BC by Panini, the great grammarian of India, it came to be called Samskrta (Sanskrit), meaning a synthesised or refined language, as opposed to Prakrta (Prakrit), the language of commoners. The term Samskrta occurs for the first time in the *Ramayana.*

Not only the language but even the literary style of the Rig-veda is peculiar. 'In the hymns,' notes Piggott, 'the transition from the more or less literal to the wholly metaphorical is often sudden, and frequently almost imperceptible.' Similes abound. One Vedic poet speaks of having 'adorned his song of praise like a bride for her lover.' There are also, as O'Flaherty points out, numerous cognitive paradoxes in the Rig-veda – such as: Aditi gave birth to Daksa, and Daksa gave birth to Aditi – and 'in places the metaphors are incomplete or jagged, the language elliptic or dense ... Not only is each hymn a separate statement ... but each verse stands on its own and often bears no obvious relationship with the verses immediately preceding and following it; indeed, each line of two-line verses – and sometimes each half-line – may contain a thought not only grammatically distinct from what surrounds it but different in tone, imagery, and reference.' The Vedic poets often composed under the psychotropic influence of Soma, the sacred drug of ancient Aryans, and this perhaps accounts for some of the oddities of the text. Prays Visvamitra in a Rig-vedic hymn addressed to rivers:

Stop in your course a moment, O true ones,
listen to my Soma-sweet speech.

Poetry works best through the free association of ideas and images, but the passage of time snaps these links. Many of the Vedic hymns therefore seem to the modern reader to be inane or nonsensical. Ralph Griffith, the translator of the Rig-veda, speaks of 'the intolerable monotony of a great number of hymns ... Many hymns are dark as the darkest oracle ... there are whole verses which ... yield no sense whatever ...' Max Müller makes the same point: The Rig-veda is 'sometimes true, genuine, and even sublime, but frequently childish, vulgar and obscure.' It is also endlessly repetitive, though this would not have mattered in its original cultural context, for the hymns were not meant to be read one after the other, but to be selected and chanted at particular religious rites. As for their banality, that is to be expected in any ancient religious text, and is counterpointed, in the Rig-veda, by a few hymns of great lyrical beauty and profound thought.

The Rig-veda is not today an easily accessible work. In fact, it was not easily accessible even in ancient times, for many of its words had become obscure within a short time after its compilation, perhaps within a couple of centuries, because of the rapid changes in Aryan language at this time. Etymologists then had to grope for the meanings of these hazy words. The earliest known exegetical work on the Rig-veda is of Yaska in the fifth century BC, but Yaska himself acknowledges that he had seventeen predecessors. If Yaska's figure is right, we should assume that the process of investigating Rig-vedic etymology began in the ninth century BC, soon after the final compilation of the text.

The explanations of obscure Vedic verses provided by ancient scholiasts are often contrived, forcing 'elaborately metaphorical interpretations on the misunderstood original,' as Piggott puts it. Further, the commentators at times contradicted each other or gave inconsistent meanings to words in different places in the same commentary. Even Sayana of Vijayanagar, who wrote the voluminous and definitive commentary on the Rig-veda in the fourteenth century, was guilty of these faults. One of Yaska's predecessors, Kautsa, even questioned the very value of the exegetical exercises, asserting that 'the science of Vedic exposition was useless, as the Vedic hymns and formulas were obscure, unmeaning, and mutually contradictory.'

As literature, the most appealing section of the Rig-veda is the seventh book (attributed to Vasistha) which has a broad emotional sweep and a pleasing unity of tone. But there are several evocative hymns in the other books as well, such as these lines in the tenth book:

Aranyani, spirit of the forest,
who seemest to vanish at sight,
How is it that thou seekest not the village?
Art thou not afraid?

When the grasshopper replies
and swells the shrill cicada's call,
Seeming to sound with tinkling bells,
the Lady of the Wood exults ...

Here one is calling to his cow,
another there hath felled a tree:
At eve the dweller in the wood fancies
that somebody hath screamed.

The goddess never slays, unless
some murderous enemy approach.
Man eats of savoury fruit and then takes,
even as he will, his rest.

Such delicacy of sentiment as in this hymn is rare in the Rig-veda, for it is a liturgical, not a literary work. But even as sacred chants, not many of the Rig-vedic hymns are inspiring. This is hardly surprising, for the Rig-veda is, after all, the work of a nascent civilisation, which would take several more centuries to attain maturity. The hymns, all except a handful of them, do not pertain to spiritual matters at all, but to mundane concerns of a rather basic nature. Some of the hymns, as B.K. Ghosh writes, are of 'extreme obscenity,' and are so explicitly and unabashedly sexual that they shock even the modern reader.

For the believer, none of this matters. They see in the Rig-veda only the exalted spirituality they wish to see in it. Indeed, the very ambiguity of many Rig-vedic passages has prompted scholiasts to read into them diverse super-subtle notions through fantastic intellectual contortions and by projecting backward into them the ideas of much later ages. This is vanity. The contention that the Vedas cannot be understood just by the sense of their words is hardly tenable. The direct meanings of the Vedic hymns, wherever they are lucid, are quite simple, and perfectly match the culture of the ancient people who composed them. To attribute transcendental metaphysics to the hymns is to impose on them a spirit that is not truly their own.

*

Around the time that the Rig-veda received its final form, Aryan tribes moved a short distance south-eastward from the banks of the drying Saraswati, to settle in the region of Kurukshetra along the Yamuna. In this new setting, the Vedic priests in their professional enthusiasm (and also, no doubt, in their eagerness for material advancement) elaborated the rather simple Rig-vedic rites and sacrifices into an incredibly complex ritual system. This in turn led to the composition of specialised liturgical texts – the Yajur and Sama Vedas – by extracting, embellishing and rearranging a number of hymns from the Rig-veda, and by adding some fresh material to them, to serve the needs of the new sacrifices.

Of the two new Vedas, the Yajur-veda is a manual of sacrificial prescriptions, built on a grid of Rig-vedic hymns by adding a few new hymns of its own and a number of prose mantras called *yajus*, from which this Veda derives its name. The mantras – to be muttered inaudibly and in a particular manner during sacrifices – constitute about half of the Yajur-veda. It has two major recensions, Krishna and Sukla. The Krishna (black) version is a miscellany of hymns, mantras, explanations and sacrificial instructions, while the Sukla (white) version, a later compilation, separates explanations and instructions from the text and organises them in a Brahmana appendix. The Yajur-veda has precedence over Sama-veda in scriptural hierarchy, but historically it is the later work, and portrays a society that has evolved an incipient caste system and has made several advances in technology and crafts. It is a work of considerable value to historians, because of the incidental light it throws on Vedic society by its descriptions of the arrangements for sacrifices.

The Sama-veda – a book of chants and melodies to be recited by Udgatr (chanter) priests at Vedic sacrifices – on the other hand yields no social or historical information whatever, and is of interest only to the specialist in Vedic rites and music. It has hardly any original material in it, as all but 99 of its 1,603 stanzas are taken from the Rig-veda. But the Rig-vedic hymns, as Griffith notes, are so 'altered [in the Sama-veda] by prolongation, repetition and insertion of syllables, and various modulations, rests, and other modifications' that they are hardly recognisable. These alterations resulted in the total loss of the sense of the hymns, but that did not matter, for the value of the chants is in their form, not in their substance. Their words, like musical notes, are only keys to sounds.

In contrast to the first three Vedas, which belong together, the Atharva-veda is in a class by itself. Consisting of 730 hymns in 20 chapters, it has a total of about 6,000 stanzas, of which some 1,200 are taken from the Rig-veda. About a sixth of the text is in prose. The distinctiveness of the Atharva-veda is that, while the other Vedas deal with grand public rituals, its own concern is with domestic rites and the mundane problems of everyday life, though it also has a few philosophical and mystical hymns similar to those in the tenth book of the Rig-veda. 'A heterogeneous collection of spells ... [the] most salient teaching [of the Atharva-veda] is sorcery,' comments Macdonnell, 'for it is mainly directed against hostile agencies, such as diseases, noxious animals, demons, wizards, foes, oppressors of Brahmans.' The Atharva-veda does not, unlike the other Vedas, work through prayers and sacrifices to gods, but through sympathetic magic. From the historian's point of view, this is the most valuable of the Vedas, for reconstructing the lifestyle of the Vedic people.

Because of its occult practices and plebeian concerns, the Atharva-veda was not initially accorded canonical status in Indian religion, and many early texts refer only to three Vedas – the Yajur-veda, for instance, does not notice the Atharva-veda at all when it speaks of scriptures:

I take refuge in the Word as the Rig-veda
in the Mind as the Yajur-veda,
in the Breath as the Sama-veda ...

The Atharva-veda gained recognition as a scripture only around the sixth or fifth century BC; the *Mahabharata* fully recognises its status, and the Puranas always speak of the four-fold Vedas.

With the passage of time and the growing complexity of rites, the significance of many Vedic sacrificial practices became obscure, so it became necessary to have guides to explain their mysteries and to interpret the relationship between the sacred texts and the rituals. This need was met by the Brahmanas, a collection of voluminous prose texts, some with different recensions, all orally composed and transmitted and appended to the different Vedas. Of these, six are of importance, the best known of them being the *Aitareya Brahmana* of the Rig-veda and the *Satapatha Brahmana* of the Yajur-veda.

The Brahmanas are the oldest prose works in Indo-European literature. With them, pedagogues took over the formulation of religion from seers and poets, and they diverted their creative energies from composing sacred poetry to the elaboration of sacrificial ceremonies. By doing so, they created, as Macdonnell notes, 'a ritual system far surpassing in complexity of detail anything the world has elsewhere known,' and earned for the Indian priestly class power and prestige as in no other civilisation.

The Brahmanas give minutely detailed directions about when and where and how to perform particular rituals, about the setting up of sacrificial fires, the deities to be invoked, the Vedic hymns and the ritual formulas to be chosen, the oblations to be offered, the utensils to be used, the priests to be engaged, the fees to be paid to them, and so on. There are also some metaphysical speculations in them. To justify these surmises and ceremonial specifications, the Brahmanas offer various occult, interpretative or etymological explanations, which often turn out to be either unverifiable or false. Or they offer mythical stories as proof. As Keith comments, the authors of the Brahmanas interpreted everything 'at their pleasure.' Typical of the Brahmanas is this exposition of transubstantiation in the *Satapatha Brahmana*: 'When it (the rice-cake) still consists of rice-meal, it is the hair. When he (the priest) pours water on it, it becomes skin. When he mixes it, it becomes flesh ... When it is baked, it becomes bone ... and when he is about to take it off [the fire] and sprinkles it with butter, he changes it into marrow.'

The Brahmanas are priestly fancy gone berserk. These works, instead of clarifying Vedic practices, often make them more obscure, by their 'pedantic and cruel pursuit of detail,' and over-elaborate, involuted and ponderous narrative style. As Macdonnell says in a harsh but essentially valid comment, the Brahmanas 'form an aggregate of shallow and pedantic discussions, full of sacerdotal conceits, and fanciful, or even absurd, identifications.'

In time the literature on Vedic rituals became so voluminous and scattered that new guides had to be prepared to present sacrificial procedures and traditional practices in a succinct and systematic manner. These handbooks, called Sutras (clues), were composed between 500 and 200 BC, and fall into two categories – the *Sruta-sutras* attached to the four Vedas and dealing with the high rituals performed by priests, and the *Grihya-sutras* of rites performed by the householder.

The Sutras are matter-of-fact works with no literary affectations, no commentaries or speculations, but are so precise in their descriptions that 'it is possible,' says Macdonnell, 'to reconstruct from them various sacrifices without having seen them performed.' There was however a problem with the Sutras – while the Brahmanas erred in being over-elaborate, the Sutras erred in being over-concise, 'almost algebraic [in their] mode of expression.' It has been said that 'the composers of grammatical Sutras delight as much in the saving of a short vowel as in the birth of a son.' The brevity of the Sutras that facilitated their memorisation also made it necessary to have commentaries to explain their formulas, adding to the incredible prolixity of Vedic literature.

By far the most valuable sources of information on life in ancient India are the two epics, the *Ramayana* and *Mahabharata*, but the material in them has to be used selectively, as they are overlaid with encrustations of much later periods. Some of the social and political conditions as well as religious beliefs and philosophical concepts that the epics deal with belong to the post-Mauryan period, and many of the details of incidents in them are clearly fictional. But the central events of the epics probably did take place in Vedic times, and it is possible that many of the heroes mentioned in them have some historical basis. It is however impossible to cull facts from fiction in them, or to assign their cultural data to any specific period.

The epics are not the original works of particular authors. Their core stories probably had their origin in bardic lays, but that beginning was like the trickle at the source of a great river. Over time the epics swelled prodigiously in size, as numerous folk tales, religious notions and philosophical concepts flowed into them from the evolving society, like tributary streams draining into a river from a vast catchment area. The *Ramayana* however remained a fairly cohesive work, and is traditionally designated as a *kavya* (poem), while the rather gallimaufric *Mahabharata* is called an *ithihasa* (history). Both the epics were composed orally, and for several centuries transmitted orally. And, being oral compositions, they – especially the *Mahabharata* – lack literary rigour, clarity and directness. They meander on, digressing endlessly, and their language is 'obscured by a cloud of qualifiers and rhetorical figures,' as Goldman puts it.

The stories of the epics are set in a time in which Aryan tribes had moved into the Gangetic Plain, and had begun to coalesce into kingdoms. Of the two epics, the *Mahabharata* contains the oldest material. The work probably began to take form around the ninth or eighth century BC, but its oldest preserved portions are hardly older than 400 BC, and fresh materials continued to be added to it even as late as AD 400, by which time the 24,000 stanzas of the original poem grew into nearly 100,000 stanzas of (usually) thirty-two syllables, a mammoth work that is nearly eight times as long as the *Iliad* and *Odyssey* combined, and is the longest poem in world literature. A few portions of the epic are in prose, and the whole text is organised in eighteen sections (*parvans*).

The locale of the story of the *Mahabharata* is the Doab, the tongue of land between the Yamuna and the Ganga, and its central event is an eighteen-day war between cousins, the Kauravas (headed by Duryodhana) and Pandavas (headed by Yudhishthira), for the throne of Kurukshetra, an extensive kingdom in the upper Doab, with its capital at Hastinapura on the right bank of the Ganga, about 90 kilometres north-east of Delhi. According to tradition, the Kurukshetra war took place in 3102 BC, but that clearly is impossible, as Aryans were not even in India at this time. The war probably took place sometime between 1400 and 800 BC, most likely towards the end of this period, as indicated by the archaeological evidence from the flood-destroyed Hastinapura.

Fortune initially favoured Duryodhana, and even when he was eventually obliged to give half the kingdom to Yudhishthira and allow him to set up a separate capital at Indraprastha (modern Delhi), he managed to win it all back in a game of dice, and send his cousins on a thirteen-year exile, promising to reinstate them on their return. Duryodhana's unwillingness to keep his promise led to war, in which the Pandavas exterminated all their adversaries with the help of Krishna, a crafty and resourceful Yadava chieftain later deified as an incarnation of Vishnu. Yudhishthira then took the throne, but subsequently abdicated in favour of his nephew Parikshit, and he with his brothers and their common wife retired to the Himalayas, where they climbed Mount Meru and entered the city of the gods.

To this core story was added, over time, all sorts of random material, numerous tales about gods, sages, kings and heroes, discourses on religion, philosophy, law, morality, social dynamics, statecraft, and so on, including the long philosophical poem, the *Bhagavad Gita* – in short, virtually every matter known to the many bards who contributed to the final shaping of the epic over the centuries – making it encyclopaedic in scope. Says the *Mahabharata* about itself: 'Whatever is found here may be found somewhere else, but what is not found here is found nowhere.'

The authorship of the *Mahabharata* is traditionally ascribed to Vyasa, who in the style of Veda-vyasa was credited with the compilation of the Vedas, but he was no more the real author of the epic than of the Vedas. The labour of a very many poets, from different parts of the land and over several generations, had gone into the making of the epic, though it is possible that its root story was initially composed by some unknown bard.

There is less ambiguity about the authorship of the *Ramayana*. Valmiki, the poet to whom this epic is credited, seems to have been a historical figure, and probably lived around the sixth century BC. It is very likely that he composed the core section of the epic, its middle five *kandas* (books), drawing his inspiration from some popular ballad or folk-tale. The Bala and Uttara *kandas*, the opening and closing books of the epic, were added later. The political setting of the *Ramayana* is more advanced than that of the *Mahabharata*, and its literary style more sophisticated. In its final version, the Valmiki *Ramayana* has about 24,000 couplets, which makes it about one-fourth the length of the *Mahabharata*. The oldest extant manuscript of the *Ramayana* is of the eleventh century AD and was found in Nepal, but the epic probably was first written down many centuries before that. The earliest epigraphic reference to the *Ramayana* is in an inscription in Cambodia dated about AD 600.

The *Ramayana*, like the *Mahabharata*, is a tale of a kingdom lost and regained, but it is more a story of the tribulations of a family than a political saga, and is therefore more poignant, its tone and spirit gentler than that of the other epic. Rama, the crown prince of Kosala, a kingdom on the river Ghaghara, was deprived of his patrimony by the machinations of his stepmother Kaikeyi, who insisted that Dasaratha, the king, should fulfil his old promise of a boon to her, and make her son Bharata the heir. Though Dasaratha demurred, and Bharata was unwilling to accept the crown, Rama went on a voluntary exile along with his wife Sita and brother Lakshmana, so that his father would not have to break his word. While they were living as hermits in the Dandaka forest, Sita was abducted by Ravana, the king of Lanka. She was eventually rescued by Rama with the help of a motley horde of monkeys and bears, and the couple returned to Ayodhya, the royal capital, where Rama accepted the throne gladly vacated by Bharata.

But there was no fairy tale happy ending to this story, for public sentiment doubting Sita's chastity compelled Rama, as a righteous ruler, to cast her out of the palace. Leaving Ayodhya, Sita lived for a while in the hermitage of Valmiki, but eventually disappeared into the bowels of the earth (her own mother, for she was born from the furrow of a ploughed field) which opened up when she cried out to protest her innocence.

This high moral tone of virtue wronged, but shining ever more brightly when drawn through the inferno of suffering, distinguishes the *Ramayana* from the *Mahabharata*. There is nothing particularly edifying about the brutal power struggle in the *Mahabharata*, and, in terms of virtue, there is little to choose between its adversaries, even the best of them being occasionally devious. In contrast, the *Ramayana* is an inspiring tale of princely nobility. The divine protagonists in both the epics were incarnations of Vishnu, but Rama, unlike Krishna, was the very embodiment of goodness. This is emphasised in the opening passage of the epic itself, in which the poet Valmiki asks the divine sage Narada: 'Is there a man in the world today who is truly virtuous? ... Who is mighty and yet knows both what is right and how to act upon it? Who always speaks the truth and holds firmly to his vows ... exemplifies proper conduct and is benevolent to all creatures ... is learned, capable, and a pleasure to behold? Who is self-controlled, having subdued anger ... is both judicious and free from envy? Who, when his fury is aroused in battle, is feared even by the gods?'

Rama was all that and more. There were only a few minor lapses in his impeccable conduct – once he shot an antagonist (Valin) from ambush, and on another occasion he allowed his bitterness to boil over in anger against his father, charging, 'All he thinks about is sex ... it seems to me that sex is a more potent force than either statecraft or righteousness. For Lakshmana, what man, even a fool, would give up an obedient son like me for the sake of a woman?' But these are minor blemishes, and they only add the shading necessary to give depth to the portrait of this effulgent hero. Rama was fatalistic – almost masochistic – in his acceptance of suffering. He, unlike the Pandavas, would not fight for his rights. He would live out his karma, not struggle against it.

Rama was the Indian ideal, Krishna the Indian reality. But both the epics, though divergent in moral tone, served to promote Brahminical values among the masses. The *Mahabharata* explicitly states that its object is to edify the lower castes that are barred from studying the Vedas. In this role, the *Ramayana* was even more effective – the very hearing of the epic 'effaces evil,' claims the *Garuda Purana.* The *Ramayana* acquired this soteriological potency as a result of its transmutation from a secular tale into a scripture through the deification of Rama. Though he was not presented as a god in the central five books of the epic, its first book, the Balakanda, a later addition, categorically proclaimed him to be an incarnation of Vishnu. Thus the epic, a moving and immensely popular tale on its own to begin with, became infused with devotional fervour, and this transformed its cathartic power into salvational grace. And it endured. 'The poem,' notes Goldman, 'in all its versions and representations in the literary, plastic, and performing arts has constituted traditional India's most pervasive and enduring instrument of acculturation.'

The Puranas, like the *Mahabharata*, are called *ithihasas*, and are a vast miscellany of material on religion, society and history. They were the storehouses of folk memory, and as such have a fair amount of genuine historical data in them, including several genealogical lists of kings and sages. Unfortunately, these are indiscriminately mixed up with all sorts of fanciful tales and expedient myths. Their dynastic lists, for instance, are all jumbled up, and were sometimes revised (falsified, really) to accommodate new dynasties and to give them appropriate genealogical antiquity, or to efface the memory of the rulers whom the Puranic authors disfavoured. As Kosambi comments, these works 'in their present form are only religious fables and cant, with whatever historical content the works once possessed heavily encrusted by myth, diluted with semi-religious legends, effaced during successive redactions copied by innumerable, careless scribes.' The Puranas therefore are not of much use in reconstructing political history. They are, however, valuable in exploring another kind of history, the story of the inner life of ancient Indians, their beliefs and values, and their social psychology. As Thapar observes, the 'social underpinnings' of the Puranic myths reveal 'the integrating values around which societies are organised.'

Over the centuries a large number of Puranas came to be composed, but they vary greatly in quality, and only eighteen of them are considered to be of any importance, more especially the *Vayu, Vishnu, Agni, Bhavihsya* and *Bhagavata Puranas.* These are attributed to various ancient sages, but only as a ruse to claim venerable authority for the texts. It is not known who compiled them and when. Some of the material in them is of considerable antiquity and probably goes back to Vedic times, but they also contain a great amount of much later data. The actual recording of the Puranas probably began only from about the third century AD, and they took their present form around the fifth century AD, during the Gupta period. But the process of adding fresh material and recasting them to suit the changing social, political, religious and geographical environment went on for many more centuries, even into medieval times.

It is generally believed that the Puranas originally belonged to the Kshatriya rather than Brahminical tradition, and that they grew out of the folk-tales and folk-songs of Sutas and Magadhas, the traditional castes of chroniclers and bards. Later, however, Brahmin scholars took over from bards the task of preserving these traditional stories. They systematised the tales and created the Puranas as we know them, by shifting their emphasis from heroic chronicles to religious tales and legends, and imposing their own world-view on the old material. The Puranas then came to be regarded as of divine origin, and became the scriptures of popular Hinduism, 'the Veda of the laity,' as Rapson calls them.

A peculiarity of the Puranas is that they give the king-lists of the period after the Kurukshetra war in the form of prophecies, apparently to claim both antiquity and prophetic credibility – in them, as Rapson says, 'history has been made to assume the disguise of prophecy.' The Puranic prophecies were always fulfilled, as what they forecast had already happened. 'I will now enumerate the kings who will reign in future periods ...' is how the *Vishnu Purana* begins its post-war king-list. There is even a Purana titled *Bhavishya-purana*: future past!

From the point of view of the Puranas, none of these oddities mattered, for their objective was not to record the past accurately, but, as Thapar points out, to write about the past to serve 'the goals and purposes of the Hindu tradition.' They are propaganda material.

THE DOMESTICATION OF ARYANS

India was the last frontier for the wandering Aryans, a cul-de-sac from which there was no exit. Nor did Aryans any more have the urge to seek fresh pastures, for agriculture now tethered them to the land and domesticated them. This was a crucial development, for the transition from nomadic pastoralism to settled agrarian life brought on a whole series of other changes in its train that fundamentally transformed Aryan civilisation. Society now became hierarchically organised, territorial states ruled by kings began to supplant the old kinship units headed by chieftains, and people adopted new customs and practices, new beliefs and values, even new gods, appropriate to their new way of life. Further, agricultural prosperity created an unprecedented demand for goods and services, and this in turn stimulated the growth of crafts and trade, so now, a millennium after the collapse of the Indus Civilisation, towns once again began to appear in India, this time in the Gangetic Valley.

These changes, though fundamental, came about very slowly, almost imperceptibly, so that from decade to decade, perhaps even from generation to generation, no one would have noticed any dramatic alterations in the pattern of Aryan life in India. Though agriculture now steadily gained in prominence, society still remained substantially pastoral during the entire Vedic period. There was as yet no private ownership in land, though the farmer who made a tract of land productive by his labour held the field and its yield as his own. Arable virgin land was freely available, and had no value, so the parental wealth that was divided among sons in Vedic times was only the moveable property, not land. In rural India, wealth continued to be measured in cattle.

The cow was the most valued domestic animal of Rig-vedic Aryans, almost a sacred animal, but not quite, for beef was freely eaten by all. The Rig-vedic poet often spoke of the earth itself as a cow, and, as Macdonnell notes, 'no sight gladdened the eye of the Vedic Indian more than the cow returning from the pasture and licking her calf fastened by a cord; no sound was more musical to his ear than the lowing of milch kine.' States the Atharva-veda: 'On the cow the gods subsist; on the cow, men also.' In the later Vedic period this sentiment of esteem and affection for the cow gradually turned into reverence, and beef-eating was now condemned for the first time, though only in a passing reference, in the *Satapatha Brahmana.*

Cattle breeding was the primary occupation of Aryans when they arrived in Punjab, but it is quite probable that they had already taken to agriculture in a small way long before arriving in India, for Indian and Iranian Aryans had a common term – *krish* – for ploughing. In India, farming gradually became their primary occupation, and they adopted many local farming techniques, as indicated by the words of Dravidian or Munda origin in Vedic literature for farming implements. Vedic literature has a fair amount of information on agricultural operations, though mostly of an indirect nature, as in this metaphoric description of the sacrificial ritual in terms of farming practices in the Rig-veda: 'Lay on the yokes, and fasten well the traces: formed is the furrow, sow the seed within it ... near to the ripened grain approach the sickle ...'

Initially, when Aryans were in Punjab, farming involved no great labour, as the land was already under cultivation by the Indus people. But it took an enormous effort to establish agrarian settlements in the Gangetic Plain, into which they moved during the later Vedic period. The region was covered with dense jungles, which could be prepared for cultivation only through arduous toil, by felling the trees and burning down the forests. Fire, says the Rig-vedic poet, 'shaves the earth as a barber a beard.'

But slashing and burning, though efficient in clearing virgin forests, were not suited for settled communities, so Aryans eventually changed their agricultural practices, and adopted methods like rotating the crops and using river silt and cattle manure, to renew the fertility of the land and thus use the same land year after year for cultivation. They irrigated fields by drawing water from wells, or by diverting water from rivers and lakes through canals. 'Come ye, mighty one, by this way here, by which I am conducting thee here!' seductively chants a priest in the Atharva-veda, to coax a river to flow into a new channel. But most of all, the farmer relied on the regenerative miracle of the monsoon. Prays an Atharva-vedic priest:

> *Let the directions, full of mist, fly together;*
> *let clouds, wind-hurried, come together;*
> *let the lowing cows of the resounding misty great bull,*
> *the waters, gratify the earth ...*

Let the juices of the waters attach
themselves to the herbs;
let gushes of rain gladden the earth;
let herbs of all forms be born here and there.

Among the many titles of Indra is *apsu-jit*, water-conqueror, and he is time and again extolled in the Rig-veda for releasing water for the benefit of Aryan tribes. It is not clear exactly what he did – the hymns in different places speak differently about this feat, sometimes implying that he released water from the thunder-cloud, at other times that he cut gorges through mountains to redirect streams or to release lake water, or yet again that he demolished the barrages or dams of the Indus people. Sometimes these different notions were mixed up, as in this Rig-vedic hymn:

There darkness stood, the vault that stayed
the water's flow: in Vritra's hollow side
the rain-cloud lay concealed.
But Indra smote the rivers which the obstructer
stayed, flood flowing after flood,
down deep declivities.

Vedic farmers prepared fields for sowing by turning the soil with ploughs drawn by yoked oxen, usually a pair of them, but sometimes by teams of twelve or even twenty-four oxen, which were apparently needed to turn over the heavy virgin soil of the Gangetic Plain. The ploughshare was initially made of wood but was later replaced with iron. The Atharva-vedic poet viewed the plough as the source of all the good things of life, and, in a mantra to be recited at the commencement of ploughing, he prayed:

Let the plough, lance-pointed,
well-lying, with well-smoothed handle,
turn up cow, sheep, an on-going chariot
and a plump wench.

Everyone shared in the farm labour, and even kings were not averse to taking up the plough – Sita, the heroine of the *Ramayana*, emerged from a furrow when king Janaka was ploughing the ground to prepare for a sacrifice. There were no hired labourers or agricultural slaves in Rig-vedic times. Crops were harvested with sickles, threshed on threshing floors, winnowed in winnowing baskets, and finally measured and stored in granaries at home. After the harvest, the farmer left behind, as a propitiatory act, three sheaves of grain for the spirits of the field, and he tied together four sheaves and hung them in his house to appease the *griha-devata*, god of the house. All agricultural activities began with prayers, and there were rites to avert drought and excessive rain.

Two harvests were normally gathered in a year. The main Aryan cereal was barley, called *yava* in Vedic literature, a term that also meant grain in general. There is no mention of wheat or cotton in the Rig-veda, though both were cultivated by the Indus people. Rig-vedic Aryans had no knowledge of rice either, but they became familiar with it when they moved into the Gangetic Plain. Rice is listed along with several other grains and vegetables – barley, wheat, lentils, millets, sesame, beans, vetches, and so on – in a prayer for bountiful harvest in the Yajur-veda. Among the trees, the pipal was considered sacred – its wood was used for making soma vessels as well as the drill to produce sacred fire; gods are described as lounging under it in the third heaven – but the banyan is not mentioned in the Rig-veda, and even the Atharva-veda mentions it only twice. Among flowers, the lotus was the special favourite of Vedic Aryans.

Rig-vedic Aryans were, in general terms, a rustic and backward people, compared to the urbanites of the Indus Civilisation. Yet in some respects, especially in metal technology and wheeled transport, they were more advanced than the Indus people. It is quite probable, though not certain, that they were familiar with the use of iron when they first arrived in India, as all Indo-European languages use a variant of *ayas* as the word for iron. It is not known when Aryans acquired the art of smelting and carbonising iron, without which the metal was not of much use, but certainly by the later Vedic period the use of iron implements had become common among them.

The term *ayas* in the Rig-veda, meaning simply metal, probably originally meant copper, so when iron was introduced, the two metals were differentiated with qualifiers, terming copper as *tamara ayas* (red metal) and iron as *krishna ayas* (black metal). Later, when copper came to be commonly called *tamara*, and iron replaced it as the primary metal, the term *ayas* came to be exclusively used for iron. Copper however remained the holy metal of Aryans, and even in later times only copper vessels were used by orthodox Hindus for storing consecrated water. Among the other metals, gold is frequently mentioned in the Vedas, but silver only rarely; lead – the metal of sorcery – tin and bronze were also known to Vedic Aryans.

Metalworking was the frontier technology in Vedic society, and the smith enjoyed high social status. In contrast, the potter had low status; he does not even merit a mention in the Rig-veda. But the carpenter was honoured, and the Rig-vedic poet thought of him in terms of his own work: 'I bend with song, as bends a wright his felloe of hard wood.' The weaver also captured the poet's fancy – 'Biting cares devour me, as rats devour the weaver's threads,' he laments. The leather-worker too was an important Vedic artisan, making reins, whips, bowstrings, drumheads, and casks to store liquor or water. These crafts were practised hereditarily in families, as everywhere in the ancient world; children assisted their parents, and learned the crafts as they grew up.

The Rig-vedic economy was a subsistence economy and had not made the transition to commercial production and trade, though there would have been some barter trade among Aryans from very early times. Men had of course always lent and borrowed, and this was common in the early Vedic period too – 'Indra excels all usurers,' states the Rig-veda enigmatically – and there is even a reference to paying 'debt from debt' in Vedic literature. But these transactions were mainly associated with gambling, not trade. There was no coinage in Vedic times, though the *satamana*, a piece of gold weighing 100 *krishnala* berries mentioned in the Brahmanas, was probably used as a unit of value. *Nishka*, a gold neck ornament, also seems to have served a similar purpose. But wealth was still primarily measured in cattle, and there could not have been much trade when cattle were currency.

There was no merchant class in early Aryan society, though non-Aryan merchants like Panis continued to flourish. The term *vanik*, meaning merchant, occurs only once in the Rig-veda. But gradually, as Aryan society moved towards urbanisation in the Gangetic Valley during the later Vedic period, trade began to gain prominence, and there are several references to merchants and usurers in the later Vedic literature. Men were often caught in debt-traps, from which they sought to free themselves by performing the magical rites prescribed in the Atharva-veda.

Later Vedic literature speaks of long trading journeys, and even alludes to contacts with Mesopotamia, but it is not clear how Vedic Aryans carried out long distance trade. Presumably it was mostly overland trade, but it is likely that there was some marine trade as well. Ships, even ships 'with a hundred oars,' and voyaging for 'three nights, three days ... to the sea's further shore' are mentioned in the Rig-veda, and one hymn describes a shipwreck. But these probably refer only to river transport. It is unlikely that Rig-vedic Aryans were familiar with the sea. Though *samudra*, the common Sanskrit term for the sea, is used in the Rig-veda, it presumably meant only a collection of waters (which is what the word literally means) and referred to the lower Indus, which even in modern times was called the Sea of Sind by the local people. There is no mention of masts or sails, or of rudder or anchor in the Rig-veda – ships apparently had only paddles or oars – and 'metaphors used by a people familiar with the ocean are lacking in the Rig-veda,' as Apte notes.

For overland transport, pack-animals or porters would normally have been used to carry goods. The horse does not seem to have been used as a draught animal by Vedic Aryans; it was primarily a chariot animal. Ox carts were common, but they could not have been used much for long distance transport, as there were hardly any roads in India at this time, and journeys by cart across the country were hazardous. Rites for the safety of carts were normally performed at the commencement of long journeys.

Rig-vedic Aryans were generally contemptuous of traders and their greed, but subsequently this attitude changed radically, and later Vedic literature conferred scriptural benediction on the profit motive, with the Atharva-veda offering a model prayer for merchants:

Please pardon, O Lord, our hardness,
our long travels for gain.
May we purchase and sell with profit!

May the barter of goods make us prosperous,
successful for us be our journeys!
Do ye gods enjoy this oblation in concord.

My wealth for trading,
seeking wealth through wealth,
may it ever wax and never wane!

By this offering to the gods, O Lord,
we check and frustrate
those who would spoil our profit.

THE WAR-BEGOTTEN KING

Early Aryans had no territorial state, and hereditary monarchy, if it existed at all, was still in a gestative state. Their basic political unit was the tribe, *jana*, made up of a number of clans, *vis*, each consisting of several family clusters called *gramas*. The entire tribe was bound by kinship ties, real or imagined, and was headed by the *janapathi*, patriarch-chieftain, who functioned under the control of the Sabha and Samithi, tribal assemblies. The composition and functions of the two chambers are not clear, but it is generally thought that the Sabha was a small, select body of tribal elders and other notables, while the Samithi was open to all the adult men of the tribe or at least to the heads of all individual families. Women were excluded from the deliberations of the assemblies. The Sabha, chaired by the Sabhapathi, probably met more often than the Samithi, and had both judicial and administrative responsibilities.

The Sabha met in the moot hall, which at other times served as a clubhouse. 'Frolic truly is thy name,' says the Atharva-veda about the hall, for it was also a place for drinking, gambling and entertainment. The deliberations in the Sabha too were often spirited, as speakers took stimulants or resorted to occult Atharva-vedic rites to empower them to prevail in the assembly. Acrimony in the assembly was however a matter of grave concern to Vedic sages, for Aryans lived in an extremely turbulent world, constantly squabbling and fighting among themselves or with the indigenous people, so tribal cohesion was essential for survival. The very last hymn of the Rig-veda concludes with a prayer for tribal harmony:

Assemble, speak together,
let your minds be all of one accord ...
The place is common, common the assembly,
common the mind, so be their thought united ...

One and the same be your resolve,
and be your minds of one accord.

United be the thoughts of all
that all may happily agree.

This unity of the tribe that the sages so ardently desired became increasingly difficult to maintain with the passage of time, as socio-economic changes corroded the very basis of tribal cohesiveness, its presumed blood ties. With the adoption of agriculture and the consequent permanent settlement of tribes on particular tracts of land, neighbouring tribes tended to merge together to form territorial states, either through voluntary association or through conquest. This loosened kinship ties, which had already begun to unravel because of the growth of population, the dispersal of families over great distances, and the intermixing of tribes and races. People then came to identify themselves increasingly with the land they lived in, rather than with their tribe. The development of the caste system around this time also undermined tribal solidarity, as it created divisions within the tribe on the one hand, and, on the other, forged trans-tribal affiliations. Significantly, the term *grama*, which originally meant an extended family group, now came to mean simply a village, without any kinship associations. Tribal names now became the names of regions. And monarchy began to supersede the old tribal form of government.

These changes were gradual, and not in the nature of the displacement of one system by another. For a while tribal republics continued to coexist with kingdoms, and within the kingdoms themselves monarchs for a time had to reckon with the countervailing power of the tribal assemblies. But eventually the Sabha and Samithi would atrophy and disappear, and the tribal republics would be absorbed into the emergent kingdoms, though some of them would survive for a few more centuries. The future belonged to the territorial states ruled by kings.

It was war that begot the king. 'They who have no king cannot fight,' states the *Taittiriya Upanishad.* Even gods, according to *Aitareya Brahmana*, needed a king to win their wars against demons. 'It is because we have no king that the demons defeat us, so let us elect a king,' they said to each other, and chose Indra as their ruler, reasoning, 'This one is among the gods the most vigorous, the most strong, the most valiant, the most perfect, who carries out best any work. Let us install him in the kingship.' What was attributed to the gods was no doubt what had really happened among men. It was invariably the successful military leader who assumed the role of the king. 'He ... by his greatness became ... king,' says the Atharvaveda about royal accession.

The king was initially more a military commander than a ruler, and was chosen by tribal consensus, perhaps for temporary assignments. But tribal wars being interminable, a successful commander tended to be called again and again to lead the tribe in battle, and this enabled him to widen and entrench his power, by first making his office permanent, and then making it hereditary. By the later Vedic period hereditary monarchy had virtually become the norm. But even then the pretence that the king was ruling by the people's consent was kept up for a while, and the formal approval of the Sabha and Samithi was required to legitimise succession. Though the king now claimed himself to be the earthly representative of Prajapati, the heavenly ruler, he still placed the popular assemblies on an equal footing with himself. 'May the Samithi and the Sabha, the two daughters of Prajapati, concurrently aid me,' he prays in the *Satapatha Brahmana*. Chants the Atharva-vedic sage:

> *Firm the heaven,*
> *firm the earth,*
> *firm the universe,*
> *firm the mountains,*
> *let the king of the people be firm.*

In time however the nature of the relationship between the king and the people became inverted – instead of the king being 'of the people', it came to be that the people were of the king. People thus became subjects. Kings then gave up the formality of seeking public approval of their authority, and ruled by *danda*, the power to coerce obedience. Support of the people became irrelevant to the king when he developed a power base independent of them – his professional army, which replaced the tribal militia. Here again, the determining factor was economic, for it was the regular and substantial revenue that the king was able to collect from the people when they took to agriculture that enabled him to maintain a standing army. At the same time, the common people were only too willing to leave warring to the king and his soldiers, as they themselves, having given up hard nomadic pastoralism for sedate farming, were inclined to a soft life. Moreover, they could not leave farm work to join military campaigns, as agriculture tied them to time cycles.

In the tribal polity, and perhaps even in the early stages of monarchy, all that the chieftain received as remuneration for his services was an irregular voluntary contribution called *bali*, the traditional offering made by the people to the king for performing tribal sacrifices. But when people settled to a farming life and their income became regular, their contribution to the king also became regular. *Bali*, the occasional payment, thus became *bhaga*, a regular tax, the king's share of the produce of the land.

The Vedic people, like people at all times, were none too happy about paying tax, and they reproachfully called the king *bhagadugha*, 'he who milks the share'. The king, says the Rig-veda, 'eats the rich' like fire eats the wood. The feeling against tax collection was so intense that the Atharvaveda describes heaven as the place where no tribute is paid 'by the weak to the strong.' But people had no option but to pay up, for the king had the means to enforce tax collection – the army, for the maintenance of which tax was mainly collected, served, paradoxically, as the means to compel tax payment. War booty was yet another source of royal income, again obtained through the army. Later, when coinage was introduced in Aryan society, the power of the king became even more inviolable, for he was now able to accumulate treasure – which he could not do as long as tax and booty were collected mostly in perishable farm produce or livestock – and thus free himself from the vagaries of tax collection.

As the wealth and power of the king grew, the distance between him and the people widened, and he drew closer to the gods. Declared the *Satapatha Brahmana*: 'The Rajanya is the visible representative of Prajapati.' However, no Vedic king directly asserted divinity; at most he claimed to be a legate of god, but never himself a divine person. Even later, Indian kings hardly ever claimed divinity – though some did count divine incarnations among their ancestors – probably because Brahmins, who were to confer such honours, had appropriated divinity for themselves. The only major exception to this was the Kushana practice (in the early Christian era) of designating the king as Devaputra, son of god.

The origin of kingship, according to both Hindu and Buddhist tradition, was contractual, and reciprocity marked the relationship between the king and his subjects, at least in theory. In the beginning men lived in a never-never utopian world of harmony, perfection and contentment, says the *Digha Nikaya*, an ancient Buddhist text. There was no private property or crime then. No government either, or any need for one. But as the cosmic cycle rolled on, corruption set in, private property came into existence, and men fought among themselves for possessions. Crime then became endemic and society slid into anarchy. People tried to end the chaos by entering into an agreement among themselves to respect each other's rights, but the arrangement did not work, as there was no institution to enforce the compact. They then thought, 'What if we were to select a certain being, who should be wrathful when indignation is right, who should ensure that which should rightly be ensured, and should banish him who deserves to be banished? We will give him in return a portion of rice ...' These considerations led them to choose one among them as their ruler and invest him with authority to maintain law and order. They called him the *Mahasammata*, the Great Chosen One.

The *Mahabharata* too tells a similar story: 'It hath been heard by us that men in days of old, in consequence of anarchy, met with destruction, devouring one another like stronger fishes devouring the weaker ones in the water. It hath been heard by us that a few amongst them, then assembling together made certain compacts saying, "He who becomes harsh in speech, or violent in temper, he who seduces or abducts other people's wives or robs the wealth that belongs to others, should be cast off by us."' But human wickedness made this agreement ineffectual. People then approached Brahma for a solution to their predicament, and he appointed Manu as their first king, and people agreed to pay him taxes as remuneration for his services.

These two legends, though similar, differ in a significant detail – while Hindus saw the contract as a result of divine intervention, for Buddhists it was a purely temporal arrangement. While the Buddhist legend viewed the contract from the point of view of the subjects and laid stress on royal obligations, the Hindu legend viewed it from the point of view of the king and laid stress on royal privileges. 'In kingdoms where there are no kings, there is no rain, there are no gods,' states the *Mahabharata*. 'How can a kingdom that has no king be maintained?'

Kings naturally favoured the Hindu view, and in this they had the indispensable support of the priestly class, who devised elaborate and exalted rituals to imbue the king with divine effulgence. In place of the original royal consecration ceremony – which probably consisted of a simple anointing of the king by priests – the grand and richly allegorical Rajasuya ritual, which in its full form lasted for over a year, was now introduced. 'Him do ye proclaim, O men as ... king and father of kings ... the lordly power ... the suzerain of all creation ... the slayer of foes ... the guardian of Brahmins ... the guardian of the law,' intoned the chief priest at the royal consecration, reciting from the *Aitareya Brahmana*. He then addressed the gods with a prayer from the *Satapatha Brahmana*: 'Of mighty power is he who has been consecrated; now he is one of yours; you must protect him.'

The royal throne was called *simhasana*, lion seat. During the consecration rite, it was placed on a tiger skin, and as the king stepped on the pelt, the officiating priest chanted the Atharva-vedic hymn:

As a tiger on tiger-skin
stride unto the great quarters;
Let all the people and heavenly waters
rich in milk desire you.

The king then fitted an arrow to his bow and took a step in each of the four directions, in symbolic conquest of the four quarters. Later he played a game of dice, which he was allowed to win and thus be assured of good luck. The emphasis of the Rajasuya ceremony was on royal pomp and power, but it did not entirely neglect royal obligations. 'As a ruler, from this day onwards, judge the strong and the weak impartially and fairly,' the priest counselled the king, reciting from the Yajur-veda. 'Strive unceasingly to do good to the people and above all, protect the country from all calamities.'

Later in his reign the king would perform another great ritual, the Vajapeya (drink of potency) ceremony, to replenish his vigour and glory. But the most important royal rite, the one that every ancient Indian king was ambitious of performing, was the Asvamedha, the royal horse-sacrifice, to demonstrate the inviolability of his power. The ritual involved letting loose a consecrated horse to wander as it pleased for a year, protected by an entourage of chosen warriors to meet the challenge of any who would seize it, and then taking it back to the royal capital to be sacrificed. This rite, which originated in an unstable political environment of competing petty kings, and was the means for a king to demonstrate his sovereign power, gradually died out with the establishment of large and stable kingdoms. The growing popularity of Buddhism also militated against the slaughter of animals. The practice however was revived in the second century BC, after the collapse of the Mauryan empire, but it never regained its earlier wide popularity, though it continued to be performed occasionally until the tenth century AD.

In sharp contrast to these extravagant rituals, ancient Indian kings initially took only modest titles like Rajaka and Raja, or at most Svarat (independent king) but gradually they began to assume flamboyant titles like Samrat (emperor), or even Visvasya-bhuvanasya-raja (lord of all the universe). But these grand titles bore little relationship to political reality, for Vedic kingdoms were all petty principalities, in which, as the Sutras reveal, kings sometimes had to personally administer whippings to punish thieves. Hardly any of the kings could have been secure on his throne, being constantly menaced by rivals within the kingdom or by pugnacious neighbours, and at no time could royal succession have been smooth, if we are to go by the record of historical times. Kings were also vulnerable to being expelled by popular uprising, as the references to exiled kings in Vedic literature indicate. The *Tandya Brahmana* in fact prescribes a sacrifice for people to destroy their tyrannical king.

People needed kings to protect their life and property, but protectors often turned into predators. 'Let the fury of kings fall on others, not on me,' prays an Atharva-vedic bard. There was not, however, much scope for royal tyranny in the ancient world. The Vedic king was a minimal ruler, not interested in anything much more than the collection of revenue and the prevention of rebellion. His authority, limited by his rudimentary administrative machinery and paltry resources, could intrude into only a very small part of the lives of his subjects. He did not have the power to do any great harm. Or any great good.

The Vedic kings lived as opulently as their circumstances permitted, and maintained great pomp. The Rig-veda, no doubt taking considerable poetic liberty with truth, speaks grandly of the king living with many wives in a palace of a thousand columns and a thousand doors, its pillars carved with 'images of girls, unrobed.' The palace was built of wood, but the king sat on a throne of 'iron columns, decked with gold,' and held court 'arrayed in golden mail and shining robes, surrounded by ministers, spies, heralds ... courtiers ... and messengers,' notes Iyengar, summarising the Vedic passages on the subject. When the king attended the court, he was surrounded by his nobles as well as by prominent members of the tribe, including artisans like chariot-builders and smiths. On state occasions, bards went in the train of the king singing his praises. He rode in a gilded and jewelled chariot, and in later Vedic times probably on an elephant.

The primary duty of the king was to lead his people in war – to defend their own lands or to pillage the neighbouring kingdoms. For him as well as for his people, war was a means to replenish their resources. The Vedic term for war was *gavisti*, meaning 'desire for cows' – war meant primarily a cattle raid for early Aryans. But in India, after they took to farming, their motives broadened. They now fought, as the Rig-vedic poet puts it, 'for seed and offspring, waters, kine, cornfields,' and for 'our share of maids.' The dry winter season at the end of the monsoon was the time for wars, when kings routinely sallied forth, mostly on cattle raids, and villagers built or repaired *purs* (stockades or earthwork fortifications) to protect themselves against pillagers. The Vedic king led the army in person. It was his duty to do so.

The Aryan warrior decked himself in finery for battle, with 'anklets on feet, gold chains on breasts,' according to the Rig-veda. He wore a 'well-sewn armour,' a helmet and a shield, and rode into battle in his chariot with its pennants flying, shooting reed-shafted arrows. The arrow was, as the Rig-veda reverently describes it, 'venom smeared, tipped with deer-horn, with iron mouth ... [and] sharpened by ... prayer.'

Two horses were normally yoked abreast to the chariot, but the Aryan nobility, notes the Rig-veda, fought in richly decorated chariots 'drawn by four trained horses decked with pearls.' Knives were often attached to chariot wheels, to mow down the enemy by driving the chariot into their midst. Vedic Aryans had no cavalry, the stirrup having not yet come into use, though horseback riding is mentioned in Vedic literature. Common soldiers fought on foot, wielding a motley of weapons – lances, spears, axes, spiked clubs, swords, sling-shots firing 'darts of stone burning with fiery flame,' and so on.

The battle car was driven by a charioteer standing on a low, wooden floor with a crescent-shaped fender along its front, probably of wickerwork or of leather stretched on a wood frame. On the left side of the charioteer there was a seat for the archer to rest when not actually engaged in battle. The archer, clad in a coat of mail and riding into battle to the accompaniment of the war-drum, was a romantic hero, and the Rig-vedic poet is lyrical in singing his praise, hearing in the hum of his bow-string the amorous murmur of a woman:

Close to his ear, as fain to speak,
she presses, holding her
well-loved friend in her embraces;
Strained on the bow, she whispers
like a woman – this bowstring
that preserves us in the combat.
These, meeting like a woman
and her lover, bear, mother-like
their child upon their bosom.
May the two bow-ends, starting swift,
sunder, scatter, in unison,
the foes who hate us.

Priests accompanied the army to invoke divine blessings on the slaughter, and soldiers themselves performed propitiatory rites while going into battle. 'My nearest, closest mail is prayer,' avows a Rig-vedic warrior. Aryans knew well the value of psychological terror in warfare, and they fell on the enemy whooping bloodcurdling war-cries – 'fear-sounding shouts,' as the Rig-veda puts it – to rouse battle-frenzy in themselves and to petrify the enemy. Equally menacing was the war-drum, of which the Atharva-veda says:

As birds start back affrighted at the eagle's cry,
As day and night they tremble at the lion's roar:
So thou, O drum, shout out against our enemies,
Scare them away in terror and confound their minds.

The Vedic battle was, even for those primitive times, a singularly savage affair, with blood-crazed warriors driving lances into the vitals of their fallen foes, chopping them up, crushing their bones, flaying them alive, even cutting off their penises and splitting their testicles.

Snatch thou the hair from off his head,
and from his body strip the skin.
Tear out his sinews,
hack off his flesh in chunks.
Crush thou his bones,
strike and beat the marrow out of them.
Disjoint his limbs and smash them.

This particular Atharva-vedic incantation was directed against the 'Brahmin's tyrant, criminal, niggard, blasphemer of the gods,' but it could well be a description of the gruesome Vedic battle scene.

A major function of the Vedic king, apart from leading his people in war, was to perform the great Vedic sacrifices considered essential for the welfare of the people. Internal security and administration of justice were also his responsibilities, though in these matters, the scope for his action was limited, as much of the judicial as well as law and order matters were taken care of by local bodies at the village level. The Vedic kingdom was poorly policed, and people relied more on divine protection than on royal justice. 'We shall sleep, do thou watch; yield refuge to our kine, horses, men,' prays the Atharva-vedic poet. Their best security was in burying valuables, and this was evidently a common practice in India even in Vedic times, for there is a reference to a buried 'pitcher full of gold' in the Rig-veda.

There was no concept of cognisable offence in Vedic times. A crime was crime under law only if someone complained about it, and in most cases, including murder, the satisfaction of the injured party closed the case. To kill or rob a stranger 'was often a duty, not a crime,' for Vedic tribesmen, notes Kosambi. Only the killing of the Brahmin was really considered murder, which had to be punished with death. In all other cases, the payment of blood-money was considered sufficient penalty, the standard value of the Kshatriya being 1,000 cows, of the Vaisya 100, and of the Sudra 10. Women had the same value as the Sudra. Over and above blood-money, the offender had to give a bull to the king, as fine for disturbing his peace.

The most common crimes in Rig-vedic times were theft (of gold or garments) and cattle-lifting. There were also some incidents of highway robbery. Cheating at gambling and moral offences like incest are also mentioned in Vedic texts. The distinction between the violation of social norms and crime was vague in those days, and so was the distinction between social sanctions and judicial punishments. Ordeals by fire, water and single combat were sometimes used to establish innocence or guilt. A sound beating by the victim seems to have been the usual punishment for thieves, though there are also some vague references to fetters and prison in Vedic literature. In one instance, a case of gambling debt, the debtor was tied to a post by the creditor to make him pay up. The worst crimes in the eyes of Vedic lawgivers, the Brahmins, were those committed against them. 'Do thou with a hundred-toothed discus, sharpened, edged like a razor-blade, sever the head from the shoulders of him, the oppressor of Brahmins,' damns the Atharva-veda, and goes on to graphically describe all the dreadful things to be done with the corpse.

Vedic kingdoms were too small in size to be divided into provinces or even districts. There was no administrative need for such divisions either, for all local governmental functions were carried out by autonomous villages under the leadership of the Gramani, the village headman. Even at the king's court, governmental organisation was quite rudimentary. The mainstay of royal administration was a miscellaneous group of advisors called Ratnins, jewels, made up of the king's relatives, courtiers and officials, whose services were considered so crucial to the king that special rites were performed during the royal consecration to secure their loyalty. Several royal officers are named in Vedic texts – Purohita, the royal priest; Senani, the military commander; Sthapathi, the chief judge; the chamberlain; revenue and treasury officials; the superintendent of dicing, and a few others whose functions are not clear. The Suta, royal charioteer, was an important official, for he was also the royal bard and confidant. Spies and envoys are also mentioned.

The Purohita – usually an Atharvan priest – was a key royal functionary, for it was he who enveloped the king with the mystique of religion by organising grand sacrificial rites. He also served as the royal physician, providing occult relief to such human miseries as cough, sleeplessness, nightmares, and so on. More importantly, it was the Purohita who immortalised the king by composing memorable panegyrics about him, in the form of *dana-stutis*. He was well rewarded for these services, and he enjoyed immense prestige and power, which he sought to protect by making himself indispensable to the king. Success, the Rig-vedic poet emphatically asserts, would favour a king only if he maintained the Purohita 'well attended, and praises and honours him as (a deity) deserving the first share (of homage).' The *Satapatha Brahmana* maintains that 'it is quite improper that a king should be without a Brahmin, for whatever deed he does, unsped by Mitra, therein he succeeds not.'

There is hardly any data on political history in Vedic literature, and there are no dateable events in it. Ancient Indians, unlike ancient Chinese, wrote no specifically historical works. The earliest Indian chronicle of history, Kalhana's *Rajatarangini*, a history of Kashmir, appeared only in the twelfth century AD, though we have a few brief historical and biographical sketches of varying quality from the seventh century AD onward. A further problem in reconstructing the political history of ancient India is that till the first century BC, India had no eras by which to reckon dates, so events were dated by the regnal years of reigning monarchs. There was therefore no direct way of coordinating the dates of different kingdoms and dynasties to build a general chronology of ancient India. The subsequent adoption of the era system did not quite end the chronological chaos, for several eras then came to be used, such as the Vikrama Era of 58 BC, the Saka Era of AD 78, the Gupta Era of AD 320, the Harsha Era of AD 606, and several local eras. In addition, Hindus, Buddhists and Jains had their own religious eras. Because of these difficulties, the political history of Vedic India can be sketched only in very broad strokes.

The original group of Aryan migrants into India called themselves the *Pancha-jana*, five peoples, which probably was the generic term for the Aryan tribes that split off from their Iranian cousins. In the course of time several of these tribes coalesced to form a few small quasi-tribal kingdoms, the most prominent of which were the Purus on the lower reaches of the Saraswati, and the Bharatas further up the river in the region between the Satluj and the Yamuna. On an unknown date sometime in the second millennium BC these two kingdoms and their allies clashed in a major war on the banks of the Ravi. This event, known as the Battle of Ten Kings, is commemorated in three hymns in the Rig-veda, and is generally considered to be the first recorded incident in Indian history. The Purus lost the war, but their dynasty endured for many centuries – a king of the line would give battle to Alexander in the fourth century BC, and another would send an embassy to Augustus Caesar in the first century AD. The victorious Bharatas, however, soon faded from history, though their name endured as one of the names for India.

During the later Vedic period the Bharatas were displaced by a new dynasty called Kurus, who called themselves the 'sons of Bharata' as well as the 'sons of Puru', probably because the two old tribes had partly merged after their great war. Around this time the Panchala kingdom to the south-east of the Kurus also came into prominence. The Pandavas, the heroes of the *Mahabharata*, are not mentioned in the Vedas or the Brahmanas.

And slowly, out of the mist of pre-history, emerged a number of prominent kingdoms in northern India, bearing such names as Kamboja, Gandhara, Kasi, Kosala, Videha, Magadha, and so on. Most of these kingdoms (as well as a few later kingdoms like that of the Sakas and Yavanas) are mentioned in the *Mahabharata* as arrayed on opposite sides in the

Kurukshetra war. But Ayodhya, the Ikshvaku kingdom of the epic hero Rama, finds no mention in Vedic literature. A short-lived and insignificant principality, it disappeared from history in the sixth century BC – it was only Valmiki's poetic genius that immortalised Rama.

COLOUR AND CASTE

In primitive tribal societies, like that of the early Aryans, the only functional division was between men and women, and the only hierarchy the dominance of the strong over the weak, as there was no scope for any marked accumulation of wealth or specialisation of labour in a pastoral economy. But as Aryans took to agriculture in India, their society evolved and grew complex, first dividing itself into four functional classes, and then splitting into numerous sub-groups. This process, which began in an embryonic form among Aryans when they were still in Iran, gradually mutated, in India, into the singularly iniquitous and maddeningly complex hereditary caste system. In Iran classes did not evolve into castes. The system was unique to India.

Aryan society, as reflected in the oldest hymns of the Rig-veda, was unstructured and fundamentally egalitarian. It had an elementary status division between nobles and commoners, as in most early societies, but no hereditary class exclusivity. There were no interdining or intermarriage taboos at this time, and anyone was free to take to any profession according to his inclination and skill. Family tradition and circumstances would normally have inclined children to follow the professions of their parents, but there were no rules constraining them to do so. Says the Rig-veda about the prevailing social scene:

We all have various hopes and plans
and many are the ways of men:
The craftsman seeks for jobs to do,
the priest his folk, the healer the sick.
Flow, Indu, flow for Indra's sake.

The arrow-smith with hard dry reeds
and feathers from the birds of air,
Bronze for the tips, and glowing coals,
seeks out the man who'll pay him best.
Flow, Indu, flow for Indra's sake.

A bard am I, my father's a healer,
and mother grinds corn on the quern:
Striving for wealth, with varied plans,
we follow our desires like kine.
Flow, Indu, flow for Indra's sake.

The openness of the Rig-vedic society did not however extend to non-Aryans, who were kept segregated, primarily on the basis of skin colour, but also due to differences in language, religion and culture. This Aryan–non-Aryan divide, which was initially quite rigid, loosened somewhat with the passage of time, as the two races intermingled, and it was no longer easy to discriminate on the basis of colour or culture. Merit in any case often outshone colour, and conferred status on those who would otherwise have been damned by prejudice. Thus Badarayana Veda-vyasa, though born of a liaison between a fisherwoman and an Aryan sage and called Badarayana the Black, was nevertheless acknowledged as the compiler of the Vedas. Some Vedic sages were openly described as sons of Dasa women, while a few were named after their mothers, indicating their uncertain paternity or non-Aryan matrilineal social background. Sage Kavasha of the *Aitareya Brahmana* was the son of a slave girl. Agastya and Vasistha are said to have been born from jars, signifying their mysterious parenthood. The Kasyapa clan of Vedic seers, notes Kosambi, was known from early days to absorb 'aborigines who wanted to become Brahmins.'

In the Brahmanas and the Epics there are many instances of Aryan chieftains marrying non-Aryan princesses – the *Mahabharata* hero Arjuna married Ulupi, a Naga princess, and his brother Bhima married Hidimbi, sister of an *Asura* chief. Among the commoners such racial intermixing was, we should assume, fairly commonplace. There were even some instances of high caste Aryans deliberately seeking, for obscure occult reasons, to have dark-skinned children. 'Now if a man wishes that a son with a dark complexion and red eyes should be born to him, that this son should learn the three Vedas and should attain a full term of life, then the couple should have rice cooked in water and eat it with ghee,' advises the *Brihadaranyaka Upanishad.* 'Thus they should be able to beget such a son.'

The basic structure of ancient Indian society was the *varna* system, which divided people into four classes – Brahmins (priestly class), Kshatriyas (martial class), Vaisyas (producers: farmers, traders and artisans) and Sudras (serfs and labourers). Then, as society evolved and became progressively more diversified, and professions became hereditary and professional groups lived apart from each other in separate villages or in particular zones in towns, these classes over the centuries split into innumerable *jatis*, hereditary castes. The classes and castes maintained their exclusivity through endogamous marriages and by imposing various taboos, especially regarding whom they could eat with and what occupations they could take to. One could become a member of a caste only by birth – *jati* means birth – so no one could change his caste.

The four *varnas* (classes) were like the four floors of a four-storeyed building. Each of these floors was in turn divided into a honeycomb of cubicles, each cubicle a particular social space occupied by a particular *jati* (caste). Every individual belonged to a caste, and each caste occupied a specific cubicle, and each cubicle had its fixed place in its allotted floor in the *varna* structure.

There was however a complication in this apparently simple and neat social arrangement, for while the *varna* structure was rigid and permanent, castes, although by convention assigned to fixed social spaces, were in practice mobile, and could gradually move, over time, from one cubicle to another on the same floor, or even, in exceptional cases, to another floor in the *varna* structure. This meant that even though an individual could not change his caste, a caste could change its position relative to other castes within its *varna*, or even change its *varna* status. Sometimes castes died out while new ones were born. Furthermore, castes were region-specific, which meant that if a caste group moved to a new region in India, it had to be fitted into the caste hierarchy prevailing there, and this too gave scope for social manoeuvring. Ultimately the status of a caste was what its immediate society acknowledged as its status.

Over the centuries there was thus a good amount of caste shuffling, within and between the bottom three floors of the *varna* structure. However, the top floor was virtually sealed off to outsiders by its Brahmin occupants through innumerable prescriptions and proscriptions. But not even this floor was entirely inviolable, for non-Aryan priests of the local sects absorbed into Aryan religion were accommodated there, just as non-Aryan chieftains were absorbed into the Kshatriya class.

A further complication in Indian society was that it had, overlapping the *varna* and *jati* system, another mode of social division, the *gotra* system. The *gotra* – literally, a cow-pen – is a lineage group, a clan, like the gens of ancient Rome. Such groups had presumably existed in Indo-European society from very early times, long before the formation of castes, and were no doubt once common among all sections of society. However, as population expanded and people spread out over the subcontinent, these lineage links lost much of their relevance, especially for the lower classes. Only Kshatriyas and Brahmins really bothered about genealogy, but more so Brahmins, for whom it was a religious duty to remember their *gotra* ancestors and invoke them while consecrating their sacred fire.

Originally Brahmins were divided into eight *gotras*, each tracing its origin to a particular ancient or legendary sage. Later, in addition to this founder, Brahmin families came to count among their forebears a few other ancestor (*pravara*) sages. The inclusion of *pravara* sages in the genealogical list resulted in the main *gotras* being subdivided into forty-nine *gotras*, and these again into various families. Meanwhile, as the members of the *gotras* dispersed to different regions of India, each regional group within the *gotra* adopted the language, faith and practices particular to its region, and became closely affiliated with the members of the other *gotras* in the region having similar language, faith and practices. These trans-*gotra* affiliations resulted in the formation of a number of regional Brahmin castes. However, these castes did not displace the *gotras*, but overlaid them, and both have to be taken into consideration to determine the social position of a Brahmin. This is especially important in marriage alliances, for while castes are endogamous, *gotras* are exogamous. A Brahmin has to marry within his caste, but outside his *gotra*, marriage between couples of the same *gotra* being considered incestuous.

A distinctive feature of the *varna-jati-gotra* system is that it was a ritual hierarchy, primarily concerned with religious matters, and did not reflect the realities of wealth and power in society. One could be a vagrant and still enjoy the highest caste status; equally, one could be wealthy and powerful and still have only the lowest status. But there existed, alongside the ritual hierarchy, a temporal hierarchy, which reflected the actual power structure in society. While the ritual hierarchy was validated and held inviolable through scriptural prescriptions, the temporal hierarchy did not have any textual sanction and was fluid, a person's status changing with changes in his circumstances. The two status systems coexisted in fair harmony in their separate spheres of operation, with everyone generally deferring to the Brahmin, irrespective of his relative temporal circumstances.

How did the caste system come about? It is quite probable that it had its origin in the Aryan-non-Aryan divide, as the very use of the term *varna*, meaning colour, to define class, indicates. Says Patanjali, a second-century BC Sanskrit grammarian: 'When one sees a black man of the colour of a heap of black beans seated in the marketplace, one definitely concludes [without inquiry] that he is not a Brahmin; one is [intuitively] convinced of it.' But racial segregation, despite its likely catalytic role, is not adequate to explain the caste system, for the system as it finally evolved was primarily a division within Aryan society, not a division between Aryans and non-Aryans. Its explanation therefore has to be sought in developments within Aryan society.

The caste system has to be seen as an expression of the evolving Hindu religion, which provided it with its rationale through such concepts as karma and transmigration. The system was based solely on ritual purity. Certain occupations, mainly those involving manual labour, were considered defiling, while spiritual pursuits were regarded as ennobling. Sudras, whose work was entirely manual, were therefore placed at the bottom of society, and just above them were placed Vaisyas, who also did a good amount of manual work. Kshatriyas, who did little manual work and had some interest in religion, occupied the second highest position in society, while Brahmins, who did virtually no manual work at all and were (in theory) solely occupied with spiritual matters, occupied the top position. Further refinements in this categorisation in terms of purity and pollution on the basis of the permutations and combinations of occupation, social and religious practices, language, habitat, diet, and so on, eventually led to the formation of the over 3,000 castes in modern India.

This is the theoretical explanation for the formation of the caste system. It is a plausible account, but there is no hard evidence that this indeed was what happened. A curious aspect of the caste system is that it proliferated most among Sudras and Vaisyas, even among the untouchables, but only sparsely among Kshatriyas and Brahmins. But this is understandable, for there was far greater occupational diversity among Sudras and Vaisyas than among Kshatriyas and Brahmins.

The caste system, whatever the circumstances of its origin, crystallised into its final form only after an evolution of several centuries. The system was virtually non-existent in Rig-vedic times. *Jati* is seldom mentioned in ancient Indian sources, and even the *varna* system is described in only one hymn of the Rig-veda, the Purusha Sukta, a late hymn in the tenth book, which was probably interpolated to provide religious justification for social divisions. The Purusha Sukta is a creation hymn, and it presents the *varnas* as arising out of the creation process itself – when Purusha (the all-being who was 'all that yet hath been and all that is to be') was sacrificed by the gods to initiate creation, out of his mouth emerged the Brahmin, his arms became the Kshatriya, his thighs the Vaisya, and from his feet was born the Sudra. In the entire Rig-veda, the terms Rajanya, Vaisya and Sudra occur only in this hymn, though the term Kshatriya (a variant of Rajanya) occurs nine times elsewhere in the text. As for the term Brahmana, it occurs only eight times in the Rig-veda in the sense of a professional priest, though *brahman*, meaning a sage, is used forty-six times.

The *varna* principle as the basis of social organisation was widely accepted in later Vedic times, with the Yajur and Atharva Vedas acknowledging it as such. Birth now became the prime determinant of social status, and society became more and more fragmented, and social discrimination more and more extreme. The *Satapatha Brahmana* even specifies different degrees of politeness to be used in addressing the four classes, and also varying sizes of funeral mounds for them. Despite all this, there was still a fair amount of flexibility in class and caste relationships throughout the Vedic period, and rules about interdining, intermarriage and so on had not yet become rigidly established. Society was still in flux.

The only view that we have of the class and caste hierarchy in Vedic times is that of the religious texts. These present the Brahminical view, and inevitably exalt the Brahmin above all others. But there is good reason to suspect, on the evidence of the secular literature of the succeeding period, that Vedic society was not quite what the Brahminical texts would have us believe. In fact, even the texts themselves occasionally provide an alternate view. Though the general opinion was that the Brahmin was socially superior to the king, and that the king derived his power from the rituals performed by the Brahmin, the *Aitareya Brahmana*, looking at the class system from the perspective of Kshatriyas, describes the Brahmin as a royal factotum – the 'receiver of gifts, drinker of the Soma, a seeker of food, liable to be dismissed at will.' And the *Kathaka Upanishad* flatly states that the Kshatriya is superior to the Brahmin.

But whatever their actual social status, Brahmins undoubtedly enjoyed the highest ritual status. In contrast, the Sudras, though nominally deemed to be Aryans, were beyond the pale, and were excluded from the study of the Vedas and denied the right to wear the sacred thread, the mark of the true Aryan. The other three varnas styled themselves as *dvijas*, the twice-born, their initiation (*upanayana*) into the Aryan fold (by the investiture of the sacred thread) being their second birth. The term Brahmana (Brahmin) is derived from *brahman*, meaning sacred knowledge or magical power; Kshatriya from *kshtra*, meaning lordship; and Vaisya from *vis*, meaning settlement or clan. The derivation and meaning of the term Sudra are uncertain.

Of the four *varnas*, Brahmins and Kshatriyas constituted the leisure class, for they were not involved in economic activity directly, not to any great extent anyway, but mainly lived off the toil of Vaisyas and Sudras. This privilege they claimed as their reward for taking care of the security and well-being of society – Brahmins by keeping the gods happy and evil forces at bay to ensure good harvests for the farmer and a good life for everyone, and Kshatriyas by protecting the life and property of the people against internal disorder and external aggression.

The basic function of the Brahmin was to deal with supernatural forces, which he claimed he could control with his mantras and rites. Says the Rig-veda about the diverse priestly functions:

One sits putting forth a rich bloom of verses,
Another sings a song in skilful numbers,
A third as teacher states the laws of being,
A fourth metes out the sacrifice's measure.

These different duties marked the different categories of priests. The most respected among them were the Rishis, who composed hymns and formulated rites, and could, it was believed, summon gods by their secret names, seduce them with flattery, and induce them to grant boons. Then there were the common priests who sang the hymns and performed the rites, and were themselves divided into four groups – the Hotri, the invoker, who summoned the gods and offered them oblations; the Udgatri, the cantor; the Adhvaryu, who performed the manual part of the sacrifice; and the Brahmana, the superintending head-priest, whose name later came to be used as the general term for the priestly class. 'The Brahmana is as it were the stage-manager in the sacerdotal drama,' comments Bloomfield; 'the physician of the sacrifice when it is attacked by the disease of faulty execution.'

Priesthood was a profession, like any other profession, and priests expected to be rewarded well for their services. There was often intense competition among priests for patronage, especially royal patronage, and one Atharva-vedic hymn warns that the king who employs the wrong person as the Purohita would be 'deposed from his kingdom within a year.' Sometimes this competition led to bitter acrimony among sages, who hurled dreadful curses at each other, as Visvamitra and Vasistha did, or it led to war, as in the Battle of Ten Kings, which was instigated by rival priests.

Not all the Vedic sages were saintly personages. Quite a few of them had feet of clay, and fumed with wrath, envy or greed, like ordinary mortals. As professionals – mercenaries, one might say – they had no abiding loyalty, but served whoever paid them or honoured them, often changing sides brazenly. Stomach or ego dictated their fidelity. Thus the Vasisthas 'who cursed the Purus on behalf of the Bharatas praised them in another hymn,' notes Kosambi. Some priests in dire need even hawked celestial boons, though their own pitiful selves were a mockery of divine favour. 'Who, desirous of good fortune, will get us out of this wretched misery?' calls out a priest in the Atharva-veda. 'Who desireth sacrifice, and who is willing to give gifts? Who desireth long life from the gods?'

Giving gifts to Brahmins was the surest way to achieve prosperity and happiness – so claimed Brahmins. 'Those that give *dakshina* (gifts) dwell on high in the heavens,' assures the Rig-veda; 'they that give horses dwell in the sun for ever; they that give gold are blest with life eternal; and they that give garments ... prolong their lives.' Any misfortune (or good fortune) was a good enough occasion for the Brahmin to claim gifts for himself. The birth of twin calves was thought to portend misfortune, which could be averted only by giving one of the calves to a Brahmin. Any domestic animal born with a defect called for expiation by a Brahmin, who then received the animal as a gift. A sterile or otherwise defective cow (called 'the cow of gods') had to be given to him for his meat, and the Atharva-veda bitterly damns those who fail to do so: 'Whoever is not willing to give the cow of the gods to the sons of seers who ask for her, falls under the wrath of gods and the fury of Brahmins.'

Some sages cadged favours by holding out 'saccharine promises' of divine blessings and by telling exaggerated stories about the magnanimity of other patrons. 'Six thousand and ninety cows did we get (when we were) with Kaurama among the Rusamas! ... [Kaurama] presented the seer with a hundred jewels, ten chaplets, three hundred steeds, and ten thousand cattle,' boasts one sage in the Atharva-veda. A more modest Rig-vedic sage proclaimed: 'A hundred gold pieces from the fame-seeking king, together with a hundred horses as a present have I received. I, Kakshivant, obtained also a thousand cows from my master, who exalted thereby his fame immortal up to heaven.' There are some forty such hymns of gift-praise in the Rig-veda. Priests had no compunction even to serve – for a fee – Dasas and Panis, inveterate Aryan adversaries. Thus sage Bharadvaja in the Rig-veda praised Brbu, a Pani chief:

Brbu hath set himself above the Panis,
O'er their highest head,
Like the wide bush on Ganga's bank.

He whose good bounty, thousandfold,
swift as the rushing of the wind,
Suddenly offers us a gift.

So all our singers ever praise
the pious Brbu's noble deed ...

In practical terms the functions of common priests in Vedic India were similar to those of medicine-men in primitive societies, manipulating the anxieties and aspirations of men, but the best of them operated on a far more sophisticated plane. It would, says the Rig-veda, do no good to be a Brahmin who, 'having attained to *vac* (speech) in sinful fashion, spins out ... the thread [of prayers] in ignorance, like spinsters.' A true Brahmin was not just a priest, but a sage. Knowledge – sacred knowledge – was indeed power for the Brahmin, and he jealously guarded it as his monopoly. As Buddha once commented, 'Brahmins practise their chants secretly, not openly.' The Brahmin was essentially a poet, 'the best of all invokers of gods in song,' as the Rig-veda states. The Purusha Sukta aptly describes him as the Purusha's mouth. Words, says the Rig-veda, were his 'appropriate arms.' His power was the power of words. When the Brahmin spoke, the gods listened.

To the power of his privileged connection with the gods, the Brahmin added the terror of his own holy wrath, to keep himself unassailable at the top of society. It was fatal to provoke a Brahmin, says the Atharva-veda, for when roused 'his tongue becomes a bow-string, his voice an arrow, his windpipe fiery arrow-heads; with these the Brahmin pierces the blasphemers of gods, with bows ... speeded by gods.' Terrible would be the suffering in the hereafter for the tormentors of Brahmins, warns the Atharva-veda – instead of water, they would have to drink tears, for 'the tears wept by the Brahmin who suffers wrong, these are the share of water that gods have assigned' to them. Elsewhere the Atharva-veda states:

They who spat upon a Brahmin,
or who shot their mucus at him –
They sit in the middle of a stream of blood,
devouring hair ...

Not even kings with their mighty armies would be able to resist the fury of the Brahmin scorned, it was maintained. Several hymns in the Vedas hold out threats of dreadful consequences to those who do not respect the inviolability of the Brahmin's family and property, especially his cow – the cow, not because it was venerated, but because it was wealth. One of the longest hymns in the Atharva-veda, with seventy-three stanzas, admonishes:

Of the Kshatriya who takes for himself
the Brahmin-cow, who scathes the Brahmin,
there departs the happiness,
the heroism, the good luck,
both force, and brilliancy, and power,
and strength, and speech,
and sense, and fortune, and virtue,
and holiness, and dominion, and kingdom,
and subjects, and brightness, and glory,
and honour, and property,
and life-time, and form, and name,
and fame, and breath, and exhalation,
and sight, and hearing,
and milk, and sap, and food, and food-eating,

and righteousness, and truth, and sacrifice,
and bestowal, and progeny, and cattle –
all these depart from the Kshatriya
who takes for himself the Brahmin-cow,
who scathes the Brahmin ...

Cut thou, cut off, cut up;
burn thou, burn off, burn up
the Brahmin-scather ...

The Brahmin's claim to exclusive knowledge of the sacred law enabled him to lay down the social code, and place himself not only at the top of society but also outside most royal controls, virtually above the law. 'This man is your king, but Soma is the king of us Brahmins,' declares the officiating priest to the assembled people at the royal consecration. The Brahmin was answerable only to gods. The *Taittiriya Brahmana* sternly advises that in any dispute between a Brahmin and a non-Brahmin, the Brahmin should be deemed right. Brahmins also asserted that the god Soma had made over to them 'his right to the first mating with every woman,' and that they could claim for themselves any woman they fancied, even married women. States the Atharva-veda, 'When a woman has had ten former husbands, not Brahmins, if a Brahmin takes her hand it is he alone who is her husband.' During the later Vedic period Brahmins even claimed a sort of divinity. 'Verily there are two kinds of gods,' states the *Satapatha Brahmana*; 'for indeed, the gods are gods; and Brahmins who have studied and teach the sacred lore are human gods.' Both had to be propitiated – Brahmins with gifts, gods with sacrifices.

Not all Brahmins, of course, had it easy even in Vedic times. Many had to live in abject poverty. A sage in the Rig-veda bemoans:

In deep distress I cooked a dog's entrails;
among the gods I found none to comfort me;
My wife I beheld in degradation ...

Complains another Rig-vedic seer:

The ribs that compass me give pain
and trouble me like rival wives.
Indigence, nakedness, exhaustion press me sore:
my mind is fluttering like a bird.

Occasionally the Brahmin was the butt of scorn, even in the Vedas. The *Chandogya Upanishad* says that Brahmins, like hungry dogs ferreting for food, sit around chanting: 'Hin! Om, let us eat; Om, let us drink! Om may the god Varuna, may Prajapati and Savitri bring food here! O Lord of food, bring food here – bring it here!' And a satirical hymn in the Rig-veda, often described as the panegyric of frogs, compares the chanting of mantras by Brahmins to the croaking of frogs at the first rain:

One is Cow-bellow and Goat-bleat the other,
one frog is Green
and one of them is Spotty.
They bear one common name,
and yet they vary,
and talking,
modulate the voice diversely.

The Brahmins, sitting round the brimful vessel,
talk at the Soma-rite of Atiratra,
So, frogs, ye gather round the pool
to honour this day of all the year,
the first of rain-time ...

Cow-bellow and Goat-bleat have granted riches,
and Green and Spotty
have vouchsafed us treasure.
The frogs who give us cows in hundreds
lengthen our lives
in this most fertilising season.

The Vedic literature, being Brahminical works, is rich in information about Brahmins, but there is very little in it about the other *varnas*. The primary function of Kshatriyas was to fight in times of war and to govern in times of peace, but in Vedic India they also studied the scriptures and composed sacred hymns, such as the third book of the Rig-veda, authored by the Kshatriya family of Visvamitra. In the Upanishadic period many kings earned distinction as philosophers, from whom even Brahmins sought to learn wisdom. In temporal matters the Kshatriya lorded over everyone, including Brahmins, but especially over Vaisyas. 'The Kshatriya, whenever he likes, says, "You Vaisya, just bring me what thou hast stored away." Thus he subdues him and obtains possession of anything he wishes,' states the *Satapatha Brahmana*.

The Vaisya, though it was his labour that fed the Brahmin and Kshatriya, was usually treated with contempt by them, because he was under their power, the physical power of the Kshatriya and the spiritual power of the

Brahmin. The *Aitareya Brahmana* describes the Vaisya as the 'tributary to another, to be lived on by another, and to be oppressed at will.' But there were probably many wealthy Vaisyas in Vedic India, as there would be in Buddha's time.

Below the Vaisya in the social hierarchy was the Sudra, whom the *Aitareya Brahmana* describes as 'the servant of another, to be expelled at will, to be beaten (or slain) at will.' Sudras, though they were Aryans, had none of the privileges of the other *varnas.* While the first three *varnas* had independent functions, the Sudra had no particular function, but simply had to do the bidding of others. But the texts do occasionally speak well of him, and the *Satapatha Brahmana* even gives him a place in the Soma sacrifice.

Further down the social scale, and outside the *varna* system, was the non-Aryan Dasa, a slave in all but name. He was not entitled to own any property, 'being himself the property of the Aryan tribe as a whole, much in the same way as cattle,' as Kosambi puts it. There was not much chattel slavery in Vedic India – the Dasas provided all the labour force society needed – but slavery did exist, especially domestic slavery, and the Rig-vedic hymns speak of 'one hundred Dasas' and 'fifty female slaves' being given as gifts. The *Aitareya Brahmana* states that a gift of 1,000 slave girls was made by a king to his priests for performing the coronation rites. The Atharva-veda also mentions female slaves.

Such then was society in Vedic times. It was a fairly well-organised society, though not quite the idyllic world of peace and happiness that the romantics would have us believe it was. Society was still turbulent. And there was still quite a bit of the savage in man. But he was also a dreamer, and his noblest aspirations were for peace and harmony and love, as in this singularly gentle and moving hymn in the Atharva-veda:

Alike in heart, of like intent
non-hostile do I make you;
One another you should love,
as the cow loves her new-born calf.

May the son do the father's will
and be of one mind with his mother,
May wife to husband be gentle,
and honeyed words ever speak.

May not brother his brother hate,
or sister her own sister;
In full accord, with duty same,
should they speak words gently . . .

Same be your drink and common your food,
to the same yoke together I bind you,
Worship Agni together in harmony
like spokes round the hub of a wheel.

'CHANT AM I, VERSE THOU'

Man am I, woman thou;
chant am I, verse thou;
heaven am I, earth thou;
so will we dwell together,
parents of children yet to be.

Thus sang the Atharva-vedic poet in a rare moment of romantic lyricism. This was a new sentiment, for there was not much romance in the life of ancient man, his nascent imagination not yet quite awake to what would be its eventual fatal obsession. In primitive societies the relationship between man and woman was a simple affair of casual sex, without the comforting, tormenting complexities of love. There was no monogamous exclusivity in the pairing of couples, no sexual possessiveness. The family as a closed unit did not exist. In former times, says the *Mahabharata*, women were free to have sex with anyone who desired them. Though some form of sexual teaming to rear children presumably did exist among even the most primitive people, as indeed it did among animals, the family evolved as a stable social unit only when society itself became stable after man settled in farming communities.

In Vedic times the family structure was still fluid, but the patrilineal joint family headed by the *grihapati*, lord of the house, was clearly emerging as the norm. Most Vedic couples were probably monogamous, but polygamy was fairly common, and polyandry not unknown. Vedic kings were certainly polygamous, obligatorily so, for coronation ritual required the participation of four wives. As for the commoner, more wives meant more children, more work-force, and therefore greater prosperity, though with several wives jostling for his favours – being pressed by 'rival wives on every side,' as the Rig-veda puts it – the poor husband would have had little peace at home or rest in bed. In that competitive conjugal environment frustrated wives used all sorts of ploys to entice their men, from blatant sexual flaunting – with 'their breasts, hips and heads quivering with passion,' says the Rig-veda – to sorcery, for which the Vedas obligingly provide several rites. 'From out of the earth I dig this plant, a herb of most effectual power,' chants a distraught wife in the Rig-veda, who wants to 'quell the rival wife and gain the husband for oneself.' Then, under the hypnotic spell of the mantra's auto-suggestion – or perhaps to induce self-hypnosis – she exults:

Stronger am I, O Stronger One, yea,
mightier than the mightiest;
And she who is my rival wife
is lower than the lowest dames.

Among men too there was competition to possess the desired woman, and the Atharva-veda has several occult rites to enable a man to prevail, by making him irresistibly virile, or turning his rival impotent. 'As women split reeds with stone for a cushion, so do I split thy member on yon woman's loins,' gloats a shaman in the Atharva-veda, while another chants:

Up, the energies of herbs,
the essences of bulls,
the virility of men be thou put together
in him, O Indra, self-controller ...

I make thy member taut,
like a bowstring on a bow;
mount as it were a stag a doe
unrelaxingly always.

Of the horse, of the mule, of the he-goat
and of the ram, also of the bull
what vigours there are – them do thou
put in him, O self-controller.

Marriage came to be considered in Vedic times as essential for the happiness of the individual and the welfare of society. To remain unmarried was considered misery, especially for women – one of the most spiteful curses a Vedic woman could hurl at her rival was the Atharva-vedic imprecation, 'May she long sit with her relatives until her hair drops from her head!' The horror of that prospect would later lead to the practice of child marriage in India, but this was not prevalent in Vedic times. Nor was there any bar on the remarriage of widows. Society frowned on women taking husbands from lower social classes in *pratiloma* (against the grain) marriages, but men taking wives from the lower classes in *anuloma* (with the grain) marriages was common. Marriage between close relatives was forbidden, but there was no prohibition of marriage within the *gotra* at this time.

In sexual matters, what Vedic Aryans most frowned upon was incest, between parents and children and between brothers and sisters. Incest was probably common among Aryans in very early times, as evident in the Buddhist tale *Dasaratha Jataka*, which presents Rama and Sita as brother and sister, and in the Rig-vedic reference to the intimacy between the god Prajapati and his daughter. Incest is also the theme of a long, dramatic dialogue in the Rig-veda between Yama and his sister Yami, who tries to seduce him.

YAMI:
Even in the womb God Tvastr, vivifier,
shaping all forms, creator,
made us consorts ...
I, Yami, am possessed by love of Yama,
that I may rest
on the same couch beside him ...

YAMA:
Sure there will come succeeding times
when brothers and sisters
will do acts unmeet for kinsfolk.
Not me, O fair one – seek another
husband and make thine arm a pillow
for thy consort ...

YAMI:
Forced by my love these many words
I utter. Come near,
and hold me in thy close embraces.

YAMA:
I will not fold mine arms about thy body:
they call it sin
when one comes near his sister ...

YAMI:
Alas! thou are indeed a weakling, Yama;
we find in thee no trace
of heart or spirit ...

YAMA:
Embrace another, Yami;
let another, even as the woodbine
rings the tree, enfold thee ...

There is no mention of divorce in the Vedas, but as marriage bonds were fairly lax, it would not have been uncommon for couples to separate and form fresh alliances. Adultery was regarded as only a venial sin in Vedic times. During religious sacrifices, which the husband and wife had to perform together, it was customary for the officiating priest to ask the wife to name her lovers or at least indicate their number by holding up as many stalks of grass as she had lovers. 'Now when a woman belonging to one man carries on intercourse with another, she undoubtedly commits (a sin) against Varuna,' states the *Satapatha Brahmana*, but goes on to contend that when she confesses, the deception becomes truth and therefore less of a sin. To absolve herself, all that the woman had to do was to make an offering of barley porridge to Agni with the words, 'Whatever sin we have committed in the village, in the forest, among men, and in ourselves, that by this sacrifice we remove here.' The *Taittiriya Brahmana* prescribes a similar ceremony for adulterous men.

Different forms of marriage, including marriage by abduction or seduction, were probably current in Vedic India, as in later Indian society, but the common practice was for the man to seek the girl's hand from her father through an intermediary. The marriage broker was already around in Vedic society, and was an object of much drollery, as in this description in the Atharva-veda: 'With forelock loosened over his brow here comes the wooer, the man in search of a wife for his friend, in quest of a husband for this bride, a wife for this unmarried man.' Some grooms had to pay bride-money, while others received dowry; sometimes a girl was simply sold by her father, or gifted to a man for services rendered.

There are several hymns in the Vedas giving details of marriage ceremonies, but their sequence has to be conjectured on the basis of later practices. The wedding ceremony, it seems, was usually held in the bride's home. On the morning of the wedding, the girl was ceremonially bathed in consecrated water, and the gods were invoked to favour her 'with the splendour of the dice, strong drink, and the buttocks of the courtesan,' states the Atharva-veda. She was then dressed, her hair coiffured, her eyes lined with kohl, and led to the nuptial ceremony. There, at the sacred fire prepared by priests, she was first symbolically married to Soma, then to Gandharva, then to Agni, all propitious deities, and finally to the groom, while a yoke, symbolic of marital union, was held over their heads. The groom then took the bride's arm and together they circumambulated the nuptial fire in the auspicious clockwise direction, and, in the concluding act of the ceremony, took seven steps in the north-east direction, the quarter of victory.

Afterwards the groom led the bride to stand on a stone, the symbolic 'lap of the earth', and, holding her hand, muttered a few stanzas of the wedding hymn, promising to cherish her all his life. He then presented her with a set of clothes and jewels, which she put on, and the couple mounted the canopied wedding chariot decorated with flowers, while an Atharva-vedic benediction was pronounced on the bride: 'As from its stalk a cucumber, from here I sever thee ... I make her softly fettered there ... May she live blest in fortune and sons ... Go to the house to be the household's mistress and speak as a lady to thy gathered people.' A chest containing her dowry was then placed in the chariot, and the couple, accompanied by friends and relatives, and with priests chanting mantras, went in a procession to the groom's house.

On entering his house, the couple sat before the household fire, on a buckskin spread over with a layer of *balbuja* grass, and worshiped Agni, as the priest chanted a Rig-vedic blessing:

Be ye not parted; dwell ye here;
reach the full span of human life.
With sons and grandsons sport and play,
rejoicing in your own abode ...
O bounteous Indra, make this bride
blest in her sons and fortunate ...

A feast was then served to guests. At night the maiden was led to the bridal chamber, while the priest invoked an Atharva-vedic blessing: 'Mount the couch with favouring mind; here give birth to progeny for this husband. Like Indrani, waking with a good awakening, mayest thou watch ... dawns tipped with light. The gods in the beginning lay with their spouses; they embraced bodies with bodies. Like Surya, O woman ... unite here with thy husband ... as male and female ... make ye progeny.' Then, turning to the groom, the priest chanted, 'Mount the spread out thighs ... embrace thy wife with a well-willing mind; ye two make progeny here, enjoying.' The next day the semen-and-blood-soiled bridal garment, the proof of the consummation of marriage, was presented to the officiating priest – it was his privilege to receive it as a gift – so that the evil spirits enviously hovering around the blissful couple might depart with it.

The primary purpose of Vedic marriage was procreation, to sustain the line. 'May I be immortal through my children,' prays the Rig-vedic poet, and describes the son as the 'cancellor of [the father's] debt' to his ancestors for giving him life. The Atharva-veda describes begetting children as 'spinning out the thread of life.'

Vedic Aryans preferred sons to daughters. Not having sons was regarded as a form of indigence – and that, in a sense, was what it really was. Sons, as hunters, warriors and farmers, were economic assets in ancient societies, and parents needed sons to take care of them in their old age. On the other hand, 'to have a daughter was misery,' according to the *Aitareya Brahmana*, and it is possible that female babies were sometimes exposed to death, of which there is a faint hint in the Yajur-veda. The desire to have sons was so strong among the Vedic people that a childless widow was allowed to cohabit with her brother-in-law until a son was born to her. Typical of the numerous Atharva-vedic rituals and charms for the birth of a son is this invocation:

Into thy womb shall enter a male sperm,
as an arrow into a quiver ...
The plants whose father was the sky,
whose mother the earth,
whose root the ocean,
may these divine herbs aid thee
in obtaining a son.

In the occult rite associated with this mantra, an arrow was broken to pieces over the woman's head, and one piece fastened on her as an amulet. Then the priest poured the 'milk of a cow which has a calf of a colour identical with her own' into a cup made from a plough, mashed some rice and barley along with the leaves of certain plants into it, and put the paste into the woman's right nostril with his right thumb. As the pregnancy progressed, other rites were performed, and in the tenth month a special ceremony was held for easy delivery, at which the priest chanted the Atharva-vedic hymn:

As the wind, as the mind,
as fly the birds,
so do thou, O ten month's child,
fly along with the afterbirth ...

The attitude of Vedic society towards women was ambivalent, but on the whole their position was much better than in later periods. The wife, though definitely subordinate to her husband, was respected as the *grihapatni*, mistress of the house, and was considered, according to the *Satapatha Brahmana*, half her husband, an equal partner. 'A wife ... is home and dwelling,' proclaims the Rig-veda. There was no seclusion of women in Vedic times – 'From olden time,' states the Rig-veda, 'the matron goes to feast and general sacrifice.' Widows could remarry. As for sati – the practice of a widow immolating herself on her husband's funeral pyre – the Brahmanas are silent about it, but it was probably prevalent in pre-Vedic times, for the Atharva-veda does mention it as an ancient practice. And it was still performed symbolically during the Vedic age, with the widow lying down for a while with the body of her husband on the funeral pyre, before taking the hand of another man. The Atharva-veda describes the scene:

This woman, choosing her husband's world,
lay down by thee that art departed, O mortal,
continuing to keep her ancient duty ...

Go up, O woman, to the world of the living;
thou liest by this one who is deceased: come!
to him who grasps thy hand, thy second spouse,
thou hast now entered into the relation of wife to husband.

Vedic women had no role in public affairs, and were not allowed to attend the meetings of the tribal assembly. But they were not barred from religious studies, and some twenty-odd of them are named in the Rig-veda as composers of its hymns. Vedic scholarship, according to the Atharva-veda, was a desirable attainment in women that could even win them good husbands. Women had at this time an important role in rituals, for the householder could perform Vedic sacrifices only if he had his wife beside him, and it was she who sang the Sama-veda hymns, though later this function was taken over by professional priests. There were also certain Vedic sacrifices exclusively performed by women, such as the Sita sacrifice intended to promote rich harvest, the Rudrabali sacrifice to promote fecundity in cattle, and the Rudrayaga sacrifice to secure good luck to maidens in marriage. The role of women in religion however declined in the later Vedic period, as rituals grew complicated and the language of the hymns became archaic and obscure.

Simultaneously, the role of women in society, and their status within the family, also declined. The *Aitareya Brahmana* warns the wife not to talk back to her husband, and the *Satapatha Brahmana* enjoins her to eat only after her husband has eaten. A woman's blood-money in Vedic India was the same as that of a Sudra, and she, again like the Sudra, was denied the right to own property. According to Sayana, the Rig-vedic rule was that, if sonless, the father's property would be inherited by his grandsons who would be treated as his sons, and that daughters had no right to it. In later Vedic times the notion that the wife was the property of her husband took hold, for the *Satapatha Brahmana* decrees that women can own neither themselves nor any legacy. They were usually taken as prizes of war, along with cattle and other property.

Vedic poets generally viewed women with distrust, as fickle, libidinous, perverse and untrustworthy. They were irresistibly alluring and yet utterly repugnant. The Rig-veda describes women as 'hardened sinners of evil conduct who deceive their husbands, in whose hearts no truth or faithfulness is found,' and thoughtfully allots a special hell for depraved wives. The *Mahabharata* echoes the same sentiment:

The fire has never too many logs
the ocean never too many rivers,
death never too many souls,
fair-eyed woman never too many men.

'The woman, the Sudra, the dog, and the crow are falsehood,' warns the *Satapatha Brahmana.* 'Indra himself hath said this: the mind of woman brooks no discipline; her intelligence is slight,' states the Rig-veda, and bemoans that 'the foolish woman sucks dry the panting wise man.'

Later, among the ascetic sects of the sixth century BC, this distrust of women would find expression in the practice of celibacy, but Vedic Aryans had no abhorrence of sex. Rather, they viewed sex as an ordinary biological need, and had no squeamishness in talking candidly about it. Says the Rig-veda:

The horse likes a light-laden cart,
gay hosts attract laugh and jest:
Penis longs for pudenda, natural as
parched frogs longing for rain.

Some of the passages in the Vedas are so graphically sexual that their Victorian translators omitted them altogether or rendered them into Latin, such as the bawdy banter in the Yajur-veda between the queen and the officiating priest during the Asvamedha-yaga, in which he teases her with a lewd description of sexual intercourse, as she lies naked with the sacrificial horse. More quotable, though not in its entirety, is Indrani's boast about her sexual prowess in the Rig-veda:

No woman has finer loins than I,
or is better at making love.
No woman thrusts against a man better than I,
or rises and spreads her thighs more ...

Indrani gets ever more alarmingly raw and graphic as she warms to the subject. Such open talk was a throwback to the time when sex was free of inhibition, as indeed it continued to be among some wild Aryan tribes even at this time. Vedic literature often speaks of unwed mothers, bastard children and paramours, and the *Vajasaneyi Samhita* notes the prevalence of illicit unions between men and women of different *varnas.* The spring festival of Mahavrata was quite a bacchanalian and promiscuous affair in Vedic times. As for the oldest profession, it was probably quite old even in Vedic times, for the nuptial hymn in the Atharva-veda speaks with admiration of the splendorous buttocks of the courtesan, here called the Mahanagni, The Great Naked Woman.

The commonplace physical craving of man for sex spun into another orbit altogether when it was ignited by his psychological need for love. A poet in the Atharva-veda speaks of his ardour as 'an arrow, winged with longing, barbed with love, whose shaft is unswerving desire,' while another celebrates a more tender emotion: 'The eyes of us two be honeyed; our face be ointment; put thou me within thy heart; may our mind verily be together.' There is even a charm in the Atharva-veda to allay the pangs of those tormented with jealousy:

As the earth is dead in spirit,
in spirit more dead than the dead,
and as the spirit of him that has died,
thus shall the spirit of the jealous be dead!

For the lovelorn, the Atharva-veda has several mantras, in one of which the suitor chants:

Consumed by burning ardour,
with parched mouth, do thou come to me,
pliant, thy pride laid aside, mine alone,
speaking sweetly and to me devoted!

For this charm to work, the man had to perform an elaborate and rather incoherent rite spread over three nights and involving the use of diverse occult devices. Somewhere along the way, perhaps at the end of the rite, he was also required to jab the woman with his thumb while reciting the above hymn. It was a lot of hard work for man to win a woman's love. The rites prescribed for a woman to ensnare her man were much simpler. Even her mantra was short, direct and simple, though hypnotic in its repetitive frenzy. She chanted:

Craze him, O Maruts;
O Akas, craze him;
O Agni, do thou craze him;
let yon man burn for me.

While chanting this hymn, all that she had to do was to throw some beans (considered a stimulant) upon the man's head – or on his couch, or on the ground he walked on, authorities helpfully suggest – then kindle the points of a few arrows and cast them around the effigy of the man. In a gentler mood, another Atharva-vedic woman prays softly:

At the tip of my tongue honey,
at the root of my tongue honeyedness
mayest thou be altogether in my power,
mayest thou come unto my intent.

UNTO US A HAPPY MIND

'Fair wealth, O Savitr, today, tomorrow, fair wealth produce for us each day that passes,' supplicates a priest in the Yajurveda. 'May we, through this our song, be happy gainers, god!' Similarly, a Rig-vedic sage seeks 'great glory ... heroic strength ... reward and riches.' The frank materialism of these hymns is not an aberration. Rather, it is the overwhelming tone of the Vedas. The Vedic Indian had none of the fatalistic, life-negating attitudes favoured by later Indian sages, but lived a positive, lusty and exuberant life, delighting in the thin yield of earthly pleasures. Even his desires for the afterlife were mundane. Pleads a Rig-vedic poet:

Make me immortal in that realm
of eager wish and strong desire,
The region of radiant moon,
where food and full delight are found.

There are however a few hymns in the Vedas that evoke a more refined sentiment, in which man withdraws his mind from the clamour of the temporal world to seek within himself a gentler vision of life. 'Send unto us a good and happy mind,' prays a Rig-vedic poet. And in the same vein an Atharva-vedic poet chants:

The earth upon which the noisy mortals
sing and dance,
upon which they fight, upon which resounds
the roaring drum ...

The earth holds people of manifold
various speech,
of diverse customs, according
to their habitations ...

The earth holds the fool and holds the wise,
endures the good and the bad;
she keeps company with the boar,
she gives herself to the wild hog ...

O mother earth, kindly set me down
upon a well-founded place!
With heaven aiding, O thou wise one, do thou
place me into happiness and prosperity!

Yet another Atharva-vedic poet offers a touching holistic prayer for peace on earth – peace not just among men, but for all the things on earth, animate and inanimate, the total earthly environment:

Peaceful be heaven, peaceful the earth,
peaceful the broad space between,
peaceful for us be the running waters,
peaceful the plants and herbs! ...

Peace be to earth and to airy spaces,
peace be to heaven, peace to the waters,
peace to the plants and peace to the trees –
may all the gods grant me peace ...

May peace prevail, happiness prevail!
May everything for us be peaceful!

One of the most endearing qualities of the Vedic Aryan was his high regard for hospitality. He esteemed a guest as *pratyaksha-Brahma*, visible Brahma, and treated him with great courtesy, even reverence. Etiquette required the householder to greet his guest graciously, give him water to wash his feet, spread a mat for him to sit, offer him a drink, arrange for his bath, and serve him a feast. The Atharva-veda views hospitality as a form of sacrifice to the gods: 'Verily when a host looks at his guests he looks at the place of sacrifice to the gods. When he salutes them reverently he undergoes preparation for a religious ceremony; when he calls for water, he solemnly brings sacrificial water ...'

There was a similar emphasis on *dana*, charity, in Vedic literature, though these pleas for charity often degenerated into entreaties for gifts. In Rig-vedic times, gifts consisted mainly of cattle and horses, food and clothing, also chariots, measures of gold, and slave-girls, but not land, or even grain, reflecting the essentially pre-agrarian nature of the prevailing economy.

There are several hymns in praise of gifts in the Rig-veda, mostly shameless panegyrics on the giver of gifts, but we do occasionally find in them a noble, compassionate sentiment:

Who has the power should give unto the needy,
regarding well the course of life hereafter:
fortune, like two chariot wheels revolving,
now to one man comes nigh, now to another.

Life in Vedic India was entirely pastoral. There were no towns or cities in India at this time, and even celebrated kings of the age ruled from villages, living in wood and thatch cottages. Masonry structures were unknown, and, as Kosambi points out, the Sanskrit word for brick, *ista*, does not occur at all in the Rig-veda, though sun-dried bricks were probably used for making fire altars. Carpenters, not masons, built the Vedic houses.

The typical upper-class Vedic house, standing in its own fenced compound, was a large rectangular structure with several rooms and a pen for domestic animals. The house was built on wooden pillars, which were, says the Atharva-veda, 'strong as elephant's feet.' Its walls were of wood and mud, and its roof, built on a frame of beams, crossbeams and props of bamboo, was covered with wickerwork mats and 'a robe of grass.' The floor was of mud, but spread over with reed mats or grass, on which reed cushions were placed. Every home had a central hearth, where the household religious rites were performed.

The Aryan house was a slight structure, which could be easily dismantled and carried away – 'Like a woman, O dwelling, we carry thee where we will,' says the Atharva-vedic poet. Houses were sometimes gifted to priests, who, notes Iyengar, 'took down their various parts with the recitation of ... mantras ... and refixed them with mantras on their own sites.' There was a ritual to begin the construction of a house, at which the Atharva-vedic priest recited:

Right here, do thou, O house, stand firmly,
full of horses, full of cattle,
full of abundance,
full of sap, full of ghee, full of milk ...

Hither to the house hath come the tender child,
hither the calf and other domestic animals;
hither the vessel full of liquor,
together with a bowl of sour milk!

The poor probably lived in clusters of mud and wattle circular huts, and slept on the bare mud floor, as they would in India in later times, but the rich, according to Iyengar's study, 'slept on beds spread on benches or cots made of a framework of wood tied with strings or tapes and provided with bolsters, coverlets and blankets.' The household furniture and utensils mentioned in Vedic literature are chairs and boxes; leather casks, bowls and buckets; ladles of wood and stirring-sticks; sieves, spits, pots, mortars and pestles; bellows and grinding stones; and rope slings to hold pots. Food was served on leaf platters, usually the lotus leaf. Goblets were made of wood.

The diet of Vedic Aryans consisted of grains, meats, vegetables and fruits, along with milk and milk products. Their main cereal was barley; they would take to rice during the later Vedic period, but only much later to wheat, which was the staple food of the Indus people. Sanskrit texts sometimes even describe wheat as *mleccha-bhojana*, alien, unclean food. Barley and rice were eaten parched, or ground into flour and made into cakes with milk and butter, or boiled in water or milk, sometimes mixed with sesame and vegetables. Milk mixed with honey was a special delicacy.

Among meats, beef 'was a normal article of contemporary Brahmin diet,' notes Kosambi. A guest in ancient India was called *goghna*, one for whom the cow was killed. To serve a feast of beef to guests, especially to revered guests like sages, was a matter of honour for the Aryan gentry. The great sage Yajnavalkya is said to have had a particular weakness for the tender flesh of the milch cow, but normally only sterile or old cows or oxen were slaughtered for meat, for the milch cow, termed *aghnya*, not to be killed, was too valuable an economic asset to be squandered. These considerations also applied to horse-flesh. Other meats were more commonly eaten. 'Cook ye the goat and the five rice dishes,' bids an Atharva-vedic sage. Meat was roasted on spits or cooked in metal or earthenware pots, and the aroma of roasting meat was as irresistible to gods as to men. Notes the Rig-veda:

They, observing that the horse
is ready, call out and say,
the smell is good; remove it;
And, carving meat, await the distribution ...

Vedic Aryans had no taboos against intoxicants. 'What may I bring to thee – curds, stirred drink, or liquor?' a solicitous wife asks her husband in the Atharva-veda. Sura, probably a beer-like drink prepared from fermented grain and herbs, was the common spirituous liquor of Aryans, and Surakara, the maker of Sura, was a recognised professional among them. Drunkenness was common in Vedic society, and was not considered a serious matter. Though Vedic texts do sometimes condemn Sura-drinking as the cause of depravity and discord, and prescribe a ritual to expiate the sin of over-indulging in it, the liquor, kept in skins, was usually served at the public hall, as an essential complement to the gambling that went on there. Another common Vedic drink was Madhu, probably mead.

The drink most often mentioned in the Vedas is Soma, a psychotropic beverage of Aryans dating back to their Central Asian days. Extracted from a rare and unidentified mountain plant, Soma was drunk only at rituals – or perhaps its drinking was always turned into a ritual. Indra was a lusty Soma drinker, and sometimes suffered hangovers in consequence; men too often overindulged in it, and the Yajur-veda has a mantra to atone for this sin. The scriptures generally viewed the effect of Soma as good intoxication, but that of Sura as base. States the *Satapatha Brahmana*: 'Soma is truth, prosperity, light, but Sura is untruth, misery, darkness.' The *Taittiriya Brahmana* however takes the indulgent view that 'Soma is male and Sura is female; the two make a pair.'

Men as well as women in Vedic India wore the same kind of dress. There are no sex-specific words for attire in Vedic literature. The common dress in Rig-vedic times consisted of two pieces of cloth, a lower garment tied around the waist, and a mantle-like upper garment that passed over the left shoulder and under the right arm. Later Vedic literature however mentions a third piece, an undergarment, probably a strip of cloth fixed to a girdle and drawn between the legs and tucked at the back. Turbans are mentioned for the first time in the Brahmanas, and both men and women wore them, perhaps in imitation of the Indus people. There is some uncertainty about whether stitched clothes were worn by Vedic Aryans or not. The probability is that they were not, though needle and sewing are mentioned in the Rig-veda, and the *Aitareya Brahmana* refers to two pieces of cloth being sewn together. Tailored dresses became popular in India only after the Turkish occupation of Delhi in the twelfth century AD.

The everyday dress material of Vedic Aryans was wool, but on ceremonial occasions an upper garment of deerskin or silk was worn. Garments were usually plain, but the rich often wore variegated cloth, embroidered or adorned with gold. Clans had their distinctive preferences in the colour of the clothes they wore; the Vasisthas, for instance, favoured white, while some others wore blue or red. Shoes made of boar-skin are mentioned in the *Satapatha Brahmana*.

Though their dress was simple, Vedic Indians, both men and women, were loaded with jewellery – necklets, earrings, anklets, bracelets and rings, all preferably of gold – and even the warrior rode into battle heavily bejewelled. Amulets were worn for good luck. People were fond of perfumes and flower garlands, and boys and girls are described in the Vedas as wearing lotus-garlands and playing on swings.

Vedic women took elaborate care in dressing. They, notes the Rig-veda, wore fresh clothes after bathing – sometimes they bathed in milk! – oiled and dressed their hair, 'decked themselves with gay ornaments' and flowers, applied scents and unguents, and, 'fair to look on and gently smiling,' attended public gatherings. Men – and gods – commonly wore beards, but shaving is also mentioned in Vedic literature. 'Sharpen us like a razor in the barber's hands,' prays a Rig-vedic poet. Personal grooming was at times turned into a ritual, especially on ceremonial occasions. Thus the *Satapatha Brahmana* specifies that the king getting ready for consecration should trim his nails (beginning with the thumb of his left hand) and shave (beginning with his right whisker) while chanting mantras.

Aryans paid particular attention to grooming their hair. Women, according to the Atharva-veda, braided their hair in broad plaits or dressed it in three different styles – like a horn, a net or a pot – and decorated it with flowers. Men also wore elaborate coiffures. Here again, distinctive hairstyles were used as clan identities – thus Vasisthas wore their hair braided or coiled on the right side of the head, while most others wore it on the left. The quill of the porcupine was generally used for parting the hair (and for applying make-up to the eyes) though the Atharva-veda also mentions combs of a hundred teeth. There is no record of tonsure as a ritual in Vedic times, but it was, as in the case of bathing or paring the nails, a means of making the body pure.

Occult rites were important beauty aids in Vedic times, as the means to clear blemishes, or to promote hair growth. Typical of this was the Atharva-vedic cure for baldness, which involved grinding together various plants and pouring the concoction on the head of the bald man by a shaman while chanting a particular mantra. The shaman was required to eat black food and wear black clothes, and perform the rite early in the morning, before sunrise. Apali in the Rig-veda had a somewhat different hair-raising problem, and prayed:

O Indra, cause to sprout again
three places, these which I declare –
My father's head, his cultured field,
and this the part below my waist.
Make all of these grow crops of hair,
yon cultivated field of ours,
my body, and my father's head.

Vedic Aryans were a fun-loving people, and their days were filled with music and dance, chariot-racing and dicing, drinking and carousing. Indians, as Alexander's officers would note in the fourth century BC, had a passion for songs. This was a marked characteristic of Vedic Aryans too – even of their gods: Indra is described as a 'lover of the song' in the Rig-veda – and music played a major role in their secular and religious life. Several musical instruments – such as the veena, cymbal, drum, reed flute, harp with a hundred strings, and a few other unidentified instruments – as well as specialist musicians like drummers, flute-players and conch-blowers are mentioned in Vedic literature.

Music developed into a highly systematised discipline in the later Vedic period, to meet the intricate chanting specifications of the Sama-veda. There were professional singers in Vedic times – a hymn in the Rig-veda speaks of Dawn as showing 'sweet things like a new song-singer' – possibly also professional actors, if the term *sailusha* in the Yajur-veda can be taken to mean an actor. The long Yama-Yami dialogue in the Rig-veda indicates that some form of ritual drama was prevalent at this time. By the later Vedic period, notes Basham, 'a rudimentary entertainment industry ... with professional acrobats, fortune-tellers, flute players and dancers' had come into existence. Professional women dancers, a common feature of later Indian society, were already present in Vedic times. Notes the Rig-veda:

She, like a dancer,
puts her embroidered garments on:
as a cow yields her udder,
so she bares her breasts.

Dancing was very much a part of the everyday life of Aryans. The Atharva-veda describes the earth as the place 'where men sing and dance,' and the Rig-veda refers to men 'going forth for dancing and for laughter.' They loved exuberant, stomping outdoor dances – the Rig-veda notes that 'thick dust arose ... from men who dance,' and the Atharva-veda speaks with deep contempt of men who dance languorously, 'like impotent men.'

Hunting was yet another pastime of Vedic Aryans – they hunted for sport as well as for food, and to protect their herds from wild animals. The 'thought-fleet' deer was their favourite game animal, but they also hunted boar, wild bulls and other animals, using bows and arrows, traps and snares. Birds were hunted with falcons, or were shot with arrows, or caught with nets spread on the ground. Dogs were used for guarding as well as boar hunting. There does not seem to have been much fishing in the early Vedic period, the rivers of Punjab being poor in fish – fish are mentioned only once in the Rig-veda – but the Yajur-veda is familiar with fishing.

The Vedic people were compulsive gamblers. For them, gambling was not a secret thrill, but a socially accepted pastime, indeed a quasi-sacramental activity, integral to rituals like the Rajasuya, as a test of divine favour. The tribal assembly hall doubled as the gambling den in Vedic times, and the regulars there were ironically called *sabha-sthanu*, pillars of the assembly. Even children seem to have gambled, for the Rig-veda mentions parents chastising them for it.

Apsaras, temptress goddesses, were the presiding deities of the dice. We do not know exactly how the game was played, but it is stated that the brown nuts of the Vibhitaka tree were used as dice, and that the gambling board had fifty-three squares – 'probably one central square and thirteen on each of the four lines radiating from the centre in the four directions,' speculates Iyengar. The Rig-veda says that four dice were used, but the Yajur-veda speaks of five, each with a name. The gambler sprinkled the dice with ghee for luck and, before throwing, muttered charms over them, such as this mantra from the Atharva-veda: 'O ye dice, give me fruitful play, like a cow rich in milk; fasten me together with a stream of winnings, as bow with a string.' To further help luck along, he often cheated, so that the Vedic term for gambler, *kitava*, came to mean a cheat in classical Sanskrit. If he won, says the Atharva-veda, the gambler exulted: 'As the wolf plucks to pieces the sheep, thus do I pluck thy winnings.' But often luck failed him, so the gamester came to be called a *dhurta*, wastrel. Laments a gambler in the Rig-veda:

She never vexed me nor was angry with me,
but to my friends and me was ever gracious.
For die's sake, whose single point is final,
mine own devoted wife I alienated.

My wife holds me aloof, her mother hates me ...
Others caress the wife of him whose riches
the die hath snatched, that rapid courser:
Of him speak father, mother, brothers saying,
'We know him not; bind him and take him with you.'

When I resolve to play with these no longer,
my friends depart from me and leave me lonely.
When the brown dice, thrown on the board, have rattled,
I hasten to play, like a fond girl to her lover.

The gamester seeks the gambling-house, and wonders,
his body all afire, Shall I be lucky?
Still do the dice extend his eager longing,
staking his gains against his adversary.

Dice, verily, are armed with goads and driving-hooks,
deceiving and tormenting, causing grievous woe.
They give frail gifts and then destroy the man who wins ...

Sad is the gambler when he sees a matron,
another's wife, and his well-ordered dwelling.
In the morning he rides the brown dice,
by evening he falls by the hearth, a beggar ...

Play not with dice: no, cultivate thy corn-land.
Enjoy the gain, and deem that wealth sufficient.
There are thy cattle, there thy wife, O gambler ...
let the brown dice snare some other captive.

Chariot racing was another favourite pastime in Vedic society and had a prominent place even in grand Vedic sacrifices like the Rajasuya and Vajapeya. The race seems to have been run on a horseshoe shaped course, for the texts speak of horses turning around a point. The winning horse was decorated and its owner presented with a prize. 'O Indra, help our chariot on, yea, Thunderer, though it lags behind,' prays a Rig-vedic poet. 'Assist our car that seeks the prize. What can be easier for thee? So make thou us victorious.'

Life was on the whole easy and pleasant for Vedic Indians. But they also had their fair share of miseries. 'My heart quakes like a rolling wheel for fear of penury,' bemoans a Rig-vedic hymnist. Famines swept the land periodically, and thousands died of starvation. Demon spirits lay in waiting to trap man at every turn of life; misfortunes hounded him, liars and cheats tripped him up, sorcerers bedevilled him. In the forest around his habitat lurked lions, tigers, wolves and hyenas. In the village itself there were deadly scorpions, and the even deadlier snakes, 'toothed ropes,' as the Atharva-veda calls them. And he was subject to many diseases – tuberculosis, haemorrhoids, abscesses, dysentery, boils, swellings, tumours, convulsions, 'fever that is spotted, speckled, ruddy like sprinkling,' ulcers, scabs, rheumatism, tearing pains, insanity, headache, heart-disease, ailments of the eye, leprosy, jaundice, cramp, venereal disease, debility, and senility – which are mentioned in Vedic literature. The most common ailment afflicting the Vedic Aryan was *takman*, probably malarial fever.

Diseases in Vedic times were considered visitations of the supernatural, and their treatment wisely worked both on the mind and the body of the patient, through medication as well as exorcism, with the surgeon using the knife as well as mantras. 'Often,' notes Iyengar, 'the treatment was based on colour merely; red objects were placed round a patient to cure him of jaundice, and Rohini, the red goddess, was worshipped.' Alternately, sympathetic magic was used, as in seeking to transfer fever to a frog 'by pouring water over the patient and putting a frog under the bed.' Diseases were often attributed to witchcraft, and were deflected by rival witchcraft. 'Bend round and pass us by, O curse, even as a burning fire a lake ... strike him down that curses us,' invokes an Atharva-vedic hymn. There are several mantras of prophylactic magic in the Vedas, such as for protection against nightmares, to expiate the ill-luck of irregular teeth, for safety from lightning, against snake-bite, and so on. Chants a physician in the Rig-veda:

The wind blows downward from on high,
downward the sun-god sends his heat,
downward the milch-cow pours her milk:
so downward go thy pain and grief.

Felicitous is this mine hand,
yet more felicitous is this.
This hand contains all healing balms,
and this makes whole with gentle touch.

The Atharva-veda – which Macdonnell describes as 'the oldest literary monument of Indian medicine' – has innumerable magical spells and rites to deal with every conceivable human malady, such as this mantra against scrofulous sores:

With urine do ye wash the tumour,
with urine do ye sprinkle it!
The urine is a potent remedy:
do thou (Rudra) with it show
mercy to us, that we may live!

The ancient Indian physician probably had a better knowledge of anatomy and physiology than his medieval successors, because of the Vedic practice of animal sacrifice. Sacrificial killing and carving of animals was done with care and according to strict prescriptions, and the slaughterer-priest was a skilled vivisectionist. The priest often doubled as the medicine-man, and in either role he was treated with respect. Lauds the Rig-vedic poet:

He who hath a store of herbs at hand,
like a king amid a crowd of men –
Physician is that sage's name,
fiend slayer, chaser of disease.

In later times, when society developed rigorous caste taboos, the physician would lose social status, because he dealt with people of all castes and conditions, and came into contact with impure body fluids. The decline in his status began as early as the later Vedic period, when Asvins, divine physicians, came to be considered as inferior gods. The *Taittiriya-samhita*, a recension of the Black Yajur-veda, warns, 'A Brahmin must not practise medicine, for the physician is impure, unfit for sacrifice.'

The Vedic age saw the rudimentary beginnings of several other branches of knowledge. The foundation for systematic astronomical studies in India was laid at this time, by the attention paid by Vedic Aryans to the calculation of time and the passage of seasons, to enable efficient farming. The early Indian calendar was lunar; the solar calendar would come into use only much later, and its widespread knowledge, observes Thapar, 'is associated with Greek contacts.'

Time, says the Atharva-veda, began when Purusha, the primeval man, 'measured out the year.' Vedic Aryans divided the year into twelve lunar months of about thirty days each, with an occasional intercalary month, which the Rig-veda designated as the thirteenth month. Day and night were each divided into thirty parts. Seasons were sometimes reckoned as three, but more often as six: Vasanta (spring), Grishma (summer), Varsha (rain), Sarad (autumn), Hemanta (winter), and Sisira (the dewy season). The Atharva-veda describes the year, the seasons, the months and the days metaphorically:

Twelve fellies, one wheel,
three hubs, who understands that?
Therein are inserted three-hundred and sixty pins,
pegs that are immovable ...

The study of geometry also began in Vedic times, out of the need to construct sacrificial altars of precise shapes and dimensions. Similarly, the rigour required in mastering the Vedas led to the various branches of linguistics. Vedic sages cherished learning very highly, and often prayed for its preservation, as in this Atharva-vedic chant:

Wisdom at evening,
wisdom in the morning,
wisdom at noon,
wisdom by the sun's rays,
by this spell,
do we make enter into us.

ACROSS THE VOID, A DIVIDING LINE

The waters listen
as they flow along:
they know the origin
of heaven and earth.

Sitting under a tree on a grassy knoll on the wooded banks of the broad and placid river Saraswati, watching the rising sun silver the false azure of its mirrored sky, the Rig-vedic poet, lost in reverie about the mysteries of life, the turning of the day and the turning of the seasons, the cycle of life and death and the beginning of beginnings, stretched his mind and took wing – so we imagine as we read these lines. Elsewhere the poet frets: 'What thing I truly am I know not. Mysterious, fettered in my mind, I wander ...' 'Where do the seasons go, where the seasons' fruits?' wonders an Atharva-vedic poet. And again:

Why does the wind not cease?
Why does the mind not rest?
Why do the waters, seeking truth,
Never ever cease?

Exploring further, another Atharva-vedic poet inquires:

Numerous things dear and not dear,
sleep, oppressions and weariness,
delights and pleasures – from where
does man bring them?

Whence comes distress, depression, decay,
mindlessness, and whence comes affluence,
success, prosperity, thought and exaltations? ...
Who set in him truth? who untruth?
Whence comes death?
Whence the immortal? ...

Who put the semen in him
so his line might be further spun?
Who brought him wisdom?
Who endowed him with music, dance?

With these tentative speculations, the Vedic sages rose to the rarefied upper realms of thought to compose some of the most evocative poems of early man, hymns of surpassing spiritual subtlety and beauty, which would, in a few centuries, lead to the solemn speculations of the Upanishads and the profound humanism of Buddhism. But in the Vedas themselves there is only a faint hint of that great potential. The Vedas are not, unlike what the orthodox pundits would have us believe, the culmination of the religious quest of man in India, but its rudimentary beginning. 'Brahmin theory,' remarks Kosambi, 'still regards the Vedas as supreme among all Indian writings; Indian culture would not have been worth writing about if the Vedas had retained that position in practice.'

The vast bulk of the Vedic hymns are coarse and trite, concerned solely with the elementary animal needs of man for food, shelter and progeny, often making crass and brazen demands on the gods in return for singing their praise and offering them oblations. The very first hymn of the Rig-veda sets the tone for this:

I laud Agni, the chosen priest, god,
minister of sacrifice ...
Through Agni man obtaineth wealth, yea,
plenty waxing day by day ...

It is only natural that these ancient texts should reflect the rusticity of thought of ancient man. The real surprise in the Vedas is not in their crudity but in the exquisite subtlety they reveal now and then, tender shoots breaking through the coarse soil and thrusting towards the sun.

But to ignore the crudity of the Vedas, as has often been done, would be to falsify Vedic civilisation, and to remove the hymns from their true socio-cultural context. It is sometimes contended that the Vedas are too subtle to be understood by merely examining the meanings of their words, and that their essential spirituality lies hidden behind the veil of the obvious. Not really. The esoteric wisdom that scholiasts claim to find in the Vedas is mostly thoughts that they themselves insert into the hymns, not the thoughts of the Vedic sages. There is indeed much that is obscure in the Vedas, but this is not because of transcendental mysticism, but largely because of the archaic nature of the Vedic language. Besides, the Vedas are mostly poetry, often composed by sages in a state of ecstasy induced by drinking Soma, and, like all poetry, they make sudden allegorical twists and turns.

All this makes the interpretation of several Vedic passages difficult. But where the meaning is explicit, as in many of the hymns, they are in such perfect harmony with the thoughts and aspirations of the primitive people who composed them, that there is no need to look in them for meanings other than what they evidently say, or to imagine that the obscure passages contain some cabalistic mystery. As for the few metaphysical hymns in the Vedas, they are as obviously metaphysical as the temporal hymns are obviously temporal. There is really no mystery.

The Vedic Indian had little awareness of anything beyond the world of his sense perceptions, and his concept of the cosmos was quite rudimentary: the earth below, the heavens above, 'two great bowls turned towards each other, each laden with treasure,' as the Rig-veda saw it. Sometimes the two parts were described as two wheels, one above the other. Occasionally a refinement was added to this simple division by treating the space immediately above the earth as a buffer zone, and placing the heavens above the vault of the sky. The heavens were not, for Vedic Aryans, an abstract idea; it was not heaven, but simply the physical place up above, visible to the eye.

The distance between the earth and the heavens is given variously in Vedic literature. It is, says the Rig-veda, 'a distance which no bird can fly.' According to the Atharva-veda the earth and the heavens are 'a thousand days' journey apart,' which the *Aitareya Brahmana* specifies as a thousand days' journey for a horse. The *Panchavimsa Brahmana* states that the distance is of a thousand cows placed one on top of the other. The first-century AD Buddhist text *Milinda Panha*, echoing ancient Indian notions, states that a stone thrown from Brahma's world 'would take four months to reach the earth, though it came down eight-and-forty-thousand *yojanas* each day and night' – that is, the two are nearly 150 million kilometres apart, about the same distance as between the earth and the sun, if a *yojana* is taken to be about 13 kilometres. The heavens are in any case beyond the reach of living men, but that is where the dead go, to join Yama (the first of the mortals) and the gods, who have their mansions there. The sun and the moon also move through that sphere. The Rig-vedic Aryans had no knowledge of the planets.

The Vedic notion was that the world was flat, and this created certain conceptual difficulties for Aryans. How were they then to explain why the sun that sets in the west rises again in the east? Vedic literature implies that while the sun travels from east to west with its light blazing, at night it makes the return journey by the same route with its light doused or turned away from the earth. But there were still many things about the world that mystified the Vedic Aryan, and there is a charming naivety about his puzzlement. Why does not the sun fall from the sky, he wonders. Where do the stars go in the daytime? Why does not the ocean ever overflow though all rivers continually flow into it? And why do 'black cows and red cows and the cows with spotted skin' all yield white milk? It is a divine miracle, thought the Rig-vedic poet.

In the eyes of the Vedic people, everything in the world was infused with divinity, and they saw the gods themselves as belonging to the everyday world of men. Their gods were not entities outside the world, but personifications of the forces of nature. And since nearly everything in nature was personified as a god, or was seen as an attribute of some god or goddess, Aryans lived, in a real sense, in the thick of divine activity.

Vedic Aryans saw the gods not as creators of the universe, but as part of the creation. However, in later Vedic times Prajapati (the Lord of Beings, here identified as Brahma) came to be designated as the creator, but not so much an active creator as the being from whom creation emanated. 'Prajapati moves in the womb,' says the Yajur-veda. 'Being unborn, he is born in many shapes ... In him all the worlds stand.' As Keith comments, 'The idea of world creation is always in the Vedic literature regarded in the light of sending out of something already there rather than of mere bringing into being.' There was really no creation, only evolution – the universe evolved out of its own latent potential.

There are several different creation myths in the Rig-veda, the most elaborate of which is of the Purusha Sukta:

A thousand heads hath Purusha,
a thousand eyes, a thousand feet;
on every side pervading the earth
he goes ten digits yet beyond.

This Purusha is all that has been
and all that is to be ...

When gods performed the sacrifice
with Purusha as their offering,
spring was the melted butter, autumn
the oblation; summer the fuel ...

From this great general sacrifice
the dripping fat was gathered up:
from this he fashioned beasts and birds,
creatures both wild and tame.

From this great general sacrifice
were born hymns and chants;
and therefrom were born metres,
and also spells and charms.

From it were horses born, from it all
creatures with two rows of teeth;
from it were the kine born,
from it the goats and sheep.

When they divided Purusha,
into how many parts did they divide him?
what were his mouth, his arms?
what were his thighs and feet?

The Brahmin was his mouth,
of his arms was the warrior made;
his thighs became the Vaisya,
from his feet the Sudra was born.

The moon arose from his mind,
and from his eye the sun,
from his mouth Indra and Agni,
and Vayu from his breath.

From his navel came the air;
the sky was fashioned from his head;
the earth from his feet, and from his ear
the four quarters – thus they fashioned the worlds.

With sacrifice the gods sacrificed to sacrifice:
These were the first holy rites ...

Elsewhere in the Rig-veda, creation is described as proceeding from Indra slaying Vritra (the dragon-demon impounding the waters and the sun) thus releasing the moisture, heat and light essential for life. Another hymn claims that Visvakarma, the All-maker, fashioned the world as a carpenter makes a chariot. Or perhaps the world was created by the gods in a sexual act – 'prolific parents, they have made the world of life,' states the Rig-veda. According to yet another Rig-vedic hymn, a primeval pair, Daksha and Aditi, formed the worlds, including the gods, by agitating the waters: 'The waters contained that earliest embryo in which all the gods were collected.'

In yet another place the Rig-veda speculates that perhaps the world tumbled out of Hiranyagarbha, the golden cosmic egg. Or perhaps the cosmos is just an expression of time. 'Time begot yonder heaven, time also these earths. That which was and that which shall be, urged forth by time, spreads out,' states the Atharva-veda. Or it could be that the world arose from *tapas*, the white heat of ascetic intensity. Or perhaps fire was all that there was in the beginning, and all that there will be in the end. 'All comes from fire and is resolved into it again,' asserts the *Aitareya Brahmana*. Or, as one of the most profound hymns in the Rig-veda would have it, the universe evolved spontaneously from an undifferentiated singularity:

Then neither non-existent nor existent was there,
no realm of air, nor the sky beyond.
Where was it all then? What covered it? In whose keeping?
Was there then cosmic water, in depths unfathomed?

There was no death then, nor immortality;
nor anything there to divide day from night.
Then the One, breathless, breathed within itself –
that One and no other was there then.

There was only darkness then, darkness wrapped
in darkness, all an undifferentiated chaos.
All was void and formless; then arose the One,
born of the heat of ascetic intensity.

Then desire arose – that was the primal seed,
desire born of the mind.
Sages in their hearts' wisdom know this:
the existent is kin to the non-existent.

Across the void they stretched a dividing line.
What was above it? And what below?
Seminal powers were there and mighty forces:
below was potential, above it energy.

But who really knows, who can say
whence it all came, how creation happened?
The gods themselves are later than creation.
So who knows truly how it all came to be?

Whence all creation had its origin,
whether it formed itself, or whether not,
he, who surveys it all from the highest heaven,
he truly knows – or perhaps even he knows not.

As the world came into being, along with it emerged Rta, the law governing its existence, 'the cosmic and moral order of the universe and man,' as Bloomfield describes it. And there appeared also Varuna, the guardian of Rta, to watch over the world and to ensure that men behaved, and that cosmic processes remained in balance.

There were no idols of Varuna or any other god in Vedic India. Nor were there any temples. There was no need for either, for the Vedic gods were visible to everyone, being personifications of the forces of nature. Besides, temples as permanent structures presuppose settled communities, and these were only just beginning to appear in India. Vedic rituals were mainly domestic, centred on the hearth, and most of them were, in Rig-vedic times, simple enough to be performed by the householder himself, without any priestly presence, though there were also a few major public rites, like the Soma, Rajasuya and Asvamedha sacrifices, for which public altars were set up when required.

Man and god were on virtually the same physical and mental plane in Rig-vedic times. 'Like [a cow] her calf, so do the poets lick [the gods] with their prayers,' says the Rig-veda. Their relationship was simple and straightforward, and was often in the nature of a barter exchange. This was explicitly stated in the Yajur-vedic mantra in which Indra tells the worshipper: 'Give me, and I give thee; bestow on me, and I bestow on thee; to me present thy merchandise, and I will give thee my wares.'

Vedic gods were conceived as persons, who could be cajoled with oblations and songs of praise to grant boons to the sacrificer. They could even be enticed away from the sacrifice of a rival and brought to one's own sacrifice. And since the gods could not be at different places at the same time to receive oblations and grant the conflicting demands of their numerous supplicants, there was at this time, as Bloomfield wryly comments, 'a scramble ... to hog the gods.'

This competitive courting of the gods was the setting in which the priestly class expanded its role in society and made itself indispensable, for priestly arts and wiles were deemed essential to extract divine favours. By the later Vedic period the number of rituals that the householder could perform without priestly assistance declined sharply.

The concept of sacrifice now acquired a portentous significance. Since the universe, including the gods, emerged from a primal sacrifice, as described in the Purusha Sukta of the Rig-veda, the continued performance of sacrifice came to be considered essential for the preservation of the universe. Sacrifice thus became an all-powerful 'supernal mystery,' to which everything in the universe, even the gods, owed their existence. The sun and the moon would not rise and these worlds would perish if sacrifices were not performed – so claimed the priests.

The central concern of religion thus shifted from devotion to the gods to the mechanics of sacrifices. These priestly rites were singularly soulless. The Vedic sacrifice, comments Sylvain Levi, was essentially a mechanical process 'operating by its own spontaneous energy.' There was no place in it for sentiment, or even faith, except faith in the potency of the sacrifice itself. There were no moral considerations whatever in the performance of sacrifices. Any sin and any crime, however heinous, could be legitimised by sacrifice; any lie could be made as good as pristine truth by uttering the appropriate mantra. The Aryan faith, as Keith observes, 'was not in the goodness of the gods, but in the efficacy of the sacrifice.'

Thus the gods, whose stature was in any case none too high in Rig-vedic religion, further lost ground, and, in a sense, came under the control of priests. The seed of this idea was in the Rig-veda itself, in its notion that it was the sacrifice, especially the Soma offering, that potentiated the gods. This idea was fully elaborated in later Vedic literature. It was no longer necessary to offer prayers to the gods, or even to bargain with them: they could be coerced by priests to do what was desired through the magical potency of sacrifice. The gods thus became mere instruments in the hands of priests to be manipulated as they pleased, and priests arrogated to themselves a position not only higher than all men, but higher than even the gods. Though the gods had supernatural powers, which priests did not have, these powers were at the disposal of priests.

Major sacrifices became enormously complicated in later Vedic times, requiring the participation of numerous priests and lasting several days, some even a year or more. Priestly professionals now replaced sages and poets as the formulators of religion, and they turned sacrifice into a highly complex and systematised process, in which every act and gesture and utterance, however seemingly trivial, was attributed high symbolic significance, from which not even the slightest deviation could be made without calamitous consequences. And, as form gained precedence over content, the meanings of mantras became irrelevant. What was important was that intonation should be precise. Often the mantras did not make any sense at all, as in this chant in the *Maitrayani Samhita*, a recension of the Black Yajur-veda: *Nidhayo va nidhayo va om va om va om ee ai om svarnajothih*, in which, as Macdonnell points out, 'only the last word, which means golden light, is translatable.'

Hymns and mantras, whether intelligible as they usually were in the Rig-vedic times, or unintelligible as they often were in the later Vedic period, were essential for the success of Vedic rites. Sacrifice without hymns was considered ineffective. 'With song will we conquer the men who sing no hymns; not easily are thou (Indra) pleased with prayerless sacrifice,' states the Rig-veda. And again: 'No [Soma] juices pressed without prayer have pleased him.' The source of the magical power of the priest was *brahman*, the mysterious potency of sacred utterance, which, it was claimed, enabled him to draw on cosmic energy. Words, syllables and rhythms had, it was believed, occult powers – 'in the rhythm of the sacred song ... echoes of the rhythm of the universe resound,' says Oldenberg.

Oblations to Vedic gods were always offered in fire altars, for it was through fire (Agni) that the gods consumed the offerings of devotees. These altars were of precise dimensions, and were constructed with bricks of prescribed measurements made in a specified manner. Sometimes Agni was bidden to carry oblations to the gods, at other times to carry messages to invite the gods to come and partake of the repast. The common items of oblation were milk, butter, grain, and cakes, as well as Soma and meat. Sometimes the offering was matched to the nature of the deity invoked, or to the object for which the offering was made. Thus the milk of a black cow with a white calf was the offering specified for Ushas (Dawn), while a black animal was required to be sacrificed in the ritual to bring rain.

The slaughter of animals for meat was always something of a ritual among primitive people, but Aryans made it into a high sacramental rite. For the rite, the sacrificial animal was led to a stake fixed on a consecrated ground spread with sacred grass and adorned with garlands and other decorations. There it was tied securely, anointed with ghee, and ceremonially slaughtered. Its joints were then carefully separated, the priests naming and praising each part. The omentum of the animal was first offered to the gods in fire – the sweet smell of the roasting omentum was considered irresistible to Vedic gods – and the rest of the meat cooked and eaten by the priests and other participants. Only the tail of the beast was kept aside, and with it was performed, as the final part of the rite, the offering to the wives of the gods. Blood and excrement were left for the demons.

It was important for worshippers to partake of the oblation, for the gods were imagined to be eating along with them, so not to eat was to exclude themselves from the sacrament of the sacrifice. Sometimes, if the oblation was butter or something like it, the worshippers, instead of eating it, might daub themselves with it. In the rite for repairing broken equipment, the oblation was rubbed on the mended part, and in the rite for victory in a chariot race, the horse was made to sniff the oblation. When the deities invoked were of a terrible aspect, the offerings were not normally eaten; nor was the oblation of rice cakes offered to dead ancestors eaten, but only smelled.

The worshipper was required to observe certain austerities while preparing to offer sacrifice – he had to abstain from sex, fast or eat only specified foods, sleep on the ground, and so on. 'The man who intends to establish the sacred fire must for the night before the performance lie awake in silence: thus he is said to secure purity and *tapas* for his approach to the gods next day,' observes Keith. The sacrificer had to take a ritual bath before the rite, but he was warned not to bathe after the rites, for that would wash away the merit of the rite adhering to him. In the case of the king, after consecration, he was not allowed to have a bath for a year but could only rub his body.

By far the most important Vedic rite was the Soma sacrifice. All the 114 hymns of the ninth book of the Rig-veda, and a few hymns in the other books as well, are devoted to Soma, the personification of the energising spirit of the Soma plant. The deity is also mentioned in numerous other hymns in the Rig-veda, and appears as Haoma in Avesta, the ancient Iranian scripture, and was apparently an Indo-Iranian innovation unknown in other Aryan cultures. The plant, described in the Rig-veda as brown, ruddy or tawny, has not been identified, though some believe it to be marijuana or a mountain mushroom. Sayana thought that it was a creeper with a milky juice.

The plant was easily available during the Rig-vedic period, for priests at this time had no difficulty in getting the vast quantities of the libation required for the Soma sacrifice. But later, when Aryans moved into the Gangetic plain, it became increasingly difficult to procure the plant; the Brahmanas speak of it being brought from a great distance, and recommend the use of various substitutes. Soma was non-alcoholic – it was drunk immediately after the juice was extracted, so there was no time for fermentation – but was evidently hallucinogenic.

Soma was the drink of divine rapture. 'We have drunk Soma, we have become immortal; we have attained the light, we have found the gods!' vaunts a Rig-vedic poet, while another invokes: 'Thou art auspicious energy ... Soma, be happy in our heart, as milch-kine in grassy meads ... In thee be juicy nutriments united, and powers and mighty foe-subduing vigour.' The juice was claimed to have miraculous curative powers, and could give sight to the blind, enable the lame to walk, even promote truth, wisdom and knowledge, and inspire poetry. The priest who had drunk Soma, it was said, could kill his foe with a mere look. One imbiber (or perhaps Indra) on a flight of ecstasy exults:

Like violent gusts of wind
the draughts have lifted me:
Have I not drunk Soma? ...

Frenzy has come upon me,
as a cow that lows to her calf:
Have I not drunk Soma?

As a wright bends a chariot-seat,
round my heart I bend this frenzy:
Have I not drunk Soma?

Not even as a mote in my eye
count the Five Tribes with me:
Have I not drunk Soma? ...

I in my grandeur have surpassed
the heavens and the great earth:
Have I not drunk Soma?

Aha! I will pick up the earth
and put it here or put it there:
Have I not drunk Soma?

The process of preparing the Soma juice is described in detail in several Rig-vedic hymns. King Soma, as the plant was called, was collected from mountains on moonlit nights, and brought to the sacrificial shed, where it was sprinkled with water and crushed between stones. It was then placed on a strainer of woollen cloth and its juice extracted, while priests, according to the Rig-veda, sang its praise 'as a lover sings to his darling.' Says the poet about the infusion:

He glideth like a serpent
from his ancient skin,
like a playful horse
the tawny steer hath run.

The juice was first offered to the gods, then distributed among priests, who, notes the Rig-veda, gathered around it 'like flies on honey.' The juice was usually drunk mixed with milk, water, honey or curds, but Indra and Vayu preferred to drink it undiluted; sometimes it was mixed with meal, cooked and offered to the gods.

The Soma sacrifice, though important in Vedic culture, was not a very elaborate ritual. That distinction goes to royal rituals like Rajasuya, Vajapeya and Asvamedha, particularly to Asvamedha, which was usually a year-long *yaga*, requiring the participation of hundreds of priests and immense quantities of supplies. The preparations for this *yaga* began early in spring, when a swift royal horse with particular auspicious marks – 'front black, behind white, with a dark mark' – was chosen and consecrated. Then the horse, escorted by a contingent of guards, was released to wander at will for a period of time, usually a year, but sometimes shortened to six months or even a couple of weeks. During this period, the horse was kept away from mares to conserve its strength, and was also prevented from bathing, so that the merit it had gained by consecration would not wash away. At the end of the specified period, the horse was brought back and sacrificed, along with numerous other animals, including bulls, cows, goats, deer and nilgais.

The horse was killed without bloodshed, by strangulation or suffocation, and laid on the consecrated ground with its head to the west and feet to the north. That night the king's wives reverently circumambulated the horse, thrice from left to right and thrice from right to left. The chief queen then lay with the dead horse under a sheet in simulated copulation, drawing the penis of the horse and placing it in her vagina, praying, 'O horse, I attract the fluid from thee which causes conception ... On this sacrificial ground let us spread our four legs. Let the horse emit his seed.' The rite also involved a rude and ribald exchange between the officiating priest and the queen about sexual intercourse, the obscene language of which, according to Oldenberg, was part of the fertility rite – or was for the amusement of the gods!

There was no human sacrifice among Rig-vedic Aryans, unlike in most other ancient societies. They sacrificed to the gods only what they themselves could eat, which was what they thought the gods too would eat. Human sacrifice however seems to have been prevalent among Aryans in earlier times, and it was still performed nominally in Vedic times. The ritual, notes Griffith, resembled the Asvamedha in many respects, with 'man, the noblest victim, being ... symbolically sacrificed instead of the horse, and men and women of various tribes, figures, complexions, characters and professions being attached to the sacrificial stakes in the place of the tame and wild animals ... These nominal victims were afterwards released uninjured, and, so far as the text of the White Yajur-veda goes, the whole was merely emblematical, a type of allegorical self-immolation of Purusha.'

With multitudinous gods and goddesses all around him all the time and involved with every aspect of his life, the days of the Vedic Aryan were crowded with innumerable rites, performed to obtain favours or to avert misfortune. These rites were centred on the domestic sacred fire, which was lighted every morning by the householder, and in which offerings were made to the gods at dawn, at midday and at sunset. Besides these, there were more elaborate rites to be performed on the new-moon and full-moon days, the Chaturmasya ritual once in four months, and the great Agnistoma ritual once a year. There were also special rituals for agricultural and pastoral activities, for marriages, conception, birth, the first feeding of solids to the child, the first shaving of the child's head, and so on.

The first important ceremony in the life of an Aryan youth was *upanayanam,* his initiation into the Aryan fold by the investiture of the sacred thread (made of three strands of cotton, each strand formed by nine threads) worn over the left shoulder and under the right arm. For those intending to adopt the priestly profession, this was an elaborate three-day ceremony, during which a girdle of *munja* grass was tied on the youth, and he took up studentship under a preceptor. For others, the ceremony was much simpler, consisting mainly of shaving the boy's head and putting on him the clothes of an adult.

Later, as a householder, he would perform numerous rituals all through his life, and they would follow him even beyond life, as there were *sraddha* ceremonies to be performed by his son to propitiate his spirit. Nearly every act in the daily life of the Aryan householder was turned into a ritual, pregnant with magical significance, yielding good if performed correctly, or evil if performed improperly. Custom hemmed him in fairly tightly, though his life was not as inflexibly bound by prescriptions and proscriptions as it would be in later times. The Atharva-veda even has a hymn to atone for the sin of urinating while standing, instead of squatting as required:

Having paid homage to heaven and earth,
to the atmosphere, to death,
I will urinate standing erect;
let not the lords harm me.

The Atharva-veda deals mainly with the private rites of the common people. These rites are believed to go back to the ancient practices of the Indo-European people, and there is in them an air of occult violence, as in this typical spell:

Arise and arm, ye spectral forms,
Followed by meteoric flames;
Ye serpents, spirits of the deep,
Demons of night, pursue the foe!

The Atharva-vedic rites are rites of magic, involving the use of spells, drugs, and various other objects in which potencies are thought to dwell. Gods play hardly any role in these rituals, but are named merely to add vigour to the spell, and are invoked in a summary manner. 'In some cases the mention of ... [individual gods] is dropped and merely the numbers are given, 99, 88, 77 and so on,' notes Keith. Sometimes strange names are used for the gods 'in accordance with the well-known rule that in magic a mysterious name is the most potent of all.'

In the beginning, as Keith observes, Vedic rites were relatively simple, and the householder was 'his own magician as well as sacrificer.' But in the later Vedic period, the priests, as specialists protecting their speciality, made many of the rituals so complicated that the householder needed priestly assistance to perform them. And the priests exacted hefty fees for their services, especially for the grand public sacrifices. 'Being anointed, he (the king) should give gold to the Brahmin who anoints; a thousand should he give, a field and quadrupeds,' prescribes the *Aitareya Brahmana*, which goes on to speak hyperbolically of the 'tens of thousands of female slaves, tens of thousands of elephants' given to a priest by a king. While the sacrificer sought to cadge favours from the gods, priests sought to cadge favours from the sacrificer.

To reinforce the obligation to give ample gifts, it was pointed out that gifts to priests were necessary to confirm the faith of the sacrificer in the rites, and that without faith there would be no benefit from the sacrifice. Thus the rewards to priests, 'instead of [being] mere appendices to the actual offering ... become in themselves offerings of the highest importance and value,' comments Keith. There was also the implied threat that a displeased priest could ruin the sacrificer by introducing intentional minor errors in the rites.

GODS OF THE MOUNTAIN

The Vedic gods, like the gods of all religions, were born of the mythopoetic imagination of man. They were the creations of the prevailing nascent culture. Conceptually, therefore, they were rather elementary beings, even though they, as personifications of the mysterious forces of nature, constituted a great advance on the gods of primitive animism. Most of the Vedic gods would later change character or fade away, and new gods and new religious concepts would take hold. As people evolved, the gods evolved with them.

The Vedic man created gods in his own image. Though called *devas*, radiant ones, these gods were quite like people, except that they had supernatural powers, were deathless, and lived in the heavens, above the vault of the sky. They, like all other beings, were subject to the unalterable laws of nature. 'The course pursued among the gods is in accordance with that pursued among men,' states the *Satapatha Brahmana*. The gods looked like people, had limbs and organs like people, though sometimes these were mere figurative representations of faculties, like the sun's rays being described as his arms. At times they appeared as warriors, in helmets and coats of mail, bearing arms – Indra even wore an amulet to boost his might. They had the same passions as people, the same joys and sorrows; they behaved like people, ate the same food as people, and had their own families. They were, again like people, mostly amoral. 'Open to adulation, they become vain; eager for advantage, they become shifty; reflecting human desires, they become sordid, and in some cases even indecent,' comments Bloomfield.

Nearly all the great Aryan gods were male, conforming to the patriarchal character of Aryan society. Their number is given as 'thrice eleven' in the Rig-veda, one set for each of the three divisions of the universe, the terrestrial, aerial and celestial spheres. But this is only a poetic expression, not a precise listing; there were in fact far more than thirty-three gods in the Vedic pantheon, though their precise number is difficult to establish because of their overlapping identities and roles.

The Vedic gods were numerous, because there were very many forces of nature to be personified. The Rig-veda even has a divinity called

Visva-devas (All-gods) – to whom forty hymns are devoted – apparently conceived so that unknown gods of the unknown forces of nature were not left out during the rites. And, because the gods were mostly personifications of the forces of nature, each having his own distinctive and autonomous sphere of activity, all the gods co-existed peaceably in the Vedic pantheon. There was no hierarchy among them, no omnipotent supreme god, and no war of the gods. Vedic religion was henotheistic – at rituals, each god was praised as the supreme god, as suited the occasion. However, the largest number of hymns of the Rig-veda, over 250, nearly a quarter of all its hymns, are addressed to Indra. He is closely followed by Agni (200 hymns) and Soma (over 100 hymns). There are in all about twenty deities to whom more than three entire hymns are addressed in the Rig-veda.

Not all the Vedic sages were happy with the disorderly, polytheistic promiscuity of the Vedic pantheon, and there are in the Rig-veda occasional expressions of monotheism, even of pantheistic monism, such as would be expounded in the Upanishads a few centuries later. 'Thou, at birth, O Agni, art Varuna; when kindled thou dost become Mitra; in thee ... all gods are centred; to the worshipper thou dost become Indra,' maintains a Rig-vedic sage, indicating that the different gods were only emanations of one basic and universal entity. States another hymn: 'To what is One, sages give many a title: they call it Agni, Yama, Matarisvan.' And again: 'Him ... though only One in nature, priests and poets with words make into many.'

Indra was the Aryan god *par excellence.* 'In him the deities have stored manliness, insight, power and might,' proclaims the Rig-veda. A swaggering, wild, boastful, flamboyant and irascible god, Indra was an impetuous and invincible warrior of colossal strength, a true Aryan hero, the hyperbolic projection of the most grandiose conceits of Aryans. His favourite weapon was the thunderbolt. 'Even the deaf will tremble at my roaring,' Indra trumpets, modesty not being a virtue of the gods. When Indra fought and killed the dragon demon Vritra, 'the heaven trembled at the birth of thine effulgence; the earth trembled at the fear of thy displeasure; the steadfast mountains shook in agitation,' claims the Rig-veda. Yet Indra, for all his lordly strutting, was human enough to get frightened at times, as the Rig-veda itself confesses in bewilderment: 'Whom sawest thou ... Indra, that fear possessed thy heart ... that, like a hawk affrighted ... thou crossedst nine-and-ninety flowing rivers?'

Tawny-bearded and grossly pot-bellied, Indra loved feasting, drinking and carousing, and once 'at a single draught drank the contents of thirty pails, pails that were filled with Soma juice,' says the Rig-veda. He could not stay away from Soma, though sometimes he got sick from drinking too much. He had, like Agni, 1,000 testicles, and was shamelessly promiscuous; he once even fell in love with an *Asura* woman 'who had unlimited organs of sex' and had intercourse with her. Because of these vulnerabilities, Indra, though the favourite Aryan god, was also the object of occasional banter in the Vedas. One Rig-vedic poet was even sceptical about his very existence: 'One and another say, there is no Indra, who hath beheld him?' On this occasion, Indra appeared before the doubting poet and declared: 'Here am I, look upon me, O singer – all that existeth I surpass in greatness.'

Varuna was another great Aryan god, but unlike the convivial Indra, he was a cold and remote god, a very godly god. As the upholder of Rta, the physical and moral order of the world, it was he who kept the heavenly luminaries from straying from their courses, and to him are addressed some of the most solemn hymns in the Rig-veda. Patriarchal, stern, implacable and omniscient, he sat steadfast on his throne of judgement, in unwinking vigilance. Nothing could be hidden from him, for his informers roamed the world and were present even at the most secret acts of man. Warns the Atharva-veda:

Whoever stands, whoever moves,
or steals from place to place
or hides in his secret cell –
the god his movements trace.

Wherever two whisper and plot,
and deem they are alone,
King Varuna is there, a third,
and all their schemes are known.

Varuna despised human weakness, abhorred sin and lies, and punished transgressors by plaguing them with horrible diseases and by consigning them, after death, to the House of Clay, the dingy and dreadful netherworld. He could not be placated, like the other gods, with sacrifices and oblations. He was incorruptible. Only true repentance could save the sinner from his magisterial wrath. Prays a penitent Rig-vedic poet: 'Loosen the bonds, O Varuna, that hold me, so in thy holy law may I be made sinless.' It was not easy for man, frail creature, to lead a righteous life. 'Whatever law of thine, O God, O Varuna, as we are men, day after day we violate,' confesses one sage in the Rig-veda. Another cries out: 'Not our own will betray us, but seduction, thoughtlessness, Varuna – wine, dice, or anger.' Every line in a Rig-vedic hymn to Varuna closes with the chorus: 'Forgive, O gracious Lord, forgive! ... Forgive, O gracious Lord, forgive!'

This yearning for moral purgation is quite unusual in Vedic religion, for the concept of sin is feeble in the Vedas. What is ordinarily considered as sin is not moral transgression, but the neglect of rituals, which does not require contrition but only expiatory rites. Not surprisingly, in the permissive environment of Vedic India, Varuna rapidly lost his position as a high god, and ended up as the lowly god of the ocean, rain and clouds. The symbol of Varuna in the horse sacrifice, as given in the *Satapatha Brahmana*, is a misshapen, hideous man! But the high moral values that Varuna represented would be revived in India several centuries later in a gentler, more compassionate form, in the teachings of Buddha.

The gods most frequently mentioned after Indra in the Rig-veda are Agni and Soma, and they, in contrast to Varuna, were familiar terrestrial deities. The very first hymn of the Rig-veda is addressed to Agni, and begins: 'I laud Agni, the chosen priest, god, minister of sacrifice ... ' Agni was ever present in the Aryan household, and was both an intermediary between man and god, and a god by himself. He is described as having 1,000 testicles and horns, and a bearded face with 1,000 eyes and many tongues. 'The forehead of the sky, earth's centre, Agni became the messenger of earth and heaven,' states the Rig-veda. Like Agni, another constant presence among the Rig-vedic Aryans was Soma, the drink of immortality by which the gods became deathless.

Shiva and Vishnu, the two great gods of later Hinduism, find little place in the Vedas. They do not seem to have been original Aryan gods, and they were not known to other ancient Aryan societies. Shiva (as Rudra) is celebrated in only three hymns in the Rig-veda; in addition, he shares one hymn with Soma and is mentioned in all about seventy-five times. A rather fearsome god, prone to violence, Shiva was an asocial, loner god who dwelt in remote mountains, and was dressed in skins. His physical appearance was quite bizarre – the Atharva-veda states that his belly and neck were blue and his back red, while the Yajur-veda states that he was copper-coloured and had a blue-black back and a white throat. The Yajur-veda dubs him as a patron of robbers, highwaymen, cheats, swindlers and ruffians.

Shiva was a god of contrasts and contradictions – he was 'fierce and destructive' as 'the ruddy boar of heaven,' but was also radiant as the sun, with firm, brown-coloured limbs and beautiful lips; he afflicted people with fever, cough and poison, but was also the guardian of the healing herbs. 'Most healing are the remedies thou givest,' states the Rig-vedic poet, and prays:

O Rudra, where is thy caressing hand,
that heals, cools, bears away god-given hurt ...
Firm his limbs, manifold his forms;

> *tawny and strong, he hath bedecked himself*
> *with ornaments of lustrous gold.*

Vishnu fared somewhat better in the Vedas, but even he gets only five whole hymns in the Rig-veda, and his name occurs not more than a hundred times in all. He is one of the several gods identified with the sun, and is called 'the wide strider' for his exploit of taking 'three strides,' the exact nature of which is not explained in the Vedas, but is probably an allegorical representation of the sweep of the sun across the heavens. Krishna is mentioned in the Rig-veda – 'the fleet Krishna lived on the banks of the Amsumati (Yamuna) River with ten thousand troops,' notes a hymn – but he has no connection with Vishnu. In fact he appears in the Vedas as Indra's foe, and there were several clashes between the two.

Among the other gods mentioned in the Vedas are Brahma – whom the Atharva-veda describes as the one who presides over the past and the future of the universe, and 'whose alone is the sky' – Prajapati (lord of creatures), Yama (lord of the dead), Maruts (spirits of storms), Asvins (morning and evening stars) and Gandharvas (guardians of celestial Soma). Asvins are helpful, ministering gods, tending the wounded in war, rescuing people from boat-wrecks, even finding husbands for spinsters. Then there are the Fathers (dead ancestors), Kshetrapati (deity of the field), Vastospati (lord of house and home), Visvakarma (all-creator: divine carpenter), and so on. Kama, the god of love, appears for the first time in the Atharva-veda.

Goddesses, unlike gods, receive scant attention in the Vedas; they are of no importance in ritual, and none of them are offered the Soma oblation. Most of them are shadowy figures of no substance, of whom nothing other than their names is known, the names themselves often formed by simply adding feminine suffixes to the names of their male consorts. There are only a handful of goddesses of independent existence in the Vedic pantheon, like Prithivi (earth mother), Aditi (mother of the gods), Ushas (dawn), Rathri (night) and Aranyani (forest nymph). The only goddess to whom the Rig-veda devotes entire hymns is Ushas, who is celebrated in twenty hymns, and is mentioned in some three hundred places. Conceived as a lovely young maiden, Ushas is greeted as the eternal renewer of life:

> *Arise! the breath, the life, again has reached us:*
> *Darkness has departed, light is coming ...*
> *We have arrived where men prolong existence.*

Aditi is mentioned about eighty times in the Rig-veda, though she has no independent hymn of her own. Saraswati – the personification of the river of that name, described as the daughter of lightning and the mother of streams – is prominent as the goddess of speech, an attribute she acquired probably because most of the Rig-vedic hymns were composed on the banks of the river. Then there are Apsaras, water nymphs, who often frequented trees, playing lutes and cymbals. One hymn in the Rig-veda invokes Sita, the furrow, seeking her blessing for a good harvest.

On the reverse side of the celestial pantheon were the *asuras*, demons, who were not, in the Vedas, much different from the gods, except that they were the adversaries of the gods and Aryans, and therefore considered evil. The term *asura* seems to have been originally used for all celestial beings, irrespective of whether they were benign or malign. When Aryans lived in Iran, both *asuras* and *devas* were considered divine beings, and even in the early parts of the Rig-veda the term *asura* was often used to denote the gods. 'The gods and the *asuras*, both of them sprang from Prajapati,' states the *Satapatha Brahmana*. *Asuras* were not creatures of the netherworld. Later, as a result of the divergence of Iranian and Indian cultures, Indians came to view *devas* as gods and *asuras* as demons, while *asuras* remained gods in Iran and *devas* became devils – Avesta in fact mentions a demon called Indra.

Rakshasas (goblins who often assumed animal forms and interfered with Vedic sacrifices) and *Pisachas* (eaters of corpses) are the other demonic creatures named in the Vedas. Also mentioned are elusive and sly devils like the incubi and succubi, who sexually harassed sleeping men and women. 'The black and hairy *asura* ... from this girl we drive, from her bosom, from her pudenda, and from her buttocks,' chants an Atharva-vedic priest to exorcise an incubus. Of the succubus, the Atharva-veda says: 'Oft, coming as a naked girl, thou hauntest people in their sleep, baffling the thought ... and the firm intention of a man.'

There is no clear concept of hell and its terrors in Vedic literature, except a vague notion that it is a place of utter darkness teeming with demons and goblins, and that this is where unchaste girls and unfaithful wives, as well as those who ill-treat Brahmins, would be consigned. The *Kaushitaki Brahmana* says that the animals a man eats in life will eat him in hell – which horrid fate can however be averted by performing certain rituals.

Heaven is described in greater detail in Vedic literature, but the concept is not unified. In some hymns, heaven is presented as a land of milk and honey and music, of Soma and Sura, a place of carnal pleasures which the Fathers enjoy in the company of the gods – where all that man desired in life but missed, would be fulfilled. But elsewhere it is stated that the Fathers and the gods live in different places – the gateway of the heaven, according to the *Satapatha Brahmana*, is in the north-east, while that of the world of the Fathers is in the south-east. In yet other texts it is said that the spirit of the dead could go to any number of different places, as if wafted by whimsical cosmic winds. As a Rig-vedic hymn has it, the spirit might go to 'the earth and heaven ... to the billowy seas ... to the beams of light that flash and flow ... to the waters and plants ... to the Sun and Dawn ... to the lofty mountain heights ... into all that lives and moves ... to distant realms beyond our ken ... far away to all that is and is to be.' Another Rig-vedic hymn scatters the dead body also:

The sun receives thine eyes, the wind thy spirit;
go, as thy merit is, to earth or heaven.
Go, if it be thy lot, unto the water;
go, make thine home in plants with all thy members.

These hymns perhaps mark the faint and tentative formulation of the later Hindu concept of transmigration, but the Vedic notions about what happens to man after death are quite rudimentary, and the idea of the dead returning to the earth to be born again is totally absent in the Rig-veda. In it, after death, it is altogether another life for man. There are no returns. 'Invested with a body of light, he (the dead man) went in a chariot or on wings to the land of eternal light; fanned by delicious winds, cooled by showers, he recovered his complete form, body, mind and life, hastened past Yama's two four-eyed, broad-nosed, brindled brown dogs ... and reached the region where Yama dwells under the Asvattha tree, drinking with the gods, while minstrels played on the flute and sang his praises,' states Iyengar, summarising the Vedic descriptions of the peregrinations of the dead. 'There he joined the company of the Fathers and led a happy life reunited with father, mother, wives and children. Life there is free from all imperfections and all desires are fulfilled.'

The Atharva-veda assures that if a man has made good offerings to the gods, the funeral pyre would not burn his genitals, so he can enjoy carnal pleasures after death. 'In the heavenly world much women-folk is theirs,' promises the text. The Atharva-vedic heaven is truly a pleasure garden:

Many lakes of melted butter abound,
banks of honey, streams of milk and
water and curds, and draughts of wine,
free-flowing like water!

May all these streams reach you
in honey-filled heaven!
Many ponds full of lotus await you!

Vedic man had thus much to look forward to in the life after death. Yet, for all the heavenly prospects that awaited him, dirges in the Vedas are often poignant, tinged with regret about the transience of life, as in this Rig-vedic hymn:

Gone are the mortals who in former ages
beheld the flushing of the earlier morning.
We living men now look upon her shining;
they are coming who shall in future see her.

The early Aryan funeral practice seems to have been to bury the dead, but later they were usually cremated, and only ascetics and children under two years of age were buried. Sometimes the dead were disposed of by casting away or exposure. In a burial hymn the Rig-veda invokes:

Open wide, O Earth, press not heavily on him,
give him easy access, gently tending him;
as with a robe a mother wraps
her child, so shroud this man, O earth.

In the normal Vedic funeral rites, the corpse was first washed and anointed, his hair, beard and nails trimmed, and laid on the ground freshly daubed with cow-dung, while the women of the house, with their hair loose, smote their thighs and breasts and wailed for the dead. The big toes of the corpse were then tied together with twigs, 'lest death should walk back to the house after the corpse was sent out.' The body was then removed to the burning ground, accompanied by professional mourners (the 'evil-wailers') and relatives, and placed on a pyre. The omentum of a cow was placed on the face of the corpse, its kidneys in his hands (this for the dogs of Yama) and the whole body covered with its skin. The dead man's staff (if Brahmin) or bow (if Kshatriya) or ox-goad (if Vaisya, as later ritual indicates) was then removed. A goat was slaughtered as an offering to Agni. Then the pyre was lit, with the priest chanting: 'Burn him not up; nor quite consume him; let not his body or his skin be scattered ... bear this man to the region of the Fathers.' It was believed that, as Keith remarks, the body of the dead would survive the cremation 'in a refined form but still unaltered in essence.' Appropriately, the dead were called *pretas*, 'the departed'.

After the funeral, the mourners left the cremation ground without looking back, washed themselves, changed garments, and returned home. They observed certain austerities for a few days, such as sleeping on the ground and avoiding sex. During this period no food was cooked in the house. On the third or tenth day after the funeral, the bones of the dead were collected, placed in an urn and buried. The obligation to the dead did not cease with the funeral – the dead needed to be comforted by the living through the performance of periodical rites of homage; if this was not done, the spirit of the dead, it was feared, would remain restless, and could even turn malevolent and harm the living.

There was, however, no prolonged mourning. After the bones were buried, mourners bathed to wash off pollution, then, returning home, resumed their normal life. States the Rig-vedic poet:

> *Divided from the dead are these, the living:*
> *now be our calling on the gods successful.*
> *We have gone forth for dancing and for laughter,*
> *to further times prolonging our existence.*

Aryan religious beliefs and practices underwent major transformation in India, as the people adapted themselves to their new physical setting and made the transition from a pastoral to an agrarian economy. Also, in India they intermingled with the older inhabitants of the land, assimilating them into Aryan society and absorbing their gods and many of their customs.

The most dramatic of the new developments was the growing popularity of fertility cults appropriate to an agrarian society, probably under the influence of Indus culture. Though the Rig-veda emphatically asserted that phallic worshippers were enemies of Aryans – 'Let those whose deity is the phallus not penetrate our sanctuary,' warned the Rig-veda – by the time the Yajur-veda was composed, phallic worship had become a recognised Aryan ritual, and the Atharva-veda sang of the splendour of 'the golden phallus standing in the waters.'

With the popularity of *linga* (phallus) worship rose the popularity of Rudra, who begins to appear in the Yajur-veda as Shiva, 'auspicious', his common appellation in later times. By the later Vedic period he became a dominant god, with the older gods cowering before him, and in a few centuries his worship in the *linga* form became widespread. Snakes were Shiva's servants, and snake worship, unknown in the Rig-veda, also became commonplace in the evolving religion. But the *linga* worship seems to have been largely confined to rural areas, for Buddhist texts, which mainly deal with urban life, do not mention it at all, though they ridicule many other common religious practices.

As fertility cults gained social acceptability, female deities, even sprites like Apsaras, gradually advanced to prominence. Dasis now appeared at rites, to dance before the sacrificial fire 'with pots on their heads, singing.' Even Vratyas, wandering sadhus of non-Vedic fertility cults – who travelled from place to place with a minstrel and a harlot, and practised ritual dancing, flagellation and prostitution – were granted semi-respectability by being treated as Aryans who had fallen from faith.

In this shifting scene, none of the old Vedic gods were able to retain their position; many disappeared altogether, and those who survived retreated to the outer fringes of the Hindu pantheon. Indra, who so decisively dominated the Rig-vedic world, now become just a king of the lower heavens – 'a debonair debauchee,' as K.M. Panikker describes him – periodically petitioning the new super-gods for help; he is no longer a war god, but a rainmaker. Varuna, once the keeper of the cosmic order, shrivelled into a god of the sea. And, as the Vedic gods lost stature, many of the grand Vedic sacrifices also became defunct, or extremely rare.

By the sixth century BC, Vedic civilisation – Vedism, as some scholars prefer to call it – was in full retreat, and classical Hinduism, very substantially different from Vedism, began to take form, as Aryans acclimatised themselves to their new home and adopted gods and rituals and social practices appropriate to their new environment and lifestyle.

Chapter Three

THE AGE OF FERMENT

TWILIGHT OF THE GODS

'I ask thee, ancient one … where the Rta of the past has gone? Who holds it now? … Where have gone the magnificent ways of Aryans? … We are fallen in misery,' a poet laments in a late Rig-vedic hymn. At the very infancy of civilisation, man was already looking back with nostalgia to the simple ways of his past!

For the romantic, nothing ever seems as good as it once was. Still, the despairing mood of the Rig-vedic poet seems rather strange, for life had never been as good for Aryans as it was at this time. The Indo-Gangetic Plain was a marvellously fertile land, and farming it generally provided the people with more than enough to eat, season after season and year after year. Life now acquired a future orientation for them. Unlike the hand-to-mouth and day-to-day existence of their pastoral-hunting days, they could now look with confidence to the months and years ahead. Further, surplus food availability enabled an ever-increasing number of people to withdraw from primary productive occupations and turn to learning and the arts. Trade flourished in this environment. And towns and cities sprouted everywhere.

These developments climaxed around the seventh century BC, which was a time of challenge and opportunity in India. But the very challenges and opportunities that held so much promise also brought in their train new tensions and anxieties. As urbanism spread and the lifestyle of Aryans changed, their institutions and the value systems underpinning them also changed. In consequence, people were torn from their old socio-cultural moorings and set adrift in a sea of change.

The very prosperity that Aryans now enjoyed seemed to breed melancholy. Previously men, ground down by the brutal drudgery of scraping out a bare living, hardly had the time or the energy, or even the words, to ponder about the meaning of life, or to worry about afterlife. But now, liberated from animal anxieties about food, shelter and survival, men turned to examine the quality of life, and found it hopelessly wanting. As civilisation evolved, the number of things about which man could be unhappy also seemed to multiply. The betterment of the material circumstances of life did not engender greater happiness, but created spiritual and intellectual disquiet, as the very ease of outer life sensitised man to the pain within.

A corrosive pessimism about life now took the place of the earlier exuberant optimism of Aryans. Some questioned the very worth of life. 'Foul-smelling and insubstantial is the body, a mere agglomeration of skin, bones, sinews, marrow, flesh, semen, blood, mucus, tears, rheum, urine, faeces, bile and phlegm – what is the good in enjoying desires in such a body?' asks King Brihadratha in *Maitri Upanishad.* 'Besides, this body is assailed by desire, anger, greed, delusion, fear, despondency, envy, separation from what one desires, union with what is distasteful, sorrow, hunger, thirst, disease, senility, death, and the like – what is the good in enjoying desires in such a body? And we see that this whole world is decaying like these gnats, these mosquitoes, this grass, and these trees that arise only to perish.' Even the greatest heroes will pass on. Why, the oceans will dry up, mountains crumble to dust, the pole star break loose, gods fall. 'Such is the round of coming to be and passing away – what then is the good in the enjoyment of desires?' the king despairs.

Death was a matter of no great moment in primitive societies, but it now became a haunting concern of man to come to terms with it. 'That which does not bring me immortality, what good is that to me?' laments Maitreyi in the *Brihadaranyaka Upanishad.* In the face of human mortality, how can man be at peace with himself?

Religion had to address these concerns. Further, the evolving urban society, based primarily on trade, required value systems and religious practices different from those of the old pastoral-farming society. Thus it was that the Upanishads, Buddhism, Jainism and a host of other radical philosophic and religious systems arose at this time, to legitimise and buttress the institutions and processes of the new society, and to provide psychological and spiritual salves to people in the changed milieu.

The leaders of these radical movements came from different sections of society, not exclusively or even primarily from the priestly class. It was not uncommon in Vedic times for Kshatriyas to take to scriptural studies, and this was not resisted by Brahmins, for it was the performance of sacrificial rites that was their exclusive prerogative, not theological exploration. And now, with philosophy gaining ascendancy in religion, Kshatriyas moved to the forefront of religious speculation. They had no inhibition to boldly innovate religious concepts, as their profession and livelihood were not dependent, unlike in the case of Brahmins, on the preservation of old beliefs and practices.

There were probably quite a few non-Aryans among the new sages, for a number of them had their mothers' names as their surnames, as in matrilineal societies. Non-Aryan spiritual leaders were in fact active in

Aryan society in earlier times also. Munis, the silent ones, devotees of Shiva, who were 'girded with the wind,' wore 'garments of soiled yellow hue,' had 'long, loose locks,' and possessed occult powers, are mentioned in the Rig-veda, and in the Atharva-veda there are references to Vratyas, itinerant priests of a non-Aryan fertility cult. These trans-cultural influences on Aryan religion deepened in the Upanishadic times, when the centre of Aryan civilisation shifted south-eastward, from the upper Doab towards Bihar, a region of strong non-Aryan cultural presence. And it was here that the heterodox sects flourished.

Royal families played a crucial role in the religious movements of this age. The founders of both Jainism and Buddhism were princes, and several kings were associated with the conceptualisation of Upanishadic philosophy, either as patrons of sages, or as sages themselves, from whom even prominent Brahmin savants took instruction in esoteric doctrines. Thus Gautama Aruni in the *Brihadaranyaka Upanishad* sought to learn the doctrine of transmigration from Panchala king Pravahana Jaivali, and the king expounded this to him as a special favour, saying, 'Although no Brahmin had ever before learned this wisdom, I shall nevertheless teach you.' Similarly, when Gargya Balaki in the *Kaushitaki Upanishad* approached King Ajatasatru of Magadha as a disciple, the king said: 'This goes against the grain, that a man of the princely class should receive a Brahmin as pupil. But come, I will teach you.'

The value of this direct textual evidence of the dominant role of Kshatriyas in formulating Upanishadic concepts is, however, somewhat diminished by the fact that, as Bloomfield points out, 'the very texts that narrate these exploits of the Kshatriyas are unquestionably Brahminic.' Indeed, there is an evolutionary continuity between the earlier Brahminical religious concepts and the new philosophy, which indicates that the same class of sages was involved with both. It is quite likely that priests sometimes attributed their own ideas to their patron kings, to curry favour. The fact that different kings are given credit for the same ideas reinforces this suspicion. Kings often conferred fabulous rewards on scholars – for instance, king Janaka of Videha presented several thousand cows to sage Yajnavalkya during a philosophical exposition, saying, 'Venerable sir, I will give you a thousand cows. Speak on.' These facts caution us against accepting the ascribed high role of kings in religion at its face value, though there were probably some philosopher-kings around in this age of philosophy in India, as indeed there would be in later times.

Brahmins in any case continued to play a major role in religious evolution, and even in Buddhism and Jainism the most influential leaders next to their founders were Brahmins. Philosophising was the most rewarding professional career for intellectuals at this time, and Brahmins deftly seized the opportunity. When Yajnavalkya presented himself at the court of

Janaka, the king asked: 'What have you come for? For cows or subtle arguments?' 'For both, Your Majesty,' answered Yajnavalkya.

Brahmins could easily move into positions of leadership in the new sects, for these sects were all offshoots of Vedic religion and held many basic ideas in common. However, the sects diverged into two broad groups in their attitude towards the Vedas. One group, comprising of Upanishadic sages, maintained that their system was the direct continuation of the Vedic tradition, in fact, its very culmination, even though they in reality disregarded the Vedic gods and rituals and deviated from many crucial Vedic beliefs. But the other group – Buddhists, Jains and other radical sectaries – boldly severed the Vedic umbilicus, pressed on further with innovative ideas, openly scorned Vedic notions of gods and sacrifices, and asserted natural law as the basis of the functioning of the universe.

The term *upa-ni-shad*, meaning 'to sit down near one', refers to the esoteric wisdom learned in secret at the feet of a guru, usually in a forest retreat. In all, there are reckoned to be 108 Upanishads, but many of them are late works of little value, some composed as late as the fifteenth century AD. The later Upanishads have hardly any connection with the Vedas, and some are more like the Puranas and Tantras. Only thirteen Upanishads – composed between roughly the seventh and fourth centuries BC – are generally acknowledged as authentic appendices of the Vedas, and are considered, like the Vedas, to be revealed wisdom. But even these vary considerably in length and style, as well as in the theories they expound. The *Brihadaranyaka Upanishad*, the longest, is about seventy printed pages in English translation, whereas the *Isa Upanishad* has just eighteen verses; the earlier Upanishads like the *Brihadaranyaka* and the *Chandogya* are in prose, while the later ones like the *Katha* and *Svetasvatara* are in verse. The oldest of the thirteen principal Upanishads is believed to be the *Brihadaranyaka Upanishad*, and the most recent the *Maitri Upanishad*.

The Upanishads mark a radical transformation in the religion of Aryans, by shifting its emphasis from gods and rituals to abstract concepts and mystic knowledge. This did not, however, involve any cultural discontinuity. The Upanishads were the efflorescence of the Vedic culture grown to maturity, after passing through intermediate development in the Brahmanas and the Aranyakas. 'As the distinction between the Brahmanas and Aranyakas is not an absolute one,' notes Keith, 'and the Aranyakas tend to contain more advanced doctrines than the Brahmanas, so the distinction between the Upanishads and Aranyakas is also not absolute, tradition actually incorporating the Upanishads in some cases in the Aranyakas.' What distinguishes the Upanishads is that metaphysical thought, which was rather like vaporous fancy in the Brahmanas and Aranyakas, acquires certain solidity and keenness in them.

But fancy too is still very much there in the Upanishads. Indeed, some of the allegorical conceits in the Upanishads are not much different from those of the Brahmanas. For instance, the *Brihadaranyaka Upanishad* describes sacrifice thus: 'Man in truth is fire, O Gautama; his open mouth is fuel, his breath the smoke, his speech the flame, his eyes the coals, his ears the sparks ... Woman in truth is fire, O Gautama; the phallus is her fuel, the hairs her smoke, the vulva her flame, sexual intercourse her coals, the ecstasy her sparks. In this fire the gods offer semen; from this oblation man is born. He lives out his allotted span. And when he dies, they carry him off to the funeral pyre. Here his fire becomes real fire, his fuel real fuel, his smoke real smoke, his flame real flame, his coal real coal, his sparks real sparks. In this very fire the gods offer up man. From this oblation arises a new man, radiant in splendour.'

The Upanishads are like a lush but wild and untended grove, marked by great profusion but not much harmony. They are exploratory works, so there are considerable divergences in the expositions of different Upanishads, divergences even within a single Upanishad. 'The thought of the Upanishads,' comments Bloomfield, 'is not systematic, but tentative, fanciful, and even romantic. It feels its way through misty, wavering, sometimes conflicting beginnings.' In most cases, the Upanishads are not the original works of single authors, but collations of various current notions, and are a mixture of subtle insights and coarse beliefs.

Often, discussions in them are not discussions at all, but camouflaged dogmatic assertions, in which propositions stand as self-evident truths, on their own authority. They frequently use the sophistic technique of seeking to substantiate propositions through their constant reiterations in slightly modified forms, not so much advancing the argument as going round and round in a tightening circle. And they use similes and metaphors profusely, not just to illustrate a point, but as clinching arguments – as proofs, in fact. When needed, more similes and metaphors are offered as additional proofs. Fanciful riddles and equally fanciful solutions often take the place of hard reasoning in them. States the *Brihadaranyaka Upanishad*: 'Gods, it seems, love the obscure and hate the obvious.' Apparently, so did the Upanishadic sages.

It is 'mystic intelligence' that characterises the Upanishads, not logical rigour. The inchoate nature of many of their theories is not surprising, for they are among man's earliest sustained efforts at philosophy. For that age, the Upanishads were indeed an extraordinarily sophisticated intellectual feat, and some of their mystical insights are in strange consonance with the findings of modern science. They certainly constituted a great advance from earlier Indian religious thought, and out of them would later rise the great Indian philosophical system of Vedanta. And their sheer spiritual radiance and seething intellectual energy would throughout history cast a magic spell on people across great cultural and religious divides. Schopenhauer, the nineteenth-century German philosopher, who came across a Latin translation of a Persian version of the Upanishads prepared by Mughal prince Dara, had this to say about them: 'In the whole world there is no study so beneficial and so elevating as that of the Upanishads. It has been the solace of my life – it will be the solace of my death.' The Upanishads do indeed open the doors of perception.

The goal of the Upanishads, as of all philosophy, is to unravel the enigma of life and examine the relationship between man and the universe. 'Whence are we born?' ponders the *Svetasvatara Upanishad.* 'Whereby do we live, and wither do we go? O ye knowers of Brahman, tell us at whose command we abide here, whether in pain or in pleasure?'

To resolve these and other ontological mysteries, the Upanishads offer several ideas. The most fundamental of these are the concepts of Brahman, Atman, karma and samsara. Brahman is the indefinable, changeless essence of the universe, while Atman is the same universal essence immanent in the individual. The two, the universal 'soul' and the individual 'soul', are in fact identical; it is only ignorance that makes us think that they are distinct. The realisation of the essential identity between Brahman and Atman, the Upanishads maintain, is the means of salvation – it is, in fact, salvation. The concept of salvation here is not of an eternal life of bliss in heaven, but of the dissolution of the individual in the universal, and the consequent release of man from samsara, the interminable cycle of transmigration, in which he is caught because of his karma, the consequences of his thoughts and deeds.

The primary concern of the Upanishads is to seek an explanation for samsara, and to mark out the path by which to escape from it. Remarkably, these issues of life and death and suffering are examined by the Upanishads without a touch of sentiment or emotion. Their reasoning is entirely cold and formal. The sages were intellectuals, not saints or saviours.

In all this, the very temper of the Upanishads is different from that of the Vedas. The Rig-vedic view was that life was on the whole good, and its ideal was a long life on earth and a blissful eternity with the Fathers after death. In contrast, the Upanishads look upon samsara – indeed, life itself – with disfavour. In temporal terms, the Upanishads offer nothing positive for man to look forward to, either here on earth or in the hereafter. There might be many good and enjoyable things in life, but these joys are evanescent. The true flavour of life is bitterness, conclude the Upanishads.

The Brahman-Atman identity, as well as the concept of samsara, are revolutionary new ideas, which are not found in the Vedas. There are, however, a few tentative speculations in the Vedas that anticipate the metaphysics and spirit of the Upanishads, as in this Atharva-vedic chant: 'Free from desire, true, eternal, self-begotten, full of joy, subject to none, he no longer fears death who knows the wise, ageless Atman.' And the Upanishads in turn, true to the perennial Indian proclivity to regard antiquity as authority, acknowledge the inviolable sacredness of the Vedas, and take care to link their abstruse gnosis to the mechanics of Vedic rituals, even though the rituals themselves had become irrelevant in the new religious environment, and the essential philosophy of the Upanishads is hardly in consonance with Vedic notions. 'The older Upanishads, through the medium of the Aranyakas, join their theosophic speculation right on to the dead ritual,' comments Bloomfield. 'To some extent the bones of the ritual skeleton rattle about in early theosophy in quite a lively fashion.'

The dominant feature of Vedic religion was sacrifice. The Upanishads do not disavow sacrifice, but bypass it and make it redundant by giving it a symbolic or mystical interpretation, and by converting the physical performance of sacrifice into an inner spiritual exercise, in which the knowledge of the symbolism of sacrifice is more important than the sacrificial rite itself. Magic is thus transformed into metaphysics.

There is thus a link between Upanishadic metaphysics and Vedic rituals. It could even be that, as Bloomfield argues, the Upanishads received their creative impulse from the study of the implications of Vedic sacrifice. On the whole, however, the Upanishads stay on a higher plane of thought than the Vedas and the Brahmanas. And they, even while acknowledging the sacredness of the Vedas, consider themselves to be superior to the Vedas. 'There are two sciences that must be known ... a higher and a lower,' states the *Mundaka Upanishad*. 'Of these, the lower consists of the Rig-veda, Yajur-veda, Sama-veda, Atharva-veda, phonetics, rituals, grammar, etymology, metre and astronomy. The higher is that by which the imperishable Brahman can be attained.' And the *Svetasvatara Upanishad* scorns: 'Of what use is the Rig-veda to one who does not know the spirit from which the Rig-veda comes?'

Vedic sacrifices, the Upanishads assert, were good only for temporal gain, for wealth, power and progeny, or at best to take man for a sojourn in 'the world of the Fathers', from where he will have to return again and again to earth through transmigration, to live and suffer endlessly. For deliverance from samsara, other means are needed. 'Frail indeed are these rafts of sacrifice,' asserts the *Mundaka Upanishad*. 'Deluded men who rejoice in them as the highest good return again and again to old age and death. Conceited, puffed up with learning, dwelling in darkness, they wander around, fools, doing themselves much harm, like blind men guided by the blind ... But those who in penance and in faith dwell in the forest, tranquil and wise, living on alms, pass on, immaculate, through the doorway of the sun, to where that deathless Person dwells.'

'The magic potency formerly ascribed to the sacrifice, now began to be attributed to asceticism,' notes Basham. But the asceticism that the Upanishads prescribe has more to do with the mind than with the body. Physical austerities and self-torture, says the *Brihadaranyaka Upanishad*, would enable man to attain only the 'lower bliss of the world of the Fathers.' The ultimate goal of escaping from the cycle of life can be achieved only through spiritual austerity, through *tapas* – calm, detached and precisely focussed meditation – which would give man not only insight into the cosmic processes but also magical, superhuman powers. This, according to the Upanishads, is the only true means of attaining the 'imperishable Brahman.'

NEYTI! NEYTI!

The Upanishads mark the twilight of the Vedic gods. 'Every embodiment of the divine idea is now abstract or symbolic,' comments Bloomfield. In the final analysis, gods do not exist, maintains the *Mandukya Upanishad*, and are in any case irrelevant. 'The essential work of Indian philosophers of the Upanishadic period was to depersonalise the old gods, and to show that in the macrocosm and the microcosm alike there existed nothing save nature powers and processes, which required no explanation by the assumption of divinities,' observes Keith. 'One of the most remarkable facts in the religion of the Vedas, when carried to its legitimate conclusion, is that these multiple gods really vanish in the end, after they have contributed their individual attributes to the great idea of unity, of the oneness at the root of the universe,' adds Bloomfield. 'This is the very negation of mythology and pantheons; of sacrificial hocus-pocus and poetic fable.' Philosophy begins at the twilight of the gods.

The Vedic gods, comments Basham, 'were too motley a company to correspond to the orderly civilisation which had ... emerged.' This chaos of gods would not have, however, mattered to the common people, who could pick and choose their favourite gods and goddesses from the great variety of deities around. In fact, even while the Upanishadic sages were seeking unity in divinity, popular religion was introducing ever more gods into its pantheon, as Aryan society took into its fold local and aboriginal people along with their deities and religious practices.

The Upanishadic path was only for the cultural elite. Indeed, some of the Upanishads themselves – the *Svetasvatara* and the *Katha*, for instance – were unable to sustain the awful burden of abstract thought, and sought refuge in the easy comfort of theism. The *Svetasvatara Upanishad* considers Rudra (Shiva) to be the supreme god, higher than even the impersonal Brahman. 'All worlds he emanates, all worlds will he roll up at the end of time,' it declares, and warns:

> *When men shall roll up space*
> *as if it were a piece of leather,*

then will there be an end of suffering
for him who knew not God!

But this is a deviant thought. In the main, god in the Upanishads is really not a god at all, but a pure abstraction called Brahman, without any attributes or potencies whatever. Tenuous speculation leading to this unique and startling concept had begun in the Rig-veda itself, but it was only in the Upanishads that the idea, as Bloomfield puts it, finally 'emerged from the stage of tremulous venture to confident and familiar statement.' In the process, the sense of the term Brahman changed totally – in the Rig-veda, it meant the magical potency of the mantra, but the Upanishads hollowed out all specific meanings from the term, so that it would resonate with mysterious metaphysical echoes. Brahman is everything and nothing. It is the irreducible essence of everything in the world, but is nothing in particular. The *Sarvasaropanishad*, a late text, states that when time, space, substance and cause disappear, 'then Brahman remains over.'

Inseparable from the concept of Brahman is the concept of Atman. Atman is 'the Brahman in ourselves,' remarks Bloomfield. 'The conviction that the Brahman without and the Atman within are one and the same – that is the real religion of the Upanishads.' The terms Brahman and Atman are often used interchangeably in the Upanishads, for they are absolutely the same, with only a contextual difference between them. Coomaraswamy explains this concept with the elegant simile of 'the identity of infinite space with the space in any closed vessel – shatter the bounding walls of the vessel ... and the identity of space is patent.'

'The Atman is indeed Brahman,' flatly declares Yajnavalkya in the *Brihadaranyaka Upanishad*. The *Chandogya Upanishad* elucidates the concept with a parable:

'Fetch me a fig from the banyan tree over there,' sage Uddalaka Aruni told Svetaketu, his son and disciple.

'Here it is, venerable sir.'

'Cut it open.'

'Yes, venerable sir.'

'What do you see inside?'

'These tiny seeds, venerable sir.'

'Cut open one of them, my son.'

'Yes, venerable sir.'

'What do you see there?'

'Nothing at all, venerable sir.'

Then Uddalaka said: 'My son, that which you cannot see is the subtle essence of the tree, and it is from that very essence that this huge banyan tree grows ... In that subtle essence is the being of everything that exists.

That is the Real. That is the Self. *Tat tvam asi* – that thou art, Svetaketu.'

Uddalaka later reinforced this lesson by having Svetaketu put a lump of salt in a pot of water one night, and asking him the next morning to take it out. But Svetaketu could not find the lump of salt in the pot, though when he sipped the water, as his father told him to do, it tasted of salt – the salt was indeed there, though he could not see it. Uddalaka then told him, 'Here also, my dear, in this body, truly is the Self, though you do not perceive it. In that subtle essence is the being of everything that exists.' States the *Svetasvatara Upanishad*:

> *As oil in sesame, as butter in cream,*
> *as water in riverbeds, as fire in the fire-sticks,*
> *so is the Self to be grasped within the self...*

On the surface everything in the world appears different from everything else, each marked by its own particularity, but the speculative imagination, as Oldenberg observes, 'strives to pierce into the depths below, in which lies the unifying bond of all diversity. Man looks for the essence in things, and essence of the essence.' But how do we define Brahman, the indefinable essence of the essence? Brahman is *nirguna*, without attributes, the Upanishads hold; it is pure consciousness, eternally changeless through waking and sleeping, through life and death and transmigration; it is both immanent and transcendent at the same time, within and outside everything. Brahman is singularity, devoid of time and space, an absolute nothingness that contains the whole universe of matter and energy.

Brahman is all that there is. But Brahman cannot be known objectively, because there is no reality outside Brahman, no 'other' to observe and know Brahman. Consciousness can exist only if there is duality, maintains Yajnavalkya. 'How would you see the seer of seeing?' he asks. 'How would you hear the hearer of hearing? ... How would you know the knower of knowing?' Evidently, Brahman can be known only in intuitive flashes. Advises the *Brihadaranyaka Upanishad*:

> *Let a wise seeker, knowing Him*
> *bend his mind towards Him:*
> *let him not meditate on many words;*
> *these can but tire the voice.*

Words are weariness. Warns the *Katha Upanishad*: 'Not through much learning is Atman reached, not through the intellect and sacred teaching.' The *Isa Upanishad* regards conventional knowledge as worse than ignorance. Adds the *Kena Upanishad*: 'He (Brahman) comes to the thought of those who know him beyond thought, not to those who imagine he can be attained by thought. He is unknown to the learned and known to the simple.'

Words and images can only hint at what Brahman is, but not describe it, for any description would limit the Brahman and violate its essential limitless quality. 'Words and mind go to him (Brahman), but reach him not and return,' says the *Taittiriya Upanishad.* The *Kena Upanishad* wonders: 'That to which no eye penetrates, nor speech, nor thought, which remains unknown, and we see it not, how can instruction therein be given to us?' The *Brihadaranyaka Upanishad* concludes that Brahman can be described only in negative terms: 'This Self, it can only be described as *Neyti! Neyti!* – Not this! Not this! It is impalpable ... indestructible ... free from attachment ... unfettered.' Centuries later, Sankara, the great Vedantic philosopher, would illustrate this point with a story – when a disciple asked a sage about the nature of Brahman-Atman, the sage at first remained silent, but on being pressed, answered, 'I teach you, indeed, but you understand not. Silence is the Atman.' You cannot point out the air with a finger.

The Upanishadic sages had difficulty in stating abstract ideas with precision, and often spoke allegorically. The results were not always happy, and there is much confusion in their attempts to define Brahman-Atman. Atman initially meant breath, not self. And, breath being considered the irreducible essence of life, a link was sought to be established through it between Atman and Brahman by maintaining that all breaths come from the universal breath. The primacy of breath, according to the *Kaushitaki Upanishad,* was once demonstrated by the great god Prajapati when the various vital powers in man quarrelled among themselves for supremacy and approached him to settle the dispute. Prajapati then asked the powers of speech, hearing, sight and mind to leave the body one after the other, but even after they all left, breath still remained. However, when breath left, all other faculties departed with it, proving that all else were dependent on breath.

'Life is breath, breath is life,' the *Kaushitaki Upanishad* states. 'Now some say that bodily organs gravitate towards unity ... When the voice speaks, all the other organs speak along with it. When the eye sees, all the other organs see along with it. When the ear hears, all the other organs hear along with it. When the mind thinks, all the other organs think along with it. When the breath breathes, all other organs breathe along with it ...' This is true, the Upanishad concedes, but goes on to maintain that there is nevertheless a hierarchy among the bodily functions, and that breath has supremacy over all else, because none of the other faculties can exist without breath. This proposition, that breath is Atman-Brahman, does not, however, find favour with Yajnavalkya in the *Brihadaranyaka*

Upanishad. Elsewhere the claim of *Om*, the mystic syllable, to be considered as Brahman is examined but rejected. The general view of the Upanishads is that it is futile to attempt to define or describe the ineffable Atman-Brahman.

Brahman certainly cannot be described in corporeal terms. Nevertheless, some Upanishads go on to furnish curious (and possibly allegorical) descriptions of the physical properties of Atman-Brahman, conceiving it as a material but very small and subtle entity. The *Svetasvatara Upanishad* gives the size of the Atman variously as that of a thumb, a needlepoint, or the ten-thousandth part of the tip of a hair. The Atman, says the *Chandogya Upanishad*, resides in the heart and is 'smaller than a grain of rice or a barely-corn, smaller than a mustard-seed or a grain of millet, or the kernel of a grain of millet ... [and yet is] greater than the earth ... greater than the sky, greater than all these worlds. All works, all desires, all scents, all tastes belong to it: it encompasses all this universe ... This my Self within the heart is that Brahman. When I depart from hence I shall merge with it.' The *Brihadaranyaka Upanishad* maintains that there are 72,000 nerves called *hita* in man and that it is through them that the Atman spreads through his body. States the *Katha Upanishad*:

> *Know this:*
> *The Atman is the master of the chariot,*
> *the chariot is the body,*
> *intellect the charioteer,*
> *mind the reins.*
> *The senses, they say, are the steeds ...*

If Atman is Brahman, and everything in the universe is nothing but Brahman, and Brahman has no attributes whatsoever, how do we account for the phenomenal world we know (and know only) by its attributes? Does it have any reality at all? Or is it just an illusion, *maya*? The general inclination of the Upanishadic sages is to consider it as *maya* – the philosophical term *maya* first appears in the *Svetasvatara Upanishad* – though the concept would be developed into an integrated philosophy only some centuries later.

The phenomenal world has no independent existence, the Upanishads hold. It exists only in our consciousness. The world is what it is only because that is the way we see it. Reality is entirely subjective. This is a simple enough proposition, but from this solid ground the Upanishads leap into a mind-spinning metaphysical vortex and argue that consciousness can become active, become conscious, only in the presence of objects (the phenomenal world), for otherwise consciousness will not have anything to be conscious of. Subject (conscious consciousness) and object are dependent on each other. One cannot exist without the other. 'If there were no objective elements, there would be no elements of consciousness,' states the *Kaushitaki Upanishad*; 'and if there were no elements of consciousness, there would be no objective elements. No form at all could be realised from either alone.' In the quantum world of the Upanishads, notes Zaehner, 'the barrier between subject and object seems magically to melt away, and experiencer, experience and the thing experienced seem to merge into one single whole.'

The Upanishads see no difference between dreams and wakeful experiences either. Both are equally unreal. Yajnavalkya in the *Brihadaranyaka Upanishad* speaks of man shuttling between the two imagined worlds: 'In dream he finds his joy, roams around, witnessing good and evil, then hastens back ... to the realm of wakefulness ... [where too] he finds his joy, roams around, witnessing good and evil. Then [again] he hurries ... to the realm of dream.' Says sage Gaudapada: 'In dreams, things are imagined internally, and in the experience that we have when we are awake, things are imagined as if existing outside, but both of them are but illusory creations of the self.' All is *maya*. States the *Katha Upanishad*:

If the killer thinks 'I killed,'
or the victim 'I have been killed,'
neither has true knowledge –
he kills not, is not killed.

All temporal distinctions vaporise in the supernal realm of Upanishadic metaphysics. But if all particularities are illusory, are we then to disregard the phenomenal world altogether? Not at all. The world, though unreal in the ultimate sense, is real enough in our temporal perception, and has to be accepted as such. But how did this world of our senses, this universe, come about? Since neither subject nor object has any independent existence, how did their dependent existence begin in the first place? And what controls this process? And how would it end? To explain these, the Upanishads offer several cosmogonic theories, not all of which are consistent with the high metaphysics they propound.

'How is the first origin to be conceived?' the *Svetasvatara Upanishad* ponders, and goes on to consider the various prevailing notions about it: 'Should time, inherent nature, fate, chance, or the elements be regarded as the cause? Or was the cause the one who is called Purusha? Or a conjunction of all these?' The *Brihadaranyaka Upanishad* in one place attributes cosmic evolution to a primal procreator: 'In the beginning this universe was the Self alone, in the likeness of a man. Looking around, he saw nothing other than himself ... He longed for a mate. Now he was of the size of a man and a woman in close embrace. He divided this Self into two, and from this arose husband and wife ... He copulated with her, and thence were human beings born. But she reflected: "How can he copulate with me, whom he generated from himself? Well, I will hide myself." She became a cow, he a bull; he copulated with her, and thence were cattle born. She became a mare, he a stallion; she became a she-ass, he a he-ass ... she became a she-goat, he a he-goat; she became a ewe, he a ram. So did he bring forth all that exist in pairs, even down to the ants.'

The *Taittiriya Upanishad* maintains that from Brahman 'space came to be, from space the wind, from wind fire, from fire water, from water earth, from earth the plants, from the plants food, from food man.' Some sages held that cosmic evolution was based on an abstract principle, while others saw it as a ripening of inherent potentialities. A few propounded atomist or other materialistic theories. Some even refused to speculate on these matters, considering that such exercises were of no value or that it was impossible to acquire ontological knowledge.

The *Svetasvatara Upanishad* rejects all these concepts and maintains that god Shiva was the primary cause of cosmic evolution: 'It is the majesty of the self-luminous Lord that causes the wheel of Brahman to turn.' But even here god is not presented as a creator – the world is his manifestation, but he did not create the world. The idea of *ex nihilo* creation is foreign to the Upanishads. And why does the universe exist? Only because that is its nature, the Upanishads hold, excluding the possibility of purpose for its existence, as firmly as they reject the concept of creation.

If the universe, as the Upanishads consistently hold, is not a created universe, then it must have always existed in some form or other, even if only as highly condensed matter or as pure energy, and it will continue to exist forever in some form or other. Time therefore is without beginning or end. The *Maitri Upanishad* exalts time as Brahman itself:

From time all creatures issue,
in time they grow and prosper
in time they attain final repose.
Time is formless. Time has form.

Brahman, the Upanishad continues, has two forms, time and timeless. 'That which existed before the sun is timeless; it cannot be divided into parts. That which begins with the sun, however, is time. And the form of this time which has parts is the year.' In other words, time (Brahman) has an earthly as well as a cosmic aspect; while the earthly time is linear and can be measured in years, and has a beginning and an end, cosmic time is cyclic, without beginning or end, and is really timeless. The cosmic time is cyclic because the cosmic process is cyclic, an endless repetition of evolution and dissolution, expansion and contraction.

*

Intertwined with this concept of cyclic cosmic process are the concepts of karma and samsara, which would fundamentally shape the Indian socio-cultural ethos, even the character and spirit of its people. Says the *Brihadaranyaka Upanishad* about karma: 'As he has acted, as he has lived, so he becomes; he who has done good, is born again as a good one; he who has done evil, is born again as an evil one. He becomes good through good action, bad through bad action ... Desire alone defines man – as is his desire, so is his will; as is his will, so will he act; as is his deed, so is his destiny.'

Karma is a deterministic system, a 'process of automatic psychic evolution,' in which, strictly speaking, man has no control over his life, for his previous karma determines his present actions. Nevertheless, the Upanishads do not propound absolute fatalism. Man has some free will, they maintain. Says the *Chandogya Upanishad*: 'Now, verily, man is possessed of an active will ... Let man exercise his will.' But on the whole the Upanishads are sceptical about the benefits of action. Any kind of action, good or bad, would keep man snared in samsara, the eternally recurrent cycle of transmigration, of life and suffering and death, over and over again. Good action would not lead to the final liberation from samsara, for, as Bloomfield notes, 'the fruit of the finite can be only finite.'

Transmigration, a revolutionary new concept in Indian religious thought, was first introduced rather tentatively in the *Brihadaranyaka Upanishad*. There is no direct mention of transmigration in the Vedas, though one passage in the Rig-veda does speak of the various organs and faculties of the dead departing to the sun, the wind, the fire and so on, and the soul to the waters or the plants. This theme is further elaborated in the Brahmanas, but does not yet quite crystallise there into the concept of transmigration, although some passages in the *Satapatha Brahmana* are sometimes doubtfully interpreted as alluding to transmigration. The world of the Fathers is the final resting place for the dead according to the Brahmanas.

But the Brahmanas do introduce a new idea – that there is death even in the world of the Fathers. This is logical, since, in the view of the Brahmanas, death on earth leads to birth in the next world – if man is born there, then he must eventually also die there. The span of a man's life of ease in the world of the Fathers is determined by the store of merit he has accumulated on earth, which in time would be exhausted, and then he would die again. But this re-death is only in the other world; there is yet no idea of the dead returning to earth to be born again. However, as Bloomfield notes, it was 'very natural to transplant the consequences of re-death to this earth ... where men, like fish, die at every wink of the eye. He who must die again comes to do it on earth where the trick is so well understood.'

The concept of transmigration is based on the notion that all living beings have souls, and that souls do migrate from one life form to another, each to be reborn as a different creature according to the individual soul's karma, till the soul is purged of all desire and all activity. On the death of a person, 'his wisdom and his karma and his accumulated experience take him by the hand' and lead him to the next life, says Yajnavalkya. 'As a caterpillar which has wriggled to the tip of a blade of grass draws itself over [to a new blade], so does this man, after he has put aside his body, draw himself over to a new existence.' But if there is thus continuity of soul from one life to another through metempsychosis, why is it that man has no memory of his previous births? According the *Garbha Upanishad*, the fully developed baby in the mother's womb remembers its previous births and experiences, but forgets it all during the trauma of birth.

The trauma of birth continues as the ordeal of life, the Upanishads hold. Life is indeed misery, and in any case ends in death, which, despite all the awfulness of life, is hardly welcome, and in any case leads to further births and deaths interminably. There is no peace in life for man, and no peace in the grave either. Total, irreversible termination of samsara alone can give the soul final peace.

A means has to be found therefore for man to break free from the distressing and endless cycle of life and death, and attain salvation. This is a major concern of the Upanishads. Knowledge, according to the Upanishads, is the key to achieve this deliverance. Invokes the *Brihadaranyaka Upanishad*:

From the unreal lead me to the real!
From darkness lead me to the light!
From death lead me to immortality!

The knowledge that the Upanishads seek is not however the knowledge of external objects and processes, but of the self within, the recognition that Atman and Brahman are one, and that there is no reality outside Brahman. 'There is really no diversity at all. Death beyond death is the lot of him who imagines he sees diversity,' warns the *Brihadaranyaka Upanishad*. The knowledge of the absolute unity of everything in the world releases man from the delusion of his individuality. He then recognises himself as one with Brahman, indeed becomes one with Brahman, like a drop of water falling into the ocean. Or, as the *Mundaka Upanishad* puts it,

Rivers all flow home to the ocean,
leaving name and form behind,

so does the knowing man seek
the beyond of the beyond,
freed from name and form.

But how does one acquire this salvational knowledge? One cannot, states the *Brihadaranyaka Upanishad*, attain this through learning and objective analysis, or by singing Vedic hymns, performing sacrifices and practising austerities, or through good deeds. One has to look into oneself to see the Brahman-Atman identity. It is not even necessary for one to become an ascetic to gain this insight. The saving knowledge can be gained while living in society, as even some kings have done, by adopting an attitude of absolute detachment, and ridding oneself entirely of earthly longings, 'like a fire that has consumed all its fuel,' as the *Svetasvatara Upanishad* puts it. Explains the *Katha Upanishad*:

When all desires that shelter in the heart
of man are cast aside
then the mortal becomes immortal –
thence to Brahman he attains.

Initially it was thought that this release could be attained only on death. The *Chandogya Upanishad* states that after death the souls of those who attain salvation would take the path of the gods and merge with Brahman, while the other souls, after a sojourn in the moon, their good karma exhausted, would return to earthly life. Later however it came to be believed that salvation could be achieved during life itself, by being awake to the knowledge of the inseparable identity of Atman and Brahman. Such a man, says the *Chandogya Upanishad*, 'becomes an independent sovereign'; entirely self-contained, he 'has pleasure in the Self, plays with the Self, lies with the Self, and has his joy with the Self.'

'Whoever knows Brahman becomes Brahman,' declares the *Mundaka Upanishad*. 'Even gods have not the power to cause him to un-Be, for he becomes their own self,' assures the *Brihadaranyaka Upanishad*. He lives, but is no longer involved with life. His actions have no karmic consequences, for they, like water on a lotus leaf, remain only on the surface. He is free of all constraints and moral imperatives, for he recognises no distinction between right and wrong, altruism and selfishness, good and evil, beauty and ugliness. Declares Indra in the *Kaushitaki Upanishad*: 'The man who knows me as I am loses nothing that is his whatever he does, even though he should slay his mother or his father, or steal or procure an abortion. Whatever evil he does, he does not suffer.'

'As the slough of a snake lies on an ant-hill, dead, cast off, even so lies his body,' says Yajnavalkya. 'Then the self becomes incorporeal, immortal spirit, Brahman ... Karma neither enhances nor diminishes him ... The man who knows Brahman will be self-controlled, calm, withdrawn into himself, patient, collected, for he sees Brahman in himself, sees all things as Brahman ... Free from evil, free from doubt, immaculate, he becomes Brahman.' He is purged of all longings, including the longing for life. He does not desire anything because he knows himself to be all; he does not fear anything or anybody because he knows that there is no 'other' around. Life then ceases to be a misery. Comments the *Svetasvatara Upanishad*:

Even as a mirror with dirt begrimed
shines brightly when cleaned,
so too the embodied soul,
once it has seen Self as it really is,
becomes one ... from sorrow free.

The state of being merged with Brahman, whether in life or after death, is a state of pure consciousness. But this is not consciousness in the mundane sense of the term, for when a man has merged with Brahman, there is no 'other' for him to be conscious of – 'no second thing other than himself that he might see it,' as Yajnavalkya puts it. The subject-object distinction disappears and there is no consciousness of particulars, for particulars do not exist.

This state of pure consciousness, in which the self abides in itself, is often spoken of by the Upanishadic philosophers as one similar to the state of dreamless sleep. In deep sleep, the spirit curls into itself, withdrawn from the chatter of the senses. In that state, the self is all-conscious, perfectly permeable and translucent, but without facets and unmarked by the awareness of particulars. All the faculties of man are open then, but he does not see, hear, smell, taste or feel anything, because, as Yajnavalkya remarks, 'there is no separation between the seer and the sight.'

Superficially, this salvation that the Upanishads envisage would seem to be negative, a peeling off of all external consciousness, a quiescence of the self in itself. But in a larger sense, it is not negative at all, for what higher prospect can there be for a mortal, whatever his transient earthly condition, than being one with the immortal, universal spirit? As Zaehner, citing the *Chandogya Upanishad*, points out, the oneness of Brahman-Atman 'is not an absolutely motionless oneness, but a true "liberation" or "release" from space and time, a form of existence that can only be compared to the wind in its freedom to roam at will, unhampered by material things ... It is an eternal mode of existence in which, paradoxically, timelessness does not preclude freedom to move in time and spacelessness does not preclude freedom to roam at will in space.'

The Upanishads consider the Brahman-Atman union as the ultimate bliss. According to the *Brihadaranyaka Upanishad*, if the greatest bliss in the temporal world is of a man who is healthy and rich, master over others, possessing all that could minister to human enjoyment, a hundred times more than that is the bliss enjoyed by the Fathers in the other world; still a hundred times more is the bliss of Gandharvas; still a hundred times more is the bliss of those who have attained divinity through karma; still a hundred times more is the bliss of the gods by birth; still a hundred times more is the bliss of the world of Prajapati; and the bliss of the Brahman world is still a hundred times more. But this bliss that the Upanishads speak of is not bliss in any temporal sense – it is bliss without form or content or attributes, without even a consciousness to register the bliss.

The Upanishadic philosophy is fundamentally asocial and amoral. The world not only has no beginning or end, it has no purpose either, and is without moral absolutes. However, the perfect freedom of action that the Upanishads sanction is only for the very few exceptional beings who attain Brahman in life, and such people, being above all desires, would also be above doing any evil, indeed, above getting involved in any action of any kind. For ordinary mortals, who can hope for the attainment of Brahman only through the transmigratory process, good karma and good behaviour are important.

The *Chandogya Upanishad* denounces self-indulgence as diabolical. 'Making oneself alone happy here, serving oneself, does one obtain both worlds, this world and the yonder ... This is the doctrine of the demons,' states the Upanishad, and goes on to recommend that men should practise austerity, liberality, truthfulness and non-violence. The *Taittiriya Upanishad* advises man to be truthful and virtuous, to study and teach, to be a responsible householder, and, far from condoning parricide, exhorts: 'Let your mother be god to you; let your father be god to you; let your teacher be god to you; let your guest be god to you. Perform only deeds to which no blame attaches, no others.' States the *Katha Upanishad*: 'The good is one thing and the pleasant another.'

Discipline, benevolence and clemency are the social virtues that the Upanishads cherish, and this is revealed in an engaging story in the *Brihadaranyaka Upanishad*. Gods, men and demons, the threefold offspring of Prajapati, in their childhood lived as *brahmacharins* (students of sacred knowledge) with their father. On finishing their studies, the gods asked Prajapati for a message.

'*Da!*' he said to them. 'Do you understand?'

'We understand,' they said. 'You said *damyata*: be self-controlled.'

'*Om*, you did understand,' Prajapati said.

Then the men said to him: 'Speak to us, sir.'

And to them also he uttered the same syllable: '*Da!* Do you understand?'
'We understand,' they said. 'You said *datta*: be charitable.'
'*Om*, you did understand,' he said.
The demons then said to him: 'Speak to us, sir.'
Again he uttered this syllable: '*Da!* Do you understand?'
'We understand,' they said. 'You said *dayadhvam*: be merciful.'
'*Om*, you did understand,' Prajapati said.
So the divine voice ever thunders: '*Da! Da! Da!* – be self-controlled, charitable, merciful.'

REBELS AND PROPHETS

'Man is formed of the four elements,' contended Ajita Kesakambala, a sixth-century BC Indian materialist. 'When he dies, earth returns to the aggregate of earth, water to water, fire to fire, and air to air, while his senses vanish into space. Four men with a bier take up the corpse; they gossip [about the dead man] as far as the burning-ground, where his bones turn to the colour of a dove's wing and his sacrifices end in ashes. They are fools who preach almsgiving, and those who affirm the existence [of non-material categories] speak vain and lying nonsense. When the body dies both the fool and the wise alike are cut off and perish. Nothing survives after death.'

Ajita was not alone in such thoughts. Of all the ages in the long history of India, the sixth-century BC was intellectually the most frenetic. The defining characteristic of the age was rationalism, not faith, and the greatest religious reformers of the age – Buddha, Mahavira and Gosala – were all rationalists, who ignored or rejected the concept of god and the authority of the Vedas. The elite of the age too were generally sceptical about afterlife and scornful of priestly conceits, as in the *Jataka* story about the king of Videha, who mockingly told the divine sage Narada: 'If thou believest ... that there is in another world a dwelling-place for the dead, then give me here five hundred [silver] pieces, and I will give thee a thousand in the next world.'

The intellectual life of this age was dominated by peripatetic polemicists known as Parivrajakas (wanderers), who constantly toured the land to propagate their radical doctrines and to engage rival theorists in public debates. There were even several women among them, and the *Jatakas* tell the story of four Jain sisters who could maintain 1,000 different theses in debate, and went from town to town challenging anyone to dispute with them. So pervasive was the addiction to philosophy in those days that it was a common civility among mendicants to greet strangers by enquiring about the doctrines they held, in the same manner as enquiring about their health.

The custom of holding public philosophical debates can be traced back to the late Vedic period – sage Uddalaka Aruni, for instance, is described in the *Satapatha Brahmana* as going about offering a gold coin to whoever could worst him in argument. In the post-Vedic period such debates became a common feature of urban life. It was high entertainment. In nearly all the towns and even in some of the larger villages in northern India there were at this time public debating halls called *kautuhala-salas* (meaning, literally, halls for arousing curiosity) where debates were regularly held, and winners were rewarded by kings and chieftains with such presents as cows with their horns adorned with gold.

These debates were virulent, gladiatorial contests. The Parivrajakas were not the sedate, contemplative, retiring philosopher types we imagine sages to be, but fiercely combative professional controversialists, who strutted about the land flinging truculent challenges at each other. One of the most colourful of them was Saccaka, who haughtily boasted that anyone who dared to face him in debate, even Buddha, would 'totter, tremble, quake and sweat. And if I attacked a lifeless pillar with my language, it would totter, tremble and quake – how much more a human being.'

Some of these wanderers – perhaps many of them – were, like the Greek sophists of about the same period, sham philosophers, who were scorned by the discerning public as 'eel-wrigglers and hair-splitters.' Probably quite a few of them were also 'unscrupulous men who initiated themselves into a profitable career of asceticism by the simple process of losing their clothes,' as Basham contends. The *Jatakas* speak of 'a shifty rascal of an ascetic, of the class which wears long, matted hair,' and states that there were many cases

Where saintliness is but a cloak
whereby to cozen guileless folk
and screen a villain's treachery ...

But equally, as the *Jatakas* themselves testify, there were many who took to asceticism 'throwing up their worldly fortune as if it were a lump of phlegm.' Asceticism had become something of a high fashion in India at this time, attracting many even (or especially) from the upper crust of society. Most of these ascetics, having dropped out of conventional society, lived austere lives in the periphery of villages and towns, concentrating on religious meditation and teaching, but there were also many who retreated into deep forests and took to bizarre practices. All these ascetics were usually held in high esteem by people and were treated deferentially by kings – even by gods, it was claimed – as persons endowed with magical or supernatural powers, whom it was dangerous to offend.

In purely materialistic terms, the ascetics were parasites. But this was their privilege as holy men, and people were generally glad to grant them that privilege. This was a time of extraordinary prosperity in India, so people could spare resources to indulge the ascetics without inconveniencing themselves. Traders, held low in the Brahminical order of society, were particularly keen patrons of the radical sages – for instance, the *Jatakas* speak of 500 Buddhist monks being fed daily in the house of Anathapindika, a merchant prince of Sravasti.

The growth of urban centres and the widening circle of education and culture provided the sages with ready and appreciative audiences. An excitement about religion now gripped the people, and they, according to the *Jatakas*, flocked to the sages clamouring, 'Tell us something worth hearing.' Though primarily an urban development – 'the villagers of those days were superstitious about gods,' scornfully comment the *Jatakas* – this passion for philosophy also frequently seized villagers, and the *Jatakas* report the case of the people of a frontier village, who were initially Buddha's followers, but later turned to 'the teachers of the permanence of matter, afterwards ... to the sect who deny immortality, and then again to the sect of the naked ascetic, for teachers of all these sects came among them in turn.'

A crucial development defining the contemporary cultural ambience was the emergence of a number of relatively stable, well-organised and prosperous kingdoms at this time, for they provided a secure environment in which learning and the arts could flourish. The kings of the age were generally liberal-minded patrons of culture, and India in the sixth century BC was very much a free society, open, syncretic and progressive. 'The most perfect freedom, both of thought and of expression, was permitted ... a freedom probably unequalled in the history of the world,' notes Rhys Davids.

Asceticism was not new to Indian tradition. In Vedic India it was common among ordinary people to practise austerities (*vrthms*) periodically, and it is not unlikely that some of them took to asceticism as a lifelong vocation. The Rig-veda also speaks of a special class of ascetics variously called *yatis, munis,* and *rsis.* The etymology of these terms, as Thapar notes, 'indicates magic, mystical rites, meditation and the ecstasy ... associated with shamanism.' These ascetics probably belonged to the non-Aryan religious tradition of India and lived at the periphery of Rig-vedic society. They, note the Brahmanas, were covered with dirt, wore long, matted hair and were dressed in antelope skins. But the ascetics of the sixth century were of a class entirely different from the shamans of the Rig-vedic age, for what they sought was not magical power, but release from the tribulations of life.

The ascetics generally laid great stress on self-torture, and many of their practices were incredibly severe. For instance, the Ajivika ascetic, according to the *Jatakas*, was 'unclothed and covered with dust, solitary and lonely, fleeing like a deer from the face of men; his food was small fish, cowdung, and other refuse; and in order that his vigil might not be disturbed, he took up his abode in a dread thicket in the jungle. In the snows of winter, he came forth by night from the sheltering thicket to the open air, returning with the sun-rise to his thicket again; and, as he was wet with the driving snows by night, so in the day time he was drenched by the drizzle from the branches of the thicket. Thus by day and night alike he endured the extremity of cold. In summer, he stayed by day in the open air, and by night in the forest – scorched by the blazing sun by day, and fanned by no cooling breezes by night, so that the sweat streamed from him.' Elsewhere the *Jatakas* mention ascetics performing 'swinging penance,' 'mortification by squatting,' lying on thorn-beds, and enduring 'the five fires.' Some practised ritual suicide, sometimes turning the private act into a public spectacle, by mounting a grand funeral pyre, as was done by an Indian ascetic before Alexander and by another before Augustus Caesar.

As many as sixty-two different philosophical or religious schools flourished in India in the sixth century BC, according to the *Digha Nikaya*, an ancient Buddhist text. And each held a widely different view. 'Eternal is the world; this is the truth, all else is delusion,' some held, according to the *Udana*, another Buddhist text. 'Others held: not eternal is the world; this is the truth, all else is delusion. Others again held: the world is finite, or the world is infinite, or again, body and soul are one and the same. Others said: body and soul are different things ... And each maintained that his own view was the truth, and that all else was delusion. So they lived quarrelsome, noisy, disputatious, abusing each other with words that pierced like javelins.' The *Acharanga-sutra*, a Jain text, states that the sages of the age held such conflicting views as: 'The world exists, the world does not exist; the world is unchangeable, the world is ever changing; the world has a beginning, the world has no beginning; the world has an end, the world has no end; ... there is beatitude, there is no beatitude; there is hell, there is no hell.'

Of these numerous sects, only Jainism and Buddhism would endure into modern times, though a third sect, the Ajivikas, would manage to survive for about two thousand years, till late medieval times. Most of the others perished soon after the death of their founders, leaving hardly any trace behind, and their genuine teachings are irretrievably lost. In most cases, nothing is known about them except their names, and even of the few about whom we have some information, all that we know is from the censorious comments of their adversaries.

These scraps of information tantalise the historian, but give him little to build on. Would not sects like Aviruddhaka (Non-enemies) and Devadhammika (Divine Order) have had worthy ideas? We do not know. We hear only the worst about most of the sects, and sometimes what we hear is hardly credible. Was, for instance, the sage mockingly called the Hen-saint – who ate pecking at food on the ground like a hen! – as ridiculous as he is made out to be? And what about the Cow-saint and the Dog-saint? We cannot even assume that the sects that survived were the best of the lot, for chance and circumstance and the capriciousness of royal patronage would have played major roles in the fate of religions.

Undoubtedly there were in the sixth century BC several sages who held complex and daringly original views, whose brilliance even now occasionally flashes through the chinks in the wrap of ridicule in which their rivals present them. One sect maintained that everything has only a momentary existence and that 'a state comes to an end the moment it comes into existence.' Sanjaya Belathiputra, the agnostic, questioned the very possibility of knowledge, and refused to affirm or deny that there was life after death, or that good and evil deeds have good and evil consequences. Many of the sages denied the very existence of the soul, and some in effect held that the only difference between god and dog is that of inverted spelling. Some were outright hedonists. 'Whoever turns in fear from the joy that he sees before him is a fool,' maintained one sage. Another advised his followers to borrow money freely and live merrily in the single-minded pursuit of pleasure, for there is only this one life to live, and they should not allow themselves to be inhibited by morality or piety, neither of which would be of any real benefit to them.

One of the most prominent sages of the age was Purana Kassapa, a disconcerting amoralist whom Buddha later won over as a disciple. Before his conversion he held views similar to those of Ajivikas, asserting that all actions are value-neutral, neither virtuous nor sinful. All beings, he maintained, are made up of seven constituents – fire, earth, water, air, pleasure, pain and the soul – which are indestructible, and are not affected in any way by any action. They cannot even be injured physically, for 'weapons pass harmless amongst these aggregates,' Kassapa asserted. And nothing can change what is and what is to be, for all beings have to pass through an unvarying and unalterable evolutionary process for a fixed number of aeons before they can attain salvation. 'Till that period arrives, however much they follow virtue, they do not become pure, and even if they commit many sins they do not go beyond that limit.'

Once, when King Angati of Videha asked Kassapa about the precepts a man should follow in life, he said: 'Hear, O king, a true, unerring utterance. There is no fruit, good or evil, in following the law. There is no other world, O king – who has ever come back hither from thence? ... All beings are equal and alike; there are none who should receive or pay honour ... All beings are predestined ... Every mortal gets what he is to get.' Another time he told King Ajatasatru of Magadha: 'If with a discus with an edge sharp as a razor he should make all the living creatures on earth one heap, one mass of flesh, there would be no guilt then resulting ... If a man makes a raid on the south bank of the Ganga, kills and lets kill, lays waste and lets lay waste, burns and lets burn, he imputes no guilt to himself; there is no punishment of guilt. If a man crosses to the north bank of the Ganga, distributes and causes to be distributed charity, offers and causes to be offered sacrifices, he does not thereby perform a good work; there is no reward for good works.' The only punishment a man suffers is that which he inflicts on himself, the torments of his guilty conscience.

Pakudha Kakkayana, the atomist, concurred with Kassapa's view that all creatures are mere aggregates of seven permanent and unchanging elements. 'So there is no slayer or slain, hearer or speaker, knower or learner,' he said. 'When one with a sharp sword cleaves a head in twain, he does not thereby deprive anyone of life; the sword has only passed between the seven elementary substances.'

In the eyes of the laity there was not much difference between the different sects of the age, and they companionably patronised all ascetics irrespective of their religious affiliations, addressing them all respectfully as Sramanas (strivers: ascetics). To them, all the heterodox sects seemed to belong to one general movement. And that indeed was how it was, for the innovators all had their spiritual roots firmly embedded in the Vedic soil, and they all shared with each other (and with the Upanishadic sages) many common ideas. It would have been difficult even for the discerning to distinguish between the bewildering number of radical sects that existed in India in the sixth century BC.

But the sects distinguished themselves from each other sharply. For all their spiritual preoccupations and life-negating attitudes, bitter rivalries existed among the sages of the age, and sometimes they – even Buddha and Mahavira – hurled dire invectives against each other, as they competed for public favour and elite patronage, though there was also a fair amount of civility and congenial interaction among the rival sects, and their members occasionally visited each other's hermitages to engage in polite debates.

Buddha found no merit in the teachings of his contemporaries, and compared their doctrines (in what was probably the earliest version of this story) to the descriptions of an elephant by the blind men who groped its different limbs. Said Buddha: 'Just so are these sectarians ... blind, unseeing, knowing not the truth, but each maintaining it is thus and thus.'

Buddha was particularly scornful of Gosala Mankhaliputta, the head of the Ajivika sect and one of the most radical and colourful religious leaders of the age, about whom we have a fair amount of information. He was the favourite target of scorn for Buddhists and Jains, but that only proves his importance. 'The hair-blanket,' Buddha once said to his disciples, 'is cold in cold weather, hot in hot weather, ill-coloured and foul-smelling and unpleasant to touch – even so, of all the theories put forward by recluses, that of Mankhali is the meanest.'

There was probably some class prejudice in Buddha's disdain, for birth had not favoured Gosala. The son of an itinerant street entertainer, he was born in a cowshed (hence the name Gosala) and had himself for a while followed his father's lowly profession. He had no high pedigree or genteel upbringing like Mahavira and Buddha, but was gross in his habits, rude and irascible. And he had a venomous, mocking tongue. Worst of all, his ideas were brilliantly unconventional, hard to refute, and he had a large following. Naturally, few of his compeers could suffer him.

Buddhists and Jains hardly have a kind word to say about Gosala. According to the Buddhist version of his life, he decided to become a naked holy man when he lost his clothes in a scuffle while fleeing from some people who had caught him for a minor offence. At one time he was closely associated with Mahavira, and for six years they travelled together, but eventually feuded and parted company. Jains claim that Gosala had attached himself to Mahavira to benefit from Mahavira's high connections and large following. This is unlikely to be the whole truth. They both belonged to the same broad ascetic group, and each had probably exerted considerable influence on the other. However, they held divergent views on chastity. The rule of chastity was an innovation that Mahavira introduced in the monastic order he led, and Gosala disapproved of this, maintaining, according to *Sutrakritanga*, a Jain text, that 'an ascetic ... commits no sin if he ... has intercourse with women.'

A few years after the two parted company Gosala asserted that he had attained omniscience, and went on to found (or lead: the sect was probably already in existence) the Ajivika sect. He set up his headquarters in the workshop of a potter woman named Halahala, in the town of Sravasti on the river Rapti, close to the Himalayan foothills in the modern state of Uttar Pradesh. There he enjoyed a great reputation as an occultist, and had a large following, as even Jain books admit. But he was, if his detractors are to be believed, foul-tempered, rude, greedy, gluttonous, lewd and clownish. He offended people by ridiculing their customs and beliefs, and was often beaten up by villagers. Once when he met the great ascetic Vesayana, whose body swarmed with lice, he mocked, 'Sir, are you a sage or a host for lice?'

Gosala also spoke contemptuously of Mahavira, his erstwhile comrade, deriding him as 'a mercenary teacher, vending his wares like a merchant,' and was deeply offended by Mahavira's claim that he was Gosala's guru.

The two friends-turned-adversaries met again, in Sravasti, towards the end of Gosala's life. Predictably Gosala turned abusive on that occasion, and, according to a Jain legend, used his magical power to burn to ashes two of Mahavira's disciples when they intervened. Then he turned on Mahavira himself and cursed him: 'You are now pervaded by my magic force, and within six months you will die of bilious fever.' Mahavira responded by saying that he was immune to Gosala's magic, and that the curse would recoil on Gosala himself. And that, according to Jain sources, was what in fact happened.

Gosala died a miserable, degrading death, again according to his adversaries. Six months after his confrontation with Mahavira, he was stricken with high fever and went into delirium, and in that state disgraced himself with all sorts of disgusting behaviour. He got drunk, sang and danced in besotted frenzy, wallowed in the potter's muddy water, and made sexual advances on Halahala, all the while holding, for some occult reason, a mango in his hand. Just before he died, Gosala instructed his disciples to bury him honourably, then abruptly changed his mind and told them to dishonour him and publicise his misdeeds. They prudently satisfied both his wishes, by first closing the doors of the building where he lay dead and roundly abusing him, then taking out the body and performing the obsequies with honour. Mahavira survived Gosala by sixteen years.

Gosala was a strict determinist, holding that human effort was entirely ineffectual to change the course of life or history. Everything is unalterably fixed. There is no free will, and man has no moral responsibility whatever for anything he does, either good or evil. '*Niyati-sangati-bhava-parinata*,' Gosala declared: our lives evolve according to our inherent nature, as modulated by chance and circumstance and governed by Niyati, the underlying cosmic principle which regulates everything in the universe, every action and all phenomena, to the smallest detail.

'There is ... no cause, either proximate or remote for the depravity of beings; they become depraved without reason or cause,' maintained Gosala. 'There is no cause, either proximate or remote, for the purity of beings; they become pure without reason or cause. Nothing depends either on one's own efforts or on the efforts of others, or on any human effort whatever ... All animals, all creatures ... all beings ... all souls are destitute of force, power or energy of their own. They are bent this way and that by their fate, their environment, and by their own individual nature.'

No one has any control over this process. All beings have to go through a transmigratory cycle of the same period, which is 8,400,000 *mahakalpas* (aeons) for all, at the end of which all, irrespective of their earthly status, will attain salvation, the saint as well as the sinner, the sage as well as the moron. This process of salvation (or purification) by transmigration (samsara-*suddhi*) cannot be altered or shortened by human effort. As a ball of thread when flung out 'will spread out just as far and no further than it can unwind,' so is the fixed cycle of transmigrations a soul has to go through. Asceticism, good works, chastity, and religious rites are all utterly useless.

'Even if a man does penance on the point of a needle he will not get more than what is destined for him,' Ajivikas declared. 'There is no short cut to bliss ... Wait on destiny. Whether [a man has] joy or sorrow, it is obtained through destiny. All beings are purified through transmigration, [so] do not be eager for that which is to come.' Why then do Ajivika monks take to asceticism? They are compelled to do so by the force of their destiny and have no choice, Ajivikas answer.

It is a long, long wait for salvation under the Ajivika scheme. The time span involved is so incredibly long that Gosala could describe it only metaphorically: 'Taking a series of seven Ganga rivers, of which each succeeding river has seven times the dimensions of the preceding river, the last of the rivers is equal to 117,649 Ganga rivers. If now every hundred years one grain of sand be removed, the time required to exhaust the whole of the sand of those seven Ganga rivers would be one saras period; and 300,000 of such saras periods make one *mahakalpa*.' And it takes 8,400,000 such *mahakalpas* for a transmigratory cycle to be completed.

There is of course no god in the Ajivika system. 'If he has form, he has no more the capacity to create all things than has the ordinary man. If he is formless, his inactivity must be greater than that of the empty space ... If he is subject to passion and other [emotions], he is not superior to us [mortals], and cannot be the maker of the universe. And if he were devoid of passion, then the variety of good and evil fortune, of lord and tramp, that we see in the world would not have come about. Therefore god is not the creator.' Such was the view of Ajivikas, as presented by Silanka, a ninth-century AD Jain commentator. The world was not created; it has always existed, and always will, turning in leaden cosmic cycles of incalculable time, each cycle a repetition of the previous cycle.

In the Ajivika cosmos of eternal repetitions, time – linear time, with its divisions of past, present and future – has no meaning. The opponents of Gosala ridiculed this notion, saying, 'If the passage of time is illusory, the food we eat must already be excreta.' In a sense, yes, Ajivikas would answer.

Ajivikas further maintained, as a corollary to their concept of a cyclic world, that the content of the universe is always the same: 'That which does not exist will not come into existence, and that which exists will not be annihilated.' But this doctrine did not mesh well with their concept of salvation through transmigration. Since salvation would take souls out of the processes of the universe, would not the content of the universe be reduced to that extent? And would not the universe eventually empty itself when all souls have attained salvation? Besides, if souls have an end, how can it be that they do not have a beginning? And if the content of the universe is constant, do new souls then take the place of those that attain salvation? If they do, that would mean souls have beginnings, and that the content of the universe changes. From where do these new souls come anyway? And how can all this be reconciled with the idea that world and time are without beginning or end? Ajivikas met these difficulties by modifying (perhaps after Gosala's death) their concept of salvation to maintain that after attaining salvation, the evolutionary process will begin again for the soul, and that the cycles will repeat endlessly, each cycle lasting the usual 8,400,000 aeons. But if salvation is not a termination, then is it really salvation? Ajivikas do not deign to answer.

Gosala had probably drawn heavily on the ideas of other sages in developing his system of philosophy, but the personality that he stamped on the sect was entirely his own. There was about Ajivikas a certain brash, growling boorishness, which repelled delicate-natured, elite-born sages like Buddha and Mahavira. Said Buddha: 'Monks, I know not of any other single person fraught with ... such loss, discomfort and sorrow to gods and mankind, as Mankhali, that infatuated man ... [He] was born into the world, methinks, to be a man-trap, for the discomfort, suffering and distress of many beings ...' He claimed that Gosala hooked men only to destroy them, like an angler catching fish.

The nauseous and socially pernicious cocktail of fatalism and amoralism that Ajivikas peddled seemed utterly repugnant to Buddha, who insisted on high moral values and required man to strive to transcend himself. Moreover, Ajivikas offended the prevailing notions of ascetic propriety by incorporating singing and dancing into their religious practice. Buddhists accused them of eating 'enormous meals in secret,' and mocked them as 'the children of a childless mother.' Jains accused them of moral laxity. The very name Ajivika seems to have had a derogatory association in the beginning – this was the name given to the followers of Gosala by their opponents and probably meant sham-monks, who took to asceticism for the ease of leading a self-indulgent life.

But Buddhists and Jains, for all their snickering scorn for Ajivikas, had no compunction to purloin several precepts and practices from the sect and quietly incorporate them into their own systems. So Gosala's ideas live on in other religions, though no Ajivika literature has survived. On its own too, the sect did fairly well for several centuries, drawing support mainly from the artisan and mercantile classes. Ajivikas had a reputation of being good astrologers – their deterministic philosophy meshed well with the postulates of astrology – and this apparently contributed to their popularity, and gave them access to royal courts. Mauryan emperor Asoka and his grandson Dasaratha patronised them, and dedicated caves to their use. Yet Ajivikas remained a minor sect, compared to Buddhism and even Jainism. After the collapse of the Mauryan empire, the sect rapidly sank into oblivion in northern India, but had by then spread into southern India, where it maintained a tenuous hold for many centuries.

Throughout their history Ajivikas had to face some persecution everywhere. In the Tamil country, for instance, a poll tax was collected from them and their patrons in the thirteenth century AD, during the reign of Rajaraja III. Village communities under Pallavas, Cholas and Hoysalas imposed special taxes on them, which sometimes amounted to as much as twenty or thirty times of what others had to pay. Despite such handicaps, Ajivikas continued to have some local influence along the Palar river in the modern states of Karnataka and Tamil Nadu till about the fourteenth century. In the end they seem to have been absorbed into Vaishnavism, during the general swell of Hindu devotionalism.

THE FORD-MAKER

'When the moon was in conjunction with the asterism Uttaraphalguni, at the confluence of the two halves of the night ... Bhagwan Mahavira entered as an embryo into the womb of the Brahmin woman Devananda ... the consort of Brahmin Rasabhadatta ... in the Brahmin village of Kundagrama,' states the *Kalpa-sutra*, a Jain text attributed (doubtfully) to Bhadrabahu of the fourth century BC. That night Devananda had fourteen auspicious dreams – 'an elephant, a bull, a lion, an anointment, a garland, the moon, the sun, a flag, a jar, a lotus lake, the ocean, a celestial mansion, a heap of gems, and a flame' – and these her husband interpreted as portending the birth of a noble son to them.

That would not be. Indra, the status-conscious chief of the gods, considered it inappropriate that a great leader of men should be born to ordinary Brahmin parents. So he sent Harinegamesi, 'the commander of the divine infantry,' to transfer the embryo from the Brahmin woman's womb into the womb of 'Trisala of the line of Vasistha, wife of Kshatriya Siddhartha, of the Jnatr-kshatriya clan of the line of Kasyapa.' The ministering spirit then stealthily extracted the embryo from one womb and transplanted it into the other by inducing deep sleep in both women. And this gave Mahavira both a Brahmin lineage appropriate to a traditional sage, and a Kshatriya pedigree appropriate to a radical reformer.

When Trisala received the embryo, she too had fourteen dreams, similar to those of Devananda, which were seen by interpreters of dreams as indicating that she would deliver a son 'calm like the moon, pleasing, pleasant and beautiful ... brave, gallant and valorous,' and that he would be either 'the master of a vast territory, with a large army and extensive wagons, or the spiritual leader of the three worlds ... the monarch of the spiritual world.' The conception indeed proved fortunate for Siddhartha, whose prosperity greatly increased around this time. So when the child was born, he was named Vardhamana, Enhancer (of fortune).

This bizarre birth story – which violates the very spirit of the teachings of Mahavira, who, as an uncompromising materialist, yielded no place for the miraculous in life – is accepted only by one sect of Jains, the

Svetambaras. There is nothing miraculous, or even out of the ordinary, about the known facts of Mahavira's childhood. He was undoubtedly a historical figure. A contemporary of Buddha, he was probably born around 540 BC at Kundagrama, a suburb of Vaishali on the river Gandak, some 44 kilometres north of Patna. His father, Siddhartha, was the chieftain of Jnatrikas, a prominent Kshatriya clan of the region, and his mother, Trisala, was the sister of Chetaka, the head of the powerful Lichchavi tribe and the ruler of Vaishali. Vardhamana was their second son. Through his mother he was connected with the kings of Videha, Magadha and Anga, who had married his uncle Chetaka's daughters.

Vardhamana was born, according to the *Kalpa-sutra*, 'at the conjunction of the moon with the asterism Uttara-phalguni, when the planets were high up in their exaltation ... bright and pure ... when all the omens were auspicious, when the favourable southerly wind kissed the ground, when the earth was full of corn, and when all the human beings were delighted and at play.' He was thus born at the same astrological configuration as at the time of his conception, and it would be at the same propitious hour that everything of any importance in his life would take place, except his death, which would be when the moon was in conjunction with the star Svati. His birth, says Bhadrabahu, was marked by a 'divine lustre' in the sky, as gods and goddesses flocked to witness the happy event. To commemorate the occasion, Siddhartha released prisoners, abolished taxes, reduced punishments, and held a ten-day celebration, during which the town was swept clean and elaborately decorated, and the public entertained with the performances of 'many players, dancers, rope-dancers, wrestlers, jesters, story-tellers, ballad-singers, actors, messengers, pole-dancers, fruit-mongers, bag-pipers, lute-players and *talakaras*.'

Not much is known about Vardhamana's youth. He was, we are told, inclined towards a spiritual life from childhood, but restrained himself from taking to asceticism during the lifetime of his parents in order to spare them anguish. As a baby, he was looked after by five nurses – 'a wet-nurse, a nurse to clean him, one to dress him, one to play with him, one to carry him,' according to the *Acharanga-sutra*, the first book of the Jain canon. He grew up in the lap of luxury, and his childhood was entirely normal for a boy of his station. He excelled in martial pursuits, and when he came of age, took a wife, Yasoda, and begot a daughter by her, Priyadarsana.

Vardhamana turned to his destined career when he was thirty, after his parents passed away and his elder brother Nandivardhana took over the fiefdom. His departure, unlike Buddha's furtive flight in the dead of night, was a celebratory public event. Before setting out for the woods, he went in a procession through the town to the accompaniment of music, sitting in a palanquin 'in all his grandeur,' dressed in scented robes and wearing garlands and ornaments. It was a winter afternoon, and the hour of his departure was chosen for its auspiciousness. The prince was followed by a large throng of people, whose 'low and pleasing murmur,' we are told, added to the solemnity of the occasion.

Outside the town, at Shandavana Park, he alighted under a giant evergreen Asoka tree. There he removed all his ornaments, garlands and finery, and 'with his own hands plucked out his hair in five handfuls ... and quite alone ... entered the state of homelessness,' says Bhadrabahu. For a year and a month he wore simple clothes, but thereafter went about stark naked – probably under the influence of Gosala, who had joined him at this time – without any possessions whatever, not even a begging bowl, receiving alms in the hollow of his hand.

He was now free of all earthly attachments, free of all feelings, including shame. 'Henceforth,' says Bhadrabahu, 'the venerable ascetic Mahavira was homeless, circumspect in his walking, circumspect in his speaking, circumspect in his begging ... circumspect in evacuating excrement, urine, saliva, mucus ... guarding his thoughts, guarding his words, guarding his acts, guarding his senses, guarding his chastity; without wrath, without pride, without deceit, without greed; calm, tranquil, composed, liberated, free from temptations, without egoism, without property; he had cut off all earthly ties, and was not stained by any worldliness ... Like the wind he knew no obstacles ... [He was] deep like the ocean, mild like the moon, refulgent like the sun, pure like excellent gold. Like the earth he patiently bore everything; like a well-kindled fire he shone in his splendour.'

Bhadrabahu exaggerates. As a person, Vardhamana does not seem to have had the charm and graciousness of Buddha, but was unkempt and taciturn. People did not take to him easily. Sometimes he was abused, ridiculed and tormented in various ways. But nothing daunted him. For over twelve years he lived thus, says the *Kalpa-sutra*, wandering from place to place, practising rigorous austerities, 'indifferent alike to the smell of ordure and of sandal, to straw and jewels, dirt and gold, pleasure and pain, attached neither to this world nor to that beyond, desiring neither life nor death ... exerting himself for the suppression of the defilement of karma.'

In the thirteenth year of his asceticism Vardhamana attained enlightenment, and took the titles Mahavira (Great Hero) and Jina (Victorious One). The *Kalpa-sutra* describes the moment of his enlightenment thus: 'In the thirteenth year, in the second month of summer, in the fourth fortnight, on the tenth day of the bright half of [the month of] Vaisakha ... on the day called Suvrata, at the hour called Vijaya, outside of the town called Grimbhika-grama, on the bank of the river Rijupalika, not far from a discarded shrine, on the farm of a householder named Syamaka, under a Sal tree, when the moon was in conjunction with the asterism Uttaraphalguni, while sitting in a milking posture, exposing himself to the full blast of the sun, with his head erect and engaged in deep mediation ... after fasting for two days without even drinking water, he attained supreme knowledge ...' Omniscient, Mahavira now 'knew all categories of gods, men and *asuras* in all the worlds; knew the conditions of all the living beings in all the worlds ... knew the ideas and the thoughts in their minds ... their doings, their open deeds as well as their secret deeds ... he knew in all respects the state of minds, words and deeds of all the living beings in all the worlds.'

At the time of his enlightenment Mahavira was forty-two years old. He spent the next thirty years in incessant missionary work, mostly in the Bihar region, preaching and winning followers. Then, at the age of seventy-two, while staying in the town of Pava near Rajagriha, the old capital of Magadha, 'in the fourth month of that rainy season, in the seventh fortnight, in the dark half of the month Karthika, on its fifteenth day ... venerable ascetic Mahavira passed away.' The year of his death is uncertain, but was probably around 468 BC. He starved himself to death, as the Jain ideal prescribed. His death – final liberation – was for his followers a joyous event, and the chieftains of the region, who had assembled at Pava for his funeral, instituted an illumination to mark the day, saying, 'The light of intellect is gone, let us then light the earthen lamps.' This, according to Jains, was the origin of Diwali celebrations.

Nothing much more than this bare outline is known about Mahavira's missionary work, but apparently he was quite successful in gathering converts, his royal connections providing him with valuable patronage and high visibility. He is said to have had the power of prophecy, and presumably that also helped him to gain devotees. At the time of his death, he had, according to the *Kalpa-sutra*, a following of 14,000 monks, 36,000 nuns, 159,000 male lay votaries, 318,000 female lay votaries, 300 great sages, 13,000 superior sages, and so on, in all totalling 545,800 followers. These are evidently imaginary figures, but Jainism certainly had become an important cult in Mahavira's own lifetime. Curiously, women far outnumbered men among his followers. Mahavira, himself a contented householder once, did not have the kind of harsh prejudice that Buddha had against women, though he too periodically issued dire warnings against their wiles, saying, 'The world is greatly troubled by women.'

The early followers of Mahavira came from all sections of society, but Jains would eventually become predominantly a community of traders and moneylenders, famed for their prudence and canniness. The insistence on absolute non-violence made almost every profession other than trade and banking unsuitable for Jains – agriculture, involving injury to plants, was barred to them, and so were all crafts, for they all involved violence of some sort in the eyes of Jains, who believed that fire, water and air were endowed with life. A military career was, of course, out of the question. On the other hand, there was excellent synergy between Jain prescriptions and trade practices, both emphasising discipline, caution, frugality and humble living. 'Though others sleep, be thou awake! Like a wise man, trust nobody, but be always on the alert,' Jain teachers exhorted. This advice, though meant primarily for monks, found a ready echo in the hearts of traders.

Jains had no feelings of guilt about being mercenary. The pursuit of profit being an abstract pursuit (even though its results were material) the accumulation of profit seemed to them almost like the accumulation of religious merit. And the Jain emphasis on individual salvation was taken by traders as the validation of self-seeking – if the ascetic could spend all his energies in acquiring religious merit, then it was legitimate for the trader to spend all his energies in acquiring wealth. Thus it came to be that the main followers of this religion that scorns earthly possessions are a people who specialise in accumulating earthly possessions. This seeming paradox is however somewhat relieved by the altruism that Jainism inculcates in its followers – the most hard-hearted Jain businessmen often turn out to be the most philanthropic, richly endowing charities and even maintaining asylums for old and diseased animals.

Jainism, like all religions, eventually split into several sects. Schism had in fact raised its head even during the lifetime of Mahavira, when his son-in-law, Jamali, opposed him on doctrinal grounds, and this was closely followed by a revolt headed by Tisagutta, a senior monk. Nothing came of these early challenges, but a major split occurred a couple of centuries later. Towards the end of the fourth century, according to Jain tradition, the Bihar region suffered a severe famine lasting some twelve years, and this threatened the Jain way of life, because of the corruption and degradation that inevitably prevails in times of prolonged distress. Further, it was impossible for mendicant monks to live among an impoverished people, who were unable to feed themselves, let alone give alms to monks. It thus became imperative for Jains to leave the Gangetic Plain and find some other more congenial place to live.

In that predicament, Bhadrabahu, the head of the community, led a large group of monks and lay followers in a long trek southward, finally to settle in Karnataka. But not all the Jain monks joined the exodus, and those who remained in the north made several changes in the traditional Jain ascetic customs, giving up the custom of nudity to wear simple garments and admitting women into the order, presumably to blend more smoothly into society in that time of hardship. When Bhadrabahu and his followers returned to Bihar they refused to accept or condone the new ways of their northern brethren. Over the decades the gap between the two groups widened, and in the first century AD the religion formally split into two sects, Digambaras (the space-clad: naked) and Svetambaras (the white-clad). In time Svetambaras, and to a lesser extent Digambaras too, further split into several sub-sects.

All this weakened Jainism in Bihar, the state of its origin, and from there it ultimately vanished altogether, despite the support of some Mauryan emperors. Meanwhile, however, it found new homes in Madhya Pradesh, Orissa, western Rajasthan, Gujarat and Karnataka. Jain fortunes varied from place to place – while Svetambaras thrived in Gujarat under royal patronage, Digambaras in Karnataka were not so fortunate; they had to face strong opposition from Hindu devotional sects like Shaivism and Vaishnavism, and suffered sporadic violent persecution. And nowhere and at no time did Jainism gain the kind of prominence that Buddhism enjoyed.

But it did not die out in India either, as Buddhism eventually did. This in itself was remarkable, for every other religion in India perished in the tidal wave of resurgent Hinduism in early medieval times. In a way, the very smallness of the community proved to be a strength, as this enabled it to remain tightly knit and well-integrated. Moreover, being a self-sustaining religion, supported by its own affluent lay members, Jainism was not much buffeted by the vagaries of royal patronage. But perhaps the most important reason for Jainism's survival was that it virtually became a Hindu caste, and so could find refuge in the commodious lap of Hindu society.

Jains had always looked to Brahmin priests to perform their domestic ceremonies – of marriage, birth, death, and so on – as Jainism had no priests, but only monks, who, having renounced the world, could not officiate at worldly functions. Moreover, Jainism has no fixed rituals of its own, being essentially an ethical system rather than a religion. Around the first century AD Jains drew closer to Hindus, when they built temples, placed in them the idols of Tirthankaras (Ford-makers: Jain saints), and worshipped them with rituals similar to those in Hindu temples, often with Brahmin priests officiating. In time Jains also took to venerating Hindu gods; perhaps they had done so always, though these practices did not quite harmonise with the fundamentally atheistic Jain metaphysics. The worship of Tirthankaras was especially incongruous, for they, having attained nirvana, had nothing more to do with the affairs of the world, and could not in any way help the worshipper.

These changes in Jain religious practices did not however lead to any substantive changes in Jain precepts. A deeply conservative religion,

Jainism did not go through the kind of philosophical mutations that Buddhism went through, even though its original scriptures, called Purvas, Old Texts, had become, over several generations of oral transmission, hopelessly corrupt or lost. Bhadrabahu was the last sage who is said to have known the whole scripture. After his death, a council was held at Pataliputra towards the end of the fourth century BC to reconstruct the canon as best as possible. This exercise was probably also necessary because, as Jacobi conjectures, the original scriptures, composed in an environment of fierce philosophical disputation, were polemical in nature, and had become unsuitable for a settled religion. But even the reconstructed scriptures became corrupted over the centuries, because they were still being transmitted orally. So when a great Jain council was held by Svetambaras at Valabhi in Gujarat in the mid-fifth century AD, nearly a thousand years after Mahavira's death, the scriptures were revised again, and some additions made. They were then reduced to writing. But these reworked scriptures were not accepted by Digambaras, who devised their own texts. There are, however, hardly any serious doctrinal differences between the two sects, and their core beliefs, despite all the transmutations their scriptures have gone through, are generally believed to be true to the original teachings of Mahavira.

The Jain faith in fact goes further back than Mahavira himself, who, according to tradition, was the last of a line of twenty-four Tirthankaras, beginning with the mythical Rishaba. Mahavira was the reformer and populariser of Jainism, rather than its founder. His enlightenment, unlike that of Buddha, did not involve a new revelation, but only the perfection of his understanding of the precepts of the sect. Jains consider their religion to be eternal, revealed over and over by Tirthankaras in every one of the endless cosmic cycles.

That, however, is a matter of faith. The factual probability is that Jainism (whose followers were originally called Nirgranthas, the Bond-free) was founded by Parsva, the twenty-third Tirthankara, who is said to have lived some 250 years before Mahavira. The teachings of Parsva and Mahavira, indeed their very lives as given in the *Kalpa-sutra*, have many similarities. Mahavira's parents were probably followers of Parsva, and it is believed that they had fasted to death.

Mahavira, like many other contemporary radical sages, was an atheist, who held that the world evolved out of its own inherent nature, its 'primeval disposition', without any divine involvement. He did acknowledge the existence of supernatural beings, but did not consider them to be the creators or rulers of the universe. This view was lucidly expounded by Jinasena in the *Mahapurana*, a ninth-century AD Jain work:

No single being has the skill to make this world –
how can immaterial god make the material world? ...
If god is ever perfect and complete,
how could the will to create have arisen in him?
If, on the other hand, he is not perfect
he could no more create the universe than a potter could ...
If you say he created to no purpose,
because it is his nature to do so, then god is pointless.
If he created in some kind of sport,
it was the sport of a foolish child, leading to trouble ...
If he created out of love for living things and need of them,
why did he not make creation wholly blissful ...?
If he were transcendent he would not create,
for he would be free;
Nor if involved in transmigration,
for then he would not be almighty ...
And god commits great sin in slaying the children
whom he himself created.
If you say he slays only to destroy evil beings,
why did he create such beings in the first place? ...
Uncreated and indestructible, the world endures
under the compulsion of its own nature ...

The Jain universe is without beginning or end, revolving idly in the stillness of space, in a time without beginning or end. Time revolves, but does not advance. Jainism visualises the universe allegorically as a stationary but perpetually revolving wheel, turning in endless cycles of progression and regression through eternity, the twelve spokes of the wheel marking the six ascending and the six descending phases of the cosmic revolution. A half turn of the wheel carries man to the pinnacle of progress through expanding stages of knowledge, happiness, longevity and physical stature, and then, smoothly, without even a momentary pause, carries him, through six contracting stages, back to the bottom.

Then the next cycle begins. At the peak of progress, men are giants, have astounding life-spans, and live in perfect harmony and contentment, for wishing-trees (*kalpa-vrikshas*) instantly satisfy all their desires. Mankind, Jains hold, is now in a 40,000-year-long declining phase of the evolutionary cycle. This process is marked by regression in the mental and physical abilities of men, and it will, when it reaches the bottom of the cycle, turn them into dwarfs with a life-span of just twenty years, brute creatures living in caves, all advances of civilisation lost, even the use of fire.

*

Jainism, in contrast to the monistic view of the Upanishads that sees everything in the world as Brahman, holds a dualistic view that divides the world into two independent categories, Jiva (life or soul), and Ajiva (non-life or non-soul). As *Istopadesa*, a Jain text of the fourth century AD, puts it:

> *The soul is one thing, matter another –*
> *that is the quintessence of truth.*
> *Whatever else may be said*
> *is merely its elaboration.*

Jiva and Ajiva, though fundamentally different, have nevertheless a similarity of sorts, in that they are both *dravyas*, substances, and are indestructible and eternal. But they are entirely dissimilar kinds of substances. Jiva is non-material, Ajiva is material. And Jiva, being non-material, has no physical limitations – it is, as Jains are fond of saying, like a lamp that can light up either a small room or a big room – but Ajiva is limited by its very materiality. Further, Jiva is immutable, is ever the same, but Ajiva is mutable, is 'a something that may become anything.' Yet another difference between the two is that while Jiva is homogeneous and cannot be divided into categories, Ajiva is divided into two categories, gross and subtle. The difference between the gross and subtle Ajiva is that whereas the gross entity – called *pudgala* – can be perceived by the senses, the subtle entity is incorporeal and cannot be perceived. Moreover, while gross Ajiva has independent existence, subtle Ajiva – itself divided into four categories: ether (*akasa*, the medium or space in which all things exist), energy (*dharma*, meaning, in this context, the motive force of action), inertia (*adharma*) and time (*kala*) – can exist only in combination with itself and with gross matter.

The essential characteristic of Jiva is consciousness, *chaitanya.* Ajiva has no consciousness. Jiva in its pure, uncontaminated form, is all-knowing and all-powerful, and exists in a state of infinite and ineffable bliss. But Jiva loses its perfection when it somehow – it is not clear how – gets entangled with Ajiva. This produces karma, and starts off the evolutionary process.

In Jainism, this karmic evolution is not limited to the 'living' – the 'non-living' are equally involved in it. There is no distinction between prebiotic chemistry and life. Jivas are present not only in animals, plants and micro-organisms, but even in the four elements – earth, water, air and fire – and all inanimate substances. Says the *Acharanga-sutra*: 'Of a truth, to the monks water has been declared to be living matter.' As the quantum physicist would say, the more closely we examine particles, the more alive they seem. The still, adamantine rock is seething with life.

There is nothing that is not matter, and there is nothing that has not life. Jiva, however, is not a unified entity like Brahman. Each Jiva is different, and there are an infinite number of Jivas. Yet, though infinite in number, different Jivas are all identical to each other in their pure state – they acquire individual characteristics and become distinct from each other only through their karmic involvement with Ajiva.

Karma in Jainism is not just a process, as it is in the Upanishads, but is a substance, a subtle matter that accretes to Jiva and envelopes it like a sheath and gives it individuality, its distinctive character. A particular karma can spend itself by producing its particular effect; but new karma will bind on to Jiva all the time, action breeding karma and karma breeding action. The process will go on eternally in an endless series of chain reactions – unless something special is done to get rid of karma altogether.

The goal of Jainism is to devise the means to do that – to scrape off the encrustation of accumulated karma and to prevent its further accretion by closing the 'channels through which karma finds entrance into Jiva,' thus to free Jiva from Ajiva and return it to its original state of purity and bliss. This, Mahavira believed, was possible only through the practice of rigorous austerities and self-torture. In normal life, however good be one's actions, one would continue to accumulate karma, for even good action produces karma, and the process would go on for ever through transmigration. Liberation therefore can be achieved only by the few who take to asceticism. Ordinary people have to reconcile themselves to keep on transmigrating, living and suffering over and over again. But the Jiva of the ascetic, when liberated, would rise 'at once to the top of the universe, above the highest heaven,' where it would remain in 'inactive omniscience through all eternity.'

To achieve that liberated state in the hereafter, man has to pay a very heavy price here on earth. 'One should mortify (one's flesh) in a low, high and highest degree,' advises the *Acharanga-sutra.* On his initiation, the Jain novice is required to pull out the hair on his head by the roots with his own hands, and take the five vows binding on all monks and nuns: not to kill, steal, lie, have sex, or possess property. 'I renounce all killing of living beings, whether subtle or gross, whether movable or immovable,' he pledges. 'I renounce all vices of lying speech [arising] from anger or greed or fear or mirth ... I renounce all taking of anything not given ... I renounce all sexual pleasures, either with gods or men or animals ... I renounce all attachments, whether little or much, small or great, to the living or the lifeless ...' Each of these vows has several sub-clauses, and together they bind the monk virtually immobile in thought and action.

The monk has to take particular precautions against sexual temptation, and there are many cautionary warnings against women in Jain texts. 'Do not desire women, those *rakshasis* (she-devils) on whose chests grow two lumps of flesh, who continually change their mind, who entice men, and then make a sport of them as of slaves,' warns the *Uttaradhyayana.* Among the Jain sects, Svetambaras are relatively liberal towards women, and they even maintain that one of the Tirthankaras, Malli, was a woman. Digambaras deny this, and hold that women can never attain salvation except by first being reborn as men.

The Jain command to monks to abjure killing is absolute: it extends to all living beings, even to plants and micro-organisms. The monk has to take care to avoid involuntarily killing tiny organisms in water or air while drinking, breathing or talking, and should be careful not to step on insects or larvae while walking – he has to strain the water he drinks, wear a veil over his mouth, and sweep the ground before him as he walks. He has to be careful about lighting lamps and fires, for fear of killing moths. He should not even step on grass, to avoid injuring plants. However, since he has to eat to live, vegetarian food is permitted to him – all Jains are vegetarians – but he has to be very circumspect about receiving and eating food, to avoid harming any living thing.

The only life the monk is allowed to take is his own. 'Death against one's will is the way of ignorant men, and [among them] it happens [to the same individual] many times. Death with one's will is the way of wise men, and at best it happens but once,' states the *Uttaradhyayana.* But this ritual suicide has to be done through slow starvation and in a state of complete dispassion, desiring neither life nor death. Jainism condemns impulsive suicide out of passion or desperation as a terrible sin, which would result in the person being reborn as a demon.

Mahavira sought to regulate every detail of the life of the monk through elaborate rules – on how he should dress, how he should seek alms, what food he can accept, when and how he should eat, where he should excrete (absolutely not on grass), where he should stay and for how long, and so on. Jainism regards cooked food as the most acceptable alms for monks, probably because it cannot be stored and accumulated. Monks are forbidden to accept food specially prepared for them, to prevent begging from 'degenerating into indulgence.' They should not eat after sunset, and should sleep only three hours a day. They are required to recite sacred texts regularly, as this would help to destroy karma and also contribute to the preservation of the sacred lore. They have to lead a wandering life, except during the rainy season, and are not allowed to remain in a village for more than a day and in a town for more than three days, to prevent them from overstaying their welcome or developing attachments.

Jainism, for all its renunciatory ethics and non-violence, is often accused of being a cold-hearted, selfish religion, in which the individual is solely concerned with his own salvation, and does not make any sacrifice to help others. The Jain monk might be altruistic, but only out of calculation, for his own spiritual benefit. Caring for others is a weakness, a bondage. 'The heart of Jainism is empty,' it is said. In a sense this is true. But it is important to note that the egoism of the Jain monk is not grasping selfishness; he is entirely without passion, wants nothing and takes nothing from anyone, nothing indeed from the world.

The disciplinary demands of Jainism on laymen are, relatively speaking, mild, but still quite considerable, for the life of the householder is considered to be a preparation for eventual asceticism, after he is reborn as a monk through transmigration. The vows and practices of laymen and monks are similar, and differ only in rigour, not in kind. Thus the absolute injunction to the monk not to kill any living beings, for the layman becomes a directive only not to kill intentionally. Roots, honey, and spirits and non-vegetarian food are forbidden to laymen and monks alike, and none are allowed to eat after sunset. 'A pious man should eat little, drink little, talk little; he should always exert himself, being calm, indifferent, a subduer (of his senses), and free from greed,' advises the *Sutrakritanga*. Jainism encourages laymen to take to temporary asceticism periodically, as this helps to integrate the life of monks with that of laymen.

The social code of Jainism is egalitarian. Status depends on what one does, not on birth. 'One does not become a monk by the tonsure,' declares the *Uttaradhyayana*, 'nor a Brahmin by the sacred syllable Om, nor a *muni* by living in the woods, nor an ascetic by wearing [clothes of] *kusa*-grass and bark. One becomes a monk by equanimity, a Brahmin by chastity, a *muni* by knowledge, and an ascetic by penance. By one's actions one becomes a Brahmin, or a Kshatriya, or a Vaisya, or a Sudra.'

Chapter Four

GEM IN THE LOTUS

A SAVIOUR IS BORN

'In this city there is neither king nor people; it is like a great desert,' writes the fifth-century AD Chinese pilgrim Fa Hsien about Kapilavastu, Buddha's hometown. 'There is simply a congregation of priests, and about ten families of lay people.' But a thousand years earlier, in the sixth century BC, Kapilavastu was a populous and wealthy town, the capital of the proud Aryan tribe of Sakyas. The Sakya country, straddling the common border of the modern states of India and Nepal, and nestling against the Himalayan foothills between the rivers Rapti and Rohini, was a small but fertile valley of gurgling streams, lush sal forests, mango and tamarind groves, and golden rice-fields.

Sakyas were at this time an obscure people, probably late Aryan migrants. There is no mention of them in pre-Buddhist literature, and not even later authors like Kautilya and Panini refer to them. They were, according to *Digha Nikaya*, a small tribe of 80,000 families totalling probably about half a million people, mostly farmers. A fair-skinned, handsome people – 'the moon-like faces of their women ... put lotuses to shame,' claims Asvaghosha, the first-century AD author of *Buddha-charita* – they grandiosely traced their descent from Ikshvaku, the mythical founder of the solar dynasty of Ayodhya, and were quite vain about their lineage. They were however no longer an independent people in Buddha's time, but were subject to the overlordship of the king of Kosala. But the loss of independence had not broken their tribal pride – they would not eat with anyone but their equals, and their chieftains considered themselves socially superior even to the kings of Kosala, and would not give their daughters in marriage to them. 'Sakyas are a proud and stiff-necked race ... desperately proud in the matter of birth,' the *Jatakas* candidly admit.

This overweening pride of Sakyas was resented by the other tribes of the region, who questioned the very legitimacy of their claims to superiority, and derided them, according to the *Jatakas*, as 'men who like dogs, jackals, and such like beasts cohabited with their sisters.' Buddha himself was once told to his face about the rude ways of Sakyas. 'Rough is this Sakya breed of yours, Gautama, and rude,' said Ambattha, a Brahmin.

'Touchy is this Sakya breed of yours and violent.' He complained that when he once visited Kapilavastu, the Sakyas showed him no civility. 'It is not seemly that the Sakyas, menials as they are, mere menials, should neither venerate, nor value, nor esteem, nor give gifts to, nor pay honour to Brahmins.' Buddha, for all his forbearance, could not bear this slur, and he met insult with insult, by tracing the inferior ancestry of Ambattha, and by claiming, on the basis of various social practices, superiority for Kshatriyas over Brahmins. 'Even when a Kshatriya has fallen into the deepest degradation, still it holds good that the Kshatriyas are higher, and Brahmins inferior,' Buddha declared.

Sakyas had no great reverence for Brahmins, because they, being a hill-country people, were not well integrated into the mainstream Aryan society. They hardly ever performed the high Vedic rituals, and had no strong caste or class divisions. Further, in contrast to the monarchic norm prevailing in the Gangetic valley, their government was a form of primitive democracy, headed by a chieftain elected by rotation from the leading families of the tribe.

Suddhodana, Buddha's father, was one such chieftain. Late Buddhist texts would glorify him as a universal monarch – he was, Asvaghosha says, 'the kindred of the sun, anointed to stand at the head of earth's monarchs' – but in reality he was only a petty chieftain. Early texts do not speak of him as a king at all. His main profession was agriculture, and, like the other clan heads of his tribe, he worked the field himself, for Buddha in a discourse speaks of watching 'the Sakyan my father ... ploughing,' though it could be that, as the head of the tribe, he only had to ceremonially plough the first furrow.

Suddhodana, like most of the chieftains and kings of the age, was a polygamist, and had married two daughters of Anjana, another Sakyan chieftain. Buddha was born to Mayadevi, the older of the two sisters. She was, according the *Lalitavistara*, a Mahayana Buddhist text, 'beautiful as a heavenly daughter, of well-proportioned body ... There was no mortal or celestial being who could be satiated by beholding her ... [She was] placid, soft, frank and pleasing of speech. Modest and bashful, virtuous and decorous, neither dull nor fidgety, neither envious nor intriguing, but guileless and benevolent ... There existed not in the region of mortals, nor in that of Gandharvas, nor even that of the *Devas*, a lady who could be compared to Mayadevi.' The text further states that 'for five hundred generations, she had been the mother of the Bodhisattvas, and so did the Suddhodana become the father on those occasions.'

With parents such as these, Buddha's conception and birth could not be anything but miraculous. The first intimation that her baby would be something very special came to Mayadevi in a dream one early spring night, in which she saw herself being carried by the four guardians of the heavenly quarters to a lake in the Himalayas, and there bathed and laid down on a divine couch in a golden mansion on a silver hill. In the dream, a white elephant with a pink lotus in its trunk approached her from the north and penetrated her. 'A noble elephant, white as silver or snow, having six tusks, well-proportioned trunk and feet, blood-red veins, adamantine firmness of joints, and ease of pace, entered my belly,' Mayadevi said to Suddhodana, describing her dream. He then summoned seers to interpret the strange dream, and they said that it signified that she had conceived a child who would become either a universal ruler or universal sage.

When her time approached, Mayadevi, as was the custom among her people, set out for her parents' home for delivery, accompanied by a large retinue of guards and attendants. On the way, at Lumbinivana, some 16 kilometres east of Kapilavastu, in a grove of sal trees (the totem tree of Sakyas) dedicated to goddess Lumbini, she halted to rest and refresh herself. Here there was a sacred pond where Sakyas performed their investiture ceremonies – a lovely pond, which Chinese pilgrim Hsuan Tsang, who saw it in the seventh century AD, described as 'bright and clear as a mirror, its surface covered with a mixture of flowers.' When Mayadevi saw it, a desire to sport in the water came upon her.

After frolicking in the water for a while, Mayadevi emerged from the pond and walked some twenty paces towards an Asoka tree in full bloom. As she approached, the tree 'lowered its head and saluted her,' says the *Lalitavistara.* This was the moment of destiny. 'As the queen supported herself by a bough which hung laden with the weight of flowers,' states Asvaghosha, 'the Bodhisattva suddenly came forth, cleaving open her womb.'

'When the Bodhisattva was born,' writes Hsuan Tsang, 'he walked without assistance in the direction of the four quarters, seven paces in each direction ... Where his feet had trod there sprang up great lotus flowers. Moreover, two dragons sprang forth, and, fixed in the air, poured down streams of cold and warm water from their mouths, to wash the prince.' Says Asvaghosha: 'The Yaksha-lords (of the four quarters of the universe) stood round guarding him with golden lotuses in their hands ... and the great dragons ... gazing with eyes of intent devotion, fanned him and strewed Mandara flowers over him ... When he was born, the earth, though fastened down by the monarch of mountains (the Himalayas), shook like a ship tossed by the wind, and from a cloudless sky there fell a shower of lotuses and water-lilies, perfumed with sandalwood ... The flowering trees at once produced their blossoms ...' Then the child, turning to each of the four directions, declared, 'in a voice full of auspicious meaning,' the purpose of his birth: 'I am born for supreme knowledge, for the welfare of the world. Thus this is my last birth.'

Such is the fable of Buddha's birth. There are many such myths about nearly every major event in Buddha's life, and Buddhist literature weaves fabulous tapestries with them. But these can be appreciated only with the eyes of the believer. To the outsider the myths seem like an ornamentation of trinkets that obscure rather than enhance Buddha's true effulgence. His real life seems to have been miraculous enough without these pious fancies, and his teachings profoundly inspiring. But we cannot be absolutely certain of anything much in Buddha's life, for legends and facts about him are so thoroughly intermixed that it is impossible to separate them. The story we tell here is therefore the story as given in Buddhist literature, which may contain a fair amount of facts, but has little that can be verified. All that can be said with certainty is that Buddha was a Sakya, that he was born in the mid-sixth century BC, probably around 563, and died aged about eighty in the first quarter of the fifth century, probably around 486, after many years of missionary work in the eastern Gangetic tracts. His *gotra* was Gautama, and it was by this name that he was commonly known in his lifetime. As a sage, he was also called Sakya-muni, the Sakya seer. His own followers reverentially called him Tathagata, an obscure term probably meaning The Perfect One or The Emancipated One.

Buddha, according to tradition, was born on the full-moon day of the lunar month of Vaisakha (April-May) – 'on the eighth day of the second half of Vaisakha,' says Hsuan Tsang with the conviction of a devotee. The constellation Pushya was in auspicious conjunction with moon at the time of his birth, claims Asvaghosha, and the *Lalitavistara* states that thirty-two good omens marked his birth. But his birth, though lucky for the world, was unlucky for his mother – she died seven days later, so the baby was brought up by her sister, Mahapajapati Gautami, Mayadevi's younger sister and the second wife of Suddhodana.

Soon after the child's birth there arrived at Suddhodana's court the great sage Asita, who, says Asvaghosha, had 'learned by signs and through the power of his penances about this birth of him who was to destroy all birth.' The baby, Asita noticed, had on his body every sign of greatness – there was a circle of downy hair between his eyebrows, his soles were marked with spoked wheel emblems, his fingers and toes were webbed, and there was about him an aura of majesty and vigour, 'like that of an elephant.' The *Lalitavistara* elaborates this list to state that Asita found on the baby thirty-two major and eighty subsidiary signs of sublimity – a coil of curly dark-blue hair on his head 'like the neck of a peacock'; a large and even forehead; black eyes; forty uniform, close-set, white teeth; a Brahman-like voice; a large, slender and moist tongue; a lower jaw like that of a lion; a golden complexion; long arms, fingers and toes; concave nails; bright red lips; deep navel; joined eyebrows; high-bridged nose; and so on. 'Every hair on his body was detached, ascending upwards, and turned on the right side ... his bottom was covered with hair,' and his 'organs were well apparent and perfect,' notes the text.

The baby was named Siddhartha, meaning, loosely, 'child of destiny'. Asita prophesied that the prince would become a great sage, and a soothsayer added that four signs would reveal to him the essential miseries of earthly existence and turn him into an ascetic. But this was not the destiny that Suddhodana desired for his son – he wanted him to be a great king, not a great sage. So, to prevent the augured fate, he enveloped the prince in a cocoon of luxury and indulgence, and insulated him from all the bitter realities of life. Still Siddhartha grew up to be a contemplative, introverted child, who preferred to sit under a tree and meditate, rather than take delight in martial games and other princely pursuits. He was, however, by no means a weakling, and it was in a contest of strength and skill that he won the hand of Yasodhara, his bride, defeating several rival youths, including his cousin Devadatta. It was not weakness but strength that made him quiet.

Yasodhara, whom Asvaghosha describes as 'fair-bosomed ... truly glorious in accordance with her name,' was Siddhartha's cousin, and he married her when he was in his mid-teens. There is nothing in the texts to indicate any marital problems that could have soured Siddhartha's domestic life, though it was probably worrisome to his parents that no child was born of the marriage for ten years. The prince seemed to have led a fairly contented life at this time, and in his old age would speak of those years with some nostalgia: 'Monks, I was delicately nurtured, exceeding delicately nurtured, delicately nurtured beyond measure ... No sandalwood powder did I use that was not from Kasi; of Kasi cloth was my turban made, of Kasi cloth was made my jacket, my tunic, my cloak. By night and day a white canopy was held over me, lest cold or heat, dust or chaff or dew should touch me. Moreover, monks, I had three palaces: one for winter, one for summer, and one for the rainy season. In the four months of the rains I was waited on by minstrels, women all of them. I came not from my palace in those months. Again, whereas in other men's houses broken rice together with sour gruel is given as food to slave servants, in my father's home they were given rice, meat and milk-rice as food.'

Siddhartha lived a secluded life in his palace, with minimal contact with the outside world. And on the few occasions when he went into the town or countryside, great care was taken by his father to remove from his path all those with 'mutilated limbs or maimed sense, as well as the decrepit, the sick and all squalid beggars,' to prevent anything unpleasant from upsetting him, says Asvaghosha. But the gods would not let Siddhartha be cheated out of his destiny, and they used their supernatural powers to show him, on four successive days when he rode out to the royal park, the sights he needed to see to turn his life in the direction it needed to turn – an old man, a sick man, a corpse, and finally a serene, yellow-robed ascetic, radiating calm joy.

As Asvaghosha tells the story, on the first day, the prince, who had never seen a frail and bent old man, asked Channa, his charioteer, what that creature was. And Channa said: 'He too was once a baby suckled by his mother; in course of time he learned to grope on the ground, and, having step by step become a vigorous youth, he has step by step in the same way reached old age.' And the prince said: 'O charioteer, turn back the horses ... How can I enjoy the pleasure-garden when the thoughts of old age overpower me?' The next day he rode out again to the countryside, hoping to quieten his mind haunted by the image of the old man. But now he saw another disturbing sight, a sick man; on the following day he saw a corpse; and on the fourth day an ascetic. Thus, for all the precautions taken by his father, the prince came to see the four sights he was destined to see. That could not be prevented, for those sights were illusions created by the gods and were visible only to the prince and his charioteer.

The sights opened Siddhartha's eyes to the reality of life. 'All that buoyancy of youth, which dwells in the young, [then] sank within me,' Buddha would later recall. He now made up his mind to become an ascetic. This grieved Suddhodana, and he said to the prince, 'O my son, keep back this thought. It is not the time for thee to betake thyself to dharma. They say that the practice of religion is full of evil in the first period of life when the mind is still fickle ... To a man who has enjoyed the pleasures of his prime, it is delightful to enter the penance-forest. But thy religion, O firm-striding hero, is to be accomplished by heroism; it would be irreligion if thou were to leave thine own father.' But the prince replied: 'If thou will be my surety, O king, against the contingencies of disease, old age and death, I will not betake myself to the forest ... If this is impossible, then this course of mine is not to be hindered. It is not right to lay hold of one who would escape from a house that is on fire.'

The king had no answer to that, but still would not let the prince leave. 'He shall not go,' he decreed, and held him a virtual prisoner in the palace. But eventually, as the prince longed for a breath of fresh air in the open countryside, one spring morning, when 'the forest was carpeted with tender grass, and the trees were resounding with cuckoos,' the king gave his reluctant permission for him to ride out. This was quite an event in Kapilavastu, the public appearance of the mysterious prince after a long absence, and Asvaghosha describes it in great detail, incidentally revealing the ambience of ancient Indian urban society.

As the prince rode out, women crowded the doorways, balconies and roofs along the way to have a glimpse of him, states the poet. 'Some of these women, even in their haste as they rushed longing to see, were delayed in their going by the weight of their hips and full bosoms.' Many thought that Siddhartha was 'Kama incarnate.' And in the royal park, where he alighted, young women mobbed him. 'Then, surrounded by troops of women, the prince wandered in the wood like an elephant in a Himalayan forest accompanied by a herd of females ... There some of them, urged by passion, pressed him with their full, firm bosoms in gentle collisions. Another violently embraced him while pretending to stumble, leaning on him with her shoulders drooping down, and with her gentle, creeper-like arms clinging. Another with her mouth smelling of spirituous liquor, her lower lip red like copper, whispered in his ear, "Let my secret be heard." Another, all wet with unguents, as if giving him her command, clasped his hand eagerly and said, "Perform thy rites of adoration here." Another, with her blue garments continually slipping down in pretended intoxication stood conspicuous with her tongue visible like the night with its lightning flashing. Others, with their golden girdles tinkling, wandered about here and there, showing to him their hips veiled with thin cloth. Others leaned, holding a mango-bough in full flower, displaying their bosoms like golden jars ... Another sang a sweet song ... with proper gesticulations, rousing him, self-subdued though he was ... Another, with beautiful bosom, and having her earrings waving in the wind, laughed loudly at him, as if saying, "Catch me, sir, if you can!" Some, as he was going away, bound him with strings of garlands; others punished him with words like an elephant-driver's hook, gentle yet reproachful. Another, wishing to argue with him, seizing a mango-spray, asked, all bewildered with passion, "This flower, whose is it?" Another, assuming a gait and attitude like those of a man, said to him, "Thou who art conquered by women, go and conquer this earth!"'

Thus went on the bacchanalian play. But Siddhartha remained calm and detached. He, says Asvaghosha, 'his senses guarded by self-control, neither rejoiced nor smiled, thinking anxiously, "One must die ... What rational being, who knows of old age, death and sickness, could stand or sit down at his ease or sleep, far less laugh? ... I do not despise worldly objects, I know that all mankind is bound up therein; but remembering that the world is transitory, my mind cannot find pleasure in them. Old age, disease, and death – if these three things did not exist, I too should find my enjoyment in the objects that please the mind."'

Siddhartha's final decision to renounce the world came, appropriately, on an occasion that would have been to worldly beings a time of great joy – the birth of his son, Rahula. When the news was brought to him one morning, his first thought was, 'A son is born to me, a fetter has been forged on me.' If he allowed paternal love to bind him, it would mean life-long bondage. He had to break free. That night he made up his mind.

It was the full-moon night of Ashadha (June-July), a night of joyous celebration in the palace, and several singing and dancing girls were in Siddhartha's bedchamber to entertain him. But the prince, indifferent to their seduction, soon fell asleep, and, seeing him sleep, the singers and dancers also curled up and slept. As they slept, Siddhartha woke up. The scented oil lamps in his room were still burning, and in their dying light he saw the damsels, who had seemed so marvellously alluring in the evening, now sprawled grotesquely in slumber. Some were talking in their sleep, some were slavering, others were sleeping in uncouth postures, their hair dishevelled, their clothes disarranged, exposing hideous deformities of the body, like women 'crushed by an elephant,' as Asvaghosha puts it. This again was a scene created by the gods to turn Siddhartha's life to its destined course. The sight overwhelmed the prince with revulsion, and he mused, 'Such is the nature of women, impure and monstrous ...; but deceived by dress and ornaments man becomes infatuated by a woman's attractions.'

The incident steeled Siddhartha's resolve to flee. He then roused Channa and had his horse Kanthaka saddled. But before he left, he wanted to have one look at his son, and went to Yasodhara's chamber, where she lay with Rahula on a jasmine-strewn bed. He was tempted to hold the baby for a moment, but checked himself, for Yasodhara's hand was on Rahula's head, and he thought, 'If I lift her hand to take up my son, she will awake, and my departure will be hindered. I will return and see him after I have attained enlightenment.' So he turned back and departed, quietly riding out of the palace and the slumbering city, with attending demigods cushioning the hoofs of his horse to prevent its hoof-beats from alerting the guards. 'Till I have seen the further shore of birth and death I will never again enter the city called after Kapila,' the prince vowed on leaving the city. On reaching the woods, he removed his dress and ornaments, cut off his hair and beard, and donned saffron robes.

This is essentially the story told in the *Buddha-charita* and the *Lalitavistara.* Many of its particulars are clearly late embellishments. The account of Siddhartha's disgust at the sight of sleeping women, for instance, is lifted out of another ancient Buddhist story – of the merchant prince Yasa leaving home to become a monk – and patched on to Buddha's life. All that the earliest Pali texts say about Siddhartha's renunciation is this: 'The ascetic Gautama has gone from home into homelessness, while still young in years ... The ascetic Gautama, although his parents did not wish it, although they shed tears and wept, has had his hair and beard shaved, has put on yellow garments, and has gone from his home into homelessness.' Or, as another account has it, he left home reflecting,

'Distressing is life at home, a state of impurity. Freedom is in leaving home.'

Siddhartha was around twenty-nine years old at this time. His renunciation, according to Asvaghosha, was watched over by gods and blessed by them. But there was also another presence there, Mara, the Buddhist tempter-devil. He was lurking in the shadows, and would follow the prince shadow-like throughout his life, watching and waiting for any sign of vulnerability, to divert him from his chosen path. We shall meet Mara again and again in this story.

THE MIDDLE PATH

When Suddhodana found that the prince had fled, he sent his family priest after him to persuade him to return. 'Religion is not wrought out only in the forests,' the priest said to Siddhartha, when he caught up with him. 'The salvation of ascetics can be accomplished even in a city. Thought and effort are the true means ... Liberation has been attained even by householders ...' Siddhartha listened to the priest courteously, but remained firm in his resolve, says Asvaghosha. So the priest tried another approach. 'This resolve of thine is an excellent counsel, not unfit in itself but only unfit at the present time,' he said. 'It could not be thy duty, loving duty, as thou dost, to leave thy father in old age to sorrow. Surely thy mind is not very penetrating, or it is ill-skilled in examining [the goals of life] ... For the sake of an unseen result thou departest, disregarding a visible end. Some say that there is another birth, others with confident assertion say that there is not; since the matter then is all in doubt, it is right to enjoy the fortune which comes to hand ... Therefore, gentle youth, if thou hast a love for liberation, follow right the prescribed rule ...'

Still the prince was unmoved. Nor was he moved when, later, Bimbisara, the king of Magadha, tried to dissuade him from becoming an ascetic, telling him that the right course for him would be to follow the *asrama-dharma*, the duties appropriate to the different stages of life, and that as a youth his duty was to pursue temporal goals and enjoy life. 'Since pleasures, however we guard them, are hard to hold, therefore, wherever pleasures are to be found, there we should seize them,' the king said. Siddhartha rejected the advice, saying, 'The fish greedy for the flesh swallows the iron hook – likewise, worldly pursuits produce misery as their end ... And since after even conquering the whole earth, one city only can serve as a dwelling-place, and even there only one house can be inhabited, is not royalty mere labour for others? And even in royal clothing one pair of garments is all he needs, and just enough food to keep off hunger; so only one bed, and only one seat; all other royal distinctions are only for pride ... I have been wounded by the enjoyment of the world, and I have come out longing to obtain peace ...'

Happiness is a chimera, Siddhartha held. The most that one could hope for in life is peace, *shanti*. Initially Siddhartha thought that the answer to his quest for peace would be found in traditional wisdom, and for a while he wandered about as a mendicant, begging food and looking for a guru. But none of the sages he met gave him the solace he sought.

One sage, explaining ascetic practices, told the prince: 'Uncultivated food, plants growing out of water, leaves, roots and fruits – this is the fare of the saints according to the sacred texts.' One has to lead an austere life and do penance to gain merit and attain heaven, the sage maintained. 'By the path of pain they eventually attain happiness – pain, they say, is the root of merit.'

Attain pleasure through pain? Happiness through suffering? Siddhartha found the notion bizarre. 'By these bodily toils ... he who does not examine the inherent evils of mundane existence, only seeks pain by pain,' he contended, and moved on. Finally he arrived at the hermitage of the renowned sage Alara (or Arada) Kalama, who welcomed him, saying, 'With the nose of a well-fed horse, large long eyes, red lower lip, white sharp teeth, and a thin red tongue, this face of thine will drink up the entire ocean of what is to be known.' Alara taught the prince the techniques of meditation and imparted to him Upanishadic (or possibly Sankhya) wisdom, but could not convince him that this was the right path to liberation. The prince then lived for a while as a disciple of Rudraka Ramaputra, another great sage, and learned from him the most advanced techniques of meditation. Still he was not content.

He had to find his own way, beyond what was already known. Leaving Rudraka, he repaired to a forest near the village Uruvela (Bodh Gaya) on the bank of the river Niranjana, about 16 kilometres south of Gaya in Magadha. 'There I beheld a lovely spot,' he would later tell his disciples, 'a pleasant forest grove and a river of clear water flowing by, easy of access and delightful. Hard by was a village where I could beg my food ... Truly a proper place ... for a clansman bent on striving for his welfare ... So, brethren, there and then I sat down, saying to myself, "A proper place is this for striving in."'

At Uruvela, the prince was joined by a group of five ascetics, and he lived with them for the next six years, practising the most rigorous austerities. 'I remember ... how I practised the four-square practice of the holy life,' he would later recall. 'I was a penance-worker, outdoing others in penance; I was rough-liver, outdoing others in roughing it; I was scrupulous, outdoing others in my scruples; a solitary was I, outdoing others in solitude. Thus far ... did I go in my penance: I went without clothes. I licked my food from my hands ... [I gave up] the practice of taking food by rule, at stated intervals ... I lived on vegetables, on millet, on wild paddy, on *daddula*, on watercress, on paddy-husk, on the scum of rice, on ground sesame, on grass, on cowdung. I lived on roots and fruits of the forest, on casual fruits [that had fallen] ... I wore coarse clothes, I wore hemp woven in with other things, grave-cloths, dust-heap rags, a dress made of bark; I wore antelope skin, a dress made of shreds of antelope skin, I wore *kusa* fibre, bark fibre, clothes made of shavings, a hair shirt of human hair, a hair shirt of horse hair, or made of owl's feathers.

'I plucked out my hair and beard, and kept the practice up. I always stood, refusing to sit down. I was a squatter on my heels, striving by the method of squatting. I was a thorn-bed man and lay upon a bed of thorns ... Thus in diverse ways did I dwell given to tormenting and again tormenting the body ... The dirt of many seasons gathered on my body just like the outer crust of tree-bark ... from forest to forest, from jungle to jungle, from marshland to marshland, from upland to upland I fled away ... lest ... [others] should see me or I should see them ... So long as my own excrements lasted ... I lived even on my own excrements. To such extremes did I go ... as to live on filth for food.

'Then ... I plunged into a fearsome forest thicket and dwelt therein ... Then those cold, frosty nights, and nights when the snow was falling, did I pass in the open air, and the days I spent in the forest covert. And in the last month of the hot season, by day I dwelt in the open air, by night in the forest covert ... Then again ... in a charnel-field I lay down to rest upon bones of corpses. And the cowherds came up to me, even spat upon me, even made water upon me, spattered me with mud, even poked straws into my ears. Yet ... I cannot call to mind that a single evil thought against them arose in me. Thus far was I gone in forbearance ...'

By these practices 'mindfulness was indeed established undisturbed,' Buddha said. 'Yet my body was perturbed – it was not made calm thereby, because I was overpowered by the stress of my painful struggling.' But he did not at that time think that his method was wrong, only that his effort was wanting. So he intensified his austerities. At mealtimes, according to Asvaghosha, the prince was content with a single jujube fruit, a single sesame seed, or a single grain of rice. 'Because of so little nourishment,' Buddha observed, 'my limbs became like some withered creepers with knotted joints, my buttocks like a buffalo's hoof, my backbone protruding like a string of balls, my ribs like rafters of a dilapidated shed. The pupils of my eyes were sunk deep in their sockets, and were like water shining at the bottom of a deep well. My scalp became shrivelled and shrunk by sun and wind ... The skin of my belly so cleaved to my backbone that if I touched my belly with my hand, I seized instead my backbone. When I wanted to answer the calls of nature, I fell down on my face then and there. When I stroked my limbs with my hand, hairs rotted at the roots fell away from my body ...' He became so shrivelled that his complexion turned from gold to a dingy dark colour, and people thought, as Buddha would recall, 'Gautama the recluse is a black man.'

Still enlightenment eluded him. 'Yet by all these bitter, woeful methods I did not achieve the truly noble excellence of knowledge and insight,' Buddha remarked. 'Wearied with hunger, thirst, and fatigue, with his mind no longer self-possessed because of fatigue, how can he who is not absolutely calm reach the end which is to be attained by his mind?' he wondered, says Asvaghosha.

Then, according to the *Majjhima Nikaya*, a thought occurred to Siddhartha: 'Maybe there is some other way to wisdom.' In this quandary, the memory of a childhood incident came to his mind, in which, when he was one day sitting in the shade of a rose-apple tree watching his father plough the field, a 'zestful ease' possessed him and he felt a strange radiance of thought glow within him. 'Why am I afraid of that state of ease, that ease which is apart from sensual desires and ill conditions?' the ascetic prince now mused. 'No, I am not afraid of that state of ease ... But it is not easy for me to reach that state of ease with a body utterly exhausted. Suppose I now take some substantial food, some rice gruel, I thought. And so I did ...'

The prince was at last on the right path to enlightenment. Resolving to change his mode of life, he went to the nearby river to bathe, and on returning, accepted a meal of milk-rice offered by Sujatha, daughter of a local farmer (or Nandabala, daughter of a cowherd, according to one text), and thereafter continued to take normal food. This disgusted his ascetic companions, for they thought that he was giving up his spiritual endeavour, and they left him and went away to Varanasi to continue their austerities.

Siddhartha remained at Uruvela. No longer at war with his body, but with his health regained, and along with it his physical and mental equanimity, he now sought enlightenment with calm deliberation. He took his seat under a giant pipal tree in a grassy meadow, and, sitting cross-legged in a yogic posture, facing east, resolved not to rise from there till he had attained enlightenment. 'Then with thought steadied, perfectly purified, and made perfectly translucent, free from blemish, purged of taint, made supple and pliable, fit for wielding, established and immovable, I bent down my mind,' says Buddha.

For forty-nine days he sat under the tree, sunk in deep meditation, surrounded by reverential gods, with Brahma himself holding the white parasol of royalty over him. During this time he was repeatedly assailed by Mara, using every wile and every terror in his power – perhaps simulating the very terrors and temptations rising within Siddhartha himself – to prevent him from attaining his goal. On Mara's approach, even the gods attending on Siddhartha fled, and he was left alone to face the fiend. Mara first tried to shame the prince into abandoning his course. 'Up, up, O thou Kshatriya, afraid of death!' he taunted. 'Follow thine own duty and abandon this pursuit of liberation! And, having conquered the lower worlds by thy arrows, proceed to gain the higher worlds of Indra.' Siddhartha was unmoved. And when Mara tempted him by saying that he (the prince) could, if he wished, turn the Himalayas into a mountain of gold, Siddhartha dismissed the prospect saying that it would not profit the wise man to have a mountain of gold. Mara then set upon the prince a host of demons, shooting fiery and poisoned darts, and tormenting him with a shower of rocks, a hurricane of burning sand, a deluge, an earthquake, and so on. Even then Siddhartha did not stir. Finally, as the last resort, Mara sent his three daughters – Desire, Unrest and Pleasure – to seduce him. They had no success either. Defeated, Mara at last retreated. Then the gods returned, singing Siddhartha's praise. He had passed the final test.

Amidst all the turmoil caused by Mara, Siddhartha had continued his meditation undisturbed, unwavering like a 'flame in a windless spot.' Then, on a full-moon day in May around the year 528, after a night of deepening ecstasy and insight, just as the day broke, Siddhartha, aged thirty-five, attained enlightenment. 'My mind was emancipated,' he would later tell his disciples. 'Ignorance was dispelled, knowledge arose; darkness was dispelled, light arose.' The earth, the heavens and the divine spirits rejoiced at the happy event – mighty rolls of thunder resounded and the earth quaked like a drunken woman, says Asvaghosha; a supernatural radiance spread over the heavens, a rain of flowers fell from the cloudless sky, and the heavenly seers proclaimed Gautama's glory. Siddhartha thus became Buddha, the Enlightened One. The pipal tree, under which he attained enlightenment, would thereafter be revered by Buddhists as the Tree of Wisdom, the symbol of Buddha.

Buddha remained at Uruvela for seven weeks after his enlightenment, reflecting on the insight he had gained and elaborating its implications. His was a radically new doctrine, a conception entirely his own. He made no appeal to authority or tradition. 'This ... the noble truth concerning sorrow was not, O monks, among the doctrines handed down,' Buddha asserted. Yet he did not claim any supernatural power or revelation for himself – the light that burned in him was not a divine light born with him, but a light that he ignited himself by the heat of resolute endeavour, the lonely, unaided quest of a mortal.

Not surprisingly, Buddha had very human doubts about himself, about what he could and should do. He was uncertain about propagating his ideas. 'I have realised this truth which is deep, difficult to see, difficult to understand ... Men who are overpowered by passion and lost in darkness cannot see this truth,' he is said to have fretted. 'Should I now preach the doctrine and mankind not understand me, it would bring me nothing but fatigue, it would cause me nothing but trouble.' The difficulty in understanding Buddha's ideas was not intellectual, but psychological. His message, like the teachings of all great sages, was marked by divine simplicity, but it was difficult to get people to look beyond their mundane preoccupations to the transcendental truths that lie beyond life and death.

As Buddha hesitated, Brahma himself appeared before him to persuade him to propagate his ideas. But Mara, ever present in Buddha's shadow, perhaps Buddha's shadow itself, advised him against it, saying that, having attained final enlightenment, he should now enter the bliss of nirvana, instead of troubling himself to enlighten mankind. The suggestion repelled Buddha. 'I shall not enter nirvana, thou wicked one, until I shall have gained monks as my disciples, who are wise and well-instructed, intelligent hearers of the word, acquainted with the doctrine,' he declared. A fortuitous incident at this time reinforced Buddha's resolve to set out on missionary work. Two merchants who were passing by, Tapussa and Bhallika, saw Buddha sitting under the pipal tree, and, impressed by the nobility of his presence, made obeisance to him and offered him his first meal after his long fasting. This was taken by Buddha as an auspicious sign, signalling him to proceed with his mission.

But the going was not easy in the beginning. Buddha in fact suffered a rebuff in his very first encounter with an ascetic. As he set out on his mission from Uruvela, he ran into Upaka, a follower of the Ajivika sect. Upaka, as the *Mahavagga* tells the story, was initially attracted to Buddha, and said to him: 'Your countenance, friend, is serene; your complexion is pure and bright ... Who is your teacher? Whose doctrine do you profess?' And Buddha, with an uncharacteristic boastfulness indicative of his early insecurity, replied: 'I have overcome all foes; I am all-wise; I am free from stains in every way; I have left everything; and have obtained emancipation by the destruction of desire. Having gained knowledge all by myself, whom should I call my master? I have no teacher; no one is equal to me; in the world of men and gods no being is like me. I am the Holy One in this world, I am the highest teacher, I alone am the absolute Sambuddha ... I will beat the drum of the immortal in the darkness of this world.' Upaka was very likely taken aback by Buddha's vehemence, and he snickered, 'It may be so, friend,' and, as the *Mahavagga* puts it, 'shook his head, took another road, and went away.'

Buddha now realised that he had to find someone who would be receptive to his ideas. 'Whom can I teach? And how shall I teach him?' he pondered. He first thought that he should go to his former teachers, Alara Kalama and Rudraka Ramaputra, but learned that they were dead. Then he thought of his five former ascetic companions. They were at this time living in the Deer Park hermitage in Saranath, a suburb of Varanasi, some 200 kilometres to the west of Uruvela, and Buddha set out to visit them. We know nothing about his journey to Varanasi, but the ascetics were guarded in receiving him. They were civil, but not deferential, and they addressed him familiarly as *Avuso* Gautama, Friend Gautama. They had not forgiven him for abandoning austerities, and were sceptical about his claim to enlightenment. But Buddha was determined to win them over as his disciples, and so he set himself on a high spiritual plane by insisting that they should address him reverentially as *bhagavat*. 'O monks, do not address the Tathagata by his name, and with the appellation "friend",' he cautioned.

He then went on to counsel them that what was required for enlightenment was discipline, not self-torture; mental effort, not physical effort. 'These so-called austerities only confuse the mind, which is overpowered by the body's exhaustion,' he told them, according to Asvaghosha. 'In the resulting stupor one can no longer understand the ordinary things of life, how much less the way to the truth which lies beyond the senses.' The force of his arguments, or perhaps the charisma of his person, in the end converted the ascetics, and they requested him to initiate them as his disciples. Buddha welcomed them, saying, 'Come near, O monks,' and delivered to them his first sermon, expounding the doctrine of the Four Noble Truths, which constitute the kernel of his teaching.

'Now this, O monks, is the noble truth about sorrow,' Buddha declared, addressing the monks. 'Birth is painful, decay is painful, disease is painful, death is painful; union with the unpleasant is painful, separation from the pleasant is painful, unfulfilled craving is painful ...

'Now this, O monks, is the noble truth about the origin of sorrow: verily, sorrow arises from craving, which leads to rebirth and thirst for sensual delights, seeking satisfaction now here, now there – that is to say, the craving for the gratification of passions, or the craving for life, or the craving for success ...

'Now this, O monks, is the noble truth about the removal of sorrow: verily, it is the complete removal of this craving, so that no passion remains ...

'Now this, O monks, is the noble truth about the way which leads to removal of sorrow: verily, it is the Noble Eight-fold Path ... '

The Noble Eight-fold Path was the path of moderation. 'There are two extremes, O monks, which a renouncer ought not to follow,' Buddha warned. One was 'the pursuit of desires and of the pleasure which springs from desires, which is base, common, leading to rebirth, ignoble and unprofitable.' Equally, the renouncer should avoid 'self-mortification, which is grievous, ignoble and unprofitable. Now there is a middle path, O monks, discovered by Tathagata, which avoids these two extremes, a path which opens the eyes, and bestows understanding, which leads to peace of mind, to the higher wisdom, to full enlightenment, to nirvana! ... Verily, it is the Noble Eight-fold Path: right views, right aspirations, right speech, right conduct, right livelihood, right effort, right mindfulness, and right contemplation.'

When Buddha enunciated his doctrine, 'the gods of the earth,' says the *Dhamma-kakka-pavathana-sutta*, 'gave forth a shout, saying: "In Varanasi, at the Deer Park hermitage, the supreme wheel of the empire of truth has been set rolling by the Blessed One – that wheel which not by any ascetic or Brahmin, not by any god, not by any Brahma or Mara, not by any one in the universe, can ever be turned back."' This chant was taken up by the guardian angels of the four quarters of the universe, and then by the gods in the highest of heavens. 'And thus, in an instant, a second, a moment, the sound went up even to the world of Brahma: and this great ten-thousand-world-system quaked and trembled and was shaken violently, and an immeasurable bright light appeared in the universe, beyond even the power of the gods!'

THE FIRE SERMON

Vishasya vishena hani, states an Indian adage. Poison is the cure for poison. Physical suffering relieves mental suffering. Is then pain, deliberate and self-inflicted, the means to end the painfulness of life? Buddha rejected the notion. Instead, he offered the golden mean of the Middle Path, between the extremes of indulgence and asceticism. In doing so, Buddha struck out on a path that was entirely his own, though nearly everything else in his teachings was a variation of the common wisdom of his time. The Middle Path alone bears the unique impress of his personality.

What sort of person was this prince-turned-sage in saffron robes who walked among the people of the Gangetic Plain two-and-a-half millenniums ago, speaking to them about the virtues of moderation and mindfulness? We have a surprisingly great deal of information about him, far more than about any other ancient Indian sage or even about any of the great rulers of the age. Much of it, the extravagant stories about him, are no doubt myths reverently invented by his devotees, but it is quite likely that the apocryphal persona of Buddha in legends retains the essential contours of the person that he really was. The substantiality of the image is confirmed by the fact that what we know of Buddha's teachings felicitously harmonises with what we know of his person. His philosophy was an emanation of his personality, and we can well visualise the man from his message. 'As the Tathagata speaks, so he does; as he does, so he speaks,' states the *Iti-vuttaka*, an ancient Buddhist text. Buddha himself once put it this way, when a devotee spoke of his happiness in seeing him: 'Hush, Vakkali! What is there in seeing this vile body of mine? He who seeth the dharma, he seeth me; he who seeth me, Vakkali, seeth the dharma.'

Buddha was undeniably a man of great charisma. Both strong and gentle, worldly-wise and yet warm and compassionate, he could win the affection and devotion of kings as well as commoners, and inspire his followers to dedicate themselves to a life of sacrifice in missionary work. Did he have a physical charm to match the charm of his personality? It does seem so. 'The recluse Gotama,' says the Brahmin Canaki in the most detailed description we have of the sage in Buddhist texts, 'is lovely, good to look upon, charming, possessed of the greatest beauty of complexion, of a sublime colour, a perfect stature, noble of presence.' Apart from this, there are no specific physical descriptions of Buddha in ancient texts. Nor are there any near contemporaneous figurative depictions of Buddha in sculpture or painting, for he was initially represented only by his symbols: the bodhi tree, his footprint, or the wheel of dharma. He was, according to the *Lalitavistara*, endowed with thirty-two distinctive bodily marks and many other subsidiary characteristics, but these constitute an iconic formula, not the description of the actual person.

The only thing that can be said with reasonable certainty about Buddha's appearance is that he had in his youth the clear, golden complexion of a highlander, to which we have several references in Buddhist texts. His skin 'shone forth in colour like gold,' says Ananda, his cousin and devoted disciple. He seems to have enjoyed excellent health throughout his life, and could swim across the Ganga even when he was nearly eighty, to the wonderment of his disciples, who had to look for a ferry to take them across. The *Jatakas* say that he moved 'with the royal gait of an elephant in the plenitude of his vigour,' and, while resting, 'stretched himself, lion-like, on his right side.' He was probably a big-made man, vigorous and bright-eyed, though Hsuan Tsang no doubt mythifies when he writes that Buddha's foot impression was 'about eighteen inches long and six inches broad,' and that his eyeball preserved in a casket was 'as large as a mango, and so bright that its rays dart forth from the box some distance outside.'

Buddha was something of an aesthete – his chambers were elegant and perfumed, even his lavatory was hung with strings of fragrant flowers. He was punctilious about the cleanliness of his person and environment, precise about his dress and manners, even rather formal, mindful of everything that he did. Thus, according to a *Jataka* story, while taking a bath he covered himself with a long piece of cloth, 'using one end to go round his waist, and covering his body up with the other,' and, coming out of the water, 'donned his two orange-coloured cloths and his girdle, adjusting his robe around him so as to leave one shoulder bare.' He always washed his feet before entering a hall, and usually sat facing the east to give discourses. His posture was always erect and dignified, wherever he was. Once, when he had to lodge in a potter's shed, on entering, he 'spread a heap of straw at one side, and sat down cross-legged, holding his body straight up, setting mindfulness before him as his aim,' notes the *Majjhima Nikaya*. He woke up early. 'The Exalted One, having risen early ... [walks] up and down in the open air,' records a *Vinaya* text.

The later portraits of Buddha always present him with a wistful, enigmatic smile, and a serene, inward-looking expression. It is a pensive face, but not sorrowful. That too seems to be in character, for though he talked incessantly about life as sorrow, he was not a mournful person. Rather, he was a well-integrated, tranquil man, contented with himself and his life, doing what he had to do and enjoyed doing.

He had a fine sense of humour. Once when he was asked how a drop of water could be prevented from drying up, he cheerfully replied: 'By throwing it into the sea.' On another occasion, when a yogi on a riverbank told him that after many years of rigorous austerities he had learned to walk on water, Buddha replied, 'What a pity to have spent so much effort – a little further on they will take you across the river for a small coin.' And when he was once abused by a young man, Buddha asked him, 'Son, if a man declined to accept a present made to him, to whom would it belong?' The man answered: 'In that case it would belong to the man who offered it.' And Buddha said: 'My son, thou has railed at me, but I decline to accept thy abuse, and request thee to keep it thyself.' As the youth remained silent, Buddha continued: 'A wicked man who reproaches a virtuous one is like one who looks up and spits at the sky; the spittle soils not the sky, but comes back and defiles his own person ... The virtuous man cannot be hurt and the misery that the other would inflict recoils on himself.'

A sober, down-to-earth realist, and no ethereal visionary, Buddha was primarily concerned with the problems of life on earth, not of life after death. It is not high metaphysics but psychological insight, compassion and practical wisdom that characterise his teachings. This is poignantly revealed in the haunting Parable of the Mustard Seed, told in the *Anguttara Nikaya.* In the town of Sravasti there was a poor, frail, simple-minded woman named Kisa Gotami, whose sole consolation in life was her only child, a son. Unfortunately he died in infancy, and this drove her clear out of her mind with grief, and she kept wandering around the town carrying the child's corpse on her hip, imploring everyone, 'Give me medicine for my son!' Seeing this, people clapped their hands and laughed at her, saying, 'Where do you ever find medicine for the dead?' She could not understand what they were saying or why they were laughing. Finally someone took pity on the poor woman and sent her to Buddha, saying that he alone would have the medicine for her.

Gotami then hastened to Buddha's hermitage and pleaded, 'O Exalted One, give me medicine for my son!' And Buddha in his compassion took her in hand and said to her, 'You did well, Gotami, in coming here for medicine.' He told her to go back into the town and fetch some mustard seeds for the medicine from a family where no one had died. She set out immediately, excited with the thought that she would now be able to revive her son. But as she went from house to house on her impossible mission, gradually the awareness dawned in her that what she was doing was absurd, that even her grief was absurd. She then left her son's body in a cremation-ground and returned to the hermitage.

'Gotami, did you get the grains of mustard seed?' Buddha asked her.

And she replied: 'Done, lord, is the business of the mustard seeds! Grant me refuge.'

The moral of the story is simple, yet profound. No predicament, no tragedy, however unique and desolating it might seem, is really unique or unbearable. In a world where everything is fleeting and transitory, we all share common fatalities. And today's endless grief dissipates altogether in the light of another dawn.

Compassion – dispassionate compassion – marked every act of Buddha. There was no hell-fire in his sermons, only gentle ministry. 'With kindly intent will I speak, not in anger,' he would often say. Buddha's caring for man was for the whole person, for the body as well as the mind, and he himself often actually nursed the sick among his folk, apart from comforting them in their spiritual and mental travails. Buddhist literature often refers to him as *arogyasaliya*, healer, and Tibetan tradition speaks of him as a great physician, as does the Chinese traveller I-Tsing. The eighth book of the *Mahavagga* records the various treatments that Buddha prescribed, and documents several incidents of Buddha personally nursing his followers, sometimes performing even the most unpleasant menial duties. Once when he came across a monk suffering from dysentery lying unattended in his own excrement, he said to Ananda who was with him: 'Go you, Ananda, and fetch water. We will wash this brother.' Later, after attending on the sick man, he went to the assembly of monks and admonished them that they should take care of each other. 'Brethren, he who would wait on me, let him wait on the sick,' he told them.

This was how Buddha worked in the world, dealing with everyday problems with wisdom, care and solicitude. He was no recluse, but very much a man of action, and he was ever active in society, preaching, offering solace to the suffering, winning disciples, training monks and looking into every detail of their discipline and organisation. He was a natural leader of men, and had phenomenal organisational skills. Equally, he was a great communicator, richly imaginative in his discourses, which were replete with similes, illustrative stories and rhetorical questions. Those who presumed to challenge him in debate were easily worsted and converted – that, at any rate, is what Buddhist sources say. We do not have the versions of his rivals.

Buddhist sacred literature has many fabulous stories about Buddha and his deeds, and in them he often speaks hyperbolically about himself and his supernatural powers. This seems out of character, for his general demeanour was modest, and his approach rationalistic and empirical. It is quite likely that many of these stories are fabrications of his overzealous votaries. Still, it is possible that Buddha's propagation of his ideas also involved some self-promotion. This was the common manner of ancient prophets in all religions, for it was the aura of the supernatural, not abstract philosophical postulations that instilled faith in people. It is therefore no surprise that Buddha did occasionally lay claim to miraculous powers. Once, when Ananda asked him whether he had the ability to travel physically to the Brahma world, he replied: 'Whensoever, Ananda, the Tathagata concentrates body in mind and concentrates mind in body, he attains the ease and buoyancy that abides therein. At such time, Ananda, the body of the Tathagata is more buoyant, softer, more pliable, more radiant ... and with but little effort [it] rises from the earth into the sky, and in diverse ways enjoys magic power, to wit: being one he becomes many, and so forth, and he has power over the body even up to the world of Brahma.'

On another occasion he told the monks, 'I, brethren, when I so desire it, can call to mind my various states of birth: for instance, one birth, two births, five, ten ... a hundred thousand births; the various ... destructions and renewals of aeons, thus: I lived there, was named thus, was of such a clan, of such a caste, was thus supported, had such and such pleasant and painful experiences, had such a length of days, disappeared thence and arose elsewhere; there too I lived, was named thus, was of such a clan, of such a caste ... This I can recall to mind in all their specific details, in all their characteristics ... I, brethren, when I so desire it, can behold with the divine vision, clarified and surpassing that of men, beings falling and rising again, both mean and excellent, fair and foul, gone to a happy state, gone to a woeful state, according to their deeds ...'

Buddha is said to have performed a number of miracles in Sravasti, even gone to heaven to preach dharma to his mother, while a likeness of himself that he created continued to work on earth. Once when Buddha was told that a renegade monk had defamed him, saying that 'there was nothing superhuman about the sage Gautama, who was not distinguished from other men by preaching a saving faith; that the sage Gautama had simply worked out a system which was the outcome of his individual thought and study; and that the ideal for the attainment of which his doctrine was preached did not lead to destruction of sorrow in those who followed it,' Buddha responded: 'In me ... dwell the Six Knowledges, and herein am I more than human. The Ten Powers are within me, and the Four Grounds of Confidence. I know the limits of the four types of earthly existence and the five states of possible rebirth after earthly death. This too is a superhuman quality in me; and whoso denies it must retract his words, change his belief, and renounce his heresy, or he will without ado be cast into hell.'

There was something of what one might call saintmanship in these posturings of Buddha. But it was more a characteristic of the age than that of the man. Worldly action in any case did not taint him, Buddha claimed, saying, 'Just as, brethren, a dark-blue lotus or a white lotus, born in the water, comes to full growth in the water, rises to the surface and stands unspotted by the water, even so, brethren, the Tathagata, [having been born in the world and] having come to full growth in the world, passes beyond the world and abides unspotted by the world.'

In the world, but not of the world – that was how Buddha saw himself. Yet he did work tirelessly and purposefully for the good of the world. For about forty-five years, from his enlightenment till his death at the age of about eighty, he travelled incessantly in the eastern Gangetic Plain – mainly in the kingdoms of Kosala and Magadha – to propagate his ideas and to organise his followers.

Buddha usually travelled in pontifical style, attended by some 500 brethren. This would have been quite a spectacle in that age, the solemn and majestic procession of the towering and radiant sage at the head of a large body of monks, all dressed in identical saffron robes and maintaining the same discipline and reverential demeanour. The awe roused by scenes such as these was undoubtedly a factor in Buddha's growing prestige and popularity. Also helpful were the demonstrations of – or the legends about – his supernatural powers. He is once said to have converted a hundred Brahmin hermits by a display of miracles. His aristocratic connections were also advantageous. The *Mahavagga* records that the Malla chieftains at Kusinara once issued an ordinance that on Buddha's visit to the town 'whoever goeth not to welcome the Exalted One should pay a fine of five hundred pieces.' Bimbisara and Prasenajit, the kings of Magadha and Kosala, who were about the same age as Buddha, were his patrons – Prasenajit was so reverential towards him that, says a Buddhist text, 'he kissed his feet and stroked them with his hands.'

For a holy man, Buddha was quite a public relations genius, ever sensitive to the impression that he and his monks were making on people. In his discourses to monks he often stressed that their good behaviour, apart from being meritorious in itself, was essential to sustain the faith of their followers and to attract new converts. 'This is not conducive to the conversion of the unconverted, or to the advancement of the converted,' was his constant rebuke to monks, whenever he came across their objectionable acts.

Buddhism, unlike Hinduism, was a proselytising religion, 'one of the greatest missionary religions on earth,' as Weber observes. Buddha's first converts were his old ascetic associates, but the real turning point in his missionary career came when Yasa, a young merchant prince of Varanasi, unexpectedly turned up to meet Buddha and entered his order. Soon after, Yasa's parents as well as his wife became Buddha's votaries, his first lay followers. That set a trend, and it soon became fashionable for the urban elite to be Buddha's followers. Several of Yasa's friends entered the order and many others became lay devotees.

As the number of monks with him grew, Buddha sent them off to different parts of the land to work as his missionaries, telling them, 'Go ye now, O brethren, and travel from place to place ... out of compassion for the world ... for the welfare of gods and men. Let not two of you go the same way. Preach, O brethren, the doctrine which is noble in the beginning, noble in the middle, noble in the end, in spirit and in letter. Proclaim a consummate, perfect, and pure life of holiness.'

And so they set off, with neophyte faith and fervour, to spread the good word. Thus what began as the lonesome private quest of an individual for release from the ordeal of life turned into a public religious movement.

As his disciples fanned out, Buddha himself along with several monks returned to Uruvela, and there won over sage Kassapa along with his many followers. And it was to them that he preached the impassioned Fire Sermon, the most stirring of his discourses: 'All things, O brethren, are on fire ... The eye, O brethren, is on fire ... the impressions received by the eye are on fire; and the sensations ... arising out of these impressions are likewise on fire.

'And with what are these on fire?

'With the fire of passion, say I, with the fire of hatred, with the fire of infatuation; with birth, old age, death, sorrow, lamentation, misery, grief, and despair are they on fire.

'The ear is on fire, sounds are on fire ... the nose is on fire ... the tongue ... the body ... the mind ... ideas are on fire ... And with what are these on fire? With the fire of passion, say I ...

'Seeing this, O brethren, the true disciple conceives an aversion for the eye ... and for the impressions received by the eye, and for the sensations arising therein ... [So also for the ear and sounds, for body and tangible things, for the mind and its sensations.] And in conceiving this aversion, he becomes divested of passion, and by the absence of passion he becomes free, and when he is free he becomes aware that he is free, and he knows that rebirth is exhausted ... and that he is no more of this world.'

The conversion of Kassapa was of great advantage to Buddha, for Kassapa was a renowned sage on his own right. Initially, when the two went about together, there was some confusion about who was whose disciple, but the public acknowledgement of Buddha as his guru by Kassapa considerably enhanced the stature of Buddha in the eyes of people. Buddha then proceeded to Rajagriha, where King Bimbisara along with his retinue and a large number of people went in procession to pay him homage, and presented him the extensive Veluvana (Bamboo-grove) park to set up a monastery. An equally important gain for Buddha in Rajagriha was the conversion of Sariputra and Moggallana, two Brahminical agnostics, who would in time rise to become his chief apostles.

From Rajagriha, Buddha went on to Kapilavastu, his hometown, accompanied by 20,000 disciples, according to Buddhist tradition. His reception there was mixed – though the proud people of the town flocked to greet him with flowers in their hands, showing him the respect due to their prince, they would not treat their familiar old lord as a new saviour and would not bow down at his feet. Buddha then, understanding their reservations, performed a miracle – he rose in the air, sat on a jewelled throne in the sky, and delivered a sermon, according to Buddhist texts – upon which all naturally fell on their knees and acknowledged Buddha's sanctity.

Buddha camped in a grove near Kapilavastu for a few days, then entered the city to beg for food, as was his custom. When his father remonstrated against this, saying, 'Not one of all our ancestors has ever begged his food,' Buddha replied, 'O king, thy descent is in the succession of kings, but mine is in the succession of Buddhas, and every one of these has begged his daily food, and lived on alms.'

Suddhodana then escorted Buddha and his disciples to his palace and feasted them grandly. There the inmates of the palace paid homage to Buddha – all except Yasodhara. She refused to go to him, saying that he should go to her 'if he thought she had any virtue.' And Buddha did go to her. She then, continues the legend, fell on her knees, clasped his ankles and adored him by laying her head upon his feet. A few days later his son Rahula approached him, as Yasodhara had told him to do, saying, 'O father, I am thy son. Give to me my inheritance.' And Buddha said to Sariputra: 'Well, then, Sariputra, receive Rahula into our Order.' This greatly upset Suddhodana, as Buddha had also ordained his step-brother, the crown prince, as well as his cousin Devadatta, so the line was in danger of becoming extinct, and he pleaded with Buddha to lay down a rule that no child should be ordained without the consent of his parents.

From Kapilavastu the sage returned to Rajagriha, and then went on to Sravasti, the capital of Kosala, on the invitation of Anathapindika, a fabulously wealthy merchant prince of the city. Anathapindika made grand preparations for the reception of Buddha and his entourage, setting up resting-places for them at every league all along the road between the two cities. And when Buddha arrived in Sravasti, the merchant presented to him the monastery he had built for the sangha in the Jetavana grove in the city. The grove originally belonged to a local chieftain, who was reluctant to part with it and agreed to sell it only when Anathapindika offered to pay for it by covering the entire ground with gold pieces. Jetavana was a particularly charming place, and it became Buddha's favourite monsoon retreat. Chinese pilgrim Fa Hsien, who saw it in the early fifth century BC, writes: 'The clear water of the tanks, the luxuriant groves, and the numberless flowers of variegated hues, combine to produce the picture of what is called the *vihara* of Chi-un (Jeta).' Sravasti was lucky for Buddha, and he gained many followers there, including Visakha, the munificent wife of another wealthy merchant. From then on the number of Buddha's followers grew rapidly, and Buddhist monasteries, mostly huts of bamboo and reed, came up in many of the major towns of the eastern Gangetic valley, most of them gifted by Buddha's rich patrons and maintained by charity.

Buddha's decision to organise his followers into a monastic order and to set up cloisters for their monsoon retreat helped to fortify the solidarity of the sect, and contributed greatly to its early success. The Buddhist sangha, as R.C. Dutt maintains, was probably 'the first organised monastic system in the world.'

But the sangha was quite unlike any other monastic order; it was more like an extended family, and its ethos was egalitarian. Monastic discipline, though fairly strict, was lovingly imposed by Buddha, like the authority of a father over his children. There was a great psychological distance between Buddha and the monks, yet there was also familial intimacy between them. 'Ye are mine own true sons, brethren, born of my mouth,' he once told them. 'Now the Master through all the six divisions of night and day keeps continual watch over the brethren, even as … a father his only son,' state the *Jatakas*.

Buddha considered himself to be a good herdsman, knowledgeable about his folk and taking intelligent and loving care of them, and he tried to instil in his monks the same attitude of affectionate and proud responsibility. He trusted them and conferred on them high responsibilities. Monks were even empowered to ordain new monks. 'Brethren, I grant you this permission – hereafter do you yourselves give ordination and full orders in such and such districts, and in such and such countries,' Buddha told them. The self-discipline of the monk, as well as the trust and responsibility that Buddha reposed in him, turned each Buddhist monk into an autonomous and fervent proselytising institution.

Buddha's advice to his monks was to preach in the language of the common people, as he himself did. Once a monk, a Brahmin by birth, told Buddha: 'At the present time, Lord, monks differing in name, differing in lineage, differing in birth, differing in family, have gone forth. These corrupt the word of Buddha by their own dialect. Let us, Lord, put the word of Buddha in hymnal (Sanskrit) verse.' Buddha rejected the suggestion and warned: 'You are not, O brethren, to put the word of Buddha into verse … I direct you, O brethren, that each should learn the word of Buddha in his own tongue.'

Buddha was equally careful to infuse his ideas into novices through measured doses and to guide them gradually through the complex techniques of meditation. He, as Kassapa once remarked, 'does not force maturity on that which is unripe ... [but] being wise, waits for maturity.' Even then Buddha was not always successful with his disciples.

'Tell me, master Gautama – do the disciples of the worthy Gautama ... do all of them win the absolute perfection which is nirvana, or do some fail ...?' a Brahmin once asked Buddha.

'Some of my disciples, Brahmin, advised and trained by me do so attain,' said Buddha. 'Others do not.'

'What is the reason ... why some disciples ... do attain, while others do not attain?' persisted the Brahmin.

Buddha replied that he could only show people the way to nirvana, but not carry them across. 'The Tathagata is one who shows the way.'

THE JOURNEY'S END

'I may teach dharma in brief, and again I may teach it in detail ... It is those who understand that are hard to find,' Buddha once lamented, despairing over his disciples, notes the *Anguttara Nikaya*. His own insight into what life was all about and how it should be lived was absolutely clear, but how many would understand him fully, and how many would follow him truly? And if he could not really carry people with him, what would be the point of his missionary endeavour at all? These doubts had assailed Buddha soon after he attained enlightenment, and they would continue to distress him till the end of his life.

Over the years Buddha did win a large number of followers, but his very success carried with it the seeds of corruption in the sangha, by attracting to it men who had no serious spiritual interest, but found that becoming a monk was an easy way to shed social and familial responsibilities and lead a carefree life. This was frankly admitted by monk Nagasena in *Milinda-panha*. When king Menander asked him whether all those who joined the sangha were motivated by the high ideal of attaining nirvana, the monk replied: 'Certainly not, Sire. Some have done so for ... [noble] reasons, but some have left the world in terror of the tyranny of kings, some have joined us to be safe from being robbed, some have come being harassed by debt, and some perhaps to gain a livelihood.'

On the whole, however, Buddha was lucky in his disciples. Most of his early devotees, both lay followers as well as monks and nuns, were earnest seekers of spiritual solace, genteel intellectuals from the cultured upper crust of urban society, Brahmins, Kshatriyas and wealthy merchants. The younger members of the newly prominent and socially insecure mercantile and artisan classes were particularly attracted to Buddha, as his Middle Path, which required discipline but not austerities, meshed well with the work ethic and lifestyle of traders and artisans. Besides, Buddhism was a very decorous religion, and this was no doubt a factor in its appeal to the elite.

Sanskrit texts often present Buddha as addressing his audience as *kula-putras*, sons of noble families. This probably was a common literary convention, but it was also, in this case, a statement of fact, for although Buddha welcomed men of all classes and castes equally into the sangha, his was essentially a religion of the upper classes. His ideal of voluntary poverty and renunciation of the material world would not have made much sense to the common people, who hardly had anything material to renounce and were already living in a state of (involuntary) poverty. Besides, Buddha mainly operated in towns and cities, and his approach was cerebral. 'To the wise belongs dharma, not to the foolish,' he asserted.

The most distinguished of Buddha's immediate disciples were Sariputra and Moggallana, who were originally followers of Sanjaya Belathiputra, the renowned agnostic, and were already quite well known at the time of their conversion. Ananda, Buddha's cousin, whom the *Jatakas* describe as the Treasurer of the Law, was another prominent devotee; he was Buddha's personal attendant and always accompanied him, taking loving care of his person and his daily needs. Buddha's son Rahula was also there, but he did not rise to prominence in the sangha or enjoy any special privileges – there would be no dynastic succession in Buddhism.

But not all the close associates of Buddha were patricians. A few were indeed from the lowest strata of society, like Sunita the sweeper and Upali the barber, whom Buddha took particular care to honour. 'I have come from a humble family, I was poor and needy,' says Sunita about his emancipation, as quoted in the *Theragatha*. 'The work I performed was lowly, sweeping off withered flowers [in temples and palaces]. I was despised by men, looked down upon and lightly esteemed. With submissive mien I showed respect to many. Then I beheld Buddha with his band of monks, as he passed, the great hero, into the most important town of Magadha. Then I cast away my burden and ran to bow myself in reverence before him. From pity for me he halted, the highest among men, [and admitted me into the sangha].'

Buddha recognised no social distinctions, and was scornful of those who claimed status by birth. However, he never directly challenged the caste system – his attitude towards it was of detachment, not of rebellion. Buddhism was not a social reform movement – it was not a movement against the established order, but outside it; its concerns were of another plane altogether.

All men, irrespective of their caste origins, can attain nirvana if they are compassionate, maintained Buddha. 'If unrighteous, all castes are sure to sink to hell,' the *Jatakas* quote him as saying; 'all castes are purified if they are righteous and act well.' In exact opposition to what the *Bhagavad Gita* would later hold, Buddha asserted, again according to the *Jatakas*, that the lives of the lowly would be transformed by their association with the wise, just as 'sweet frankincense when wrapped in a leaf, the leaf itself will smell sweet.' The distinctions between man and man on the basis of class and caste, race and tribe, are all superficial and transitory, Buddha contended. As the *Jatakas* would have it:

> *With canvas of many a tint pavilions may be made ...*
> *But the shades of all are always of one colour.*

The egalitarianism of Buddha did not, however, extend to women. He was implacably prejudiced against them, reflecting the common bias of ascetics everywhere, though he welcomed the patronage of wealthy women and accepted the hospitality even of courtesans. Once, while camping in Sravasti, Buddha spoke to monks at length on the fatal craving of men for women. 'Brethren, I know of no other single form by which a man's heart is enslaved as it is by that of a woman,' *Anguttara Nikaya* quotes him as saying. 'Brethren, a woman's form obsesses a man's heart. Brethren, I know of no other single sound by which a man's heart is enslaved as it is by the voice of a woman ... Brethren, I know of no other single scent ... savour ... touch by which a man's heart is so enslaved as it is by the scent, savour and touch of a woman ...'

Women are of the earth, men of the spirit. Buddha saw women as the perpetuators of life that is sorrow, the cause of birth, of rebirth too. Moreover, women, and the family ties they epitomise, are the chief impediments to the attainment of spiritual goals by men. Worse, women are in themselves evil – they are 'lustful, profligate, vile and degraded,' contend the *Jatakas*. 'Like the course of a fish in water is the character of women. Robbers with many artifices, with them truth is hard to find. To them a lie is like the truth, and the truth is like a lie ... No heed should be paid either to their likes or to their dislikes.' Further, Buddha once told Ananda, 'Women are soon angered, Ananda; women are full of passion, Ananda; women are envious, Ananda; women are stupid, Ananda. That is the reason, Ananda ... why women have no place in public assemblies, do not carry on any business, and do not earn their living by any profession.'

Buddha was equally harsh in his comments on the other religious leaders of the age, orthodox as well as heterodox sages. He set himself apart from them all. 'Whereas some recluses and Brahmins, while living on food provided by the faithful, are tricksters, droners out of holy words for pay, diviners, exorcists, ever hungering to add gain to gain, Gautama the recluse holds aloof from such deception and patter,' state the *Silas*. Buddha found it ridiculous that Brahmins should claim special sanctity for themselves, simply because they could recite the compositions of Vedic sages – that, he said, was like an actor imagining himself to be a king because he plays the role of a king on stage. Buddha was equally scornful of their blind acceptance of Vedic tenets as immutable wisdom. 'Like a chain of blind men ... is the discourse of Brahmins,' he said. 'He who is in front sees nothing, he who is in the middle sees nothing, he who is behind sees nothing ... Is not then the faith of the Brahmins vain?'

Brahmins, we should assume, did not take kindly to such comments. Moreover, the spread of Buddha's non-ritualistic sect threatened their very profession and livelihood, and his rejection of the caste system imperilled their dominant social position. Yet the opposition between Buddhists and Brahmins led to no serious direct confrontation. Brahmins, operating mainly among the rural folk, generally ignored the radical sects as transient urban fads of little consequence. There is hardly any mention of Buddha in the extant Brahminical literature. As for Buddhists, they did not consider Brahmins as their real opponents – their rivalry was mainly with radical sectarians like Jains and Ajivikas, and between these three groups there was intense competition, and some amount of intrigue, to win public patronage.

'The heretics were like fireflies after sunrise,' charge the *Jatakas*. 'No honours and gifts had they. In the street they stood, and cried out to the people: What, is the ascetic Gautama the Buddha? We are Buddhas also.' In their desperation they once enticed a beautiful Buddhist nun – 'full of all grace, a very sylph' – named Cincamanavika to pretend intimacy with Buddha, and accuse him of making her pregnant. They had her tie some padding on her abdomen under her clothes to make it appear as if she was with child, and denounce Buddha publicly when he was giving a discourse. But Buddha said to her calmly, 'Sister, whether thy words be true or false, none knoweth save thou and I.' The instant he spoke, the strings she had tied around her waist gave way, so that the padding fell off, exposing the hoax, and she herself (as the *Jatakas* tell the story) was swallowed up by flames miraculously bursting forth from the earth while she was fleeing from Buddha's angry devotees.

His own disciples sometimes created problems for Buddha. A recurrent source of annoyance was a boisterous band of young monks, the notorious Gang of Six, who, say the *Jatakas*, paid scant respect to the elders of the sangha and were ever 'inclined to quarrelling and strife and disputation.' No amount of admonition would make them change their ways. Even among senior monks violent disagreements erupted occasionally, disrupting the peace and harmony of the sangha. But these were minor irritants compared to the challenge to Buddha's authority by his cousin Devadatta. 'The base and wicked Devadatta,' state the *Jatakas*, won over King Ajatasatru of Magadha and 'got gain and honour for himself.' The king built a monastery for him, and Devadatta set himself up as a rival centre of power in the sangha, enticing a good number of monks to join him. This was a serious development, though Buddha made light of it, saying, 'To his own harm, brethren, have gain, favours and flattery come to Devadatta.'

The clash of the cousins was not just a power struggle. Major religious issues were involved in it, as is evident even from the highly biased reports in Buddhist texts. Their basic disagreement was over monastic discipline – while Buddha favoured moderation in ascetic practices, and permitted monks to live near towns and villages and even to accept laymen's invitations to dine, Devadatta wanted them to lead a more austere and reclusive life, camp only in jungles, live exclusively on alms, and dress 'only in clothes made of gathered rags.' Devadatta was also critical of the growing laxity of discipline in the sangha.

These differences eventually led to an open confrontation between the two. As the *Vinaya Pitaka* tells the story, one day some eight years before Buddha's death, at a gathering of monks, Devadatta 'rising from his seat and throwing his upper robe over one shoulder,' bowed to Buddha with folded palms and said: 'My Lord, the Exalted One is now grown old, is ... far gone in years ... Let now My Lord live without worry. Let Him dwell, given to such happiness as this life contains. Let Him hand over the care of the Order of Brethren unto me, and I will take charge of the Order of Brethren.' Buddha would not hear of that. 'Enough, Devadatta,' he said. 'Seek not to take charge of the Order of Brethren!'

Then, continues the text, 'a second time and yet a third time did Devadatta make the same request and get the same reply.' In the end Buddha, exasperated by Devadatta's persistence, closed the matter curtly, declaring rudely, 'Not even to Sariputra and Moggallana would I hand over the care of the Order of Brethren, much less to one like thee, a vile lick-spittle!' He then peremptorily expelled Devadatta from the sangha. Devadatta is said to have subsequently made several attempts on Buddha's life, all of which Buddha overcame with his miraculous powers. 'He that is born into his last existence cannot be killed,' Buddha claimed, according to the *Jatakas*. 'For like a lamp within a jar, even so securely within his breast burns the flame of his destiny to become an Arahat.'

It is difficult to see Devadatta as quite the villain that Buddhist texts make him out to be. He had, it does seem, good reason to want to take over the sangha. Monastic discipline had certainly grown slack towards the end of Buddha's life, when, for all his great physical vigour, age told on him. 'O brethren, I am now advanced in years, and some brethren, when they have been told "Let us go this way," take another way, and some drop my bowl and cloak on the ground,' complained Buddha once when he was in his late fifties. The worst was yet to come. Twenty years later he told Ananda: 'I am now a broken-down old man, aged, far gone in years, I have reached the journey's end ... My age is turning now eighty years. Just as, Ananda, a worn-out cart is kept going by being tied together with braces, even so, methinks, Ananda, the Tathagata's body is kept going with braces. Only at times when the Tathagata withdraws his attention from all externals, by the ceasing of his several feelings, by entering on and abiding in the objectless concentration of mind – only at such times, Ananda, is the Tathagata's body at ease.'

There were now clear signs of physical decline in Buddha. Ananda once remarked on this when Buddha was staying at Sravasti. 'Now on that occasion,' notes *Samyutta Nikaya*, 'the Exalted One, having risen at the eventide from His solitude, was sitting in the westering sun, letting it warm His back. Then the venerable Ananda came to the Exalted One and, while chafing His limbs with his hands, thus addressed the Exalted One: "A marvel it is, Lord! Strange it is, Lord! Now, Lord, the Exalted One's complexion is no longer clear and translucent; all his limbs are loosened and become wrinkled. Formerly His body was radiant, but now is seen a change of every organ – of sight, hearing, smelling, savouring, and body-feeling – all is changed, Lord." "Even so, Ananda, the nature of decay is inherent in youth," said Buddha.'

Buddha would however, despite his failing health, continue his missionary work till the very end. On his last tour, he travelled north from Rajagriha, and, crossing the Ganga at Pataliputra then under construction, proceeded to Vaishali, the capital of the Lichchavis. Vaishali was a dazzling city those days, rich and fun-loving, and was the home of the renowned courtesan Ambapali. Buddha in fact camped in Ambapali's mango grove in the suburbs of the city, and she, on hearing about it, hastened to pay him homage, and invited him and his monks to dine at her mansion. Buddha indicated his acceptance of her invitation by remaining, as was his custom, silent. A while later, Lichchavi nobles too arrived there, and they tried to persuade Buddha to dine with them instead, but he refused to change his mind, and Ambapali too declined to cancel her invitation, even though the nobles offered her a large sum of money as inducement. So it was that the last major public reception for Buddha was at the courtesan's house. Ambapali served Buddha with her own hands. After dining, Buddha delivered there a discourse, which, says the text, 'instructed, aroused, incited and gladdened' Ambapali, and she presented to the sangha the grove in which Buddha was camping.

Leaving Vaishali, Buddha paused once to look back at the gay city. 'This will be the last time, Ananda, that I will behold Vaishali. Come, Ananda, let us go.' He then proceeded to the village of Beluva to spend the rainy season in retreat. There he sent off the disciples with him, telling them, 'O mendicants, do you take up your abode for the rainy season roundabout Vaishali, each one according to the place where his friends and near companions may live. I shall enter upon the rainy season here at Beluva.'

At Beluva, in the change of season, Buddha fell ill. 'There fell upon him a dire sickness, and sharp pains came upon him, even unto death,' says the *Mahaparinibbana Sutta*, which describes Buddha's last days. 'But the Blessed One, mindful and self-possessed, bore them without complaint.' His only anxiety was that he should not die just then, thinking, 'It would not be right for me to pass away from existence without addressing the disciples, without taking leave of the sangha.' Death – nirvana – was the easier choice for him, than dragging on with life and continuing his missionary labours, but this was a temptation that he would resist. In fact, as Buddha lay critically ill, Mara appeared before him once again, to tempt him for the last time, telling him that, as his life's mission had been accomplished, he should reward himself with nirvana. Buddha spurned him, saying that he still had work to do, in training disciples who, 'having themselves grasped their master's teaching ... may proclaim, teach ... analyse, and make it plain; so that they may refute any wrong view arising ...'

Mara however argued (according to a Buddhist tradition recorded by Hsuan Tsang) that since Buddha had already saved innumerable souls, he could choose nirvana with a clear conscience. Buddha then took some grains of dust on his nail and asked Mara, 'Are the grains of dust on my nail equal to the dust of the whole earth or not?' Mara answered, 'The dust of the earth is much greater.' And Buddha said, 'Those who are saved are as the grains of earth on my nail; those not saved are like the grains of the whole earth. But after three months I shall die.'

When Buddha recovered, Ananda, who was with him, being anxious about the future of the sangha, requested him to lay down rules to guide his followers after his death. Buddha refused to do so. He would not claim that his teachings constituted the final and definitive truth. 'Be ye to yourselves, Ananda, your own light and your own refuge,' Buddha advised. 'Seek no other refuge. Whosoever now, Ananda, or after my departure, shall be his own light, his own refuge, and shall seek no other refuge, whosoever taketh the truth as his light and his refuge and shall seek no other refuge, such will henceforth, Ananda, be my true disciples, who walk in the right path.'

When the rains ceased, Buddha and his disciples set out again and proceeded to Kusinara. On the way he camped for a while at Pava, in the mango grove of a metalsmith named Cunda, a devotee of Buddha. Cunda invited them for a meal, and when Buddha accepted, he 'made ready choice food, both hard and soft, together with a quantity of fat hog's flesh, and sent a message as to the time to the Exalted One,' records *Digha Nikaya*. 'Then the Exalted One rose at early dawn and robed himself, and, taking the outer robe and bowl, started off for the house of Cunda ... attended by the Order of Brethren. When he got there, he sat down on a seat made ready. There sitting the Exalted One called to Cunda and said: "Cunda, as to that fat hog's flesh which you have prepared, serve me with it, but serve the brethren with whatsoever food, both soft and hard, you have prepared." "Very well, Lord," said Cunda ... and did accordingly.'

Buddha, it seems, had a weakness for pork – his favourite food, says *Milinda-panha*, was 'tender boar's flesh, and the rice porridge boiled in milk' – but that was not the reason why he asked Cunda to serve the meat only to him. He apparently had a premonition that the meat had spoiled. So when he had eaten, he called Cunda to him again and said, 'Cunda, whatever of the fat hog's flesh is remaining, bury that in a hole in the ground. For I can see no one in this world, Cunda, together with the world of the *devas* ... by whom that food when eaten can be digested, save only by the Tathagata.' 'Very well, Lord,' replied Cunda. He did what he was told, and went and sat near Buddha, who then delivered a discourse to him and left.

'Now when the Exalted One had eaten the food given by Cunda ... a grievous sickness came upon him, a dysentery, and strong pains set in, like to end in death. Those pains did the Exalted One endure unflinchingly, calm and composed.' He knew his end was near, so he called Ananda to him and said, 'Let us go, Ananda, towards Kusinara.' Kusinara, now called Kasia, was a small town on the river Chota Gandak, about 130 kilometres east of Kapilavastu. Buddha was going home to die.

But he barely made it to Kusinara. On the way, quite ill now, he stepped aside from the road, to rest under a tree. 'Come now, Ananda! Prepare my robe by folding it in four. I am weary. I will sit down.'

'Even so, Lord,' said Ananda, and folded the robe into four for Buddha to sit.

'Come now, Ananda! Do you bring me water to drink. I am thirsty.'

Ananda was reluctant to leave Buddha's side, on the excuse that the water in the nearby stream was muddy as a caravan of 500 carts had just then crossed the ford. Buddha had to ask him thrice before he would go. 'So be it, Lord,' he said at last, and taking a bowl went down to the stream, which he found to his surprise to be running clear. Buddha's thoughts now turned to Cunda. He did not want the poor man to blame himself for his death. He therefore asked Ananda to assure Cunda that serving the last meal to him was a meritorious deed, which enabled him to 'utterly pass away' – to attain nirvana – and so he should not have any regrets about it.

After resting for a while under the tree, Buddha and Ananda, along with a few other monks, crossed the stream and went on to Kusinara. When they reached the Sala Grove at the outskirts of the town, Buddha said to Ananda: 'Look you, Ananda! Get ready a couch between the twin Sala trees. I am weary, Ananda. I will lie down.' When the bed was got ready, 'then the Exalted One lay down on His right side in the posture of a lion, with one foot resting on the other, calm and composed,' continues the *Digha Nikaya.* 'Then said the Exalted One to the venerable Ananda: 'See, Ananda! All-abloom are the twin Sala trees; with unseasonal blossoms do they shower down upon the body of the Tathagata ... in worship of the Tathagata. Moreover, heavenly frankincense comes falling from the sky ... And heavenly music sounds in the sky ... and heavenly songs are wafted from the sky in worship of the Tathagata. Yet not thus is the Tathagata truly honoured, revered ... Whosoever, Ananda, be he brother or sister, or lay-brother or lay-sister, whosoever dwells in the fulfilment of dharma ... whosoever walks uprightly in accordance with dharma, he it is that truly honours, reveres ... the Tathagata in the perfection of worship ...'

It was the full-moon day of the month of Vesakha (May), as it was on the day of Buddha's enlightenment. Ananda noticed that Buddha's skin had now once again 'become clear and exceeding bright,' as on the day of his enlightenment, and he knew that his master's death was near. It saddened Ananda that Buddha should die in an obscure town, and he, according to the *Jatakas,* pleaded, 'O Blessed One, suffer not your end to be in this sorry little town, this rough little town in the jungle ... Shall not Rajagriha or some other great city be the death-place of Buddha?' Buddha consoled him saying that Kusinara was a fitting enough place for him to die, for it was once a 'a mighty city encompassed by jewelled walls twelve leagues round.'

As Buddha lay dying, Ananda began to weep. 'Not so, Ananda. Weep not, sorrow not,' Buddha consoled him. 'Have I not ere this said to thee, Ananda, that from all that man loves and from all that man enjoys, from that he must part ... It may be, Ananda, that ye shall say: the world has lost its master ... Ye must not think thus, Ananda. The dharma and *vinaya* (discipline) which I have taught and preached unto ye, these are your masters when I am gone hence.'

Soon after that Buddha gave his final instructions on sangha matters. He then asked the assembled monks whether they had any last doubts or questions. He asked this thrice, but each time they remained silent. Finally Buddha said: 'Hearken, O brethren, I do remind ye: everything that cometh into being passeth away. Strive without ceasing.' These were his last words.

When Buddha died, 'the earth quaked and thunder rolled,' it is said. When some of the brethren began to wail, they were cautioned against it by an elder – to mourn the dissolution of a composite being, as all creatures are, was against the very spirit of Buddha's teaching. And Brahma himself, according to the *Mahaparinibbana Sutta*, had on that occasion consolingly chanted:

They all, all beings that have life, shall lay
Aside their complex forms – that aggregation
Of mental and material qualities,
That gives them, in heaven or on earth,
Their fleeting individuality.

What was to be done with Buddha's mortal remains? Buddha had given no instructions about it. 'How, Lord, are we to deal with the body of the Tathagata?' Ananda had asked Buddha on his deathbed. 'Worry not about the body-rites of the Tathagata, Ananda,' Buddha had replied. 'Look you, Ananda! Strive for your own welfare ... dwell heedful, ardent, and resolute. There are discreet nobles, discreet Brahmins and heads of households, Ananda, believers in the Tathagata – they will see to the body-rites of the Tathagata.'

Now it so happened that a number of chieftains of the local tribe of Mallas had gathered at Kusinara at this time to pay their last respects to Buddha. They assumed the responsibility for his funeral. 'And the Mallas of Kusinara,' says *Mahaparinibbana Sutta*, 'took perfumes and garlands, and all musical instruments, and five hundred suits of apparel, and went to ... where the body of the Blessed One lay.' They perfumed the place and adorned it with garlands and canopies, and 'there they passed the day in paying honour, reverence, respect, and homage to the remains of the Blessed One with dancing, and hymns, and music.' This went on for six days. On the seventh day they decided to take the body and perform the cremation at a spot to the south of the city. 'And thereupon eight chieftains among the Mallas bathed their heads, and clad themselves in new garments with the intention of bearing the body of the Blessed One. But, behold, they could not lift it up.' The reason they could not lift it, Anuruddha told them, was that the spirits wanted the body to be taken into the city through the northern gate, and, passing through the city in solemn procession, carry it out through the eastern gate to 'the shrine of the Mallas called Makuta-bandhana, to the east of the city,' and there perform the cremation. When the chieftains agreed to this, states the *Sutta*, a shower of flowers fell from the skies over the city covering 'even the dustbins and rubbish heaps knee-deep with Mandarava flowers from heaven!'

The chieftains asked Ananda how they should treat Buddha's remains. 'As men treat the remains of a king of kings,' said Ananda, and explained: 'They wrap the body of a king of kings ... in a new cloth. When that is done, they wrap it in cotton wool. When that is done, they wrap it in a new cloth, and so on till they have wrapped the body in five hundred successive layers of both kinds. Then they place the body in an oil vessel of iron, and cover that close with another oil vessel of iron. They then build a funeral pile of all kinds of perfumes, and burn the body of the king of kings. And then at the four crossroads they erect a monument to the king of kings. This ... is the way in which they treat the remains of a king of kings.'

After the funeral, there was nearly a battle between the Mallas and the other chieftains and kings of the region who by then had gathered there, for sharing Buddha's relics. The Mallas initially refused to share them with anyone, saying that Buddha had died in their land. But Dona, a venerable old Brahmin, intervened in the dispute, reminding them of Buddha's message of peace and forbearance. The chieftains then peacefully divided the relics into eight portions and distributed them among the claimants, and each of them built monuments over them in their own domain.

In time all these monuments would turn to dust, leaving no trace. Even the teachings of Buddha would be forgotten in his homeland. And that, in a perverse sense, was a vindication of Buddha's philosophy. 'Everything that cometh into being passeth away,' he had taught. All existence is transitory.

MONKEY AND THE PITCH-TRAP

Once, soon after his enlightenment, when Buddha was asked by an ascetic who his teacher was, he replied, 'I had no teacher,' claiming absolute originality for his ideas. This was an overstatement. Some of the key concepts of his teaching were indeed unique and his own, but there was also much in it that was drawn from the ideas swirling about in India during the intellectual ferment of the sixth century BC. Buddha would, as part of the then normal training of Kshatriyas, have acquired some Vedic scholarship in his childhood, and later, while living in the hermitages of Alara Kalama and Rudraka Ramaputra, and during his wanderings with ascetics, would also have become conversant with the innovative philosophic notions of the age. All these went into the shaping of Buddha's philosophy, and he often indirectly acknowledged his link with the Vedic tradition by claiming himself to be a true Brahmin, by virtue of his lifestyle and vocation. 'Brethren, I am a Brahmin given to begging,' he often said of himself.

Buddhism was as much an offshoot of the old faith as its repudiation. 'Brahminical speculation,' notes Hermann Oldenberg, 'anticipated Buddhism in diction as well as in thought ... [and provided it with] not merely a series of its most important dogmas, but ... [also] the bent of its religious thought and feeling ... If in Buddhism the proud attempt has been made to conceive a deliverance in which man delivers himself, to create a faith without god, it was Brahminical speculation [in the Upanishads] which prepared the way for this thought ... [having] thrust back the idea of a god step by step.'

This debt cannot be denied. But equally, it cannot be denied that there are fundamental conceptual differences between Buddhism and the Upanishads, and that in ethical temper they are altogether unlike each other. Buddha adopted the Upanishadic concepts of samsara and karma with some modifications, but rejected its crucial belief in the eternal, all-pervasive and changeless Atman-Brahman. Instead, he conceived a world without any permanent core of self or soul, in which everything is ever in flux and mutation, and is never the same from moment to moment, and from life to life. To hush this incessant turbulence, and thus attain a self-contained state of calm bliss, is the goal of Buddhist spiritual endeavour unlike the merging of Atman in Brahman propounded by the Upanishads. Further, while the Upanishadic sages coyly and somewhat incongruously accepted the sacred authority of the Vedas, Buddha rejected it outright, and questioned the value of prayers and sacrifices. As the *Jatakas* candidly observe,

> *The Vedas have no hidden power to save …*
> *None, however zealously he prays,*
> *Or feeds fuel to the sacrificial fire,*
> *Gains merit by his mummeries …*
> *These greedy liars propagate deceit,*
> *And fools believe the fictions they repeat …*
> *Why does not Brahma set his creatures right,*
> *If his wide power no limits can restrain?*
> *Why is his hand so rarely spread to bless?*
> *Why are his creatures all condemned to pain?*
> *Why does he not to all give happiness?*
> *Why do fraud, lies, and ignorance prevail?*
> *Why does falsehood triumph, truth and justice fail? …*
> *These cruel cheats, as ignorant as vile,*
> *Weave their long frauds the simple to beguile …*

Elsewhere the *Jatakas* state that, 'failing just works, a thousand Vedas will not bring safety, or save one from evil plight.' The Vedas, whatever their original spiritual potency, had by Buddha's time become calcified wisdom, incapable of throwing any fresh light to illumine the evolving human predicament. Worse, the dead hand of Vedic tradition had become an actual impediment to spiritual growth. 'Worst of all, perhaps, from Buddha's standpoint, religion was straying … away from the insistent, poignant, practical needs of men and women,' observes Brutt. 'It was not leading them toward true fulfilment and more dependable happiness; it was becoming mired in obstructive tradition, repetitious rite, and dead or cantankerous dogma.'

Ethics take the place of faith in Buddhism. Often Buddha derided the very concept of god as an omniscient, omnipotent entity. Has any Brahmin versed in the Vedas – or his teacher, or the teacher of his teacher, or even the original composers of the Vedic hymns – 'ever seen Brahma face to face?' Buddha once asked Vasettha, a learned Brahmin. Obviously not. This being so, continued Buddha, 'the talk of these Brahmins … turns out to be ridiculous, mere words, a vain and empty thing.' The Brahminical practices of worshipping gods and performing sacrifices are of no use whatsoever, Buddha maintained; self-mastery and purity are what are needed for salvation. One should be 'free from anger, free from malice, pure in mind, and master of himself.'

'As the echo belongs to the sound, and the shadow to the substance, so misery will overtake the evil doer without fail,' Buddha warned. Man should lead a moral life, not because gods have ordained it, but because it is the only sensible way to live. Buddha however did not altogether deny the existence of gods as supernatural beings – Buddhist texts do occasionally mention Brahma and several other Vedic gods – but he denied that they had any power over worldly affairs. Gods did not create the world; they do not control the world. They are only special forms of life and are, like all other forms of life, ever subject to mutation.

In these core concepts, Buddha remained consistent in all his discourses. There are, however, many incongruities and contradictions in Buddhist texts. Buddha's discourses, always given extemporaneously, were not in every case consistent with each other, as his ideas evolved and changed in time, and were in any case variously remembered and preserved by his disciples according to their particular predilections. The texts suffered further corruption while being transmitted orally from generation to generation, and when interpolations were added to them to suit the changing environment or to serve sectarian interests. The language that Buddha used in his discourses was probably Ardha-Magadhi, the dialect of ancient Bihar, but none of his sayings is preserved in its original language. 'All we have,' observes Conze, 'are translations of what may have been the early canon into other Indian languages, chiefly Pali and a particular form of Buddhist Sanskrit.'

No one wrote down Buddha's discourses as he delivered them. Though writing probably had been introduced into India well before Buddha's time, it could not possibly have been used at this time to transcribe lengthy discourses. Ananda and Upali, senior monks and close associates of Buddha, are said to have repeated from memory many of his discourses at the great council of monks held in Rajagriha soon after Buddha's death, but the veracity of this tradition, indeed the historicity of the council itself, is in doubt. Buddhist texts often begin with the phrase *evam maya srutam*: 'Thus have I heard.' The texts are recollections, or presumed recollections, of what Buddha said and did.

Nevertheless, despite all these uncertainties about Buddhist scriptures, it is quite probable that the *Tripitaka*, the three earliest extant Buddhist texts, truly present the substance of Buddha's original teachings, though perhaps not their exact tone and phraseology. These ancient texts deserve credence because of the extreme care usually taken in India to preserve scriptures orally, and also because these different texts are generally in consonance with each other. But even in the case of the *Tripitaka* it cannot be established, as Woodward comments, 'how much of this is the genuine utterance of the Buddha, and how much is worked up and put into the Master's mouth.'

Later, when Buddhism split into various sects, many of Buddha's original teachings were radically modified, sometimes beyond recognition. This would not have surprised – perhaps not even displeased – Buddha. In a mutable world, how could ideas possibly remain immutable! Buddha in any case never claimed that he was expounding a divinely revealed final wisdom. Rather, he saw himself as a questing mortal, a guide who removed mental blinkers and pointed out new avenues for gnostic exploration. He did not profess to be a saviour, one who would carry mankind on his shoulders to salvation. Each man had to find his own way. 'You yourself must strive,' Buddha told his followers; 'Buddhas are but sign-posts.'

'Lord,' said Kalamas of Kesaputta, a lay inquirer, to Buddha one day, 'there are here some recluses and Brahmins ... [who] extol and magnify their own views, but the views of others they spitefully abuse, depreciate, and pluck bare.' And Buddha said: 'Now, Kalamas, do not ye go by hearsay, nor by what is handed down by others, nor by what people say, nor by what is stated on the authority of your traditional teachings.' Do not even depend on abstract reasoning, Buddha warned. Each man has to choose for himself, out of his own experience, what is good for his spiritual welfare. Practicality should be the main consideration. 'Kalamas, when you know of yourself ... [that certain teachings] when followed and put in practice, conduce to loss and suffering, then reject them,' Buddha counselled.

Even faith in Buddha by itself would not save anyone, any more than mere faith in the physician would cure a patient. 'A man must take medicine to be cured; the mere sight of the physician is not enough,' Buddha is quoted by Asvaghosha as saying. 'Likewise the mere sight of me enables no one to conquer suffering; he will have to meditate for himself about the gnosis I have communicated.' Buddha considered even dharma, the central doctrine of Buddhism, to be only of transitory value, and compared it to a boat one uses to cross a river and abandons to move on – dharma is useful to cross the river of woe that is life, but one should not burden oneself with it after getting across. Dharma, he cautioned his disciples, 'is something to leave behind, not to take with you.'

Such commonsensical, pragmatic advice was characteristic of Buddha. He had little interest in abstruse metaphysical speculations, but was primarily concerned with the everyday problems of everyday life. King Ajatasatru of Magadha, during his only meeting with Buddha, is reported to have asked the sage: 'What in the world is the good of your renunciation, of joining an Order like yours? Other people ... by following ordinary crafts get something out of them. They can make themselves comfortable in this world, and keep their families in comfort. Can you, Sir, declare to me any such immediate fruit, visible in this world, of the life of a recluse?' Buddha answered the king at length – it runs to over nineteen printed pages in English translation – pointing out that a recluse enjoyed contentment, self-confidence, joy, peace, supra-human wisdom, and so on, and that even a slave who becomes a recluse would be venerated by his former master. This particular answer was probably modulated by Buddha to suit the ears of his worldly questioner, but his teachings, though not concerned with material gains, had much to do with temporal life, the all too real and vexing problems of the psychological health of man and society. Buddha was really a counsellor in the garb of a prophet.

'There is no path in the sky,' Buddha used to say. We have to find our passage here on our poor earth, picking our way through the garbage of the world and morasses of life. Solutions to the problems of life have to be found in life itself, not in metaphysical fancies.

The basic problem of life, as Buddha saw it, is transience. 'Even down to a tiny seed of sesame, there is no such thing as a compound thing which is permanent; all are transient, all must break up,' state the *Jatakas*. All must break up, because all, even the most seemingly homogenous and adamantine objects, are agglomerations of different elements, and these elements eventually detach from each other as the energy that holds them together is depleted. Not only that, even the apparent integrity of objects during their brief existence is illusory, for the elements that constitute the objects are for ever realigning, and the balance between these elements, as well as the potency (*prapti*) of the individual elements themselves, are ever fluctuating.

Life is an endless stream of chain reactions. All that exists, every being and every object is always, in every passing moment, in the process of becoming something else. We, as individuals, in our mental and physical constitution, are not the same from instant to instant, nor is anything else in the world the same from instant to instant. Becoming never leads to being. Nothing, absolutely nothing, is permanent, and there is no unchanging entity underlying the world, no Atman or Brahman. There is no soul. Nor is there an enduring self. The so-called self, an individual's particular identity, is nothing but a passing configuration of the elements of which he is constituted. The self changes when the constituent elements reconfigure, as they constantly do, and the self disappears when the elements finally break up, as all compound things inevitably do. 'The body, as well as the soul, exists only as a complex of manifold interconnected origination and decease, but neither body nor soul has existence as a self-contained substance, sustaining itself per se,' comments Oldenberg.

Our sense of self, and the seeming continuity of self – our feeling that we are the same person from day to day and year to year – is an illusion created by memory. Similarly our bodies too, which seem distinctive and identifiable to us, are not really the same from day to day. *Nama* and *rupa*, name and form, are merely identification tags that we accept as a pragmatic convention. The tag is not the person. In body and mind we are not what we from memory imagine ourselves to be, or what others believe us to be. We are, as Anuruddha, a modern Buddhist says, 'like a river which maintains one constant form, one seeming identity, though not a single drop remains today of all the volume that composed the river yesterday.' We cannot, as the saying goes, step into the same river twice. Nor can we ever meet the same person twice.

Something in us dies every passing moment, and something new comes to life in its place. But ultimately it is death, not life, that prevails. Everything that lives is born doomed to die. 'How can we ever feel secure, when from the womb onwards death follows us like a murderer with his sword raised to kill us?' asks Asvaghosha in *Buddhacharita*. 'Not in the sky, nor in the depths of the sea, nor in mountain clefts is there a place on earth where a man can be and death cannot overcome him,' observes the *Dhammapada*. Or, as the *Jatakas* would have it,

He who draws his mortal breath
forfeit every hour to death.
Be he standing, sitting still,
moving, resting, what he will,
in the twinkling of an eye,
in a moment death is nigh.

Nothing lasts. The final result of every gain and achievement and of every happiness – 'the short-lived pleasure of the frightened in the arms of the frightened,' as the *Dhammapada* puts it – is loss and desolation and sorrow. This simple, commonplace, yet terrifying fact of life was what engaged Buddha during his many years of spiritual quest, and led him eventually to formulate the concept of the Four Noble Truths. 'A withered leaf fell before him. In it he came to see the principles of decay and death,' the *Jatakas* state. Life is sorrow because everything in life, material as well as mental states, including life itself, is transient.

Yet hope lives eternally, eternally breeding despair. Buddha illustrated this point with the telling parable of the monkey and the pitch-trap. When a hunter sets up the trap, said Buddha, wise monkeys keep well away from it, 'but a greedy, foolish monkey goes up to the pitch and handles it with one paw, and his paw sticks fast in it. Then, thinking "I'll free my paw," he seizes it with the other paw, but that too sticks fast. To free both paws he seizes them with one foot, and that sticks fast. To free both paws and one foot, he lays hold of them with the other foot, but that too sticks fast. To free both paws and both feet, he lays hold of them with his muzzle, and that sticks fast. So, brethren, that monkey, thus caught in five ways, lies down and howls, a prey for the hunter.'

Such too is the human predicament. The pursuit of happiness does not bring happiness. All human endeavours are ultimately counterproductive. 'The iron itself createth the rust which slowly consumes it,' notes the *Dhammapada*. As Santideva, a sixth century AD Buddhist philosopher wrote, 'Eager to escape sorrow, men rush into sorrow; from desire for happiness they blindly slay their own happiness, enemies to themselves.' The consequences of all this are not confined to just this one life, but go on endlessly, life after life, as the karmic web of our own making binds us to the ever-spinning wheel of samsara.

There is no end to life. Or death. There is no end to sorrow. But how did man ever get into this predicament? The root cause, according to Buddha, is desire – *tanha*, he called it: thirst. 'Driven on by craving men run round and round like a hunted hare,' states the *Dhammapada*. We are, said Buddha, held hostages for life by 'the brigands of the five senses.' The answer to the problems of life, it seemed to him, was simple and obvious. Since desire is the cause of misery, the means to end misery is to snuff out desire altogether. If the candle does not burn, wax will not melt.

Buddha often compared the world to a house on fire, from which sensible people should flee. 'Why this laughter, why this jubilation, when this world is burning, burning?' he demanded. Unfortunately, few see themselves as living in a house on fire, and do not therefore seek the means to escape from it.

The *Jatakas* compare the plight of man to that of 'a hawk that seized a piece of meat in a butcher's shop and darted up into the air. The other birds surrounded him and struck at him with feet, claws and beaks. Unable to bear the pain he dropped the piece of meat. Another bird seized it. It too in like manner being hard pressed let the meat fall. Then another bird pounced on it, and whoever got the meat was pursed by the rest, and whoever let it go was left in peace ... These desires of ours are pieces of meat. To those that grasp at them is sorrow, and to those that let them go is peace.' This lesson is reiterated in another story in the *Jatakas*, about a woman who makes an assignation with her lover, and sits up waiting anxiously for him through the night on the threshold of her house, hoping that he will come at any moment, but finally, at daybreak, realising that he will not come, lies down and slumbers peacefully. 'While hope ... brings sorrow, hopelessness brings peace,' comments the text. Said Buddha: 'From yearning cometh sorrow; from yearning cometh fear; whosoever is free from yearning, for him there is no sorrow.'

The complete annihilation of desire is essential for man's psychological and physical well-being, and to free him from the cycle of samsara. 'Cut down the whole forest of desire, not single trees; danger lurks in that forest. Having cut down trees and uprooted the weeds of desire you are free, O monks,' advised Buddha. Free from sorrow, man then achieves perfect serenity. 'Tranquil is his thought, tranquil are his word and deed ...'

The means for extinguishing desire, as enunciated by Buddha in his first sermon, is the Noble Eight-fold Path. This is the path of moderation, which avoids the extremes of both renunciation and indulgence, and views even the over-anxious pursuit of goodness and virtue as harmful. 'A blade of *kusa* grass wrongly handled cuts the hand; asceticism wrongly practised leads downward, to hell,' warns the *Dhammapada.* This counsel for moderation applies to the discipline of the body as well as of the mind. Buddha, contrary to the common attitude of ascetics, did not hold the body in contempt, or advocate its mortification for spiritual gain. Neither the body nor the mind is better or worse than the other. And just as we have to be attentive to the welfare of the mind, so also we should take good care of the body, for physical health and comfort are essential for spiritual serenity. 'Health is the greatest of gifts; contentment is the greatest wealth; trust is the best of relationships; nirvana is the highest happiness,' Buddha proclaimed. The pursuit of physical and mental health is not, however, a goal in itself in Buddhism, but only the means to attain nirvana.

But what is nirvana? It is a mystic rather than a philosophic concept, and Buddha, uncomfortable with abstract speculations – and also perhaps because of the ineffability of mystical experiences – never defined it with precision. There is ambiguity not only about what nirvana really means, but also about when and how it is attained. While some Buddhist philosophers held that nirvana is attained on death, others claimed that it is a state that can be attained in life itself. Buddha was once questioned by 'the venerable Radha,' a senior monk, about the purpose of Buddhist discipline. The object, said Buddha, was 'to bring about dispassion.'

'But dispassion, Lord – for what purpose is it?' asked Radha.

'Dispassion, Radha, is to get release.'

'But release, Lord – what is it for?'

'Release, Radha, means nirvana.'

'But nirvana, Lord – what is the aim of that?'

'This, Radha, is a question that goes too far ... Rooted in nirvana, Radha, the holy life is lived. Nirvana is its goal. Nirvana is its end.'

Another time, when Buddha was in Sravasti, he said that 'the destruction of craving is nirvana,' and again that 'the ceasing of becoming is nirvana.' Buddha seems to have conceived nirvana as the termination of karmic mutation, a state of absolute stillness that presumably can be achieved by man at any stage of his life, or on his death. 'Illusion utterly has passed from me; cool am I now, gone out all fire within,' sings a monk in *Thera-theri-gatha*, about the state of beatitude he achieved. Early Buddhists compared nirvana to a flame being extinguished, the complete cessation of the subjective being and of the temporal hankerings that cause sorrow and bind one to samsara. Nirvana is often described as a state of enlightenment or super-consciousness. 'Nirvana is where it is recognised that there is nothing but what is seen of the mind itself; where there is no attachment to external objects, existent or non-existent,' maintains the *Lankavatara Sutra.* Max Müller considered nirvana to be 'a completion but not an extinction of being ... the entry of the spirit upon its rest, an eternal beatitude.' The *Dhammapada* puts it this way: 'If you make yourself still like a broken gong, you have already reached Nirvana.' And again: 'A tamed man riding on his tamed self arrives there (Nirvana).'

These are vain attempts to define what is essentially undefinable. Nagasena in *Milinda-panha,* when asked by king Menander to describe nirvana, said, 'One cannot say of nirvana that it arises or that it does not arise, or that it is to be produced, or that it is past or future or present, or that it is cognisable by the eye, ear, nose, tongue or body.' In that case, said the king, 'nirvana is a thing that is not; nirvana is not.' Said Nagasena, 'Sire, nirvana is; nirvana is cognisable by mind.' The king wanted this point to be elucidated.

'Is there, sire, what is called wind?' Nagasena asked.

'Yes, revered sir.'

'Please, sire, show the wind by its colour or configuration or as thin or thick or long or short.'

'But it is not possible, revered Nagasena, for the wind to be shown ...'

'If, sire, it is not possible for the wind to be shown, well then, there is no wind.'

'I, revered Nagasena, know that there is wind ... but I am not able to show the wind.'

'Even so, sire, there is nirvana, but it is not possible to show nirvana by colour or configuration,' said Nagasena.

Nirvana can be known only from within itself, not from outside it. It can be known only by attaining it, not otherwise. It cannot be known from others, by hearsay. Nor can nirvana be attained as the automatic result of any spiritual exercise – one cannot by will and action set the course and calendar of nirvana, any more than one can by will and action set the course and calendar of the wind. In fact, the very hankering for nirvana, like the hankering for anything else, would prevent its realisation. To attain nirvana, one simply has to lead a dharmic life – and wait. Nirvana comes in the fullness of its own time. Buddha once compared this process to farming – though the peasant takes every care in preparing his field and in sowing the seeds, he can do nothing to get the seeds to germinate according to his will. The seeds will sprout on their own, according to their nature and in the maturity of time.

Of all forms of life, man alone, Buddha maintained, is capable of achieving nirvana, for he, being a rational creature, has the free will to choose the quality of his life, instead of being a helpless victim of karmic forces. The critical factor here is the rationality of man, to which Buddha attributed his own enlightenment, saying that 'through rational thinking and insight arose comprehension.'

'Ignorance is the worst taint,' Buddha held, and placed great emphasis on acquiring right knowledge and insight, maintaining that it was essential to know why samsara goes on, in order to be able to stop the process. 'Not to know [that life is] suffering, not to know the cause of suffering, not to know the [cause of the] cessation of suffering, not to know the path which leads to the cessation of suffering, this is called ignorance,' states the *Majjhima Nikaya*. The qualities of mind required to gain knowledge are, according to Buddhism, clear memory, intellectual stamina, concentration, empathy, and lucid, unbiased and tranquil investigation. Early Buddhism was an intellectually elitist religion, and Buddha generally shunned fools, saying, 'A fool associating himself with a wise man all his life sees not the truth, even as the spoon enjoys not the taste of the soup.'

The inquiry into the nature of existence led Buddha to formulate the law of dependant origination, which explains phenomena in terms of causation. The chain of causation, as given in the *Mahavagga*, is a complicated process. What started off this process was ignorance, which initially caused subject and object to come together. Out of this pairing was born consciousness. From consciousness sprang the six senses (including mind), and these enabled links between subject and object to be established. The links in turn engendered sensations, thus rousing desire. Desire led to attachment, and from attachment sprang existence with its concomitant misery. One thing led to another, and thus evolved, over the aeons, our infinite world and its complex, ceaseless processes.

Nothing in this world happens in isolation. Everything that happens and every circumstance and every form of existence arises out of what has already happened and out of previous circumstances and forms of existence. Everything is caused, everything is a cause. But this is not a simple matter of direct cause and effect, but a process of incredible complexity, for the thoughts and actions of even those with whom we are not in contact and who are far from us in time and space – in this life and in this world as well as in previous lives and in other worlds – affect us through untold intermediaries or through their general effect on life on earth.

Everything is connected with everything else, through all time and all space.

Buddha, unlike some of his contemporaries, did not wholly deny the reality of the temporal world, but took, as in everything else, a middle position, between the extreme views of asserting the total reality of the temporal world and of its total denial. The temporal world exists, Buddha held, but because it is ever in instantaneous transition, no precise and meaningful observation or description of anything in it is possible. We can only know the process, not particular states. The world we think we know, the world of particulars, is a representation or image of reality, but is not itself real, for it is a purely mental construction stored in memory, and has no existence outside our consciousness. If consciousness ceases, the world as we know it would also cease.

Each of us makes up his own world. And we keep recreating this imaginary world to suit each passing moment. The only unchanging reality is the ceaselessness of change. This is the knowledge – the knowledge of the chain of causation, of the transitoriness of everything, and of the primacy of consciousness in the perception of reality – that Buddha considered as essential to release man from the clutches of karma and samsara, from the life that is sorrow.

What began with ignorance can be ended only by the elimination of ignorance. If the chain of causation is not severed with the scalpel of knowledge, life (and suffering) will go on for ever and ever, through transmigration, impelled by karma. There will be no end to it, because there is no end to time itself. Buddha, like many other thinkers of his age, considered time to be cyclic, a process of expansion and contraction, progress and decline, without beginning or end. Aeons (*kalpas*) were considered to be of incalculable length, which Buddha once described with engaging poetic fancy thus: 'Just as if, brother, there were a mighty mountain crag, four leagues in length, breadth, and height, without a crack or cranny, not hollowed out, one solid mass of rock, and a man should come at the end of every century, and with [the superfine] cloth of Varanasi should once on each occasion stroke that rock: sooner, brother, would that mighty mountain crag be worn away by this method … than the aeon.'

'Now what think ye, brethren? Which is the greater, all the mother's milk that ye have sucked in this long journey, for ever running through the round of rebirth, or the water in the four mighty oceans?' Buddha once asked his disciples. 'Greater is the milk sucked by us, Lord,' they answered. Only those who attain nirvana are released from the cycle of samsara. The unliberated, like the coward, dies again and again.

But what is it that transmigrates? Since Buddhism denies the existence of

Atman, what survives the perishing of the body? How can there be rebirth when there is no permanent entity to be reborn? Buddha explained this by stating that the consequences of karma do not cease just because the body ceases, but lead to a new creature being formulated according to the unfinished karma. 'The history of the individual,' Coomaraswamy observes, 'does not begin at birth.' Nor does it end with death. 'The new being,' Basham comments, 'suffers as a result of the action of the old one.'

The unfinished karma, like a chemical residue, sustains the chain of reactions that is samsara. Transmigration is then fundamentally no different from the process of mutation to which everything is subject in life, and is its continuation in another dimension. The dead man and the new creature are not of course the same entity, but then the living being is also not the same from day to day either. The only difference between the transmigratory mutation and the mutation in life is that the persistence of memory gives an illusion of continuity of identity to the living, and this sense of continuity is lost in the transmigrant being, as memory does not survive death. Buddhists often used the analogy of one lamp lighting another lamp to explain transmigration without soul. There is continuity here, but no continuity of identity – one flame produces the other flame, but they are not the same flames.

This explanation does not however close the issue. The analogy of the flame is in fact not quite appropriate, for the quality of the new flame is not determined by the quality of the old flame, while the quality of the new life is determined by the quality of the old life. In fact, transmigration as Buddha conceived it does not seem to be transmigration at all, since nothing transmigrates, neither soul nor personality. There is continuity from life to life, but it is only a continuity of the process.

There are other difficulties too with the Buddhist concept of transmigration. Since there is no continuity of individuality from life to life, and memory does not persist from life to life, there is also no continuity or accumulation of suffering from life to life. Suffering begins anew with each birth. The intensity of the suffering of the new being might depend on the karma of the old being, but this is of no concern for the old being, as the old being does not suffer in the new being. This being so, how does the eternal cycle of life and suffering matter to the individual? Why should he in this life be concerned with samsara at all, the sufferings of other lives in other times? Nirvana might be worthwhile for him as the means to gain equanimity in this life, but why should he seek to end samsara? It makes sense only as an altruistic concern, as an expression of compassion for the beings that are yet to be born, to prevent their suffering by preventing their birth, by means of terminating one's own karmic process. Here there is a convergence of utter selfishness and total altruism – the means to end one's own suffering is also the means to prevent the sufferings of other lives in other times.

Conceivably all creatures on earth will eventually attain nirvana. But what would happen then? Doubtless another cosmic cycle would then begin, since the cycle of time never ceases. But how can samsara begin again when the chain of causation has totally ceased with all creatures having attained nirvana? And how did the karmic process begin in the first place? Ignorance was the first cause, Buddhists maintain. But what caused ignorance? Since every action is also a reaction, how can there be an uncaused first action?

But is nirvana really a terminal state? In a world of ceaseless change, how can nirvana be permanent? Buddhists sometimes meet this paradox by claiming that nirvana is 'outside the universe.' But this is just a jugglery of words, a made-up explanation that explains nothing. Some later Buddhist sects would in fact deny the permanence of nirvana. But how can nirvana that is not permanent be nirvana at all? How can the flame be considered extinguished if it flames again?

There are many such puzzles in Buddhism. For instance, does not Buddha's exhortation to men to strive for nirvana violate the spirit of karmic determinism that he professed? If karma predetermines everything – what we are, what happens to us, and what we do – does it not also predetermine whether we would strive for nirvana or not, and whether we would attain it or not? On the other hand, if, as Buddha maintained, rationality frees man from being a passive subject of karma, then karma is not inescapable, is not absolute. But how can karma that is not absolute be karma at all? And is not the Buddhist idea of the momentariness of personality an overstatement? Is not the persistence of memory really the persistence of self? And finally, if consciousness is all, as Buddha held, then suffering is an illusion of the mind, and all that we need to do to end suffering is to switch off the mind. Is this what Buddha meant by nirvana, the disengagement of the mind from all sensations and feelings?

There are no clear answers to these puzzles. Like all religions, Buddhism too bristles with ambiguities and contradictions. But they really do not matter. It is not high metaphysics that distinguishes Buddhism, but the psychological solace it offers to man and the moral authority it imposes on him.

Buddha did not have the common vanity of philosophers to explain the cosmos and its processes. It was not that he had no views on these matters, but considered such mental excursions to be of no practical value. He mainly concentrated on life as we know it and on what needed to be done to improve its quality. Human conduct was what primarily concerned

Buddha. Once when he was in Kosambi, camping in a Sinsapa grove, he took a few Sinsapa leaves in his hand and asked his disciples: 'What think ye, brethren, which are more, these few Sinsapa leaves that I hold in my hand, or the other leaves yonder in the Sinsapa grove?' Those in the grove, they answered. And Buddha said, 'So also, brethren, is that much more, which I have learned and have not told you, than that which I have told you. And why, brethren, have I not told you that? Because, brethren, it brings you no profit, it does not conduce to progress in holiness, because it does not lead to the turning away from the earthly, to the subjugation of all desire, to the cessation of the transitory, to peace, to knowledge, to illumination, to nirvana.'

Another time, when Buddha was living in Sravasti, he was asked by Malunkyaputta, a monk, why he did not discuss questions about the ultimate nature of the world, the connection between body and soul, about life after death, and so on. Buddha answered him with a parable. 'Suppose, Malunkyaputta,' he said, 'a man were pierced with an arrow smeared with poison, and his close friends and relatives were to summon a physician, a surgeon. Then suppose the man says, "I will not have this arrow pulled out until I know of the man by whom I was pierced, his name and caste and clan, and whether he is tall or short or of middle stature, whether he is a black, dusky or sallow-skinned man; whether he is from this or that village or suburb or town. I will not have the arrow pulled out until I know of the bow by which I was pierced, whether it is a long-bow or a cross-bow ... not until I know of the bow-string by means of which I was pierced, whether it is made of creeper, or reed, or tendon, or hemp ... [not until I know whether the arrow is made] of a reed-shaft or a sapling ... [not until I know whether its feathers are] of a vulture or a heron, or of a kite or a peacock or of a hook-bill ... [not until I know whether the arrow] is bound with the tendon of an ox or a buffalo or a deer or a monkey ... [not until I know whether the arrow is] just an arrow, or a razor-edge or a splinter or a calf-tooth or a javelin-head or a barb-headed arrow." Well, Malunkyaputta, that man would die, but still the matter would not be found out by him.

'Just so, Malunkyaputta, he who should say, "I will not follow the holy life under the Exalted One until he declares unto me whether the world is eternal or not; whether what is the life, what is the body; whether one thing is the life, another is the body; whether the Tathagata is beyond death or not ..." Such a one would come to his end, but that thing would not be declared by the Tathagata ...

'The religious life, Malunkyaputta, does not depend on the dogma that the world is eternal; nor does the religious life ... depend on the dogma that the world is not eternal ... Whether the world is eternal or not, nevertheless there is birth, there is decay, there is death, there are sorrow and grief, woe, lamentation, and despair; and it is the destruction of these things that concerns me.'

Buddhism is usually considered to be a pessimistic, life-negating religion. It is indeed true that its philosophy does not place much value on temporal existence. And the Buddhist doctrine that everything in the world is impermanent has nihilistic overtones – if nothing is permanent, how can there be permanent values? And if all distinctions are illusory, how can there be any difference between right and wrong? And does not Buddhism's preoccupation with the individual and his pursuit of nirvana exclude public service and civic ethics? The Buddhist monk, as Burtt observes, does seem to 'show himself a selfish person, in forsaking ordinary social relationships and responsibilities so that, by the freedom from distraction of the homeless life, he can enter nirvana by himself.'

All this is true. But it is true only if we push Buddhist theory to its most extreme limit. Theory moreover does not have primacy in Buddhism. It is practice that counts. And in practice Buddhism is a life-affirming, altruistic, and socially active religion. It is a compassionate religion, though its compassion is dispassionate. As Burtt comments, 'By love ... Buddha meant no dependent attachment to a person or object ... but an unlimited self-giving compassion flowing freely toward all creatures that live.' The seeming egocentrism of the Buddhist monk is not selfishness, but self-reliance. The pursuit of nirvana is indeed a solitary pursuit that each man has to undertake in the loneliness of spirit. But the result of this pursuit is not without benefit to others and to society at large. As Buddhists would say, the purification of society begins with the purification of man. And it is this concern of Buddhism for people at large, for society, which finds expression in its missionary work. Buddhism, unlike Hinduism, is not content to leave things as they are, but seeks to perfect man and society.

'In guarding themselves, sir, do men prove guardians of others?' a lay follower once asked Buddha. And Buddha replied, 'Yes, lay-brother. In guarding himself a man guards others; in guarding others, he guards himself.' Each man is his own keeper, but equally he is also his brother's keeper. Good works 'is another name for happiness,' Buddha held. Notes Thapar: 'The constituents of merit for the layman [in Buddhism] are activities motivated by the need to further social good, such as harmonious social relationships and charity, but above all sexual control and non-violence. Harmony in social relationships referred not only to those between parents and children, but also between master and slave, and employer and employee ...' Though Buddha viewed the caste system, as well as attachment to family and private property, as detrimental to spiritual welfare, he never sought to subvert these institutions. Rather, he supported social peace, stability and harmony. 'No preacher of the dharma, brethren, quarrels with anyone in the world,' Buddha declared. 'Enduring patience is the highest *tapas* ... He who oppresses another is no recluse; he who harms another is no ascetic,' states the *Dhammapada*. 'Never is enmity appeased by hatred; love alone can appease hatred. This is the Law Eternal.'

These are values of life-affirmation, not of life-negation. Death certainly is not the goal of life in Buddhism. If life is undesirable because it is sorrow, so is death. What Buddha wanted was to end the cycle of life, not particular lives. In fact, he specifically prohibited suicide. 'A monk who preaches suicide, who tells man, "Do away with this wretched life, full of suffering and sin; death is better," in fact preaches murder, is a murderer, is no longer a monk,' declared Buddha. 'The body ... has been declared by the Blessed One to be like a wound,' expounds Nagasena in *Milinda-panha*. But suicide is not the means to heal the wound. What is needed is an attitude of detachment. 'Therefore ... without cleaving to it, do the recluses bear about the body.'

By rejecting extreme austerities and choosing the middle path of moderation, Buddha was in fact saying yes to life – not with an exultant shout of joy, but in quiet, gentle acceptance. 'Not nakedness, nor matted hair, nor filth, nor fasting, nor lying on the ground, nor besmearing the body with dust and ashes, nor practising [yogic] *asanas* can cleanse the mortal who is full of doubt,' Buddha held. 'But he who is tranquil and serene and calm and lives a tamed and restrained life of holiness and has ceased to injure living things, though richly attired, he is a Brahmin, a *samana* (ascetic), a *bhikkhu* (monk).' Buddha's ideal, as Weber states, was 'the cool, stoic equanimity of the knowing man.'

Buddha did, it is true, encourage asceticism, but this was only for exceptional persons. For lay followers, his emphasis was on dharmic life, not renunciation. The dharma he decreed was indeed exacting and constituted in itself a form of asceticism, but this was not a negation of life, but an affirmation of life on a higher plane, beyond the awful ordinariness of everyday life.

The Eight-fold Path is a way to live, not a way to flee from life, and it presents man with a sensible, practical means to cope with living in society, by leading a good, productive and contented life. If it had been otherwise, Buddhism would not have been patronised by rulers, traders and artisans, the most active and dynamic sections of society. 'Buddhism is, in its essence, a system of self-culture and self-restraint,' remarks R.C. Dutt. 'Doctrines and beliefs are of secondary importance in this system ... Holy peace, the sinless, tranquil life ... is attainable on this earth; it is the Buddhist's heaven, it is nirvana. Gautama's religion offers no glowing rewards in a world to come; virtue is its own reward ... It knows of no higher aim among gods or men than the attainment of a tranquil, sinless life; it speaks of no other salvation than virtuous peace, it knows of no other heaven than holiness.'

The acquisition of wisdom and the cultivation of virtue are the means to achieve this holiness, Buddha maintained, not worship of the gods, prayers and rituals. 'Better than a man who offers, month after month for a thousand years, a thousand sacrifices is that man who pays homage to one grounded in wisdom,' states the *Dhammapada*. 'Better than a man who tends the sacred fire in the forest for a hundred years is that man who pays homage to one grounded in wisdom ... Better than a man who offers an oblation and a sacrifice for a whole year in order to gain merit is that man who pays homage to the righteous.' Elsewhere the text states: 'Abstention from sin, doing good works, and purifying one's mind, this is the teaching of Buddhism.' Warn the *Jatakas*, 'Well now, watch and guard the three avenues of the voice, the mind, and the body; do no evil whether in word or thought or deed.'

Buddhism is primarily concerned with showing man how to set his body and mind in order, and lead a serene life, despite all the enduring miseries and evanescent pleasures of life. Buddha 'sought to put a new temper into men, to imbue them with a new spirit, give them a new heart,' comments Woodward. Man does not feel at home in the world. He does not in fact feel at home in himself. Buddha sought to put him at peace with the world and at peace with himself.

Buddha was a messenger of hope. Perhaps the best summing up of the spirit of Buddhism is this moving peace chant in the *Sutta-nipata*:

May all be happy and safe; may all
be blessed with peace always;
great or small, subtle or gross,
seen or unseen, dwelling far or near,
born or yet unborn –
may all be blessed with peace.

May none deceive another,
nor scorn another,
nor, in anger or ill-will,
desire another's sorrow ...
Let all-embracing thoughts
for all that live be thine,
an all-embracing love
for all the universe
in all its heights and depths
and breadth, unstinted love,
unhindered, free from hate and ill-will.

EHI BHIKKHU!

Sakyaputtiya Samanas, ascetics of the Sakya prince – this was how Buddhists were known in Buddha's lifetime. Theirs was essentially a monastic order rather than a religion. 'The monks alone, not the lay adherents, were exclusively members of the church,' observes Oldenberg. At one time monks were in fact forbidden to recite the Buddhist canon to laymen, and even Anathapindika, one of the most prominent early patrons of Buddhism, was granted the privilege of hearing it only on his deathbed, after persistent requests. This restriction on access to the canon was not, however, because it was esoteric wisdom, but rather because it was thought that laymen had no practical need for that knowledge in their lives.

Pragmatism was a distinctive quality of Buddha's precepts and practices, and he invariably adapted his teachings to suit the needs of different classes of people, as he himself once explained to a village headman.

'Is the Tathagata compassionate towards all living, breathing creatures?' asked the headman.

'Yes, headman,' said Buddha.

'But does the Lord teach dharma in full to some, but not likewise to others?' continued the headman.

'Now, what do you think, headman? Suppose a farmer has three fields, one excellent, one mediocre, and one poor with bad soil – when he wants to sow the seed, which field would he sow first?'

'He would sow the excellent one, then the mediocre one,' said the headman. 'When he has done that, he might or might not sow the poor one with the bad soil ...'

'In the same way, headman, my monks and nuns are like the excellent field,' Buddha responded. 'It is to these that I teach dharma ... in spirit and letter ... completely fulfilled, utterly pure. And why? It is these that dwell with me for light, me for shelter, me for stronghold, me for refuge.' The turn of his lay followers, who were 'like the mediocre field,' came next, said Buddha, and only lastly did he turn to 'recluses, Brahmins and wanderers of other sects,' for they were 'like the poor field with bad soil.'

Buddhist laymen and monks lived in entirely different worlds. While

Buddha's guidelines for laymen consisted of just a few cardinal rules and supplementaries, and their lifestyles were not significantly different from that of the rest of society, monks formed a clearly distinctive group, being subject to over 250 rules and very many supplementaries. These rules were initially laid down by Buddha one by one and case by case over several years as he went on, often modifying them to meet changing circumstances, always keeping in mind convenience and usefulness as his guiding principles, but they were later codified in a text called the *Patimokkha*.

There were no class or caste distinctions in the sangha; all were brothers and comrades to each other, and all freely mingled and ate together, in total disregard of conventional social taboos. The monks, having renounced the world, were not concerned with worldly institutions and hierarchies. Said Buddha: 'Just as, brethren, the great rivers Ganga, Yamuna, Asirvati, Sarabhu, and Mahi, on reaching the mighty ocean renounce their former names and lineage and one and all are reckoned as the mighty ocean, even so, brethren, do the four classes – Kshatriyas, Brahmins, Vaisyas and Sudras – go forth from home to the homeless life under the dharma discipline of the Tathagata and renounce their former names and lineage.'

The sangha was open to all, except to certain categories of people who were, for practical reasons, considered ineligible. Habitual criminals, escaped prisoners, and those who sought to take refuge in the sangha to evade punishments, were denied admission, though Buddha did once ordain a notorious brigand named Angulimala, who sported a necklace of fingers cut off from his victims. Runaway slaves and those fleeing from creditors, as well as government servants, especially soldiers, were also not allowed to join the sangha. Those with serious bodily deformities and sicknesses too were denied admission, perhaps because it was thought that their physical distress would impede their spiritual pursuit.

Only children over fifteen years were normally admitted into the sangha as novices, but sometimes they were admitted from the age of eight. 'I allow you, brethren, to give ordination to lads ... even under the age of fifteen years,' ruled Buddha. Children, however, could be admitted into the sangha only with the consent of their parents, a condition that Buddha laid down on the insistence of his father. Novices had to undergo several years of training before they could be ordained as monks, the minimum age for which was twenty years. 'Let no one, brethren, give full orders ... to one under twenty years of age,' Buddha decreed.

Initiation into the sangha was in two stages, a preparatory ordination (*pabbajja*: departure) for the novice and, after several years of probation, the full ordination (*upasampada*: arrival) for the monk or nun. In the sangha 'the training is gradual, progress is gradual, it goes step by step; there is no sudden penetration to insight,' states the *Majjhima Nikaya*. The novice had to pass a test by reciting part of a Buddhist canonical text – the length of which was shorter for nuns, keeping in mind their presumed lower mental capacity – before receiving full ordination.

Ordination was originally performed by Buddha personally, but later he delegated the authority to his disciples, with the stipulation that they should do so only in the presence of a certain number of monks, usually ten. For the rite of confirmation, the novice, his head and beard shaved, and wearing saffron robes, would sit cross-legged before the officiating elder monk with palms joined reverently, and repeat three times the formula *Buddham saranam! Dharmam saranam! Sangham saranam!* – In Buddha I take refuge! In dharma I take refuge! In sangha I take refuge! – and then recite the ten basic ethical precepts of Buddhism. The elder would then propose his ordination to the attending monks, repeating it thrice, and if they gave their assent by remaining silent, the novice would be inducted into monkhood. The old Pali formula for ordination was simple and direct, true to the spirit of early Buddhism. '*Ehi bhikkhu*' – Come O monk! – was all that the ordainer had to say to confirm the monk. On becoming a monk, the novice had to adopt a new name, symbolising his rebirth in the sangha.

The monk was required to lead a life of strict discipline. He had to abjure violence of thought, word and deed, taking special care not to knowingly deprive any creature of life, 'not even of a worm or ant.' He was entirely forbidden to have sex, 'even with an animal,' and he had to abstain from all false speech – lying, backbiting or abusive speech and idle babble. He was not allowed to take anything not given to him voluntarily, 'not even a blade of grass'; and he was forbidden to take intoxicants, or to eat after midday. It was improper for him to attend music, dance and drama performances. The use of garlands, perfumes, unguents and jewellery was taboo for him, and he was not allowed to use a high or broad bed. He was forbidden to handle gold and silver. These ten precepts constituted the basic monastic prohibitions. In addition, the monk was subject to innumerable minor regulations – some 250 of them, as given in the *Patimokkha* rules.

'Brethren,' cautioned Buddha, 'there is no such thing as a petty sin.' The monk had to shun all pleasures of the senses and avoid all displays of emotions. 'In the noble discipline, brethren, music is lamentation,' Buddha declared. 'In the noble discipline, dancing is sheer madness. In the noble discipline, laughing that displays the teeth is childishness ... Enough for you just to smile if you have any cause to show your pleasure.' Going 'to see an army drawn up in battle-array, except for a cause thereto sufficient,' 'emission of semen by design, except by a person sleeping,' 'poking [another person] with a finger ... sporting in water ... bathing at intervals of less than half a month, except on proper occasion' – these are some of the prohibitions in the long *Patimokkha* list. The monk is warned not to go about laughing, 'swaying body ... arms ... [and] head'; or hold his arms akimbo or leave his head uncovered. Self-glorification, such as exhibiting miraculous powers or boasting about superhuman perfection, was considered a serious violation of monastic discipline.

Detachment, benevolence, and, more than anything else, thoughtfulness, were the high qualities required of a Buddhist monk. 'And how does a monk become thoughtful?' Buddha once asked rhetorically in one of his discourses, and continued: 'He acts ... in full presence of mind whatever he may do, in going out and coming in, in looking forward and in looking back, in bending his arm or stretching it forth, in wearing his robes or carrying his bowl; in eating, drinking, chewing, swallowing; in relieving nature's needs; in walking or standing or sitting; in sleeping or waking; in talking and being silent. That, brethren, is how a brother becomes thoughtful and self-possessed.' Everything should be done with deliberation and dispassion. The *Lotus of the Wonderful Law*, a late Buddhist work, avows:

> *Upon all I ever look*
> *everywhere impartially,*
> *without distinction of persons*
> *or mind of love or hate.*
> *I have no predilection*
> *nor any limitations.*

Buddha's emphasis was on self-culture. 'Irrigators lead the water; fletchers make the arrows straight; carpenters carve the wood; good people discipline themselves,' Buddha maintained. 'Better than a man who conquers in battles a thousand times a thousand men is he who conquers himself. He indeed is the mightiest of warriors.' Discipline has to be internalised, Buddha stressed; it is not enough to seem to be outwardly disciplined. 'He is not a monk simply because he carries the begging bowl,' he asserted. 'Nor even because he adopts the whole law outwardly. But he who is above good and evil, is chaste, who comports himself in the world with understanding, he, indeed is called a monk ... What avails thy matted hair, O fool? What avails thy deer-skin? Outwardly you clean yourself, within you there is ravening.' The mind, which is the source of all karma, has to be rigorously controlled. 'All that we are is the result of what we have thought,' says the *Dhammapada*. But 'thinking is difficult to discipline. Mind is flighty, alighting where it listeth. Good it is to tame it. The tamed mind brings happiness.'

The only possessions the Buddhist monk was allowed to own were an alms-bowl, three pieces of plain cloth, a girdle, a razor, a needle and a water-pot. All these had to be obtained by begging. No hoarding of provisions was permitted, either by the monk or in the monasteries, though later a storehouse was allowed to be built outside the monastic campus. Agriculture and all labour for profit were forbidden to the monk. He should not handle money. Further, he had to renounce all emotional and sentimental ties. He had no family, no social affiliations whatsoever.

It was a hard, austere life. But not too hard, especially when compared to the mortifications advocated by sects like Jainism. Buddha disapproved of every kind of excess, even excessive religious zeal. He once explained this to Sona Kalivisa, a rich man's son who was ordained, and who in his ardour to gain merit kept walking up and down abstractedly all the time, so that the soles of his feet were lacerated and the ground was 'all dabbled with blood like a butcher's shambles.' Yet he was not able to free himself from worldly attachments. As he despaired over his predicament, Buddha visited him in his lodging and spoke to him.

'Now how say you, Sona? Formerly when you dwelt at home, were you not skilled in playing stringed music on the lute?' Buddha asked.

'Yes, Lord,' Sona replied.

'Now how say you, Sona? When your lute strings were over-taut, did your lute then give out a sound, was it fit to play upon?'

'No, Lord.'

'Now how say you, Sona? When your lute-strings were neither over-taut nor over-slack, but evenly strung, did your lute then give out a sound; was it fit to play upon?'

'It was, Lord.'

'Even so, Sona, excess of zeal makes one liable to self-exaltation, while lack of zeal makes one liable to sluggishness. Therefore do you, Sona, persist in evenness of zeal, master your faculties, and make that your mark.'

Buddha was particular about the conduct of monks in society. 'As one who has no shoes walks over a thorny ground, watchfully picking his steps, so let the wise man walk in the village,' advises the *Teragatha*. High decorum characterised every action of the monk, even his mode of begging. 'Enveloped in his shawl, with downcast look, without bustle, and in neither hasty nor careless fashion, the monk is to enter the houses,' notes Oldenberg. 'He is not to stand too near nor too far off; he is not to stay too long nor to go away too quickly. He is to wait in silence, until something is given to him; then he is to hold out his bowl, and without looking at the face of the giver, receive what she gives him. Then he spreads his shawl over the alms-bowl, and goes slowly away.' He is not to look back. Monks were required to seek alms from house to house in sequence, without any differentiation about the caste and status of the households, though they were not allowed to seek food from the very poor who could not give alms without depriving themselves of sustenance. 'As the bee damages not the colour or the perfume of the flower, but sucks its juice and flies on, so let the wise man walk in the village,' counsels the *Dhammapada.*

Buddha and his monks lived entirely on alms, and considered it an honourable way to live. Once Bharadvaja, a Brahmin, seeing Buddha going about seeking alms, ridiculed him, saying: 'I, O ascetic, both plough and sow, and having ploughed and sown, I eat; thou also, O ascetic, shouldst plough and sow, and having ploughed and sown, thou shouldst eat.' Buddha had a ready answer to the reproach. 'I also, O Brahmin, both plough and sow, and having ploughed and sown, I eat,' he said. 'Faith is the seed, penance the rain, understanding my yoke and plough, modesty the plough-shaft, mind the tie of the yoke, mindfulness my ploughshare and goad … Exertion is my beast of burden, carrying me to nirvana.' For the Buddhist monk, begging was not simply a means of livelihood or even of freeing oneself from temporal concerns, but a religious duty, to cultivate humility and non-attachment. A monk never sought (or rejected) any particular food, but gratefully accepted whatever was given.

After his morning round of begging, the monk returned to his retreat, where he was required to eat his only meal of the day before noon. He ate without pleasure, often mixing together the scraps of food he had received to make it less tasty. As Nagasena told King Menander, 'The lustful man, O king, in eating his food enjoys both the taste and the lust that arises from taste, but the man free from lust experiences the taste only, and not the lust arising therefrom.'

Traditionally monks were not allowed to prepare their own food, or to take any food that was not given to them as alms. They were not even allowed to pick fallen fruit, except to ward off starvation. 'I allow you, O monks, wherever edible fruit is seen and there is no one to make it allowable, to pick it of your own accord and take it away,' Buddha ruled. But the monk was not permitted to eat the fruit until he found someone to perform the ceremony of giving it to him. 'And when you see one who can make it allowable, you are to place it on the ground, and eat it [only] after you have received it again.' Buddhist monks were not vegetarians, but they were forbidden to eat the meat of an animal specifically slaughtered to feed them, for that would indirectly make them the killers of the animal. Said Buddha: 'Let no one, O monks, knowingly eat the meat [of an animal] killed for that purpose … I prescribe, O monks, that flesh (or fish) is pure to you in three cases: if you do not see, if you have not heard, if you do not suspect [that it has been caught or killed specially to prepare food for you].'

The *Patimokkha* even specifies the manner in which food is to be eaten.

Rice, says the text, should be made into 'round mouthfuls,' but not 'too large balls.' And while eating, the monk had to remind himself: 'Not till the ball is brought close will I open ... my mouth ... Not the whole hand, when eating, will I put into my mouth ... When the food is in my mouth will I not talk ... Without tossing the food into my mouth will I eat ... Without nibbling at the balls of food will I eat ... Without stuffing my cheeks out will I eat ... Without putting out my tongue will I eat ... Without smacking my lips will I eat ... Without making a hissing sound will I eat ... Without licking my fingers will I eat ... Without licking my bowl will I eat ... Without licking my lips will I eat ... Not with a hand soiled with food will I take hold of the water-jar ...' And so on.

Similar detailed rules were laid down about the monk's dress, which consisted of three plain cloths dyed yellow, preferably made of rags sewn together – a loincloth secured by a girdle, a lower cloth tied around the waist, and an upper robe wrapped around the waist and drawn from the right hip over the left shoulder. Silk was forbidden to monks, as its manufacture involved the killing of larvae. Monks were not normally allowed any footwear, and were specifically forbidden to wear ornamental footwear. Except during the rainy season, when they went into retreat in some rude shelter, Buddhist monks were required to tour around on foot to preach. During their wanderings, they were not ordinarily permitted, save in emergencies, to lodge in towns and villages, or even to enter them between noon and dawn. They had to reside outside human settlements, in a grove or a cave.

Buddha made it a special point to warn monks to guard against the wiles of women.

'Master, how shall we behave before women?' Ananda once asked Buddha.

'You should shun their gaze, Ananda,' advised Buddha.

'But if we see them, master, what then are we to do?'

'Not speak to them, Ananda.'

'But if we speak to them, master, what then?'

'Then you must watch over yourselves, Ananda.'

Not surprisingly, Buddha was most reluctant to admit women into the sangha, concerned as much with how that would alter the ethos of the sangha, as with the social repercussions of women renouncing family life. When his foster-mother Mahapajapati, the widowed queen of Suddhodana, wanted to join the sangha along with several other Kshatriya women, Buddha rejected her appeal on three separate occasions, and it was only after Ananda's persistent plea that he finally acceded to her request. Ananda was a champion of women, and his clinching argument in their favour was to ask Buddha, 'Are the Buddhas born into the world only for the benefit of men?' Buddha could not deny that it was for the benefit of all, and that trapped him.

But he had dire forebodings about the consequences of ordaining nuns, and he warned Ananda: 'As a field of rice, Ananda, which is full of vigour, loses its vigour when mildew breaks out in it, so also, Ananda, if women be admitted [into the sangha] ... holy living does not last long.' If women were not admitted, the sangha would have remained pure and strong for a thousand years, Buddha said, 'but now that ... [women are admitted] holy living will not be long preserved. Only five hundred years, Ananda, will the doctrine of the truth abide.'

To mitigate the harm of admitting women into the sangha, Buddha laid down stringent and harshly discriminatory rules for the conduct of nuns. 'A sister, even if she had been a hundred years in the robes, shall salute, shall rise up before, shall bow down before, shall perform all duties of respect unto a brother, even if that brother has only just taken the robes. Let this rule never be broken, but be honoured, esteemed, reverenced, and observed as long as life doth last,' Buddha decreed. 'Secondly, a sister shall not spend the rainy season in a district where there is no brother residing. Let this rule never be broken ...' There are in all eight rules in this set, which concluded, 'Seventhly, a sister shall not in any case abuse or censure a brother. Let this rule never be broken ... Eighthly, henceforth is forbidden the right of a sister to have speech among brethren, but not forbidden is the speaking of brethren unto sisters. Let this rule never be broken ...'

These regulations reflected the prevailing social values, and there is no record of women resenting them. Quite the contrary, the most zealous followers of Buddha turned out to be women, and they played a major role in sustaining the sangha with their munificence. Some of the most charming Buddhist hymns were composed by nuns, and a few of them went on to make substantial reputations for themselves for wisdom and spiritual merit. Ananda, naturally, remained the favourite sage of nuns. 'The nuns principally honour the stupa of Ananda, because it was Ananda who requested the lord of the world to let women take orders,' notes Chinese pilgrim Fa Hsien.

The Buddhist monks, for all their ascetic discipline, were not hermits, but a community of seekers, who interacted among themselves and with society. Theirs was an organised brotherhood, a sangha, consisting of novices and monks who were, as an old Buddhist confessional formula has it, 'so bound together that one exhorts the other, one stabilises the other.'

The sangha was fundamentally egalitarian and democratic in all its processes. Buddhism was neither dogmatic in its beliefs nor pontifical in its organisation – Buddha did not nominate a successor, and in early Buddhism there was no apostolic succession, no permanent and hierarchical power structure, and no central authority to mandate doctrines and practices. It was an open religion, its possibilities changing and expanding with time and place.

The Buddhist monks, as Ananda Coomaraswamy notes, were not 'required to take vows of obedience to superiors: all were equal, with due allowance for seniority and degree of spiritual attainment: even in large monasteries, the head was merely *primus inter pares*.' All issues before the sangha, including doctrinal matters, were decided, as in tribal oligarchies like Buddha's own clan, at formal meetings of monks, from which only nuns and novices were excluded. At these meetings, presided over by a chosen senior monk, resolutions were moved with due legislative decorum, and decisions taken either by consensus or majority opinion. The meetings required a quorum (of nine monks normally, of five in exceptional cases) for their decisions to be valid.

Seniority was the only basis for rank in the sangha, so there was no jostling for power and position among monks. 'In the religion which I teach, the standard by which precedence in the matter of lodging and the like is to be settled, is not noble birth, or having been a Brahmin, or having been wealthy before entry into the sangha; the standard is not familiarity with the rules of the sangha, with the canonical texts, or with metaphysical books; nor is it either the attainment of any of the four stages of mystic ecstasy, or the walking in any of the four paths of salvation,' Buddha ruled, according to the *Jatakas*. 'Brethren, in my religion it is seniority which claims respect of word and deed, salutation, and all due service; it is seniors who should enjoy the best lodging, the best water, and the best rice.'

It was not that merit was not valued in Buddhism. Among the monks there were in fact a few called Arhats, the Worthy, who were held in the highest esteem in the sangha and symbolised the spiritual ideal of orthodox Buddhism, having by relentless self-discipline subdued desire, the demon within. But the very fact that they had overcome temporal passions meant that they did not see themselves in relation to others as better or worse. The Arhats were revered, but they did not rule over monks.

In Buddhism, discipline was self-administered, by each monk or by peer groups of monks. It was in any case impossible to organise the monks in ranks, or discipline them from the outside, as they constantly travelled around on their own, without anyone sending them anywhere or controlling their movements. Groups of monks came together only during the rainy season retreat, that too in shelters scattered all over the land. It was only when, a couple of centuries after Buddha's death, permanent monastic settlements replaced rain retreats, that Buddhism developed an administrative organisation. The establishment of rainy season retreats itself was an innovation that Buddha introduced rather late in his life. In the early days, states the *Khuddaka Nikaya*, 'the retreat during the rainy season was not yet appointed ... So the brethren went a-roaming in the cold, the hot, and the rainy season alike.'

Once the retreats were established, Buddha specified the guidelines for choosing their sites and laying out their structures, and set down the rules for their maintenance, with emphasis on sanitation and cleanliness. The retreat, he stipulated, should 'not be too far from, nor yet too near the town, well provided with entrances and exits, easily accessible to all people who inquire after it, with not too much bustle of life by day, quiet by night, far from commotion and crowds of men, a place of retirement, a good spot for solitary meditation.' Taking care of monastic property was now made a part of monastic discipline. Monks were required to share in housekeeping chores, cleaning their own cells as well as the common rooms, and sweeping the courtyard. They were also enjoined to take care of each other. Said Buddha: 'You, O brethren, have neither a mother nor a father who could nurse you. If, O brethren, you do not nurse one another, who, then, will nurse you?'

Buddhist monks were expected to maintain decorum, even certain ceremoniousness, in all matters, however trivial they might be. Thus the *Vinaya Pitaka* specifies that a monk arriving at a retreat or monastery should, 'having taken off his sandals, turn them down, beat them together, take them up again, lay down his umbrella, uncover his head, put his upper robe over one shoulder, then enter the residence heedfully and without undue haste ... In washing his feet, let him hold the water with one hand and rub down his feet with the other hand.' In the monasteries, senior monks usually spent a good amount of their time teaching novices. 'The priests,' notes Fa Hsien, 'ever engage themselves in doing meritorious works for the purpose of religious advancement, or in reciting the scriptures, or in meditation.'

These were the ideals. Reality was often quite different. Monks were not angels, so violations of monastic discipline were common. 'Many who wear the yellow robe are ill-natured and uncontrolled,' sadly admits the *Dhammapada*. Sometimes monks expelled each other in pique. There was much gossiping, quarrelling and backbiting, and Buddha had to repeatedly admonish them about it. 'In whatever quarter monks dwell in strife and uproar, given to disputes and wounding each other with the weapons of the tongue,' said Buddha, ' it is unpleasant for me even to think of such a quarter, much more unpleasant for me to go to it.' When a schism once broke out in the sangha, Buddha cried out in exasperation: 'The *bhikkhu* sangha is divided! The *bhikkhu* sangha is divided!'

Monks often indulged in prohibited luxuries. Thus, according to a story in the Jatakas, a rich merchant, on joining the brotherhood, 'caused to be built for himself a chamber to live in, a kitchen, and a store-room; and not till he had stocked his store-room with ghee, rice, and the like, did he finally join. Even after he had become a brother, he used to send for his servants and make them cook him what he liked to eat. He was richly provided with requisites, having an entire change of clothing for night and another for day; he dwelt aloof on the outskirts of the monastery.'

Some monks, according to the *Mahavagga*, were in the habit of wearing colourful and ornate shoes, and using plush furniture, divans with luxurious coverings and cushions. Some even used to cavort on heifers, and 'touch with lustful thoughts their privy parts.' And certain monks, continues the *Mahavagga*, 'used to rise up in the night towards dawn, and, putting on wooden shoes, walk up and down in the open air talking in tones high, loud and harsh, of all kinds of worldly things – such as tales of kings, or robbers, or ministers of state; tales of armies, of terror, of war; conversation respecting meats, drinks, clothes, couches, garlands, perfumes, relationships, equipages, villages, towns, cities, provinces, women, warriors, and streets; tales about buried treasure, ghost stories; various tales; discussions on the world; disasters by sea; things which are and things which are not.'

Though Buddha proscribed all such behaviour as improper, Buddhist monks had at one time the reputation of leading an easy life, and this sometimes attracted self-indulgent people to the sangha. Thus the *Mahavagga* tells the story of a Brahmin who, seeing the monks being invited for meals at rich households, got himself ordained, hoping for a life of ease and comfort. But when the invitations ceased, and monks called him to go with them for alms, he said: 'I have not embraced the religious life for that purpose – to going about for alms; if you give me [food], I will eat; if you do not, I will return to the world.'

'What, friend, have you indeed embraced the religious life for your belly's sake?' the monks asked.

'Yes, friends,' said the Brahmin.

Seeing that men were joining the sangha for worldly comfort, Buddha ruled that the candidate seeking to become a monk should be told of 'the four resources' before he was ordained – that normally he had to live on 'morsels of food given in alms,' dress in 'robes made of rags taken from a dust heap,' live under trees, and make do with 'decomposing urine as medicine,' and that all else were exceptions, 'extra allowances.' Later, however, when Buddha found that these dire warnings frightened off many from taking monkhood, he modified the procedure and specified that the warning about 'the four resources' should be given immediately after full ordination.

Buddha sensibly did not require monks to take life-long vows. Anyone could leave the sangha at any time, if worldly thoughts held him. He could leave quietly, or, more properly, declare his intention before a witness and leave. Indeed, those who had no true vocation for monastic life were encouraged to return to the world, so that they would not trouble themselves or others. Monks who violated discipline were punished with various penances, and those who committed serious offences were expelled from the sangha. Disciplinary actions were usually taken at the fortnightly meetings of monks, on the basis of the confession or proven guilt of the erring monk. In a sense, it was the guilty monk who punished himself.

Every fortnight, on the full and new moon days, the monks of a region assembled in one place for a ceremony called Uposatha, at which the *Patimokkha* rules were recited, and the guilty confessed their transgressions and received punishments. No one except the insane was permitted to absent himself from these meetings. The sick had to assure that they had not transgressed, otherwise they had to be brought to the assembly; if they could not be moved, then the assembly had to go to them.

The fortnightly confessional meetings were solemn affairs, and the mood that prevailed in them, as in other assemblies of Buddhist monks, was, as Oldenberg puts it, 'calm, composed, one might say, ceremonious ... [more] in quiet transport than in ecstatic excitement.' After reading each set of offences in the *Patimokkha*, the presiding monk would ask, 'Whosoever has incurred a fault, let him declare it. If no fault has been incurred it is meet to keep silence.' This would be repeated thrice. The monks would also be warned that remaining silent about transgressions was itself a grave offence.

The monks, though living outside society and free from social concerns and responsibilities, nevertheless lived in close association with society. Buddha, it is important to note, returned to society to preach after attaining enlightenment. Buddhist monasteries were usually located close to population centres such as towns or prosperous villages, to enable monks to live on alms and to interact with society. The monk and the layman, though they lived in worlds apart, were interdependent, the monk providing the rationale of life for laymen, and laymen providing the material means of life for monks. Often Buddha and his monks were invited for meals by wealthy householders or by groups of individuals, and he invariably accepted such invitations, for that (as well as the begging routine) served to integrate the sangha with the community. 'The monasteries,' notes Thapar, 'irrespective of sectarian differences, acted as networks of acculturation and contact within the Indian subcontinent reaching out into the remotest corners, monks travelling either in isolation or accompanying the traders.' Further, the monasteries served as education centres – the

Buddhist monks were, apart from Brahmins, the dominant literate group in ancient India.

The monk's role in the everyday life of people was, however, limited. As Coomaraswamy points out, the monk did not have any sanctity or authority other than what was derived from his own good living; nor did he have the 'power to save or condemn, to forgive sins or to administer sacraments.' Warned Buddha: 'No man can purify another.' The monk was not a priest, and he could not officiate at domestic rituals; these functions continued to be performed by Brahmin priests in Buddhist households, as Buddhism prescribed no religious rites of its own. 'The Buddhist lay persons,' observes Basham, 'were always simultaneously in some measure Hindu lay persons.' Laymen, unlike monks, were not required to abjure their traditional religious practices or even to give up their caste affiliations.

Buddha's lay followers were therefore hardly distinguishable as Buddhists in ancient India. They were devoted to Buddha, but often not exclusively so. There was no bar on their being simultaneously devoted to other sages, just as there was no bar on a Hindu being a devotee of different gods. However, Buddhism, like Jainism, encouraged its lay followers to retreat into a monastery periodically for short periods for instruction and meditation. On Uposatha days laymen usually visited monasteries to give alms to monks. But generally the lives of monks and laymen did not intermingle, and monks often discouraged those with strong social ties or responsibilities from taking to monastic life. Thus Buddhist elder Maha Kakkayana advised lay disciple Sona Kutikanna (Sona of Conical Ears)not to become a monk, telling him that monkhood would be too hard for him. 'Do you, therefore, Sona, remain in the state of a householder and practise only for a time the higher life,' advised Kakkayana.

The emphasis of the Buddhist guidelines for laymen was on leading an intelligent, disciplined and productive life in society. Indeed, the lay followers could fulfil their role as patrons of Buddhism and offer gifts to the sangha only if they were successful in their temporal pursuits. But it was hoped that whatever they did, their actions would be infused with Buddhist ideals. 'The wise and moral man shines like a fire on a hilltop, making money like the bee which does not hurt the flower,' states the *Digha Nikaya*. 'Such a man makes his pile as an anthill, gradually. The man grown wealthy thus can help his family and firmly bind his friends to himself. He should divide his money in four parts: on one part he should live, with two expand his trade, and the fourth he should save against a rainy day.'

Buddhist laymen were generally expected to follow the basic ethical precepts of Buddhism. They, warns the *Digha Nikaya*, should avoid the four vices of action ('injury to life, taking what is not given, base conduct in sexual matters and false speech'), the four motives of evil deeds ('deeds committed from partiality, enmity, stupidity and fear') and the six ways of squandering wealth ('addiction to drink, carelessness, roaming the streets at improper times, frequenting fairs, gambling, keeping bad company and idleness'). If he avoids all these fourteen evils, 'then he ... is ready for the conquest of both worlds ... this world and the next, and when his body breaks up on his death he is reborn to bliss in heaven,' assures the text.

Devotion to parents and teachers, loving care of wife and children, faithfulness to friends, looking after the welfare of servants and workers, reverence for sages – these are the other qualities that a layman should cultivate, according to the *Digha Nikaya*. In turn, parents should take care of children, wives should be devoted to their husbands, servants should be true to their masters, sages should minister to the spiritual welfare of laymen. Further, according to Asvaghosha, laymen should abjure 'duplicity, slander, frivolous talk, contrariness, malice, currying favour, and false devotions.' The *Khuddaka-patha* advises laymen not to take 'unseasonable meals,' or indulge in music and dance, or go to see entertainments. Adds the *Sutta Nipata*: 'Let him not wear wreaths or use perfumes.'

What would laymen gain from practising the Buddhist dharma and by giving alms to monks and gifts to the sangha? Primarily they gain merit. And that is no small matter. 'The scent of flowers travels not against the wind, be it tagara or jasmine or even of the sandalwood tree. But the fragrance of the good wafts even against the wind,' observes the *Dhammapada*. According to Buddha, the practise of dharma also enabled men to lead productive lives, gain serenity and self-confidence, face death without anxiety, and attain heavenly bliss in the hereafter.

To whom did all this appeal? Mostly to cultured urbanites, evidently. A religion without the psychologically protective magic of rituals, and without gods to turn to in times of tribulation, but which required each man to bear full responsibility for his own life and actions, and demanded of him high spiritual endeavour and rigorous moral discipline, would hardly have appealed to the poor and illiterate masses ground down by the stark and numbing toil for bare physical survival. What the common people needed of religion was an opiate. Buddhism did not offer them that solace.

The religious needs of the common people were better served by their simplistic faith in gods and rituals. Not surprisingly, Buddhism remained a relatively minor sect for about two and half centuries after its founding. It was Asoka's imperial patronage that transformed it into an all-India religion, and set it on the path of becoming a world religion. Thereafter, for a good many centuries Buddhism remained the dominant religion of India. But it was dominant only in the sense that it was the religion of the dominant classes in India during most of this period – it is doubtful whether it ever had a broad base in India, even at the height of its popularity.

In the process of its growth and expansion, Buddhism split into several sects, and transformed itself almost beyond recognition. It adopted, on the one hand, many elements from popular beliefs to accommodate the religious needs of the common people, and, on the other, developed complex metaphysical systems as in high Hinduism. These changes eroded Buddhism's distinctive moral tone and identity, the very reason for its existence, and paved the way for its eventual extinction in India. Further, Buddhism was heavily dependent on the patronage of the urban elite, and when that patronage dwindled with the decline of trade and urban culture in India in early medieval times, Buddhism too declined.

Buddha had initially estimated that his sect would thrive in India for a thousand years, but later, after the admission of nuns into the sangha, he lowered the figure to five hundred years. He was not far wrong in his first estimate. Buddhism remained strong in India for over a thousand years. Its decline began around the fifth century AD, and is reflected in this melancholy lamentation of the contemporary Buddhist writer Vasubandhu:

The times are come when
submerged in the rising tide of ignorance
Buddha's religion seems to breathe its last.

Not quite. Not yet. Buddhism, though clearly on the wane, managed to survive in a few pockets in India for several centuries more, and utterly perished only in the thirteenth century, following the ruthless destruction of monasteries by Turkish invaders. But that is another story.

Chapter Five

THE FIRST EMPIRE

THE PATRICIDES

Magadha was the land of destiny in ancient India. By about the seventh century BC the great tidal surge of Aryans across the Indian subcontinent had subsided, and they had mostly settled to sedentary farming life in permanent tribal habitats in the Indo-Gangetic Plain. Then began a process of political amalgamation and consolidation leading to the rise of a number of prominent states, the *mahajanapadas* (literally, footholds of the great tribes), sixteen in number according to the conventional reckoning of Buddhist texts. And from among them rose, by the fourth century BC, the dominant power of Magadha, the first empire of India. 'In this eastern quarter,' says the *Aitareya Brahmana*, 'whatever kings there are of the eastern people, they are anointed for imperial rule. "O Samrat," they style him when anointed.'

The process of post-Vedic political consolidation was mostly through conquests by aggrandising monarchs, but there were also a few instances of tribes peacefully coalescing to form oligarchic confederations ruled by councils of chieftains. But in every one of these instances – in the rise of kingdoms as well as of tribal republics – the protagonists in the political arena at this time were entirely different from those who played the lead roles in Vedic times. The scene had in fact begun to shift during the later Vedic period itself, when most of the renowned Rig-vedic tribes – the Tritsus, Purus, Yadus, Turvasas, Anus, and Druhyus – sank into oblivion, and their places were taken by parvenu tribes like the Kurus, Panchalas, and so on, whose names do not even figure in the Rig-veda. Later, even these tribes lost ground, yielding place to an entirely new set of rulers, the Magadhans, Kasis, Kosalans, Vatsas, Vrijis, and Avantis, some of them of doubtful Aryan origin.

Meanwhile, the centre of dominant political activity in India, which had shifted from its Rig-vedic locale in Punjab to the middle Gangetic basin in later Vedic times, shifted again further to the east, to the frontier Aryan settlements in the region of the modern states of Uttar Pradesh and Bihar. This shift coincided with (or resulted in) a change in the make-up of the ruling class. Political authority, though theoretically still vested with Kshatriyas, was no longer their exclusive preserve. Many of the prominent new rulers were Sudras, some even of non-Aryan or mixed racial origin.

The very nature of the government now changed. While the Vedic monarch was a minimal ruler, with virtually no bureaucratic organisation, and was primarily a military chief who also performed some elementary judicial and police functions, a complex administrative system now began to take form, with emphasis on systematic revenue collection. The provision of internal and external security was still the primary function of the government, but control of the economic resources of the state now became one of its major concerns, as productive activities in society – agriculture, crafts and trade – grew phenomenally in importance. This is reflected in the Buddhist text *Digha Nikaya*, which counselled that kings, in addition to protecting people from external enemies and maintaining law and order, should supply seeds to peasants, capital to traders and employment to craftsmen, and undertake public works like the construction of wells and ponds, and the planting of trees along highways. To do so was as much in the interest of the rulers as of the people – if the people prospered, so would the rulers, by harvesting a part of the increased production as tax. As for the people, especially traders, it was to their advantage to support strong governments and large states, which could protect private property and secure roads, thus facilitating trade and the accumulation of wealth.

Indian history now begins to gradually emerge from the haze of ancient myths. Facts solidify. Individual rulers become recognisable as distinctive persons. Events, some of them at least, are now datable, and the general contours of the history of the period can be drawn with fair accuracy, though there is yet considerable confusion about the details of events, and much of the chronology remains uncertain. Religious texts are still our main sources of historical information, and they are invariably coloured by bias, not only in their views on particular rulers and dynasties, but even in recording the lengths of their reigns – favourites reign long, while adversaries are given short reigns or are ignored altogether. There is hardly any archaeological evidence to substantiate the textual data.

A curious and rather anachronistic political development of this age was the reversion of some kingdoms to oligarchic rule. Megasthenes, the Greek ambassador at the court of Mauryan Emperor Chandragupta, described the development in terms of Greek notions – these states, he writes, 'dissolved [monarchies] and set up democratic governments.' The remark is misleading. What came into existence were oligarchies, not democracies, with chieftains and petty kings becoming oligarchs when small tribal units merged to form confederacies. Non-Kshatriyas had no political role in these 'republics', and the office of chieftains, who constituted their ruling council, was hereditary, not elective.

These tribal republics were mostly in the hill country in the north-west and along the Himalayan foothills north of the Ganga, and nearly all of them were small congeries of related tribes, ruled by petty chieftains who, as Kosambi puts it, 'did not disdain to set their hands to the plough.' Most of these tribes, like the Sakyas under Kosalan overlordship, could retain their identities only by accepting the suzerainty of some neighbouring king.

The only major independent tribal power of this age was the Vrijian Confederacy of some eight or nine tribes, with Vaishali on the Gandak River as its capital. The dominant tribe of the confederacy were the Lichchavis, a people not known before this time – they were probably non-Aryans, possibly Tibetans or Turanians, who had been absorbed into the Aryan cultural fold and treated as Kshatriyas. Panini, the Sanskrit grammarian of the fourth century BC, describes the Lichchavis as a people living by their arms. It was evidently their fierce martial spirit that enabled the Vrijian Confederacy to preserve its independence against powerful, aggressive and expansionist kingdoms, though, as Buddha held, the cultural cohesiveness of the confederacy and the strength of its 'republican' institutions were also crucial factors.

'Have you heard, Ananda, that the Vrijians hold full and frequent public assemblies?' Buddha once asked.

'Lord, so I have heard,' replied Ananda.

'So long, Ananda, as the Vrijians meet together in concord, and rise in concord, and carry out their undertakings in concord, so long as they enact nothing not already established, abrogate nothing that has been already enacted, and act in accordance with the ancient institutions of the Vrijians established in former days, so long as they honour and esteem and revere and support Vrijian elders, and hold it a point of duty to harken to their words, so long as no women or girls belonging to their clans are detained among them by force or abduction, so long as they honour and esteem and support Vrijian shrines in town and country, and allow not the proper offering and rites, as formerly given and performed, to fall into desuetude, so long as the rightful protection, defence and support be fully provided for the Arhats among them ... so long may the Vrijians be expected not to decline, but to prosper,' said Buddha.

The primary political institution of the tribal oligarchies was the general assembly, constituted of the heads of all the Kshatriya families in the confederacy. Its meetings were held in the town-hall, and its business was conducted according to clearly prescribed rules about quorum and voting. Chips of wood were used for casting votes in the assemblies, and there were officers specifically appointed to collect and count the votes. Unanimous decisions or decisions by consensus were normally preferred, but if differences persisted, then a vote was taken and the issue decided according to the majority will. The tribal republics thus had several democratic features, though they were not democracies in the modern sense of the term.

The general assembly was an unwieldy body in the larger confederacies like that of the Vrijians, among whom it probably met only once a year, during the spring festival, while the routine functions of government were carried out by an executive council of nine chieftains (rajas), of whom an elected member acted as the president. In smaller tribal states like that of the Sakyas, the general assembly met more often.

The tribal republics were really archaic political entities. None of them, small or big, had any political future, and in time most of them would be absorbed by their neighbouring kingdoms, though some of the tribes would manage to retain their identity and prestige, perhaps some political influence as well, for very many centuries. Thus Gupta emperor Chandra Gupta I in the fourth century AD, nearly a thousand years after Magadha subjugated the Lichchavis, still considered it so great an honour to have a Lichchavi princess as his queen that he flaunted his marriage with her on his seals and coins. But it was only the status of these tribes that endured, not their power.

The future really belonged to the monarchies. The major kingdoms of India in Buddha's time were Kosala, Vatsa, Magadha and Avanti. Of them, Kosala was the largest and most powerful state, occupying the extensive tract between the Ganga and the Gandak. The original core of the kingdom was probably around its capital Sravasti on the river Rapti, near the Nepalese border, but in time it expanded southward up to the Ganga and absorbed the prosperous kingdom of Kasi. Kosala, however, was not an integrated state, but an amalgam of tribal domains and vassal kingdoms, so its effective power was far less than its apparent size. Nor did Prasenajit, who ruled the kingdom in the time of Buddha, have the ruthlessness essential to prevail in that brutal age.

Prasenajit, like many other kings of that age, was philosophically inclined, and was a friend and patron of Buddha. His admiration for the sage prompted him, in a well-meaning move, to seek the hand of a Sakyan princess, but this in its ultimate consequences proved to be calamitous to the Sakyas as well as to the king himself. The king's request for a bride put the Sakyas in a quandary. Being Kosalan subjects, they could not reject Prasenajit's request without provoking royal wrath; on the other hand, their tribal pride would not let them accede to the request, as they considered the Kosalan dynasty to be of low social status. Prasenajit was not, as Kosambi points out, 'a Kshatriya in the Vedic-Brahminical sense. He was of low tribal origin. His family is given as the Matangakula, which is equivalent to the present untouchable Mang caste ... Mallika, his chief queen, was the daughter of a flower-vendor.'

The Sakyas had to find some means to please the king and yet not offend their own tribal honour. The solution they found was to play an elaborate ruse before the Kosalan envoy who came with the king's request, and palm off a daughter born of a slave to the Sakyan chief as a true princess. A son, Virudhaka, was born out of the marriage, and he accidentally learned the truth about his mother when, as a youth, he visited the Sakyas.

The story of Virudhaka's visit to Kapilavastu is told in detail in the *Jatakas*, and is illustrative of the social and political ethos of the age. The Sakyas, though they entertained Virudhaka grandly, would not return his greetings, he being a slave girl's son. And when he set out to return to Sravasti, they had the seat on which he sat washed with milk. By chance this was seen by a member of the Kosalan retinue, and he informed the prince about the outrage. Virudhaka said nothing, but he would never forget the slight or forgive the Sakyas. 'Yes,' he thought, 'let them pour milk and wash the seat I sat on! When I am king, I will wash the place with their hearts' blood.'

A few years later, when his father was away visiting Buddha, Virudhaka, who had been appointed as the military chief of the kingdom, usurped the Kosalan throne, and soon after, his smouldering grudge now in full blaze, led his army into Kapilavastu. 'King Virudhaka slew all the Sakyas,' note the *Jatakas*, 'beginning with babes at the breast, and with their hearts' blood washed the seat [on which he had once sat] and returned.' A few Sakyas however managed to escape the slaughter, and the clan would survive long enough to give a bride to a Sri Lankan Buddhist king some centuries later. Virudhaka's savage revenge is the last known incident of Kosalan history. We do not know when and how its power collapsed, but the kingdom was eventually absorbed by Magadha.

Magadha lay immediately to the south-east of Kosala, a long and narrow strip of land in southern Bihar along the eastern bank of the Son, from the Ganga in the north to the wilderness of the Chota Nagpur Plateau in the south. In the beginning it was a much smaller kingdom than Kosala, and it hardly seemed destined to an imperial career. Located near the extremity of Aryan settlements in India, a good part of its land was rough, hilly tracts unsuitable for agriculture. Its original capital, Rajagriha in southern Magadha, surrounded by several hills, seemed to huddle for safety in the mountain fastness, and was better suited for defence than for imperial endeavour. However, Magadha had a plentiful supply of forest timber and elephants, and its position bordering the Ganga was an advantage in controlling trade. Furthermore, the state had vast deposits of iron and copper in its southern districts, and this gave it a decisive advantage over its rivals, for, as the *Arthasastra* would later state, 'the mine is the womb of war materials.' But more than anything else, Magadha's triumph was the triumph of human resourcefulness and enterprise.

The rise of Magadha began with Bimbisara of the Sisunaga clan, its first known dynasty. Its history before him is obscure. There is no mention of Magadhans in the Rig-veda, but the Atharva-veda names them as a people living on the confines of Aryan civilisation, and early Brahminical literature describes them as a mixed caste. The term Magadhan originally meant a bard, but later also came to mean a trader.

The kings of Magadha, like those of Kosala, 'were of low birth,' observes Kosambi. 'Bimbisara's lineage is not given in Pali records, but Sanskrit Puranas ascribe him to the Sisunaga line ... The termination *naga* for the name would be impossible in Vedic usage; here, it would indicate aboriginal blood, or at least aboriginal cults. The Brahmin records speak of the dynasty with contempt as the lowest of Kshatriyas, *kshatra-bandhu*.' But lineage was of little consequence in the fluid society of the sixth century BC, so Bimbisara was readily accepted by the other rulers of the Gangetic basin as their peer, and several of them, including the chieftain of the race-proud Lichchavis, gave their daughters to him in marriage.

The Buddhist text *Mahavamsa* states that Bimbisara was anointed king by his father at the age of fifteen, but does not mention his father's name or title. He ascended the throne around the middle of the sixth century BC, and is believed to have reigned for fifty-two years. A ruler of exceptional ability, he developed Magadha into the most powerful and best-organised state in India, by setting up, for the first time in India, a complex administrative organisation, with the objective of collecting revenue systematically. This enabled him to maintain a professional army, and thus rule as an absolute monarch, free of tribal restraints. He was probably the first Indian king to maintain a standing army – he sported the title *seniya*, meaning 'one with an army' – while other rulers mostly depended on temporary recruits or tribal militias enlisted in times of war.

A tireless and thorough ruler, Bimbisara rigorously controlled every aspect of administration, minutely supervising the work of his officers, regularly summoning village headmen – who were in charge of collecting the dues to the state – for conferences, and periodically touring the kingdom for inspection. He is also said to have built roadways and causeways, to integrate his kingdom with a transportation and communication grid. All this turned Magadha into a tightly organised state, its effective economic and military power far greater than indicated by its physical size and outward resources. Bimbisara was an autarch, unlike the other kings of the age who were dependent on the fickle support of chieftains. The state belonged to him, absolutely. Bimbisara thus laid the foundations of a form of government that would, in a couple of centuries, find its ultimate expression in the totalitarian administrative system of the Mauryas.

From the very beginning Bimbisara worked patiently and systematically according to a well-conceived plan of conquest. First, he entered into a series of marriage alliances – the *Mahavagga* gives the number of his wives as 500, a conventional figure of little value – deliberately planned to gain political and strategic advantages. Particularly beneficial were his marriages to the sister of Prasenajit of Kosala, and to the daughter of the Lichchavi chieftain Chetaka. His Kosalan bride brought him the rich tract of Kasi as her dowry, and the alliance secured his western frontier, while his alliance with the Lichchavis secured his northern frontier. This security enabled Bimbisara to turn to the east and conquer the kingdom of Anga that bordered the right bank of the Ganga on its southern course. The annexation of Anga, with its capital at Champa, a river port of considerable commercial importance, greatly enhanced Bimbisara's wealth and power, as he now controlled the trade down the lower Ganga to the seaports of the Bengal delta.

A sagacious monarch, Bimbisara made much of patronising sages, and both Buddhists and Jains claimed him as their devotee. He was related to Mahavira through his Lichchavi queen, who was the sage's maternal first cousin. But Bimbisara was equally devoted to Buddha, to whom he gifted the Veluvana Park, and lent to the sangha the services of Jivaka, the legendary royal physician. Perhaps he had a genuine interest in spiritual quests, but showing favours to these sages was good policy too, for the king thus won the support of their influential urban followers.

Bimbisara died about eight years before Buddha. His kingdom, according to the stock figures given in the *Mahavagga*, extended to 300 leagues and had 80,000 villages. Whatever its actual size, Magadha had by the end of Bimbisara's reign become the most powerful state in the Gangetic Plain. But his half-century-long reign made his son Ajatasatru fretful, and, impatient to rule himself, he finally imprisoned his aged father and usurped the throne. Buddhist sources state that Ajatasatru later starved his father to death – that he, on the advice of 'the base and wicked Devadatta,' Buddha's rebel cousin, 'slew the good and virtuous old king his father.' Jain sources absolve Ajatasatru of patricide; they admit that he imprisoned his father and seized the throne, but maintain that Bimbisara died of his own hand, by taking poison.

Bimbisara's tragic fate, according to the *Jatakas*, had been foreseen by soothsayers. At the time of Ajatasatru's conception there arose in his mother, Chellana, the Kosalan princess, 'a chronic longing to drink blood from the right knee of king Bimbisara, her husband,' the *Jatakas* state. Diviners interpreted this to mean that the child would kill his father and seize the kingdom, so they named him Ajatasatru, because he was his father's enemy while still in the womb.

Bimbisara however disregarded the dire prediction, and brought up the prince with affection, refusing to take any precaution against possible treachery, though his courtiers warned him that every prince was a potential patricide. 'Great king, formerly kings when suspicious of their sons had them kept in a secret place, and gave orders that at their death they were to be brought forth and set up on the throne,' they told him. But Bimbisara, perhaps weary after his long reign and stupendous military and administrative endeavours, was ready to passively accept whatever fate had in store for him. In a way, he brought about his own death.

Soon after Bimbisara's death, his grief-stricken queen, Chellana, also died. Suspicions about the circumstances of their death prompted Prasenajit to repossess Kasi, Chellana's dowry. This led to war, in which Kosalans, though initially defeated, ambushed and captured Ajatasatru. Prasenajit however released him and restored him to his throne, and even gave his daughter Vajira in marriage to him with Kasi as her dowry. Peace with Kosala enabled Ajatasatru to advance against the Vrijian Confederacy, which lay to the north of Magadha, across the Ganga. 'I will root out and destroy these Vrijians ... and bring them to utter ruin,' he declared. But the war dragged on for many years – sixteen years, according to Jain sources – and it was only by fomenting squabbles among the Vrijian clans that Ajatasatru was finally able to subdue the confederacy.

It was for the campaign against the Vrijian Confederacy that Ajatasatru built Pataliputra – as a forward outpost at a strategic location on the right bank of the Ganga – which would later grow to become the Magadhan imperial capital, and would remain the chief city of India for about a thousand years. Ajatasatru also made a few innovations in military technology during his wars against the Vrijians, such as catapults to shoot huge stone balls, and an armoured vehicle called Rathamusala – which was manoeuvred by soldiers secure inside it, and had projecting blades, probably attached to its wheels and sides – to scythe down enemy soldiers, like a mechanical Grim Reaper, while it hurtled through the enemy ranks.

Ajatasatru, according to Sinhalese chronicles, ruled for thirty-two years and died in the mid-fifth century BC, leaving an extensive kingdom which, says Buddhaghosha, measured 500 leagues. He was a just and efficient ruler, as even Buddhist sources acknowledge, though they damn him as a patricide. Like his father, he was a keen patron of religion, and it was under his aegis, according to Buddhist tradition, that the first Buddhist council was held at Rajagriha. 'He with all expedition had a magnificent hall constructed ... It was like the assembly hall of the gods themselves,' says the *Mahavamsa*. 'When it was adorned in every way, he caused precious rugs to be spread according to the number of monks. For the presiding monk was prepared a lofty and noble seat, while for the reciting monk was placed another high seat in the middle of the hall.'

Ajatasatru was succeeded by four kings, all patricides, Buddhist sources state. The last of them, Kalasoka, was, according to Greek chroniclers, murdered by his wife's paramour, who then usurped the throne and founded the Nanda dynasty. He was, says Curtius, 'a barber, scarcely staving off hunger by his daily earnings, but who, for his being not uncomely in person, had gained the affections of the queen, and was by her influence advanced to too near a place in the confidence of the reigning monarch. Afterwards, however, he (or the queen herself, according to Diodorus) treacherously murdered his sovereign; and then, under the pretence of acting as guardian to the royal children, usurped the supreme authority, having put the young princes to death.'

There is much confusion about the lineage of the Nandas. According to the Puranas, theirs was not even a new dynasty, but the continuation of the Sisunaga rule through a son born of a liaison between Sisunaga king Mahanandin and a Sudra woman. 'The son of Mahanandin will be born of a woman of the Sudra class: his name will be Nanda (called) Mahapadma, for he will be exceedingly avaricious,' states the *Vishnu Purana* in its oracular style. Jain sources maintain that the founder was the son of a barber and a courtesan. Buddhist texts speak of Nandas as *annatakula* – of unknown lineage. Even the founder's name is uncertain. The Puranas refer to him as Mahapadma, while Buddhists call him Ugrasena, which is probably the same as Agrammes mentioned by Greek writers as the Nanda king ruling at the time of Alexander's invasion of Punjab. The Nandas were called Nava-Nandas, which could mean either 'nine Nandas' or 'new Nandas'. The Pali Buddhist text *Mahavamsatika* states that Ugrasena and his brothers were dacoits before they became kings.

The only thing that is certain about the Nandas is that they were not Kshatriyas. The Puranas speak of them as Sudras, and damn them as *adharmikas* (irreligious), probably because they were patrons of Jainism. 'After him (Mahapadma Nanda) the kings of the earth will (be Sudras),' declares the *Vishnu Purana*. Indeed, most of the leading dynasties of India from then on till the establishment of Rajput kingdoms a thousand years later would belong to non-Kshatriya castes, and even the claims of Rajputs to be Kshatriyas are not always credible.

The Nandas were unpopular rulers – at least, so claimed their adversaries. According to Plutarch, Chandragupta, the founder of the Mauryan dynasty that overthrew the Nandas, told Alexander when he was in Punjab that the Nanda king 'was hated and despised by his subjects for the wickedness of his disposition and the meanness of his origin.' There might be some truth in these charges, for the Nandas seem to have tightened administrative rigour, especially in revenue collection, which was already quite stringent under the Sisunagas, and this would have alienated the people. Buddhist sources state that Dhana Nanda was 'addicted to hoarding treasure ... [and that] he collected riches to the amount of eighty crores,' and the *Kathasarit-sagara*, a Sanskrit work of the eleventh century AD, states that he accumulated 990 million gold pieces. So widespread and enduring was the legend about the fabulous wealth of the Nandas that even Sangam poets in the faraway Tamil country extolled it, and people were still talking about it a thousand years later, as Hsuan Tsang in the seventh century AD noted.

The expansion of Magadha continued under the Nandas, and by the end of the Nanda rule, two centuries after the process began under Bimbisara, the kingdom assumed the proportions of an empire. Nanda power stretched over the entire Gangetic basin, perhaps even extended into southern India as far as northern Karnataka. The Puranas refer to Mahapadma as the exterminator of Kshatriyas, probably because he overthrew many old dynasties – 'Like another Parasurama, he will be the annihilator of the Kshatriya race,' says the *Vishnu Purana*. 'He will bring the whole earth under one umbrella ... He and his sons will govern for a hundred years.' In the end the Nandas had become *chakravartis*, universal monarchs, having accomplished the Indian imperial ideal of *digvijaya*, the conquest of the four quarters.

A GREEK INTERLUDE

For about 1,500 years, after they parted company in Central Asia and went their separate ways, there was no significant interaction between Indian and Iranian Aryans. They were neighbours, but were kept well apart by the great mountains, though the trickle of people into India through the mountain passes never ceased entirely. But in the second half of the sixth century BC the destinies of the two nations once again became intertwined, when Cyrus the Great, having unified Persia into an empire, sent his armies rolling westward towards the Mediterranean and eastward towards India. His campaigns along the Indian borderland brought Bactria under his power, and possibly also the narrow ribbon of land between the Indus and the western mountains. Xenophon, a fourth-century BC Greek historian, states that the empire of Cyrus stretched from Syria to the Indian Ocean. But much of the evidence about the eastern campaigns of Cyrus is contradictory, and it is probable that it was only Darius I, the second ruler after Cyrus, who extended the Persian empire up to the Indus.

If it was indeed Darius who annexed the Indus Valley, he did so quite early in his reign, probably around 518 BC. It is not certain how far into India his power extended. Direct Persian rule probably reached only up to the Indus, for Alexander when he invaded India did not come across any Persian satrap after he crossed the river. But Persian hegemony, though not Persian rule, very likely extended as far as the Jhelum, for here there were officials and chieftains sporting Persian titles. Even the king of Taxila seems to have acknowledged Persian suzerainty. But whatever the actual extent of the Persian satrapy in India, it yielded the largest revenue in the empire. Says Herodotus: 'The population of Indians is by far the greatest of all the people that we know; and they paid a tribute proportionately larger than the rest: 360 talents of gold dust.' This was about a third of the total revenue from Persia's Asian provinces, and probably amounted to close to nine tons of gold, as Kosambi conjectures.

The empire of Darius, the greatest the world had known till then, lasted barely a century, as his later successors, taking their power for granted, slackened vigilance and effort, and took to a life of ease. Once a hardy, austere people, Persians now sank into a life of wanton luxury and dissipation, even languorously prolonging their customary single meal of the day from noon to night.

For a while, however, Persian expansion continued under the successors of Darius. Xerxes I, who succeeded Darius, pursued his father's expansionist policy, and it was during his invasion of Greece that Indian soldiers fought in Europe for the first time. Indian infantrymen were, notes Herodotus, 'clad in garments made of cotton [and] carried bows of cane and arrows of cane, the latter tipped with iron.' Indian cavalrymen too were 'armed with the same equipment as in the case of the infantry, but they brought riding-horses and chariots, the latter being drawn by horses and wild asses.' A vast number of Indian dogs, known for their ferocity, followed the Persian army, says Herodotus.

The Persian invasion of Greece was a disaster, and with its failure began the decline of the Persian empire. But the immense mass of the empire, by its sheer gravitational force, prevented the provinces from breaking away altogether, and even its farthest regions generally yielded to the will of the emperor till the very end, as evident from the fact that Darius III, the last Persian emperor, could field an Indian contingent along with a small elephant force in his final stand against Alexander.

The long Persian occupation of the Indus Valley had cultural and political consequences of great importance. The Achaemenids introduced Aramaic, their official language, into their Indian territories, and from this was derived the Kharoshthi script that Asoka used in some of his inscriptions, and possibly even the Brahmi script from which all the different Indian scripts later evolved. Indian coinage was also influenced by Persians, and probably, as Thapar conjectures, Asoka's inscriptions were inspired by the rock inscriptions of Darius.

It was inevitable that Alexander's invasion of Persia should lead him into India, to complete his conquest of the Achaemenid empire. In 334 BC, a mere two years after his accession to the throne of Macedonia, Alexander, aged twenty-two, crossed into Asia to begin what would be the greatest and most romantic military saga in the history of mankind.

Alexander would, during his Asian campaign, proclaim himself to be a god, but even the ancients found the notion rather laughable, as indeed he himself sometimes did. But there certainly was something very special about him, even if we find it hard to believe Plutarch's claim that his body and breath 'were so fragrant as to perfume the clothes that he wore.' He was handsome, and was a superb athlete, brilliant in martial arts. In his personal life, he was the very embodiment of moderation; he was abstemious in sex, ate and (until his last years) drank in moderation. A disciple of Aristotle, he enjoyed the company of scholars, and often stayed up late into the night conversing with them, even in the midst of his campaigns; he loved poetry and music, and used to play the harp in his youth. He was also a tireless adventurer, who 'liked ... dangerous enterprises, and could not bear to rest.' On the negative side, he was blindly superstitious, and often allowed portents to sway his judgement, and was much given to performing magical rites. At times he was utterly savage, butchering even women and children in the thousands in cold blood. He had a vicious temper and was subject to 'paroxysms of cruelty.' But more than anything else, he was a matchless military genius, who did the right thing instinctively, every time. He might not have been a god, but the gods were certainly with him.

Yet no one could have presaged Alexander's grand destiny when he set out to wage war against Persia. It would in fact have seemed a doomed enterprise to most people. In material terms there was no comparison between the two contenders. Macedonia, even after its conquest of Greece, was an insignificant little kingdom, while Persia was ten times as large, stretching well over 4,000 kilometres east-west, all the way from the Indus to the Aegean Sea, and about 2,000 kilometres north-south, from the Aral Sea to southern Egypt. Persia's resources in men and materials were immeasurably greater than those of Macedonia. Alexander had an army of just 30,000 infantry and 5,000 cavalry; Darius opposed him with 600,000 soldiers. Yet Macedonians easily vanquished Persians, for Persians lacked discipline and spirit and, more than anything else, leadership. Alexander routed Darius at Issus, and then again at Gaugamela; he took Babylon and Susa, bestially ravaged and burned down the noble city of Persepolis, and finally advanced to the borderland of India.

The Greeks had at this time only the vaguest notion about the geography of India. Asia for Alexander meant essentially the Persian empire, and he thought that India was a peninsula stretching eastward into the sea as an extension of the Persian landmass. The Greeks had no knowledge of any land beyond India, and Alexander believed that by conquering India he would be reaching the very end of the earth, the shore of the far ocean which he thought lay at India's eastern border.

It is impossible to trace precisely Alexander's path into India, as he criss-crossed the land, seldom taking the direct route from one place to another. The original chronicles of his campaigns written by his officers are all lost, and what is available are the condensed and sometimes garbled versions written by later Greek and Roman historians. This evidence indicates that Alexander arrived in Seistan in the winter of 330, from where, as the snows began to clear, he moved into southern Afghanistan for a few months, and then swung north-eastward to cross into the Kabul Valley. From there he headed for Bactria, the farthest north-eastern province of the Persian empire. After nearly a year-long campaign there, he returned to Kabul, and finally began his preparations to advance into India.

This was in the summer of 327. From Kabul he sent heralds to the various principalities of the old Persian domain in India, summoning their rulers to meet him, their new overlord. He already had with him an Indian ruler – one Sasigupta, probably a tribal chieftain – who had joined him in Bactria, and he had received assurances of co-operation from the king of Taxila, whose emissaries had trekked through the Hindu Kush mountains to meet him in Central Asia. The Taxilan king was probably a vassal of the Persian emperor, in which case it would have been natural for him to offer his allegiance to Alexander as the successor to Darius. But he had a more urgent reason to ally with Alexander, for he was being threatened with annihilation by King Porus, his powerful neighbour to the east across the Jhelum. His survival depended on Alexander's support. The king, whom Plutarch describes as 'a shrewd man,' found it prudent to submit to Alexander, as the Macedonians were transients and were not likely to dispossess him of his lands.

In the Kabul Valley, Alexander divided his army into two, and sent one division under Hephaestion, his boon companion, directly to the Indus, probably through the Khyber Pass, to build boats to cross the river. He himself then struck north into the hills to subdue the hostile tribes there and to secure his rear. This involved much hard fighting. Alexander was absolutely ruthless in extirpating his adversaries, and no considerations of compassion or honour restrained him. Sometimes he was even perfidious, as in his massacre of enemy soldiers at Massaga in the Swat valley, after agreeing to let them depart in peace. He would not leave any potential enemies behind him.

Some of the hardest battles that Alexander ever fought were in India, that too not against organised kingdoms, but against obscure hill tribes, where the fight was not against paid armies but against people defending their hearth. The harder the fight, the more brutal was Alexander's retaliation, and his passage through India was marked by some of the most thorough, deliberate and systematic carnages the country had witnessed in its history of numerous invasions. There was an awful and unquenchable blood-thirst in this disciple of Aristotle.

After subduing the tribes, Alexander descended from the hills and joined his main army at Ohind on the Indus, about 25 kilometres north of Attock. 'When Alexander arrived at the river Indus, he found a bridge [of boats] made over it by Hephaestion, and two thirty-oared galleys, besides many smaller crafts,' records Arrian. 'He moreover found that 200 talents of silver, 3,000 oxen, and 10,000 sheep for sacrificial victims, and 30 elephants had arrived as gifts from Taxiles the Indian; 700 Indian horsemen also arrived from Taxiles as a reinforcement, and that prince sent word that he would surrender to him the city of Taxila, the largest town between the river Indus and Hydaspes (Jhelum). Alexander there offered sacrifice to the gods to whom he was in the habit of sacrificing, and celebrated a gymnastic and horse contest near the river.'

At the Indus Alexander gave his army a well-earned thirty-day rest. Then, at daybreak one day early in the spring of 326, finding the omens auspicious, he with his army crossed 'into the country of the Indians,' as Arrian puts it. 'When Alexander had crossed to the other side of the river Indus, he again offered sacrifice there, according to his custom.'

Here King Ambhi of Taxila, who had earlier, as prince, negotiated the kingdom's submission to Alexander, and had now, on the death of his father, succeeded to the throne, advanced with his army some 6 kilometres from Taxila to meet the Macedonians. For a moment, when Alexander saw the Indian forces deployed in battle formation across his path, he suspected treachery and ordered his own army to prepare for battle. Seeing this, Ambhi rode up with a few officers to clear up the misunderstanding – he had, he explained through an interpreter, come only to escort Alexander to Taxila. Ambhi then placed his army and his kingdom at Alexander's disposal. And Alexander in turn confirmed him on his throne.

For three days Alexander was royally entertained in Taxila, and the two rulers exchanged gifts. Around this time he also received a number of ambassadors from the kings and chieftains of the region, bearing presents and offering submission. Only Porus, who ruled over the kingdom across the Jhelum, and was probably a scion of the ancient and proud Aryan clan of Purus mentioned in the Rig-veda, stood aloof and haughty. When Alexander's messenger told him 'in peremptory terms that he must pay tribute and come to meet his sovereign at the very frontiers of his own dominions,' he, according to Curtius, replied that he would indeed comply with the second of these demands, and that 'when Alexander entered his realm he would meet him, but come armed for battle.' Alexander responded to the challenge by cutting short his stay in Taxila and hastening to the Jhelum to confront Porus.

He was, as usual, in a tearing hurry, impatient to move on, racing against time to get to the end of the earth before time itself ran out for him. In the spring of 326 the Macedonian army assembled on the west bank of the Jhelum. Across the river, probably near the town of Jhelum, was drawn up the army of Porus. In numerical strength, the rival forces were fairly evenly matched. According to Arrian, Porus deployed in the battle against Alexander 4,000 cavalrymen, 300 chariots, 30,000 infantry and 200 war elephants; in addition, he had some advance guards and reserves. Alexander is said to have had 120,000 people in his camp, but these included camp followers and other non-combatants, including 'the

Asiatic wives of the Macedonian soldiers and their children.' His soldiers probably numbered only around 35,000, about the same strength he had when he was encamped in the Kabul Valley. He too had some elephants with him, but used them only for transport, not in battle, for elephants often ran out of control during battle, and control was everything in his meticulous battle plans.

For Porus, on the other hand, there was a major advantage in deploying elephants, for the Macedonian horses, unfamiliar with these towering black behemoths, usually bucked in fright and bolted at the very sight of them. Porus had a few other advantages too. Though the two armies were about the same size, Porus had a substantial numerical advantage over the Macedonians when they actually engaged in battle, as Alexander could cross the river with only about a third of his army. Further, the Indian army was all of one people, while Alexander's was a polyglot army, its core composed of Macedonian regiments, but the rest formed of mercenaries from Greek cities, Balkan hill-men, Persians, Phoenicians, Egyptians, Central Asians, recruits from Afghanistan, and the regiments of his Indian allies, many of whom did not even speak each others' language.

Alexander's immediate problem was to cross the Jhelum safely. The river, like all Himalayan rivers in summer, was in flood due to the melting of snows in the mountains. It could not be easily forded. Nor was it possible to build a bridge of boats across it, for Porus had posted scouts up and down the river to monitor and challenge every move of Alexander. In the face of such vigilance, and the strong force gathered on the opposite bank – with elephants to scare off horses – any attempt to cross the river openly would have been suicidal.

Alexander somehow had to steal a passage and take the enemy by surprise. He used a stratagem for this. To distract and confuse Porus and to get him to lower his guard, Alexander divided his army into many divisions, and 'himself led some of his troops now into one part of the land, and now into another, at one time ravaging the enemy's property, at another looking out for a place where the river might appear easier for him to ford it,' says Arrian. 'The rest of his troops he entrusted to his different generals, and sent them about in many directions. He conveyed corn from all quarters into his camp from the land on his side of the Hydaspes, so that it might be evident to Porus that he had resolved to remain quiet near the bank until the water of the river subsided in the winter, and afforded him a passage in many places. As his vessels were sailing up and down the river, and skins were being filled with hay, and the whole bank appeared to be covered in one place with cavalry and in another with infantry, Porus was not allowed to keep at rest ...'

All this thoroughly bewildered Porus. He did not know what to expect.

Alexander had seized the initiative. 'In the night,' continues Arrian, 'Alexander led most of his cavalry along the bank in various directions, making a clamour and raising the battle-cry ... as if they were making all the preparations necessary for crossing the river. Porus also marched along the river at the head of his elephants opposite the places where the clamour was heard, and Alexander thus gradually got him into the habit of leading his men along opposite the noise. But when this occurred frequently, and there was merely a clamour and a raising of the battle-cry, Porus no longer continued to move about to meet the expected advance of the cavalry; but perceiving that his fear had been groundless, he kept his position in the camp ... Alexander ... [thus] brought it about that the mind of Porus no longer entertained any fear of his nocturnal attempts.'

Meanwhile Alexander located a place where he could cross the river unobserved by the enemy, a bend of the river some 28 kilometres from his camp, where there was a fair-sized wooded island which concealed the crossing point from the enemy scouts. An additional advantage of the place, says Curtius, was that there was 'a deep hollow [there] ... not far from the bank, capable of hiding not only foot soldiers but also mounted cavalry.' In this wooded gully Alexander secretly assembled and hid a number of the dismantled boats he had brought from the Indus, and collected there all the materials he needed for crossing the river. Then on a night of storm and rain in June 326, Alexander, keeping well away from the bank of the river to avoid detection, moved with a select band of soldiers to his chosen crossing point. He left a good part of his army in his main camp opposite the Indian position and the elephants had been withdrawn. Another division was stationed half way to the crossing point with similar instructions. The royal tent was left standing at the main camp, with the royal guard stationed around it as usual; Alexander even got a man who roughly resembled him to wear the royal mantle and move about, 'to make it appear as if the king in person was guarding that part of the bank,' says Curtius.

The stormy night suited Alexander's plan perfectly, says Arrian, for 'the claps of thunder and the storm drowned ... the clatter of the weapons and the noise which arose from the orders given by officers.' At dawn, as the sky cleared, Alexander with some 6,000 infantry and 5,000 cavalry crossed the river, the infantry in boats and the cavalry swimming across on skins filled with hay. Alexander himself, along with his top generals, embarked in a thirty-oared galley. Everything went off according to Alexander's plan – nearly everything. He had one unexpected problem: when he landed on what he took to be the opposite bank, it turned out to be a large island separated from the riverbank by a rain-swollen channel. With some difficulty the army managed to cross the channel, but in the delay Alexander lost valuable time and the chance to surprise Porus. Furthermore, as the Macedonian flotilla rounded the first island, they were spotted by the Indian scouts, who galloped to warn Porus.

The news put Porus in a quandary. Right opposite to his own position, he could see the Macedonian army still in place along with a large number of boats. The reported landing, he feared, could be a manoeuvre to draw him away from his position to enable the main Macedonian army to cross over. He needed time to decide what to do. So he despatched one of his sons with a small cavalry contingent and some chariots to block the path of those who had landed. This small force was easily routed by Alexander and the prince killed.

The vanquished Indian cavalrymen sped back to inform Porus that it was indeed Alexander who had crossed the river. It was only then that Porus advanced with his main army to give battle, leaving behind a small contingent and a few elephants at his original position to thwart the Macedonian army on the opposite bank from crossing over. On reaching a broad, level and fairly firm sandy ground a little away from the marshy riverbank, he halted, and drew up his army in the traditional Indian battle formation. He deployed his elephants in front, spacing them out about 30 metres apart. Immediately behind the elephants and extending somewhat beyond them he arrayed his infantry, and placed his cavalry on its outer flanks with chariots in front of them. Porus himself took up a central and commanding position, mounted on an enormous elephant and wearing an intricate armour that was 'embellished with gold and silver, setting off his supremely majestic person to great advantage,' Curtius notes.

Presently Alexander too reached the field. But he did not rush into battle. Instead, he halted the army, to give them some rest before engaging the enemy, and to give himself time to survey the Indian battle order and choose a suitable strategy. After careful consideration, he decided to avoid the Indian centre defended by elephants, but to storm its exposed wings with his cavalry. The cavalry was his strength, and he intended to win the battle with it. He therefore concentrated the bulk of his cavalry on his right flank under his personal command, with a contingent of Central Asian horse archers in front of him, leaving only a small cavalry force on his left flank. In between the two cavalry positions he placed his phalanx, the soldiers resplendent in bronze armour. And 'on each side, at the extremities of the phalanx, his archers, Agrianians and javelin-throwers were posted,' writes Arrian.

Alexander then worked out a detailed battle plan, rehearsing in his mind his response to every contingency that might arise in the course of the encounter. For all his personal impetuosity, he was a meticulous general, who prepared for every battle with thoroughness, patience and precision, leaving nothing to chance. He foresaw every eventuality, therefore could meet every battlefield emergency with lightning speed. There were never any surprises for him.

According to the fairly cogent account of the encounter given by Arrian, Alexander opened the action by sending his Central Asian cavalry archers, a thousand of them, against the Indian left, showering it with arrows, while they themselves remained out of range of the Indian weapons. Here again the overnight storm worked to Alexander's favour. The one distinct advantage that Indians had over the Greeks was in archery, for their bow was a formidable, six-foot-long weapon, which could shoot an arrow with such force as to pierce through shield and armour. But on this particular day, the rain-soaked field made it difficult for the Indian archers to rest their bows firmly on the ground, as they needed to do, to draw them effectively. Their chariots too proved useless, for, as Curtius notes, they got stuck 'in the muddy sloughs and proved almost immovable from their great weight.'

As the Central Asian horse-archers attacked, the left wing cavalry of Porus rode out to meet them. But they were immediately taken on by the main Macedonian cavalry charging into the battle under the direct command of Alexander, tilting their enormous wooden lances tipped with sharp metal heads. To relieve his beleaguered left wing, Porus then swung his right wing cavalry into action. But as the horsemen advanced across the battlefield, Alexander, who had anticipated the move, attacked them from the rear with his left wing cavalry. To save the situation, Porus pushed forward his elephants, his main battle division, while Alexander tried to neutralise the elephants by attacking them with his phalanx, 'the men casting darts at the riders and also striking the beasts themselves, standing around them on all sides,' says Arrian. But this was an unequal fight, men against mammoths, and the Macedonian infantry took very heavy losses in the action – as Arrian puts it, the elephants 'demolished the phalanx of the Macedonians, dense as it was.' The Indian cavalry too rallied at this point.

The outcome of the battle now lay in fine balance. But presently the elephants, many of them wounded and several without mahouts, began to run amok – 'rushing forward at friends and foes alike, they pushed about, trampled down and killed them in every kind of way,' Arrian says. It was in fact the Indian army which suffered the greater loss from the elephants, for the Macedonians, 'attacking the beasts in an open space in accordance with their own plan, got out of their way whenever they rushed at them, and when they wheeled round to return, followed them close and hurled javelins at them. But the Indians retreating among the elephants received greater injury from them.' Eventually the elephants fled, 'uttering a shrill piping sound.'

As the elephants fled, the Macedonian phalanx formed again into their usual tight array and advanced against the Indian centre, while at the same time their cavalry charged the wings. This combined onslaught utterly routed the Indian army. But there was no escape in flight for the Indians, as the retreating soldiers were taken on by the Macedonian divisions that had crossed the river from their main camp during the battle. The Indian soldiers were soft targets, for, as Kosambi points out, 'a relative shortage of metal led Indians to fight with no other protection than a shield and leather cuirass with, perhaps, a metal helmet.'

The slaughter was terrible. 'Of the Indians little short of 20,000 infantry and 3,000 cavalry were killed in this battle,' states Arrian, perhaps vastly exaggerating the figures. All the top commanders of Porus and two of his sons were slain. His chariots were all destroyed. The Macedonian loss, very likely understated, is given by Arrian as 80 infantry, 10 horse-archers, and 220 cavalry. Diodorus, another ancient Greek historian gives quite different figures – while 12,000 Indians fell, Macedonians lost 280 horsemen and 700 foot soldiers. The battle, which began early in the morning, 'was so obstinately maintained that it was fully the eighth hour of the day before the Indian renounced all attempts at further resistance,' says Plutarch.

It was Alexander's military genius that won the day for the Macedonians. But Porus was not found wanting in comparison. The Greek chroniclers, not given to lauding their adversaries, use only superlatives to describe the Indian king. 'Porus,' says Arrian, 'exhibited great talent in the battle, performing the deeds not only of a general but also of a valiant soldier.' He was a giant of a man. 'In stature he measured five cubits (well over seven feet), while his girth was such that his breastplate was twice the size required for a man of ordinary bulk,' says Diodorus. 'His courage matched his bodily vigour,' says Curtius, 'and his wisdom was the utmost attainable in a rude community.'

Porus, though severely wounded – he had received nine wounds – fought on till the end, 'as long as any body of Indians remained compact in the battle,' says Arrian. But in the end, his army totally scattered, he turned his elephant around and left the field. Alexander then sent Ambhi, the king of Taxila, after him, asking him to surrender and presumably promising him good treatment. 'Alexander,' says Arrian, 'having seen that he was a great man and valiant in battle, was very desirous of saving his life.' Porus initially spurned the offer and flung a javelin at Ambhi. But when Alexander sent a second messenger (the Greeks call him Meroes, and some scholars think it was Chandragupta Maurya) who happened to be a friend of Porus, the king, weakened by his wounds and overcome with thirst, stopped the elephant and got down. He was given a drink of water and escorted to Alexander.

On his approach, Alexander galloped up with a few officers to meet him. Alexander, Arrian says, 'was surprised that he (Porus) did not seem cowed in spirit, but advanced to meet him as one brave man would meet another brave man, after having gallantly struggled in defence of his own kingdom against another king.' The emperor asked Porus how he wished to be treated.

'As befits a king,' said this proud and taciturn Indian.

'For my own sake thou shalt be thus treated,' responded Alexander, referring to his own sense of honour. 'But for thy own sake do thou demand what is pleasing to thee!'

But Porus would only say that his demand to be treated as king covered all that he desired. And Alexander, states Arrian, 'being still more pleased at this remark, not only granted him the rule over his own kingdom, but also added another country to that which he had before, of larger extent than the former.' Alexander evidently wanted to turn the dangerous enemy into a powerful ally. It could be also that Alexander had no plan to incorporate into his empire the lands beyond the Jhelum, which had not formed part of the Persian empire, but merely wanted to establish his suzerainty over them. Alexander's generosity certainly paid off. Porus would prove to be the staunchest and most energetic of Alexander's allies in his further advance into India. He was also the chief beneficiary of Alexander's Indian campaign.

The Greeks immortalised Porus. He is not mentioned in any Indian source whatever – we know of him only from Greek chronicles. While his name was well known to Europeans throughout history, he was entirely unknown to Indians till modern times.

LIVE SHORT, LIVE MUCH

The battle of the Jhelum was a landmark victory for Alexander, which he memorialised by founding two cities on the opposite banks of the river, one named Bucephala, after Bucephalus, his favourite horse which died there, and the other Nicaea, City of Victory. Later he also issued coins from his Babylonian mint to commemorate the battle, showing himself on a rampant horse attacking Porus on an elephant.

After celebrating the victory with thanksgiving sacrifices as usual, Alexander resumed his eastward advance, keeping close to the Himalayan foothills, where there was some relief from the searing heat of the Indian plains, and the rivers were narrow and fordable. He believed that somewhere there in the east, not too far away, along India's eastern frontier, lay the 'outer ocean', the very end of the earth. This was where he was headed. To stand on the shore of the vast terminal ocean, from beyond which the sun rose, and to be acclaimed as the conqueror of the whole world – this, says Plutarch, was Alexander's ultimate ambition. He had come a long, long way from home, faced and overcome formidable adversaries, encountered countless dangers, all for this one moment of supreme triumph.

It was a possible dream. The 'whole world' that Alexander wanted to conquer was really only a small part of the earth, the band of civilised human habitats stretching from the Mediterranean to the Ganga. He knew nothing of the great civilisation of China, did not even know of the country's existence, and he ignored Europe and northern Asia and the whole of Africa beyond Egypt as primeval wilderness where there were no nations to conquer. The goal that Alexander had set for himself was therefore not chimerical, though based on faulty knowledge. He believed that this goal was now close at hand. The thought quickened his steps. He was certain of success. Ever victorious, Alexander considered himself invincible. His spirit never flagged.

He now crossed the Chenab, probably near Sialkot, then crossed the Ravi, and within a month was on the Beas. To the east of the Beas lay the Satluj, the last of the Punjab rivers. Beyond this, Alexander was told, 'there were two nations, the Gangaridae and Prasii, whose king Agrammes kept in the field for guarding the approaches to his country 20,000 cavalry and

200,000 infantry, besides 2,000 four-horsed chariots, and, what was most formidable force of all, a troop of elephants which ... ran up to the number of 3,000,' states Curtius.

The prospect of encountering such a stupendous adversary, far from daunting Alexander, only 'excited ... [in him] an ardent desire to advance further,' says Arrian. Danger was nurture for Alexander. Besides, he himself had quite a large army now, as he was accompanied by several Indian kings, including Porus, with their armies, and had received some reinforcements from Persia soon after the battle of the Jhelum. The only problem that troubled him was the need to cross innumerable rivers in the Gangetic Valley, especially now that the monsoon had set in and the rivers were in flood. But still 'his avidity for glory and his insatiable ambition forbade him to think that any place was so far distant or inaccessible as to be beyond his reach,' observes Curtius.

But his men did not share his grand vision. They had had enough of warring. They were nearly 5,000 kilometres and eight years away from home; they had fought innumerable battles, amassed vast quantities of booty, but now they were weary. All that they now wanted was to get back home to Greece and Macedonia to be with their loved ones and enjoy their fortune. Very many of their comrades had perished along the way, many of them in battles but many more of disease. They knew that the same grim fate awaited everyone if they went on with Alexander, especially in view of the great armies they would have to encounter in the Gangetic Valley. They had to stop Alexander. On the banks of the Beas, perhaps near the modern town of Gurdaspur, the soldiers refused to advance any further.

'The battle with Porus,' says Plutarch, 'depressed the spirits of the Macedonians, and made them most unwilling to advance further into India.' It was hard enough to cross the Jhelum and defeat the relatively small army of Porus, but now Alexander wanted them to cross further rivers, fight other battles, even to cross the Ganga – which, they were told, 'had a breadth of two and thirty stadia and a depth of 100 fathoms' – and fight armies that were several times larger than that of Porus. This they most resolutely opposed.

Alexander was well aware of the mood of his men. 'Overflowing and laden with booty, they would rather, he judged, enjoy what they had won than wear themselves out in getting more,' notes Curtius. 'They could not of course be of the same mind as himself, for while he had grasped the conception of a world-wide empire and stood as yet but on the threshold of his labours, they were now worn out with toil, and longed for the time when, all their dangers being at length ended, they might enjoy their latest winnings.' Reason told Alexander that he should heed the feelings of his soldiers and turn back, but 'in the end ambition carried the day against reason.'

Alexander thought that he could win his men over with arguments or by appealing to their sense of honour. He knew that they were troubled by the stories they had heard of the dangers ahead. These tales, he told them, were hollow exaggerations, just like the many other similar tales they had heard all along the way. There could be a large number of elephants in the Gangetic army, he conceded, but he saw no reason for his soldiers to fear them. 'For myself, I have such a poor opinion of these animals that, though I had them, I did not bring them into the field, being fully convinced that they occasion more danger to their own side than to the enemy,' he said. As for the vast armies they would have to face, he reminded them of their own experience in easily routing the 'undisciplined multitudes.'

Abide with him just a little longer, Alexander pleaded with his men. They did not have far to go. 'We are not standing on the threshold of our enterprise and our labours, but at their very close ... and unless your sloth and cowardice prevent it, we shall ... [soon] return in triumph to our native land, having conquered the earth to its remotest bounds ... The prizes before you are greater than the risks ... I, who never ordered you upon my service in which I did not place myself in the forefront of the danger, I who have often with mine own buckler covered you in battle, now entreat you not to shatter the palm which is already in my grasp, and by which, if I may so speak without incurring the ill-will of heaven, I shall become the equal of Hercules and Father Bacchus. Grant this to my entreaties, and break at last your obstinate silence,' Alexander beseeched. 'Where is that familiar shout, the wonted token of your alacrity? Where are the cheerful looks of my Macedonians?'

His men remained glum and silent. Alexander was disgusted. 'I do not recognise you, soldiers, and methinks, I seem not to be recognised by you,' he said. 'I have all along been knocking at deaf ears. I am trying to rouse hearts that are disloyal and crushed with craven fear.'

Alexander was wrong. His men were not disloyal; they were only battle-weary. At the words of Alexander, his hardened veterans wept, we are told, out of pity for themselves. They, says Curtius, 'did not refuse the duties of war, but were simply unable to discharge them,' being 'exhausted with their wounds and incessant labours in the field.' Alexander tried to rally their spirit. 'To a brave man there is no end to labours except the labours themselves,' he reminded them. 'Glorious are the deeds of those who undergo labour and run the risk of danger; and it is delightful to live a life of valour and die, leaving behind immortal glory.'

When they still remained silent, he implored them to speak their minds.

Finally Koinos, a veteran cavalry commander, spoke up, telling Alexander about the sufferings and privations of his men. 'We have conquered all the world, but are ourselves destitute of all things,' he said. 'You are preparing to go to a sphere altogether new – to go in quest of an India unknown even to the Indians themselves ... so that you may traverse as a conqueror more regions than the sun surveys. The thought is altogether worthy of a soul so lofty as thine, but it is above ours; for while thy courage will be ever growing, our vigour is fast waning to its end.' He advised Alexander to return home, and, if he wished, to start afresh on another expedition with new recruits. 'Do not lead us now against our will,' he pleaded.

As Koinos spoke, the soldiers cheered. But Alexander, annoyed, 'leaped down from the tribunal and shut himself up in the royal pavilion, into which he forbade anyone to be admitted except his ordinary attendants,' says Curtius. Alexander could not possibly retreat, for he regarded retreat as 'tantamount to a confession of defeat.' He had to go on, whether his men followed him or not. According to Arrian, he called the generals together again the next day, and told them of his resolve to advance further into India, but said that he would not force anyone to follow him. They were, he said cuttingly, free to return home and tell the people that they had 'deserted their king in the midst of his enemies.'

But neither cajolery nor taunts moved his men. Alexander then returned to his tent, and sulked there for three days, waiting to see whether there would be a change of heart in them. There was not. On the fourth day he emerged from his tent to begin preparations for his advance. As usual, he offered sacrifices for the passage of the river, and took omens. Opportunely, the omens turned out to be most unfavourable – the gods were still with him in his moment of humiliation, granting him a face-saving excuse to retreat. Alexander would never turn back in the face of men, but there would be no shame in yielding to divine will. He then summoned his generals and ordered retreat.

The order to retreat electrified the army, as no victory had ever done. 'Then they shouted as a mixed multitude would shout when rejoicing, and most of them shed tears of joy,' reports Arrian. 'Some of them even approached the royal tent, and prayed many blessings upon Alexander, because by them alone he suffered himself to be conquered.' Alexander marked the farthest point of his conquest by building twelve massive towers – fifty cubits (over twenty-five metres) in height, according to Diodorus – on the bank of the Beas, offered sacrifices on them and, as at every turning-point of his campaign, held gymnastic and equestrian contests and rewarded the winners. He is also said to have built a few giant-sized quarters there, in which everything – rooms, couches, stalls – was made twice the normal size, to give the impression 'that supermen had been there,' says Curtius.

Time and the humid climate of Punjab would in a few centuries reduce the great towers to rubble and dust. Though Plutarch, writing in the first century AD, claimed that 'the king of the Praisiai (Magadha) even to the present day hold [them] in veneration ... [and] offer sacrifices upon them in the Hellenic fashion,' no trace of them has been found. Not even the memory of Alexander's campaign would endure in India.

The Greek retreat began in July 326 BC. Alexander marched back to the Ravi, then to the Chenab. Here his broken, bedraggled army received from Babylon reinforcements and supplies it badly needed – 5,000 cavalry and 7,000 infantry, and 25,000 suits of armour. He then moved on to the Jhelum.

But Alexander was not yet done with adventuring. By the time he got to the Jhelum, he had formulated a plan to transform his retreat into an advance – though thwarted in his dream of reaching the eastern ocean, he now set his sights on advancing to the southern ocean. So, instead of returning by the secure and familiar route by which he had come, he decided to sail down the Indus to the sea, before finally turning homeward. For this new adventure he assembled a massive fleet on the Jhelum, the size of which is given variously in different accounts, from 800 to about 2,000 ships. There were, says Arrian, eighty thirty-oared galleys, 'but the total number of vessels, including the horse transports and boats, and all the other river crafts ... fell not far short of 2,000.' The ships, says Nearchus, were equipped with great splendour.

At dawn one day in October 326, when everything was ready, and the soldiers chosen for the odyssey along with their horses had boarded the ships, and the vessels had been marshalled in perfect order, Alexander offered sacrifices to the gods and, escorted by his guard of honour, boarded the royal flagship. Then, with his army drawn up on both banks of the river, he stood at the high prow of his ship and ceremonially poured a libation into the river out of a golden goblet, invoking the spirits of the Chenab, Jhelum and Indus to bless the voyage. A trumpet was then sounded, and the fleet began to sail majestically down the river, all the ships keeping their places in exact formation. 'He did not allow even the fast-sailing ships to get out of rank,' notes Arrian. The people living along the banks of the river, who had never seen such a grand spectacle in their lives, ran along the banks for a good distance, 'singing their native songs.'

But this was not a recreational excursion. There was much hard fighting ahead. And the river itself held many terrors. Alexander's ship almost foundered at the confluence of the Chenab and the Jhelum, where 'one very narrow river is formed out of the two,' and the current was swift and there were 'prodigious eddies in the whirling stream.' Alexander would have been in mortal danger if the ship had capsized. 'As death itself stared him in the face, he (Alexander) stripped off his clothes, and in his naked condition clung to anything that offered a chance to safety,' while his friends swam alongside the ship, ready to rescue him if the ship sank, notes Diodorus. Fortunately the danger passed, and Alexander continued his voyage down the Indus. His army, split into three divisions, marched along the riverbanks, two on one side at three days' interval from each other, and the third on the opposite bank. The army had to fight its way all the way, initially against tribal oligarchies, then, further down the river, against petty kings. The land was swarming with combative people who fought desperately in self-defence, for they did not know that the Macedonians were leaving India, and feared that they had come to take their homes and lands from them.

Alexander very nearly lost his life in one of these encounters, in a fight against the Malavas, an obscure tribal people living in what Plutarch describes as a 'contemptible town' north of the junction of the Chenab and the Ravi. The town was protected only by a mud citadel, which should have been easy for the Greeks to storm, without the emperor having to personally take part in the fight. But Alexander, possessed by demon fate, grew annoyed at the slow progress of the assault, and, snatching a scaling ladder from a soldier, himself began to mount the citadel wall, accompanied only by two bodyguards and the bearer of his sacred shield. This was an act of fatal bravado. In fact, says Curtius, 'a soothsayer [had] warned him not to undertake the siege, or at all events to postpone it, since the omens indicated that his life would be in danger.' But Alexander, with adrenaline surging in him, 'sharply rebuked him for hampering the valour of men in the heat of action,' and pressed ahead with the assault, says Diodorus.

As Alexander got on to the top of the citadel wall, he came under direct attack, a conspicuous target for enemy missiles. This threw his men into frenzy, and a number of them madly clambered on to the ladder to rush to his aid. But their very haste wrecked their effort, as the ladder, with too many soldiers on it, broke. Alexander was thus left on the battlement of the citadel with only a couple of Macedonian soldiers with him.

According to Curtius, Alexander's men at the foot of the wall then shouted to him to jump back, and stood ready to catch him and break his fall. But to retreat in the face of danger was not in Alexander's character. So, instead of jumping to safety, he leapt into the midst of the enemy in the citadel, 'thinking that it would be unworthy of his characteristic good fortune if he retired from the walls,' says Diodorus. He was now in mortal peril. The enemy soldiers, says Justin, now rushed at him 'to finish, if possible, the wars that embroiled the world by one man's death.'

Luckily, Alexander landed near a large tree, which shielded his flank.

This, and the fact that he stood against the citadel wall, prevented him from being closely surrounded. Still the enemy showered him with arrows, javelins and stones, while he tried to protect himself by crouching on his knees behind his shield. Soon 'his buckler was ... loaded with darts, and his helmet shattered by stones,' says Curtius. Meanwhile the three men who had climbed the ladder along with Alexander also jumped into the citadel, and fought in front of him. But one of them fell, and the other two were severely wounded. Then Alexander himself, all alone and surrounded by the enemy, was hit and gravely wounded by an arrow. 'One man, who stood a little further off, shot an arrow from his bow at full bent, and with such a force that it pierced through his corselet and lodged itself in the bones of his breast,' says Plutarch, who also claims that Alexander received a severe blow on his neck from a club.

Critically wounded, Alexander fell swooning. But by then several Macedonian soldiers, now frantic to save Alexander, had managed to enter the citadel by diverse means, by climbing on pegs driven into the earthen wall or by mounting one upon the other. 'Then ensued a desperate conflict around his fallen body, one Macedonian after another holding his shield in front of him,' notes Arrian. Meanwhile the citadel gates were broken open, and the main body of Macedonians entered. Alexander's guards then laid him on his shield and carried him out to safety, while his army rampaged through the town, vengefully slaughtering all they came across, 'sparing not even a woman or a child.'

The arrow that hit Alexander was over a metre long, says Curtius, and its head, says Plutarch, was three or four fingers wide and four or five fingers long. The attending surgeon, Critobulus, 'who was famous for his surgical skill,' cut off the arrow's wooden shaft, but finding that its head was barbed and that he would have to open the wound to remove it, hesitated to proceed, fearing that he might not be able to staunch the flow of blood. But Alexander urged him to go ahead. 'For what and how long are you waiting that you do not set to work as quickly as possible?' he scolded. 'If die I must, free me at least from the pain I suffer.' The surgeon then 'begged Alexander to suffer himself to be held while he was extracting the point, since even a slight motion of his body would be of dangerous consequence.' Alexander replied that there was no need for anyone to hold him, and true to his word remained absolutely still – 'did not wince in the least,' says Curtius – during the operation.

'When the wound had been laid wide open and the point extracted, there followed such a copious discharge of blood that the king began to swoon, while a dark mist came over his eyes, and he lay extended as if he were dying,' continues Curtius. But eventually the bleeding stopped and Alexander gradually recovered consciousness. 'All that day and the night which followed, the army lay under arms around the royal tent. All of them confessed that their life depended on his single breath.'

Alexander was laid up for seven days. At this time a rumour began to spread through the army that he had been killed, and when the rumour reached his base camp, it created much consternation among the soldiers. 'They were,' says Arrian, 'in a state of perplexity about how to get back in safety to their own country, being quite enclosed by so many warlike nations ... Besides, they seemed then ... to be in the midst of impassable rivers, and all things appeared to them uncertain and impracticable now that they were bereft of Alexander.' When they were told that Alexander had survived and was recovering, they refused to believe it 'on account of their excessive fear.'

Alexander then had himself carried in a ship to the main camp at the confluence of the Ravi and Chenab, though his wound had not yet healed. But such was the state of anxiety of his soldiers that when they saw the royal ship arriving, they thought that it was carrying Alexander's body. They were reassured only when, as the ship neared the bank, Alexander stood at its prow and raised his hand in greeting. 'Some of the shield-bearing guards brought a litter for him when he was conveyed out of the ship; but he ordered them to fetch his horse. When he was seen again mounting his horse, the whole army re-echoed with loud clapping of hands, so that the banks of the river and groves near them reverberated with the sound,' says Arrian.

Some days later, when Alexander was still recovering from his wound, a group of his special friends got together and went into his tent to caution him against taking similar risks in future. Craterus, their chosen spokesman, told Alexander that in risking his life he was also imperilling the lives of many others, who would be left leaderless in a dangerous foreign country if he died. 'Under your conduct and command we have advanced so far that there is no one but yourself who can lead us back to our hearths and homes,' he said. In any case, why should he have risked his life for 'an obscure village?'

Alexander thanked them for their solicitude, but said: 'I measure myself not by the span of age, but by that of glory ... Had I been contented with my paternal heritage, I might have spent my days within the bounds of Macedonia, in slothful ease, to an obscure and inglorious old age ... I, however, who do not count my years but my victories, have already had a long career of life, if I reckon aright the gifts of fortune ... Wheresoever I shall be fighting I shall imagine myself to be on the world's theatre with all mankind for spectators ... I am bound to prefer living much to living long ... We consider nothing little in which there is room for great glory to be won.'

When Alexander fully regained his strength, the army and the fleet resumed their southward journey. On the way he sent part of his army with his elephants homeward via Kandahar, but himself proceeded down the river to Pattala, a city at the head of the Indus delta. From Pattala, Alexander explored the two branches of the Indus leading to the sea and offered sacrifices on the islands at the mouth of the river. Then he sailed for a while into the open sea so that, says Arrian in a snide aside, 'he might be able to say that he had navigated the great outer sea of India.' In the sea Alexander sacrificed bulls to Poseidon and cast them into the sea, poured out libations in gold goblets and bowls, and threw the vessels too into the sea, praying to god for the safety of his fleet that would sail to the Persian gulf.

In September 325, Alexander left Pattala and, striking south-west, crossed the Hab River into the Makran seacoast to proceed to Persia. A while later his navy, under the command of Nearchus, also set sail. The Macedonians thus finally left India, a little over two years after they first entered it. It was a quiet departure.

The Makran coast is one of the most inhospitable regions on the earth, but Alexander decided to take that route, so that he might dig wells and leave provision depots for his coasting fleet – and perhaps also, as some claimed, so that he might earn renown for having successfully traversed a land which none had dared to pass through before. But this final passage out of India was the greatest hardship that his army had to endure anywhere in all their endless campaigns and wanderings. There was hardly any human habitation along this tract, except for some primitive fishermen on the seashore. The entire stretch was a barren desert of 'lofty ridges of deep sand ... so loose that those who stepped on it sunk down as into ... untrodden snow,' notes Arrian. The army marched only at night to avoid 'the heat which scorched like fire' in daytime. Sometimes guides lost their way, so the army strayed helplessly over long distances. There were many mishaps along the route, in one of which the royal baggage itself was lost. Often provisions ran out. 'Many perished from malignant distempers, wretched food, and scorching heat, but most from sheer hunger,' says Plutarch. Adds Arrian: 'The majority [of men] perished in the sand like shipwrecked men at sea.'

Alexander shared in all the woes of his men. He refused to ride, but walked with common soldiers. Once when 'the army was prosecuting its march through the sand under a sun already blazing high because a halt could not be made till water ... was reached ... and Alexander himself, though distressed with thirst, was nevertheless with pain and difficulty marching on foot at the head of his army,' a little water was found by some soldiers, and they brought it in a helmet and gave it to Alexander. 'He took it and thanked the men who brought it, but at once poured it upon the ground in the sight of all,' records Arrian. 'By this deed the whole army was inspired with fresh vigour to such a degree that one would have imagined that the water poured out by Alexander supplied a draught to the men all round.'

After sixty days of toil, the Macedonian army emerged from the 'waterless inferno' and reached southern Persia, where they were joined by the army division that took the Kandahar route. Presently Nearchus also arrived there, to report the safe voyage of the navy. Alexander's army celebrated their happy return from India with a week-long revelry. 'He (Alexander) himself sat at table with his companions mounted on a lofty oblong platform drawn by eight horses, and in that conspicuous position feasted continually both by day and night ... There was not a helmet, a shield or a pike to be seen ... Wherever they passed might be heard the music of the pipe and the flute and the voices of women singing and dancing and making merry ... Soldiers ... indulged in ribald jests,' notes Plutarch censoriously. 'The army for seven days advanced in this Bacchanalian fashion,' during which they could easily have been put to sword by a small enemy force, comments Curtius. 'But fortune, which assigns to everything its fame and value in the world's estimation, turned into glory this gross military scandal.'

Alexander finally reached Susa a year and a half after turning back at the Beas. From Susa he went on to Babylon. There, while preparing an Arabian expedition, he, weakened by the rigours of his campaigns and by the heavy drinking to which he had lately taken, fell ill with high fever, and was barely able to speak. Knowing that his end was near, the Macedonian generals asked him to whom he left his empire.

'To the strongest,' Alexander said.

He was by now nearly comatose. His generals then carried him into Nebuchadnezzar's sixth-century palace and laid him there, so that the veterans of his army could pay their last respects to their dying king. On the eleventh day of his illness, 13 June, 323 BC, at sunset, Alexander, thirty-three, passed away. He was now truly an immortal.

India would soon forget Alexander entirely, just as it would forget Porus and many other of its own great kings, preferring to honour mythical rather than real heroes. There is no mention of Alexander in ancient Indian literature. Nor are there in India any material remains of his invasion. The many towns he founded in India as strategic bases have all disappeared, along with the great towers he built on the Beas. Alexander had meant his towns to be permanent settlements, not just temporary military cantonments; they were part of his grand plan for unifying and Hellenising his world empire. But the Greek and Macedonian garrisons he left in these towns looked upon them as penal settlements, and abandoned them as soon as they could, though here and there, in Afghanistan for instance, there remained a significant Greek-speaking population.

On Alexander's death, his vast empire disintegrated as rapidly as he had built it. Superficially therefore, for India, his invasion seems just a brief and passing event in a remote corner, a minor and insignificant episode in the long haul of its history. But in reality it did bring about major changes on the Indian cultural and political scene. Hellenism would remain a dominant factor in the politics and culture of north-western India for several centuries, leading to the formation of Indo-Greek kingdoms and the evolution of Gandharan art. Equally important, Alexander's chroniclers give us for the first time relatively precise historical information about India, in contrast to the contradictory and mythical stories generally found in ancient Indian sources. Further, trade between India and the western lands expanded in consequence of Alexander's campaigns, and this in turn contributed to the spread of urbanisation in India. And, more immediately, the political upheaval that Alexander wrought in north-western India facilitated the establishment of the Mauryan empire. The Macedonian invasion was too great an event not to have enduring consequences in India. After Alexander, things in India – indeed, in the world – could not remain just as they were.

KAUTILYA'S REVENGE

Alexander had willed his empire to whoever had the strength to seize it. This meant that the issue had to be settled in the battlefield. But the Macedonian generals, worn out by their long campaigns, were not yet ready for major wars, so they divided the provinces among themselves after some squabbling, to rule as satraps. Alexander had a posthumous son by a Bactrian princess he had married, and the generals raised the baby and a half-witted illegitimate stepbrother of Alexander to the throne, as a provisional arrangement. These cipher kings were later murdered, and the satraps proclaimed themselves as independent rulers. Then, as expected, they turned on each other. Out of the wars that followed emerged three fairly stable kingdoms: the Macedonian monarchy in south-eastern Europe, the Ptolemaic monarchy in Egypt, and the Seleucid monarchy in Asia.

The Seleucid kingdom, founded by Seleucus Nicator, Alexander's great infantry general, was the most extensive of the three realms, covering virtually the entire Asian territory of the old Persian empire, including its Indian provinces. Initially Seleucus, preoccupied with his adversaries in the west, paid no attention to his Indian territories, and we know little about what happened there in the years immediately after Alexander's death. Even the structure of the provincial organisation that Alexander left behind is not clear. He probably had four satrapies to the east of the Hindu Kush, with Ambhi in charge of the territory from the Indus to the Jhelum, and Porus ruling the extensive domain from the Jhelum to the Beas as a subordinate ally.

This arrangement began to unravel even as Alexander was leaving India, and collapsed altogether around the time of his death. The satrap he left in the Kabul Valley was murdered by his own officers, Ambhi became an independent ruler, and Porus extended his kingdom southward to the sea. Presently the Macedonian officers stationed in India began to desert their stations, hurrying off one after the other to join in the battles of the generals, often without bothering to put anyone in charge of their posts. None of them returned. Sometime around 317 BC Ambhi and Porus too disappeared from the scene, probably murdered by the departing Greek officers, who seized their war elephants.

The scene of action now shifted to the eastern Gangetic valley, where a young adventurer, Chandragupta Maurya, and his canny mentor, Kautilya (also known as Chanakya), were laying the foundations of the greatest empire in ancient India. Unfortunately there is very little reliable information about this enterprise, for most of the stories about its protagonists are unverifiable legends drawn from folklore. No contemporary or near contemporary accounts about them exist, except a few stray references to Chandragupta by classical Greek and Roman chroniclers. They do not mention Kautilya at all. The Indian literary sources on the founding of the Mauryan empire are of a much later period, and the stories they tell are not consistent.

Nothing is known for certain about Chandragupta's background. Late Buddhist sources state that he was the son of the chieftain of the Kshatriya clan of Moriyas of Pipphalivana – probably in the Himalayan foothills – and that this clan was related to Buddha's Sakya tribe. When the chieftain died in a brawl (so goes the story) his pregnant wife fled to Pataliputra, the Magadhan capital, to seek the protection of her relatives. Chandragupta was born there, but for some reason she abandoned the child at the door of a cattle-pen, so the baby was brought up by a cowherd. Later however he was carried away by a hunter, and this gave him the appropriate background for a soldierly career. Jain tradition gives Chandragupta a lesser but nevertheless quite respectable pedigree – it says that he was the son of the daughter of the headman of a village of peacock breeders, *mayura-poshakas.*

Hindu sources are generally silent about Chandragupta's lineage, but a commentator of the *Vishnu Purana* derives (through false etymology) the name Maurya from Mura, a Sudra wife or concubine of the Nanda king. The *Markandeya Purana* even brands the Mauryas as *asuras*, demons, aborigines by implication. In Visakhadatta's *Mudra-Rakshasa*, a Sanskrit play of about the sixth century AD, Chandragupta is called *vrshala* and *kulahina*, which indicates his low origin. Roman historian Justin states that Chandragupta 'was born in humble life.' The Mauryas, observes Kosambi, 'though Aryanised, were of aboriginal or mixed descent. The name Maurya ... indicates the peacock totem and could not be Vedic-Aryan.' Thapar argues that Chandragupta was probably a Vaisya, as 'the suffix *gupta* is known to have been used largely by the Vaisya caste, although Brahmin and Kshatriya names ending in *gupta* also occur.'

The one point on which nearly all the sources agree is that Chandragupta came from the eastern Gangetic Valley. But this cannot be taken as established. There are other possibilities too. The Greek sources, for instance, mention a tribe called Morieis that they came across in India.

And the chieftain whom Alexander sent as a messenger to Porus after the battle of Jhelum was named Meroes, according to Arrian. Further, Curtius says that Alexander confronted a king named Moeres in the Indus Valley. Are all these similarities in names mere coincidences? Possibly. Probably not. Significantly, the Chinese pilgrim Hsuan Tsang in the seventh century AD associated the Mauryas with the Mora Pass in the Swat Valley. And there is the fact that Chandragupta recruited his first army from the hill-tribes of the north-west, which therefore must have been a region familiar to him. And his ally in the conquest of Magadha was Parvataka, a mountain king, as his name means, again presumably from the north-west. None of this proves that Chandragupta really came from the north-west, but it is a possibility that has to be kept in mind, as we grope to establish his lineage.

We know even less about the background of Kautilya, the Brahmin advisor who is said to have masterminded Chandragupta's rise to power. No Greek source, not even Megasthenes, who attended Chandragupta's court for several years, mentions his name. He was also totally ignored by Brahminical writers for many centuries, and is first mentioned only in the Puranas, late Sanskrit works of about the fifth century AD. But the legend about him lived on in folklore, and provided the theme for the *Mudra-Rakshasa.* There is also internal evidence in the *Arthasastra*, the great political treatise attributed to Kautilya, to link him with the overthrow of the Nandas. 'This work,' states the text, 'has been composed by one who, resenting the misrule of the Nanda kings, rescued this neglected science and used it as a weapon to destroy them and save the kingdom.'

It is generally believed, and Buddhist sources specifically maintain, that Kautilya came from Taxila, though Hemachandra, a Jain writer of the twelfth century AD, says that 'Kautilya, son of Chanaka, was a Dramila' – that is, a Dravidian from south India. In all probability he studied in Taxila, a renowned centre of learning to which scholars from all over India flocked in ancient times. The Buddhist text *Mahavamsa-tika* of about the tenth century AD (but based on earlier sources) states that Kautilya was hideously ugly, with deformed limbs and a repulsive complexion, but was proficient in the Vedas and occult practices, and in the use of stratagems, intrigue and diplomacy. The text further says that when Kautilya was a child, physiognomists had divined from the structure of his teeth that he was destined for royal power, and that he then deliberately broke off his teeth to thwart the destiny, for he was devoted to his mother and did not want be drawn away from her.

Hemachandra tells a variation of this story. Kautilya, according to him, was the son of Chani (a Brahmin who lived in a village called Chanaka and was a devout Jain) and his wife Chanesvari. His destiny, says

Hemachandra, was evident in him even as a baby, for he was born with all his teeth fully developed, which was considered a portent of royal power. This, instead of pleasing his father, alarmed him with the thought that his son would lead a life of sin and perdition, and he sought to alter that fate by breaking off all his teeth. But this only modified his fate, not annulled it, for seers then foretold that the boy would rule by proxy.

Kautilya's mind, it turned out, was as convoluted as his body was deformed. He was, says Visakhadatta, a 'crooked genius.' But it is easy to make too much of this reproach. The power game is seldom played according to dharmic principles, and even Rakshasa, Kautilya's supposedly upright rival in the *Mudra-Rakshasa*, was not above using 'assassins, poisoners and others' to gain political advantage. Morality and personal likes and dislikes have no role in the pursuit of power. Says a Nanda courtier in the *Mudra-Rakshasa*: 'Prince, in the case of those who are actively engaged in political affairs it is the exigency of political goals which determines the grouping of belligerents, allies and neutrals; it does not depend on personal inclinations, as with the common people.' Kautilya's uniqueness was not in being just crafty or deceitful, but in being unrivalled in the use of stratagems. Concedes Rakshasa in the *Mudra-Rakshasa*:

> *Sowing, at the outset, a tiny seed of the plot,*
> *He plans for its further elaboration;*
> *When the seed germinates, its eventual fruition,*
> *Hidden and mysterious, is gradually revealed.*

But what did Kautilya have against the Nandas? He had apparently gone to Pataliputra to seek the patronage of Dhana Nanda, who was, for all his reputation for greed and miserliness, a liberal patron of learning and a great philanthropist, according to the *Mahavamsa-tika* and the *Brihatkatha*. Pataliputra under the Nanda rule had become the abode of Saraswati and Lakshmi, the goddesses of learning and wealth, says the *Brihatkatha*. Dhana Nanda had, according to Buddhist sources, set up an institution called Danasala to promote learning by granting awards to scholars. This institution was administered by a sangha, whose president (by convention a Brahmin) was authorised to sanction awards of as much as ten million coins out of the funds of the Danasala. Kautilya, it appears, became the president of the sangha, and by virtue of it took a seat of honour at the royal court, presumably without being granted that privilege by the king. In any case, Dhana Nanda took an instant dislike to the unprepossessing and ill-mannered savant, and had him unceremoniously ejected from the seat. Infuriated by this, Kautilya cursed the king and openly vowed to destroy his dynasty, and then fled from the city in the guise of a naked ascetic, to escape punishment.

Kautilya, continues the *Tika*, 'fled into the wilderness of Winjjha where, with the view of raising resources, he converted (by re-coining) each Kahapana (the coin of Magadha) into eight, and amassed eighty crore (800 million) Kahapanas.' He had, according to late Jain sources, studied metallurgy, perhaps for this very purpose. It could legitimately be asked how he got the initial 100 million Kahapanas. If we are to judge Kautilya by his later actions, it is not improbable that he had misappropriated the money from the funds of the Danasala, which could very well have been the real reason for his expulsion from the royal court.

'All undertakings depend on finance,' Kautilya would write in the *Arthasastra*. It is not then surprising that he should begin preparing for his vendetta by securing the funds needed for his project by counterfeiting money. But he still needed a medium through which to act – he had the brain and the funds, but he needed brawn too. So 'he next searched for a person who was entitled by birth to be raised to sovereign power and lighted upon Chandagutta of Moriyan dynasty,' states the *Tika*. It seems that Chanakya one day came across the boy playing king with a gang of friends, and, taking it as a sign from the heavens, bought him from his hunter master for a thousand Kahapanas. According to Jain sources, Chanakya, to test the mettle of the boy, asked him for a gift, and the boy royally pointed to a herd of someone else's cattle grazing nearby and told the Brahmin to take them, saying, 'The earth is for the enjoyment of heroes.' Chanakya at once knew that this was his man of destiny.

Chanakya then took Chandragupta to Taxila, and spent the next six or seven years there, educating and training him. Meanwhile, the political situation in north India turned opportune for their daring enterprise. They were in the right place at the right time. Alexander's campaigns in India, by wrecking the old political structure in the Indus Valley, had opened up opportunities for new power configurations. Chandragupta seized the opportunity. Initially he seems to have thought of seeking Macedonian help against Magadha. He met Alexander in Punjab, and tried to entice him eastward by telling him, according to Curtius, that the Magadhan king 'was detested and held cheap by his subjects.' But the refusal of the Macedonian army to advance beyond the Beas aborted that prospect. According to Plutarch, Chandragupta 'afterwards used to declare that Alexander could easily have taken possession of the whole country,' because of the unpopularity of the Nanda king.

But when one door of opportunity closed, another opened, for Alexander's premature death left a power vacuum in the north-western tribal lands, which Chandragupta could occupy to launch his career. The tribesmen were at this time in an unsettled state, because the Macedonian invasion had scattered them from their lands and had ruined their pastoral economy by taking away their cattle. These were mostly predatory tribes, the *aratta* (kingless) people, whom Panini calls *ayudhajivi-sanghas*, gangs that live by arms. Chandragupta found plenty of eager recruits for his rebel force among these tough, fractious, battle-hardened highlanders, and Kautilya used his counterfeit hoard to pay them. Chandragupta, says Justin, 'collected a band of robbers.' According to Justin, portents – a lion licking the sweat of his body like a pet animal one day as he lay asleep in the forest, and a huge wild elephant offering itself as his battle-mount – favoured and inspired Chandragupta.

On Alexander's death, says Justin, Indians 'put his prefects to death. Sandrocottus (Chandragupta) was the leader who achieved their freedom.' This action was evidently in the tribal tracts of the north-west. From that power base, and presumably with the connivance of the kings of Punjab, Chandragupta led his troops against the Dhana Nanda, opening his campaign with harassing forays against Magadhan towns and villages. The campaign was a disaster. His forces were too small, his tactics all wrong. 'In the course of their warfare, the population rose all together, and surrounding them, and hewing their army with their weapons, vanquished them,' says the *Mahavamsa-tika*. According to Jain sources, Chandragupta nearly lost his life in one such raid. He certainly was not being welcomed by the people as their saviour from the alleged oppressive rule of the Nandas.

After this initial setback, Chandragupta changed his strategy. The *Tika* (as well as Hemachandra) says that he took his cue from a woman whom he overheard scolding her son for eating from the centre of a hot dish, comparing it to the folly of Chandragupta who, she said, 'invaded the heart of the country and laid towns waste, without first subduing the frontiers. On that account, both the inhabitants of the towns and others, rising, closed in upon him, from the frontiers to the centre, and destroyed his army.' The rebels took that lesson to heart. They also realised that they needed help to win against Magadha. Kautilya then 'went to Himavatkuta and entered into an alliance with Parvataka, the king of that place,' says Hemachandra. It is probable that Chandragupta also received some help from the kings of Punjab, possibly from Porus, who had much to fear from his powerful eastern neighbour, the Nanda king. It is even possible that he had some Greek mercenaries in his army and had adopted in his own army Greek methods of military training and discipline.

When Chandragupta resumed his campaign, he systematically reduced the provinces and secured them by stationing garrisons at strategic places, then attacked and captured Pataliputra, the imperial capital. What happened to Dhana Nanda is not clear. According to Hemachandra, he was allowed to leave the city with his family and whatever treasure he could load into a chariot, but the *Tika* says that he was put to death.

The initial consequence of the dynastic war was chaos in the kingdom. Both Buddhist and Jain sources state that there was an outbreak of lawlessness in Magadha at the commencement of Chandragupta's reign, and that Kautilya suppressed it with an iron hand. For the common people, the Mauryan rule was likely to have been no different from that of the Nandas; indeed, it probably was more burdensome, being more efficient. Says Justin: 'After his victory, he (Chandragupta) forfeited by his tyranny all title to the name of the liberator, for he oppressed with servitude the very people whom he had emancipated from foreign thraldom.'

Chandragupta was probably aged about twenty-five when he took Pataliputra, for when he met Alexander in Punjab he 'was then but a youth,' according to Plutarch. There is no record of the year of his accession, but it probably was around 321 BC. Popular legend holds that it was in the dead of night that he made his formal entry into the royal palace – at the midnight hour, 'as indicated by the augurs,' says the *Mudra-Rakshasa*. Some months (or years) later, after Chandragupta had settled down as monarch, Kautilya, his awful vow of vengeance fulfilled, returned to his hermitage, where he presumably devoted himself to writing his magnum opus, the *Arthasastra*. Late Buddhist and Jain sources however maintain that Kautilya survived Chandragupta, and served his successor, Bindusara.

Once his position in Magadha became secure, Chandragupta turned to conquer Punjab. This could not have been before 317 BC, for Eudamus, the Greek commander, was in Punjab till then, and Porus and Ambhi were both still in power. Around the time Eudamus left, the two Punjab monarchs also vanished from the scene. Their disappearance favoured Chandragupta's invasion of Punjab – or, possibly, it was a consequence of his invasion. We just do not know. Either way, Punjab came under Magadhan rule, probably between 317 and 312. According to the *Mudra-Rakshasa*, Chandragupta and Kautilya also contrived the death of their ally Parvataka and annexed his kingdom. When a few years later Seleucus Nicator and Chandragupta confronted each other, the Indus was the boundary of their empires.

While Chandragupta was building his empire, Seleucus Nicator, who had become the master of the vast Asian provinces of the Macedonian empire, ignored him altogether, himself being engaged in a struggle for survival against his fellow generals on his western frontier. To wage wars on two fronts at the same time would have been fatal for him. But by about 311 BC his position in the west became sufficiently secure for him to turn to the developments along his eastern frontier. Even then, Central Asian campaigns occupied him for a while, and it was only by about 305 that he reached the Indus.

This led to some sort of engagement between Seleucus and Chandragupta. Classical Western sources give no details of their confrontation. 'He (Seleucus) then passed over into India ... [and] having made a treaty with him (Chandragupta) and otherwise settled his affairs in the east, returned home,' is all that Justin says. Some scholars even doubt whether there was a battle between the two kings, but Roman historian Appian clearly states that Seleucus 'crossed the Indus and waged war with Androcottus, king of the Indians.' It is in any case unlikely that there was no battle – Seleucus had come a long way with his army to regain his Indian territories, and he would not have turned back, or ceded extensive new territories to Chandragupta, without a trial of strength. The contest was in all probability won by Chandragupta, who, according to Plutarch, had an army of over half a million men, backed no doubt by numerous war elephants and chariots. There was no way that Seleucus could defeat such an army. Besides, he could not have waged a prolonged war in India, as he could not stay away for too long from his western frontier and from his ongoing conflict with Antigonus, the ruler of Macedonia.

Whatever be the nature of the collision between Seleucus and Chandragupta, the two rulers parted on good terms. According to Appian they 'came to an understanding with each other and contracted a marriage relationship.' It is not clear what this marriage contract meant, and nowhere is it explicitly stated that a Seleucid princess was given in marriage to Chandragupta or his son Bindusara. Some scholars hold that all that was involved was 'a general agreement of a matrimonial right between the two peoples.' But it is more probable that a marriage was indeed arranged between the two royal families, for it was a common practice in India as well as in Greece to seal a treaty between two kings with a marriage alliance. And since it is usually the loser who gives a daughter in marriage to the victor, it is likely that Chandragupta or Bindusara took a Seleucid princess as bride – Chandragupta would have been in his mid-forties at this time, young enough to take a new bride; and Bindusara would have been in his late teens, old enough to marry. As for the territory Seleucus ceded to Chandragupta, it is not described clearly anywhere, but it certainly was extensive, probably all the lands from Herat to the Indus. Indians, says Strabo, 'held much of Ariana, having received it from the Macedonians.' Seleucus perhaps viewed the lands he gave away as his daughter's dowry.

In exchange, Seleucus received 500 war elephants from Chandragupta, which, from his point of view, was probably not a bad bargain. The elephants were more valuable to him than the territory he ceded, for he could not possibly have held on to those lands, as his arm was 'neither long enough nor strong enough to govern India from Babylon.' The war elephants, on the other hand, gave him a decisive advantage over Antigonus, whom he in fact overthrew in 301 BC.

The peace between the Mauryas and the Seleucids endured for a long time, and the two kingdoms remained in close friendly contact with each other for many decades. Soon after the departure of Seleucus, he sent an ambassador, Megasthenes, to Pataliputra, who remained there for several years. Chandragupta probably returned the courtesy, and he is known to have sent Seleucus a present of some potent aphrodisiac drugs. Antiochus, the successor of Seleucus, also sent an ambassador to Pataliputra. At one time there was also present at the Mauryan court an ambassador from Ptolemaic Egypt, presumably sent to counter the Seleucid influence in India. There were probably other unrecorded missions too.

The treaty with Seleucus was advantageous to Chandragupta, as it freed him to pursue his policy of conquest in the subcontinent, without worrying about his vulnerable north-western frontier. He then 'overran and subdued the whole of India with an army of 600,000 men,' states Plutarch. We do not know what territory Chandragupta acquired as part of the Nanda empire, or what new territories he conquered, and when. Chandragupta's empire in all probability extended from the Afghan highlands all the way across the Indo-Gangetic Plain to the Bay of Bengal, and from the Himalayas southward as far as central Karnataka, possibly even further south, for ancient Tamil works speak of the invasion of the Tamil country by a people called Vamba Moriyar (Maurya Upstarts). The empire was so extensive that Chandragupta needed, apart from Pataliputra, two subsidiary capitals, Taxila in Punjab and Ujjain in Malwa, where royal princes served as viceroys.

We do not know how or when Chandragupta's reign ended. According to Buddhist sources he reigned for twenty-four years, in which case he must have been about fifty when he abdicated or died. Jain tradition maintains that he became a follower of Mahavira towards the end of his life, and that he abdicated power to join the Jain monks led by sage Bhadrabahu in their migration to Sravana Belgola in Karnataka during a twelve-year-long famine in the Gangetic Valley. Inscriptions of the early medieval period in Karnataka speak of Chandragupta and Bhadrabahu living in Sravana Belgola. There is a hill there known as Chandragiri, where Chandragupta is said to have lived, and this has a cave named after Bhadrabahu, and a temple called Chandragupta-basti, supposedly erected by the emperor. Chandragupta is said to have fasted to death, in the Jain manner.

All this is possible, and is very much in the Indian tradition of men renouncing temporal pursuits in their old age to take to religious life. It was probably only towards the end of his life that Chandragupta became a Jain. He seems to have been a champion of Brahminism during the early phase of his rule, and there is good reason to believe that he and Kautilya represented the orthodox reaction against heretical sects, of which the Nandas were patrons. Strabo states that Chandragupta took part in religious sacrifices, which marks him out as a follower of Vedic practices. Further, Buddhist sources state that he persecuted Buddhist elders at the instigation of Kautilya, and Jain writer Hemachandra charges that Chandragupta at one time patronised heretical (non-Jain) teachers. Presumably Chandragupta sought, after a long career of war and aggrandisement, peace in renunciation.

Chapter Six

THE FORGOTTEN EMPEROR

THE WICKED PRINCE

'As long as the sun and moon shall shine' – this was how long that Emperor Asoka, the grandson of Chandragupta Maurya and the most renowned of the ancient Indian kings, expected his successors to uphold and implement his dharmic policies. As it happened, his dynasty would last for barely half a century after his death, and not even his memory would endure for long. This noble king, whose *dharma chakra*, the wheel of virtue, adorns the national flag of the Republic of India, was virtually unknown until about a century ago. He was just a name in the Puranic dynastic lists. There was no hint of his greatness in any source.

The process of the discovery of Asoka began in 1837, when amateur philologist James Prinsep, a British officer at the Calcutta mint, deciphered Brahmi (the earliest known Indian script) and came across a king named Devanam-piya Piyadassi in the inscription he was reading. The name was a puzzle. It was not found in any of the other known Indian sources. Fortuitously, around this time the name was also found in the ancient Pali chronicles of Sri Lanka, in which Piyadassi was given as the title of the Mauryan king Asoka. Finally, clinching evidence to identify Devanam-piya Piyadassi with Asoka was found in 1915, on a rock edict of the emperor found at Maski in north Karnataka, in which the king identified himself as Devanam-piyasa Asokasa. And slowly, as more and more Asokan inscriptions were discovered all over the Indian subcontinent and beyond, and literary references from many sources and different countries were collated, a fairly detailed portrait of this great emperor began to emerge from the mist of time.

Asoka was the son of Bindusara, the son and successor of Chandragupta Maurya. Bindusara appears to have been a man of broad intellectual interests and urbane lifestyle, and he probably kept a brilliant court. He, like his father, maintained cordial relations with the Greek kingdoms of Asia and Africa – ambassadors of Antiochus of Syria and Ptolemy Philadelphus of Egypt were present at his court, and there were no doubt several Greek and Persian women in his palace as the entourage of the Seleucid princess in the royal harem. Diodorus quoting Iamboulos (a

Greek writer who claimed to have visited India) states that the king of 'Polibothra' (quite likely Bindusara) 'had a great love for Grecians, and was very studious in the liberal sciences.' Bindusara certainly had Hellenic tastes – Greek chroniclers state that he once sent a request to Antiochus, asking him to buy and send him a stock of dried figs and sweet wine, and a sophist to teach him to argue. Replied Antiochus: 'We shall send you figs and wine, but in Greece the laws forbid a sophist to be sold.'

Beyond this, we know little about Bindusara. The Greeks called him Amitrochates – Amirtra-khada: foe-devourer – and this dread title, an epithet of Indra, is sometimes taken by scholars as indicative of his belligerence. But no particular conquest has been credited to him, and it is unlikely that he added any extensive territory to his inherited empire. He could not, however, have rested on his father's laurels, for constant vigilance was essential to preserve the nascent empire menaced by provincial revolts. Tradition speaks of at least one major uprising, in Taxila, that he suppressed, and there were probably several other similar incidents. Late Buddhist and Jain sources hold that Kautilya served Bindusara for a time as his chief counsellor, but was eventually succeeded by one Radhagupta. Bindusara reigned for about twenty-five years.

Like most kings of the age, Bindusara was a polygamist, and is said to have had sixteen wives and 101 sons. Asoka's mother, according to Buddhist legends, was Subhadrangi (also called Dhamma and Janapadakalyani in some sources), the beautiful daughter of a Brahmin of Champa. She was introduced into the royal harem by her ambitious father in his energetic endeavour to fulfil a prophecy that her son would become a universal monarch. Bindusara's other wives resented her presence, and they 'debarred her from royal embraces and assigned to her menial duties,' but she eventually managed to unite with the king and bear him two sons, the first of whom was named Asoka, and the second Vitasoka or Tisya.

It is not known when Asoka was born, but there are several mythical stories about his birth in Buddhist texts. Pali chronicles claim that when Asoka's mother was pregnant with him she had some very curious cravings – she wanted to 'eat up the forests' and stride over the moon and the sun and play with the stars – and these were interpreted by augurs to mean that her son would kill his brothers and rule over the land, destroy heretical sects and be a patron of Buddhism. Indeed, a couple of centuries earlier, Buddha himself, while interpreting a dream of the early Magadhan king Bimbisara, is said to have prophesied, according to Chinese pilgrim I-Tsing, that 'more than a hundred years after his nirvana, there will arise a king named Asoka, who will rule over the whole of Jambudvipa.' More credible is the statement in the *Divyavadana* that Asoka's grand destiny was foretold by an Ajivika fortune-teller at the time of his birth.

But what splendour the stars bestowed on Asoka's fortune, they subtracted in the same measure from his bodily form. 'Now Asoka's body was rough and unpleasant to the touch, and he was not at all liked by his father, king Bindusara,' states the *Divyavadana.* Bindusara however recognised Asoka's talents and sent him, when he was around eighteen, to Ujjain as viceroy. He was apparently a tough and competent ruler, so when a serious rebellion broke out in Taxila around this time, he was deputed by the emperor to suppress it. Taxila was at this time a Persianised city, culturally rather distinct from the Gangetic cities, and its citizens were resentful of Mauryan rule. But the rebels submitted tamely on Asoka's menacing approach, saying that they 'were not opposed to the prince or even to king Bindusara,' but only to the wicked local officials – in the eyes of the people the distant king was always just, and the local officer always oppressive.

Asoka's Ujjain viceroyalty was touched with romance. On his way to Ujjain, while he was at Vidisa, a nearby town, he, according to tradition, fell in love with a young maiden named Devi, daughter of a local merchant, and a son (Mahinda) and a daughter (Samghamitta) were born of this liaison. Devi probably was a Buddhist, for Vidisa was a Buddhist centre, and the merchant class generally favoured Buddhism. Asoka's relationship with Devi does not seem to have been legitimised, for when the prince eventually returned to Pataliputra, Devi and her children were left behind, though this could have been also because of the hasty nature of his departure from Ujjain.

Asoka had to leave for Pataliputra abruptly, for news had reached him that Bindusara was seriously ill, and this had put his future, indeed his life itself, in jeopardy. He had to win the crown even to save his life. The crown was not his by right. Bindusara's choice of successor was Susima, his eldest son, who was at this time the viceroy of Taxila. But Susima, arrogant and tactless by nature, was unpopular with the royal ministers, so they hatched a plot to bypass him and raise Asoka to the throne. A war of succession followed, which Asoka won, proving by his ruthlessness his fitness to rule the empire. He then consolidated his position and ensured the safety of his crown by the only means possible – by liquidating his brothers, each a potential claimant to the crown. Buddhist sources maintain that he killed ninety-nine of his brothers, sparing only Vitasoka, who later retired to a religious life, perhaps as the best way to save his head. 'Having killed his ... brothers, alone continuing his race, Asoka was anointed king,' states the *Dipavamsa.*

There was nothing unusual in these events. Fratricide, even patricide, was fairly common in royal families everywhere in the ancient world. Asoka in any case had, as prince, a reputation for cold-blooded efficiency. It is therefore not inconceivable that he did kill some of his brothers to secure the throne, though the numbers mentioned in the Buddhist chronicles are evidently gross exaggerations.

Hyperboles like these greatly reduce the value of Buddhist texts for reconstructing the history of Asoka. Though these texts are our main sources of information on Asoka's life, they are grossly tainted by religious bias. That apart, they are all quite late works. The *Divyavadana*, a collection of legends, was probably put together around the third century AD, the *Dipavamsa* a century later, and the *Mahavamsa* in the fifth century, while the commentary on *Mahavamsa* was written as late as the tenth century. And these works often differ widely in the details of events, and even on the identities of the persons involved.

The Buddhist texts are not history. They are primarily meant for religious edification, and tell the story of Buddhism, only incidentally dealing with secular events, which they often modify to suit their message. Thus, in describing Asoka's transformation under the influence of Buddhism, the texts spin outrageous fables about his earlier evil ways, which are difficult to believe even if we willingly suspend disbelief. However, as Nilakanta Sastri observes, we have no alternative but to 'accept as fact whatever is not intrinsically improbable [in the legends], though we have no means of deciding between contradictions in the rival versions.'

Brahmin records completely ignored Asoka for several centuries, before including his name in the Puranic lists of kings. Not even Patanjali, who wrote in the second century BC, refers to him. Nor do ancient Greek and Roman chroniclers mention him. There are many references to him in the writings of Chinese pilgrims, but the earliest of them, Fa Hsien, was in India only in the fifth century AD. The only contemporary sources of information on Asoka are his own inscriptions. But the edicts, though they tell us a great deal about Asoka's ideals and aspirations, have very little information on the events of his reign. Indeed, even in their totality the inscriptions do not add up to much data, for all of them put together run to only about sixteen printed pages in English translation, and many of the statements in them are repetitive. Often the evidence in them is ambiguous. For instance, in one of his edicts Asoka speaks about taking care of the families of his brothers and sisters, which probably means that some of his brothers were still alive – on the other hand, it can also mean that his brothers were not alive, since he does not mention his brothers, but only their families. We cannot in any case take what Asoka says about himself entirely at his word, without corroboration.

Still, despite all the deficiencies of the sources of information on Asoka, the story of this greatest ruler of ancient India is also the first detailed history of an Indian ruler that we have. Asoka's chronology, however, remains uncertain. We do not know when Asoka ascended the throne or how long he reigned. Kosambi places his accession in about 270 BC. J.F. Fleet maintains, on the basis of the many references to the asterism Tishya in Asokan inscriptions, that he was born under that star sign, and that his *abhisheka* (anointment) as emperor was on 25 April 264 BC. Some scholars take 269 as the year of his accession, others place it between 277 and 270. According to Thapar's calculation, Asoka was probably around thirty-four years old when he gained power.

Asoka dates his inscriptions from the year of his formal accession, which, it is believed, took place about four years after his de facto assumption of power. The delay in formalising his rule was probably due to prolonged succession struggles, but, as Vincent Smith remarks, there is no independent evidence of such a struggle. If we may hazard other possibilities on the basis of the history of other Indian dynasties – the story of Ajatasatru in Magadha itself – the delay could have been because Bindusara, though incapacitated, was still alive during this period. Or perhaps the reasons were astrological.

There was a strange transformation in Asoka on his consecration, according to the *Dipavamsa*. 'When Piyadassana was installed,' says the chronicle, 'the miraculous faculties of royal majesty entered into him; he diffused the splendour which he had obtained in consequence of his merits.' Divine beings on that occasion brought him water infused with medicinal herbs, 'fragrant teeth-cleaners made of the betel vine ... fragrant myrobalans ... divine drinks and ripe mangoes ... upper and under garments dyed with five colours ... sugar-cane, quantities of areca-nuts, yellow towels ...' Further, Naga kings brought him 'fragrant powder for washing the head, and also unguents, and fine seamless clothes to put on ... and precious collyrium.' So goes the fabulous tale.

It was presumably on his accession that Asoka assumed the royal title Devanam-piya Piyadassi Raja, by which he would thereafter identify himself in all but one of his edicts. Devanam-piya (dear to the gods) seems to have been a common title of kings in the Mauryan period, and Asoka himself in an edict refers to other kings as Devanam-piyas. The term Piyadassi (of pleasing mien) particularised the title and identified the emperor, so Asoka's full title as it appears in his edicts may be translated accurately, though not literally, as His Sacred Majesty, King Piyadassi. Asoka never called himself Chakravarti, emperor; in fact, in one of his edicts he described himself modestly as the king of Magadha.

The title Piyadassi has an ironical ring to it, considering the unprepossessing appearance that tradition attributes to Asoka. No one would have dared to snicker, though. Especially as Asoka in the early years of his reign had the grim reputation of being cruel and vindictive. Buddhist sources call him Candasoka (cruel Asoka) in this early phase, and there might be some truth in the charge, for without ruthlessness he could not have fought his way to the throne against his many brothers. But the elaborate and ghoulish tales of his cruelty in Buddhist legends are no doubt grotesque inventions.

'At first when Asoka raja ascended the throne, he exercised a most cruel tyranny; he constituted a hell for the purpose of torturing living creatures,' states Hsuan Tsang. According to Buddhist sources, the 'hell' was run for Asoka by one Chandagirika, 'a wretch of unexampled cruelty, who loved to torture animals, and had slain his father and mother.' The king, according to Fa Hsien, told Chandagirika: 'You must enclose a square space with high walls, and within this enclosure plant every kind of flower and fruit [trees], and make beautiful alcoves, and arrange everything with such taste as to make people anxious to look within. Make a wide gate to it, and then when anyone enters, seize him at once and subject him to every kind of torture.'

But one day it so happened that a holy ascetic unwittingly entered the gate, says the *Divyavadana.* The jailer at once seized him and 'cast him into a seething cauldron of filth, beneath which a great fire was kindled,' but the sage miraculously remained unscathed by the fire. When this was reported to Asoka, he came to witness the marvel, and was 'converted by the sight and the preaching of the holy man, and he embraced the true religion and forsook the path of wickedness. The prison was demolished and the jailer burnt alive.'

Buddhist chronicles speak of several other instances of Asoka's wickedness. 'One day,' again according to the *Divyavadana,* 'when five hundred of his ministers ventured to resist the royal will, Asoka, transported with rage, drew his sword, and with his own hand cut off the heads of all the offenders ... Another day, the women of the palace, whom Asoka's rough features failed to please, mocked him by breaking off the leaves of an Asoka tree in the garden. The king, when he heard of the incident, caused the five hundred women to be burnt alive.' This streak of manic savagery remained in Asoka for a while even after his conversion to Buddhism, according to the *Divyavadana* – once when some ascetics spoke scornfully of Buddha, Asoka placed a price on the head of every non-Buddhist ascetic!

These stories are incredible, but incredible only in detail. They might have some basis in truth. If Asoka was once even remotely as evil as the Buddhist chronicles make him out to be, his transformation from Candasoka to Dharmasoka (virtuous Asoka) was indeed remarkable.

'ALL MEN ARE MY CHILDREN'

Asoka could reign in peace, having liquidated his brothers. But he could not live in peace with himself. This perhaps was why he turned to Buddhism soon after his consecration, to seek solace for his troubled conscience. According to the *Dipavamsa*, in the fourth year after his consecration Asoka assembled the exponents of various sects in a conclave, and asked them 'an exceedingly difficult question' to ascertain 'where truth and where falsehood was.' But none of them could answer him satisfactorily. Then one day he spotted a young Buddhist ascetic passing by on the street, and, impressed by his calm bearing, called him in and asked him to expound his beliefs. And the ascetic, a mere boy, just seven years old, stated: 'Earnestness is the way to immortality, indifference is the way to death; the earnest do not die, the indifferent are like the dead.'

The answer dazzled Asoka. If Buddhism could make one so young so wise and serene, what would it not do to the great emperor! This, according to Pali texts, was the beginning of Asoka's association with Buddhism. But there was more to Asoka's encounter with the boy than the obvious. In it was also a subtle play of the ironies of fate. The young monk, though this was not known to Asoka, was Nigrotha, the posthumous son of Asoka's slain elder brother Susima – the agent of the emperor's conversion, the one who set him on the path of renown, was none other than the son of the chief victim of his ruthless pursuit of power!

Asoka was at this time a patron of Brahmins – 60,000 Brahmins had for three years 'enjoyed the bounty of Asoka, as they had enjoyed that of his predecessors on the throne,' claim Pali chronicles. The Brahmins 'were now dismissed, and in their place Buddhist monks in equal number were constantly entertained.' But apart from this there does not seem to have been any immediate outward change in Asoka. Conversion did not turn him into a pacifist. In fact, his early involvement with Buddhism was rather casual. 'I have been a lay Buddhist for more than two and a half years, but for a year I did not exert myself well,' Asoka states in an early edict. 'But now for a year – indeed, for more than a year – I have drawn close to the sangha and have become ardent.'

It would however take a few more years and another traumatic event, the Kalinga war, for Asoka's Buddhist sensitivity to find expression in royal policy and action. The thirteenth major rock edict of Asoka directly links his growing zeal for Buddhism to the Kalinga war: 'Immediately after conquering Kalinga, His Sacred Majesty became earnest in the practice of dharma, the desire for dharma, and the inculcation of dharma.' But the war was not the cause of Asoka's conversion, as commonly believed – he was already a Buddhist (of a sort) at the time of the Kalinga war.

Kalinga was Asoka's only conquest. It was not an easy victory, for Kalinga was a powerful kingdom, having, according to Pliny, an army of '60,000 foot-soldiers, 1,000 horsemen, 700 elephants, always caparisoned, ready for battle.' Besides, the Kalingas were an obstinately independent-minded people. The Nandas had once occupied the kingdom, but could not keep it for long. Asoka nevertheless ventured on the conquest, for the annexation of Kalinga was necessary to round off the frontiers of his empire and to secure the sea and land routes to southern India.

The Kalinga war took place in the thirteenth year of Asoka's reign – the ninth after his consecration – and it would altogether change his life. 'When he had been consecrated eight years, His Sacred Majesty, King Piyadassi, conquered Kalinga,' states Asoka. 'A hundred and fifty thousand people were deported, a hundred thousand were slain, and many times that many perished' in the war. In addition, many hundreds of thousands of innocent people suffered grievously from 'violence, murder, and separation from their loved ones ... [and from] the misfortunes of their friends, acquaintances, colleagues and relatives.' This widespread suffering weighed 'heavily on the mind of His Sacred Majesty,' continues Asoka. 'Thence arises the remorse of His Sacred Majesty for having conquered Kalinga ... a matter of profound sorrow and regret to His Sacred Majesty.' He would wage no more wars, Asoka resolved. The war drum, *bheri-ghosha*, would be stilled, and in its place *dharma-ghosha*, the drum of virtue, would be beaten.

With the conquest of Kalinga, Asoka's empire stretched uninterruptedly all the way from the Hindu Kush in the north-west to the Pennar river in the south. Kashmir too was probably a part of his empire, and he is said to have built there a city called Srinagari. Only the small principalities of the far south – the Cholas, Pandyas and Keralaputras – and the tribal lands of the north-east beyond the Ganga remained outside his empire. These were not worth the trouble to conquer. 'The wheel of his (Asoka's) power,' says the *Dipavamsa*, 'rolled through the great empire of Jambudvipa.' The Asokan empire, observes Basham, was 'the mightiest empire in the world' in its time.

Soon after the Kalinga war, Asoka unequivocally declared himself to be a

Buddhist, and went on to record in a rock inscription his 'reverence for and faith in Buddha, Dharma and Sangha.' This did not however turn the Mauryan empire into a theocratic state. Asoka would remain tolerant of other sects, and would even patronise them, as he did by dedicating a cave retreat to Ajivikas, the bitter adversaries of Buddhists. Still, an emperor's faith could not be a mere private affair. His religious observances were state ceremonies. Thus, once on going out to meet Buddhist monks, the emperor, according to the *Dipavamsa*, ordered, among other things: 'Let them beat the drums in the city, let them sweep the roads, let them scatter white sand and flowers of the five colours; let them place here and there garlands and triumphal arches, plantain trees, auspicious brimming jars ... Let all people procure heaps of perfumed garlands and flowers, many flowers, parasols, flags, lamps burning in the daytime ... Let all [people living] in the city, the merchants from the four quarters of the horizon, and all the royal officers, with their oxen, troops, and vehicles, follow me to meet the congregation of monks.'

With each passing year, Asoka drew closer and closer to Buddhism, but it is unlikely that he ever became a monk, though an ambiguous phrase – *sanghe upete*: visiting or entering the monastery – in one of his edicts is sometimes interpreted to mean that he took the order, and confirmation of this is thought to be found in the Chinese pilgrim I-Tsing's seventh-century AD statement that he once saw an image of Asoka dressed as a monk. It could be that Asoka lived for a while in a monastery, as Buddhist custom encouraged lay followers to do, but he could not possibly have taken the order, for the essential condition for becoming a Buddhist monk was to give up all temporal pursuits and become homeless. One could not be a king and a monk at the same time.

The year after the Kalinga war Asoka went on his first Buddhist pilgrimage, to Bodh Gaya, to venerate the Bodhi-tree. 'From this arose the practice of dharma tours,' states Asoka, 'visiting sramanas and Brahmins and bestowing gifts on them, visiting the aged with largess of gold, meeting with people of the countryside to instruct them on dharma and to hold discussions on dharma. His Sacred Majesty, King Piyadassi derives much pleasure from this, more than from anything else.' These tours, which took Asoka to all parts of the empire, including the far south, probably served an administrative purpose as well, to check on the local officers of the empire.

In the twenty-first year of his reign, Asoka went on a pilgrimage to the Lumbini garden, where Buddha was born, probably as part of the extensive pilgrimages to Buddhist sacred sites that he is believed to have undertaken as a propitiatory act following the solar eclipse that year. 'His Sacred Majesty, King Piyadassi, when he had been consecrated twenty years, came in person and reverenced the place where Buddha Sakyamuni was born,' states Asoka. 'He caused a stone enclosure to be made and a stone pillar to be erected.' According to the *Divyavadana*, Asoka 'bestowed a hundred thousand gold pieces on the people of the place, and built a stupa there.' The text further claims that he built 84,000 stupas at this time with the help of the genii summoned by Saint Upagupta. 'At the moment of the solar eclipse the genii, in obedience to the commands of the king and the saint, simultaneously deposited the relics [of Buddha] in all the stupas.'

As a Buddhist, one of Asoka's major concerns was to maintain discipline in the sangha, for fear that fissures in it would undermine his goal of propagating dharma and achieving peace and harmony in society. Schisms had bedevilled the sangha even during the lifetime of Buddha, but now they became rampant, as adherents of several different sects flocked to Buddhism, like flies descending on a bowl of honey, attracted by its ascendancy under royal patronage. 'Ajivikas and sectarians of different descriptions,' several thousands of them, began to wear the yellow robes and live with Buddhist monks, states the *Dipavamsa*. They caused much disturbance and confusion in the sangha by their unruly behaviour and by proclaiming their own various tenets as Buddhist doctrines. This went on for some seven years, and it so vitiated discipline in the sangha that even such absolutely obligatory ceremonies like the Uposatha were casually and imperfectly performed, prompting many of the revered elders of the sect to disassociate themselves from these ceremonies.

At this point Asoka stepped in to stop the slide. At first, he deputed his officers to restore order, but their coercive and violent methods proved counter-productive. The sangha, it was evident, had to discipline itself. Asoka then summoned the revered septuagenarian sage Moggaliputta Tissa from his solitary retreat to convene a council of monks and restore legitimate practices. At this, the Third Buddhist Council, said to have been held in the seventeenth regnal year of Asoka (236 years after Buddha's death), dissidents were defrocked, made to wear white robes, and expelled. Asoka personally, with Tissa's assistance, is then said to have selected 'a thousand orthodox monks of holy character' to form a council, which, following the Buddhist tradition, 'recited and verified the whole body of the scriptures, and, after a session lasting nine months, dispersed.' The orthodox faith (Theravada Buddhism) was firmly established at this council, and the Pali canon codified. 'At the conclusion of the council the earth quaked, as if to say "Well done," beholding the re-establishment of religion,' claim the Pali texts.

The historicity of the Third Buddhist Council has been doubted by some scholars, as it is reported only in Pali chronicles, and Asoka does not mention it in any of his edicts. But there is a persuasive internal consistency in the chronicles, and the story they tell about the council fits well with the other known facts of Asoka's reign. If the council was held in his seventeenth regnal year, then the flocking of non-Buddhists to the sangha that had begun seven years earlier would have started in his tenth regnal year, the year he began to actively patronise Buddhism. The dates match perfectly. This apart, Asoka's Schism Edict, which indicates that the orthodox tenets of Buddhism had by then been well established, presupposes that a council was held to promulgate them. It is not surprising that non-Pali (Mahayana) sources should ignore the council, for this was a gathering of orthodox Theravada monks. There is therefore good reason to believe that the Third Buddhist Council was indeed historical.

Still, the silence about the council in Asoka's edicts is puzzling. All we have is a faint echo of it in the Schism Edict. This edict, issued about a decade after the council, and addressed specifically to the royal officers assigned to the sangha, warned, 'No one shall cause dissension in the sangha. Whoever creates schism in the sangha, be it monk or be it nun, shall be dressed in white garments and expelled from the monastery ... [so that] as long as my sons and great-grandsons shall reign, and as long as the sun and moon shall shine ... the sangha may remain united.' In another edict, addressed to fellow Buddhists, he advised: 'Sirs, whatever was spoken by the Lord Buddha was well spoken ... These sermons ... I desire that many monks and nuns should hear frequently and meditate upon, and likewise the laity, male and female, should do the same.' Asoka even specified the sermons he desired monks and nuns to study.

No one in Buddhism had the ecclesiastical authority to give such directions, certainly not Asoka, but presumably royal authority made up for it. Buddhists in any case had no cause to complain about this political intervention in religion, for their sect, however great its inherent merit, would probably have faded away but for Asoka's patronage, as so many other sects of considerable merit in ancient India had faded away. Asoka saved Buddhism from that fate, partly through the prestige of imperial patronage, but also by emphasising Buddhism's ethical content and thereby broadening its appeal and transforming it from a primarily monastic movement to a religion of the masses.

The Kalinga war was in every respect the turning point in Asoka's reign. But it is not clear why he was so distressed by the human suffering that the war caused. He certainly was no stranger to war and bloodshed. Could it be that it was crafty policy rather than contrition which turned Asoka to pacifism? We should note that it was easy for Asoka to give up conquest after annexing Kalinga, for there was no more any worthy territory in India left for him to conquer. Nor did Asoka's professed remorse induce him to return their homeland to the Kalingas. Moreover, pacifism now served the emperor's political goals better than militarism. Wars were expensive, and the obligation to maintain a vast standing army was an unacceptable drain on the empire's resources. It was less expensive, and probably more efficient, to keep the people pacified with dharma.

We cannot ignore these considerations. But we do not know enough about Asoka to pass verdict on his motives. There is therefore no alternative but to judge Asoka by his professions and actions. And here there is no ambiguity. No monarch had ever set nobler goals for himself, or had worked as hard as Asoka did to achieve them. His entire value system underwent a radical change when he became an earnest Buddhist, to such an extent that he himself was pleasantly amazed by this transformation. 'It is hard to do good, and he who does good does a difficult thing,' he states. 'And I have done much good.'

Monarchs in all ages have held that the only rewards they sought for their ordeals and exertions were fame and glory. Asoka too sought fame and glory, but in a field outside the normal concerns of kings. 'His Sacred Majesty does not regard that fame and glory bring much profit, unless my people obediently hearken to dharma and conform to its precepts, now and in the future,' he states. 'For this purpose only does His Sacred Majesty ... desire fame and glory.' Elsewhere he states that while 'in the past, kings went on pleasure tours, which consisted of hunts and other similar amusements,' he himself went on tours only to promote dharma. And again: 'Nothing is more important than promoting the welfare of all the people. And whatever work I do, it is done to discharge my debt to all beings, for their happiness in this life and the attainment of heaven in the life beyond.' And he exhorted himself: 'I must work for the welfare of the whole world.'

Nearly every one of Asoka's edicts speaks of his overriding concern for the welfare of the people. This concern also found expression in the many public welfare measures that he initiated. 'Everywhere in the dominions of the Beloved-of-the-Gods ... and likewise among the rulers on his frontiers, such as the Cholas, the Pandyas, the Satiyaputra, the Keralaputra, even Tamraparni (Sri Lanka), the Greek king Antiochus, and also the kings who are neighbours of this Antiochus – everywhere two kinds of medical services have been instituted by the Beloved-of-the-gods, for the treatment of men and for the treatments of beasts,' states Asoka. 'And wherever there were no herbs that are beneficial to men and beneficial to beasts, everywhere they were caused to be brought and planted; similarly, roots and fruits, wherever lacking, have been everywhere brought and planted.'

Elsewhere he states: 'On the highways I have had banyan trees planted, to give shade to beasts and men, and I have had mango-groves planted, and I have had wells dug and rest houses built at every half-kos (probably about four kilometres). And numerous watering-places have been provided by me here and there for the comfort of man and beast.' Other rulers before him had provided similar facilities to the people, acknowledges Asoka, but he says that his own objective was different from theirs: 'I have done these things so that my people may conform to dharma.'

'All men are my children,' proclaimed Asoka – '*savve munisse paja mama*.' He laboured for the welfare of the people, as a father would for his children. This humanistic orientation that Asoka gave to governance was a radical departure from the precepts of the *Arthasastra*, which was solely concerned with administrative efficiency in promoting the power of the king, without any real regard for the wellbeing of the people or any consideration whatever for ethical values. With Asoka, welfare of the people was an end in itself, not just a means to promote the welfare of the monarch. And dharma was an absolute obligation, for the king as well as for the people.

These welfare and ethical concerns of Asoka further broadened the paternalistic (or totalitarian) role of the Mauryan government – and also considerably increased the burden of work on the emperor. But Asoka welcomed the work and delighted in it. 'I never feel contented in my exertion and dispatch of business,' states the perfectionist emperor. 'Work I must for the welfare of all the folk, and for that energy and dispatch of business are essential.' And again: 'It is hard to obtain happiness in this world and the next without utmost love for dharma, utmost self-examination, utmost obedience, utmost fear of sin, and utmost effort.'

Asoka was always available for administrative work, always accessible to his officers. 'In times past there has been no quick dispatch of business, or receipt of reports at all times. But I have now arranged that at all times, wherever I may be – whether I am eating, or I am in the harem or my inner apartments, or in the animal stalls, or in my carriage or pleasure-grove – my intelligence officers should keep me informed about the affairs of the people,' he says. 'In all places do I attend to the affairs of the people.'

The tireless endeavour that Asoka demanded of himself, he also demanded of his officers. He delegated great powers to them, but insisted on their accountability. 'My Rajukas (district officers) are appointed over many hundred thousands of people,' he states. 'To them I have granted independence in the award of honours and penalties, so that they may perform their duties confidently and fearlessly, and promote the welfare and happiness of the people of the country. They shall ascertain what causes happiness and misery, and, together with those devoted to dharma, they will admonish the people of the country so that they may obtain happiness in this world and the next ... Just as a man, having entrusted his child to a skilful nurse, feels confident that the nurse would take good care of the child, even so my Rajukas have been appointed for the welfare and happiness of the people of the country.'

In another edict he advised his officers thus: 'You are in charge of many thousands of living beings. You should win their affection. All men are my children, and just as I desire for my children that they should obtain prosperity and happiness both in this world and the next, the same do I desire for all men ... Reflect on it well ... You should strive to practise justice. But this is not possible for one who is envious, lacks perseverance, is cruel and heedless, wants application, is lazy and slack. You should avoid such faults. The root of the whole matter lies in perseverance and patience in [work] ... The indolent man cannot rouse himself to move; yet one needs to move, advance, go on ... Ill performance of duty can never gain my regard ... whereas in fulfilling my instructions you will gain heaven and also discharge your debt to me.'

In all this Asoka was fulfilling his duty as a king, as his enlightened vision perceived it. As king, his primary responsibility was to enforce law and order, and this involved the stern repression of criminals and rebels. Asoka could not possibly rule without exercising this coercive power. But he did what he could to mitigate the rigour of the Mauryan penal system. He would not tolerate crime, but he would be humane towards criminals. 'His Sacred Majesty desires for all beings security, self-control, peace of mind, and happiness,' he announced, and went on to state that he 'believes that even one who does wrong should be forgiven as far as it is possible to forgive him.' In the same spirit he advised his officers that there 'should be impartiality in judicial proceedings and impartiality in punishments.' He even sought to 'conciliate and convert' the criminal forest tribes. But his compassion was counterbalanced with sternness, and he advised the tribesmen to desist from their evil ways, 'lest they be killed.'

Asoka did not abolish the death penalty – that would have been impractical – but he ordered that 'men in prison who are sentenced to death are to be given three days respite. Thus their relations may plead for their lives, or, if there is no one to plead for them, they may give alms or undertake a fast for the sake of the other world.' Even torture was not given up by Asoka, but he warned his officers not to torture or imprison anyone 'without due cause.' And, like his predecessors, he continued the practice of annually releasing a number of prisoners – he had, he states, released prisoners twenty-five times up to the twenty-sixth anniversary of his consecration.

Concern for the propagation of dharma also governed Asoka's relationship with his neighbours. 'If the unconquered peoples on my borders ask what is my will, they should be made to understand that this is my will with regard to them: The king desires that they should have no trouble on his account, should trust in him, and should have in their dealing with him only happiness and not sorrow,' he advised his frontier officers. 'They should understand that the king will bear patiently with them, and that through him they should follow dharma and gain this world and the next.'

'The Beloved-of-the-gods considers the conquest by dharma to be the foremost conquest,' declared Asoka. And he claimed that this victory for dharma he had 'repeatedly won both here (in his own dominions) and among all his neighbours as far as 600 *yojanas*, where the Greek king Antiochus reigns, and beyond the realm of this Antiochus where rule four kings named Ptolemy, Antigonos, Magas, and Alexander, and towards the south among the Cholas and Pandyas, as far as Tamraparni. Likewise here in the king's dominions, among the Greeks and Kambojas, among the Nabhakas and Nabhitis, among the Bhojas and Pitinikas, among the Andhras and Pulindas – everywhere people conform to the dharma instructions of the Beloved-of-the-gods. Even where the envoys of the Beloved-of-the-gods have not gone, people, hearing of ... [his] practice, ordinances and injunctions on dharma, follow dharma ... [It] is victory everywhere ...'

There might be some self-serving exaggeration for a good cause in all this. Asoka did indeed send missions to several lands – mainly to the Hellenistic world closely connected with the Mauryan empire through trade and political ties – but with what success we do not know. There is no reference to these missions in any ancient Greek or Roman chronicle. The only certain Buddhist missionary success in a foreign country during Asoka's reign was the conversion of the king of Sri Lanka, though there is also some evidence that Buddhism was already present in the island before the conversion of its king. Curiously, there are only a couple of passing references to Sri Lanka in Asoka's edicts, nothing at all about any specific mission, and no mention of the Sri Lankan monarch.

Asoka's silence about the mission to Sri Lanka is more than made up for by Pali chronicles, which tell the story in epic detail. The king of Sri Lanka, Devanampiya Tissa, and Asoka 'were both intimate friends, united by faithful affection though they never had seen each other,' states the *Dipavamsa*. The initiative for establishing the relationship was taken by Tissa, who sent an embassy to Asoka bearing, as presents, 'three resplendent gems, eight excellent pearls and three bamboo poles, besides a collection of the most precious *chanks* (large shells, used for offering libations), together with many valuable objects.' Asoka returned the courtesy and sent to Tissa 'a royal parasol ... a diadem, ear ornaments, water from the Ganges, and an anointing vase; a *chank* trumpet, a palanquin, a right hand *chank* and a virgin ...; a suit of clothes (which are cleansed by being passed through fire, without being washed) and costly towels; most precious yellow sandal wood, a measure of rouge ... myrobalan ...; a *chowry* (fly-whisk made of the tail of the Tibetan Yak), a turban, a sword ... slippers ...'

Shortly after this embassy, Asoka's son (brother, according to some sources) Mahinda (son of Devi, the emperor's first love) arrived in Sri Lanka – he came flying through the air, 'as flies the king of swans,' according to Pali legends. Mahinda informed Tissa that Asoka had become a Buddhist, and suggested that Tissa too should become an *upasaka.* The king accepted this advice and embraced Buddhism – along with 40,000 of his followers, according to Pali sources, which also state that Queen Anula and 500 of her attendants were later converted by Asoka's daughter Samghamitta. Tissa then sent a second mission to Pataliputra, to fetch a branch of the Bodhi-tree (its seeds, according to Fa Hsien) for planting in the island. So goes the legend.

BELOVED OF THE GODS

Asoka adopted a dual strategy to propagate dharma. 'The advancement of dharma amongst men has been achieved through two means, legislation and persuasion,' he states. 'But of these two, legislation has been less effective, and persuasion more so.' He had no hesitation in using the administrative machinery of the state to propagate dharma, for he considered this an essential function of the government. 'Asoka,' Sastri observes, 'bent the entire machinery of the state towards the practical realisation of the ideal of good life among men.'

The emperor shrewdly calculated that incessant propaganda was the best means for the dissemination of dharma. 'In times past kings had sought to make men grow with the growth of dharma in due proportion; men however did not in due proportion grow with the growth of dharma. By what means, then, can men be induced to conform?' Asoka wondered. 'Then this thought occurred to me: I shall issue proclamations on dharma, and shall order instruction in dharma, so that men hearkening thereto may conform, lift themselves up, and mightily grow with the growth of dharma. For this purpose proclamations of dharma and various kinds of religious injunctions have been issued ... [My officers have been] ordered by me: "In such and such a manner exhort ye the people," ... [And to further promote dharma] I have set up pillars of dharma, appointed Mahamatras (officers) of dharma ...'

Royal officers were required to go on regular tours to propagate dharma. 'When I had been anointed twelve years, I commanded as follows: Everywhere in my dominions the Yuktas (subordinate officers), the Rajukas, and the Pradesikas (provincial officers) shall go on tours (throughout their territory) every five years to instruct people in dharma as well as for other (government) business,' he states. And he himself went on regular tours through the empire, interacting with people and expounding dharma.

To oversee the propagation and observance of dharma, Asoka appointed, in an important administrative innovation, a group of special officers titled Dharma-mahamatras. 'In times past there were no Dharma-mahamatras. It was I who first instituted the office, when I had been consecrated thirteen years,' Asoka records. 'They are busy in all sects, establishing dharma, promoting dharma, and attending to the welfare and happiness of those who are devoted to dharma, [even] among the Greeks, Kambojas, Gandharas, Rashtrikas, Pitinikas, and the other peoples on my western frontier. Among servants and masters, Brahmins and the wealthy, the destitute and the aged, they (the Dharma-mahamatras) are working to alleviate their distress. They are also busy in promoting the welfare of prisoners, causing their fetters to be taken off, setting free those who have children, or are bewitched, or are in advanced years ... Everywhere throughout my empire the officers of dharma are busy in all matters concerning dharma, in the establishment of dharma and in the administration of charities among those devoted to dharma.'

These enforcers of virtue roamed all over the empire and had access to all homes, even to royal harems. 'They are busy everywhere, here [in Pataliputra] and in all the outlying towns, in all the harems, whether my own, those of my brothers and sisters, or those of other relatives,' states Asoka. Through such measures Asoka hoped that 'compassion, liberality, truthfulness, purity, gentleness, and virtue' would spread among mankind.

History would not have known of any of these idealistic policies and actions of Asoka but for the fact that he engraved his edicts on pillars and rock. But it was not to memorialise himself that Asoka inscribed these edicts on stone; he did so only because this was the best available means in those days for publicising his ideas and keeping them in the public eye. The inscriptions gazetted the edicts. The fact that they would remain intact for many centuries was incidental, though Asoka did often express the hope that the dharma he propagated would endure for long. 'This inscription of dharma,' states Asoka, 'has been engraved so that my sons or great-grandsons that I may have should not think of gaining new conquests ... They should consider conquest by dharma to be a true conquest, and delight in dharma should be their whole delight, for this is of value in both this world and the next.'

The inscriptions spoke of dharma in simple, clear terms, and described what the emperor was doing to propagate it. They were mostly of an advisory nature, though they also laid down a few rules that were mandatory. There were no philosophical or religious discourses in the edicts. Asoka's interests were primarily ethical.

The emperor had probably derived the idea of the inscriptions from Persia, though an independent development of the tradition in India cannot be ruled out. North-western India was for long a Persian province, and Persian cultural influence was strong there. When the Achaemenid empire collapsed, many Persian aristocrats and artisans migrated to India, and a number of them were employed by the Mauryas in government service, some even in very high positions, as for instance Tushaspa, undoubtedly a Persian, who was Asoka's governor in Gujarat. Persian influence in India is also indicated by the use of Kharoshthi, the Aramaic script of Persia, in a couple of Asokan inscriptions.

Whether Asoka borrowed the idea of the inscriptions from Persia or not, the content and tone of his edicts were uniquely his own. While Darius, with an eye on history, boasted of his conquests in his inscriptions, Asoka spoke only about the propagation of dharma, for his objective was to promote the welfare of the people, and not to perpetuate royal glory. The edicts, he states, were 'engraved for the welfare and happiness of the world.' Asoka's tone was quiet and gentle, in contrast to the blaring, grandiloquent style of Darius.

Asokan inscriptions fall into two major clusters. The earliest of these, the major rock inscriptions, mostly belong to his thirteenth and fourteenth regnal years. Then there was a long gap of about thirteen years during which only minor edicts were issued, after which, around his twenty-seventh and twenty-eighth regnal years, were issued the major pillar edicts. The last pillar edict, the seventh, was issued in his twenty-eighth regnal year. In the last ten years of his reign he issued no major edicts. In their contents, the edicts fall into two categories – those addressed to the general public, and those (a very small number) addressed specifically to the Buddhist sangha. In addition to inscribing the edicts on stone, it is possible, as Thapar posits, that they were also inscribed on media like wood and sent to all parts of the empire; these, if they did indeed exist, have been lost because of the perishable materials used.

The edicts vary in length and importance, and copies of most of them were inscribed at diverse locations in the empire, with some variations. They exist, states Asoka, 'in condensed, medium-length, and expanded versions, for each clause has not been engraved everywhere. Since the empire is extensive, much has been engraved and much has yet to be engraved. Certain phrases have been used again and again because of the charm of particular topics, and in order that people may conform to them. In some places it may be inaccurately engraved, whether by omission of a passage or by lack of attention, or by the error of the engraver.' The sites for inscribing the edicts were carefully chosen for maximum publicity effect – near towns or places of religious importance, and on important trade and pilgrimage routes, all over the Mauryan empire.

The language that Asoka used in edicts was the dialect of Magadha, a form of Prakrit, with some local variations in spelling, wording and grammar. The decision not to use Sanskrit was probably deliberate and in conformity with Buddha's injunction to his monks to use only the vernacular, to make their message accessible to common people. For the same reason, Asoka kept the language of the edicts plain, almost rustic, without any literary flourishes. Nevertheless the edicts have, as Vincent Smith observes, 'considerable amount of force and simple dignity ... The accuracy of the texts is wonderful. A clerical error or engraver's blunder very rarely occurs.'

Most of the edicts were engraved in the Brahmi script, but Kharoshthi was used for two major edicts in the north-west, and the Kandahar inscription is bilingual, in Greek and Aramaic. The inscriptions were meant to be read out to people, who were, we must assume, mostly illiterate. 'This edict must be read out [to gatherings] on every day of the constellation Tishya (every four months),' ordered Asoka. 'In the intervals also it may be read out frequently. On occasion it may be read out even to a single person.'

'This is my principle – to give protection [to people] through dharma, to give them happiness through dharma, to rule through dharma, and to guard the empire through dharma,' Asoka declared, summarising the goals of his reign. The constituents of Asokan dharma were social and familial virtues, and had nothing to do with piety or observance of religious prescriptions. 'Dharma is having few sins, but many good deeds, compassion, liberality, truthfulness and purity,' Asoka maintained. And sin, he clarified, is 'cruelty, harshness, anger, pride, and envy' – all offences against man, not against any god.

The Beloved of the Gods was not particularly interested in the gods. He, like Buddha, was concerned primarily with man in society. His dharma was not based on any divine law, was not even specifically Buddhist, though there was good synergy between his goals and Buddhist ideals. Dharma, as Asoka conceived it, was essentially 'an attitude of social responsibility,' comments Thapar. One did not have to be Buddhist to conform to Asoka's dharma. In fact, contrary to the teachings of early Buddhism, Asoka often spoke of heaven as the reward for dharmic life, because that was something that people could easily understand, and that could motivate them to live sensibly. On the other hand, he never mentioned transmigration, a key Buddhist concept, presumably because it was a complex idea and had no immediate bearing on human conduct. It was good sense and practicality that marked Asoka's edicts, not religious fervour; he was only concerned with what would benefit the individual, society, and the state. 'Asoka's approach to Buddhism,' comments Sastri, 'was that of a profound humanist; it was practical, pragmatic, and intensely ethical.'

For all his idealism, Asoka was a realist. He knew that he had to reckon with human frailty, and that it 'is difficult for men, whether humble or highly placed, to free themselves from evil inclinations, and it is particularly difficult for the highly placed, save by utmost exertion, giving up all other aims.' He did not therefore seek to force perfection and absolute conformity on people. 'Mastery over the senses, purity of mind, gratitude, and steady devotion are ... commendable,' he advised, but added philosophically: 'Men have varying desires and varying passions, so they may perform [their duties] wholly or only in part.'

And, just as he acknowledged the intractability of human nature, so did he accept the diversity of beliefs among his subjects. Asoka was no fanatic. In fact, the noblest and most endearing qualities of Asoka were humaneness and tolerance. 'The Beloved-of-the-gods, King Piyadassi, desires that all sects may dwell everywhere, for all seek self-control and purity of mind,' he proclaimed. It was in this spirit of tolerance that Asoka, though himself a firm Buddhist, showed favours to all sects and included them all in the welfare work of the Dharma-mahamatras.

'The beloved-of-the-gods ... honours all sects ... with gifts and various forms of recognition. But the Beloved-of-the-gods does not consider gifts or honour to be as important as the advancement of the essential doctrines of all sects,' Asoka declared. Different sects might take different paths, but it was essential that one should 'control one's speech, so as not to extol one's own sect or disparage that of another without reason, or at least to do so only mildly and for specific reasons, because the sects of other people all deserve reverence for one reason or another. By thus acting, a man exalts his own sect, and at the same time does service to the sects of other people. For whosoever honours his own sect while condemning the sects of others wholly from devotion to his own sect ... in reality ... inflicts the severest injury on his own sect. Hence concord alone is meritorious, so that men may willingly hearken to one another's doctrines ... Wherefore the adherents of all sects, whatever they may be, must be informed that the Beloved-of-the-gods does not care so much for gifts or external reverence as that there should be growth of the essential doctrines and breadth of outlook of all sects.'

Asoka's abhorrence for violence in thought, word and deed, implicit in his plea for religious tolerance, found yet another expression in his advocacy of *ahimsa*. Buddhism and other heterodox sects had long opposed the practice of animal sacrifice, which had in any case become, as Kosambi observes, anachronistic with the supersession of the pastoral-hunting economy by the agrarian economy. Asoka now banned animal sacrifice and restricted even the slaughter of animals for meat. 'Here no living thing is to be slaughtered for sacrifice,' ordered Asoka. The royal family itself virtually gave up meat eating. 'Formerly in the kitchens of the Beloved-of-the-gods ... many hundred thousands of living animals were slaughtered daily for meat,' continued Asoka. 'But now, at the time of writing this inscription ... only three animals are killed, two peacocks and a deer, and the deer not regularly. Even these three animals will not be slaughtered in future.' Further, Asoka gave up the common royal pastime of hunting wild animals.

Asoka in one of his pillar edicts gives a long and seemingly arbitrary list of over two dozen creatures forbidden to be killed: parrots, minas, red ducks, swans, doves, bats, ants, tortoises, boneless fish, porcupines, squirrels, deer, lizards, rhinoceroses, and so on. 'Capons must not be made,' Asoka further ordered. 'Chaff which contains living things must not be set on fire. Forests must not be burned down wantonly or to kill living things. The living must not be fed with the living.' And on certain sacred days, particularly on days associated with the stars Tishya and Punarvasu, various restrictions were imposed on the slaughter, castration, and branding of animals, as well as on fishing. Strangely, the cow and the bull are not on Asoka's list of protected animals, though they were probably covered by the general term 'domesticated animals' in the list. Beef, Kosambi notes, continued to be 'sold openly in the market and at the crossroads, like any other meat.'

There was nothing particularly unconventional about the values that Asoka sought to inculcate in society, nothing that would have given offence to non-Buddhists, except his stress on *ahimsa* and the prohibition of animal sacrifice. What distinguished Asoka was his resolute endeavour to get people to conform to the values they generally accepted in principle but violated in practice. 'Meritorious is obedience to mother and father. Liberality to friends, acquaintances, and relatives, to Brahmins and ascetics is meritorious. Abstention from killing animals is meritorious. Moderation in expenditure and possessions is meritorious,' he counselled. He also commended 'compassion, liberality, truthfulness, purity, gentleness, and virtue' as values to be cherished. In edict after edict he emphasised these values, especially purity in domestic life, presumably viewing the stability of the family as the basis of social order. Equally, he laid great stress on fairness in all dealings, on man's responsibilities to his fellow-beings, and on the 'proper treatment of slaves and servants, reverence to teachers, gentleness towards all living beings.'

It was not faith that mattered to Asoka, but conduct. Though he did impose certain restrictions on traditional religious practices, his objective in doing so was to reorder society rather than to gain advantage for Buddhism. It was in this spirit that he forbade animal sacrifices as well as certain festivals and 'merry-makings' – presumably saturnalian orgies like Mahavrata – in which he saw 'much evil'. Men must 'give up their old ways,' he ordered.

Asoka particularly disapproved of superstitious and wasteful rituals. 'In sickness, at the marriage of sons and daughters, at the birth of children, when going on a journey – on these and on other similar occasions people perform many ceremonies. Women especially perform a variety of ceremonies, which are trivial and useless,' observed Asoka. Such ceremonies bore little fruit, he maintained, and went on to suggest that 'what bears great fruit is the ceremony of dharma ... Other ceremonies are doubtful in their effectiveness ... The results of the ceremony of dharma are not confined to the temporal world, for ... endless merit is produced for the life beyond ... There is no gift or favour comparable to the gift of dharma or the favour of dharma.'

Curiously, though Asoka generally disapproved of superstitious practices and religious fairs, he himself promoted certain religious spectacles that he considered as edifying and conducive to the promotion of dharma. 'The sound of the drum has become the sound of dharma,' he claimed, 'showing the people displays of divine chariots, elephants, illumination, and other divine manifestations.' These displays were apparently baits to hook the common people and turn them towards dharma, and were perhaps similar to the grand Buddhist processions that Chinese pilgrim Fa-Hsien says he saw in India in the fourth century AD.

Dharma was for Asoka a matter of deep personal conviction, but we should also note that the ideals of Buddhism eminently suited his political objectives, by providing him with a unifying ethic to integrate and pacify the diverse peoples of his vast empire. He probably believed, as Thapar maintains, that 'the new faith and its active propagation would act as a cementing force.' The monastic organisation of Buddhism was of particular advantage to Asoka in inculcating values that would promote law and order in society. If people could be made to lead a civilised life through the propagation of dharma, and thus be made law-abiding without the use of force, it would be of the greatest value in transforming the harsh business of governance into a humane process. This was a revolutionary notion – that people could be governed through dharmic persuasion, and not by coercion – and a repudiation of Kautilyan ideology. 'The real Asokan conversion,' Kosambi remarks, 'was not merely of the king but of the whole system.'

These policies and practices of Asoka were in all probability not sustained by his successors. Within a few centuries the very origin and purpose of his inscriptions were forgotten, and no one could any longer read them, as the script had changed. Asokan pillars however 'came to be treated as a kind of historical palimpsest,' notes Thapar; the pillar at Allahabad, for instance, carries the inscriptions of the fourth century AD Gupta emperor Samudragupta and of the seventeenth century Mughal emperor Jahangir, as well as numerous other scribblings. Astonishingly, for about two thousand years, until the mid-nineteenth century, no serious effort was made by anyone to decipher the inscriptions. Some of the Asokan pillars in fact came to be revered simply as *lingas*, phallic icons. In Bihar a couple of the pillars are said to have been used by a Mughal general for cannon practice; in Sanchi a pillar was broken into two and used in a sugarcane press, and in Allahabad a pillar was used as a road-roller by a British engineer. One pillar near Varanasi was destroyed in a riot in the early nineteenth century; some others were presumably broken up for use in later constructions. One inscribed slab was used as a pedestal in a Hindu temple.

The only person known to have shown any serious interest in Asokan pillars in pre-modern times was Sultan Firuz Tughluq of Delhi in the mid-fourteenth century. The pillars intrigued him, and he had two of them, one from near Ambala and the other from near Meerut, transported to Delhi and erected there with great care and enormous labour. 'Many Brahmins and Hindu devotees were invited [by the sultan] to read them, but no one was able to,' records contemporary chronicler Shams-i-Siraj Afif. 'It is said that certain ... Hindus interpreted them as stating that no one should be able to remove the obelisk from its place till there should arise in the latter days a Muhammadan king, named Sultan Firuz.' Some claimed that the pillars were the walking sticks of Bhima, the hero of the *Mahabharata*!

ASOKA'S END-LIFE CRISIS

The voice of Asoka that we hear in his edicts is soft, serene. There is nothing in it of the usual gloating, swaggering flamboyance of monarchs. Asoka does occasionally sing his own praise, but only about the good that he has done by propagating dharma, not about his power and glory. 'The gift of spiritual insight I have bestowed in manifold ways,' he says; 'I have conferred many benefits on men, animals, birds and fish, even unto the boon of life, and many other good deeds have I performed.' He does not, he says, seek the adulation of the world, but only the beatitude of the soul, for himself and for all the people. 'Whatever exertions the Beloved-of-the-gods ... makes are all for the sake of the life hereafter, so that all men may be freed from peril, the peril of vice.'

Asoka's goal, says Sastri, was 'the moral regeneration of a whole nation.' He wanted man to transcend himself, society to transcend itself. 'This, the instruction in the law, is the most valuable activity,' Asoka held. 'Men should make progress in this matter, and not be satisfied with their shortcomings.' But was it not chimerical for the emperor to imagine himself to be, as Rhys Davids alleges, '*a deus ex machina*, able and ready to put all things and all men straight'? Quite so, for Asoka did indeed fall far short of his goals. But then, this is true of every great reformer in history. The pursuit of the possible is the stock in trade of those who are content with making do; it is by aspiring for the impossible that the reformer brings about a possible improvement in the human condition.

Asoka was a dreamer, but he considered his dreams realisable, and worked tirelessly at them. He believed he was succeeding. 'For a long time past, even for many hundred years, the killing and injuring of living beings, discourtesy towards relatives, Brahmins and ascetics have been growing. But today, thanks to the practice of dharma on the part of the Beloved-of-the-gods ... [and] by reason of the inculcation of dharma by the Beloved-of-the-gods ..., abstention from killing animals, non-injury to living beings, courtesy to relatives, Brahmins and ascetics, obedience to mother and father, and obedience to elders, have all increased as never before for many centuries,' states Asoka. 'The gods, who in Jambudvipa up to this time did not associate with men, now mingle with them, and this is the result of my efforts,' he states in another edict, perhaps meaning that people had, because of his endeavours, gained godly virtues. 'Moreover,' continues Asoka, 'this is not something to be obtained only by the great; even the humble, if they exert themselves earnestly, can achieve heavenly bliss.'

His main achievement, Asoka claimed, was in changing the disposition of the people. But there was also much else for which he could take credit. His edicts, for instance, are the first written documents of Indian history, and to his reign belong the earliest extant stone monuments and art objects of India after the collapse of the Indus Civilisation more than a millennium earlier. Asoka was probably also the first ruler to use stone instead of wood for construction in a big way, though wood continued to be his chief construction material. Asoka's own palace was built of stone, according to Fa Hsien, who claims he saw it in the early fifth century AD, some six and a half centuries after it was built. 'The royal palace and halls in the midst of the city, which exist now as of old,' writes Fa Hsien, 'were all made by spirits which he employed, and which piled up the stones, reared the walls and gates, and executed the elegant carving and inlaid sculpture-work, all in a way which no human hand of this world could accomplish.' Two centuries after Fa Hsien, Hsuan Tsang found Pataliputra in ruins, destroyed by fire and flood, as archaeological evidence indicates. None of Asoka's buildings exists today, though the stone columns in the ruins of Pataliputra have been tentatively identified as part of Asoka's palace. Of Asoka's monuments, only the rock-cut retreat he built for Ajivikas and a few of his pillars remain intact.

Asoka is believed to have built a large number of stupas to house Buddha's relics – 84,000 of them 'were completed within three years, and in a single day the news of their completion reached the court,' claim Pali sources. 'By means of the supernatural powers with which he was gifted, King Asoka was enabled to behold at one glance all these works throughout the empire.' The number 84,000 was not impressive enough for the Nepalese Buddhist work *Avadana*, which raised the figure to 3,510 million stupas. Closer to the truth, Hsuan Tsang says he saw more than eighty stupas and monasteries built by Asoka.

The stupa is a large but architecturally simple hemispherical dome of unburnt bricks faced with burnt bricks and covered with a thick layer of plaster, with a circumambulatory path around it enclosed by a railing. It had apparently evolved from primitive burial mounds raised over the revered dead, and had existed even before the time of Asoka. Asoka built them specifically to enshrine the relics of Buddha, the relic – a bone fragment or a tooth, and such – being usually placed in a small, carved crystal casket in the central chamber of the dome. At Sanchi, the original brick stupa is believed to have been built by Asoka, but was subsequently, about a century later, expanded to double its size. None of the stupas that Asoka built exists today in its original form.

But the Asokan pillars, the finest works of Mauryan art, remain, a good number of them having surprisingly survived the ravages of time and the vandalism of men. In them, says Vincent Smith, 'the skill of the stone-cutter may be said to have attained perfection, and to have accomplished tasks which would, perhaps, be found beyond the powers of the twentieth century. Gigantic shafts of hard sandstone ... were dressed and proportioned with the utmost nicety, receiving a polish which no modern mason knows how to impart to the material. Enormous surfaces of the hardest gneiss were burnished like mirrors ...' Because of its brilliant polish, Thomas Coryat, the British traveller who saw it in Delhi in the early seventeenth century, mistook it to be 'a brazen pillar,' and Bishop Heber in the early nineteenth century thought it was a 'pillar of cast metal.'

The pillars are beautifully proportioned, and crowned with animal sculptures of outstanding artistic merit. The most renowned of them is the Saranath pillar, its capital of four snarling lions being the emblem of the Republic of India. The lions are set back to back on an abacus, which in turn is mounted on an inverted bell-shaped lotus. The entire capital, made up of these three elements, is 2.1 metres high, and is carved out of a single block of stone. A polished stone dharma wheel once surmounted the lions, but it has since broken off. The abacus is adorned with fine bas-relief carvings of animals – an elephant, a horse, a bull, and a lion, with wheels separating them – all executed with a sure hand somewhat reminiscent of the Indus seals. John Marshall considered the Saranath pillar sculptures to be 'masterpieces in point of both style and technique – the finest carving, indeed, that India has yet produced, and unsurpassed ... by anything of their kind in the ancient world.'

The stone for Asokan pillars came mainly from Chunar near Varanasi – a fine grained buff-coloured sandstone speckled with tiny dark spots – but some also from around Mathura. Incomplete cylindrical monoliths, apparently hewed for making Asokan pillars, were found at the ancient quarries of Chunar. The quarried stones were transported by river and land to the sites where the pillars were to be erected, and there chiselled to their final shape and carved. The uniformity of their artistic style indicates that they were all sculpted under the supervision of a single school of master craftsmen.

The Asokan pillars are massive, some towering nearly as high as a five-storeyed building, their height varying from 12 to 15 metres. The diameter of the pillars at the base varies from nearly a metre to a metre and a quarter, tapering smoothly to the top, where the diameter varies from 56 to 89 centimetres. An average Asokan pillar probably weighed about 50 tons, so transporting the pillars over great distances through trackless countryside and uneven terrain would have required considerable engineering skill and immense labour. When Firuz Tughluq moved one of these pillars from near Ambala to Delhi, it was carried to the Yamuna in a cart of 42 wheels, drawn by 8,400 men, and then down the river to Delhi in a raft made of a large number of boats.

The Asokan sculpture does not quite fit the ambience of mainstream Indian art tradition. 'Compared with later figural sculptures in the round ... the art represented by these crowning lions [of the Asokan pillar] belongs to an altogether different world of conception and execution, of style and technique, altogether much more complex, urban and civilised,' comments art historian Niharranjan Ray. Their rather formal and almost frozen appearance suggests, according to Ray, 'that this style and convention came from outside where they were already fixed and well established.'

There was hardly any stone carving in Aryan India before Asoka. Then suddenly appears the highly sophisticated and mature art form of Asokan sculptures. How did this come about? Since it was impossible for Indian artisans to have acquired, all by themselves and in just a few decades, a new skill of such a high standard, it is generally assumed that craftsmen with a long tradition of stone quarrying and carving, in all probability Persians, were employed in making the pillars. This assumption is borne out by the brief Kharoshthi inscription found on one of the cylindrical monoliths at the Chunar quarries. Certain minor rock edicts in Karnataka also have the engraver's Kharoshthi marks.

The Saranath pillar, observes Thapar, definitely 'shows a Perso-Hellenistic connection.' Persian influence is believed to be evident also in the structure of the royal palace in Pataliputra, where the pillared hall – which is 'outside the line of Indian architectural development' – bears resemblance to the Hall of a Hundred Columns in Persepolis, and was perhaps consciously adopted, as Ray maintains, 'as a part of the paraphernalia of imperialism.' A mason's mark on a stone column in the Pataliputra palace even bears a close resemblance to similar marks in Persepolis.

All this is no surprise. India had maintained close contacts with West Asia even from the time of the Indus Civilisation, and these ties strengthened with the Aryan occupation of India and Persia. Later, when western Punjab became a satrapy of the Achaemenid empire, the two sister civilisations became closely interlinked. Naturally then, when the Achaemenid empire collapsed under Alexander's onslaught, many Persian artisans migrated to India for safety or employment. And later, when Chandragupta extended the Mauryan empire into Afghanistan, Graeco-Persian lands became part of the Indian empire, and the cultural interaction between India and West Asia quickened. 'India and Iran,' notes Ray, 'participated in a common politico-historical process ... Early Indian art can be viewed and understood fully only against the background of age-old but very potent and effective Indo-Sumerian and Indo-Iranian contacts maintained through long centuries.' Observes Ananda Coomaraswamy: 'India, in the centuries and perhaps millenniums BC was an integral part of an 'Ancient East' that extended from the Mediterranean to the Ganges Valley.'

The role of foreign artisans in sculpting Asokan pillars is also indicated by the fact that the high craftsmanship in stone was lost after the Mauryas, which would not have happened had it been a native skill. Comments Kramrisch: Mauryan art 'was a hot-house plant reared up by the will, care and patronage of a court heavily under the influence of foreign culture and ideology.' The Mauryan style of architecture and sculpture, even the Mauryan style of government, did not survive the collapse of the empire, because, as Ray maintains, they 'lacked deeper roots in the collective social will, taste and preference' of Indians.

Thus it was that all the noble aspirations of the great emperor, and all the good work he had done, turned to ashes soon after his death. Nothing came of the pious hope expressed by Asoka in his fifth major rock edict, and repeated in several other edicts, that 'my sons, my grandsons and my descendants after them until the end of the world, if they will follow my example, they too will do good.' The Mauryan empire itself would not long survive Asoka. Indeed, its decline began towards the close of his reign.

In the last ten years of his life Asoka was virtually inactive as a ruler, and was beset with family problems and personal misfortunes. It was not a peaceful old age for him. When he was in his mid-sixties, his chief queen and good companion, Asandhimitra, died. With that began his troubles. About four years later, Asoka, in some sort of an end-life crisis – or probably 'prompted by sensual passion,' as Pali chronicles would have it – elevated a young and wanton woman, Tissarakha, to the rank of chief queen. According to the *Divyavadana*, she gained ascendancy over him by curing him of a dangerous and revolting disease.

'Now it happened that King Asoka became very ill; excrement began to come out of his mouth, and impure substance oozed out of all his pores,' says the text. 'No one was able to cure him.' But Tissarakha cured him on a diet of onions. And that, according to the text, brought the emperor under her spell. Whatever the circumstances of her ascendancy, it led to domestic intrigues. Tissarakha, it is said, had a vicious streak in her, and once tried to destroy the Bodhi-tree, resenting the tree as her rival for the affections of the emperor. She also tried to form an amorous liaison with Asoka's son Kunala, being infatuated with his beautiful eyes, and when he spurned her, she had him blinded by forging a royal order. When at last Asoka woke up to the enormity of Tissarakha's crimes, he had her burnt to death.

Could all this be true? We cannot be certain. But it does seem likely that Asoka, weak with age, perhaps ill, was no longer the man he had been in his youth. Legend says that he was forced by his ministers to abdicate power to Samprati, his grandson. There is a poignant story, told in different versions, that towards the end of his life Asoka tried to empty his treasury – give away a thousand million gold pieces, according to the *Divyavadana* – and even mortgage the empire to the Buddhist sangha to gain religious merit, but was prevented from doing so by Samprati and the ministers. Fa Hsien claims he saw in Pataliputra a stone pillar bearing the inscription: 'Asoka gave Jambudvipa to the general body of all the monks, and then redeemed it from them with money. This he did three times.' Says Hsuan Tsang: 'King Asoka having fallen sick and lingering for a long time, felt that he would not recover, and desired to offer all his possessions to the sangha so as to crown his religious merit. The minister who was carrying on the government was unwilling to comply with his wish.'

One day around this time, while Asoka was eating a mango, the minister in playful ceremoniousness put half the fruit in the emperor's hand, as if making an offering. Asoka, according to Hsuan Tsang, held the fruit in the palm of his hand in silence for a while, then looked up at the minister 'with a sigh' and asked: 'Who now is the lord of Jambudvipa?'

'Only your majesty,' the minister replied.

'Not so!' said the weary old emperor. 'I am no longer the lord, for I have only this half fruit to call my own! Alas! The wealth and honour of the world are as difficult to keep as it is to preserve the light of a lamp in the wind! My widespread possessions, my name and high renown, at the close of life are snatched away from me, and I am in the hands of a minister violent and powerful. The empire is no longer mine; this half fruit alone is left!'

Asoka, continues Hsuan Tsang, sent that half fruit as an offering to the Buddhist monastery, and asked his officer to tell the priests, 'All that I have is gone and lost, only this half fruit remains as my little possession. Pity the poverty of the offering, and grant that it may increase the seeds of his religious merit.'

There is nothing inherently improbable in these stories. Emperors are not immune to old age and senility. And it was common for princes in ancient

India to seize power from their aged parents, and for ministers to collude with them. Death finally released Asoka from his troubles around 232 BC, when he was about seventy years old. He had reigned for thirty-seven years.

The Mauryan empire was probably partitioned on Asoka's death, maybe into western and eastern halves. Asoka's long ailment at the end of his life would have given his ministers ample time to accommodate the rival ambitions of his heirs by negotiating a division of the empire. But once the empire broke into two, further fragmentation, and eventually total disintegration, with provinces becoming independent kingdoms, was only a matter of time.

It is impossible to reconstruct the history of the later Mauryas, or even to identify the rulers, as the names of Asoka's successors are given variously and in different sequences in different sources. 'Upon the cessation of the race of the Nandas, the Mauryas will possess the earth, for Kautilya will place Chandragupta on the throne. His son will be Bindusara; his son will be Asoka Vardhana; his son will be Suyasas; his son will be Dasaratha; his son will be Sangata; his son will be Salisuka; his son will be Somasraman; and his successor will be Brihadratha. These are the ten Mauryas who will reign over the earth for a hundred and thirty-seven years,' says the *Vishnu Purana* about the Mauryan dynasty, losing count along the way. Other sources give the names of other kings as the successors of Asoka. There is no certainty about any of these lists.

After Asoka's death, the Mauryan dynasty lasted only for about fifty years, till the early second century BC, that too only as rulers of a severely truncated kingdom, 'more or less confined to the province of Magadha.' The total span of the dynasty given as 137 years in the *Vishnu Purana* is probably correct.

The last of the Mauryan rulers, according to the Puranas, was Brihadratha. Described by Bana as a gullible and foolish young man, he was assassinated during a military parade by his commander-in-chief, a Brahmin named Pushyamitra, who then assumed royal power and founded the Sunga dynasty. It is however possible that the descendants of Brihadratha retained their dynastic identity for several centuries, though only as petty chieftains, for Hsuan Tsang says that one Puranavarman of the Mauryan lineage, who was the feudatory king of Magadha, replanted the sacred tree at Bodh Gaya in the seventh century.

Can the collapse of the empire be blamed on Asoka? The charges are that his pacific policy softened the martial vigour essential to sustain the empire; that law and order suffered because of his compassion towards criminals and rebels; that his patronage of Buddhism antagonised the powerful community of Brahmins; and that his softness towards the frontier people emboldened them to make incursions into the empire.

All these are plausible. But much can be said also in defence of Asoka. His Buddhist affiliation is unlikely to have alienated other sects, for he was tolerant towards all religions and extended patronage to all. The fact that Pushyamitra, who overthrew the Mauryas, was a Brahmin does not necessarily mean that he was heading a Brahminical counter-revolution. There is no evidence of vigorous persecution of Buddhists by the Sungas. The allegations in Buddhist literature that Pushyamitra, on learning that Asoka had gained fame by building 84,000 stupas, decided to gain an equal fame for himself by demolishing 84,000 stupas, and that he put a price on the head of every Buddhist monk, are in all probability stories invented by Buddhists to illustrate the wickedness of non-Buddhist rulers. The Sungas were indeed patrons of Brahminical religion, but the charge of the destruction of stupas is not supported by archaeological evidence. Quite the contrary, it was during the Sunga period that the great stupa at Bharhut was built, and the Sanchi stupa renovated and enlarged. The Sungas themselves, we should note, were in the end overthrown by a Brahmin minister, Vasudeva.

The Mauryan army probably had lost some of its martial spirit and fitness during the long years of peace under Asoka, but there was no serious external aggression during the time of his immediate successors. The incursion of Bactrian Greeks began towards the end of Mauryan rule, but this was the consequence, not the cause, of the collapse of the empire. Further, though Asoka was a pacifist, he was careful not to weaken the authority of the state – he did not abolish the death penalty, or even torture, and the hill tribes within his empire and the people along his frontiers were sternly warned under threat of punishment to maintain order.

It is likely that there was some slackening of administrative efficiency during Asoka's last years, as he had grown too old to rule. The Mauryan empire was in any case too extensive to be governed efficiently, given the limitations of the ancient means of transportation and communication. As power stretched over a vast area, it stretched thin. In a sense, the empire collapsed under its own weight, as its administrative structure, though remarkably elaborate and strong for that age, could not support the weight of the immense empire. There are indications that the empire was under financial stress under Asoka, certainly so under his successors. 'Silver coins after Chandragupta show a sudden increase in the copper content, with less accurate minted weights,' notes Kosambi. Though the Indian economy would have prospered during the nearly three decades of peace under Asoka, the state might not have gained from it, because of its administrative laxity. At the same time, the financial burden of the empire would have greatly increased under Asoka, as its bureaucracy proliferated monstrously to serve the vast new (and, in purely financial terms, unproductive) responsibilities that Asoka assumed for the propagation of dharma.

All these contributed to the decline of the empire. But perhaps the primary reason for its collapse was that it had simply lost its *elan vital.* In the beginning, nothing could harm the empire, because of its sheer vitality; in the end, nothing could save it, because it had grown old and weary. Spengler is probably right: empires, like living organisms, are subject to old age and decay. They too have a life span.

Chapter Seven

THE CLOCKWORK STATE

ALL FOR THE KING

Praja sukhe sukham rajnah prajanam ca hite hitam –
In the happiness of his subjects is the happiness of the king,
in their welfare is his welfare.

Thus proclaims Kautilya piously in the *Arthasastra*, and then proceeds, with cold, grim detachment, to expound practices that are the exact opposite of this precept. Equating the good of the people with the good of the king, the pundit examines all the innumerable ways by which the king can enslave, dupe and mulct his subjects for his own aggrandisement. He then goes on to discuss, again with the same stern dispassion, the artifices and deceits that the king should use to subdue neighbouring states, and the precautions he should take to protect himself against corrupt officials and treacherous sons. But there is not a word in this prodigious treatise of well over 5,000 verses about what people should do to protect themselves against royal tyranny. The *Arthasastra*, as its title indicates, is solely concerned with acquiring and preserving *artha* – wealth and power. It is, states Kautilya, 'the science by which territory is acquired and maintained; it is the science of wealth and welfare.'

Kautilya understood power. Nothing else really interested him. And he would allow neither sentiment nor morality to sway his professional objectivity in matching ends and means. Dharma is one thing, politics quite another, Kautilya held. Considerations of honour, chivalry and fair play have no place in the pursuit of power. Any means is good means if it succeeds. 'There is not [in the *Arthasastra*] the least pretence at morality or altruism,' observes Kosambi. 'The only difficulties ever discussed, no matter how gruesome or treacherous the methods, are practical, with due consideration of cost and possible after-effects.'

There are, however, a few passages in which Kautilya outwardly professes concern for the welfare of the people. 'Whenever danger threatens, the king shall protect all those afflicted like a father,' he enjoins. 'The king shall maintain, at state expense, children, the old, the destitute, those suffering from adversity, childless women and the children of destitute women. The village elders shall act as trustees of ... the inheritance of minors. Every man has an obligation to maintain his wife, children, parents, minor brothers and dependent sisters ... No one shall renounce the life of a householder in order to become an ascetic without providing for the maintenance of his wife and children.' During famines, the king was required to distribute food and seeds from the royal stores at subsidised rates, undertake food-for-work programmes, take over and distribute hoarded private stocks, seek assistance from other kings, and encourage people to migrate to another district or even to another country.

Sentiments like these are extremely rare in the *Arthasastra*. And even in these instances, Kautilya's real concern, it turns out on close examination, is not so much to alleviate the sufferings of the people as to protect the interests of the king through a policy of enlightened self-interest. 'When a people are impoverished,' he warns, 'they become greedy; when they are greedy, they become disaffected; when disaffected, they either go over to the enemy or kill their rulers themselves.' The king should keep the people contented, so as to keep them docile. This was Kautilya's view. 'This kind of protection was nearer to the care of the master for his cattle than of a father for his children,' comments Kosambi. 'It is much easier to be a despot in practice while claiming a paternal attitude.'

The primacy that Kautilya gives to the pursuit of power, and the baseness of the means he recommends, make the *Arthasastra* a most perverse and repellent book, if we judge it from a moralistic viewpoint. But it is also an utterly fascinating book, the untrammelled play of relentless logic and crafty imagination on the intractable problems of governance. Kautilya was a man of forbiddingly complex intelligence, and compared to the monumentality, detached professionalism and surgical precision of the *Arthasastra*, Machiavelli's pamphlet, *The Prince*, written about 1,800 years later, seems rather like the work of an ardent amateur.

The very name Kautilya means 'crooked', hardly an epithet by which a sage would have wanted to be known. Perhaps his real name, as some scholars maintain, was Kautalya, derived from Kautala, his *gotra*, which got corrupted – or was deliberately distorted – into Kautilya. Kautilya was also known as Chanakya (son of Chanaka) and Vishnugupta (very likely his personal name). A verse in the *Arthasastra* connects him to the overthrow of the Nandas, and there is a strong possibility that he was Chandragupta Maurya's guru and minister. Kautilya's Mauryan background is also indicated by the close correspondence between the data in the *Arthasastra*, the accounts of Megasthenes, and the edicts of Asoka.

Yet, curiously, there is no reference in the *Arthasastra* to Chandragupta or Pataliputra. And the political environment it deals with is of competing small states, not of a large empire like that of the Mauryas. Kosambi persuasively argues that 'a good deal of the work ... rests solidly upon previous administrative practice, and a theory of statecraft which can only be pre-Mauryan.' Could then the author of the *Arthasastra* really have been the mentor of Chandragupta? The book, Nilakanta Sastri points out, 'is so full of pedantry and schematic classifications that it could only have been written by a pundit,' and not by one who had clawed his way up through the rough and tumble of politics. But then, Kautilya was a man of thought as well as of action. According to tradition, he began his career as a scholar before taking to *realpolitik*, and he retired from politics early in the reign of Bindusara to revert to scholarly pursuits. The *Arthasastra* was the labour of love of Kautilya's retirement, summarising all he had learned about life and politics.

But why did not Kautilya deal with imperial administration? The reason could be that he was almost exclusively concerned with royal power, and therefore with central administration. Furthermore, the *Arthasastra* is essentially a critical digest of the political wisdom accumulated over several generations, and therefore limited in its scope to what had been covered in previous texts. The very opening line of the book states, 'This *Arthasastra* is made as a compendium of almost all the *Arthasastras*, which, in view of acquisition and maintenance of the earth, have been composed by ancient teachers.'

The *Arthasastra* is a *sastra*, a theoretical treatise. It is a prescriptive, not just a descriptive work. But undeniably the precepts of the *Arthasastra* are based on thorough knowledge of administrative practice. Indeed, it is highly probable that what it prescribes are, in broad terms, what was practised by the central government in the Mauryan empire. This is evident from the fact that the accounts of Mauryan administration in other sources generally match the accounts in the *Arthasastra*. Kautilya did no doubt go beyond descriptions of practice to examine theoretical possibilities – 'for the completeness of the *sastra*,' as Nilakanta Sastri puts it. But we have no sure means of separating prescriptions from descriptions, and therefore have to proceed on the assumption that the text presents – except where it is obviously speculative – a more or less true picture of Mauryan administration.

A lengthy work of 5,348 verses in 150 chapters, the *Arthasastra* meticulously analyses the teachings of several authorities and offers its own sober advice. The work – especially its fourteenth book, dealing with poisons, alchemy and occult practices – was meant for the specialist, not for the general reader. Fairly large portions of the original work – 'between a fifth and a quarter of the original,' according to some – were in later times lost or taken out, and probably some new material interpolated. The earliest specific reference to the book belongs to about the third century AD. The book was well known in medieval times, and commentaries on it were written in regional languages, including one in Malayalam in the twelfth century. It was even translated into Arabic. But the original text itself was subsequently thought lost, until a pundit in Mysore, R. Shamasastry, discovered a manuscript of the book in the Grantha script in 1904.

The *Arthasastra* has many of the flaws of ancient Indian scholarly writing, and is full of pedantic minutiae and ponderous, tiresome lists, and suffers from the common scholastic affliction of over-elaboration. However, it is refreshingly free of the pious platitudes and specious reasoning common to the works of Indian sages. Unlike most other texts of the period, which used Prakrit, the *Arthasastra* was written in Sanskrit, and its literary style, Kosambi notes, is 'unique in Sanskrit for its compression, lack of flourishes, and terse prose.'

Kautilya was no respecter of tradition; he would not blindly accept the given wisdom, and had the unprecedented audacity to question even the judgement of his own guru, stating, 'My teacher says that ... Not so, says Kautilya ...' He exalted reason above textual prescriptions, and was contemptuous of superstitions like astrology, maintaining that man should act with faith in himself and not in the stars. He had little interest in religion, except in manipulating it to promote royal power, and the only use he found for ascetics and holy men was to employ them as spies. He did occasionally speak of philosophy and ethics – 'Philosophy is the lamp that illuminates all sciences; it provides the techniques for all action; it is the pillar which supports dharma,' he says in one place – but apparently what he meant by philosophy in this context was the theoretical framework needed to give coherence to policy, not abstract thought inquiring into fundamental reality.

Kautilya broke with tradition in another respect too. Comments Nilakanta Sastri: 'The mass and variety of detailed statistical information which the *Arthasastra* requires the officials of the state to collect and arrange for ready reference ... is something unique in all Indian political literature. We are tempted to suppose that the model for Kautilya ... was furnished by the practice of Persian kings and satraps ...' However, the Persian model was not just 'borrowed, but assimilated to the indigenous scheme so as to produce a harmonious whole ... The polity of the Mauryan empire was ... in part a culmination of the development of an indigenous tradition of imperialism which began to take shape under the Nandas and in part comprised wise borrowings and adaptations from contemporary foreign models, immediately Hellenistic, but ultimately traceable to the Achaemenid empire of Persia.'

The Kautilyan monarch was an absolute ruler, with all the enormous powers and responsibilities of the government concentrated in his person. The reach of his authority extended far beyond the limits set by Indian political tradition. The conventional concept of royal power in India was that the king should rule in conformity to dharma as given in the sacred texts and expressed in social usage. He had no legislative powers. 'With Kautilya, on the other hand, the royal decree has an independent validity of its own; moreover, its validity is of so overriding a character that it must be taken to prevail against dharma, private treaty or contract, and social usage,' Sastri observes. 'This view of the supremacy of the royal decree is exceptional among Indian writers,' and was similar to the position in Persian and Hellenistic monarchies.

Society cannot exist without a king, according to Kautilya. 'Where there is no *danda-dhara* (sceptre-bearer) the strong eat up the weak, as it is among fish,' he observed, conveniently overlooking the fact that in the Kautilyan system the king eats all. The king protects social order and promotes public welfare, and 'is thus the fountain of favours and justice, like Indra and Yama, and is entitled to the loyalty of his subjects,' he argued, and went on to warn that since kings perform divine functions on earth, 'they should never be slighted, for divine punishment will be visited on whoever slights them.' He even recommended that, to awe his subjects, the king should disguise his secret agents as gods, and allow himself to be seen mingling with them.

Kautilya did concede that the relationship between the king and the people was one of reciprocity, for mutual benefit. 'Subjects who do not pay fines and taxes take on themselves the sins of kings, while kings who do not look after the welfare of the people take on themselves the sins of the subjects,' he held. But this seeming reciprocity in practice worked solely for the benefit of the king. People were required to meet their obligations to the king, not so much in their own interest as in the interest of the king, while the king was required to meet his obligations to the people primarily in his own interest. The people were the king's source of wealth and power, and it was in his self-interest to take good care of them.

The Kautilyan king had to be something of a superman, and lead a life of unremitting vigilance and relentless exertion, and the *Arthasastra* gives a long list of the qualities needed in a king to meet these arduous obligations. Most of all, he had to practise strict self-discipline, eschew passion, anger, greed, obstinacy and capriciousness, and also 'avoid daydreaming.' States the *Arthasastra*:

Readiness in action is the king's sacred vow,
Discharge of duty, his sacrifice.

Kautilya prescribed a punishing daily routine for the monarch. 'The king should be always energetic. He shall divide the day and the night each into eight *nalikas* (periods of one and a half hours) and perform his duties as follows,' he directed, and went on to lay down a detailed schedule about what exactly he should do during each of the sixteen periods. The king was allowed four and a half hours of sleep at night, and was allotted three hours for bath and meals and one and a half hours for recreation. The rest of his time had to be spent on public business, every particular of which was specified, hour by hour.

The king was woken up at 1.30 a.m. with the sound of music. On waking, he meditated for one *nalika* on political affairs and reviewed the day's schedule of work. The next *nalika* was spent in consulting councillors and in assigning tasks to spies, and this was followed by the period when he received blessings from his guru and priest, and met with his physician, chief cook, and astrologer. At daybreak he proceeded to the audience chamber 'after circumambulating a cow, its calf and a bull,' and spent most of the rest of the day on administrative work, reviewing finance and defence matters, receiving petitions from the public, dispatching messengers, inspecting the armed forces, and so on, till he retired to bed at 9 p.m. ('The palace,' says Curtius, 'is open to all comers, even when the king is having his hair combed and dressed. It is then that he gives audience to ambassadors, and administers justice to his subjects.')

The strait-jacket discipline of the royal timetable was not very practical, Kautilya knew, so he added a rider to the schedule to allow the king to 'divide up the night and day according to his own strength and tastes.' But whatever his actual schedule, the king was always under relentless pressure of work. Comments Kosambi: 'Far from wallowing in oriental luxury, the *Arthasastra* monarch was the hardest-worked person in his realm.' While everyone and everything in the empire was yoked to the royal will, the emperor himself was yoked to work, a harried slave of the pursuit of power. He could enjoy power, but not enjoy life. There was no place for emotions and sentiments or for the gratification of whims in the life of the Kautilyan monarch. As the fictionalised Chandragupta Maurya says in the play the *Mudra-Rakshasa*, 'Kingship is, for the ruler of men who is intent on acting in pursuance of the duties of royalty, an office of mighty discomfort.'

One reason for the king's 'mighty discomfort' was that he lived in a state of perpetual insecurity, for fear of being poisoned, assassinated or overthrown. He could never, ever relax. And he had no privacy, being always surrounded by his security detail. The *Arthasastra* has an extensive section on the innumerable precautions the king should take for his personal safety, and the security requirements that had to be met in the construction of his palace. His private apartment, at the centre of the royal complex in a fortified citadel, was required to be built in the 'middle of a labyrinth with concealed passages in its walls' leading to an underground chamber, and from there to a nearby shrine. Kautilya stipulated that convicts should be used to build the secret structures, and that they should be executed after the work was done. Various occult and other measures were taken to protect the palace complex against fire, serpents and poison.

(Further, according to Strabo, the king had to 'change his bed from time to time because of the plots against him.')

'Every object which comes into the palace complex or goes out of it shall be examined, its arrival and departure recorded and sent to its destination [only] after affixing the [appropriate] seal,' warned Kautilya. 'The king shall eat only freshly cooked food, after first making oblations to the sacred fire and offering food to birds ... Barbers and valets shall wait on the king only after they have had a bath and put on clean clothes. They shall receive, with clean hands, implements [of their trade], toilet articles and dresses, in a sealed condition from the concerned officer.' Attendants had to apply cosmetics first on themselves before applying them on the king. Physicians and experts in treating poisoning were required to be always in attendance on the king.

The personal guards and servants of the king were all women. 'The care of the king's person is entrusted to women, who are bought from their parents' and trained in their profession, writes Strabo. 'The bodyguards and the rest of the military force are stationed outside the [palace] gates ... [When the king goes out] he is surrounded by women, and outside them by spear-bearers. Drum-beaters and gong-carriers precede them. The road is lined with ropes, and death is the penalty for anyone who passes inside the ropes ... Some of the women ride in chariots, some on horse-back, some on elephants, and they are equipped with all kinds of weapons, as they are when they go on military expeditions with men.' Kautilya prescribed that 'courtesans shall be appointed to attend on the king in one of the three grades, according to their beauty and the splendour of their make-up and ornaments. The lowest grade ... shall hold the umbrella over the king; the middle grade ... shall carry his water jug, and the highest ... shall be his fan bearer.'

The king's mount, horse or elephant, had to be certified as safe, and when he travelled by water, a specially selected sailor piloted the royal barge. Kautilya directed that the king 'shall inspect fully armed troops only when fully armed himself and riding a horse, an elephant or a chariot.' Ascetics could turn out to be disguised spies or assassins, so the king was advised to receive them only in the presence of trusted armed guards, and to be 'particularly careful with anchorites and those expert in magic, for such people are easy to anger.' Foreign envoys were to be received by him only in the presence of ministers. He had to be careful even with his wives. 'The king shall visit the queen in her own apartment only after an old [trusted] maidservant assures him that there is no danger from the queen.'

Of particular danger to the king were his own sons, and the *Arthasastra* has a long and lively discussion on how he should protect himself against filial treachery, with Kautilya quoting various authorities and finally giving his own sane and moderate advice. 'Princes, like crabs, eat their begetters,' held one sage. 'A king should therefore guard himself against them right from their birth. It is better to kill them quietly if they are found wanting in affection.' This view was condemned by others as inhuman, and they in turn suggested various other measures, including 'letting him (the prince) free to dissipate himself, because a son engrossed in pleasures does not hate his father.' None of these suggestions found favour with others, or with Kautilya.

Finally one sage proposed that the loyalty of the prince should be tested by secret agents by tempting him to seize the kingdom, after winning his confidence by indulging him in the pleasures of hunting, gambling, wine and women. Kautilya opposed this, saying, 'There can be no greater crime or sin than making wicked impressions on an innocent mind. A prince should be taught what is true dharma and *artha*, not what is unrighteous and materially harmful.' According to him, the best policy would be to keep the suspect prince under the constant guard of secret agents, who should also direct him along the right path. 'If the disgruntled son has good personal qualities, he shall be made the chief of defence or heir-apparent [to assure him of his succession].'

It was not kindness that prompted Kautilya to prescribe this policy, but expediency. This is evident from the fact that the *Arthasastra* has a section that advises the prince on how to overthrow and kill his father, if unjustly treated. With equal impartiality, it also advises the king how to entrap and eliminate a disgruntled prince. 'When he is brought before the king, an only son shall be pacified by promising him the kingdom after the father's death but kept in confinement. If there are other sons, the disgruntled prince shall be killed.'

Ordinarily, royal succession was by primogeniture, but Kautilya warned that a wicked son should not be crowned, even if he was the only son. If there was no heir, 'an old or sick king shall get a child begotten on his wife by one of the following: his mother's kinsman, a close relation or a virtuous neighbouring prince.' In case there was uncertainty about succession, and the king was seriously ill, his condition should be concealed, and a double used to give the public the impression that the king was well and was performing his duties. Similarly, the death of the king should be kept secret until precautionary measures were taken. If there was no suitable heir, the councillor should set up a regency by placing on the throne a child prince or a princess or a pregnant queen, but he should not himself usurp the throne.

On the training of princes, Kautilya recommended: 'A prince should learn the alphabet and arithmetic as the tonsure ceremony is performed [in his third year]. Later, when the ceremony of the sacred thread is performed, he should learn philosophy and the three Vedas from authoritative teachers, economics from the heads of departments, and the science of government from political theorists and administrators. He should remain a *brahmachari* till he is sixteen. He should then have the second tonsure ceremony and get married. With a view to improving his self-discipline, he should always associate with learned elders ... During the first part of the day he shall be trained in martial arts ...; in the latter part of the day he shall listen to *itihasas*; in the remaining part of the day and at night, he shall prepare new lessons, revise old lessons and listen repeatedly to things which he had not understood clearly.'

If the life of the king was one of endless toil and bother, why would anyone ever want to be a king? Evidently, the reward for the pursuit of power was primarily in the enjoyment of power. But there were other compensations as well. The Mauryan emperor, according to Greek sources, lived in great luxury. 'Neither Memnonian Susa with all its costly splendour, nor Ekbatana with all its magnificence can vie' with the glory of the palace where 'the greatest of all the kings' of India lives, says Aelian, an ancient Roman chronicler, on the authority of Megasthenes. The royal mansion stood in an extensive park full of 'tame peacocks and pheasants, shady groves and trees set in clumps with branches woven together by some special cunning of horticulture, trees that are always green, that never grow old and never shed their leaves. Some of them are native, and some are brought from other lands with great care, and these with their beauty enhance the charms of the landscape.' Many different species of birds and animals were stocked in the park, especially parrots. 'In this royal pleasance, there are also artificial ponds of great beauty in which they keep fish of enormous size, but quite tame.'

'The luxury of their kings ... is carried to a vicious excess without parallel in the world,' writes Curtius. 'When the king condescends to show himself in public, his attendants carry in their hands silver censers, and perfume with incense all the road by which it is his pleasure to be conveyed. He lolls in a golden palanquin, garnished with pearls which dangle all around it, and he is robed in fine muslin embroidered with purple and gold. Behind his palanquin follow men-at-arms and his bodyguards, of whom some carry boughs of trees on which birds are perched, trained to interrupt business with their cries ... He rides on horseback when making short journeys, but when bound on a distant expedition, he rides in a chariot mounted on elephants, and, huge as these animals are, their bodies are covered completely over with trappings of gold.'

'That no form of shameless profligacy may be wanting, he is accompanied by a long train of courtesans carried in golden palanquins,' continues Curtius, 'and this troop holds a separate place in the procession from the queen's retinue, and is as sumptuously appointed. His food is prepared by women, who also serve him with wine, which is much used by all Indians. When the king falls into a drunken sleep, his courtesans carry him away to his bedchamber, invoking the gods of the night in their native hymns.'

Hunting, as usual, was the chief royal pastime. 'The king hunts in fenced enclosures, shooting arrows from a platform in his chariot (with two or three armed women standing beside him), and also in unfenced hunting grounds from an elephant,' says Strabo. Kautilya considered hunting to be a good pastime for kings, to get rid of phlegm, bile and fat, to improve marksmanship, and to acquire knowledge of the tempers of wild animals. For exercise the king was also massaged 'by four men who stand around him and rub him with smooth sticks of ebony,' says Strabo. And his feet, says Curtius, 'are rubbed with scented ointments.'

To revive the jaded royal spirit there were also public spectacles, like gladiatorial contests and animal fights. Says Aelian: 'The great king of the Indians appoints a day every year for fighting between men ... and also between brute animals ... wild bulls, tame rams ... unicorn asses (rhinos?), hyenas ... Before the close of the spectacle, elephants come forward to fight ... One infrequently proves the stronger, and it often happens that both are killed.' The royal menagerie was another source of relaxation for the king, and was kept stocked with the animals and birds presented to him by his subjects. Participation in religious festivities was yet another royal diversion, and no doubt he was entertained every day by singing and dancing girls. It does thus appear that the Mauryan emperor, despite his burdensome workload and Kautilya's austere injunctions, did manage to get some fun out of life.

THE LEVIATHAN

The Kautilyan state was a Hobbesian leviathan, which sought to control every aspect of the life of the individual and society through complex bureaucratic procedures, with hordes of officers keeping track of everything that happened and overseeing every transaction, from births and deaths and the movements of individuals, to the total control of all economic activity – all mining, farming and pastoral operations, even hunting; all manufacturing processes and the prices of commodities, all transport and trade; the rates of interest, the wages of workers and artisans, the fees of professionals, including those of prostitutes; the standards of weights and measures – as well as the conduct of religious festivals and social functions, the movements of ascetics, the performances of public entertainers, and so on *ad infinitum*. It was as totalitarian as a state could be in ancient times, and it has been said of it without too much exaggeration that one could not even sneeze there without it being noted and recorded by some official.

The nucleus of Kautilyan administration, indeed the very reason for its existence, was the king. But, as Kautilya pointed out, 'a single wheel cannot turn, nor is government possible without assistance.' The monarch, however absolute his power, had to have an administrative organisation. The apex body of this organisation, as Kautilya conceived it, was the privy council, which advised the king on policy. *Mantrapurvah sarvarambhah* – policy should precede action, decreed Kautilya. The success of the government, he believed, was critically dependent on the wisdom and efficiency of the royal advisors, so he prescribed detailed rules for choosing councillors and testing their integrity, and gave advice on how the king should conduct deliberations with them. He recommended that the privy council should have only three or four members, for 'with more than four, secrecy is rarely maintained.' Strict confidentiality was expected of the councillors, so persons prone to 'carelessness, intoxication, talking in one's sleep, indulgence in amorous pursuits and similar bad habits' should not to be taken into the council, he warned. 'Anyone who betrays a secret shall be torn to pieces.'

The high status and responsibility of the privy councillor was reflected in his salary, which was the highest in the state, and was equal to that of the crown prince, principal queen, chief of the army, Purohita (royal chaplain), chief priest and royal guru. The role of the crown prince in government is not clearly stated in the *Arthasastra*, but he was usually appointed as the head of the army. The chief priest and the royal guru would have had no direct administrative role, but they – as well as the queens – would have indirectly influenced the modulation of policy, through their close daily interaction with the king.

The Purohita had a more obvious role in government – he mediated between the king and the gods, a crucial function in ancient societies – and Kautilya emphasised that great care should be taken in his appointment. 'The king shall appoint as the Purohita one from the very highest family, of the most exemplary character, learned in the Vedas and their branches, expert in reading omens, well-versed in the science of politics and capable of performing the correct expiatory rites against acts of god and human calamities,' he advised. 'The king shall follow him as a pupil does his teacher, as a son his father, and a servant his master.' The presence of the Purohita was required when the king received Brahmins and ascetics, and he accompanied him on his tours and wars.

The privy council, as Kautilya conceived it, was a policymaking body, not an executive body. The implementation of policy was the responsibility of the Mantri-parishad, the council of ministers. This body included, among others, the chancellor, treasurer, royal chamberlain, commander of the royal guards, an officer of unknown functions titled Prasastar, and the chief comptroller and auditor. The actual number of ministers varied – while some sages recommended a ministerial council of twelve or sixteen, Kautilya directed that 'the number shall be according to need.' The council met regularly, and normally took decisions by consensus, but if differences could not be reconciled, decisions were taken by majority vote. Absent ministers were consulted by letter. The king, according to the requirements of the issue at hand, consulted the entire council, or a section of ministers, or even just one minister.

The organisation of officers beneath the ministers is given haphazardly in the *Arthasastra*, indicating that the administrative system had not yet evolved fully. Even at the highest levels, designations and ranks given in the *Arthasastra* are often confusing – the titles Amatya and Mantri, for instance, are often used interchangeably, and their ranks and functions indicated differently in different places. A variety of high officials are designated as Mahamatras. In all, thirty-two departments are mentioned in the *Arthasastra*, according to the enumeration of Sastri – treasury, mines, metals, mint, salt, gold, storehouses, trade, forest produce, armoury, weights and measures, measurement of space and time, tolls, spinning and weaving, agriculture, alcoholic beverages, slaughter houses, courtesans, shipping, cattle, horses, elephants, chariots, infantry, passports, pastures, elephant forests, spies, religious institutions, gambling, jails, and ports – each headed by an Adyaksha. The *Arthasastra* does not say anything about how the royal officers were to be recruited. The actual method was probably casual. India, unlike China, had no tests for bureaucratic appointments, though fresh recruits seem to have been put on probation for a period.

Megasthenes, in a passage quoted by Strabo, speaks of the diverse functions performed by Mauryan officers: 'Of the great officers of the state, some have charge of the market, others of the city, others of the soldiers. Some superintend the rivers, measure the land ... and inspect sluices by which water is let out from the main canals into their branches, so that every one may have an equal supply of it. The same persons have charge also of the huntsmen, and are entrusted with the power of rewarding or punishing them according to their deserts. They collect the taxes, and superintend the occupations connected with the land, as those of woodcutters, carpenters, blacksmiths, and miners. They construct roads, and at every stadia set up a pillar to show the by-roads and distances.'

The Mauryan bureaucracy was a mammoth organisation, its members numerous enough for Megasthenes to reckon them as a social class by themselves. 'The seventh class consists of councillors and assessors, of those who deliberate on public affairs,' he writes. 'It is the smallest class as regards to number, but the most respected on account of the high character and wisdom of its members. From their ranks the advisers of the king are taken, and the treasurers of the state, and the arbiters who settle disputes. The generals of the army also, and the chief magistrates usually belong to this class.'

Kautilya, who knew from personal experience all the vicissitudes of royal service, offered sound advice to officials on how they should conduct themselves, for their own good as well as for the good of the state. 'Service under a king has been compared to living in a fire ... [The king] may either confer prosperity or may have the whole family, including wives and children, killed.' So a wise officer should make 'self-protection his first and constant concern ... He shall watch carefully the king's gestures and expressions,' and 'shall never say anything that is unwelcome to or is likely to provoke the king.' Omens too should be heeded. The *Arthasastra* records several instances of courtiers saving themselves from royal wrath by minding portents – one took care when the 'king's dog barked at him,' another heeded the peril indicated by the 'the flight of a heron from right to left,' and so on.

If the risks of royal service were high, so were the rewards. Royal officers constituted the only elite in the Mauryan empire, as it had no feudal aristocracy. They enjoyed fabulous salaries, especially the top officers. Kautilya assigned to the privy councillors, the army chief, the Purohita, the chief priest and the royal guru an annual salary of 48,000 panas (silver coins), 'enough to prevent them from succumbing to the temptations of the enemy or rising up in revolt.' In contrast, the lowest grade royal servant received just 60 panas, which apparently was enough to maintain a family in comfort – so the top officials received 800 times more than what was necessary for subsistence. And, presumably, they also enjoyed various perquisites and other benefits. They could live like princes.

The *Arthasastra* lists the salaries of various categories of government servants, from senior ministers down to menial servants, revealing, incidentally, how Mauryan society valued different services. The royal physician, for instance, is ranked with second grade courtesans and gets only 2,000 panas; the court poet receives even less, 1,000 panas, the same as astrologers and third grade courtesans, while musicians and accountants are put on the same scale as assassins and get 500 panas. Sculptors are given just 120 panas. Select scholars are granted an honorarium of 500 to 1,000 panas, less than the salary of third grade courtesans.

The *Arthasastra* gives only bare figures as salaries, without specifying the period for which the amount was to be paid or the coin in which it was to be paid, but it is generally assumed that the payment indicated was for a year, and that it was to be paid in panas. Besides salaries, officers who had to travel on official duty were sanctioned travel allowances. Salaries were to be normally paid in cash, but sometimes officials were allotted holdings of crown land, to collect their revenues as salaries. 'If the [cash in] treasury is inadequate, salaries may be paid in forest produce, cattle or land, supplemented by a little money,' suggested Kautilya.

The Kautilyan state was a good employer, and Kautilya directed that 'if a government servant dies while on duty, his sons and wives shall be entitled to his salary and food allowance.' Those who were disabled in service and those who retired from service in old age were also provided for. Even prostitutes, 'when they can no longer work under a madam in an establishment, shall be given work in the pantry or kitchen.'

Bureaucratic corruption – the fence eating the crop – was a matter of grave concern to Kautilya. 'Just as it is impossible not to taste honey ... that one may find at the tip of one's tongue, so it is impossible for one dealing with government funds not to taste, at least a little bit, of the king's wealth,' observed Kautilya. He despaired over this problem, acknowledging, 'Just as it is impossible to know when a fish moving in water is drinking it, so it is impossible to find out when government servants in charge of undertakings misappropriate money.' And again: 'It is possible to know even the path of birds flying in the sky but not the ways of government servants who hide their [dishonest] income.'

No one could be trusted, Kautilya held. Frequent transfer of officials was one of the measures that he recommended for curtailing corruption. 'Permanent service by its security is liable to make its incumbent independent and mischievous, while the country people have no interest in reporting his defects,' he warned. 'Heads of departments shall not remain permanently in one job and shall be rotated frequently.' Corrupt or heedless officers were to be severely punished. 'An officer negligent or remiss in his work shall be fined double his wages and expenses incurred ... If an official is accused of defrauding a large amount, and if the accusation is proved even for a small part of it, he shall be held liable for the whole.' The informer who reported on the corrupt official was to be given protection and offered a part of the amount involved as his reward. At the same time, to prevent false charges being levelled against honest officers by their rivals or enemies, Kautilya laid down that if a charge was not proved, the informer should be given 'corporal punishment or fined, and no mercy should be shown to him.'

But there was no way to eliminate bureaucratic corruption entirely. The most that could be done was to contain the damage. Kautilya's best means for doing this was to cover the entire state with a close network of intelligence agents and spies. Megasthenes states that there was in the Mauryan empire a class of officers who kept watch over all that went on in the empire and made reports secretly to the king. Engaging spies to gather information was an old practice in India – even the Rig-veda mentions spies, and in the *Ramayana*, it was spies who reported to Rama that people were talking ill of Sita – but the Kautilyan state, in its fantastic and almost incredible elaboration of the intelligence network, was unlike any other known in history. Spies and informers were everywhere in the Mauryan empire, among householders, in the market places, at social and religious gatherings, at government offices, at river crossings and along the highways, at the frontiers of the state, even in the forests. Double-agents and *agents provocateurs* infiltrated into neighbouring kingdoms, and even operated within the empire, to ferret out traitors and cheats, to ascertain or manipulate public opinion, or to facilitate some ploy of the king to swindle his subjects. They tested the integrity of ministers and other high officials, maintained tabs on all officers, watched over all economic transactions, kept the general public under surveillance, and trapped criminals, bandits and anti-social elements.

Secret agents used every conceivable cover, as astrologers and palmists, farmers and traders, ordinary householders, vagrants, cooks, nurses, prostitutes, mendicant women, and so on. Kautilya mentions 'twenty-nine distinct categories of cover with fifty subtypes ... [Secret agents] could even act out the parts of gods and evil spirits,' notes Rangarajan. Some lived in the guise of ascetics and holy men of supernatural power, performing sham miracles with the connivance of other secret agents, who helped to make their 'predictions' come true. The state had its own assassins and poisoners, to quietly liquidate troublesome relatives or traitorous high officials.

In rulers, suspicion; in subjects, fear – this was the political ambience of the Mauryan empire. The state would not trust even its own secret agents. Those who watched over everyone themselves had to be watched over. Every secret report had to be confirmed by other secret reports. Only 'the information corroborated by three [different] spies shall be taken to be true,' the *Arthasastra* cautions. 'The intelligence gathered from roving spies shall be collected together in the establishments of spies based in one place and shall be transmitted by code. The transmitters shall not know who the gatherers were.'

The *Arthasastra* does not deal with the provincial organisation of the empire. For this, we have to turn to the edicts of Asoka and the report of Megasthenes, but these are not of much help either. The Nandas were the first to run an imperial government in India, and the Mauryas elaborated and refined the system, and this turned the Mauryan empire into one of the most tightly organised states in the history of India. Still, it was not a fully integrated state, but an amalgam of several autonomous or semi-autonomous units. The core area of the empire in all probability had a highly centralised government of the Kautilyan model, but the outlying provinces seem to have retained their pre-existing forms of government, and were often governed by their former rulers as vassal kings. Megasthenes states that there were different types of government in the Mauryan empire – vassal kings, self-governing cities, and semi-independent tribes.

A major weakness of the Mauryan empire was that it had no unifying force other than the military might of the emperor. It was not a nation state. Indeed, the very idea that people constituted the state faded in India with the decline of tribal republics on the one hand, and the emergence of the caste system on the other. By according a higher status to the social order than to the state, the caste system diverted loyalty from the state to the caste, and this, as well as the trans-border affiliations of castes, prevented the emergence of nationalist feeling in India as a whole, or even in any of its regions. The fate of the state and its ruler was of little concern to the common people, and they, as Megasthenes records, often stood by and watched with utter indifference – as indifferent as the cows grazing placidly in the pasture nearby – the battle raging between their king and his enemy. Even in the core area of the empire, where 'a common language, common customs and a common historical tradition were present ... the idea of the state was not known ... [In the *Arthasastra*] the loyalty of the subject is to the individual king and not to the state ... the state as an entity above the government, symbolised in the king, does not exist,' observes Thapar. Asoka made a noble attempt to integrate the empire into a nation by propagating a common dharma, but without success. The empire was too extensive, and too diversified in race, language, customs, material culture and history to congeal into a nation, or even into an administratively integrated state.

Asokan edicts mention four provinces in the Mauryan empire: a northern province with Taxila as its capital, a western province with its capital at Ujjain, an eastern province with its capital at Tosali, and a southern province with Suvarnagiri as its capital. Special care was taken to protect the frontiers of the empire with well-garrisoned forts. All the major ferries and highways were guarded. 'Ferries,' Kautilya enjoined, 'shall cross waterways only at fixed points, in order to prevent traitors to the king crossing [into the country].'

Mauryan provinces were ruled by viceroys, generally princes, who had, according to Megasthenes, their own councils of ministers. At the top, the provincial administration seems to have replicated the organisation of the central government, but further down there were in all probability considerable local variations in the system. In the far-flung empire, the provinces seldom conformed strictly to the central administrative regulations. Communications between the imperial capital and its outlying centres usually took several weeks to reach their destinations, so the emperor seldom interfered in provincial administration, as long as the governors met their revenue obligations and adhered to the broad administrative guidelines of the empire. It was viceregal whim, rather than administrative orderliness, that usually prevailed in the provinces, and this often led to major popular uprisings. Chandragupta, Bindusara and Asoka all had to deal with this problem.

The Mauryan provinces were huge, each the size of a large kingdom, so they were further divided into manageable administrative districts called Janapadas, under officials titled Sthanikas. The land being sparsely populated, the Janapadas were separated from each other by broad swaths of forestland, and the frontiers of the Janapadas, like the frontiers of the empire itself, were well guarded. 'These ... internal frontiers of the kingdom,' notes Kosambi, 'were as important as its boundaries with other kingdoms ...Trade caravans between Janapadas had to pay customs duties at the points of entry and of exit. Every individual crossing the Janapada frontier had to produce a duly stamped official pass, to be obtained only for good reasons by paying a heavy fee.'

The Janapadas were again divided into groups of five to ten villages in charge of Gopas (guardians) who maintained records of all the human and material resources of the villages under them. Individual villages were separated from each other by pastures and forests, and each village was headed by a government official titled Gramini, who regulated land and water rights, and collected taxes and fines. Cultivable land in the village was parcelled out to individual families, but pasture and forest were held in common. District and provincial officials periodically visited villages on inspection tours, and secret agents reported to them all the unusual happenings in villages.

Villages in Mauryan India enjoyed a considerable amount of autonomy, and were largely left to their own devices as long as they paid taxes regularly and maintained law and order. Village polity, as R.K. Mookerjee observes, was really 'independent of state-politics and of the vicissitudes of the political fortune affecting the state or the sovereign at the top.' Village elders managed the day-to-day affairs of the village, though even here the state did lay down certain guidelines. Participation in community activities, especially in productive undertakings, was compulsory. Anyone who failed to contribute, whether labour, money or food, had to pay as fine twice the amount he should have contributed. This rule applied even to village festivals and public entertainment. 'Anyone who does not contribute his share of the cost of production of a performance shall not be allowed to see it; his family shall also be banned. Watching or listening to it secretly is a punishable offence,' Kautilya ruled.

The most fascinating aspect of the Mauryan administration was its complex and meticulously organised system of urban government. Pataliputra, the imperial capital, was ruled by a committee of thirty divided into six groups, says Megasthenes. 'One group looks after everything relating to the industrial arts. Another group attends to the entertainment of foreigners, assigning them lodgings, keeping watch over their modes of life by means of those persons whom they give to them as assistants. They escort them on the way when they leave the country, or, in the event of their dying, forward their property to their relatives. They take care of them when they are sick, and bury them if they die. The third group consists of those who inquire when and how births and deaths occur, with a view not only of levying a tax, but also in order that births and deaths among both high and low may not escape the cognisance of government. The fourth group superintends trade and commerce. Its members have charge of weights and measures, and see that the products in their season are sold by public notice. No one is allowed to deal in more than one kind of commodity unless he pays a double tax. The fifth group supervises manufactured articles, which they sell by public notice. What is new is sold separated from what is old, and there is a fine for mixing the two together. The sixth and last group consists of those who collect the tenths of the prices of the articles sold. Fraud in the payment of this tax is punished with death. Such are the functions which these bodies separately discharge. In their collective capacity they have charge ... also of matters affecting the general interest, as the keeping of public buildings in proper repair, the regulation of prices, the care of markets, harbours and temples.'

The *Arthasastra* does not mention this committee of thirty. The head of the city administration in the Kautilyan system was the Nagarika, the city governor. He was responsible for the maintenance of law and order in the city, as well as for cleanliness and sanitation; he enforced curfew regulations and fire precautions, and took custody of lost property. Further, he controlled trade and ensured that goods were sold at fixed prices, at specified places and at specified times, and that stolen goods were not sold. The supervision of cremation grounds and prisons was also his responsibility.

The Nagarika had to ensure that visitors lodged only at the places specified for them. 'Artisans and artists,' Kautilya regulated, 'shall provide accommodation in their own places of work to visitors following similar professions; merchants shall stay with other merchants, on the basis of reciprocity. Merchants providing accommodation shall be responsible for informing the authorities if the visitor sells goods of which they are not full owners or at an unauthorised time or place. Those in charge of drinking places, vegetarian and non-vegetarian eating houses, and brothels shall allow only those well known to them to stay with them. They shall report to authorities anyone spending extravagantly or behaving rashly.' Ascetics of the heretical sects were not ordinarily allowed to stay in the city, and required special permission to stay in a lodge.

The Nagarika divided the city into four parts, each under a Sthanika. The Sthanikas were in turn assisted by Gopas, each of whom was in charge of a certain number of families, and maintained records of 'the number of people in each family, their sex, caste, family name, occupation, income and expenditure.' They registered all births and deaths in their wards, reported on the movements of strangers, including visiting traders, and inquired into the circumstances of anyone acquiring sudden wealth or behaving in a suspicious way. Every house-owner had to report to the Gopas the arrival and departure of his guests.

Elaborate precautions were taken to maintain law and order in the city, and night curfew – from six *nalikas* after sunset to six *nalikas* before dawn: from about 8.30 p.m. to about 3.30 a.m. – was strictly enforced. 'A bugle shall be sounded to mark the beginning and the end of the curfew period,' Kautilya prescribed. 'Only the following shall be permitted to move about during the curfew period: midwives attending to delivery, doctors attending to illness, those who have to go about due to a death in the family, those who go [openly] with lamps in their hands, visitors to the city officials for official purposes, those summoned by a trumpet call, fire-fighters and those having a valid pass.' All others had to stay indoors. However, free movement of people was allowed on festival nights, though even on such nights those going about with their faces covered, or wearing unbecoming dresses (such as a man in a woman's dress or a woman in a man's dress), ascetics, and those bearing weapons were required to be retained and examined by officials. Kautilya further directed that, whether in the day or in the night, 'no one shall move about carrying arms, unless they have a special permit, with proper seal.'

The civic duties and courtesies that the Kautilyan system required of citizens were quite elaborate and in some cases surprisingly modern, especially in protecting the privacy of individuals against prying neighbours – though not against the prying government – and in promoting good neighbourliness. 'No one shall interfere in the affairs of a neighbour, without due cause. However, every one has the duty to run to the help of a neighbour in distress,' warned Kautilya. Those who interfered in a neighbour's affair without reason, and those who did not hasten to help a neighbour in distress, were punished with a fine as high as 100 panas.

Kautilya laid down precise rules for dividing the city into zones for occupation by different communities, professions, trades and crafts, and even specified the width of the city roads – 15 metres for royal highways and major roads, 8 metres for other city streets. Building regulations are given in great detail in the *Arthasastra*. 'The boundaries of every residential property shall be clearly demarcated by pillars at the corners with lines strung between them. Houses shall be built in conformity with the [nature and] extent of the land. There shall be adequate rain-water drainage. The house and its various facilities shall be built at a suitable distance from a neighbour's property so as not to cause inconvenience to the neighbour. The roof of a house may either be three inches away from the roof of a neighbour's house or may [even] overlap it. There shall be a lane between two houses with a side door for access to repair damage and to avoid overcrowding. Rain-water falling from the roof of a house should not damage the veranda [of the neighbouring house]; if it is likely to do so, it shall be protected either by a wall or a mat. The doors and windows shall be so made as not to cause annoyance by facing directly a door or window of a neighbouring house, except when the two houses are separated by a wide road such as the royal highway. Any window made for lighting shall be high up. No part of the house (ditch, step, water channel, ladder or dunghill) shall be built in a manner which will cause obstruction and prevent the enjoyment of others. When the house is occupied, the doors and windows shall be suitably covered.'

The *Arthasastra* further specifies the distances that two neighbouring houses have to maintain in building various facilities, such as 'dung hill, sewage channel, well ... places for carts, domestic animals, fire, water jar, grinding mill, pounding mortar,' and so on, but thoughtfully adds a rider: 'Neighbours may, by mutual agreement, modify the above [building regulations] so long as they avoid the undesirable. The regulation about sewage channels does not apply to temporary facilities provided for child-birth and lying-in for ten days after delivery.' Failure to provide houses with adequate rain-water drainage was an offence punishable with a fine of twelve panas. Similarly, causing damage to another house by letting rain-water collect, or causing nuisance to neighbours by letting urine and dung collect – or letting them drain through improper places – entailed a fine of twenty-four panas.

On public hygiene, Kautilya directed that 'no one shall throw dirt on the streets or let mud and water collect there. This applies, particularly, to the royal highways. No one shall pass urine or faeces in [or near] a holy place, a water reservoir, a temple or a royal property, unless it is for unavoidable reasons like illness, medication or fear. No one shall throw out dead bodies of animals or human beings inside the city. Corpses shall be taken out of the city only by the prescribed route and gate, and cremation or burial done only in the designated places.'

The Mauryan cities were provided with various civic amenities, far better than in later times in India, assuming that the injunctions of the *Arthasastra* were actually executed. 'Each group of ten houses shall be provided with a well,' Kautilya decreed. Cities were to be adequately stocked with essential supplies like 'oils, grains, sugar, salt, perfumery, medicines, dried vegetables, fodder, dried meat, hay, firewood, metals, hides, charcoal, gut, poisons, horns, bamboo, yarn, strong timber, weapons, shields and stones. Old items in storage should be constantly replaced by new ones.'

Cities in Mauryan times were largely built of wood, so Kautilya laid down detailed and thorough fire safety regulations: 'The Nagarika shall make all those who work with fire [e.g., blacksmiths] live in one locality and shall remove any thatch found in that locality. He shall arrange to have thousands of water jars kept in the following places: main roads, crossroads, city gates and all royal dwellings [including the treasury and commodity warehouses] ... In the summer, citizens shall take appropriate precautions against fire. They shall not light fires during the [two] middle quarters of the day; if food has to be cooked during this period, it shall be done outside the house. Every household shall ... [be equipped, for fire-fighting, with] five water pots, a big jar, a trough, a ladder, an axe, a winnowing basket, a hook, a hooked rake, and a skin bag. During the night householders shall stay near the front doors of their houses ... If a house catches fire, every occupant, owner and tenant, shall take immediate steps [to put it out].' Even villagers were required to 'do their cooking during the summer months outside their houses,' and they had to always keep fire-fighting implements at hand. Violations of these regulations were punished with fines – one-eighth pana for lighting a fire during the prohibited hours, a quarter pana for not providing fire-fighting equipment, 12 panas for not hastening to put out the fire in one's house, and 54 panas for letting the house catch fire through negligence.

Fire was the peril of the summer months, but even more devastating than that were the river floods of the rainy season. There was nothing that the state could do to prevent floods, but Kautilya with his usual thoroughness laid down the precautions to be taken to minimise damage. 'During the rainy season,' he cautioned, 'villagers living near river banks shall move to higher ground; they shall keep a collection of wooden planks, bamboo and boats. Persons carried away by floods shall be rescued using gourds, skin bags, tree trunks, canoes, boats and thick ropes. Owners of canoes shall be punished if they do not try to save someone in danger.'

The *Arthasastra* even has detailed traffic regulations, though Mauryan city traffic consisted mainly of pedestrians and a few ox- or horse-drawn carts. 'A cart shall not [be allowed to] move without a driver in it. Only an adult can be in charge of a cart; a minor driver shall be accompanied by an adult.' About traffic accidents, the rule was that if a charioteer warns pedestrians by shouting '*Apehi! Apehi!*' – Make way! Make way! – he would not be guilty in case of collision.

Kautilya protected tenants from unfair eviction by landlords, and equally protected landlords from troublesome tenants, by prescribing a fine of 12 panas on either for violating tenancy regulations. 'A tenant shall not continue to occupy forcibly a house from which he has been asked to leave; nor can a landlord evict a tenant who has paid his rent, except when the tenant is involved in a case of verbal or physical injury, theft, robbery, abduction or wrongful possession. A tenant who leaves of his own accord shall pay the balance of the annual rent.'

Similar rights and duties were laid on nearly every class of people. 'Any doctor who is called to a house to treat a severely wounded person or one suffering from unwholesome food or drink shall report the fact to the Gopa and Sthanika. If he makes a report, he shall not be accused of any crime; if he does not, he shall be charged with the same offence [which he helped to conceal].'

Environmental protection was a major concern for Kautilya. 'Damaging plants and trees in city parks, sanctuaries, holy places and cremation grounds, particularly those which bear fruits or flowers or provide shade,' entailed a fine as high as 48 panas. For urinating near a holy place the fine was half a pana, for doing so near a water reservoir it was one pana; urinating near a temple was punished with a fine of one and a half panas, while doing so near a royal building attracted a fine of two panas.

MAURYAN STATE CAPITALISM

'All undertakings depend on finance,' maintained Kautilya. 'Therefore, the king shall devote his greatest attention to the treasury.' This was common political wisdom, which was usually interpreted by kings to mean that they should maximise tax collection, but Kautilya took the application of the principle to another dimension altogether, by having the government occupy the commanding heights of the economy as the dominant producer of goods and services, and by controlling all economic activities in the state. It was state capitalism many centuries before its time.

'The root of wealth is [fruitful economic] activity,' Kautilya held; 'without it ... both current prosperity and future growth will be destroyed. A king can achieve desired objectives and abundance of riches by undertaking economic activity.' One has to sow wealth to harvest wealth. Or, as the *Arthasastra* puts it, 'Just as elephants are needed to catch elephants, so does one need wealth to get more wealth.'

A full treasury, Kautilya maintained, was essential not only for the preservation of royal power, but for the good of the people as well. 'A king with a depleted treasury,' he warned, 'eats into the very vitals of the country.' Such a king would destroy the country, and destroy himself too. Kautilya sought to prevent this contingency by turning the government into a mammoth business corporation, with vast and diversified holdings in agriculture, industry, trade and services. The state dominated agricultural production by reserving for itself extensive areas of the kingdom as crown lands and by clearing new lands for cultivation with indentured labour; it monopolised all natural wealth and many essential services, ran numerous production units, and traded in many commodities.And what it did not own directly, it controlled tightly for its own profit. Indeed, wherever even the faintest clink of money was heard, royal officials were there, watching, recording, and claiming dues for the king.

This was not a mere utopian fancy, but an actual operational plan that was to a large extent implemented by the Mauryan state, as Greek writers confirm. However, comprehensive state control of the economy was in all probability confined to the core area of the empire, not extended over its entire vast territory, which would have been impracticable in ancient times. Even if thus limited in its application, the system would have required an enormous amount of bookkeeping, and there would have been at one time in Pataliputra and the other administrative centres of the Mauryan empire mountainous piles of records about all the resources of the empire in men and materials, and about how these were being utilised, and what the emperor was getting out of them.

Typical of the thoroughness of the system was Kautilya's instruction to Gopas in charge of groups of villages: 'Villages shall be classified as best, average or lowest. They shall also be classified according to whether they are [tax-paying or] tax-exempt, whether they supply soldiers [in lieu of tax], and whether they supply [fixed amounts of] grain, cattle, gold, forest produce, labour or other commodities. [Within each village,] every plot of land shall be numbered and its use recorded according to the classification: cultivated or fallow, dry or wet cultivation, park, vegetable garden, cremation ground, rest-house, public drinking-water facility, holy place, pasture or road. These records shall be used for determining the location of fields, forests and roads, and to record transactions such as gifts, sales, charitable endowments and tax exemptions. [Likewise,] each house shall be numbered and classified as to whether it is tax-paying or tax-exempt. Records of the inhabitants shall also be kept under the following headings: 1. *varna*; 2. occupation (such as farmer, cowherd, trader, craftsman, labourer or slave); 3. the number of males and females as well as the number of children and old people, their [family] history, occupation, income and expenditure; 4. livestock and poultry owned; 5. the amount of tax payable in cash or in free labour; and 6. tolls and fines that may be due.' Gopas in charge of city wards were also required to keep similar records.

In the conventional view, kingdom is territory. Kautilya knew better. 'It is the people who constitute a kingdom,' he held; 'like a barren cow, a land without people yields nothing.' Territory by itself was of no use to the king. He had to have people to make the land productive. Kautilya therefore laid down various measures to preserve and expand the population of the state. 'No one,' he decreed, 'shall induce a woman [still capable of bearing children] to become an ascetic.' Just as fields were not allowed to lie fallow, women were not allowed to remain barren. As for men, they too could renounce family life only after they had 'passed the age of sexual activity,' and that too only 'with the approval of the judges. But if the judges do not approve, he shall be prevented from doing so.' Kautilya further recommended that, if necessary, the land should be stocked with people through forced migration. 'The king shall populate the countryside by creating [new] villages on virgin land or by reviving abandoned village sites. Settlement can be affected either by shifting some of the population of his own country or by immigration of foreigners [by inducement or force]. The settlers in the villages shall mainly be Sudra agriculturists with a minimum of a hundred families and a maximum of five hundred.'

Nothing in the economy mattered to Kautilya more than agricultural production, with the possible exception of mining. 'All economic activities have their source in the countryside,' he observed. The king, he advised, should grant tax concessions and provide loans to farmers during times of scarcity and natural calamities, and should 'protect agriculture from being harassed by [onerous] fines, taxes and demands for labour.'

By the Mauryan age agriculture had completely displaced the traditional Aryan pastoral economy and was rapidly expanding. Extensive tracts of virgin lands were now cleared for cultivation, by the state as well as by private farmers, but mainly by the state, which was by far the largest land-clearing agency, using prisoners of war and deportees from newly conquered lands as indentured labourers, as Asoka did after the Kalinga war, forcibly resettling 150,000 Kalingas. The state also provided various incentives to private farmers to expand cultivation, and Kautilya recommended that in new settlements 'cultivators shall be granted grains, cattle and money which they can repay at their convenience.' Even royal officers posted to virgin settlements received special favours, by having 'all their salaries ... paid in cash,' instead of partly in kind.

In all this, Kautilya's motive was to promote the interest of the king – he counselled that farmers should be protected and favours shown to them, because the state could later extract taxes from them in good measure. Similarly, his objective in giving land to Sudras was not social upliftment, but royal gain. He preferred Sudras for farming only because, being poor and illiterate – and having no interest in life other than to feed and procreate – they could be made to grind on mindlessly in the rut of agricultural routine, like yoked farm animals. 'As for settling a land with the four castes, the one where the lowest castes predominate is better because it will permit all sorts of exploitation,' he states with brutal candour. The Sudra farm labourer, though legally not a slave, lived a life not much different from that of a slave. In fact, his life was not much different from that of the farm cattle.

These men were shackled to the fields. They could not leave the land. Nor could they remain idle. They were the productive assets of the state, and the state would not let them be wasted in any way. Nothing was permitted in villages that would distract the farmer from his work. 'There shall be no grounds or buildings intended for recreation [in new settlements],' Kautilya decreed. 'Actors, dancers, singers, musicians, raconteurs, and bards shall not disturb the work [in the fields]. In villages which provide no shelter [to outsiders], the people will be [fully] involved in the work of the fields. [Consequently] there will be an increase of taxes, labour supply, wealth, and grain.' Heretic ascetics were not permitted to enter crown villages, for fear that they would disturb the bovine placidity of rural life.

'The idiocy of village life,' comments Kosambi, 'was deliberately fostered by state policy.' And it was accepted fatalistically by peasants and farm labourers. There is no evidence of any peasant uprising in Mauryan India, and the *Arthasastra* does not make any provision for dealing with such an eventuality. According to Megasthenes, peasants in Mauryan India lived a contented though monotonous life, never leaving their village to go to town, 'either to take part in its tumults or for any other purpose.' They were exempted from military service, and were not normally affected by political and military convulsions. 'Tillers,' Arrian quotes Megasthenes as reporting, 'are neither furnished with arms, nor have any military duties to perform ... In times of civil war, the soldiers are not allowed to molest the husbandmen or ravage their land; hence, while the former are fighting and killing each other as they can, the latter may be seen close at hand tranquilly pursuing their work ...'

To maximise agricultural production, the Mauryan state took the initiative in building infrastructural facilities like dams and canals, and at least one of the Mauryan dams – the Sudarsana lake at Girnar in Gujarat built by Pusyagupta, Chandragupta's governor – remained in service for many centuries, the last known repairs to it being carried out in the mid-fifth century AD by a local officer of Gupta emperor Skandagupta. According to Megasthenes, Mauryan royal officers in charge of water resources regularly inspected rivers, canals and sluices, and ensured that water was shared equitably by agriculturists and was not wasted. Those who neglected, misused or damaged irrigation systems were severely punished. Equally, it was obligatory for people to participate in civic work. 'If anyone refuses to participate in a co-operative effort to build a reservoir, his labourers and bullocks shall [be made to] do [his share of] the work,' Kautilya decreed. 'He shall pay his share of the cost but shall not receive any share of the benefits.'

Agricultural land in the Mauryan empire was divided into two ownership categories: *rashtra*, the privately owned tax-paying properties, and *sita*, the crown lands. The *sita* lands were either directly farmed by the crown or leased out to sharecroppers. In the *rashtra* tracts, land belonged to the cultivator. There were no feudal lords in the Mauryan empire. Megasthenes was clearly mistaken when he states that 'all India is the property of the crown, and no private person is permitted to own land.' The king was entitled to a share of the produce of all the land, but he did not own all the land.

The king possessed territory, not land. Land in itself had little value in Mauryan India, as there was plenty of virgin land to be had for free. The *Arthasastra* does not even mention land in its list of inheritable property. Land became valuable only when made productive by human labour. 'The value of land is what man makes of it,' held Kautilya. And the ownership of productive land belonged to the man who made it productive. He could sell it or mortgage it as he wished. But when a piece of land became productive, the king also acquired an interest in it, claiming a portion of its produce as tax in return for the security he provided to the farmer.

This consequential right of the king was however turned on its head by Kautilya, by making it a primary obligation for the peasant to cultivate land and pay tax. In his view, it was as much a crime not to cultivate land as it was not to pay tax. 'The lands of those who do not cultivate their fields shall be confiscated and given to others,' Kautilya ruled. 'The loss suffered by the state due to non-cultivation shall be made good by the offending householder.' In this sense, the cultivator had no absolute right of ownership of land. But then, the king had no absolute right of ownership either – he could not legally take away the land of a farmer who cultivated his fields and paid his taxes. 'The land prepared for cultivation by anyone [by his own effort] shall not be taken away from him,' Kautilya specifically stated.

The state did not even normally intervene in property disputes – these, Kautilya directed, 'shall be decided by the elders of the neighbourhood' – and entered the scene only to deal with tax related matters, and to regulate land use and transactions. The rule was that a taxpayer should sell or mortgage his land only to another taxpayer, and that those who held tax-free lands should sell or mortgage them only to similar gift holders. A taxpayer was not allowed to settle in a village exempt from tax.

Next to agriculture, Kautilya paid the greatest attention to trade and industry, which had by Mauryan times emerged as a major field of economic activity. Craftsmen in Vedic India were few, and were respected professionals, but in Mauryan India, with the spread of urbanisation and the growth in the demand for goods and services, they became ubiquitous in towns, and gradually turned into petty manufacturers, thus gaining in wealth but losing in social status. The relative social standing of different groups of artisans and traders is indicated by Kautilya's allocation of residential areas to them – jewellers lived among Brahmins to the north of the royal palace, while dealers in scents, garlands, and grains lived among Kshatriyas on the east; on the south, among Vaisyas, lived dealers in cooked food, liquors and flesh; weavers and armourers lived with Sudras on the west.

A significant new economic development in Mauryan India was the emergence of artisan and trade guilds, the *srenis*, which protected their members from competition and gave them bargaining power in dealing with their customers and the state. Occupations had long been hereditary in India, but now they gradually congealed into castes, and this facilitated the stability and consolidation of the guilds. 'Each *sreni*,' notes Thapar, 'had its own professional code, working arrangements, duties and obligations and even religious observances.' In towns each guild occupied a different zone.

Kautilya looked on guilds with dour suspicion – 'Artisans are dishonest,' he declared – but probably found it convenient to deal with them, as guilds facilitated the collection of taxes and the regulation of industry. Craftsmen sometimes combined to strike work, to raise their wages or to gain other advantages, but Kautilya regarded such manoeuvres as punishable offences. He also prescribed punishments for frauds by craftsmen, as well as for shoddy workmanship and for delays in completing a contracted work. At the same time, employees who withheld from artisans their just dues were also fined. Kautilya, whatever he thought of the character of artisans, greatly valued their economic contribution, and prescribed fines as high as 100 panas for the theft of even small articles belonging to them. If a man 'causes an artisan to lose his hand or his eye, he is put to death,' says Megasthenes.

The state itself was the largest commodity producer in Mauryan India, and certain categories of craftsmen – those who made weapons and military equipment – were required to work exclusively for the state. 'The armour-makers and ship-builders receive wages and their victuals from the king, for whom alone they work,' states Megasthenes. Those who produced implements for industrial or agricultural production were also favoured by the state – 'This class,' notes Megasthenes, 'is not only exempt from paying taxes, but even receives maintenance from the royal exchequer.' The state ran its own spinning and weaving establishments, employing indigent women. This was succour to the women, but the state also extracted good work from them. Kautilya recommended that 'women who spin shall be given oil and myrobalan cakes as a special favour; they shall be induced to work on festive days [and holidays] by giving them gifts ... Weavers ... shall be given gifts of perfumes, flowers and similar presents of encouragement.'

Mining received special attention in the Mauryan state, because of its revenue and military potential. 'From mining comes the treasury, from the treasury the army has its origin; through the treasury may the earth, full of treasures, be conquered,' maintained Kautilya. He therefore recommended that the state should retain all mines, as well as salt pans, pearl and conch fisheries, as state monopolies. These were generally worked directly by the state, but where the mines or fisheries were difficult to run and were of uncertain profitability, they were leased out to private operators. All metals, observes Kosambi, 'from the ore to the finished article, were ... state monopoly' managed by the ministry of mines, 'which controlled also other minerals, salt, and coinage and circulation of money.'

Forests and everything in them, all timber and game, even firewood, but especially elephants, were state property. Elephant forests were not allowed to be cleared, and those found guilty of killing elephants were put to death. The state also claimed for itself all treasure-troves; finders were rewarded with one-sixth of the value of the treasure, but only if the value of the find (and therefore the reward) was small. All treasure-troves valued over 100,000 panas were fully taken over by the state without any compensation for the finder. Sweepers and cleaners who found objects of high value were rewarded with one-third the value of the object, but gems were taken over by the treasury without any reward.

The Mauryan age was a period of rapid trade expansion, as urbanisation and rural prosperity vastly expanded the market in India, and the opulence of the imperial court and the lavish lifestyles of the top Mauryan officials created a high demand for luxury goods. At the same time political integration swept away many of the old impediments to the flow of trade, such as territorial fragmentation and diversity of administrative practices. The gradual monetisation of the economy, the standardisation of weights and measures, and the trade regulations of the Mauryas, all helped to invigorate the market. The missionary activities of Jain and Buddhist monks also helped to open up new areas for trade, as missionaries and traders worked in tandem, traders being generally champions of the reformist sects.

The Mauryas were great road builders, and they provided various amenities along the road and improved travel security, to facilitate trade. 'Trade routes shall be kept free of harassment by courtiers, state officials, thieves and frontier guards, and from being damaged by herds of cattle,' directed Kautilya. 'Frontier officers shall be responsible for the safety of the merchandise passing on the roads and shall make good what is lost.' Trade caravans were required to camp only at specified sites in villages for their own safety, 'after letting the village officers know of the value of their merchandise.' Village headmen and district officers had to make good the loss if any goods were stolen in the areas under their control. If no official could be held responsible for the loss, all the villages close to the place of theft together had to pay for the loss. Ultimately, 'if a king is unable to apprehend a thief or recover stolen property, the victim of the theft shall be reimbursed from the treasury,' Kautilya advised.

To encourage sea trade, the *Arthasastra* laid down that the superintendent of shipping should extend 'fatherly protection' to vessels, and authorised customs officers to reduce by half the duty on the goods of the vessels that were weather-damaged or had strayed off course. Goods meant for domestic or public religious rituals, and items beneficial to the country, such as rare seeds, were permitted to be imported free of duty at the discretion of the controller of customs. On the other hand, the export of weapons and armour of all kinds, metals, chariots, jewels and gems, grains and cattle was absolutely prohibited.

An important and unusual aspect of the economic scene in Mauryan India was that the state itself entered the market as a dominant and monopolistic trader, selling the output of its numerous manufacturing units and mines, the yield of its forests, the harvest of the crown lands, and the produce it received through tax collection. These goods were stocked in state warehouses maintained throughout the empire, and were sold either directly through royal officers or through private agents.

There was in all probability a substantial increase in foreign trade during the Mauryan period, since much of the civilised world was economically interlinked at this time, consequent to Alexander's invasion of Persia and India. India's trade with the Middle East was not, however, a new development. The Indus Civilisation had traded with Sumer, and Indian traders were active in Iran and Mesopotamia in the sixth and fifth centuries BC – it is even said that a tavern in southern Iraq was run by an Indian businesswoman. This traditional trade received a great boost under the Mauryas, as they maintained close commercial, cultural and political ties with the Hellenistic kingdoms of Central Asia and the Middle East. There were at this time a fair number of foreigners living in the major cities of India, engaged in trade; in Pataliputra their number was so large that the government had to set up a special department to look after them.

Long distance trade, however, was still a high-risk activity in the Mauryan age, as indicated by the very high interest rates charged on loans for such trade. Roads, notwithstanding all the police measures of the Mauryas, were not really safe; brigands – and ogres, according to folklore – lurked in the forests to entrap caravans, as the *Jatakas* recount vividly. Corrupt royal officials were equally troublesome – Kautilya's warning that royal officers should not harass traders indicates that such harassment was common. District borders were virtually treated as interstate frontiers, and traders were required to pay road taxes and other tolls at each of these borders. Their passports had to be cleared by officials, who recorded the details about them and their merchandise. At the city gates they had to pay octroi. There were no bridges at all across rivers in India, and goods were often lost during the numerous river crossings. A good part of western India was a trackless desert, which, because of the burning heat, could be traversed by caravans only at night, with the help of land-pilots who guided them by the stars, and at such crossings caravans were vulnerable to raids by bandits.

These, however, seem to have been taken as normal occupational hazards by Mauryan traders. If risks in trade were high, so were profits. The Mauryan traders, as the *Jatakas* reveal, made incredible fortunes, lived like princes in grand mansions, and often dominated urban life. They had little to complain about.

Kautilya, cynical about human nature, was deeply suspicious of traders. 'Merchants ... are all thieves, in effect, if not in name,' he held, charging that they 'form cartels to raise prices [for the goods they sell] or lower them [for the goods they buy]; they are profiteers making one hundred panas on one pana.' To prevent such practices Kautilya set up an elaborate market-regulatory mechanism, run by the chief controller of private trading, who regulated prices, adjusted supply and demand, controlled product quality, and maintained the standards of weights and measures. Spies on the trade routes reported to officials on merchants trying to defraud the state. Local merchants had to stand surety for their visiting foreign trade associates.

These measures were intended to regulate trade, not to curb it, for it was very much in the interest of the state to promote private trade, as it stood to gain much from its imposts on trade and from the general economic prosperity generated by trade. Kautilya therefore gave every encouragement to traders and provided them with every needed facility, and recommended several measures to protect trade during difficult times. 'Whenever there is a glut in the supply of a commodity, the chief controller of trading shall build up a buffer stock by paying a price higher than the market price; when the market prices reaches the support level, the buying price shall be changed according to the situation,' he prescribed. He further specified that the sale of commodities in excess supply should be channelled through controlled outlets and that merchants should sell only from the accumulated stock until it was exhausted. Similarly, to prevent competitive reduction of prices, it was laid down that when a group of traders was granted the licence to sell a particular product, no one else should be given the licence to sell it, so long as the goods in stock remained unsold.

While the state thus sought to protect fair trade, it also took precautions to protect itself and the public against short-changing by traders. Standardisation of weights and measures, probably first introduced by the Nandas, was strictly enforced by the Mauryas, with officials periodically inspecting the weights and measures used in markets, and imposing fines for deficiencies. 'Weights shall be made of iron or stone from Magadha and Makala or of such materials that will neither increase in weight when wet nor decrease in weight when heated,' Kautilya directed. To prevent fraud, all balances and weights were required to be bought from the chief superintendent of weights and measures. Prices of everyday goods were fixed by the state and announced to the public by officials. The legal profit allowed to the trader was set at 5 per cent on local goods, and 10 per cent on imported goods, and merchants taking higher profits were fined.

With his eyes ever peeled for every revenue opportunity, Kautilya specified that 'commodities and products [of the countryside] shall not be sold [by private traders] in the places of their production [but sold only at the designated markets or brought into the city],' so as to add value to goods by transport, and to ensure that no merchandise was sold without the payment of octroi. However, ordinary household necessities like milk and vegetables were permitted to be sold at any time and place. Finished goods were stamped by royal officers and the state dues immediately collected, to prevent manufacturers and traders from mixing up old and new goods.

As trade grew, so did the business of financing trade – Megasthenes was entirely mistaken in stating that 'Indians neither put out money at usury, nor know how to borrow.' Moneylenders were common in Mauryan India – even the state lent out money from the treasury on interest – and there were elaborate rules to control credit. The lawful rate of interest for personal borrowings was 15 per cent per annum; for commercial transactions the rate was 60 per cent, but if the enterprise involved travel through forests, the rate was doubled to 120 per cent, and for sea trade it was again doubled to 240 per cent. 'No one shall charge or cause to be charged a rate higher than the above, except in regions where the king is unable to guarantee security; in such a case, the judges shall take into account the customary practices among debtors and creditors,' decreed Kautilya. Overcharging usurers were fined; even witnesses to such transactions were fined. Creditors were not allowed to collect interest on unpaid interest. Debts became time-barred if not recovered within ten years.

One of the most important developments of the Mauryan age was the growing monetisation of the economy. Coinage was first introduced in India in the Indus region, probably sometime between the sixth and the fourth centuries BC, presumably under Iranian influence, as this region was at this time a province of the Achaemenid empire. Coins seem to have been originally issued by merchants to facilitate trade, but minting was later taken over by the state. Panini in the early fourth century BC was familiar with coins. From the Indus Valley, the practice of minting coins rapidly spread to the Gangetic Valley, and it became widespread under the Mauryas.

The Mauryan society, as Allchin observes, 'revolved around money and monetary values.' The stamped coin is termed in the *Arthasastra* as rupa (or *rupya*, meaning 'beautiful': money is beautiful), and it designates the standard currency of the Mauryas as pana. Pana was a punch-marked silver coin alloyed with 25 per cent copper and 6 per cent hardening metal. The minting of coins itself was a business in Mauryan India, and private manufacturers were allowed to mint coins, on condition that they met the currency standards laid down by the state and paid due fees to the royal treasury.

The art of coining was not particularly advanced in India at this time, and counterfeit coins were common. Kautilya cautioned the royal treasurer to 'accept into the treasury only such coins as have been certified genuine by the chief coin examiner. All counterfeit coins shall be cut into pieces.' The punishment for minting and circulating counterfeit coins was rather light, only 1,000 panas. But those paying counterfeit coins into the treasury were punished with death!

THE GREAT TAX HEIST

The basis of state power, Kautilya held, was financial power. In administration, nothing was therefore more important to him than revenue collection, and in this he had no ethical inhibitions whatsoever. Brothels, taverns and casinos were, in his view, excellent sources of revenue, and were to be run as state monopolies. It was also perfectly legitimate for the state to trick and cheat the public, even commit theft and murder, for the sake of revenue.

Kautilya paid particular attention to taverns, bordellos and gambling dens, as these paid good returns without any great investment or risk. The chief controller of alcoholic beverages 'shall make arrangements for the manufacture of alcoholic beverages in the city, the countryside and the camps, with the help of experts in brewing and fermenting,' he directed. 'Women and children shall be employed in searching for special ingredients used in the industry and in processing them ... The chief controller shall organise, through appropriate persons, the sale of liquor in as many places as are necessary. [He] shall be responsible for the construction of drinking places. These shall have many rooms, with beds and seats in separate places. The drinking rooms shall be made pleasant in all seasons by providing them with perfumes, flowers and water.'

Only the liquors not made by the state, such as fermented fruit juices, were permitted to be made by private manufacturers, but they had to give 5 per cent of what they produced as royalty to the state. Householders were allowed to make *arishtas* (restorative liquors) for medicinal purposes, and also 'white liquor' for special occasions. During festivals, fairs and pilgrimages, permission was given to people to make and sell liquor for a period of four days, but those who made liquor without permission were fined. Kautilya abhorred disorderliness, and punished drunkenness, even though he encouraged the sale of liquor as a profitable business. 'No one shall move about while drunk,' he decreed.

The head of the department of prostitutes was an important personage in the Kautilyan bureaucracy; he was responsible for training courtesans and prostitutes, and for looking after their interests as well as the interests of their clients. There was no prudery about prostitution in Mauryan

India – it was deemed a profession like any other, a valued service. In urban centres, Kautilya allotted the north-eastern part of the city for brothels, and the state itself provided this service. 'The state,' Kautilya advised, 'shall bear the expenditure of training courtesans, prostitutes and actresses in the following accomplishments: singing, playing musical instruments, conversing, reciting, dancing, acting, writing, painting, mind-reading, preparing perfumes and garlands, massaging and making love. Their sons shall also be trained [at state expense] to be producers of plays and dances.'

The treasury received substantial regular revenues from the state-run brothels, so Kautilya laid down strict financial controls for their administration. 'Every prostitute shall report the persons entertained, the payments received and the net income to the chief controller. The chief controller shall keep an account of the payments and gifts received by each prostitute, her total income, expenditure and net income. He shall ensure that prostitutes do not incur excessive expenditure.' Even private courtesans – *rupajiva*, as Kautilya elegantly calls them: those who live by their beauty – had to pay as tax one-sixth of their earnings.

A prostitute, trained at government expense, was an income-earning asset of the state, and she was not allowed to remain idle or to be kept as a mistress by anyone, except by compensating the state for its loss of revenue. And it was obligatory for a prostitute to provide pleasing service to everyone, so as not to lose customers. 'A prostitute shall not show dislike to a client after receiving payment from him,' Kautilya ruled. 'She shall not abuse a client, disfigure him or cause him physical injury. She shall not refuse to sleep with a client staying overnight, unless the client has physical defects or is ill.' Violations of these rules were punished with fines. Equally, Kautilya sought to protect prostitutes from being abused by clients: 'No one shall abduct a prostitute, keep her confined against her will, or spoil her beauty by wounding her.'

State-run gambling houses were another regular source of revenue for the Mauryan emperor. Casinos were a state monopoly, and gambling in an unauthorised place was a punishable offence. 'The chief controller of gambling shall be responsible for ensuring that gambling is carried out only in designated places under the supervision of honest gambling masters,' Kautilya instructed. 'Gambling masters shall hire out to the players gambling equipment (such as dice, cowries, ivory rollers and leather cups) and provide water and other necessities. They can levy an entrance fee, hire charges for the equipment, and charges for water and accommodation, and can accept articles as pledges which may be sold [if not redeemed].' Gambling masters took 5 per cent of all winnings as tax, and were advised to be particularly careful in dealing with gambling disputes, because 'all gamblers, winners as well as losers, cheat as a matter of course.'

The Mauryan state exercised similar controls on all public entertainments. One of its major concerns in regulating entertainers was to make sure that they did not divert the attention of farmers from agricultural work during the rainy (farming) season. 'Entertainers shall not move from place to place during the rainy season,' warned Kautilya. This prohibition also applied to beggars and mendicants. 'The punishment for transgression shall be whipping with an iron rod.' The reason for these restrictive measures was purely economic. Where this consideration was not involved, Kautilya was surprisingly liberal in permitting freedom of speech and expression. Entertainers in their performances might, 'if they wish, make fun of the customs of regions, castes or families, and the practices or love affairs [of individuals],' he granted. But they were not allowed to 'praise anyone excessively or receive excessive presents.'

A pleasing aspect of the Kautilyan system was its concern for consumer protection. Artisans, traders and professionals who cheated customers were severely punished. 'Both locally produced and imported goods shall be sold for the benefit of the public,' Kautilya advised. 'Hoarded stock in the hands of merchants shall be sold for the benefit of the public ... No artificial scarcity shall be created by hoarding commodities constantly in demand.' The sale of shoddy goods, hoarding, overcharging of customers, adulteration of provisions, medicines, perfumes and similar products, were all punishable offences. And so were deficient professional services, including medical malpractice. 'Physicians shall inform authorities before undertaking any treatment which may involve danger to the life of the patient,' warned Kautilya. 'If, as a result of the treatment, the patient dies or is physically deformed, the doctor shall be punished.'

Even trivial problems of everyday life received Kautilya's attention. 'Washermen and tailors,' he cautioned, 'shall not wear, sell, hire out, mortgage, lose or change a customer's garment. They shall return the garments within the time prescribed. Loss due to washing [shrinkage, loss of colour, etc.] shall be allowed at the rates of one-fourth of the value for the first wash and one-fifth for the second and subsequent washes. Washermen shall wash garments only on wooden boards or smooth stone slabs. If they damage clothes by washing them on rough surfaces, they shall pay compensation and fine.' He also specified the time allowed for various types of washing and dyeing, and the fees to be charged. As for foodstuffs, a typical regulation stated that 'only meat from freshly killed animals shall be sold ... Fish without head or bones shall not be sold.'

Kautilya protected labourers from exploitation by punishing officials who delayed the payment of wages, and at the same time protected the interests of the state by punishing officials for paying wages for work not done. The modesty of women workers was required to be respected.

'When women who do not [normally] move out of their houses come to the yarn shed early in the morning, there shall only be a lamp for the inspection of the yarn.' Sexual harassment at work was punished. An official 'looking at the face of a woman or talking to her about anything other than work shall be punished.'

Unfortunately, these noble sentiments vanished the moment the interests of the king entered the scene. People were not allowed to cheat each other or the king, but the king was free to cheat all. Indeed, Kautilya encouraged him to cheat the public, and advised him on the ways and means to do so. Weights and measures as well as quality tests were all set higher for what was received into the treasury, and lower for what was paid out of it. The trade measure for liquids, for instance, was about 6 per cent smaller than the revenue measure. And on the use of touchstones, Kautilya recommended: 'A greenish-grey stone shows a higher carat and is better for sale, whereas a stone of uneven colour shows a lower carat and is better for buying gold.' The king even cheated his own employees, by having his secret agents in the guise of merchants sell goods at double the normal price to soldiers during campaigns.

Kautilya would let the state defraud its own staff, for he was not concerned with righteousness, but only with sustaining state power by maintaining its financial health. The Kautilyan strategy for ensuring this health had three elements: profitable operation of state enterprises, maximisation of tax collection, and prudent financial management. In revenue collection the Mauryan government was both cautious and ruthless at the same time. It would unhesitatingly swindle the public, but would not overtax them, for fear of ruining the economy. 'He who ... produces double the [anticipated] revenue eats up the country,' Kautilya held, and punished officers for collecting excess tax, especially if they misappropriated part of the collection. He was equally careful with expenditure, and specified that the establishment charges of the government should not be more than one-fourth of its revenue.

The Mauryan fiscal year was from Ashadha (June-July) to Ashadha. Accounts closed on the full moon day of the month. The year was reckoned as 354 days, with provision for separate accounting for the intercalary month. The entire financial operations of the empire, revenue collection as well as expenditure, were supervised by a minister titled Samaharta, the chancellor of the exchequer, who periodically reviewed the finances of the state at joint meetings with ministers and the top financial officials of departments and provinces.

The accounting procedures laid down by Kautilya were precise and elaborate, and stipulated punishments for irregularities. Each department had to maintain its own accounts according to prescribed rules, and clerks had to post accounts daily and submit the cash balances and ledgers to the chief accountant for checking. They also had to prepare weekly, fortnightly, monthly, four-monthly and annual abstracts of accounts. State manufacturing units were required to maintain stock and wage registers, and state warehouses had to keep detailed records of their stores, indicating their price, quality and quantity, as well as the 'description of the containers in which they were stored.' From these various accounts a consolidated statement about the state's financial position was prepared for submission to the king. 'The chief comptroller and auditor shall compile, for every department, the estimated revenue, the actual revenue, the outstanding revenue, income, expenditure and balance,' Kautilya directed.

Annual account statements were required to be submitted by all units to the central government strictly on time. 'On the closing day for accounts, all accounts officers [of the regions, undertakings, etc.] shall present themselves with sealed account books and with the [net] balance [of revenue over expenditure] in sealed containers,' Kautilya instructed. 'The officers shall be kept separate and shall not be allowed to talk [to each other]. The chief comptroller and auditor shall have the accounts audited, checking daily entries as well as weekly, fortnightly, monthly, four-monthly and annual totals.' As an essential additional precaution, royal spies watched over the functioning of all offices. Irregularities in accounts were severely punished, the fine being eight times the amount involved.

Revenue rules were not however uniform throughout the Mauryan empire. Kautilya would have preferred uniformity, but that was not possible in the vast and diversified empire. He therefore made allowances for local variations in customs and practices, and instructed the chief comptroller-auditor to maintain 'for each region, village, caste, family and guild, a rule book of customary laws regarding social customs and economic transactions.' He also provided – rather reluctantly, it seems – various tax concessions in deference to public sentiment. Brahmins, ascetics, and religious institutions were thus exempted from taxes, although he was, as Kosambi notes, 'systematically against standard Brahmin practices and financial privileges,' despite being himself a Brahmin. Brahmins – and pregnant women – were allowed to use ferries free of charge, and Brahmins were entitled to a free supply of salt.

Of all the revenue sources of the Mauryan empire, the most important was land revenue, collected as a share of the produce of the land. The traditional tax on private farmers was one-sixth of the gross produce of the land, but the rate varied from place to place and time to time, with Kautilya recommending a quarter and even one-third of the produce as tax for fertile lands. The tax rate in crown lands was higher than in private farms, and varied from a minimum of one-fifth to a maximum of one-third of the harvest, the higher rate being for land irrigated by state facilities. However, if the state provided cultivators with plough-oxen, implements and seeds, they had to give half of the harvest to the state. In addition to this, sharecroppers in crown lands had to pay a land rent. 'They pay a land-tribute to the king ... besides [this] ... they pay into the royal treasury a fourth part of the produce of the soil,' reports Megasthenes. Agricultural tax was usually collected from individual farmers, but in some cases the tax was imposed on the village as a whole, leaving it to the villagers themselves to determine the individual shares. In times of distress, tax concessions or remissions were granted to farmers, in crown lands as well as in private farms.

Every aspect of agricultural production was taken into consideration in making tax assessments. 'All land,' notes Kosambi, 'was measured, its yield of every crop estimated for every class of soil, type of irrigation, and rainfall. Every royal storehouse and state granary had a rain gauge, which helped in the classification.' Land was graded as high, middle and low yielding, and records were maintained about each cultivator in every village, and villages themselves were categorised as those exempt from taxes, those that paid taxes in grain, cattle, gold or raw material, and those that supplied labour or soldiers or dairy produce.

Special incentives were granted to those bringing virgin land under the plough. 'Anyone who brings new land under cultivation shall be granted exemption from payment of agricultural taxes [on the newly cultivated land] for a period of two years,' Kautilya directed. Even in crown lands, if the settlement was new, tax remission was allowed. Tax exemption for five years was given for building new tanks and embankments, for four years for renovating ruined or abandoned water works, for three years for clearing water works overgrown with weeds. On the other hand, payment had to be made to the state for using the waterworks built by the king. 'No one,' Kautilya laid down, 'shall let water out of dams out of turn, obstruct ... the use of water by others, obstruct a customary water course ... [or divert water from it].' For breaking a water reservoir, the punishment was 'drowning in the same place.'

Every product and every transaction and every service was taxed in the Mauryan state. Artisans were required to provide free services to the state for a specified period of time, one or two days in a month, but this was probably commuted to a payment in cash or kind. Traders had to pay import and export duties at the customs offices located at the main gates of towns, and there were harbour dues to be paid by ships touching the Mauryan ports. The tax rate on trade varied from commodity to commodity – while some items of everyday consumption were taxed at one-twentieth of their value, in some cases the tax was as high as one-fifth. To prevent tax evasion, commodities were required to be sold only at designated markets. Octroi was charged on goods brought into towns. In addition, traders had to pay a road tax, to compensate the state for protecting caravans from thieves. Ferrymen collected tolls at river crossings. In the case of traders who became bankrupt, the state had the first claim on their assets, to recover the dues to the state.

During financial emergencies, the Mauryan state took some extraordinary measures to replenish the treasury, and the *Arthasastra* devotes a whole chapter to this subject. These measures included forcing craftsmen and traders to make special contributions, and imposing virtually confiscatory levies on many items. Further, one-third to one-quarter of the farmer's harvest was collected as tax, and they were coerced to cultivate an extra summer crop. In addition, 'actors and prostitutes shall pay half their earnings [to the state] ... Brothel keepers shall make use of the young and beautiful women sent by the king to collect [more revenue].' Kautilya however warned that these exceptional demands 'are to be made only once, never a second time.'

In addition to these overt special imposts, the Mauryan state used several covert (and fraudulent) means to collect funds in emergencies. People, for instance, were pressed to make 'voluntary contributions' to the state, with secret agents starting off the collection with huge sham donations. Honours and status symbols (umbrella, turban and decorations) were bestowed on the rich in return for gold. Temple properties were expropriated on some pretext or other. Funds were also collected by performing simulated miracles (such as 'building a temple or a sanctuary overnight, as if it happened by a miracle') and by exploiting unusual incidents ('such as the appearance of an unseasonal flower or fruit, by making it into a divine phenomenon'). Further, people were induced to make offerings by frightening them about evil spirits, and by 'playing tricks on people by showing a cobra apparently with many heads, or a stone cobra coming alive.' 'Selling remedies against evil occult manifestations' was yet another means of collecting funds. 'If people are not taken in so easily, they should be frightened into doing so,' Kautilya urged. 'Secret agents should give unbelievers an anaesthetic in water and blame their condition on a curse of the gods; or, a condemned man shall be killed by poison and his death blamed on divine retribution.'

This was not all. Merchants could be cheated of their wealth by secret agents pretending to be traders collecting deposits or loans. Or they could be got drunk and their goods and money stolen. 'In a family quarrel, arrange for one member of the family to be killed by a poisoner and blame it on another,' and confiscate the property of both, Kautilya advised. So goes the sordid list. But these measures, he piously added, were to be used 'only against the seditious and the wicked, never against others.'

*

It is surprising that the Mauryan empire had to resort to these extraordinary measures once in a while to extort revenue. Clearly the empire, for all its extensive farming and business interests, and its elaborate and thorough system of revenue collection, was not always able to pay its way. The very administrative machinery that was to bring in revenue, it seems, turned out to be a voracious and wasteful devourer of revenue, its salary expenses presumably far exceeding the limit of one-fourth of the revenue set by Kautilya. Maintaining the opulence of the royal court also would have been a major and unproductive drain on state resources. But more than anything else, the military adventures of the empire, which had in the initial stages substantially contributed to the expansion of revenue, in the end turned out to be counterproductive, as the cost of conquering and administering far away and marginal lands was greater than their revenue potential.

The financial difficulties of the empire are indicated by the gradual debasement and coarseness of Mauryan coins. Asoka's silver coins, for instance, were two-thirds or more copper. Possibly, as Kosambi speculates, Mauryan control over metals had weakened at this time, because the south Bihar mines had reached the water level and could not be effectively exploited, and it was difficult to make up the loss with the yield of the south Indian mines, as these were too far away and in tribal tracts.

THE KAUTILYAN COMMANDMENTS

'Only the rule of law can guarantee the security of life and welfare of the people,' declared Kautilya. 'It is the power of punishment alone, when exercised impartially in proportion to the guilt, and irrespective of whether the person punished is the king's son or an enemy, that protects this world and the next.' But in a society that did not recognise equality of men even in the eyes of God, the rule of law could not possibly mean equality of men in the eyes of law. In Mauryan India, law discriminated between man and man according to class and caste, and Kautilya specifically and repeatedly directed that the caste and social standing of persons should be taken into account in making judicial decisions.

'Any matter in dispute shall be judged according to the four bases of justice,' enjoined Kautilya. 'These ... are dharma, which is based on truth; evidence, which is based on witnesses; custom, which is tradition accepted by the people; and royal edicts, which is law as promulgated.' Of these, Kautilya gave pre-eminence to royal decree, on the ground that the dictates of dharma and custom were not always apparent. The scope for royal decree was, however, limited, for the king was normally content to let custom rule, intervening only when the interest of the state was involved. Custom varied from community to community, caste to caste, guild to guild, and place to place, and was administered autonomously by each guild and caste and community without reference to the government, though the king had the general responsibility to oversee that customary laws were not violated. There were no common laws applicable to all, except in the narrow field of crimes against the state, and even there punishment varied with caste. This dominance of customary law in the Mauryan empire misled Megasthenes into believing that Indians 'regulate every single thing from memory ... Their laws, some public and some private, are unwritten.' He was wrong. The decrees of the state were certainly written down and codified, of which the very existence of the *Arthasastra* is proof.

Megasthenes had a tendency to romanticise and idealise, even mythify, certain aspects of life in India, either because of genuine misunderstanding or because he wanted to contrast these with the practices he disapproved of in his own society. 'They dislike a great undisciplined multitude, and consequently they observe good order,' he writes. 'Theft is a very rare occurrence ... They seldom go to law. They have no suits about pledges or deposits, nor do they require either seals or witnesses, but make their deposits trusting each other. Their houses and property they generally leave unguarded ... Truth and virtue they hold in high esteem.'

The *Arthasastra* presents an entirely different picture. The society we see in it is one that is struggling to bring some order into human affairs, by curbing man's all too common predilections for violence, fraud and crime. The book deals at length with matters of crime and punishment, and incidentally provides a great amount of information on Mauryan social life, on such diverse matters as women's rights, treatment of various castes, treatment of slaves, marriage customs and sexual practices, conjugal rights and duties, defamation, suicide, inheritance laws, tenancy rights, and so on.

In matters of social norms and penal law, Kautilya, for all his deviousness, often appears quite fair, even rather liberal. The treatment of slaves and bonded labourers that he prescribed is a case in point. Slavery was on the whole mild in India, so mild in fact – and the number of slaves so few – that Greek writers thought that there were no slaves at all in India. 'The lowest order in the social scale of Mauryan society,' Thapar observes, 'was not the slave but the outcaste.' Unlike in Greece, slaves did not constitute a class in India, and there was no unbridgeable gap between them and freemen. Anybody could be a slave – even an Aryan – and anybody could be free. However, Kautilya laid down that 'an Aryan minor shall never be sold or mortgaged into slavery,' though he did not consider it 'a crime for a *mleccha* to sell or mortgage his child.' Forcing a man into slavery was a very serious crime in Mauryan India, and Kautilya prescribed one of the highest fines in the *Arthasastra* – 1,000 panas – for that offence.

Slaves were classified into four categories by Kautilya: 'born in the house, inherited, bought, or obtained in some other way [such as captured in war or received as a present].' Most of the slaves in India were domestic servants, though some were also employed in mines, industrial units and large farms. Sometimes people pledged themselves as slaves to pay off debts, but such persons could redeem themselves, or could be redeemed by their relatives, by paying off their debts. Similarly, a man captured in war had to be freed if he paid his ransom, or earned his freedom through labour. 'Anyone who fails to set free a slave on receipt of redemption money shall not only be fined but the culprit shall be kept in detention until the slave is freed,' Kautilya directed. There was no slavery for life in Mauryan India.

The slave, though himself a property of another, had property rights of his own. 'A slave's property shall pass on to his kinsmen,' Kautilya ruled; it would go to the master only if the slave had no heirs. A man giving himself to bondage did not thereby lose his social status, and Kautilya laid down that a pledged person should not be deprived of his civic rights or made to do demeaning work or be cheated of his due wages. At the same time Kautilya protected the interests of the slave-owner by prescribing that a pledged person 'shall forfeit the right to redemption if he or she runs away.'

Female slaves received particularly considerate attention from Kautilya. 'A female bonded labourer shall not be beaten, treated violently, made to give a bath to a naked man or deprived of her virginity,' he charged. 'Raping a pledged woman is a punishable offence. If a master himself rapes or lets someone else rape a virgin girl under his control, he shall not only forfeit the amount owed but shall also pay the dowry for her marriage and a fine of double the dowry.' Similarly, it was laid down that a man who deflowers the daughter of a slave should be fined, and also made to pay her dowry and give her ornaments.

In Mauryan times a girl was deemed to have come of age at twelve, and a boy at sixteen. It was the responsibility of the girl's father to give her in marriage soon after she attained puberty, and if he was unable to do so, she was free to choose a husband on her own. 'It shall not be an offence for a daughter, remaining unmarried for three years after her first menstruation, to marry a man [of her own choice] of the same *varna*, and she shall be free to marry a man of [even] another *varna*, provided that she does not take with her the ornaments [given to her by her father],' Kautilya declared.

Parents sometimes resorted to deception to get a daughter (or a son) married off, but Kautilya considered that a crime. 'Giving away a girl [or a boy] in marriage by hiding the fact of her [or his] having a sexual defect is a punishable offence,' he maintained. 'The bride shall be a virgin at the time of the consummation of marriage; if she is not, she shall pay the dowry and marriage expenses and a fine. Pretending to be a virgin and deceiving by substituting some other blood [to indicate falsely the rupture of the hymen] shall be a punishable offence.'

The purpose of marriage, according to the *Arthasastra*, was 'to beget sons.' This was a duty that the couple owed to their family – and to the state. 'A wife shall not conceal her fertile period and her husband shall not fail in his duty to try to get a son with his wife in this period ... Failure to carry out marital duties is punishable,' warned Kautilya, and prescribed fines ranging from 12 to 96 panas for the offence. Further, 'a wife who ... refuses to adorn herself and does not let her husband sleep with her for seven menstrual periods' had to return to him the endowment and gifts he had given her. Under the circumstances the husband was free to sleep with another woman.

'If more than one wife has her fertile period at the same time, the husband shall lie with that wife to whom he had been married longer or with one who has living sons,' Kautilya regulated. However, 'a husband shall not have intercourse with a wife against her will if she has already borne him sons, wants to lead a pious life, is barren, has given birth to a stillborn child, or has reached her menopause. A husband is not obliged to have intercourse with a wife who is either insane or is a leper. But a wife can have intercourse with a leprous or mad husband, in order to beget a son.' Kautilya considered abortion a grave crime, and declared that even 'procuring the abortion of a pregnant slave is a punishable offence.'

Polygamy was the norm among ancient Indian kings, probably among the upper classes too, and it was not uncommon among the ordinary folk. There are many references in the *Arthasastra* to polygamous households of the commoners. Kautilya normally preferred large families, to augment the population of the state. Yet he laid down (could this be a later interpolation?) stringent rules for a man to take a second wife – he had to wait for eight years if his first wife happened to be barren, ten years if she had given birth to stillborn babies, twelve years if her children were all daughters. If he violated these rules, he had to return to his first wife her dowry and her property and pay her a compensation equal to half the total of her dowry and property. In addition, he had to pay a fine to the state – the state had to get something out of everything.

Women in Mauryan India clearly enjoyed greater rights than they did for centuries afterwards, and Kautilya was generally protective towards them. They had the right (though limited) to own property, and in some cases even the right to choose their husbands, or to seek divorce. Widows could remarry. A man could use his wife's dowry or other property only in absolute emergencies. Law protected her against violence by her husband in word or deed – and equally, it protected the husband against violence by his wife. 'A wife shall be taught proper behaviour, but the husband shall not use abusive language against her,' Kautilya directed. 'Breach of this rule is a punishable offence. Physical punishments shall be [limited to] slapping on her buttocks three times with the hand, a rope or a bamboo cane. Any beating exceeding this shall be a punishable offence.' To be fair, he also ruled that 'a woman who is known to abuse or beat her husband shall be subject to the same punishments as a cruel husband.'

Sexual mores were rather lax in Mauryan times, and there are several references in the *Arthasastra* to the children of unmarried girls, girls pregnant at the time of marriage, and men having wives of different *varnas.*

Kautilya's own attitude was, however, puritanical, and the sexual norms he prescribed were highly restrictive. 'A man and a woman [not married to each other] shall refrain from gestures or secret conversations with a view of sexual intercourse,' he warns. 'Neither a man nor a woman shall touch the hair or the knot of the lower garment of another of the opposite sex. Marking another with teeth or nails is forbidden. Neither a man nor a woman shall give presents to anyone to whom the giving of presents is prohibited. A woman shall not have dealings [such as buying and borrowing] with anyone with whom having such transactions are forbidden. A wife shall not indulge in drinking or unseemly sports, if so prohibited [by her husband]. She shall not go [without her husband] on pleasure trips or to see performances, with other men or even with other women, either by day or by night. She shall not leave the house when the husband is asleep or intoxicated, or refuse to open the door to her husband. No man shall give asylum to another man's wife except to save her from danger ... A wife shall not go on a journey to another village without her husband, particularly if she is with a man with whom she could have sexual intercourse.' Violation of these rules entailed fines, the fine on the man being double of that on the woman.

Punishments for sexual transgressions varied with caste as well as gender. While the Aryan man was only branded for having sex with an outcaste woman, the outcaste man was executed for having sex with an Aryan woman. And it was a capital offence for a woman to have 'sexual relations with a slave, a servant or a pledged man.' The punishment for a man for having sex with the queen was to be boiled alive. For committing adultery with a Brahmin woman, a Kshatriya only had to pay a fine, but a Vaisya had all his property confiscated, and a Sudra was burnt alive. The punishment for a wife caught in adultery was cutting off her nose and one of her ears or a fine of 500 panas, while the punishment for her lover was cutting off his nose and both ears or a fine of 1,000 panas. The lover could even be put to death. A person helping an adulteress was also similarly punished.

The proofs of adultery given by Kautilya are: 'finding the hair of one person on another, marks of carnal enjoyment, the opinion of experts, or the woman's admission.' However, adultery became a punishable offence only if there was a complaint. 'If ... the husband does not raise any objection, neither the woman nor her lover shall be prosecuted; otherwise the wife shall suffer mutilation and the lover death,' Kautilya decreed. Kautilya further granted that 'a man may, with her consent, enjoy a woman unknown to him, if he rescued her from robbers, enemy troops or jungle tribes; protected her during famine or civil disturbance; saved her from being carried away in a current; or found her abandoned or lost in a forest, or left for dead.' But if she was unwilling to have sex with him, or if she was a woman of a higher caste or already a mother, he had to restore her on payment of a ransom.

Kautilya viewed rape as a grievous crime. 'Even a prostitute shall not be enjoyed against her will,' he held. The punishment for the rapist of a minor girl was cutting off one of his hands or a fine of 400 panas, but death if the girl died; for raping a virgin, the punishment was cutting off the man's middle and index fingers or a fine of 200 panas. Even sex between two consenting adults was forbidden, if the girl happened to be a virgin, and both were fined. But by far the most serious sexual transgression was incest. 'For a man,' states Kautilya, 'sexual relations with the following are prohibited, under pain of punishment of cutting off his penis and both testicles, and death thereafter: aunt ... daughter-in-law, daughter or sister. Any woman who permits such a relationship shall also be sentenced to death.' It was also forbidden for a man to have sex with his guru's wife – that amounted to incest, and, like incest, was punished with death. Policemen who misbehaved with a woman detained during curfew hours were severely punished, and could even be executed if the woman involved was 'respectable'.

The purpose of sexual intercourse, in Kautilya's view, was procreation, so he made deviant sexual practices punishable offences. Intercourse other than through the vagina was punished, and so was homosexuality. Virginity being cherished, it was a crime for a girl to deflower herself, or to let another woman deflower her. Bestiality was also punished. 'He who forgets himself so much that he has sex with beasts shall be fined,' Kautilya ordained.

The *Arthasastra* recognises eight forms of marriage – Brahma, in which the father endowed his daughter and gave her away in marriage; Prajapatya, in which ceremonies were performed without the consent of the girl's father; Aarsha, in which a cohabiting couple regularised their relationship by giving a gift of two cows to the girl's father; Daiva, in which the householder gifted his daughter to the officiating priest during a sacrifice; Gandharva, the clandestine marriage of lovers; Asura, marriage by paying bride-money; Rakshasa, marriage by abduction; and Paisacha, sexual intercourse with a sleeping or drunken girl.

Kautilya frowned on any disruption of family life, viewing the stability of the family as essential for the stability of society and state, but realistically permitted the annulment of marriage and divorce under certain circumstances. 'In the case of the three higher *varnas*, a marriage agreement can be revoked up to the stage of *panigrahana* [bride and groom joining hands during the marriage ceremony],' Kautilya held. 'It can be revoked even after this if a sexual defect [such as loss of virginity or impotency] is discovered after it. Inthe case of Sudras, a marriage agreement can be revoked until consummation. Under no circumstances can an agreement be revoked if the girl has conceived a child by the man.'

As for divorce, Kautilya did not permit it in any of the first four kinds of marriages. Even in the other cases, 'a marriage can be dissolved only when there is mutual hatred,' he ruled. 'Neither a husband nor a wife may seek a divorce on the grounds of unilateral hatred, if the other is unwilling to end the marriage.' Further, to discourage divorce, Kautilya laid down rules to prevent the person seeking divorce from benefiting by it: 'If a husband seeks a divorce on the grounds of his wife's misconduct, he shall return to her all he has received from her. However, if a wife seeks a divorce on the grounds of her husband's misconduct, he need not return to her whatever he has received from her.'

A virgin wife whose husband was away from home for a long time was 'free to remarry as she wishes after she has waited for the prescribed period (varying from three to twelve menstrual periods) and with the approval of judges,' Kautilya held. Even after the consummation of marriage she was free to remarry after waiting for a prescribed period, which in this case was counted in years, not in menstrual cycles. The waiting period, like everything else, varied with caste, the lowest being one year for a Sudra woman with no children and no maintenance, and the highest ten years for a Brahmin woman who had children and had been provided with maintenance by her husband. It was mandatory for the husband to provide maintenance to the separated or superseded wife, unless the woman was financially independent.

Kautilya permitted widow remarriage, but imposed certain restrictions on it. 'Women who do not expect to remarry shall receive, on the death of her husband, the support endowment, her jewellery, the balance dowry (if any) and whatever had been given to her by her husband,' he ruled, but went to qualify this by stating that 'if a window remarries after receiving all the above, she shall forfeit what was left to her by her [previous] husband and shall also be obliged to return the rest with interest. If, however, she marries [someone from her late husband's family] with a view of begetting a son, she shall retain whatever was given to her by her late husband and father-in-law. If the remarriage is without the consent of the father-in-law, she shall forfeit whatever was given to her by him and her late husband.'

Kautilya required householders to take their family responsibilities seriously, and punished neglect. 'No man shall renounce his marital life [to become an ascetic] without providing for his wife and sons,' he ruled. In the matter of inheritance, the Mauryan practice was to follow 'the customs prevalent in the region, caste, tribe, or village.' However, outcastes, the progeny of outcastes, eunuchs, the impotent, the insane, the blind, and lepers were not granted any inheritance rights. Further, only sons could inherit the father's property, not daughters, for the reason that the continuity of the line was through sons, and it was they who performed the funeral rites and annual death ceremonies. The widow had no share in the property of her husband, though she could retain her dowry, her jewellery and whatever her husband had given her during his lifetime, but only if she did not remarry. Daughters could inherit the family property only if there were no male heirs, though they had equal claim with the sons on the property of their mother, and also had the right to a share in the 'bronze household utensils and their mother's jewellery.'

In dividing the property, the father 'shall neither show special favour to anyone nor exclude any rightful heir from the inheritance without good reason,' Kautilya directed, but added that 'if a man from any of the three higher *varnas* had wives from different *varnas*, the shares of the sons shall be according to the *varna* of the mother,' with the children of the lower-caste mothers getting lesser shares. Kautilya further observed that 'the laws of inheritance do not apply to self-acquired property ... When there is no ancestral property ... the eldest son shall support his younger brothers, except those of bad character ... Liabilities shall be divided just like assets ... Anyone who brings the ancestral property to a prosperous condition shall receive a double share. If there are no heirs, the property shall go to the king, except for the amounts needed for the maintenance of the widow and for the funeral rites.'

Business and trade laws are described in detail in the *Arthasastra*. Contracts had to be witnessed to be valid. They were not valid if concluded in the absence of any of the parties involved, or concluded secretly inside a house, at night, or in a forest, or with fraudulent intention. Exemptions were however granted for each of these conditions – secret agreements were valid in the case of the members of secret organisations, and even fraudulent agreements were valid if made by the king's secret agents. But 'contracts entered into when one of the parties was angry, intoxicated, mad or under duress shall be invalid,' Kautilya laid down. Similar rules governed promises of gifts.

Regarding property ownership, Kautilya prescribed that 'in the case of owners who cannot produce proof of ownership of goods, proof of continuity of possession shall be enough to establish title.' On the other hand, 'owners who have neglected their property and let it be enjoyed by others for a period of ten years shall lose their title to it ... Owners shall lose the title to buildings which they have neglected and in which they have not lived for twenty years.' As for the property entrusted to others, the person to whom it was entrusted was not obliged to return it if it was lost in circumstances beyond his control, such as a natural calamity, civil strife, or in acts of rulers or brigands.

In regulating religious practices, Kautilya ruled that heterodox ascetics should be barred from entering crown villages, and that fines should be imposed on those who entertained such ascetics at orthodox religious ceremonies. 'Heretics and Chandalas shall stay in land allotted to them beyond the cremation grounds,' he stipulated. He also regulated the work of Brahmin priests, specifying their fees for various rites and imposing fines on priests who did not properly conduct the rites. 'No celebrant shall abandon a ritual ... once it has started; doing so is a punishable offence,' he warned. 'It is not an offence to expel a priest from a ritual who is found to have been guilty of any of the following: not performing his daily rituals, not performing his special rituals, being drunk, marrying a heretic, killing a Brahmin, having immoral relations with the wife of his guru, taking gifts from evil persons, stealing, and performing rituals for a degraded person.' He further decreed that 'anyone associating with those who perform forbidden rites shall lose the right to perform rites, to teach and to give or receive gifts for a year. This shall extend to the associates of the associates.'

Kautilya viewed suicide as a most heinous sin, and directed that 'if any person under the influence of passion or anger, or any woman captivated by sin, were to commit suicide ... the body shall neither be cremated with rites nor shall the relatives perform the subsequent ceremonies. The body shall be dragged by a Chandala on a royal highway. Any kinsman performing the funeral rites shall meet the same fate on his death or be declared an outcaste by his relatives.'

'Cases of suicide by hanging shall be investigated to ascertain whether any injustice had been done to the deceased ... The magistrate shall conduct a post-mortem on any case of sudden death after smearing the body with oil [to bring out bruises, swellings and other injuries],' Kautilya ordered, and went on to give clinical descriptions of the symptoms of various kinds of unnatural deaths. In the case of strangling, 'urine and faeces are thrown out, skin of the abdomen is inflated with wind, hands and feet are swollen, eyes are open, and there are marks on the throat,' he observed; in the case of hanging, in addition to the above symptoms, there would be 'contraction of arms and thighs.' Asphyxiation should be suspected if 'hands, feet or abdomen are swollen, eyes sunken, and navel inflated,' while drowning was indicated by 'protruding eyes or anus, bitten tongue, and swollen abdomen.' Symptoms of poisoning were 'dark hands, feet, teeth or nails; loose flesh, hair or skin, and frothy mouth.' And so on. If poisoning was suspected, 'the undigested parts of the meal shall be tested by feeding it to birds,' Kautilya directed. 'If these parts, when thrown in fire, produce a crackling sound and turn multicoloured, poisoning is proved. If the heart [or stomach] does not burn when the body is cremated, then also poisoning is proved.'

Kautilyan criminal law was, for that age, relatively humane. No one could be arrested for a crime committed more than three nights earlier, unless he was caught with the tools of the crime. However, it was legitimate to lay traps for cheats. The use of torture to elicit confession was also permitted, but Kautilya warned that 'only those about whom there is a strong presumption of guilt shall be tortured.' Those suspected of minor offences, minors, the aged, the sick, the debilitated, the drunken, the insane, and those suffering from hunger, thirst or fatigue after a long journey, as well as those who have eaten too much, were not allowed to be tortured. It was further laid down that 'a person can be tortured only on alternate days and only once on the permitted days. Torture shall not result in death; if it does so, the person responsible shall be punished.' Brahmins learned in the Vedas and ascetics were not to be tortured at all, but only investigated through secret agents. Nor were pregnant woman allowed to be tortured. 'Women shall [preferably] be only interrogated; if tortured, they shall be subjected to half the prescribed scale.' The *Arthasastra* mentions eighteen methods of torture, four for ordinary offences and fourteen for serious crimes, and these ranged from giving seven lashes with the whip and pouring salt water through the nose, to thirty-two lashes, pricking with a needle under the fingernails, and making the accused stand in the sun for a day after being made to drink oil.

There is no precise information in the *Arthasastra* on judicial organisation and procedures. 'There is no reference in the text to a hierarchy of courts or to appeals from the decisions of a lower court to a higher one,' notes Rangarajan. Kautilya also does not make a clear distinction between the judicial and executive functions of the government. The king was, as usual in monarchies, at the apex of the judicial system. Beneath him there were, according to Sastri's analysis, two sets of royal courts – the Dharmasthiya (upholder of dharma) and the Kantakasodhana (remover of thorns), but the distinction between the two is not stated clearly in the *Arthasastra.* Possibly, as Rangarajan maintains, the difference was that 'while the former dealt with all cases concerning transactions between two parties, the latter was concerned with crimes against society in general.' Apart from these royal courts, there were also several other categories of judicial bodies in Mauryan India, such as village tribunals that dealt with petty cases, and caste and guild courts that administered the laws of communities and professions.

Kautilyan justice was quick – the defendant was given only a maximum of seven days to file his defence, and the plaintiff had to submit his rejoinder the very day the defendant submitted his answer. Delays entailed fines.

'Except in cases of riots, forcible seizure or trade disputes among merchants, the defendant shall not have the right to file a countersuit against the plaintiff,' Kautilya held. Some of the Kautilyan judicial provisions were remarkably liberal, progressive and humane. For instance, judges were required to 'take charge of the affairs of gods, Brahmins, ascetics, women, minors, old people, the sick and those that are helpless, [even] when they do not approach the court. No suit of theirs shall be dismissed for want of jurisdiction, passage of time or adverse possession.'

The probity of judges was periodically tested by *agents provocateurs.* No private interviews were permitted between judges and litigants. 'Judges,' enjoined Kautilya, 'shall discharge their duties objectively and impartially so that they may earn the trust and affection of the people.' They were warned not to 'threaten, intimidate, drive away or unjustly silence any litigant, or abuse any person coming before the court. They should not fail to put relevant and necessary questions, but not ask unnecessary or irrelevant ones, or leave out answers relevant to his own questions.' Nor should they in any way coach witnesses, misrepresent the statements of witnesses, 'fail to call for relevant evidence, or call for irrelevant evidence.' They were cautioned not to dismiss cases on some pretext, or to make people abandon cases 'by making them tired of undue delays.' The judge was also not allowed to 'rehear a case which had been completed and judgement pronounced.' Violations of these regulations were punished.

Normally cases were decided on the basis of the evidence of witnesses, but trial by ordeal was permitted in the absence of witnesses. Unwilling witnesses and those who lived far away were summoned by royal writ. Three witnesses were usually required to decide a case, but if the parties so agreed, two were enough. 'Judgements in cases involving debt shall never be based on the testimony of only one witness.' The close relatives of the claimant, his business partners, dependants, creditors, debtors, and enemies were not allowed to give evidence. Cripples and those with earlier convictions were also disqualified.

'Witnesses shall take the oath in the presence of a Brahmin, a water jar or fire. The judge shall caution the witnesses to tell the truth and point out the consequences of not doing so.' Here again the caste of the witness determined the warning administered. Brahmins were simply exhorted to tell the truth, but Kshatriyas and Vaisyas were warned that bearing false witness would result in the loss of all their accumulated merit and that they would be reduced to beggary, and Sudras were told that all their merits would go to the king and all the king's sins would fall upon them if they did not speak the truth. False witnesses were common in Mauryan India, and were severely punished. 'Anyone caught guilty of false-witness has his hands and feet cut off,' reports Megasthenes.

*

In assigning punishments, Kautilya took the middle course between excessive harshness and excessive clemency, noting that 'a severe king is hated by the people he terrorises, while one who is too lenient is held in contempt by his own people. Whoever imposes just and deserved punishment is respected and honoured.' Punishments were carefully graded to match crimes as well as the social status of the criminal. 'Magistrates shall,' he advised, 'determine the propriety of imposing the first, the middle or the highest penalty, taking into consideration the [social position] of persons, the nature of the offence, the motive and its gravity, the circumstances prevailing [at the time of the offence], including the time and place as well as the consequences ...'

Mauryan punishments were meant to deter crime, not just to punish the criminal. 'The maintenance of law and order by the use of punishment is the science of government,' states the *Arthasastra*. 'It is the power of punishment alone ... that protects this world.' Even the most trivial offences should be punished, 'as proof of the [omniscient] power of the king,' Kautilya held. Criminals were often paraded through cities and villages to warn people that they should 'keep under control any relative with criminal tendencies, because all thieves were bound to be caught.' Government officials caught in criminal acts were publicly humiliated by smearing them with cow dung and ashes, or by putting on them garlands of broken pots, or by shaving their heads.

The *Arthasastra* does not normally provide imprisonment as a punishment, presumably because there was no merit in feeding the criminal at state expense. Jails are however mentioned in the text, which also refers to prisoners being released on occasions of national rejoicing, such as the birthday of the king, the installation of a crown prince, the birth of a prince, or the conquest of a new territory. Suspects during investigation, and criminals when they were unable to pay the fine imposed on them, were kept in confinement.

Convicted criminals were permitted, perhaps encouraged, to commute physical punishments, such as mutilation and amputation, into fines. And fines could be commuted into services. 'Whenever *brahmacharis*, *vanaprasthas* or *sanyasins* have to pay fines, they may instead perform rituals and penances for the benefit of the king, for as many days as the amount of the fine,' Kautilya stated. 'Likewise, heretics without money shall observe a fast for the number of days equivalent to the fine. This rule does not apply to [serious crimes such as] defamation, theft, assault and abduction; in such cases the prescribed punishment shall be implemented.' Kautilya was particularly strict in the matter of sexual offences, and he provided 'no monetary equivalent to the cutting off of the penis and testicles.'

ENEMY AND THE ENEMY OF THE ENEMY

A *Vijigishu*: the seeker of conquest – this is how Kautilya defined the monarch. The field of the king's operations, the *chakravarti-kshetram*, was, according to him, the whole earth, by which he meant the entire Indian subcontinent, which he described as 'the land stretching from the Himalayas down to the sea, a thousand *yojanas* from corner to corner.' This was however only a theoretical projection. Kautilya did not deal with the strategic and foreign policy concerns of a vast empire, but only of a small state battling with its neighbours for survival. But in dealing with these issues, Kautilya looked, as he did in the case of many other aspects of polity, beyond actual and realistic situations and possibilities to purely theoretical situations and possibilities. This explains many of the book's bizarre elaborations.

'The welfare of a state depends on an active foreign policy,' Kautilya maintained, and advised the king to be always vigilant against his neighbours, for they were his natural enemies, whom he had to dominate to save his own crown. But domination did not necessarily mean annexation, though this was an option. The *Arthasastra* classifies conquests into three types: *dharmavijaya* (righteous conquest, in which the conquered territory is returned to its ruler after receiving his homage and tribute), *lohbhavijaya* (conquest for gain, in which booty is claimed and part of the kingdom is annexed), and *asuravijaya* (demonic conquest, in which the conquered kingdom is annexed). These terms have moralistic overtones, but Kautilya used them entirely as value-neutral categories on the basis of their practicality in given situations.

There is not a word about honour or political morality in the whole of the *Arthasastra.* Treaties can be made without faith and broken with impunity. Nor does the book give chivalry any role in war, perhaps rightly so – if a strong man can use his strength to crush an adversary, why should not a clever man use stratagems for the same objective? As Kautilya put it, 'An archer letting off an arrow may or may not kill a single man, but a wise man using his intellect can kill even reaching to the very womb.'

Expediency determines policy, not morality. According to the *Arthasastra,* there are six foreign policy options for a king, each related to the six possible situations (*gunas*) he is likely to encounter. If he is weaker than the enemy, he should opt for a conciliatory peace treaty. But if stronger, he should wage war and subjugate the enemy. In a situation of balance of power, he should remain in a state of peaceful vigilance. If he is in the process of gaining advantage over the enemy, he should make preparations for war and adopt a threatening posture. On the other hand, if he is in danger of being annihilated, he should seek the protection of another king. And if threatened from two sides, he should make peace with one adversary and wage war on the other. When the enemy 'is in trouble he must be attacked, when he has little or no help he may be uprooted, otherwise he must be harassed and weakened,' Kautilya advised.

But Kautilya was not a warmonger. He saw no glory in war, and accepted it only as a painful necessity in a volatile political environment. 'When the benefits accruing to kings under a treaty ... are fair to each one, peace by agreement shall be the preferred course; if the benefits are to be distributed unfairly, war is preferable,' he declared. 'One should neither submit spinelessly nor sacrifice oneself in foolhardy valour. It is better to adopt such policies as would enable one to survive and live to fight another day.' War was hazardous even for the strong, its results chancy, so 'when the degree of progress is the same in pursuing peace and waging war, peace is to be preferred.' At the same time Kautilya acknowledged that 'one cannot make peace with an enemy,' and went on to advise: 'An enemy's destruction shall be brought about even at the cost of great losses in men, material and wealth.'

In Kautilya's scheme of foreign relations, the immediate neighbour of a king is his inevitable enemy. And the neighbour of his neighbour is his natural ally, being the enemy of his enemy. It is this simple and essentially sound concept that Kautilya elaborated into the celebrated but much misunderstood Mandala Theory, which depicted a kingdom as being surrounded by concentric circles of alternating friends and enemies. But the concept of concentric circles was not meant to be taken literally, as representing actual alignments on the ground; it was only an illustrative or metaphoric idea.

Kautilya reserved some of his most diabolic stratagems for the destruction of oligarchic tribal republics, many of which were still powerful in his time. These turbulent and intractable states not only disrupted the orderly conduct of external policy that Kautilya envisaged, but also provided an alternative form of government opposed to the centralised absolute monarchy which he ardently championed.

The tribal republics were difficult to subdue, for in them the conquering king was up against not just another king, but against a people. The strength of the republic was in its tribal solidarity. This had to be broken before it could be conquered. And the best means to do this, according to the *Arthasastra*, was to spread dissension among the oligarchs. '*Agents provocateurs* should gain access to all these tribes, discover the possible sources of jealousy, hatred and contention among them, and should disseminate the seeds of progressive dissension,' counselled Kautilya. 'Public decisions and tribal customs should be brought to dissolution by insistence upon the contrary.' Secret agents should spread lies and rumours, and even use sly assassinations, to cause confusion, disarray and mutual suspicion among the chieftains. They should use 'young women of great beauty' to infatuate the chieftains and to provoke them to fight among themselves for the women's favours. Similarly, they should write fake conspiratorial letters to some of the chieftains and should contrive these to fall into the hands of others, to spread mutual distrust. 'Miraculous results can be gained by practising the methods of subversion,' Kautilya held. 'A single assassin can achieve, with weapons, fire or poison, more than a fully mobilised army.'

Feigned defection was one of Kautilya's favourite ploys. 'The conqueror shall ostensibly banish a chief official of a fort, province or army accusing him of treachery. The banished official shall [then take shelter with the enemy and] use the opportunity of a battle, a sudden assault, a siege or a calamity to outmanoeuvre the enemy. [While waiting for an opportunity] he shall set out sowing dissension among the supporters of the enemy.'

'In all cases of strife among the members of an oligarchy, whether they arise by themselves or are incited by assassins, the conqueror shall assist the weaker party with money and arms, make them fight the hostile group, and urge them to kill their rivals,' advised Kautilya. As for the turbulent forest tribes, he suggested that they should be ambushed and slaughtered, or killed off with poisoned liquor.

In contrast to these singularly vile methods for subduing enemy states, Kautilya was very fair in his recommendations on how to treat a conquered people, though even here his ultimate objective was to serve the interests of the king. 'Having acquired a new territory, the conqueror shall substitute his virtues for the enemy's vices, and where the enemy was good he shall be twice as good,' he counselled. 'He shall follow policies which are pleasing and beneficial to the constituents by acting according to his dharma and by bestowing favours and exemptions, giving gifts and honours ... He shall adopt the way of life, dress, language and customs of the people [of the conquered territory], show the same devotion to the gods of the territory [as to his own gods] and participate in the people's festivals and amusements.' These measures, Kautilya believed, would enable the king to win over the conquered people. Benevolence too was a stratagem.

But stratagems by themselves could not give victory. They would work only when backed by credible military power. Kautilya therefore paid great attention to the organisation of the army. The core of the Mauryan army was a standing professional body of soldiers maintained by the state. This was supplemented in times of need with militias, as well as with mercenaries recruited from warrior clans, jungle tribes and foreigners. The emperor could also draw on the military resources of allied kings. There was no general conscription in Mauryan India, the traditional compulsory military service having been by this time commuted into a military provisions tax.

The standing army was kept in constant battle-readiness. 'Fighting men are maintained at the king's expense and hence they are always ready, when occasion calls, to take the field,' notes Megasthenes. These soldiers formed a privileged group; they were well paid – even the foot soldier got as much as 500 panas a year – and in active duty got double the normal wages and were allowed to keep whatever booty they seized. 'They have only military duties to perform,' states Arrian. 'Others make their arms, and others supply them with horses, and they have others to attend on them in camp, who take care of their horses, clean their arms, drive their elephants, prepare their chariots, and act as their charioteers. As long as they are required to fight, they fight, and when peace returns they abandon themselves to enjoyment – the pay which they receive from the state being so liberal that they can with ease maintain themselves and others.'

According to Pliny, Chandragupta had an army of 600,000 infantry, 30,000 cavalry and 9,000 elephants. In addition, he had, according to Diodorus and Curtius, 2,000 chariots, while Plutarch puts the number of chariots at 8,000. Whatever its actual size, the Mauryan army was a formidable force, equipped with the best possible arms and mounts. The weapons and the mount of the soldier were provided by the state, which he had to return to the state at the end of each campaign, notes Megasthenes. 'No private person is allowed to keep either a horse or an elephant.'

The chief of the Mauryan army was the Senapati, one of the highest officers of the empire, who received a salary equal to that of the crown prince. He was assisted by a war office which, according to Megasthenes, was made up of six boards of five members each, each board in charge of one of the six corps of the army: infantry, cavalry, chariots, elephants, commissariat, and transport. The Mauryas did not have much of a navy, though Megasthenes speaks of an 'admiral of the fleet,' and the *Arthasastra* mentions a superintendent of ships. Each division of the army, according to Kautilya's prescription, had to have more than one chief, 'for, with many chiefs, mutual fear will prevent them from succumbing to the temptations of the enemy.'

There were four battle divisions in the Mauryan army – the cavalry, the infantry, the elephant corps, and chariots. Elephants, though not used in war in Vedic times, had now become the main battle-arm of the Indian army. Kautilya believed that they were capable of achieving victory in battle all by themselves, without the help of the other limbs of the army. The war-elephant, according to Megasthenes, carried, in a howdah or on its bare back, four men: 'three who shoot arrows, and the driver.' Elephants were essential to smash through walls, stockades and other obstacles, and to scatter massed infantry formations. They were also used to haul heavy equipment, to clear paths through jungles, to cross rivers, and to construct log bridges. Bullocks were used by the army for transporting equipment and also to draw chariots during the march, so as not to fatigue the war horses.

Second in importance were the chariots. Unlike the light, fleet, two-wheeled war chariots of early Aryans, Mauryan chariots were huge, four- or eight-wheeled cumbersome wagons, which made up for the loss of speed and manoeuvrability by being able to carry a larger number of soldiers and weapons. They, according to Kautilya, also added magnificence to the army, and made 'an awesome noise.' The chariots of Porus in the battle of Jhelum, says Curtius, were each drawn by four horses and carried six men, and the *Arthasastra* speaks of chariots carrying ten or twelve men.

The third in rank were the cavalrymen, who, according to Arrian, were 'equipped with two lances ... and with a shorter buckler than that carried by foot soldiers.' And finally, there was the infantry. 'The foot soldiers carry a bow made of equal length with the man who bears it,' writes Arrian. 'This they rest upon the ground, and pressing against it with their foot thus discharge the arrow, having drawn the string far backwards ... There is nothing which can resist an Indian archer's shot – neither shield nor breastplate, nor any stronger defence if such there be.' Not surprisingly, Indians were in ancient times known as great archers, though Curtius, a near contemporary of Arrian, was scornful of their effectiveness. 'The arrows,' he writes, 'which are two cubits (about three feet) long, are discharged with more effort than effect, for though the force of these missiles depends on their lightness, they are loaded with obnoxious weight.' The foot soldiers, continues Arrian, carry 'in their left hand ... bucklers made of undressed ox-hide, which are not so broad as those who carry them, but are about as long. Some are equipped with javelins instead of bows, but all wear a sword, which is broad in the blade, not longer than three cubits; and this, when they engage in close fight (which they do with reluctance), they wield with both hands, to fetch down a lustier blow.'

The Mauryan army also used a variety of war machines, which are described in some detail in the *Arthasastra* – machines to throw stones and shoot arrows, a rotating machine to throw logs, water pumps to put out fire, a machine called the hundred-slayer, and so on. There was even 'a machine to raise wind dust.'

The advance of the Mauryan army across the plains in a cloud of dust would have been an awesome sight, a vast horde spread out as far as the eye could see, for the army, itself a mammoth body, was accompanied by a far greater multitude of non-combatants, consisting of the harems of the king and the great officers, the families of soldiers, women as well as children, traders and hawkers and menials and various professionals and their families, and a large troupe of prostitutes. Inevitably, the army marched slowly, covering a maximum of about 16 kilometres a day, but often only half that distance.

Sappers marched ahead of the army, clearing the way and digging wells. Kautilya ordered that 'food-stuffs and provisions should be carried in double the quantity that may be required in any emergency,' and that the route of the army should be carefully chosen to ensure adequate supply of fodder, firewood and water. The Mauryan military camp was about the size of a city, and was laid out like a city. Particular attention was given to security in the camp. 'Guards, stationed at eighteen [designated] points in the camp shall be changed [at stated times],' Kautilya specified. 'Watch shall be kept during the day, in order to uncover spies. Disputes, drinking, parties and gambling shall be prohibited. A system of passes with seals shall be instituted. The perimeter-commander shall arrest any soldier trying to leave the camp without a written order.'

The basic battle unit of the Mauryan army had an elephant or a chariot at its centre, with a protective ring of five cavalrymen, each cavalryman in turn being protected by a ring of six foot soldiers. In the battlefield, clusters of these core units were deployed in the traditional battle formation of a centre, two flanks and two wings. Depending on the terrain and tactical requirements, the army was tightly or loosely grouped, but Kautilya specified the minimum distance to be maintained between two foot soldiers – about 26 centimetres – and also between archers, cavalrymen, chariots and elephants. He also directed that the army should not be deployed facing the south, and that it should have the sun behind it, and that the wind should be favourable.

The minimum battle array prescribed by Kautilya consisted of 45 chariots (or elephants), each chariot with its complement of protective cavalry, and each cavalry soldier with his retinue of infantrymen, thus making a total of 45 chariots (or elephants), 225 horsemen and 1,350 infantrymen. 'Every division of the formation shall have its own distinguishing trumpet sound, flags and banners,' Kautilya specified. 'These shall be used to signal the commands to that division.' At the rear of the army were stationed 'physicians with surgical instruments, equipment, medicines, oils and bandages; women with cooked food and beverages and women to encourage the men to fight.' A strong force made up of the pick of the army was held in reserve – the king, warned Kautilya, should not attack 'without having reinforcements in the rear, since these are essential for rallying broken ranks.'

The king stationed himself with the reserve force about half a kilometre behind the main army. Kautilya took special care to protect the king, for he knew that if he fell, the battle would be lost instantly. The king 'shall take his place, bare of flags and distinguishing features and surrounded by warrior kinsmen,' he prescribed. 'He shall ride a chariot or an elephant and be guarded by cavalry ... A double shall impersonate the king at the head of the battle formation.' Further, as a matter of abundant caution, Kautilya suggested that the king 'shall make secure a mountain or forest fort at the rear of his own country as a refuge and a place for recoupment, and then only establish a base camp for fighting the battle.' It was also stressed that the king should mentally (or spiritually) prepare himself for the battle. 'The king shall observe a fast the night before the battle and sleep beside his chariot and weapons,' Kautilya advised. 'He shall make oblations in the fire according to the Atharva-veda. He shall have prayers said for victory in the battle and for attainment of heaven [by those who fall]. He shall entrust himself to Brahmins.'

The battle itself, like the preparations for it, was a methodical, formulaic affair in the Kautilyan scheme, not the chaotic, blood-and-guts savage affair that one would imagine ancient warfare to be. Kautilya prescribed four basic tactical movements to meet different military situations – a truncheon style advance with the forces held in rigid conventional formation; a snake type attack in undulating surges; a radiating attack with the army advancing in all directions simultaneously from a compact circular formation; and a dispersed attack in which the various units of the army acted independently. These four basic tactics were again divided into thirty-two sub-types, with distinctions so subtle in some cases as to be almost non-existent. Kautilya further directed that 'the infantry shall be attacked by horses, horses by chariots, and chariots by elephants,' and that three infantrymen should be assigned to oppose a horse, fifteen to oppose a chariot, and five horses to oppose an elephant. 'The enemy's warriors may be kept awake by night forays and then attacked during the day when they are drowsy or asleep ... The ranks of the enemy's horses and elephants may be broken by letting loose frightened cattle, buffaloes or camels, which are made to run helter-skelter with contraptions which make a lot of noise tied to their backs.'

The outcome of battles ultimately depended on the spirit of men, Kautilya knew, so he considered it essential that a propaganda war to crush the morale of the enemy should precede the engagement in the battlefield. Gullible people should be made to believe through various tricks that the conqueror had the special favour of the gods, he suggested. 'Soothsayers, readers of omens, astrologers, reciters of Puranas, intuitionists and clandestine agents ... [shall help] the king perform ... "miracles" and ... shall advertise them.' Similarly, they had to spread the word among the enemy's subjects that the conqueror had received his army and treasury from divine sources, and interpret omens and dreams to proclaim the inevitability of his victory. 'Any appearance of a meteor in the enemy's zodiacal sign shall be proclaimed by a beat of drums [as an omen of his imminent defeat].' Further, Kautilya recommended that the king should strike terror in the enemy forces by such means as witchcraft, fake miracles, provocative assassinations, incitement of traitors, and by spreading lies about revolts and defections in the enemy's kingdom.

At the same time, measures should be taken to rouse the ardour of the king's own men, Kautilya directed: 'Astrologers and similar professionals shall inspire the troops by proclaiming the king to be omniscient and divinely aided and shall fill the enemy troops with dread ... Bards and praise-singers shall describe the heaven that awaits the brave and the hell that shall be the lot of cowards. They shall extol the clan, group, family, deed and conduct of the warriors. Assistants of the Purohita shall speak of the spells and incantations they have used against the enemy, and astrologers of the good omens for their side and the bad ones for the enemy. Technicians and carpenters shall speak about the [powerful] machines they have built.' And finally, to inflame the warrior's frenzy with greed, Kautilya prescribed that a price should be set on every enemy head – 100,000 panas for killing the enemy king, 50,000 for a prince or army chief, 10,000 for a division chief, 5,000 for an elephant or chariot warrior, 1,000 for a cavalier, 100 for an infantry section leader, and 20 for a foot soldier.

As in everything else, careful matching of ends and means characterised Kautilya's military strategies. He would be ruthless, but no more than was absolutely necessary. 'The following,' he directed, 'shall not be harmed when the enemy fort or camp is attacked: anyone falling down in the fight, those turning their backs, anyone surrendering, anyone who unties his hair or throws his weapons down; anyone contorted by fear, or anyone who does not fight.' He also advised against pursuing a routed enemy, for reasons of prudence. 'The fury of a desperate king returning to battle with no thought for his own life is irresistible; therefore, a routed army shall not be further harassed,' he warned. Nor did he allow the scorched earth policy against the enemy. Says Megasthenes: 'Whereas among other nations it is usual, in contests of war, to ravage the soil and reduce it to an uncultivated waste, among the Indians, on the contrary, by whom husbandmen are regarded as a class that is sacred and inviolable ... combatants on either side ... allow those engaged in husbandry to remain quite unmolested. Besides, they neither ravage an enemy's land with fire, nor cut down the trees.'

For defence, Kautilya laid the greatest emphasis on building a strong royal fort, stating, 'The treasury is kept safe there and the army is well protected in it. It is from the fort that secret war is waged, one's own people controlled, allies received and enemy troops and jungle tribes kept at bay.' He prescribed that the citadel of the king should be located at the centre of his kingdom, at a confluence of rivers or at a perennial lake or other good water sources, and that it should be well served by land and water routes. 'The fort shall be surrounded by three moats, either filled by natural springs or by water brought in from elsewhere; they shall have adequate drainage and be filled with lotuses and crocodiles, [and the bridge over them shall be removable]. There shall be a rampart all round the fort ... planted [on the outward side] with thorny bushes and poisonous creepers.' When under siege, the defenders should, Kautilya suggested, 'burn all grass and wood for a distance of one *yojana* around the fort [to improve visibility and deny the enemy any cover]; spoil or divert all [nearby] water works; and lay traps such as deep well-like holes, concealed pits and thorny obstructions.'

Storming the fort was the most difficult of ancient military tasks, and Kautilya recommended that, before attempting to storm a fort, every possible stratagem should be used to force its peaceful surrender. Spreading panic among the defenders, assassinating their king, bribing the enemy officers, infiltrating soldiers into the fort by some trick, or luring the enemy out of the fort with a feigned retreat, are some of the measures he suggested for this. 'The work of laying a siege shall be preceded by actions designed to deplete the resources of the enemy,' Kautilya enjoined. 'These are: destroying his sowings and crops, cutting off his supplies through foraging raids, making his people run away, and killing the leaders secretly.' However, Kautilya did not favour setting fire to the fort to capture it. 'When a fort can be captured by fighting, fire shall not be used at all,' he warned. 'A fort whose stores are burnt down only gives rise to further losses.' Only if there was absolutely no other alternative, should the fort be burned down, by catching birds nesting in the fort and releasing them with fire-balls tied to them, by shooting fire-arrows into the fort, and by tying lighted torches on animals like monkeys, cats and dogs and releasing them into the fort.

Kautilyan politics was *realpolitik* pushed to its very limits. Beyond its limits, in fact. It had absolutely no moralistic concerns at all, no trace of idealism. Success alone mattered. And success was defined by Kautilya in purely materialistic terms. '*Artha* (material gain) alone is the principal aim,' he declared, 'for dharma and *kama* are both rooted in the gain of *artha*.' He did now and then laud dharma – 'When dharma is transgressed, the resulting chaos leads to the extermination of this world,' he says in one place – but nowhere in the *Arthasastra* are any measures suggested to promote dharma.

'The sole purpose of every action [in the *Arthasastra*] was the safety and profit of the state,' comments Kosambi. 'Abstract questions of ethics are never raised or discussed in the whole book. Murder, poison, false accusations, subversion were to be used at need by the king's secret agents, methodically and without qualm. At the same time, the normal mechanism of law and order continued to function for the common man with the utmost vigilance and severity. Such a state could have no firm basis except its own administration – and even that had to be kept under the most careful observation by spies.'

Inevitably the Kautilyan system failed in the long run, failed even in its stated exclusive objective of promoting the interests of the king, for it based royal power solely on the army and bureaucracy, a far too narrow base to provide stability. The Kautilyan state had no genuine interest in the welfare of the people, and the people in turn had no interest in the welfare of the state. So, if the army failed the king, he had nothing to fall back on. The people did not care what happened to him. The much-lauded scene of peasants labouring peacefully in the field while a battle raged within their sight is, if looked at from a different perspective, a shocking picture of public indifference to the fortunes of their king.

Perhaps the greatest failing of the *Arthasastra* is that, though there is much in it that is sensible and practical and wise, its system, taken in its entirety, was impractical in an ancient Indian state, impractical even in a modern totalitarian state. The Kautilyan government tried to do too much, was over-organised, and was too exacting in its prescriptions and expectations. It required the king to be a superman, the bureaucrats to be perfectly programmed robots, and subjects to be toiling zombies.

Not surprisingly, Kautilya was repudiated in his own age, when Asoka abandoned the policy of internal and external aggression, against his own subjects and against other kingdoms. Asoka then reintroduced dharma into politics, from which Kautilya had unceremoniously banished it. And he brought to centre stage the heretical sects that Kautilya had driven to the outcaste periphery of society.

Under the later Mauryas the complex jigsaw of the brave new world that Kautilya had so patiently and carefully assembled fell apart, never to be put together again. Expedient amorality would no doubt continue to mark politics. And rulers would continue to exploit their subjects pitilessly. But never as systematically and efficiently as Kautilya envisaged.

Chapter Eight

THE NEVER-NEVER LAND

GREEK FABLES

Ancient Greek travellers in India, like ancient travellers everywhere, were brazen fabulists. India was an exotic land such as the Greeks had not seen anywhere else, and the sheer intoxication of their experience set them on fantastic flights of fancy, aided no doubt by the antic tales that Indians, matchless mythmakers themselves, told them. Moreover, the Greek chroniclers, being literary men, could not resist the temptation to add frills to facts to dramatise their accounts. Some of them – Megasthenes, for instance – also idealised the conditions in India and coloured their reports in the hope of influencing Greek ideas and institutions.

But their readers were not always easily taken in. They questioned the truthfulness of the reports, and the chroniclers themselves often charged each other with mendacity. Thus Megasthenes cautioned his readers 'to have no faith in the ancient stories about the Indians,' but was himself censured by others. 'Generally speaking, the men who have hitherto written on the affairs of India were a set of liars,' asserted Strabo, and included Megasthenes in his list of liars. Strabo was even more caustic about Onesicritus: 'He may as well be called the master fabulist as the master pilot of Alexander.' Roman scholar Pliny in the first century AD thought that the early reports about India were all 'diverse and incredible.'

Sometimes even the plain facts about India seemed improbable to the Greeks, because of their inability to accept the unfamiliar as true. Strabo puts the problem in perspective: 'It is necessary for us to hear accounts of this country (India) with indulgence, for not only is it farthest away from us, but not many of our people have seen it; and even those who have seen it, have seen only parts of it, and the greater part of what they say is from hearsay; and even what they saw they learned from a hasty passage with an army through the country. Wherefore they do not give out the same accounts of the same things, even though they have written these accounts as though their statements had been carefully confirmed. Some of them were on the same expedition together, like those who helped Alexander to subdue Asia; yet they all frequently contradict one another. If they differ thus about what was seen, what must we think of what they report from hearsay? ... So, in cases like these, one must accept everything that is nearest to credibility.'

So must we. Though the Greek chroniclers generally tended to fantasise quite a bit about India, there were among them a few who had the curiosity to study the land and the people empirically, and were blessed with a robust scepticism that enabled them to keep their vision clear, and their feet firmly on the ground. To them we owe the earliest factual descriptions of India. This information is invaluable, for the period that the earliest Greek records cover, the fifth and fourth centuries BC, is a blind period in Indian history, on which we have virtually no Indian literary records, none at all of dated inscriptions or archaeological evidence. That apart, foreign travellers usually record matters of everyday life that the natives overlook as commonplace, but which the passage of time has made fascinating to later generations. After Megasthenes, some six centuries would pass before we get another foreign account of India, from Chinese pilgrim Fa Hsien in the early fifth century AD.

India and Greece were some 4,500 kilometres distant from each other, at the eastern and western extremities of the ancient civilised world. Outside this narrow band there was only one other great civilisation, that of China, but the Chinese lived in wilful isolation from the rest of the world. India, on the other hand, was always, even from the time of the Indus Civilisation, closely linked with other ancient civilisations. And when the great Aryan racial tide engulfed most of the ancient world, the links became even stronger, as the entire stretch of land from the Mediterranean to the Gangetic valley came under the domination of related Indo-European peoples. However, there was no direct contact between India and Greece for many centuries, and the Greeks in early times had only a vague awareness of India as a faraway mysterious land. This changed with the establishment of the Achaemenid empire in Persia in the sixth century BC, which stretched up to Greece in the west and to India in the east, and had both Greeks and Indians in its imperial service.

The first Greek to write a book on India was Scylax, a Greek mercenary sea-captain in Persian service, who was deputed by emperor Darius, towards the close of the sixth century BC, to explore the Indus down to the sea. With Scylax began the fabulous European legends about India, and it was from him that Herodotus in the mid-fifth century drew much of his information about India, though he generally (but not altogether) ignored the mythical stories. A few decades later, Ctesias, a Greek physician who served for seventeen years in the Iranian court, wrote a substantial book on India. He was in a position to write authoritatively and realistically, but chose to sensationalise India as a land of wonders. This won him a large readership and greatly influenced the common Greek perception of

India, but did not advance factual knowledge. The Greeks would never entirely shake off these fantasies, even after they gained direct knowledge of the country following Alexander's invasion of Punjab.

Alexander had broad intellectual interests, and there were in his army several scholars who recorded the peculiarities of the lands and peoples they came across, and some of them wrote books on their experiences. Unfortunately, these records are all lost, and are today known only from the extracts quoted by later writers. Also lost is Megasthenes's four-volume *Indica*, by far the fullest and most authentic ancient Greek account of India. It too survives only in fragments quoted by later writers, who so edited and paraphrased the original text that even the same extracts in different books vary in detail.

The loss of *Indica* is irreparable. But even Megasthenes, who stayed longer in India than the other chroniclers, and travelled more extensively, could write with authority only about a small portion of the subcontinent. India was too vast a land, and too diverse in peoples and cultures, to be compacted into any one man's report. Besides, the Greek chroniclers had a major disadvantage in not knowing the languages of the country. They received their information second hand, through interpreters, and this entailed considerable risk of misinterpretation. The problem was further complicated by the total strangeness of Indian culture to the Greeks. Often, we should assume, what the Greeks were told was one thing, and what they understood was something rather different.

Because of all this, and the eccentricities of individual perception, Greek accounts of India are often at variance with each other, somewhat like the fabled description of the elephant by six blind men. Some wrote grisly tales of primitive, cannibalistic men, who had sexual intercourse in the open, like animals, and of men who wore marsh grass skirts and ate raw fish and meat, while others wrote of sophisticated urbanites belonging to another cultural aeon altogether, men who dressed in fine cottons and silks embroidered with gold, and had complex socio-political institutions and advanced philosophical ideas. These divergent accounts, though elaborately embellished and rather confusing, were all probably not without some factual basis, given the great diversity of India. But of a class wholly different from them were the entirely fictional descriptions of India by the Greek literati, who waxed eloquent about the country without ever having visited it. Such is the Elysian portrait of India presented by Dion Chrysostom, a first century AD Greek rhetorician of Asia Minor.

'No men,' writes Dion, 'live more happily than [Indians] ... for in their country, it is said, the rivers flow not ... with water, but one river with pellucid wine, another with honey, and another with oil ... So then they pass each day in the society of their children and their wives ... by the streams of the rivers, playing and laughing as if at a festival. Along the riverbanks there flourishes in great vigour and luxuriance the lotus – and this is about the sweetest of all comestibles ...'

'They have besides at hand water-baths of two kinds,' continues Dion, 'that which is hot and clearer than silver, and the other dark blue by reason of its depth and coldness. In these the women and children swim about together – all of them models of beauty. Emerging from the bath, I can fancy them lying down in the meadows, commingling their sweet voices in mirth and song. And there the meadows are of ideal loveliness, and decked by nature with flowers, and with trees, which from overhead cast a protecting shade, and offer fruit within reach of all who would pluck it from the descending branches. Of birds, again, there is a great plenty, which make the hills where they have their homes resound with their songs, while others, from the spray of overhanging boughs, warble notes more melodious than those played by our instruments of music. The wind, too, blows gently, and there is always an equable temperature, such as prevails at the beginning of summer, and besides all this, the sky is there clearer ... and surpasses in the multitude and splendour of its stars. Their span of life is not less than forty years, and for all this time they are in the bloom of youth and they know neither old age nor disease nor want.'

'These statements,' Dion boldly concludes, 'are not fiction, for some of those who come from India have ere now asserted them to be facts.' India, in the seductive imagination of Dion, was literally a heaven on earth. Unfortunately, it existed only in his imagination.

Such fantasies about India are not surprising, considering the time and circumstances in which they were written. What is surprising is that the Greeks got quite a few things right about India. Though none of them had travelled over the whole subcontinent, and so had to conjure up the image of the regions they had not seen from what people told them, they had a fair knowledge of the general lie of the land. 'The shape of the country is rhomboidal,' says Megasthenes. 'India,' Diodorus writes, 'which is in shape quadrilateral, has its eastern as well as its southern side bounded by the great sea, but on the northern side is divided by Mount Hemodos ... while the fourth or western side is bounded by the river called the Indus.' One Greek writer, Patrocles, in a fluke guess even got the north-south measure of India fairly close when he stated that it was 15,000 stadia – 2,775 kilometres, the actual length being about 3,200 kilometres. 'A considerable portion of India,' Arrian correctly notes, 'consists of a level plain, and this ... has been formed from the alluvial deposits of rivers.' Most Greek writers considered the Indus as the western boundary of India.

The Greeks believed that India was at the very extremity of the inhabited world, beyond which was a limitless desert or a limitless ocean. 'Of all the inhabitants of Asia of whom we have any reliable information, the Indians are the most easterly,' Herodotus writes. 'Beyond them the country is uninhabitable desert.' The Greeks generally exaggerated the size of India. Comments Arrian on what his compatriots had to say on this: 'Ktesias of Knidos says that India equals in size all the rest of Asia, which is absurd, while Onesicritus as absurdly declares that it is the third part of the whole earth.' The Greeks were also wrong in describing the orientation of India – they thought that peninsular India extended east-south-east from the mouth of the Indus, and that Cape Comorin was to the east of the mouth of the Ganga.

The sheer number and size of Indian rivers filled the Greeks with amazement, but the Greeks themselves amaze us with the outrageous hyperbole they used to describe Indian rivers. Notes Arrian: 'Megasthenes asserts that ... the Ganga ... has a breadth where narrowest of one hundred stadia (18.5 kilometres), while in many places it spreads out into lakes, so that when the country happens to be flat and destitute of elevations the opposite shores cannot be seen from each other.' Aelian gives the Ganga's width as 400 stadia – 74 kilometres! And he gives its depth as 107 metres. Even in the modest estimate of Pliny, the Ganga had a depth of 30 metres.

Indian skies too seemed different to the Greeks – here the Great Bear was visible only for a couple of weeks in the year, that too 'only at the early part of the evening,' and in summer shadows fell to the south in some regions of India. The heat in the plains of India was oppressive, and during the monsoon it rained there as nowhere else in the world. The Greeks believed that this environment of high humidity and baking heat, though irksome to man, was also most beneficial to him, as it turned India fertile beyond imagination and nurtured plants and animals of gigantic size. 'India,' Diodorus writes, 'has many huge mountains which abound in fruit trees of every kind, and vast plains of great fertility, which are remarkable for their beauty, and are supplied with water by a multitude of rivers. The greater part of the soil, moreover, is well watered, and consequently bears two crops in the course of the year.'

There were, the Greeks reported, dense forests everywhere in India, abounding in strange trees and stranger animals and birds. The banyan tree particularly aroused their curiosity, with Strabo comparing it to an immense 'tent with many supporting columns.' Pliny stated that several squadrons of cavalry could take cover under it, and Nearchus claimed that it could shelter 10,000 men. The cotton tree was also a marvel to them. 'Certain wild trees there bear wool instead of fruit, that in beauty and quality excels that of sheep, and the Indians make their clothing from these trees,' writes Herodotus. Then there was this amazing reed, the sugarcane, which, Strabo says, had honey as its sap. And it was from the reports of Alexander's officers that Europe first learned about rice, where it then came to be valued for its supposed medicinal properties.

Even more marvellous than the flora was the fauna of India. 'All animals, both quadrupeds and birds, are much larger than they are in other countries, with the exception of horses,' states Herodotus. The strangest of all Indian animals was the elephant. What dazzled the Greeks about the elephant, apart from its mammoth size and crucial role in battles, was its intelligence. 'The elephant,' Arrian writes, 'is of all brutes the most intelligent ... I have myself actually seen an elephant playing on cymbals, while other elephants are dancing to his strains.' Says Strabo: 'They are naturally so mild and gentle in their disposition that they approximate to rational creatures. Some of them take up their drivers when fallen in battle, and carry them off in safety from the field. Others, when their masters have sought refuge between their forelegs, have fought in their defence and saved their lives. If in a fit of anger they kill either the man who feeds or the man who trains them, they pine so much for their loss that they refuse to take food, and sometimes die of hunger.' Alexander, though he did not care to use elephants in war, nevertheless acquired a good number of them in India, and is believed to have sent one to Athens as a gift. On his death, his elephants were divided among his generals, and the elephant corps thereafter became an important division of Hellenistic armies.

Alexander was fascinated by the ferocious hunting dogs of Punjab – they were, reports Diodorus, 'remarkable for their size and strength ... [and were] said to have been bred from tigresses.' Another object of curiosity for the Greeks was the small but spirited species of Indian oxen – they looked like 'very big goats,' says Aelian, but were 'not inferior in speed to horses.' The tiger, the lion, the one-horned rhinoceros, and the monkey were some of the other marvels noted by the Greeks. Snakes greatly troubled Alexander's men in India, the small ones because they were hard to notice and highly poisonous, the large ones because they were powerful enough to crush and swallow men and large animals. Some Indian snakes, according to credulous Onesicritus, were as large as 140 cubits – about 70 metres! Among the birds, the peacock so charmed Alexander that, according to Arrian, he decreed severe punishment for those who killed the bird. The parrots in India were 'as talkative as children,' Aelian says. And, as if reality was not fabulous enough, the Greeks attributed to India many imaginary creatures, like gold-digging ants the size of dogs, dog-faced men, pygmies two feet tall, men without mouths who lived on fragrances, others with such enormous ears that they could curl up inside them, and so on.

The vastness of India's population, and its sheer diversity of races, languages and cultures baffled the Greeks, who came from a nation of one race, language and culture. 'Of the Indians the population is by far the greatest of all nations whom we know of,' writes Herodotus, and goes on to state that 'there are many tribes of Indians who speak different languages.' Indians, Dionysios states, 'do not form a single community bearing a common name.' According the Megasthenes, there were 118 tribes in India, a number which Arrian thought was too precise to be correct. 'I am at a loss to conjecture how he arrived at it,' comments Arrian, 'for the greater part of India he did not visit, nor is mutual intercourse maintained between all the tribes.'

Of all Indians, the Greeks were most impressed by the strength and valour of the men of Punjab. 'The inhabitants,' says Megasthenes, 'having abundant means of subsistence, exceed in consequence the ordinary stature, and are distinguished by their proud bearing.' In war, adds Arrian, they were 'far the bravest of all the races inhabiting Asia.' Some of them, Dionysios claims, were 'so tall that they could mount elephants with as much ease as they mount horses.' But in general Indians were not heavily built, but were, according to Arrian, 'slender and tall, and of much lighter weight than other men.' Onesicritus would have us believe that the life span of Indians was over 130 years.

It was skin colour rather than facial features that distinguished Indians from other people. 'As for the people of India,' Strabo observes, 'those in the south are like the Ethiopians in colour, although they are like the rest in respect to countenance and hair ... whereas those of the north are like the Egyptians.'

This was the age of rapid urbanisation in India – the second urbanisation, as historians call it, the Indus Civilisation being the first – and we have a fair amount of information on Indian cities from classical European sources, though archaeological evidence is scanty. The land, for that age, was dotted with towns, and the Greeks, ardent urbanites themselves, were surprised by the large number of cities and towns they came across, though, as usual, they tended to exaggerate what they saw. 'The number of cities in India is so great that it cannot be stated with precision,' remarks Megasthenes. 'The country of Porus, extensive and fertile ... [contains] about 300 cities,' states Strabo. This incredible figure multiplies magically in Plutarch, who states that the kingdom of Porus had '5,000 considerable cities, and villages without number.'

Most of the Indian cities were administrative centres, but there were also a fair number of commercial cities and pilgrim centres. City houses were usually built around a central courtyard, and the affluent lived in opulent two- or three-storyed mansions with several courtyards, one behind the other, as early Buddhist literature and sculpture show. All these grand mansions were largely built of wood, as stone was scarce in the alluvial plain, and sun-dried bricks were impractical, for they, as Megasthenes observes, 'would never hold out for any length of time with the rains on the one hand, and, on the other, the rivers which rise above their banks and spread a sheet of water over the plains.' Hence only 'those cities which stand on commanding situations and lofty eminences are built of brick and mud.' Even the palace complex in Pataliputra was built mainly of wood. It had, Kosambi notes, 'flooring, ceiling, roof, substructure, and even drains of heavy timbers; its beautifully polished stone pillars rested securely upon heavy logs sunk vertically into the soil with a mat of clay.' The fortifications of the city were also of timber, covered with earth. Timber was plentiful in this region in ancient times, as evidenced by the fact that 'roads built of corduroy of trimmed logs ran for miles through Bihar even in the seventh century AD.'

The greatest city in ancient India, indeed one of the greatest cities in the ancient world, greater than anything the Greeks had built, was Pataliputra, the imperial capital of the Mauryas at the confluence of the Ganga and the Son. Megasthenes has given a fairly detailed description of the city, and the measurements he gives roughly correspond to the actual measurements indicated by archaeology. 'The inhabited part of the city,' he says, 'stretched on either side to an extreme length of eighty stadia (about 15 kilometres), and its breadth was fifteen stadia (about 2.8 kilometres). A ditch encompassed it all round, which was six *plethra* (about 182 metres) in breadth and thirty cubits (about 13 metres) in depth. The city wall was crowned with 570 towers and had 64 gates.' Strabo says that the city was 'in the shape of a parallelogram, and surrounded by a wooden wall that is perforated, so that arrows can be shot through the holes, and ... in front of the wall ... there lies a trench used both for defence and as a receptacle for the sewage that flows from the city.' The city probably had a population of about 270,000, according to Allchin's estimate.

Pataliputra continued to be the imperial capital under the successors of the Mauryas. Chinese pilgrim Fa Hsien, who visited the city in the fifth century AD, some 800 years after its founding, saw it still flourishing. But the city rapidly decayed thereafter, and Hsuan Tsang in the seventh century found it in ruins. It regained some prosperity a couple of centuries later under Pala kings, but collapsed again soon after, and today its debris lies under some four metres of alluvium.

Another city the Greeks have described in some detail is Taxila, which, according to Strabo, had 'most excellent laws.' It was 'a large and prosperous city, in fact the largest of those situated between the rivers Indus and Hydaspes (Jhelum),' says Arrian. According to the doubtful testimony of Philostratus, an early third century AD Greek biographer of Apollonius, a Greek savant who visited India, 'Taxila was about the size of Nineveh, walled like a Greek city ... divided by narrow streets, well arranged ... [rather like] Athens. From the streets, the houses seemed of only one storey, but they all had an underground floor ... [The king's] palace was distinguished by no extraordinary magnificence, and was just like the house of any citizen of the better class. There were no sentinels or bodyguards and but few servants about, and perhaps three or four persons who were waiting to talk with the king. The same simplicity was observable in the courts, halls, waiting and inner rooms ...' Outsiders, says Philostratus, were not allowed to stay in Taxila for more than three days.

Somewhere to the east of Jhelum, perhaps along the Salt Range, was the well-administered domain of a most unusual people, of whom we have a fascinating but tantalisingly brief account in Greek chronicles. The people there, says Diodorus, 'were governed by laws in the highest degree salutary,' but their true uniqueness was in that 'beauty was held among them in the highest estimation.' Onesicritus claims that such was their preoccupation with physical elegance that when they came to choose their ruler, they disregarded valour and other normally esteemed regal qualities, but crowned the handsomest man among them as king. When Alexander passed through this land after his battle with Porus, their king, whom the Greeks call Sopeithes (probably Saubhuti), came out of his city and surrendered to the emperor. He was, Curtius says, a 'tall and handsome figure. His royal robe, which flowed down to his very feet, was all inwrought with gold and purple. His sandals were of gold and studded with precious stones, and even his arms and wrists were curiously adorned with pearls. At his ears he wore pendants of precious stones which from their lustre and magnitude were of an inestimable value. His sceptre too was made of gold and set with beryls, and this he delivered up to Alexander with an expression of his wish that it might bring him good luck, and be accepted as a token that he surrendered into his hands his children and his kingdom.' Alexander graciously returned the kingdom to the king. Diodorus adds that 'Sopeithes with utmost cordiality feasted the whole army in splendid style for several days.'

This good life of the subjects of Sopeithes was probably somewhat exaggerated by the Greeks, but the India that the Greeks encountered was generally a prosperous and progressive society, with rapidly expanding agriculture, industry and trade. There was, Thapar comments, 'considerable material improvement in the culture of the time.' Nature had richly endowed India, and human endeavour had added greatly to that wealth. Its climate was congenial, man and beast robust and healthy, the soil bountiful in agricultural and mineral wealth.

'Famine has never visited India,' claims Diodorus; 'there has never been a general scarcity in the supply of nourishing food.' This was not quite true. The ravages of famine are described in the *Jatakas*, and the last years of Chandragupta's reign, according to tradition, were marred by a famine lasting several years. Still, relatively speaking, sustenance was not normally a great problem in India, and the countryside produced enough surpluses of provisions to feed the rapidly growing urban population.

The double crop that the soil yielded was the main insurance against food scarcity. 'Even should one of the sowings prove more or less abortive, they are always sure of the other crop,' says Diodorus. Rice, millet and sesame were cultivated in summer; wheat, barley and pulse in winter. Astrologers, perhaps no less dependable than modern meteorologists, provided farmers with annual weather forecasting, so they could plan their farming pattern.

'The fruits ... of spontaneous growth, and the edible roots which grow in marshy places and are of varied sweetness, afford abundant sustenance for man,' Megasthenes reports. 'The fact is, almost all the plains in the country have a moisture which is alike genial, whether it is derived from the rivers, or from the rains of the summer seasons, which are wont to fall every year at the stated period with surprising regularity; while the great heat which prevails ripens the roots which grow in the marshes, and especially those of the tall reeds.' The beneficence of nature was supplemented by the benevolence of rulers. Cultivators were not normally harmed or their fields damaged during political and military upheavals. 'The land thus remaining undamaged, and producing heavy crops, supplies the inhabitants with all that is requisite to make life very enjoyable.'

There was plenty of mineral wealth too in India. Diodorus reports that 'while the soil bears on its surface all kinds of fruits which are known to cultivation, it has also under ground numerous veins of all sorts of metals, for it contains much gold and silver, and copper and iron in no small quantity, and even tin and other metals, which are employed in making articles of use and ornament, as well as the implements and accoutrements of war.' Writes Herodotus: 'There is abundance of gold there, partly dug, partly brought down by the rivers, and partly seized [from gold-digging ants].' Gold, Macdonald comments, was in fact 'so abundant [in India] that for many centuries its value relatively to silver was extraordinarily low.' India was also rich in pearl fishery. 'The pearl in India is worth thrice its weight in refined gold,' says Arrian. And, Strabo adds, 'in the country of Sopeithes there is a mountain of mineral salt sufficient for the whole of India.'

The Greeks were generally impressed by India's wealth and prosperity, but economic conditions varied so dramatically from region to region that the accounts of Greek writers who visited different regions of India seem like reports about altogether different countries. While Megasthenes wrote of a flourishing and advanced economy, and Diodorus spoke admiringly about the skill of Indian craftsmen, others wrote of primitive economic and technological conditions, presumably because their experience was confined to the tribal belt of the north-west. According to Strabo, Indians did not even know the technique of smelting metals. 'Since the Indians are inexperienced in mining and smelting, they also do not know what their resources are, and handle the business in a rather simple manner,' he writes. He was evidently mistaken in this. The Indus Civilisation was familiar with the use of metals, and Aryans carried the technology further. The *Jatakas* also speak of metal industries, and the *Arthasastra* describes in detail various metals and the manufacturing processes of different metal wares.

The Indian product that the Greeks most admired was cotton cloth. The tradition of cotton weaving, which began with the Indus Civilisation and continued through the Vedic period – weaving is mentioned in the Rig-veda and the Atharva-veda – reached a high degree of refinement at this time, and early Buddhist texts speak of the fine cloth manufactured in Varanasi. There are references to embroidered cloth even in the Rig-veda, and the *Jatakas* have descriptions of the golden turbans of kings and the golden trappings of royal elephants. Kautilya lists several varieties of cotton, silk and woollen cloth, and mentions the places where these were manufactured. Indian kings, says Curtius, were 'robed in fine muslin embroidered with purple and gold.'

Cotton cloth was very likely a major item of trade between India and the Greek kingdoms of the Middle East. Much of this trade was carried overland, but sea trade between these countries by way of the Red Sea and Alexandria was now rapidly growing in importance. Initially, sea trade was in the hands of Indian and Arab traders; the Greeks were not directly involved in it, and very few Greek ships went beyond south Arabia in Mauryan times. It was only towards the close of the first century BC that the Greeks established direct sea trade with India. This trade was originally carried 'in small vessels which kept close to shore and followed its windings,' but it received a great boost when Greek sailor Hippalus in the first century AD discovered the direct course across the Arabian Sea to India, by taking advantage of the monsoon winds. Thereafter Greek traders became very much a part of the bustle and polyglot hubbub of Indian ports, as vividly described by ancient Tamil poets, who sang of the 'good ships' of the Yavanas (Ionian Greeks) that arrived at their ports 'making the water white with foam,' bringing 'cool and fragrant wines,' and returning laden with pepper.

WOMEN, SOPHISTS AND CANNIBALS

India in the eyes of Greek writers was a whole world all by itself. And it was a very strange world, where everything – plants and animals as well as society and culture – was wholly different from what they had known elsewhere. Especially confusing to them was the Indian caste system. Even Megasthenes, who spent a long time in Pataliputra, had no clear understanding of it.

In Mauryan times the caste system had not yet acquired the complexity and rigidity of the later periods, but was rapidly congealing into that state. 'The custom of the country,' notes Megasthenes, 'prohibits inter-marriage between castes … Custom also prohibits any one from exercising two trades, or from changing from one caste to another. One cannot, for instance, become a husbandman if he is a herdsman, or become a herdsman if he is an artisan.' Megasthenes, confusing castes with professions, divided Indian society into seven exclusive classes: philosophers, cultivators, herdsmen-hunters, artisans and merchants, warriors, superintendents, and assessors-councillors.

At the apex of Indian society were those whom the Greeks called sophists, in the original Greek sense of the term – sages and learned teachers. Their superiority was not of wealth or power, as of the aristocracy in other societies, but of learning and sanctity, and their only privilege was freedom from all temporal concerns and constraints. 'The sophists,' says Megasthenes, 'being exempted from all public duties, are neither the masters nor the servants of others.' They were exempt from all taxation, did not have to pay road or ferry tolls, and were allowed to take salt free. They could not be subjected to corporal punishment even for the most heinous crimes, but only be branded and banished. Says Apollonius: 'the Brahmins dwell on the earth, and yet not on the earth … [they] possess nothing and yet all things.'

Megasthenes divided sophists into two groups, priests and ascetics. The priests, he writes, 'are not so numerous as the others, but hold the supreme place of dignity and honour, for they are under no necessity of doing any bodily labour at all, or of contributing from the produce of their labour anything to the common stock, nor indeed is any duty absolutely binding on them except to perform the sacrifices offered to the gods on behalf of the state. If any one, again, has a private sacrifice to offer, one of these sophists shows him the proper mode, as if he could not otherwise make an acceptable offering to the gods.' Most of the priests were Brahmins, but not all Brahmins were priests. 'Brachmanes,' says Strabo quoting Nearchus, 'engage in affairs of the state and attend the kings as counsellors.' Many Brahmins, especially in north-west India, were warriors.

Unlike the priests, the ascetics among the sophists had no caste exclusiveness. They, says Megasthenes, could be 'from any caste, for the life of the sophist is not an easy one but the hardest of all.' They belonged to diverse sects and practised different kinds of austerities. Some ascetics, continues Megasthenes, 'go naked, living during winter in the open air to enjoy the sunshine, and during summer, when the heat is too powerful, in meadows and low grounds under large trees. They live upon the fruits which each season produces, and on the bark of trees, the bark being no less sweet and nutritious than the fruit of the date palm.'

The ascetics were greatly esteemed as oracles. 'To this class the knowledge of divination among the Indians is exclusively restricted and none but a sophist is allowed to practice that art,' Megasthenes states. 'They predict about such matters as the seasons of the year, and any calamity which may befall the state, but private fortunes of individuals they do not care to predict.' Megasthenes was evidently wrong in the matter of private predictions, perhaps because his experience was confined to the royal court. Other sources speak of mystics making uncannily accurate predictions about individuals. Greek sage Apollonius once had, according to Philostratus, the singular experience of being told his entire past in graphic detail by an Indian ascetic – 'who his father was, who his mother, all that happened to him at Aegae, and how Damis (his companion) joined him, and what they had said and done on the journey, and this so distinctly and fluently, that he might have been a companion of their route.'

At the beginning of every year, the king, according to Diodorus, summoned the sophists to assemble in the capital city and 'forewarn the assembled multitudes about droughts and wet weather, and also about propitious winds, and diseases, and other topics capable of profiting the hearers.' Adds Strabo: 'He who is thrice found false [in his predictions] is required by law to keep silence for life, whereas he who has proved correct is judged exempt from tribute and taxes.'

A peculiarity of Indian society in the eyes of some Greek chroniclers was what they considered to be the absence of slavery. 'All the Indians are free, and not one of them is a slave,' says Megasthenes. According to Diodorus, 'the law ordains that no one among them shall, under any circumstances, be a slave, but that, enjoying freedom, they shall respect the principle of equality in all persons.' This was clearly a misconception.

Strabo in fact contradicts Megasthenes and quotes Onesicritus to state that there was indeed slavery in India, at least in some regions. There are also numerous references to slaves in Indian sources, in the *Jatakas*, the *Arthasastra*, and Asokan edicts.

There were quite a large number of Greeks living in Mauryan India, especially in Pataliputra, women as well as men, the entourages of Hellenistic ambassadors and of the Seleucid princess in the Mauryan harem, as well as traders, artisans and various adventurers. Persian emperor Xerxes is believed to have established a colony of Ionian Greeks in the borderland of India, and Alexander is reported to have come across people in India who claimed Greek ancestry. And Apollonius claims that he met villagers in India who spoke Greek. We do not know how the Greeks fitted into Mauryan society. Presumably they were designated as *mlecchas*, ritually impure but not socially inferior.

The Mauryan aristocracy was essentially an official aristocracy, and was therefore an ephemeral class dependent on royal will and fortune. But they did live an opulent life. Their robes, Strabo writes, 'are worked in gold and ornamented with precious stones, and they also wear flowered garments made of the finest muslin. Attendants walking behind hold up umbrellas over them.' Curtius adds that 'they cover their persons down to the feet with fine muslin, are shod with sandals, and coil round their heads cloths of cotton. They hang precious stones as pendants from their ears, and persons of high social rank, or of great wealth, deck their wrist and upper arm with bracelets of gold. They frequently comb, but seldom cut, the hair of their head. The beard of the chin they never cut at all, but they shave off the hair from the rest of face, so that it looks polished.' 'Their favourite mode of exercising the body,' says Strabo, 'is by friction, applied in various ways, but especially by passing smooth ebony rollers over the skin.' The nobles rode on elephants when they travelled. 'The animals used by the common sort for riding on are camels and horses and asses,' Arrian reports. 'But the wealthy use elephants, for it is the elephant which in India carries royalty. The conveyance which ranks next in honour is the chariot-and-four; the camel ranks third; while to be drawn by a single horse is considered no distinction at all.'

'They marry many wives, whom they purchase from their parents, and they get them in exchange for a yoke of oxen, marrying some of them for the sake of prompt obedience and the others for the sake of pleasure and numerous offspring,' says Strabo. Indians, he claims, desired to have many children through many wives because 'they have no servants,' and hence 'it is necessary for them to provide for more service from children.'

Ancient Indians, according to Strabo, had some rather curious marriage customs. 'Aristobulus mentions some novel and unusual customs in Taxila,' he writes. 'Those who by reason of poverty are unable to marry off their daughters, lead them forth to the marketplace in the flower of their youth to the sound of trumpets and drums ... thus assembling a crowd. And to any man who comes forward, they first expose her rear parts up to the shoulders and then her front parts, and if she pleases him, and at the same time allows herself to be persuaded, on approved terms, he marries her.' Arrian mentions a variation of this practice: 'They marry without either giving or taking dowries, but the women, as soon as they are marriageable, are brought forward by their fathers and exposed in public, to be selected by the victor in wrestling or boxing or running, or by some one who excels in any other manly exercise.' In the kingdom of Sopeithes in Punjab, according to Diodorus and Curtius, men do not look for high birth or dowry in selecting their brides, but only for the girl's 'beauty and other advantages of the outward person.'

The Greeks had no direct knowledge of the customs of southern India, but reported what they learned from hearsay. 'In that part of the country ... it is said that women when seven years old are of marriageable age, and the men live at most forty years,' claims Arrian on the authority of Megasthenes, and goes on to rationalise the practice. 'If the age at which the women there are marriageable is correctly stated, this is quite consistent, it seems to me, with what is said of the men's age – that those who live the longest die at forty; for men who come so much sooner to old age, and with old age to death, must of course flower into full manhood as much earlier as their life ends earlier. It follows hence that men of thirty would there be in their green old age, and young men at twenty would be past puberty, while the stage of full puberty would be reached by fifteen. And, quite compatibly with this, the women might be marriageable at the age of seven. And why not, when Megasthenes declares that the very fruits of the country ripen faster than the fruits elsewhere, and decay faster?'

The Greeks considered Indian women to be wanton. Wives, claims Strabo, 'are permitted to prostitute themselves' if their 'husbands do not force them to be chaste.' According to Arrian, even a lady 'possessed of uncommon discretion' would, for the gift of an elephant, 'let the giver enjoy her person. Nor do the Indians consider it any disgrace to a woman to grant her favours for an elephant, but it is rather regarded as a high compliment to the sex that their charms should be deemed worth an elephant.' And among the primitive tribes of India, writes Herodotus, 'the intercourse ... takes place openly like cattle ... The seed they emit is not white as that of other men, but black as their skin ... These Indians are situated very far from the Persians, towards the south, and were never subject to Darius.'

Except in sexual matters, the Greeks generally lauded Indian values, often unrealistically idealising them. 'It is against use and wont for Indians to give in a false report,' states Megasthenes, himself not reporting quite truthfully. 'Indeed, no Indian is accused of lying.' And Strabo has this to say about Indians: 'All Indians live a simple life ... and ... they behave in an orderly manner. But their greatest self-restraint pertains to theft; at any rate, Megasthenes says that when he was in the camp of Sandrocottus, although the number in camp was forty thousand, he on no day saw reports of stolen articles that were worth more than two hundred drachmae ... Further, they respect alike virtue and truth ...' This angelic characterisation of Indians is wholly contradicted by the evidence of the *Jatakas* and the *Arthasastra*, which speak of a people barely held in restraint by the rigour of law and the threat of punishment. The Greeks mythified the good as well as the bad in India.

The accounts of the Greeks are more reliable on value-neutral matters like food and dress. Megasthenes was impressed by the 'simplicity and frugality' of Indians, and he wrote: 'Indeed they do not drink wine, except at sacrifices, but drink a beverage which they make from rice instead of barley ... Their food consists for the most part of rice porridge.' Athenaeus, a Greek writer of the second-third century AD, writes: 'Megasthenes in the second book of his *Indica* says that when the Indians are at supper a table is placed before each person, this being like a tripod. There is placed upon it a golden bowl, into which they first put rice, boiled as one would boil barley, and then they add many dainties prepared according to Indian recipes.' The custom among Indians, according to Strabo, was 'of always eating alone and of not having one common hour for all for dinner and breakfast,' and this he disapproved, 'for eating in the other way is more conducive to a social and civic life.'

Most Indians were non-vegetarians. Strabo says that they 'partake of meats of animals that are of no help to man in his work, but abstain from pungent and seasoned food.' On the other hand, there were some primitive tribes in India, who, according to Herodotus, 'neither kill anything that has life, nor sow anything, nor are they wont to have houses, but they live upon herbs, and they have a grain the size of millet in a pod, which springs spontaneously from the earth, this they gather, and boil it and eat it with the pod.'

Some Indian tribes were shockingly barbaric according to Greek accounts. 'Other Indians,' states Herodotus, 'are nomads, and eat raw flesh; they are called Padaeans. They are said to have the following customs. When one of the community is sick, if he be a man, the men who are his nearest connections put him to death, alleging that if he is wasted by his disease his flesh would be spoilt. But if he denies that he is sick, they, not agreeing with him, kill and feast upon him. And if a woman be sick, in like manner the women who are most intimate with her do the same as the men. And whoever reaches to old age, they sacrifice and feast upon. But few among them attain to this state, for before that they put to death every one that falls into any distemper.'

Ancient Indians loved to bedeck themselves with ornaments. 'Contrary to their simplicity in general, they love finery and adornment,' Strabo remarks, but goes on to state that 'Indians (presumably the common folk) in general wear white clothing, white linen or cotton garments, contrary to accounts of those who say that they wear highly coloured garments.' Arrian also speaks of the preference of Indians for white clothes. 'The dress worn by the Indians,' he states, 'is made of cotton ... This cotton is either of a brighter white colour than any cotton found elsewhere, or the darkness of the Indian complexion makes their apparel look so much the whiter. They wear an undergarment of cotton which reaches below the knee halfway down to the ankles, and also an upper garment which they throw partly over their shoulders and partly twist in folds round their head. The Indian wears also earrings of ivory, but only such of them do this as are very wealthy ... Their beards, Nearchus tells us, they dye of one hue and another, according to taste. Some dye their white beards to make them look as white as possible, but others dye them blue; while some again prefer a red tint, some a purple, and others a rank green. Such Indians ... as are thought anything of, use parasols as a screen from the heat. They wear shoes made of white leather, and these are elaborately trimmed, while the soles are variegated, and made of great thickness, to make the wearer seem so much the taller.'

Men dyeing their beards 'with many most florid colours' was the custom in the kingdom of Sopeithes, says Strabo, but he goes on to quote Onesicritus to maintain that 'this practice is carefully followed by numerous other Indian peoples also (for the country produces marvellous colours ...) who dye both their hair and their garments ... The people though shabby in every other way, are fond of adornment.' Elsewhere he states that men 'all wear long hair and long beards, and they braid their hair and surround it with a head-band.' The ornaments of an affluent woman, according to Diodorus, 'consisted of a multitude of finger-rings, set with precious stones of diverse colours; upon her head there was no small number of little golden stars, between which were placed sparkling stones of all sorts; about her neck she wore many rows of jewels, some small, others large, and increasing in size gradually as they were placed on the string.'

Gambling was a common addiction of the people in Mauryan times, as in the Vedic age. Bull races were popular, and 'both the king himself and many of the greatest nobles take contending views of their swiftness, and make bets in gold and silver,' says Aelian. Affluent families took special pride in grandly celebrating family functions like marriages and births. For the common people, the celebratory occasions were fairs and festivals, at which, as the *Jatakas* tell, they wore flower garlands, drank liquor freely, and enjoyed themselves in the company of women. Acrobats, actors, bards, singers, conjurers, dancers, clowns, jugglers, musicians, prostitutes, reciters of Puranas, storytellers, minstrels and trumpeters were the common entertainers of the age, and are listed in the *Arthasastra*. Jugglers were common in Taxila, according to Apollonius; he mentions in particular one juggler who was 'so good a marksman, that he set up his own son against a board, and then threw his darts, so aiming that, fixed in the board, they traced out his son's outline.'

The position of women in Mauryan India varied from region to region, but was generally on the decline, though it was much better than in later periods. Brahmins, says Strabo, 'do not share their philosophy with their wives, lest they should divulge any of the forbidden mysteries to the profane if they become depraved, or lest they should desert them if they become good philosophers: for no one who despises pleasure and pain, as well as life and death, wishes to be in subjection to another ...' In the north-west, tribal women were warlike, and Diodorus reports that in one place they, 'taking the arms of the fallen, fought side by side with the men' against the Macedonian army. In some regions women ruled. 'The Pandaean nation is governed by females,' states Solinus.

Sati was practised among some communities at this time, especially among the Kshatriyas in the north-west. Kautilya does not mention sati, but Greek chroniclers do. Strabo quotes Aristobulus as stating that in the region of Taxila 'among certain tribes wives were glad to be burned up along with their deceased husbands, and that those who would not submit to it were held in disgrace.'

The earliest known graphic description of sati is in the chronicle of Diodorus. 'When Eumenes (a Greek general) was interring the slain (in a battle in Persia) with splendid obsequies, a marvellous thing occurred, of a nature quite contrary to what is customary among the Greeks. For Keteus, the commander of those who had come from India, was killed in the battle when fighting gloriously, and he left two wives who had accompanied him in the expedition, one lately married, while the other had been for a few years his helpmate, but both of them devotedly attached to him ...

'Although by the law only one was to be burned with the husband, yet at the funeral of Keteus each of his wives strove for the honour of dying with him, as if this were the noblest crown of virtue. When the matter was brought to the generals for decision, the younger wife represented that the other was pregnant and could not therefore take advantage of the law.

The elder pleaded that as she was before the other in years, she should be preferred before her in honour also, for in every other case it was the rule that more honour and respect should be accorded to the elder than to the younger. The generals being informed by the midwives that the older was with child, decided in favour of the younger; whereupon the one who lost her cause went away weeping and wailing, rent the veil from her head, and tore her hair as if some terrible news had been told her.

'The other, overjoyed at her victory, set forth for the funeral pile, crowned with mitres by the women of her house, and richly attired, as if she were going to some marriage festival, escorted by her kindred setting forth in songs the praises of her virtues. When she came near the pyre she stripped off her ornaments and distributed them to her servants and friends, bequeathing them, so to speak, as tokens of remembrance to those she loved ...

'At length she took farewell of her domestics, and was assisted by her brother to mount the pyre, and, to the great admiration of the people, who ran together to see the spectacle, she made her exit from life in heroic style. For the whole army under arms marched thrice round the pile before fire was set to it, and the victim, having meanwhile laid herself by her husband's side, scorned to demean herself by uttering shrieks, even when the flames were raging around her – a sight which affected the onlookers variously. Some were filled with pity, others were profuse in their praises, while there were not wanting Greeks who condemned the institution as barbarous and inhuman.'

The reason for sati, Diodorus was told, was the perversity of women. 'Now, it was an ancient law among the Indians that when young men and maidens were minded to wed, they did not marry according to the judgement of their parents, but by mutual consent,' writes Diodorus. 'But when in these old times espousals were made between persons of immature age, mistakes of judgement were of frequent occurrence, and when both sides repented their union, many of the women became depraved, and through incontinence fell in love with other men, and when at last they wished to leave the husbands they had first chosen, but could not in decency do so openly, they got rid of them by poison, a means of destroying life which they could readily procure in the country, which produces a great quantity and variety of drugs of fatal potency, some of which cause death if merely introduced as a powder into food or drink. But when this nefarious practice had become quite prevalent, and many lives had been sacrificed, and when it was found that the punishment of the guilty had no effect in deterring other wives from their career of iniquity, they passed a law ordaining that a wife, unless she were pregnant, or had already borne children, should be burned along with her deceased husband, and that if she did not choose to obey the law that she should remain a widow to the end of her life, and be for ever excommunicated from the sacrifices and other solemnities as being an impious person. When these laws had been enacted, it came to pass that women changed to the very opposite disposition ... [and] willingly submitted to the death ordained, rather than endure the excess of infamy which would attend its refusal ... They not only provided for the safety and welfare of their husbands in which their own were equally involved, but they contended with each other for this (sati) as the highest of all honours.' On this explanation of sati, Strabo comments: 'The law is not stated in a plausible manner, nor the cause of it either.'

No less dreadful than sati was the practice of infanticide among the dandies in the kingdom of Sopeithes, though the Greeks speak of it admiringly, probably because it was similar to Spartan customs. The people of this kingdom, according to Diodorus, placed the greatest value on physical beauty, and 'for this reason a discrimination between the children born to them is made at the stage of infancy, when those that are perfect in their limbs and features, and have constitutions which promise a combination of strength and beauty, are allowed to be reared, while those that have any bodily defect are condemned to be destroyed as not worth rearing. It follows that the inhabitants of these cities are generally held in higher estimation than the rest of their countrymen.' Adds Curtius: 'Here they do not acknowledge and rear children according to the will of the parents, but as the officers entrusted with the medical inspection of the infants may direct.'

MLECCHAS AND SAGES

The Greeks had a problem in India. They needed two sets of interpreters to talk to Indians – to translate Greek into Persian, then Persian into the local language, and back again. That made the discussion of abstract ideas virtually impossible.

This was Alexander's experience. He was keen to inquire into Indian thought, so when at Taxila he heard of the presence of some Indian sages at the outskirts of the city, he sent one of his top officers, Onesicritus, to summon them for a discussion. According to Strabo, Mandanis, the leader of the sages, declined the invitation, disregarding with scorn both the lure and the threat held out by the Greek. He wanted nothing from Alexander, and was not afraid of anything that Alexander would do to him. He could not, he said, in any case discuss philosophy by 'conversing through three interpreters, who ... knew no more than the masses ... For that, he added, would be like expecting water to flow pure through mud.'

Not surprisingly, there is very little information in the reports of Alexander's officers about the culture and religion of India, except for some stray curiosities. Megasthenes had a good opportunity to study Indian culture, but unfortunately much of what he wrote on the subject has been lost. There is no mention at all of the Vedas or the Upanishads in the extant Greek accounts. Buddhism and Jainism are alluded to only in passing.

Nor is there anything much in them on art and architecture, for in these fields India had nothing that could rouse the interestof the Greeks, nothing that was even remotely comparable to Greek achievements. There were no grand monuments in India, as wood was still being used almost exclusively for construction. The fortifications of Pataliputra were noted by Megasthenes, but they are of little artistic interest. The earliest surviving post-Harappan stone monuments and sculptures belong to the reign of Asoka, the period after the Greek reports on India were written. The skill of Indian craftsmen was however acknowledged by the Greeks. Diodorus writes that Indians were 'well skilled in the arts, as might be expected of men who inhale a pure air and drink the very finest water,' and Nearchus, quoted by Strabo, speaks of the 'skill of the Indians in handiwork.'

The Greeks held divergent views on the state of music in India. 'Writers say that India has no wine,' states Strabo, 'and therefore ... it also has no flutes, or any other musical instruments except cymbals and drums and castanets, which are possessed by the jugglers.' This obviously was not true, for music, song and dance were very much a part of everyday life in ancient India even from the days of the Indus Civilisation. The *Arthasastra* too indicates that Indians widely cultivated music. 'No nation is fonder of singing and dancing than the Indian,' remarks Arrian.

Strabo is also wrong in quoting Megasthenes as stating that Indians 'have no knowledge of written letters,' for the context of Megasthenes's statement makes it clear that he meant only that Indians had no written laws, which itself was not quite true. Megasthenes could not possibly have missed noticing the wide prevalence of writing in India and the innumerable records kept by the Mauryan government. Even Nearchus, during his brief passage through Punjab with Alexander, noted that Indians were familiar with writing, and stated that they 'write missives on linen cloth that is very closely woven.'

In Buddhist and early Magadhan times, Taxila was the greatest centre for higher education in India, and it was through this city that Persian influence filtered into India. It was only later, with the establishment of the Mauryan empire, that the centre of culture shifted to the Gangetic valley, with the migration of Taxilan intellectuals to Pataliputra. Jivaka, the renowned Magadhan court physician, had his education in Taxila, and so did Kautilya. And it was there too that Panini, one of the greatest linguists the world has known, wrote his Sanskrit grammar towards the close of the fourth century BC, at around the time of Alexander's invasion. Strangely, Alexander's chroniclers say nothing of the intellectual vibrancy of Taxila, though the emperor spent three leisurely days in the city. Apollonius is however said to have discussed philosophy with the king of Taxila.

There is very little data in the Greek accounts about scientific learning in India, except for some passing references to medical practice. 'By their knowledge of pharmacy they can make marriages fruitful, and determine the sex of the offspring,' says Strabo, quoting Megasthenes. 'They effect cures rather by regulating diet than by the use of medicines. The remedies most esteemed are ointments and plasters. All others they consider to be in a great measure pernicious in their nature.' Medicine in India had made substantial progress at this time under the rationalist influence of Buddhism, but it did not displace the old Atharva-vedic system of occult medicine, which continued to be popular. There were, Strabo writes, certain ascetics who 'wear deer skins and carry wallets full of roots and drugs, pretending to cure people with these, along with witchery and enchantments and amulets.' Physicians, he says, were esteemed in India next only to sophists.

Alexander is reported to have been greatly impressed by the skill of Indians in curing victims of snakebites, which killed a number of Greek soldiers. 'No cure for the bite of the Indian snake has been found out by any of the Greek physicians,' writes Arrian, 'though the Indians, it is certain, can cure those who have been bitten.' Strabo states that '[snake] charmers go around who are believed to cure the wounds [inflicted by snakes], and ... this is almost the only art of medicine [among Indians], for the people do not have many diseases on account of the simplicity of their diet and their abstinence from wine. But ... if diseases arise, they are cured by the Wise Men.'

Life was on the whole easy in India, as the Greeks saw it. They were therefore all the more surprised by the life-negating attitude of Indian religions. 'Though India is actually in the enjoyment of all ... blessings,' observes Dion Chrysostom, 'there are nevertheless men called Brachmans, who, bidding adieu to the rivers and turning away from those with whom they had been thrown into contact, live apart, absorbed in philosophic contemplation, subjecting their bodies to suffering of astonishing severity, though no one compels them, and submitting to terrible endurances. It is said, further, that they possess a remarkable fountain, that of truth, by far the best and most divine of all, and that any one who has once tasted it can never be satiated or filled with it.'

Indians were morbidly preoccupied with death, states Strabo on the authority of Megasthenes. 'Death is with them a very frequent subject of discourse,' he writes. 'They believe that life here is, as it were, that of an evolving babe still in the womb, and that death, to those who devote themselves to philosophy, is birth into the true life, that is, the happy life. On this account they undergo much discipline as a preparation for death. They consider nothing that befalls men to be either good or bad, and that to suppose otherwise is a dream-like illusion. If it were not so, how could it be that some are grieved and others delighted by the same thing, and that the same things affect the same individuals at different times with opposite emotions?' Bardaisan, a Syrian sage of the second century AD, says that Indians 'take such a view of death that they endure life unwillingly ... They weep [at funerals], but it is for themselves, because they must continue to live.'

Life being of little consequence, Indians treated death with casualness. 'Indians do not rear monuments to the dead, but consider the virtues which men have displayed in life, and the songs in which their praises are celebrated sufficient to preserve their memory after death,' says Arrian. 'Their funerals are simple and their mounds small,' adds Strabo.

Aristobulus states that in Taxila 'the dead are thrown out to be devoured by vultures.' Elsewhere, according to Herodotus, 'when any of them falls ill, he goes and lies down in the desert, and no one takes any thought about him, whether dead or sick.'

The Greeks have little to say about Indian gods. 'Indians worship Zeus and the Ganga river and the local deities,' is all that Strabo says on the subject. 'They regard as gods whatever objects they value, especially trees,' says Curtius. In Punjab, according to Aelian, Alexander came across a people who worshipped a snake kept in a cave. 'It was said to be seventy cubits long,' Aelian says. 'Its eyes ... are reported to have equalled the size of the large round Macedonian shield.'

There are no reports of the Greeks seeing any great temples in India, though an early third century AD work claims that Apollonius came across a stone temple of many columns in Taxila, around the sanctum of which 'were hung pictures on copper tablets, representing the feats of Alexander and Porus.' It is doubtful whether there were any temples in India at this time, for the oldest extant Hindu temples are only of the fourth century AD, though some small Vishnu and Shiva shrines of the third and second century BC have been identified. The importance of sacrifices in Hinduism was noted by the Greeks, but Strabo was surprised that no one burned incense or poured out libations or even wore garlands at such rituals. Another oddity from the Greek point of view was that in sacrificing animals, Indians did not cut the throat of the victim, but strangled it, 'in order that it may be given to the god in its entirety and not mutilated.'

Religious fairs and carnivals were popular in ancient India, with the king himself participating in them with great pomp. 'In the processions at the time of festivals,' Strabo writes, 'many elephants are paraded, all adorned with gold and silver, as also many four-horse chariots and ox-teams. Then follows the army, all in military uniform, and then golden vessels consisting of large basins and bowls a fathom in breadth; and tables, high chairs, drinking-cups, and bathtubs, all of which are made of Indian copper and most of them are set with precious stones ... and also variegated garments spangled with gold, and tame bison, leopards, and lions, and numbers of variegated and sweet-voiced birds.' Also in the procession were 'four-wheeled carriages on which large-leaved trees are carried ... [with] different kinds of tamed birds that cling to these trees.'

Yogis were to the Greeks, as to foreigners at all times, objects of curiosity in India. But the yogic feats that Alexander was shown were rather pedestrian. One of the yogis lay on his back and 'endured the sun's rays and the rains' for a whole day, reports Macedonian general Aristobulus. Another yogi 'stood on one leg holding aloft in both hands a log about three cubits in length, and when one leg tired he changed the support to the other and kept this up all day long.' Some 'ascetics who pursue wisdom go about naked,' says Dionysios, 'and, what is wonderful, look with eyes undazzled on the sun, and, while concentrating their vision on its rays, concentrate also their minds on the holy themes, and in its light grasp the meaning of the secret signs of what is to be.' The ascetics justified their nakedness saying that the body was unimportant, as it was only a 'covering for the soul.'

The earliest known reference to Indian heterodox sects by a foreigner was by Megasthenes. Strabo quotes him as stating that there were two kinds of Indian philosophers, 'one kind called Brachmanes (Brahmins) and the other Garmanes (Sramanas: ascetics) ... As for the Garmanes ... the most highly honoured are the Hylobii, who live in forests, subsisting on leaves and wild fruits, clothed in garments made from the bark of trees, and abstaining from wine and the delights of love.' The first Greek writer to mention Buddha was Clement of Alexandria in the second century AD, who stated: 'Among the Indians are ... philosophers ... who follow the precepts of Boutta, whom they honour as a god on account of his extraordinary sanctity.'

Buddhism in early Mauryan times was a minor sect. Brahmins dominated the religious life of the country, for they were, as Strabo enigmatically puts it, 'more in agreement in their dogmas.' But heterodox creeds were clearly beginning to gain prominence, and Strabo mentions a sect called 'the Pramnae (Pramanikas), a contentious and disputatious sect' who derided Brahmins as 'quacks and fools.'

Ascetics, to whichever sect they belonged, were generally honoured in India. 'The sophists have their abode in a grove in front of the city within a moderate-sized enclosure,' reports Strabo. 'They live in a simple style, and lie on beds of rushes or skins, abstaining from animal food and sexual pleasures, and spend their time in listening to serious discourses, and in imparting their knowledge to such as will listen to them. The hearer is not allowed to speak, or even cough, and much less to spit, and if he offends in any of these ways he is cast out from their society that very day, as being a man who is wanting in self-restraint.'

Aristobulus once saw two sophists in Taxila, one with his head shaven and the other with long hair, each with his own band of followers. 'When not otherwise engaged they spent their time in the marketplace,' Strabo quotes the general as stating, 'being honoured as counsellors and being authorised to take as gift any merchandise they wished. Anyone whom they accosted poured over them sesame oil, in such profusion that it flowed down over their eyes; and that since quantities of honey and sesame were put out for sale, they made cakes of it and subsisted free of charge.' Such ascetics had, according to Onesicritus, 'the whole of a wealthy home open to them, even to women's apartments, and ... [could] enter and share in meals and conversation.'

*

Discussions of Indian philosophy in Greek accounts are cursory. Megasthenes did not think much of Indian wisdom, though he acknowledged that there were some similarities between Indian and Greek religious thoughts. 'Their ideas about physical phenomena,' he maintained, 'are very crude ... inasmuch as their belief is in great measure based upon fables, though on many points their opinions coincide with those of the Greeks ... They wrap up their doctrines about immortality and future judgement and kindred topics in allegories, after the manner of Plato.' There was probably some cross-fertilisation in philosophy between India, West Asia and Greece, and some scholars hold that the formulations of Manicheanism, Gnosticism and, especially, Neoplatonism were influenced by Indian ideas. Clement of Alexandria, a disaffected Greek, even asserted that the Greeks 'stole their philosophy from barbarians.'

Clement cannot be taken seriously. But it has been persuasively argued that Pythagorean philosophy was fundamentally influenced by Indian concepts. 'The similarities between Pythagorean thought and that of the Upanishads, and between the organisation and ceremonial of the Pythagorean fraternity and the ancient ascetic orders of India are too close to be treated as chance coincidences or the results of parallel developments,' observes Sastri. It is unlikely that Pythagoras visited India, as some claim, but he would have got to know about Indian philosophy through Persia. Later, when the Indian cultural world expanded with the spread of Buddhism, there were plenty of opportunities for Indian concepts to seep into foreign philosophical systems. As Albiruni would write at the beginning of the second millennium AD, 'In former times, Khorasan, Persia, Iraq, Mosul and the country up to the frontier of Syria was Buddhistic.'

There is an amusing story told of an Indian sage meeting Socrates in Athens, and asking him what his philosophy was. When Socrates said that he was 'enquiring into the human condition,' the Indian is said to have mocked: 'How can a man enquire into the human condition when he is ignorant of the divine condition?' The story might be apocryphal, but the exchange was typical of the two divergent civilisations – Greek thinkers were mainly concerned with understanding the temporal world, but the preoccupation of Indian thinkers was with the transcendental world. A similar exchange is said to have taken place between Apollonius and an Indian ascetic. When the ascetic claimed that Indian sages knew all things, the Greek asked, 'But did the sages know themselves?' And the Indian answered, 'They knew all things, because they first knew themselves.'

The most detailed account of a Greek encounter with Indian sages is given by Onesicritus, a disciple of Diogenes, who was sent by Alexander to meet the sages who lived at the outskirts of Taxila. Writes Strabo: 'Onesicritus says that he himself was sent to converse with these sophists, for Alexander had heard that these people always went naked and devoted themselves to endurance, and that they were held in great honour, and that they did not visit other people when invited, but bade them to visit them if they wished to participate in anything they did or said; and that, therefore, such being the case, since to Alexander it did not seem fitting either to visit them or to force them against their will to do anything contrary to their ancestral customs, he himself was sent.'

The conversation of Onesicritus with the sophists was desultory. Mandanis, the leader of the ascetics, told Onesicritus that he could not possibly discuss philosophy through three interpreters. 'At all events, all he said, according to Onesicritus, tended to this, that the best teaching is that which removes pleasure and pain from the soul; and that pain and toil differ, for the former is inimical to man and the latter friendly ...' Plutarch in his account of the encounter however says that the Indian sage did not 'enter into any discourse with the Greek, but merely asked why Alexander had taken so long a journey.'

According to yet another version of the story, Onesicritus asked Dandamis (as the sage is called here) to visit Alexander, saying, 'If you comply, he will reward you with great and splendid gifts, but if you refuse he will cut off your head.' The sage was not impressed. 'Dandamis, with a complacent smile, heard him to the end, but did not so much as lift up his head from his couch of leaves, and while still retaining his recumbent attitude returned this scornful answer ... "What Alexander offers me, and the gifts he promises, are all things to me utterly useless. The things that I prize, and find of real use and worth, are these leaves which are my house, these blooming plants which supply me with dainty food, and the water which is my drink, while all other possessions and things, which are amassed with anxious care, are wont to prove ruinous to those who amass them, and cause only sorrow and vexation, with which every poor mortal is fully fraught.

' "As for me," continued the sage, "I lie upon the forest leaves, and having nothing which requires guarding, close my eyes in tranquil slumber; whereas had I gold to guard, that would banish sleep. The earth supplies me with everything, even as a mother her child with milk. I go wherever I please, and there are no cares with which I am forced to encumber myself, against my will. Should Alexander cut off my head, he cannot also destroy my soul. My ... soul will go away to its master, leaving the body like a torn garment upon the earth, whence also it was taken ... Let Alexander, then, terrify with these threats those who wish for gold and for wealth, and who dread death, for against us these weapons are both alike powerless ... Go, then, and tell Alexander this: 'Dandamis has no need of aught that is yours, and therefore will not go to you, but if you want anything from Dandamis come you to him.' " '

Dandamis (or Mandanis) was, in a sense, speaking as much for India as for himself. And his words adumbrated the future of India. India would not go to the world. The world had to go to her. And it did. In hordes, race after race, century after century. But they went to conquer, not to learn ancient wisdom at her feet.

INCIDENTAL DATA

CHAPTER ONE: THE GENESIS

The Indian plate pushing against Asia will one day, many million years in the future, stop pushing, say geologists. Then the Himalayas, along with the Tibetan plateau, will gradually subside, and the mountain and plateau will be plain again.

As the Indian plate slid across the ocean floor, a portion of the land broke off and drifted southward, and gradually sank under the sea, leaving only the island of Mauritius as its remnant.

The *Vishnu Purana* tells an allegorical story about the eastward diversion of the Yamuna: When Sesha in the guise of Baladeva was wandering in the forests, Varuna said to his wife: 'O Madira (Wine), that mighty hero Ananta will find you desirable and beneficent. Go in joy, pure woman, and make him happy.' Baladeva smelt wine, and drank up the river flowing from the hollow of a kadamba tree. 'When he was drunk and disoriented, covered with drops of perspiration that shone like pearls, he shouted to the river Yamuna, "Come over here! I want to take a bath!"' The river ignored the call. 'Crazed with drink, he grabbed her and dragged her after him with the edge of his plough, exclaiming, "You refused to come to me, wicked woman. Now escape if you can!" Hauled around by him, the river left her course.'

The Saraswati is today a small, thready river that dries up in Haryana, but it was once one of the greatest rivers of India. Scientists at BARC, Mumbai, have mapped the dry bed of the river using satellite imagery – the river had apparently flowed through the Jaisalmer district of Rajasthan into the Arabian Sea, through the now dry bed of the Ghagghar. The abandoned course of the river is marked by Harappan settlement sites.

Many of the old life forms in India died out in the evolutionary process – the outer Himalayas, for instance, have yielded fossils of twenty species of elephants, instead of the one surviving in India. At the same time, several new species entered the subcontinent from Asia. India today has about 45,000 species of plants, of which about 35 per cent are endemic. The Indian fauna consists of 75,000 species: 2,500 species of fish, 150 of amphibians, 450 of reptiles, 2,000 of birds, 850 of mammals, and the rest invertebrates.

Nearly half the classified skulls found in Mohenjo-daro are of Mediterraneans, a brown-complexioned, medium-statured, slender, long-headed people, who today constitute a major element in the Indian population. Three skulls are of the dark-skinned, flat-nosed, thick-lipped Proto-Australoid race; a few are of the round-headed, brown-complexioned, hairy Alpine type; and one of a Mongol.

The Great Bath complex in Mohenjo-daro measures about 55 metres by 33 metres, and at least a part of it once had an upper storey, as the vertical drains in its walls and a stairway in one of the rooms prove. The outer walls of the structure are over 2 metres thick, strong enough to bear the weight of an upper storey. The abundance of charcoal at the site indicates the extensive use of timber for its construction, presumably for the upper floor.

The granary in Mohenjo-daro, covering an area of about 1,045 square metres, is built on a base of 27 solid brick platforms arranged in three rows. The platforms are 1.5 metres high and are separated from each other by narrow ventilation channels for air circulation to keep the floor of the granary dry. There is a loading platform to one side of it. The granary was enlarged even while its construction was going on, and additional storage space was built into it later, as the city's power and prosperity grew.

In Harappa the granary consists of twelve warehouses built in two neat rows separated by a 7-metre-broad passage, and has a total floor space of about 840 square metres. Built on a 1.2-metre-high platform of rammed earth, riveted by a bank of baked bricks, 'the floors of individual granaries were carried clear of the ground on sleeper-walls, three to each unit,' notes Wheeler. 'The purpose of the sleepers ... was to provide intervening air-ducts to keep the overlying building dry and so to prevent sweating and mildew.' When the ground level rose and choked the air ducts, 'small projecting air-vents, conducting from a higher level, were added at their outer ends.'

CHAPTER TWO: VEDIC INDIA

In the Rig-veda, which has a total of 153,972 words, the term Arya occurs only about 33 times. Dasa occurs about 50 times; Dasyus about 70 times.

At the western end of the Aryan world, the Celts of the British Isles also would not commit their sacred literature to writing. Noted Julius Caesar: 'It is against the principles of the Druids to commit their doctrines to writing ... During their novitiate it is said that they learn by heart innumerable verses.'

The language of the Rig-veda is considered to be the closest known offshoot of the original Indo-European tongue, but even in it there are several borrowings from the Dravidian and Proto-Australoid languages of India. These external influences grew dramatically during the later Vedic period, between 1000 and 600 BC. 'Dravidian dialects,' observes Iyengar, 'affected profoundly the sounds, the structure, the idiom and the vocabulary' of the Aryan language, which in the process 'lost the subjunctive mood, many infinitive forms, and several noundeclensions, forgot its richly varied system of real verb tenses and adopted turns of expressions peculiar to the Dravidian idiom.' The hard retroflex sounds of Sanskrit, like *th* and *dh*, are said to be derived from the Dravidian language.

In northern India the use of palm leaves for writing was abandoned when paper was introduced in the thirteenth century AD, but in the south it continued to be used well into modern times.

Ravana was a Brahmin according to tradition; 'there actually is a Ravanin *gotra* in some Vasistha lists,' notes Kosambi.

Mughal chronicler Ferishta on the *Mahabharata*: 'Gracious God, what a marvellous and out-of-the-way story is this! In no history throughout the world, excepting in Hindustan, is such a circumstance to be found.'

The *Mahabharata* on Veda Vyasa: 'The sage with his matted hair was ugly, a skinny man of a most peculiar colour, and his odour was the very opposite of sweet-smelling; he was in all ways hard to take.'

An Atharva-vedic hymn on the earth:

Tranquil, fragrant, pleasant,
with sweet drink in her udder,
rich in milk, let earth bless me,
earth together with milk.

Fratricidal clashes were so common in ancient India that the word for cousins (*bhratrivyah*) came to mean enemies.

Apart from the Vikrama, Saka, Gupta, and Harsha Eras, there were several local eras in India, such as the Kalacuri Era of Central India, the Lakshmana Era of Bengal, the Laukika Era of Kashmir, the Lichchavi Era of Nepal, the Kollam Era of Kerala, and so on. In addition, major religions had their own eras, the Kaliyuga Era of Hindus, the Buddha Era of Buddhists, and the Mahavira Era of Jains, but these were used mostly for religious purposes, seldom to date political events, except in Sri Lanka, where the Buddha Era was used.

The chariot was probably a Sumerian invention, which Aryans adopted and transformed into a light, fast, fearsome war machine, by using two spoked wheels (instead of the four solid wheels of the Sumerian model) and yoking to it the horse (instead of the ass). The spoked wheels, shod with metal tyres, gave the chariot both speed and strength.

The Stream of Riches mantra of the Yajur-veda lists well over 130 different items that a man, in the eyes of the Veda, could possibly want in life. He craved, among very many other things, for 'wrath ... angry passion ... violence ... impetuosity,' strength, fame, energy, power, and greatness. 'May my truth and my faith, and my cattle and my wealth, and my goods and my pleasure, and my play and my enjoyment, and my children and my future children ... prosper by sacrifice,' the worshipper prays. '[May] my freedom from tuberculosis and my freedom from disease, and my life and my longevity, and my freedom from enemies and my freedom from danger, and my happiness and my lying down, and my fair dawn and my fair day prosper by sacrifice. May … my knowledge and my understanding, and my begetting and my propagation, and my plough and my harrow prosper by sacrifice …'

'May my vigour and pleasantness, and my milk and my sap, and my butter and my honey, and my meal in company and my drinking in company, and my ploughing and my husbandry … prosper by sacrifice,' he continues. 'May my rice-plants and my barley, and my beans and my sesame, and my kidney-beans and vetches, and my millet … and my wild rice, and my wheat and my lentils prosper by sacrifice. May my stone and clay, and my hills and my mountains, and my pebbles and my trees, and my gold and my bronze, and my copper and my iron, and my lead and my tin prosper by sacrifice. May my fire and my water, and my creepers and my plants … and my domestic animals and my wild animals … May my treasure and my dwelling, and my religious service and my ability to perform it … and my way and my going prosper by sacrifice …'

Kosambi: There is 'good reason to believe that the first Brahmins were the result of the interaction between the Aryan priesthood and the ritually superior priesthood of the Indus culture.'

The earliest reference to *upanayana*, the initiation ceremony, is in the Atharva-veda.

For the symbolic human sacrifice, altogether 170 human types are listed in the Yajur-veda as nominal sacrificial victims. The list, which is in effect a register of the constituents of Vedic society, includes: 'For priesthood, he binds a Brahmin to the stake; for royalty, a Kshatriya; for the Maruts, a Vaisya; for penance, a Sudra; for darkness, a robber; for hell, a homicide or a man who has lost his consecrated fire; for misfortune, a eunuch … for lust, a harlot; for excessive noise, a Magadha (professional bard) … for pastime, a timid man; for sport, a chatterer … for pleasure, a woman-lover … for firmness, a carpenter; for trouble, a potter's son … for beauty, a jeweller … for death, a hunter … for motives, one demented … for homestead, a paramour; for trouble, an unmarried elder brother … for garrulity, a by-sitter … for delight, a dwarf … for sleep, a blind man; for unrighteousness, a deaf man … for insight, an astrologer … for homicide, a slanderer … for passion, an iron-smelter … for virtue, a female ointment-maker … for Yama, a barren woman … for laughter, a jester; for lust, a woman with spotty skin … for fire, a fat man; for earth, a cripple; for wind, a Chandala; for mid-air, a pole-dancer; for sky, a bald man; for the sun, a green-eyed man; for stars, a spotty man; for the moon, a leper; for day, a white yellow-eyed man; for night, a black man with yellow eyes.'

Love-crazed, a woman cries out in the Atharva-veda:

Hanker thou after my body, my feet,
hanker after my eyes, my thighs!
The eyes of thee, as thou lustest after me,
and thy hair shall be parched with love!
I make thee cling to my arm,
cling to my heart,
so that thou shalt be in my power,
shalt come to my wish!

The *Satapatha Brahmana* specifies that the wife should lie on the left (or north) side of the husband.

The Rig-veda on women:

With women there can be
no lasting friendship:
hearts of hyenas
are the hearts of women.

In Vedic literature, there is only one passing statement, in the *Satapatha Brahmana*, against cow slaughter. But Yajnavalkya in the same Brahmana says about beef: 'I for one eat it, provided it is tender.' In the *Ramayana* and *Mahabharata* the cow's sacredness is fully established.

The *Satapatha Brahmana* offers a curious explanation of why man alone among animals wears clothes. Gods, says the text, flayed man and put on the cow his skin ('because the cow supports everything on earth') so the cow can endure rain and cold and heat. But man cannot, so he has to wear clothes; they are his skin. 'For this reason none but man wears a garment, it having been put on him as his skin. Hence also one should take care to be properly clad, so that he may be completely endued with his own skin.'

Atharva-veda's interpretation of dreams: 'Whoever, in a dream, has his head cut off or sees a bloody chariot will become a general or have a long life or get a lot of money. If his ear is cut off, he will have knowledge; if his hand is cut off, he will get a son; if his arms, wealth; if his chest or penis, supreme happiness ... If he dreams that his limbs are smeared with poison and blood, he will obtain pleasure; if his body is on fire, he will obtain the earth ... If, in a dream, a flat-nosed, dark, naked monk urinates, there will be rain; if one dreams that one gives birth to a female boar or female buffalo or female elephant or female bird, there will be abundance of food. If one dreams that his bed, chairs, houses, and cities fall into decay, that foretells prosperity.'

The *Prasana Upanishad* views dreams as the process of reviewing waking experiences.

Gold represents divine semen, according to the Brahmanas.

Most of the ordinary Vedic rites were performed at the domestic fire, but sometimes this benedictory fire itself would turn malevolent – into a 'flesh-eating fire,' as the Vedas speak of it – which then had to be purified to stave off adversity.

Keith on ancient Indian moral ambivalence: 'Varuna seizes the doer of evil, and therefore, since the evening is Varuna's time, one should then on no account utter falsehood. But, having spoken truth in the evening, it makes no difference how much falsehood one speaks thereafter ... Untruth and impurity can be washed away by water, or wiped away by application of the sacred Darbha grass.'

The difference between *Devas* and *Asuras*, as given in the *Satapatha Brahmana*: 'The gods and *Asuras*, both of them sprang from Prajapati, entered upon their father Prajapati's inheritance, to wit, speech – truth and untruth, both truth and untruth: they, both of them, spoke the truth, and they both spoke untruth, and, indeed, speaking alike, they were alike. Then the gods relinquished untruth, and held fast to truth, and the *Asuras* relinquished truth, and held fast to untruth ... The gods spoke nothing but truth, and the *Asuras* nothing but untruth. And the gods, speaking truth diligently, were very contemptible, and very poor; hence he who speaks the truth diligently, becomes very contemptible, and very poor; but in the end he assuredly prospers, for the gods indeed prospered.

'And the *Asuras*, speaking untruth diligently, throve even as salt soil, and were very prosperous: hence he who speaks untruth, thrives indeed, even as salt soil, and becomes very prosperous; but in the end he assuredly comes to naught, for the *Asuras* indeed came to naught.'

Snake worship began in the later Vedic period, when serpents became recognised as the guardians of the sacred fire.

CHAPTER THREE: THE AGE OF FERMENT

The opening lines of Book Five of the *Brihadaranyaka Upanishad*:

Om! Infinite beyond, infinite here.
Infinite from infinite does proceed.
From infinite take infinite away,
yet infinite remains.

'Om!', the mystic syllable, was, according to Keith, 'originally no more than a formal word of assent.'

The *Chandogya Upanishad*: 'Verily, if there were no Word, there would be knowledge neither of right and wrong, nor of truth and untruth, nor the pleasing and unpleasing.'

The *Brihadaranyaka Upanishad*: 'Whether asleep or awake, if one should spill his semen, he should touch it and say, "That semen of mine which has today spilled on the earth, or has flowed to plants or to water, I reclaim that semen. Let virility return to me, and energy and strength. Let the fire be put in its right place, on the fire altar." Having said this, he should take [the semen] with his thumb and fourth finger and rub it between his breasts or his eyebrows.'

Modern neuroscientists concur with the intuitive perception of ancient Indian sages that the world as we know it exists only in our consciousness. Thus Dr Rodolfo Llinas of New York University Medical School states: 'Light is nothing but electromagnetic radiation. Colours clearly don't exist outside our brains, nor does sound. Is there a sound if a tree drops in the forest and none hears it? No. Sound is the relationship between external vibration and the brain. If there is no brain, there can be no sound. Being awake or being conscious is nothing but a dreamlike state.'

The Upanishads spoke of the ultimate reality as *neyti, neyti!* – not this, not this! This is somewhat like what Robert Oppenheimer said of electrons: 'If we ask ... whether the position of the electron remains the same, we must say "no"; if we ask whether the electron's position changes with time, we must say "no"; if we ask whether the electron is at rest, we must say "no"; if we ask whether it is in motion, we must say "no".'

Yajnavalkya on the Atman-Brahman union: 'Just as a man closely embraced by his beloved wife, knows nothing that is external, nothing that is internal, so does the Self, when closely embraced by the Supreme Self [in deep sleep], know nothing that is external, nothing that is internal.'

Vishnu Purana has its own version of the modern concept of expanding and contracting universe: 'I have known the dreadful dissolution of the universe, I have seen all perish, again and again, at the end of the cycle. At that terrible time, every single atom dissolves into the primal, pure water of eternity, whence originally all arose.'

Stephen Hawking in *A Brief History of Time*: 'If the universe is really self-contained, having no boundary or edge, it would have neither beginning nor end: it would simply be. What place, then, for a creator?'

Where does the soul go on death, and how does it return to earth? The Upanishads have no logical answer to this, but turn to whimsy. According to their general view, all spirits first go to the moon, from where some go on to merge with Brahman, while others return to earth. The returning soul comes down through ether and reaches earth as rain, where it enters plants and becomes food for living beings; the food then turns into the father's seed, and finally reaches the mother's womb.

A poem attributed to the mythical sage Brihaspathi:

No heaven exists, no final liberation,
No soul, no other world ...
The triple Veda, triple self-command,

And all the dust and ashes of repentance –
These yield a means of livelihood for men
Devoid of intellect and manliness …
The costly rites enjoined for those who die
Are but a means of livelihood devised
By sacerdotal cunning, nothing more …
While life endures let life be spent in ease
And merriment; let a man borrow money
From all his friends, and feast on melted butter.

Sage Jabali to Rama in the *Ramayana*:

I weep for erring mortals who, on erring duty bent,
Sacrifice this dear enjoyment till their barren life is spent,
Who to gods and to the Fathers vainly still their offerings make …
There is no hereafter, Rama, vain the hope and creed of men;
Seek the pleasures of the present, spurn illusion poor and vain.

The lifestyles of all ascetics, irrespective of their religious affiliations, were essentially the same, differing only in minor details: while Brahmin ascetics wore matted hair and received only uncooked food as alms, Jain and Buddhist ascetics shaved their head and received only cooked food as alms.

Once when a disciple asked a question, Gosala replied: 'Play the lute, man, play the lute.'

According to the *Surtrakrtanga*, some ascetics held 'that there was no more sin in having intercourse with women than in squeezing a boil.'

The Digambara and Svetambara traditions vary about the details of Vardhamana's life. Digambaras deny that Mahavira was conceived in a Brahmin womb, hold that he took to asceticism when his parents were still alive, that he adopted nudity right from the beginning, and deny that he was ever a householder.

Mahavira: 'Man, thou art thy own friend; why wishest thou for a friend beyond thyself?'

Mahavira on the horrors of hell: among many other things, 'there cruel punishers tie their hands and feet, and with axes in their hands cut them like wooden planks. And they turn the writhing victims round, and stew them, like living fishes, in an iron cauldron filled with their own blood, their limbs covered with ordure, their heads smashed.'

Apart from its complex concepts about the cosmic processes, Jainism developed, perhaps under the influence of agnostics, a subtle system of dialectics called Syadvada, the 'maybe doctrine', which maintained that 'you can affirm the existence of a thing from one point of view, deny it from another; and affirm both existence and non-existence with reference to it at different times,' and so on. Here we enter the rarefied field of hyper-logic, where it is difficult for ordinary mortals to breathe.

The Digambara monks went about stark naked till Muslim rulers forced them to cover their genitals. The British also discouraged naked monks from appearing in public.

CHAPTER FOUR: GEM IN THE LOTUS

Buddha, according to the *Digha Nikaya*, had prophesied that at the time of the advent of Maitreya, the future Buddha, 'Jambudvipa (India) will be pervaded by mankind even as jungle is by reeds and rushes.'

Buddha on the futility of self-torture: 'If the mortification of the body here is religion, then the body's happiness is only irreligion; but by religion a man obtains happiness in the next world, therefore religion here bears irreligion as its fruit in the hereafter! Since it is only by the mind's authority that the body either acts or ceases to act, to control thought is alone befitting. Without thought the body is like a log ... Neither purity of food nor the waters of a sacred river can cleanse the heart. Water without doubt is only water. The true place of pilgrimage is the virtue of a virtuous man.'

Buddha on Brahmins: 'Not by birth is one a Brahmin, nor is one by birth a non-Brahmin ... but by effort, by religious living, by self-restraint and by temperance, by this is one a Brahmin.'

Indian sages loved to indulge in Catch-22-like riddles, like this one in *Milinda-pinha*:

'Nagasena, I have a question to ask you,' said the king.
'Pray ask it, sire.'
'I have asked it, your reverence.'
'That is answered already.'
'What have you answered?'
'To what, then, does your majesty refer?'

Nagasena in *Milinda-pinha* on transmigration: 'It is like milk, which when once taken from the cow, turns, after a lapse of time, first to curds, and then from curds to butter, and then from butter to ghee. Now would it be right to say that the milk was the same thing as the curds, or the butter or the ghee?'

'Certainly not; but they are produced of it.'

'Just so, O king, is the continuity of person or thing maintained. One comes into being, another passes away; and the rebirth is, as it were, simultaneous. Thus neither as the same nor as another does a man go on to the last phase of self-consciousness.'

Buddha on subject-object relationship: Subject and object are dependent on each other for their existence, Buddha maintained, virtually paraphrasing the

Upanishads. 'Where consciousness is, there also is mind-body: mind-and-body is conditioned by consciousness ... [And] where mind-body is, there is consciousness: conditioned by mind-body is consciousness,' contended Buddha. 'By the cessation of mind-body [comes] the cessation of consciousness. By the cessation of consciousness [comes] the cessation of mind-body.' On another occasion Buddha elaborated the concept thus: 'Now, brethren, consciousness arises in dependence on a condition, and is reckoned just according to that condition. Thus dependent on eye and object arise ... eye consciousness. And so on with ear, nose, tongue, body tangibles, and mind consciousness, which arises conditioned by mind and ideas.' Keith clarifies: 'Through the eye and visible form arises visual consciousness: the collision of the two factors is contact: conditioned by contact arises feeling: what one feels one perceives ...'

Feeling is the determining factor here. As Asvaghosha would later explain, 'A sense-organ, although it may have begun to react to a sense-object, does not get caught up in it unless the mind conceives imaginary ideas about the object. Both fuel and air must be present for a fire to blaze up ... The sight of one and the same object may attract one person, repel another, and leave a third indifferent; a fourth may be moved to withdraw gently from it. Hence the sense-object itself is not the decisive cause of [attachment] ... It is the presence or absence of imagination which determines whether attachment takes place or not.'

The oldest Buddhist scriptures do not state that Buddha attained enlightenment under a tree, but it is quite probable that it indeed happened under a tree, for meditation in his time was usually done under trees. And it could very well have been a pipal tree under which he sat, for the pipal was already considered a sacred tree, so Buddha would have chosen it. He considered it especially fruitful to meditate under trees, and would often tell his disciples, 'Here are trees; think this matter out!' Trees were important in Buddha's life – his birth and enlightenment were under trees, and so was his death.

Cunningham on the condition of the pipal tree at Bodh Gaya in the late nineteenth century: 'The celebrated Bodhi tree still exists, but is very much decayed; one large stem, with three branches to the westward, is still green, but the other branches are barkless and rotten. The tree must have been renewed frequently as the present pipal is standing on a terrace at least 30 feet above the level of the surrounding country.'

Freud considered Buddha the greatest psychologist of all time.

Kosambi on the relationship between Buddhism and Hinduism: 'There is no point in arguing whether they (Buddhism and Jainism) were Hindu or not; Hinduism came into existence, with the indelible stamp of these sects, only when they had faded many centuries later.'

The Buddhist canon was first written down in Sri Lanka in the first century BC, at the order of king Vattagamani. It was revised by Buddhaghosha, an Indian monk of the fourth-fifth century AD. The language used was Pali, an

Indian dialect, which became the canonical language of Buddhists in Sri Lanka, Myanmar, Thailand, Cambodia and Laos.

Buddha in *Dhammapada*: 'Whosoever is free from merriment, for him there is no sorrow.'

The *Jatakas*: 'Sorrow must be told to him that is able to take it away, and to no other.'

Asvaghosha on relatives: 'Relatives are no more closely united than travellers who for a while meet at an inn, and then part again, losing sight of each other. This world is by nature split up into disjointed parts; no one really belongs to anyone else; it is held together by cause and effect, as loose sand by a clenched fist.'

Buddha, according to the *Mahavagga*, gained insight into the process of causation soon after his enlightenment. 'At that time the blessed Buddha dwelt at Uruvela, on the bank of the river Niranjana, at the foot of the Bodhi tree, just after he had become Sambuddha,' records the *Mahavagga*. 'And the blessed Buddha sat cross-legged at the foot of the Bodhi tree uninterruptedly during seven days, enjoying the bliss of emancipation. Then the Blessed One [at the end of these seven days] during the first watch of the night fixed his mind upon the Chain of Causation, in direct and reverse order. From ignorance spring *samkharas* (formulations), from the *samkharas* spring consciousness, from consciousness spring name-and-form, from name-and-form spring the six provinces (of the six senses, including mind), from the six provinces spring contact, from contact springs sensation, from sensation springs thirst (or desire), from thirst springs attachment, from attachment springs existence, from existence springs birth, from birth springs old age and death, grief, lamentation, suffering, dejection and despair. Such is the origination of this mass of suffering. Again, by the destruction of ignorance, which consists of the complete absence of desire, the *samkharas* are destroyed, by the destruction of the *samkharas* consciousness is destroyed, by the destruction of consciousness name-and-form are destroyed, by the destruction of name-and-form the six provinces are destroyed, by the destruction of the six provinces contact is destroyed, by the destruction of contact sensation is destroyed, by the destruction of sensation thirst is destroyed, by the destruction of thirst attachment is destroyed, by the destruction of attachment existence is destroyed, by the destruction of existence birth is destroyed, and by the destruction of birth are destroyed old age and death, grief, lamentation, suffering, dejection and despair. Such is the cessation of this whole mass of suffering.'

The *Mahaparinibbana Sutta* describes Buddha's death in psychic terms, as a process of deepening trance, in which mental functions were gradually brought to quiescence, then quickened again, before being finally stilled. 'Then the Blessed One entered into the first stage of deep meditation,' states the *Sutta*. 'And rising out of the first stage, he passed into the second. And rising out of the second, he passed into the third. And rising out of the third stage, he passed into the fourth. And rising out of the fourth stage of deep meditation, he entered into the state of mind to which the infinity of space alone is present. And passing out of the mere consciousness of the infinity of space, he entered into the state of mind to which nothing at all was especially present. And passing out of the consciousness of no special object, he fell into a state between consciousness and unconsciousness. And passing out of the state between consciousness and unconsciousness, he fell into a state in which the consciousness both of sensations and of ideas had wholly passed away.

'Then the venerable Ananda said to the venerable Anuruddha: "O my Lord, O Anuruddha, the Blessed One is dead!"

'And Anuruddha said, "Nay! brother Ananda, the Blessed one is not dead. He has entered into that state in which both sensation and ideas have ceased to be!"'

Buddha then, says the text, reversed the whole psychic process, and returned, step by step, to the first stage of deep meditation. And then again, without a pause, he advanced step by step to the fourth and last stage of deep mediation, 'and passing out of the last stage of deep meditation, he immediately expired.'

Offences requiring disciplinary action listed in the *Patimokkha*: There are four grave offences, which entailed expulsion from the sangha: sexual intercourse, theft, murder, and exaggerating one's spiritual powers. These are followed by thirteen offences to be punished with suspension. These included offences like levelling serious false charges against a fellow monk and trying to create divisions among monks, but nearly half of the offences in this group are sexual transgressions, such as 'holding a woman's hand or arm, touching her hair or any other part of her body, above or below, or rubbing or caressing it,' or telling a woman that it 'is a supreme service or gift ... to offer intercourse to monks like us.' Then there are some thirty-odd violations – accepting gold and silver, engaging in any kind of buying or selling, and so on – which are punished in various ways but generally by damning the offending monk to a degraded birth in the next life. Similar is the punishment for the next lot of ninety offences, which include 'preaching dharma in more than five or six words to a woman,' disclosing a monk's offence to outsiders, 'destroying any kind of vegetation; sitting alone with a woman in the open ... looking at an army drawn up in battle-array,' not discolouring one's new robes, 'drinking alcoholic beverages; having a chair or bed made with legs higher than eight inches.' Finally, there are 'four offences requiring confession, 113 rules of decorum, seven rules for the settling of disputes.'

CHAPTER FIVE: THE FIRST EMPIRE

According to Tibetan tradition, there was a law among the Lichchavis of Vaishali that the most beautiful woman among them (like Ambapali) should not marry, but become a courtesan, to be honoured as the wife of the whole republic. This honour was conferred at the annual meeting of the tribal assembly.

Alexander, according to Plutarch, once asked an Indian gymnosophist: 'Which existed first, the day or the night?'

The man answered: 'The day was the first by one day.'

Alexander was puzzled by the answer, so the man explained: 'Impossible questions require impossible answers.'

The rise of Magadha roughly paralleled the rise of the Achaemenid empire in Persia. Cyrus, the founder of the Persian dynasty, and Bimbisara were contemporaries, and the Magadhan monarch could not but have been aware of the Persian developments, as he was in friendly contact with the king of Gandhara (Kandahar), the immediate neighbour of Persia.

It is claimed that Mores (of Maharashtra) are descendants of the Mauryas.

CHAPTER SIX: THE FORGOTTEN EMPEROR

Scholars have calculated that the solar eclipse that prompted Asoka to undertake his extensive pilgrimages took place on 4 May 249 BC.

The earliest extant stone structures of India are the ramparts of the sixth-century BC Magadhan fort of Rajagriha. But these are just piled up stones of no architectural value.

The tradition of setting up monumental pillars, as royal symbols or as cult objects, was an ancient practice in India. Asoka states in an inscription that he ordered his edicts to be engraved also on existing stone pillars.

The first foreigner to describe the Asokan pillars was Fa Hsien in the fifth century AD.

CHAPTER SEVEN: THE CLOCKWORK STATE

Karl Marx: 'There have been in Asia, generally, from immemorial times but three departments of government: that of finance, or the plunder of the interior; that of war, or the plunder of the exterior; and finally, the department of public works.'

Hellenistic kingdoms held that 'the state was the house of the king, and its territory his estate.' The Mauryas were influenced by this precept.

Kautilya on the use of ascetics as secret agents: 'He shall pretend to practise austerities by eating very sparingly in public, just a handful of barley every month or two; he may eat secretly as much as he likes. [He shall then establish his reputation with the help of other secret agents] ... Secret agents and other clandestine operators shall make his predictions come true.'

Spies are mentioned even in the Rig-veda:

> *Send thy spies forward, fleetest in their motion.*
> *Be not deceived by him who, near or far, is bent on evil.*

Charles Metcalfe on Indian villages in the mid-nineteenth century: 'The Indian village communities are little republics, having nearly everything they can want within themselves, and almost independent of any foreign relations. They seem to last where nothing else lasts. Dynasty after dynasty tumbles down; revolution succeeds to revolution … but the village community remains the same.' This was how it was in ancient India also.

No detail missed Kautilya's attention. On the preparation of seeds for planting he advised: 'Cereals to be soaked in dew by night and dried in the sun by day for seven days and nights … root-crops to be smeared with ghee and honey, cotton seeds to be smeared with cow dung, trees to be planted in a pit in which grass, leaves etc. are burnt and then manured with bones and cow dung at the right time.'

Kautilya on the stratagems to misappropriate temple property: 'Agents appointed by the state shall first take away the property of temples … They shall then pretend that the property was lost … The chief superintendent of temples shall collect together the wealth of temples in the city and in the countryside. Then, [using a similar pretext] the property shall be taken away to the treasury.'

Kautilya: 'The frustration of a woman's fertile period is a violation of sacred duty.'

Kautilya: 'Any girl who deflowers herself shall become the king's slave.'

Some Kautilyan punishments:

Fine for the failure to save one from drowning or being attacked by a wild animal: 12 panas.

For selling human flesh: capital punishment.

Fine for the gang rape of a prostitute: 24 panas for each offender.

Defamation: highest fine for a sarcastic defamation and the lowest for a true one.

Theft: first offence: cutting off thumb and forefinger of the right hand or a fine of 54 panas; second offence: cutting off all four fingers of the right hand or a fine of 100 panas; third offence: cutting off the right hand or a fine of 400 panas; fourth offence: death. The theft of any royal property was punished with death.

Punishment for treasonable activities: burning alive.

Brahmins were not punished with mutilation or death; the highest punishment was to brand and exile them or to send them to work in mines. 'The guilt of a Brahmin shall be displayed publicly and permanently so that he may be excluded from all activities of Brahmins,' decreed Kautilya. Different brands were used for different crimes. For theft, the brand was the figure of a dog; for drinking alcohol, the vintner's flag; for murder, a headless torso; for rape of the teacher's wife, the female sexual organ.

Punishment for medical malpractice: if a patient lost a limb by a wrong operation, the same limb of the surgeon was to be amputated.

Kautilya on astrology: 'Wealth will slip away from that childish man who constantly consults the stars.'

Silver, not gold, was the standard metal in Mauryan India.

Book 14 of the *Arthasastra* deals with secret or occult measures, such as:

To prepare poisons: Make a powder of the carcasses of, among other things, frog, centipede, crab, lizard, blind snake, partridge, stinking insect and various specified herbs – 'the smoke caused by burning the above powders causes instantaneous death.'

'When the body of a man is smeared over with the serum of the flesh of a frog, it burns with fire (with no hurt).'

'Having pulled both the right and the left eyeballs of a cat, camel, wolf, boar, porcupine, vaguli (?), naptr (?), crow and owl, or of any one, two or three, or of any such animals as roam at night, one should reduce them to two kinds of powder. Whoever anoints his own right eye with the powder of the left eyeball, and the left eye with the powder of the right eyeball, can clearly see things in pitch dark at night.'

'Having fasted for three nights and having afterwards pulled out on the day of the star Pushya both the right and the left eyes of a dog, a cat, an owl, and a vaguli (?), one should reduce them to two kinds of powder. Then, having anointed one's own eyes with this ointment as usual, one can walk invisible to others.'

Preparations for causing blindness or madness, for going without food for a month, for turning hair white, for turning the body black, preparation of an ointment for smearing on feet to enable a man to walk 100 yojanas without fatigue, the means to make a vessel that would give an inexhaustible supply of food, and so on are also given in this book.

To avoid property disputes, the *Arthasastra* laid down precise procedures for selling immovable property. For the sale of houses, the regulation was that 'the owner selling a house shall proclaim its sale in front of the property and in the presence of representatives from among the [forty] neighbouring families. An owner selling a field, garden, an embankment, a tank or a reservoir shall proclaim the sale at the boundary of the property and in the presence of the elders of the neighbouring village.' Kautilya further specified that 'the owner shall name his price and ask three times: "Who is willing to buy at this price?" If, during this time, no one has challenged [the owner's right to sell the property], prospective buyers may make their bids ... If there is a competition among buyers and a higher price is realised, the difference between the call price and the sale price along with any tax payable shall go to the treasury. The tax [due on the transaction] shall be paid by the successful bidder. If the successful bidder fails to [pay and] take possession [of the property] within seven days, the owner shall be free to offer it for sale again.'

In the Mauryan age, the hub of India's overland foreign trade was Taxila, from where trade caravans proceeded west to Central Asia and east to Pataliputra.

Other trade routes passed through Ujjain to southern India, and down the Ganga to the east coast. Apart from this land trade, sea trade grew in importance at this time. Within the subcontinent itself, Asoka's conquest of Kalinga eliminated a possible impediment to the Mauryan domination of the eastern coastal trade. It is possible, as Kosambi conjectures, that Indians at this time traded with Myanmar and Indonesia, but their major sea trade was with West Asia. There were two sea routes to India from the West: along the Persian and Baluchi coasts to Sind and Gujarat, and (after the discovery of trade winds in the first century AD) across the Indian Ocean to Kerala. Buddhist texts speak of traders going on sea voyages lasting as long as six months, and there is a story in the *Jatakas* of a hundred merchants gathering to buy the cargo of a newly arrived ship.

Agricultural levies recommended in the *Arthasastra*: From the *rashtra* villages the state collected revenue under ten different heads: a village levy as a collective tax, the sixth portion of the agricultural produce, a military tax (in lieu of compulsory military service), *bali* (sacrifice tax, collected customarily, whether sacrifices were performed or not), the state's share of fruits and other perennial produce, an annual cash tax, gifts to the king on special occasions, a supplementary tax, damage tax (to compensate the loss to crops by straying cattle), and a special tax on lands irrigated by state tanks.

Kautilyan state revenue came from three major sources: from state farming and business operations, taxes, and miscellaneous income. These broad categories might be further divided into various revenue heads: agricultural tax, as a share of the produce of the land; irrigation charges and other dues collected from farmers; revenue from pastures, forests and crown lands; revenue from state-owned mines, factories and state-run trade; taxes on crafts and trade, such as customs, licence fees and octroi; taxes on professions; road and ferry tolls; treasure-troves and escheat; urban taxes such as house tax; fines imposed by law courts – a major revenue source, for the list of fines in the *Arthasastra* is long – presents received by the king on celebratory occasions, such as the birth of a son, and finally, miscellaneous incomes.

CHAPTER EIGHT: THE NEVER-NEVER LAND

The gold-digging ants mentioned by Herodotus ('bigger than a fox, though not so big as a dog') could be marmots, a species of burrowing squirrel, with thick bodies and bushy fur, found in the inaccessible regions of the Himalayas along the upper Indus. They bring up gold-bearing soil from deep underground, and from that the native people in the high plateau have for generations collected gold dust, according to modern explorers.

Pliny quotes Megasthenes to state that there were people in India 'who live merely by breathing, and the perfume inhaled by their nostrils. They eat nothing, and they drink nothing. They require merely a variety of odours of roots and flowers and of wild apples. They carry apples with them when they go on a distant journey, and they always have something to smell. Too strong an odour would readily kill them.'

Credit facilities, an essential prerequisite of trade, were well organised in Mauryan India, and Kautilya laid down rules to govern these transactions. The Greeks were entirely wrong in maintaining that Indians neither lent nor borrowed, and that, as Aelian claimed, 'It is contrary to established usage for an Indian either to do or suffer wrong, and therefore they neither make contracts nor require securities.' Nicolaus Damascenus was equally wrong in stating that 'among the Indians one who is unable to recover a loan or a deposit has no remedy at law. All the creditor can do is to blame himself for trusting a rogue.'

The ideal of female beauty given in the *Jatakas*:

Fragrant as golden sandal-wood, in brightness like the sun,
A slim and winsome maid art thou, right fair to look upon.
So soft and pure, with slender waist, and firmly springing gait,
Thy movements are so full of grace, my heart they captivate.
Thy thighs, like trunk of elephant, are finely tapering found,
Thy buttocks soft to touch and like my dice-board round ...
Twin milky breasts, like pumpkins halved, their swelling globes display,
Firm set, although without a stalk all unsupported they.
Thy lips are red as thy tongue, and, O auspicious sign,
Thy neck, long as the antelope's, is marked with triple line ...
Thy eyes are long and large of shape, a lovely sight to view,
Like gunja berries black, marked out with lines of reddish hue.
Thy tresses smooth, not over-long and bound in neatest coil,
Are tipped with gold and perfumed with the finest sandal oil ...

NOTES

For primary sources in Pali and Sanskrit, I have used several standard English translations, sometimes conflating them for clarity. For the *Arthasastra* I have mainly depended on L.N. Rangarajan's modern translation.

In several places, the spellings of names and terms in quotations have been modified to conform to the general usage in the book. I have generally (but not always) used the Sanskrit version of Pali names and terms.

Where sources differ in detail, I have melded data from different sources to tell a coherent story, for instance, about the life of Buddha. In a few instances, I have patched together Buddha's sayings from different texts.

For the description of everyday life in Vedic India, especially of marriage and funeral customs, I am indebted to Srinivasa Iyengar's meticulous cataloguing of the information in the Vedas.

Chapter Eight: This is not a description of post-Vedic Indian society. Society was in transition at this time, and the texts that describe the social conditions of ancient India are of uncertain dates. I am therefore leaving it to my next book to examine Indian society as it crystallised during the Gupta period. All that is attempted in this chapter is to collate the fragmentary, disjointed and often contradictory information in ancient Greek and Roman sources.

The title 'Gem in The Lotus' is not used in its Tantric sense, but only as a metaphor, to suggest the seeding of Indian civilisation.

Throughout this book the term India refers to the Indian subcontinent.

The sources of nearly all quotations are given in the text itself. Readers requiring clarifications are welcome to contact the author at eraly@vsnl.com.

BIBLIOGRAPHY

Allchin, F.R. (Ed.): *The Archaeology of Early Historic South Asia* (Cambridge, 1995)

Allchin, Raymond and Bridget: *The Birth of Indian Civilisation* (1968/Delhi, 1993)

Allchin, Raymond and Bridget: *Origins of a Civilisation* (Delhi, 1997)

Altekar, A.S.: *Education in Ancient India* (Benares, 1944)

Altekar, A.S.: *The Position of Women in Hindu Civilisation* (1938/Delhi, 1959)

Altekar, A.S.: *State and Government in Ancient India* (Benares, 1949)

Apte, Usha M.: *The Sacrament of Marriage in Hindu Society* (Delhi, 1978)

Asvaghosha (Tr.: T. Suzuki): *Awakening of Faith* (Chicago, 1900)

Asvaghosha (Tr.: E.B. Colwell): *Buddha-carita* (Buddhist Mahayana Texts Part I) (Oxford, 1894/Delhi, 1965)

Atre, Shubhangana: *The Archetypal Mother: A Systemic Approach to Harappan Religion* (Pune, 1987)

Balasubramanian, D: 'On the Origins of Indians' (*The Hindu*, March 14, 1996)

Barnett, L.D.: *Antiquities of India* (Calcutta, 1964)

Basham, A.L.: *History and Doctrines of the Ajivikas* (1951/Delhi, 1981)

Basham, A.L.: *The Origins and Development of Classical Hinduism* (1989/Delhi, 1992)

Basham, A.L.: *The Wonder that Was India* (New York, 1954)

Beal, Samuel (Tr.): *Buddhist Records of the Western World by Si-yu-ki* (London, 1884/Delhi, 1981)

Beal, Samuel (Tr.): *The Life of Hiuen-Tsiang by the Shaman Hwui Li* (London, 1911)

Bhadrabahu (Tr.: K.S. Lalwani): *Kalpa-sutra* (Delhi, 1979)

Bloomfield, Maurice (Tr.): *The Hymns of the Atharva Veda* (1897/Delhi, 1967)

Bloomfield, Maurice: *The Religion of the Veda* (New York, 1908)

Buitenen, J.A.B. van (Tr.): *The Mahabharata* (Chicago, 1973)

Burtt, E.A.: *The Teachings of the Compassionate Buddha* (New York, 1955)

Capra, F.: *The Tao of Physics* (Berkeley, 1975)

Cavalli-Sforza, Luigi Luca: 'Genes, Peoples and Languages' (*Scientific American*, November, 1991)

Chakravarti, P.C.: *The Art of War in Ancient India* (1941/Delhi, 1993)

Chand, Bool: *Lord Mahavira* (Benares, 1948)

Chattopadhyaya, Debiprasad: *Science and Society in Ancient India* (Calcutta, 1977/1979)
Childe, Gordon: *The Aryans* (London, 1926)
Childe, Gordon: *New Light on the Most Ancient East* (London, 1952)
Clayton, A.C.: *The Rigveda and Vedic Religion* (New Delhi, 1913/1981)
Colwell, E.B. (Tr.): *The Jataka*: 6 vols. (1895–1907/Delhi, 1993)
Conze, Edward (Tr.): *Buddhist Scriptures* (London, 1959/1966)
Conze, Edward: *A Short History of Buddhism* (London, 1980/1986)
Coomaraswamy, Ananda: *Buddha and the Gospel of Buddhism* (New York, 1916/1964)
Cunningham, A.: *The Ancient Geography of India* (Calcutta, 1924)
Das, Swaswati: *Social Life in Ancient India* (New Delhi, 1994)
Davids, T.W. Rhys: *Buddhist India* (London, 1903/Delhi, 1993)
Davids, T.W. Rhys (Tr.): *Buddhist Suttas* (SBE Vol. XI) (Oxford, 1900)
Davids, T.W. Rhys (Tr.): *Dialogues of The Buddha*, 2 Vols. (London, 1899/1977)
Davids, T.W. Rhys (Tr.): *The Questions of King Milanda Part I & II* (New York, 1894/1963)
Davids, T.W. Rhys and Hermann Oldenberg (Tr.): *Vinaya Texts*: 2 Vols. (Oxford, 1881, 1882/Delhi, 1965)
Davids, Mrs Rhys (Tr.): *Poems of Cloister and Jungle* (London, 1941)
Day, Nundo Lal: *The Geographical Dictionary of Ancient and Mediaeval India* (New Delhi, 1927/1994)
De, Sushil Kumar: *Ancient Indian Erotics and Erotic Literature* (Calcutta, 1959)
de Bary, Theodore (Ed.): *Sources of Indian Tradition* (London, 1958)
Dhammapada (Bombay, 1957/1965)
Dimmitt, Cornelia and J.A.B. van Buitenen (Tr.): *Classical Hindu Mythology: A Reader in the Sanskrit Puranas* (Philadelphia, 1978/Delhi, 1983)
Durant, Will: *The Life of Greece* (New York, 1939)
Durant, Will: *Our Oriental Heritage* (New York, 1954)
Dutt, Romesh C.: *Civilisation in the Buddhist Age* (1908/Delhi, 1993)
Easwaran, Eknath (Tr.): *The Dhammapada* (1986/Delhi, 1996)
Eggeling, Julius (Tr.): *Satapatha Brahmana* (SBE 12, 24, 41, 43) (Oxford, 1882/1897)
Embree, Ainslie T. (Ed.): *Sources of Indian Tradition* (Delhi, 1992)
Ferishta: *Tarikh-I-Ferishta*: (Elliot & Dowson: Vol. VI) (1867–1877/Delhi, 1990)
Fick, Richard: *The Social Organisation in North-east India in Buddha's Time* (Tr.: Shishirkumar Maitra) (Varanasi, 1920/1972)
Garrett, John: *A Classical Dictionary of India* (1871/Delhi, 1990)
Gazetteer of India (Delhi, 1965/1973)
Goldman, Robert P. (Ed. & Tr.): *The Ramayana of Valmiki* (Princeton, 1984)
Griffith, T.H. Ralph (Tr.): *The Hymns of the Rigveda* (1889/New Delhi, 1973)
Griffith, T.H. Ralph (Tr.): *The Sama-veda Samhita* (1893/Nag Publishers, 1991)
Griffith, T.H. Ralph (Tr.): *The White Yajurveda* (Benares, 1899)
Griffith, T.H. Ralph (Tr.): *The Hymns of the Atharvaveda* (1894/Varanasi, 1968)
Guha, B.S.: *Outline of the Racial History of India* (Calcutta, 1937)

Herodotus (Tr. Henry Cary): *History* (London, 1879)
History and Culture of The Indian People: Vol. I: *The Vedic Age*; Vol. II: *The Age of Imperial Unity* (Bharatiya Vidya Bhavan, Bombay, 1951/1988)
Iyengar, P.T. Srinivasa: *Life in Ancient India in the Age of the Mantras* (Madras, 1912)
Jacobi, Hermann (Tr.): *Jaina Sutras*, 2 vols (New York, 1884/1968)
Kalupahana, David J. (Tr.): *Mulamadhyamakakarika of Nagarjuna* (New Delhi, 1986/1991)
Kangle, R.P. (Tr.): *The Kautilya Arthasastra* (Bombay, 1965)
Karttunen, Klaus: *India and the Hellenistic World* (Helsinki, 1977)
Karve, Irawati: *Hindu Society, an Interpretation* (California, 1959–60)
Keith, Arthur Berriedale: *History of Sanskrit Literature* (Oxford, 1928)
Keith, Arthur Berriedale: *The Religion and Philosophy of the Veda and Upanishads* (Harvard, 1925/Delhi, 1970)
Keith, Arthur Berriedale (Tr.): *Rigveda Brahmanas: The Aitareya and Kausitaki Brahmanas* (Harvard, 1920)
Khosala, Sarala: *Lalitavistara and the Evolution of Buddha Legend* (New Delhi, 1991)
Konow, Sten and Paul Tuxen: *Religions of India* (Copenhagen, 1949)
Kosambi, D.D.: *The Culture and Civilisation of Ancient India in Outline* (Delhi, 1970/1976)
Kosambi, D.D.: *An Introduction to the Study of Indian History* (Bombay, 1956)
Law, Bimla Churn: *India as Described in Early Texts of Buddhism and Jainism* (Delhi, 1980)
Leslie, Charles (Ed.): *Asian Medical Systems* (Delhi, 1998)
Liu, Xinru: *Ancient India and Ancient China: AD 1–600* (Delhi, 1988)
Lorenzen, David N.: *The Kapalikas and Kalamukhas* (California, 1972)
Macdonnell, A.A.: *A History of Sanskrit Literature* (1889/Delhi, 1962)
Mackay, Ernest: *The Indus Civilisation* (London, 1935)
Majumdar, R.C. (Ed.): *The Classical Accounts of India* (Calcutta, 1960)
Malalasekara, G.P. (Ed.): *Vamsatthappakasini* (London, 1935)
Marshall, John (Ed.): *Mohenjo-daro and the Indus Civilisation* (London, 1931)
Mascaro, Juan (Ed.): *The Upanishads* (Baltimore, 1965/1967)
McCrindle (Tr.): *Ancient India as Described by Megasthenes and Arrian* (New Delhi, 1972)
Meyer, Johann Jakob: *Sexual Life in Ancient India*, 2 vols. (London, 1930)
Mitra, Rajendralal (Ed.): *Lalita-vistara* (Calcutta, 1877)
Mitra, R.C.: *The Decline of Buddhism in India* (Santiniketan, 1981)
Mookerji, Radhakumud: *Asoka* (1928/Delhi, 1962)
Mookerji, Radhakumud: *Chandragupta Maurya and His Times* (Madras, 1943)
Müller, F. Max and J. Takakuusu (Tr.): *Buddhist Mahayana Texts* Part II (Oxford, 1894/Delhi, 1965)
Nikhilananda, Swami (Tr.): *The Upanishads* (New York, 1964)
O'Flaherty, Wendy Doniger: *Asceticism and Eroticism in the Mythology of Siva* (Delhi, 1973)

O'Flaherty, Wendy Doniger: *Dreams, Illusion and Other Realities* (Chicago, 1984)
O'Flaherty, Wendy Doniger (Ed.): *Karma and Rebirth in Classical Indian Tradition* (California, 1980/Delhi, 1983)
O'Flaherty, Wendy Doniger (Tr.): *Rig Veda* (Delhi, 1981)
O'Flaherty, Wendy Doniger: *Sexual Metaphors and Animal Symbols in Indian Mythology* (Chicago, 1980/Delhi, 1981)
O'Flaherty, Wendy Doniger (Tr.): *Textual Sources for the Study of Hinduism* (Manchester, 1988)
O'Flaherty, Wendy Doniger: *Women, Androgynes and Other Mythical Beasts* (Chicago, 1980/1982)
Oldenberg, Hermann: *Buddha* (1882/Delhi, 1971)
Oldenberg, Hermann (Tr.): *Grihya-Sutras* I & II (1886/Delhi, 1964)
Oldenberg, Hermann (Tr.): *The Dipavamsa* (New Delhi, 1982)
Panikkar, K.M.: *Geographic Factors in Indian History* (Bombay, 1959)
Panikkar, K.M.: *Survey of Indian History* (1946)
Panikkar, Raimondo: *The Vedic Experience* (California, 1977)
Parpola, Asko: *Deciphering The Indus Valley* (Cambridge, 1994)
Petech, L.: *Northern India According to the Shui-Ching-Chu* (Rome, 1950)
Pichamuthu: *Physical Geography of India* (New Delhi, 1967)
Piggott, Stuart: *Prehistoric India* (London, 1950)
Randhawa, M. S.: *A History of Agriculture in India*, 4 vols. (New Delhi, 1980)
Rangarajan, L.N. (Tr. & Ed.): *The Arthasastra* (New Delhi, 1987)
Rao, S. R.: *Dawn and Evolution of the Indus Civilisation* (New Delhi, 1991)
Ratnagar, Shereen: *Enquiries into the Political Organisation of Harappan Society* (Pune, 1991)
Ray, Praphulla Chandra: *History of Hindu Chemistry*, 2 vols. (Calcutta, 1905, 1925)
Ripley, S. Dillon: *Tropical Asia* (New York, 1969)
Risley, Sir Robert: *The People of India* (London, 1915)
Ross, Philip E.: 'Hard Words' (*Scientific American*, April 1991)
Sastri, K.A. Nilakanta: *Age of the Nandas and Mauryas* (Benares, 1952)
Schotsman, Irma (Tr.) *Avaghosa's Buddhacarita* (Varanasi, 1995)
Sengupta, P.: *Everyday Life in Ancient India* (Bombay, 1950)
Shamasastry, R. (Tr.): *Kautilya's Arthasastra* (Mysore, 1929)
Sharma, J.P.: *Republics in Ancient India c.1500 BC–500 BC* (Leiden, 1968)
Sharma, R.S.: *Sudras in Ancient India* (Benares, 1959/1980)
Smith, V.A.: *Asoka* (1919 / Delhi, 1990)
Smith, V.A.: *Early History of India* (Oxford, 1925)
Spear, Percival: *India* (Michigan, 1961)
Sreedhara Menon: *A Survey of Kerala History* (Kottayam, 1967)
Stcherbatsky (Tr.): *The Conception of Buddhist Nirvana* (Translation of a section of Nagarjuna's *Madhyamaka-karika*) (Varanasi, 1969 revised edition)
Stevenson, Mrs Sinclair: *The Heart of Jainism* (Oxford, 1915)
Strong, John S. (Tr. & Ed.): *The Legend of King Asoka: A Study and Translation of the Asokavadana* (Princeton, 1983/Delhi, 1989)

Suzuki, Daisetz Teitaro: *Studies in the Lankavatara Sutra* (London and Boston, 1930/1975)
Tarn, W.W.: *Alexander the Great*, Vol. I (Cambridge, 1948)
Thapar, Romila: *Ancient Indian Social History* (Orient Longman, 1979)
Thapar, Romila: *Asoka and the Decline of the Mauryas* (Oxford, 1997)
Thapar, Romila: *A History of India*, Vol. I (Baltimore, 1966)
Thapar, Romila: *Interpreting Early India* (Oxford, Delhi, 1992)
Thapar, Romila: *The Past and Prejudice* (New Delhi, 1975)
Visakhadatta: *Mudra-Rakshasa* (Tr.: Ranjit Sitaram Pandit) (Bombay, 1944)
Wadia, D.N.: *Geology of India* (London, 1926)
Walker, Benjamin: *Tantrism* (Williamborough, 1982)
Wallbank, T. Walter: *India* (California, 1951)
Wasson, R. Gordon: *Soma* (Harcourt)
Weber, Max: *The Religion of India* (New York, 1958)
Wheeler, Mortimer: *Early India and Pakistan* (London, 1958)
Wheeler, Mortimer: *The Indus Civilisation* (Cambridge, 1953)
Whitney, William Dwight (Tr.): *Atharva-veda Samhita*, 2 vols. (Delhi, 1962)
Woodward, F.L. (Tr.): *Some Sayings of The Buddha* (Oxford, 1925/1949)
Woodward, F.L. (Tr.): *The Books of Gradual Sayings*, 2 vols. (Oxford, 1931)
Wolpert, Stanley: *An Introduction to India* (Delhi, 1991)
Yutang Lin (Ed.): *The Wisdom of China and India* (New York, 1942)
Zaehner, R.C. (Tr.): *Hindu Scriptures* (Delhi, 1992)
Zysk, Kenneth G.: *Asceticism and Healing in Ancient India* (Oxford, 1991)

INDEX